# THE
# ACQUISITIONS MANUAL

*Edited by*

## Sumner N. Levine
State University of New York
Stony Brook, New York

New York Institute of Finance

Library of Congress Cataloging-in-Publication Data

The Acquisitions manual / edited by Sumner N. Levine.
        p.    cm.
    Includes index.
    ISBN 0-13-405929-8 :
    1. Consolidation and merger of corporations--United States-
-Handbooks, manuals, etc.  2. Business enterprises, Sale of--United
States--Handbooks, manuals, etc.  3. Business enterprises--United
States--Purchasing--Handbooks, manual, etc.   I. Levine, Sumner N.
HD2746.5.A26   1989
658.1'6'0973--dc20                                          89-32615
                                                              CIP

This publication is designed to provide accurate and authoritative information in regard to the subject matter covered. It is sold with the understanding that the publisher is not engaged in rendering legal, accounting, or other professional service. If legal advice or other expert assistance is required, the services of a competent professional person should be sought.

*From a Declaration of Principles Jointly Adopted by*
*a Committee of the American Bar Association and a*
*Committee of Publishers and Associations*

New York Institute of Finance
(NYIF Corp.)
70 Pine Street
New York, New York 10270-0003

# Contents

**Appendix 6–A**
*Key Business Ratios and Their Meanings, 210*

**Chapter 7**
*Valuation and Pricing of Acquisitions, 211*

*Patrick F. Dolan*

**Chapter 10**
## *Financing Acquisitions, 349*

*John D. Carton*

**Appendix 10–A**
## *Recommended Directories of Financing Sources, 377*

**Chapter 11**
*Acquiring the Turnaround Candidate, 379*

*Ronald G. Quintero*

# Contributors

*George C. Beck* is a partner in the New York City law firm of Burns & Beck. For many years he has been involved in all aspects of business combinations. He is co-author of the book *Acquisitions, Mergers, Sales, Buyouts and Takeovers* (Prentice-Hall).

*Paul Broderick* is an attorney specializing in tax with the law firm Christian, Barton, Epps, Brent & Chappell in Richmond, Virginia. His previous positions were senior tax manager at Deloitte, Haskins and Sells in Richmond, Virginia and attorney in the Corporate Reorganization Branch of the IRS National Office.

*John D. Carton* is a vice president at MMG Petricof & Co., Inc., New York City, where he specializes in acquisitions and leveraged buyouts. Prior to his present position, he was a vice president at J. Henry Schroder Corp.

*Patrick F. Dolan* is a manager at Peat Marwick Main & Co. in New York City, where he specializes in corporate valuations.

*Erich A. Helfert* is currently a consultant. Previously, he was a vice president of Corporate Planning at Crown Zellerbach. He is the author of *Techniques of Financial Analysis* (Dow Jones–Irwin), now in its sixth edition.

*David I. Karabell* is a partner in the New York City law firm of O'Sullivan, Graev and Karabell, where he specializes in mergers, acquisitions, and divestitures.

*Sumner N. Levine* is a professor at the State University of New York at Stony Brook, New York and is the editor/author of several books including the *Financial Analyst's Handbook* (Dow Jones–Irwin), now in its second edition. He is also affiliated with Nortech Associates, specializing in the biomedical industries.

*Joseph H. Marren,* currently at Kidder Peabody, had been involved for many years in analyzing mergers and divestitures for American-Maize Products Company, Stamford, Connecticut. He is the author of *Mergers and Acquisitions* (Dow Jones–Irwin).

*Ronald G. Quintero* is a partner in Gibbons, Quintero & Co. in New York City and Tenafly, New Jersey, which provides management consulting services for troubled companies. Before founding his present company, he was with the Financial Restructuring Group at Bear, Stearns & Co.

*Fred B. Renwick* is a professor of finance at the Graduate School of Business Administration, New York University and the author of several texts on investing.

*Charles A. Scharf* was formerly a partner of Scharf & Beck in New York City. He is a co-author of the book *Acquisitions, Mergers, Sales, Buyouts and Takeovers* (Prentice-Hall).

*Edward E. Shea* is a partner specializing in acquisitions in the law firm of Windels, Marx, Davies. He was formerly a senior vice president and director of the GAF Corp., Wayne, New Jersey. He is a co-author of *Acquisitions, Mergers, Sales, Buyouts and Takeovers* (Prentice-Hall).

# Introduction

This book is intended for executives, corporate planners, and others who desire to establish an acquisition program. It is intended as a practical guide providing a step-by-step approach to the entire acquisition process. Throughout, an effort was made to avoid excess verbiage and to keep the discussion of each topic as succinct as possible without, it is hoped, sacrificing clarity.

The initial chapter provides an overview of the acquisition process including a discussion of the factors that contribute to success and failure. While no magic potion is available for ensuring success, the merits of basing acquisition decisions on a strategic plan and well-defined acquisition criteria are emphasized here.

Strategic acquisition planning requires a good deal of relevant information. Sources of industry and economic information are given in Chapter 2 and sources for screening and identifying candidates are described in Chapter 3. The convenience of using online databases for these and other purposes is so considerable that an effort was made throughout to identify available online sources.

Tactics for contacting and pursuing potential acquisition candidates are presented in Chapter 4. Emphasis is placed on the importance of the human element in keeping the process on track and moving the negotiations forward.

Subsequent chapters cover such important topics as valuation, financing, taxation, accounting, and other aspects of acquisitions. Because recent years have seen considerable interest in the acquisition of turnaround situations, a chapter is included discussing this subject.

Finally, I wish to express my gratitude to a superb group of contributors whose expertise and effort made this work possible. My very special thanks are extended to my wife, Caroline, without whose publishing experience and persistence this book would not have seen the light of day.

*Sumner N. Levine*

# Chapter 1

# Defining the Acquisition Target

*Sumner N. Levine*

Purchasing a business is generally expensive and time consuming. A prospective buyer must be clear as to what he or she hopes to achieve and whether the objectives could better be realized by other means.

As with many other business decisions, the chances of successfully acquiring an attractive candidate are greatly enhanced when the acquisition process is geared to a strategic planning program that provides a broad overview of a company's situation and alternatives. The basic elements of the strategic planning process are outlined in the appendix to this chapter.

## OVERVIEW OF THE ACQUISITION PROCESS

From an overall perspective, the acquisition process consists, with variations, of the following stages:

- establishing the acquisition objectives
- identifying potential candidates by use of screening procedures
- narrowing the initial list of target companies
- initiating contact with a target's management to determine

receptivity to an offer and possibly to acquire additional information

- on the basis of the foregoing, making a realistic evaluation of the feasibility of an acquisition
- obtaining financial statements covering the last five years and relevant contractual and leasing information
- establishing an offering price, together with the terms and conditions and the form (cash, stocks, notes, and so forth) by which the price is to be paid
- exploring the sources of financing
- issuing a nonbinding agreement in principle (usually in letter form) outlining the above pricing proposal and stating positions on such matters as maintaining continuity of management, payment of brokerage fees, and so forth
- undertaking an in-depth study (so-called due diligence) of the target
- preparing and signing the acquisitions contract
- closing (the actual transfer of assets and payment of considerations)

In practice, the above activities proceed in an atmosphere of continuous negotiations, involving interchanges of ideas, information, and positions during telephone calls and meetings, both formal and informal. The interactions continue until the negotiations fail or an agreement is reached and a closing takes place.

## TYPES OF ACQUISITIONS

The purchase of a business can take various forms. Generally, the term *acquisition* is used for any transaction occurring between willing parties, in which the buyer acquires all or part of the assets of the seller. The term *takeover* is used when the management of the selling firm is an unwilling participant in the combination of the companies. Specific forms of acquisitions include asset or stock acquisitions, statutory mergers, and consolidations.

With a *statutory merger,* two corporations combine according to the requirements set forth in the laws of the states of incorporation. Filing the merger certificate with the secretaries of state in the states of incorporation generally requires prior approval by the boards of directors and stockholders of both corporations. On completion of the merger, one corporation survives and the other is dissolved. The surviving corporation becomes heir to both the assets and liabilities of the dissolved corporation. A major convenience of the statutory merger is that the assets of the seller are automatically transferred to the buyer, eliminating the need for the numerous documents required in an asset acquisition. The latter requires that title to each asset be individually transferred.

With a *reverse merger,* the seller survives and the buying firm is dissolved. This type of merger is used if the seller has valuable assets that cannot be transferred because of legal and other considerations.

A statutory *consolidation* also involves a combination pursuant to state laws and hence requires the prior approval of the boards of directors and stockholders of both corporations. Consolidations differ from mergers in that both parties to the transaction disappear and a new, third corporation is formed. The new corporation becomes heir to the assets and liabilities of both corporations.

An *asset acquisition* is a transaction in which the buying firm acquires all or part of the assets of the seller. Generally with corporations, asset acquisition requires approval of the seller's stockholders but not that of the buyer's. Although the seller corporation may remain intact after the acquisition, it is generally liquidated. Transfer of assets is not realized by operation of the law, as with statutory mergers and consolidations, but is implemented by specific instruments for each asset. Liabilities of the selling firm are not automatically transferred to the buyer; the buyer accepts only those, if any, agreed to in the acquisition's contract. However, in order to avoid liability to various creditors of the seller, buyers should comply with the *bulk sales laws.* These laws require the seller to prepare a sworn list of creditors and of the property being sold. It is the buyer's responsibility to inform creditors of the intended sale within at least ten days before the sale. Creditors may then make appropriate arrangements with the seller.

With *stock acquisitions,* all or part of the stock of the seller is acquired by the buyer. Stock acquisitions generally involve a direct agreement between the selling stockholders and the buying corporation. After acquisition, the seller's corporation remains subject to all liabilities so that the buyer cannot limit the liabilities to those specified in the acquisition contract. When the selling corporation has only a few willing stockholders, stock acquisition is particularly simple to achieve and can circumvent the intentions of an unwilling management. However, with widely held public corporations, stock acquisition may be difficult and time consuming.

The sale of stock rather than assets is often preferred when the corporation holds certain contracts, leases, franchises, or licensing agreements that cannot be assigned to the buyer, at least on the same favorable terms. A good credit rating of the selling corporation may also favor stock acquisition.

The tax aspects of an acquisition play an important role and are discussed in Chapter 8.

## ACQUISITIONS COMPARED WITH ALTERNATIVE STRATEGIES

It is worthwhile recalling that an acquisition is only one of several alternatives for achieving the basic business objectives of a firm. Consider a company that has decided that further growth requires product diversification. Among the alternatives to acquisition are the internal development of new products, joint ventures with other companies, and licensing agreements. Ultimately, the choice depends on considerations of cost, time, and whether an alternative is available, as well as other factors.

With a joint venture, for example, problems may arise because of personality incompatibilities among key personnel as well as from differences in corporate objectives or styles. If one firm in the joint venture is of the slow, methodical school and the other is geared to a faster pace, considerable friction may develop. Joint ventures may also pose the danger of setting up a competitor if the deal subsequently falls apart.

An important advantage of an acquisition over internal development is that it usually saves time. This is particularly true for diversification into an unrelated product or service. Entry into a new product line by acquisition may require only a few months while internal development of a new product may require years. Moreover, purchasing an established business generally involves less risk than starting from scratch.

Acquisitions have been employed to completely restructure companies within a relatively short time span. National Distillers, for example, divested its original liquor business and acquired companies in the commodity chemical, polyethylene, and propane gas industries. While the commodity industries hardly seem exciting, the intent of the restructuring was to take National Distillers out of the shrinking liquor industry—in which it was far behind the leader Seagrams and losing clout with distributors—and to put the company into plastics such as polyethylene, in which it is now the leader.

In some instances, the acquisition decision is inevitable because it may be practically impossible to develop internally the resources to compete effectively. Substantial entry barriers may include the presence of a well-established brand name, proprietary technology, strong patent positions, difficult-to-penetrate distribution channels, or the need for large economies of scale (high production volume).

### Advantages of the Acquisition Approach

In addition to saving time, acquisitions may provide operating and other benefits to the buyer through synergies, particularly if the acquired company is in a related business. These benefits include added strengths derived from transferable production technology, marketing know-how, R&D capability, and managerial skills. For example, when a well-known brand name is acquired, instant market recognition is achieved. Acquiring a firm with superior production facilities can contribute to substantial cost reductions. Consolidation of staffs is often possible, permitting significant savings. Acquisitions may also result in financial and tax benefits. The acquired firm may have assets that are redundant or unrelated to the purposes of the acquisition, which may be sold to provide a source of cash. Unused debt capacity of the acquired firm may be used to increase borrowing.

Where an acquisition is structured as a purchase of assets, tax benefits may be available in the form of increased depreciation resulting from a step-up in the basis of the acquired assets. Increased depreciation results in a reduction in taxable income and hence an increase in cash flow. On the other hand, if the acquisition is structured as a stock purchase or as a tax-free reorganization (see Chapter 8) in compliance with IRS regulations, no change in basis is allowed but certain loss carryover benefits may be available to the buyer. The buyer benefits because any operating loss acquired may be offset against the buyer's taxable income either as a carryback to three preceding years or as a carryforward to the subsequent 15 years. However, under the 1986 Tax Reform Act these tax benefits have been substantially compromised.

### *Problems with Acquisitions*

Because the market for established profitable companies is highly competitive, acquisitions are expensive. According to a number of studies, most financial benefits are captured by the seller. This is hardly surprising since the market for acquisitions is well organized, involving numerous brokers, finders, investment bankers, and legal and accounting firms. Indeed, today information concerning many deals can be accessed on every desktop computer through online databases. As with all highly competitive markets, the pricing tends to eliminate excess returns to the buyer.

Another concern with acquisitions is the adverse impact on the buyer's balance sheet if substantial cash or debt financing is employed. This can restrict future borrowing capacity and downgrade the buyer's credit rating.

Purchasing a firm also involves acquiring new personnel as well as the corporate culture of the seller. As already mentioned, incompatibilities between personnel and operating styles may cause difficulties. Such difficulties can be particularly serious if the acquisition is in a business with which the buyer has little or no experience. Departure or noncooperation of key personnel from the acquired firm can be devastating if it occurs before replacement personnel are in place.

Internal approaches to new product or market development can often be accomplished incrementally so that the decision to withdraw involves a limited cost. In contrast, acquisitions often involve substantial up-front commitments, making withdrawal expensive. The costs may be not only financial. For example, the closing of a plant long-established in a community can precipitate awkward social and image problems.

Antitrust impediments may arise if the acquisition appears to limit competition or results in the capture of a large market share. Antitrust action can be taken by the Justice Department, the Federal Trade Commission, or both. However, apart from acquisitions involving the largest concerns, the number of acquisitions opposed on antitrust grounds is small.

## WHY ACQUISITIONS FAIL

Surprisingly, according to one study, between one-half and one-third of acquisitions don't work.* A common reason for failure is the leap-before-looking syndrome that results from impulsive or poorly conceived acquisition strategies. While a well-planned strategy is certainly no guarantee of success, it certainly helps in anticipating possible pitfalls.

Other causes of failure include the following:

- overpaying
- lack of experience for managing the acquisition
- failure to keep or motivate key personnel of the acquired company
- purchase of a company that is too big in terms of the resources available to the buyer
- incompatibility of corporate cultures
- fraud on the part of the seller

* *Business Week,* "Do Mergers Really Work?," June 3, 1983.

- failure of favorable forecasted events to occur
- unforeseen disasters

It is worth noting that buyers are often unable to understand fully or to preserve the key characteristics that contributed to the success of the acquired firm. This was apparently the case with Avon's unsuccessful 1979 acquisition of the New York–based jewelry and luxury retailer, Tiffany. Avon, a large mass marketer of cosmetics, failed to appreciate that much of Tiffany's appeal to its wealthy clients stemmed from an aura of exclusivity. Consequently, when Avon's management extended Tiffany's line of merchandise to less expensive items, the sense of exclusivity was compromised and Tiffany's traditional client base eroded. In 1984, losses caused Avon to sell Tiffany to private buyers.

## THE ROLE OF LONG-TERM PLANNING

Strategic planning serves a number of important purposes. Planning requires management to maintain an awareness of the company's strengths and weaknesses, as well as the opportunities and threats provided by the business environment. As a result, planning forces management to take a long-term view of the company's business. The planning process raises basic questions such as:

- What businesses are we in?
- What businesses should we be in?
- What are the pros and cons of our current strategies?

As pointed out in the appendix to this chapter, the output of the planning process is a set of objectives and strategies for achieving those objectives. Only after management has fully appraised the available strategic alternatives is it in a position to consider an acquisition. The desirability of an acquisition strategy (compared with internal development or other alternatives) should be considered in the context of achieving the following objectives:

- to develop new products for current markets
- to expand the distribution channels for existing products
- to develop new products for new markets
- to develop new markets for existing products
- to achieve economies of scale in order to lower production costs
- to increase name recognition
- to acquire new technologies, patents, or R&D capability
- to upgrade production technology
- to expand customer service facilities
- to upgrade managerial skills
- to develop new markets as well as control over sources of supply by expanding toward suppliers' product lines (backward integration)
- to develop new markets by expanding toward customers' product lines (forward integration)

Other objectives of a more or less defensive character may also motivate acquisitions. These include the need to eliminate a weak competitor which, if acquired by another rival, would result in a combination that could pose a serious threat. Acquisitions may also be considered for the purpose of reducing a firm's large cash position in order to decrease its attractiveness as a takeover target.

## FORMULATING ACQUISITION CRITERIA

Once the objectives of the acquisition have been decided, a more or less detailed set of acquisition criteria (an acquisition profile) is developed. The acquisition profile focuses on the following items:

- type of products or services sought
- price range of target
- sales volume and/or market share of target

- earnings and/or sales growth
- profitability in terms of return on investment or assets (ROI, ROA)
- degree to which target's product line is diversified
- degree to which target complements existing products or distribution channels of the buyer
- diversity of target's customer base
- willingness of target's management to remain after acquisition
- compatibility of corporate cultures
- patent position of target
- R&D strengths of target
- production strengths of target
- location of target

Acquisition criteria may also include items to be avoided, such as:

- avoid companies in highly regulated industries
- avoid companies in financial distress
- avoid competitors of existing customers
- avoid companies in industries dominated by a few large competitors
- avoid antitrust situations
- avoid labor troubles

In practice, the extent to which acquisition criteria are formally stated varies considerably. Some firms employ relatively detailed acquisition profiles, while others consider any prospects that are profitable and can take care of their own management needs. In the simplest of terms, acquisition criteria are often reduced to answering the following queries:

- Does it meet our operating objectives?
- Will it provide a return equal to or better than other available opportunities?

- Can we manage it?
- Can we afford it?

For initial screening purposes it is advisable to focus on a small subset of criteria about which information can be easily obtained. These criteria may include product type (or industry), sales volume, years in business, number of employees, and geographic location.

## REFERENCES

Gordon Bing, *Corporate Acquisitions* (Gulf Publishing Co., Houston, TX, 1980)

S.J. Lee and R.D. Colman, editors, *Handbook of Mergers, Acquisitions and Buyouts* (Prentice-Hall, Englewood Cliffs, NJ, 1981)

M.E. Porter, *Competitive Strategy* (The Free Press, New York, NY, 1980)

Milton Rock, editor, *The Merger and Acquisition Handbook* (McGraw-Hill, New York, NY, 1987)

C.A. Scharf, E.E. Shea, G.C. Beck, *Acquisitions, Mergers, Sales, Buyouts and Takeovers* (Prentice-Hall, Englewood Cliffs, NJ, 1985)

## APPENDIX 1-A:
## Strategic Planning for Acquisitions

Because the terms *objectives* and *strategies* are employed here, their definitions are in order. The specific *results* that a company seeks to achieve are its *objectives*. The *means* for achieving those objectives are the *strategies*.

An outline of the strategic planning process as it relates to the acquisition process is shown in Figure 1-1. As indicated, the strategic planning process usually consists of (a) a company self-analysis, (b) a customer analysis, (c) an industry analysis (which may include a study of competitors although competitor analysis is often done separately), and (d) a review of the relevant socioeconomic environment as it relates to the purposes of the plan. These are discussed in detail in the following sections.

The purpose of the analysis is to clarify the firm's strengths and weaknesses as well as the threats and opportunities presented by the business environment. In this way analysis provides a rational basis for formulating the firm's objectives and strategies. To be useful, objectives should be stated in clear, precise, and, as far as possible, quantitative terms. The selection of the strategic alternatives to be considered depends on available resources, opportunities, and assumptions concerning the future business environment. Acquisitions are, of course, just one of the several strategies that may be considered.

**Figure 1-1.** *Outline of strategic planning process and the development of acquisition criteria.*

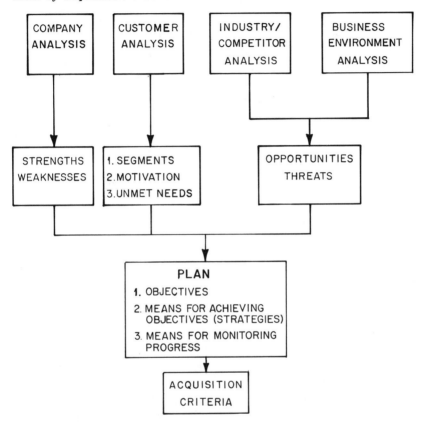

A few brief comments on the mechanics of the planning process itself may be helpful. The composition and degree of commitment of the planning committee is particularly important for the ultimate success of the effort. Active participation of the CEO and key line managers is crucial. It is important to avoid making the planning process too complex and rigid. Unless care is taken, information inputs can become so voluminous as to become unmanageable—the well-known, drowning-in-information syndrome. The background reports and data should be kept succinct and well focused on the relevant planning issues. The use of summary-type formats is helpful in this

**Figure 1-2.** *Chart for analyzing relative strengths of competitors.*

| COMPETITION ANALYSIS | | | | | | |
|---|---|---|---|---|---|---|
| NAME | SALES VOLUME ($000) | MARKET SHARE | SALES GROWTH RATE | PROFITABILITY | STRENGTHS | WEAKNESSES |
| XYZ CORP | 20 | 25% | 10% | PM=10% ROA= 5% | STRONG SALES FORCE | WEAK R/D |
| AAA CORP | 5 | 15% | 12% | PM=12% ROA= 8% | LOW PRICING | POOR QUALITY |
| | | | | | | |
| | | | | | | |
| | | | | | | |
| | PM = PROFIT MARGINS ROA = RETURN ON ASSETS | | | | | |

regard. An example of such a format intended for competitor analysis is shown in Figure 1-2.

As indicated above, the output from the strategic planning process should consist of a statement of objectives including their relative priorities, an evaluation of alternative strategies, and procedures for monitoring progress. Figure 1-1 provides a checklist of the major items usually included in a strategic analysis. All projections referred to in the figure assume that the firm continues in its present mode.

Information sources for the industry, competitor, and environmental analysis are discussed in Chapter 2. Financial terms and ratios are given in Chapter 6.

## 1. *Company Analysis*

### 1.1 *Aggregate Analysis*
- historical (past five years) and projected (three to five years) aggregate sales, earnings, profitability, and debt ratios

1.2 *Analysis by Product Type*

- historical and projected sales, costs, and contribution to company profit
- historical and projected market share
- projected sales and contribution to earnings of products under development
- characterization of buyers and (if different) users of products or services
- percentage of sales by customer type
- customer motivation for buying product
- unmet needs of customer

1.3 *Production and Cost-Related Analysis*

- trends in the firm's costs, including labor, materials, maintenance, marketing, R&D, administration, pensions, and so forth
- cost comparisons with competitors
- projected expenditures for plant and equipment
- supplier-related problems concerning costs, quality, and reliability
- quality control review (in-plant rejection rate trends, field failures, customer complaints)
- quality comparisons with competitors

1.4 *Organizational Analysis*

- degree of centralization
- formal and informal lines of communication
- decision-making procedures
- practices for encouraging and rewarding creativity and initiative
- practices for recruiting, recognizing, and holding talented individuals
- innovative record of the organization (history of new product introductions, patents, and novel marketing approaches)

1.5 *Financial Capacity*
- historical and projected cash and cash flows
- borrowing capacity and rates
- access to equity market

1.6 *Performance Review*
- Which products have been successful?
- Which products have failed?
- Which strategies and circumstances were responsible for the foregoing?
- How well has the firm responded to opportunities? to threats?

1.7 *Identification of Strengths and Weaknesses*

This section is a major output of the analysis. It attempts to identify strengths that can be exploited and weaknesses that can be eliminated or neutralized. Relevant questions to be asked here are: What are we good at? What are we bad at? What are our unique capabilities? Key items for evaluation are listed in the following. Numerical ratings are often assigned to each item, as appropriate, on a scale of, say, 1 (very poor) to 5 (excellent).

1.7.1 *Marketing Ratings*
- awareness of customer needs
- product quality
- access to distribution channels
- advertising and promotion
- sales force
- name recognition
- customer service
- customer loyalty
- diversity of customer base

1.7.2 *Manufacturing Ratings*
- quality of plant and equipment

- cost and quality of raw materials or supplies
- labor force quality and supply
- production capacity
- quality control systems

### 1.7.3 *Financial Ratings*

- cash position
- borrowing capacity
- access to equity market
- relationship with financial institutions
- investor relationships

### 1.7.4 *Creativity Ratings*

- quality of R&D
- patent record
- new product record
- record of marketing innovations
- quality of engineering

### 1.7.5 *Management and Personnel Ratings*

- ability to attract and hold talented personnel
- ability to motivate employee loyalty and initiative
- quality of training programs
- accessibility of upward communication channels within the organization
- control over operations
- ability to respond to changing circumstances
- quality of personnel at various levels

## 2. *Customer Analysis*

- definition of current buyers and users as well as of potential customers not now using product
- customer motivation for buying product
- problems experienced by customers and unmet needs

3. *Industry and Competitor Analysis*

- definition of industry segments (who uses the product and how it is used)
- current size and growth rate by segment
- cyclical and seasonal characteristics
- extent of industry consolidation
- level of manufacturing technology
- marketing and distribution practices
- threat of substitute products or new technologies
- bargaining power of suppliers and customers
- key success factors
- entry barriers
- industry trends

3.1 *Competitor Analysis*

- current sales, market share, profitability, strengths and weaknesses by competitor
- growth trend in sales and market share
- cost structure of competitors
- degree of vertical integration of competitors
- breadth of product line
- potential new competitors

4. *Environmental Analysis*

- current and forecasted state of the economy
- demographic and socioeconomic trends
- changes in government regulations
- changes in the tax law
- changes in government spending patterns
- changes in foreign markets
- technological trends

## REFERENCES

The literature on strategic planning is extensive. In the space available it is possible only to outline the subject in broad terms. Readers interested in exploring the matter in greater detail may find the following of value:

David A. Aaker, *Developing Business Strategies* (Wiley, New York, NY, 1984)

John Argenti, *Stemmatic Corporate Planning* (Wiley, New York, NY, 1974)

Richard G. Hamermesh, editor, *Strategic Management* (Wiley, New York, NY, 1983)

D.F. Hussey, *Corporate Planning Theory and Practice* (Pergamon Press, New York, NY, 1974)

William E. Rothschild, *Putting It All Together* (American Management Association, New York, NY, 1976)

George A. Steiner, *Top Management Planning* (Macmillan, New York, NY, 1969)

Chapter **2**

# *Information Sources for Acquisition Planning*

*Sumner N. Levine*

Implementation of a strategic study requires access to information. Because a large amount of information is often accumulated, at the outset, some thought must be given to how the information is to be organized and made available when needed. Of course, individuals differ as to how best to accomplish this end. Some prefer a set of indexed loose-leaf notebooks while others use ordinary files. However, with the wide availability of desktop computers, the most versatile and convenient method is to put the information on a disk employing one of the several commercially available database programs.

A representative set of headings for organizing the data follows:

A. *Companies Participating in the Industry*
   product lines
   sales volume
   market share
   growth rates
   profitability
   strengths and weaknesses

B. *Marketing Data*
   definition of market segments

current market size and potential
determinants of growth
selling strategies
distribution channels

C. *Production Data*
cost structure
level of technology
suppliers

D. *Industry Data*
technological developments
social factors
substitute products
foreign competition

E. *Regulatory and Governmental Impact Data*
government regulations affecting industry
impact of government spending and tax policies

Perhaps the best place to begin the research is with industry studies prepared by various marketing, investment, and trade associations. Sources of these are given on pages 24–26. A helpful second step is to contact trade associations and obtain copies of the major trade publications. Both of these sources also provide information about trade shows and conferences. Conferences are an excellent source of company literature as well as a means for making direct contact with industry personnel.

In the course of this research, a list should be assembled of knowledgeable individuals to be interviewed. It is advisable to begin making such contacts as soon as enough background information has been accumulated to permit intelligent questioning and discussions. Interviewees should also be asked about other individuals to be contacted and other information sources.

A number of information sources are given in this chapter. The following chapter discusses in more detail how to develop a fairly complete list of industry participants using sources such as the Dun and Bradstreet *Million Dollar Directory, Ward's Business Directory, Thomas Register of American Manufactur-*

*ers,* and *Standard & Poor's Register of Corporation Directors and Executives.* These references list both public and private companies. However, it is worth pointing out that the Dun and Bradstreet, Standard & Poor's, Thomas, and Ward's directories classify industries by SIC (Standard Industrial Classification) numbers. This classification is too broad for many purposes. More focused listings of companies by products are provided in industry-specific directories, for example, *Medical Devices Register, Directory of Chemical Producers,* and the like. Sources of specialized directories are given on pages 28–29.

## *GENERAL REFERENCES*

Several helpful general references to which analysts should have access include:

Lorna Daniells, *Business Information Sources,* revised edition (University of California Press, Berkeley, CA)

This ranks among the best general references to U.S. business and economic data, including statistics, U.S. and foreign investments.

*Encyclopedia of Business Information Sources,* sixth edition (Gale Research Co., Detroit, MI)

This massive book provides, under industry and other subject headings, information about trade associations, professional societies, periodicals, trade publications, handbooks, yearbooks, statistical sources, and online databases. Helpful to analysts who are new to an industry. The book is updated annually. A sample of the information provided is shown in Figure 2–1.

Sumner Levine (ed.), *Business and Investment Almanac* (Dow Jones-Irwin, Homewood, IL)

This annual contains much basic data on the economy, specific industries, and the financial markets. It also provides extensive listings of information sources including state and federal agencies, as well as listings of industry experts in government.

**Figure 2–1.** *Sample entry from* Encyclopedia of Business Information Sources.

## ADHESIVES

**GENERAL WORKS**

*Adhesives for Wood.* Noyes Data Corp., Mill Rd. at Grand Ave., Park Ridge, NJ 07656. (201) 391-8484. 1984. $36.00.

**ABSTRACT SERVICES AND INDEXES**

*Applied Science and Technology Index.* H.W. Wilson Co., 950 University Ave., Bronx, NY 10452. (212) 588-8400 or (800) 367-6770. Monthly.

*Chemical Abstracts.* Chemical Abstracts Service, P.O. Box 3012, Columbus, OH 43210. (614) 421-3600. Weekly. $9,200.00 per year.

**BIBLIOGRAPHIES**

*Adhesives.* Jack Weiner and Lillian Roth. Institute of Paper Chemistry, 1043 E. S. River St., Appleton, WI 54911. Four volumes, 1963-1964. Supplement I; four volumes, 1968-1969, $10.00 each. Supplement II; three volumes, 1972-, price varies for each volume.

*Cryogenic Adhesives and Sealants. Abstracted Publications Prepared for the Aerospace Research and Data Institute, NASA Lewis Research Center.* U.S. National Aeronautics and Space Administration. Available from U.S. Government Printing Office, Washington, DC 20402. 1977.

**DIRECTORIES**

*Adhesives.* International Plastics Selector, Inc., Subsidiary, 9889 Willow Creek Rd., San Diego, CA 92126. (619) 578-3910. Annual. $99.00.

*Adhesives Red Book.* 6285 Barfield Rd., Atlanta, GA 30328. (404) 256-9800. Annual. $29.50.

*Adhesives Technology.* Noyes Data Corp., Mill Rd. at Grand Ave., Park Ridge, NJ 07656. (201) 391-8484. 1983. $48.00.

**HANDBOOKS AND MANUALS**

*Construction Sealants and Adhesives. 2nd edition.* Julian R. Panek and John P. Cook. John Wiley & Sons, Inc., 605 Third Ave., New York, NY 10158. (212) 850-6465. 1984. $36.95.

*Handbook of Adhesive Bonding.* Charles V. Cagle. McGraw-Hill Book Co., 1221 Ave. of the Americas, New York, NY 10020. (212) 512-2000. 1973. $64.50.

*Handbook of Adhesives.* Irving Skeist. Van Nostrand Reinhold Co., 115 Fifth Ave., New York, NY 10003. (212) 254-3232. Second edition. 1977. $49.50.

*Handbook of Pressure-Sensitive Adhesive Technology.* Donatas Satas. Van Nostrand Reinhold Co., 115 Fifth Ave., New York, NY 10003. (212) 254-3232. 1982. $37.50.

**ONLINE DATA BASES**

*CA Search.* Chemical Abstracts Service, P.O. Box 3012, Columbus, OH 43210. Guide to chemical literature, 1972 to present. Inquire as to online cost and availability.

*PaperChem.* Institute of Paper Chemistry, P.O. Box 1039, Appleton, WI 54911. (414) 734-9251. Worldwide coverage of the scientific and technical paper industry chemical literature, including patents, 1968 to present. Inquire as to online cost and availability.

**PERIODICALS AND NEWSLETTERS**

*Adhesives Age.* Communication Channels, Inc., 6255 Barfield Rd., Atlanta, GA 30328. (404) 256-9800. $27.00 per year.

*International Journal of Adhesion and Adhesives.* Butterworth Scientific Ltd., P.O. Box 63, Westbury House, Bury St., Guildford, Surrey, England GU2 5BH. Quarterly. $150.00 per year.

*Journal of Adhesion.* Gordon and Breach Science Publishers, 1 Bedford St., London, England WC2 4HD. Two volumes per year. $244.00 per year.

**RESEARCH CENTERS AND INSTITUTES**

Center for the Study of Materials. Carnegie-Mellon University, Schenley Park, Pittsburgh, PA 15213. (412) 578-3654.

Franklin Institute. Benjamin Franklin Parkway at 20th St., Philadelphia, PA 19103. (215) 448-1000.

Ontario Research Foundation. Sheridan Park, ON, Canada L5K 1B3. (416) 822-4111.

**TRADE ASSOCIATIONS AND PROFESSIONAL SOCIETIES**

Adhesive and Sealant Council. 1600 Wilson Blvd., Suite 910, Arlington, VA 22209. (703) 841-1112.

Adhesives Manufacturers Association of America. 111 E. Wacker Dr., Chicago, IL 60601. (312) 644-6610.

Gummed Industries Association. 380 N. Broadway, Jericho, Long Island, NY 11753. (516) 822-8948.

**OTHER SOURCES**

*Adhesives and Sealants.* Business Trend Analysts, 2171 Jericho Turnpike, Commack, NY 11725. (516) 462-5454. 1985. $595.00. Market data and forecasts.

*Adhesives and Sealants.* The Freedonia Group. Available from Find/SVP, 500 Fifth Ave., New York, NY 10110. (800) 346-3787 or (212) 354-2424. 1985. $1,500.00. Market data.

*Epoxy Resin Technology.* Maurice W. Ranney. Noyes Data Corp., Mill Rd. at Grand Ave., Park Ridge, NJ 07656. (201) 391-8484. 1982. $48.00.

*Household Adhesives Market.* Packaged Facts. Available from Find/SVP, 500 Fifth Ave., New York, NY 10110. (800) 346-3787 or (212) 354-2424. 1985. $995.00. Market data.

Source: From *Encyclopedia of Business Information Sources,* edited by James Woy (Copyright ©1986 by Gale Research Company; reprinted by permission), 6th Edition, Gale Research Co., 1986, pp. 49–50.

Matthew Lesko, *Information USA* (Viking and Penguin, New York, NY, 1986)

This is an extensive listing of U.S. government information sources organized by government agencies. The index is useful in locating industry information.

## SOURCES OF INDUSTRY STUDIES

The following sources of industry studies are helpful:

*Industry Surveys* (Standard and Poor's Corporation, New York, NY)

Updated quarterly, these surveys are an excellent source of basic industry information. These reports also provide industry evaluations and projections.

*Directory of Industry Data Sources* (Information Access Company, Belmont, CA)

This comprehensive directory lists market research, investment, economic, and statistical reports covering the United States, Canada, and Western Europe.

*PTS PROMT* (Predicasts, Inc., Cleveland, OH)

Published monthly, this is an excellent service, providing continuous abstracting of many industries on a worldwide basis. It covers market research, acquisitions, and government regulations, among other topics and is available online through *DIALOG* and other vendors. A sample *PTS PROMT* record is shown in Figure 2–2.

*Find/SVP* (New York, NY)

This organization publishes *Findex,* a directory of thousands of market research reports generated by organizations here and abroad. The information is updated quarterly and is also available online through *DIALOG.*

*Investex* (Business Research Corp., Boston, MA)

This service provides full-text industry and company reports

**Figure 2-2.** PTS PROMT *sample record.*

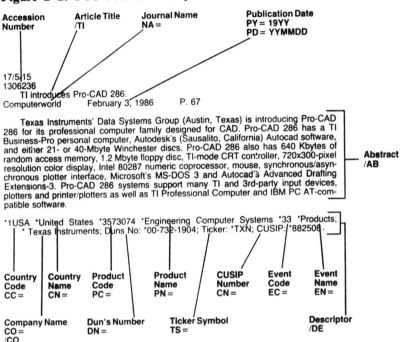

Accession Number

Article Title /TI

Journal Name NA =

Publication Date PY = 19YY PD = YYMMDD

17/5/15
1306236
    TI introduces Pro-CAD 286.
Computerworld        February 3, 1986        P. 67

Texas Instruments' Data Systems Group (Austin, Texas) is introducing Pro-CAD 286 for its professional computer family designed for CAD. Pro-CAD 286 has a TI Business-Pro personal computer, Autodesk's (Sausalito, California) Autocad software, and either 21- or 40-Mbyte Winchester discs. Pro-CAD 286 also has 640 Kbytes of random access memory, 1.2 Mbyte floppy disc, TI-mode CRT controller, 720x300-pixel resolution color display, Intel 80287 numeric coprocessor, mouse, synchronous/asynchronous plotter interface, Microsoft's MS-DOS 3 and Autocad's Advanced Drafting Extensions-3. Pro-CAD 286 systems support many TI and 3rd-party input devices, plotters and printer/plotters as well as TI Professional Computer and IBM PC AT-compatible software.

Abstract /AB

*1USA *United States *3573074 *Engineering Computer Systems *33 *Products; * Texas Instruments; Duns No: *00-732-1904; Ticker: *TXN; CUSIP: *882508 ·

| Country Code CC = | Country Name CN = | Product Code PC = | Product Name PN = | CUSIP Number CN = | Event Code EC = | Event Name EN = |

Company Name CO = /CO

Dun's Number DN =

Ticker Symbol TS =

Descriptor /DE

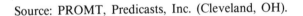

Source: PROMT, Predicasts, Inc. (Cleveland, OH).

from major brokerage firms, investment banks, and other industry analysts. Also available online through Dow Jones News Retrieval service and *DIALOG.*

*Wall Street Transcript* (New York, NY)

This weekly contains full-text reports issued by investment houses and insightful roundtable discussions by financial analysts on the current status of different industries. Each issue contains a detailed index of previously published reports. Available online through *VuText.*

*U.S. Industrial Outlook* (U.S. Department of Commerce, Washington, DC, ordered through the U.S. Government Printing Office)

Published annually, this volume contains surveys, statistics, and projections for about 300 manufacturing and service industries. At the end of each article, industry-related references are included, as well as the name and phone number of the Commerce Department expert who authored the article. A good initial source.

*Current Industrial Reports* (U.S. Department of Commerce, Bureau of the Census)
Data are shown for industries in the following categories:

- all manufacturing industries
- aerospace
- apparel
- chemicals and related products
- food
- glass products
- industrial equipment and consumer goods
- machinery and machinery components
- motors, generators, and electrical distribution equipment
- office furniture, supplies, and related products
- primary metals
- rubber and plastic products
- switchgear and industrial controls
- textile mill products
- wood and paper products

In addition to the above, major marketing research organizations such as Arthur D. Little (Cambridge, MA) and Frost and Sullivan (New York, NY) provide off-the-shelf reports on industries and products. Extensive listings of other helpful organizations are given in the following:

*Information Sources* (Information Industry Association, Washington, DC)
*The Encyclopedia of Information Systems and Services* (Gale Research Co., Detroit, MI)

## DIRECTORIES OF ASSOCIATIONS

Professional and trade associations are a valuable resource for trade information statistics, meetings, and contacts. Many associations publish directories of members as well as other helpful books and reports.

*Encyclopedia of Associations* (Gale Research Co., Detroit, MI)
This is a comprehensive listing of all types of U.S. and international organizations. For each association the directory provides the names of officers and publications, a description of activities, the number of members, and dates of meetings. It is available online through *DIALOG*.

*National Trade and Professional Associations of the United States* (Columbia Books, Inc., Washington, DC)
As the title implies, this directory focuses mainly on U.S. trade and professional organizations.

*Yearbook of International Organizations* (K.G. Saur, New York, NY)
This is another comprehensive directory of all types of international organizations.

## SOURCES OF TRADE PUBLICATIONS

Other major sources of information are the trade and professional publications. These provide a vast amount of current information including industry-wide forecasts and surveys. Subscriptions to all major publications covering a particular area of interest should be obtained. The following lists the major sources that can direct planners to relevant trade and professional publications.

*Ulrich's International Periodicals Directory* (R.R. Bowker, New York, NY)
This guide to international periodicals is especially useful.

The circulation figures given for each entry are helpful in selecting the more widely read publications. Available online through *DIALOG* and other vendors.

*The IMS Ayers Directory of Publications* (IMS Press, Fort Washington, PA)
This listing mainly covers periodicals published in the United States and Canada.

*Oxbridge Directory of Newsletters* (Oxbridge Communication, Inc., New York, NY)
This comprehensive directory of newsletters is published in the United States and Canada. Many of the newsletters listed contain information not found elsewhere.

## *SPECIALIZED DIRECTORIES*

Industry-specific directories (including special issues of trade publications) are invaluable guides to companies and products. There are many such directories, covering nearly every industry. Some examples are listed here:

- *Baker's Production and Marketing Buyers Guide*
- *ODP Chemical Buyers Directory*
- *Guide to the Health Care Field*
- *Post's Paper and Pulp Directory*
- *Progressive Grocer Marketing Guidebook*
- *Rubber and Plastics News*
- *Rubber Directory*
- *ISA Directory of Instrumentation*
- *Insurance Almanac*

The following lists sources of specialized directory information:

*Directory of Directories* (Gale Research Co., Detroit, MI)
This guide covers a wide range of business and industrial

directories. Contains mostly U.S. directories and a few foreign ones.

*Guide to American Directories* (B. Klein Publications, Coral Springs, FL)
A good annotated directory of industrial and professional directories, it is arranged by subject.

*Trade Directories of the World* (Croner Publications, Queens, NY)
This work contains industrial and professional directories arranged by continent and country.

*International Directories in Print* (Gale Research Co., Detroit, MI)
The volume provides information on a wide range of directories not published in the United States.

In addition, a number of state, local, and regional directories are published by private concerns as well as by state and local industrial development associations. Most of these directories are listed in the aforementioned guides to directories. A few examples of the many available directories of this type are:

- *California Manufacturers Registry*
- *Directory of New England Manufacturers*
- *Pennsylvania State Industrial Directory*

## INFORMATION ABOUT THE ECONOMY

Most information concerning the U.S. economy is gathered by agencies of the federal government and presented in the publications listed here, among others. As might be expected, the data in government publications is often months old. More current data is conveniently summarized in the financial section of the Sunday *New York Times* and in *Barron's National Business and Financial Weekly* (see Figure 2–3). *Barron's* also contains notification of forthcoming releases of government statistics

# Figure 2–3.

| Pulse of Industry and Trade | | | |
|---|---|---|---|

| Production—What's Made | Latest Date | Latest Period | Preceding Period | Year Ago |
|---|---|---|---|---|
| Autos, U.S. domestic units | Mar. 12 | e129,578 | r121,908 | r67,443 |
| Electric power, millions kw hrs | Mar. 6 | 50,379 | 52,159 | 47,967 |
| Paper, thousands tons | Feb. 27 | 733 | r723 | 721 |
| Paperboard, thousands tons | Feb. 27 | 737.3 | r746.4 | 727.0 |
| Petroleum, daily runs, thousands bbls | Mar. 4 | 12,805 | 12,676 | 11,554 |
| Petroleum, rated capacity, % | Mar. 4 | 82.5 | 81.3 | 75.0 |
| Rotary rigs running (Hughes) | Mar. 7 | 1,338 | r1,344 | 946 |
| Steel production, thousands tons | Mar. 5 | 1,971 | 2,002 | 1,570 |
| Steel, rated capacity, % (AISI) | Mar. 5 | 91.8 | 93.2 | 72.9 |
| Gross National Product, (adj. annual rate) | 4th qtr. | +4.5 | +4.3 | +4.1 |
| Factory operating rate, % | Dec. | 82.1 | 82.0 | 79.7 |
| Industrial Production (FRB) | Jan. | p133.8 | r133.6 | 126.5 |
| Manufacturing a | Jan. | p138.8 | r138.6 | 130.7 |
| Durable Mfg a | Jan. | p137.1 | r137.2 | 129.3 |
| Non-durable Mfg a | Jan. | p141.2 | r140.6 | 132.7 |
| Mining a | Jan. | p102.6 | r103.2 | 99.4 |
| Utilities a | Jan. | p114.0 | r112.6 | 108.0 |
| Newsprint, U.S. & Can., thousands metric tons | Jan. | 1,274 | 1,236 | 1,239 |

| Distribution—What's Sold | | | | |
|---|---|---|---|---|
| Business sales, billions $ | Dec. | 466.57 | r460.62 | 443.62 |
| Autos, U.S. domestic units | Feb. | 649,063 | 531,225 | 556,953 |
| Autos, imports | Feb. | 240,238 | 228,789 | 226,406 |
| Retail store sales, billions $ | Feb. | 127.99 | r127.28 | 124.28 |
| Factory Shipments, billions $ | Jan. | 207.69 | r211.36 | 189.96 |
| Durable goods, billions $ | Jan. | 109.26 | r113.0 | 99.3 |
| Machine tools, millions $ | Jan. | 143.0 | r288.4 | 147.7 |

| Inventories—What's Left on Hand | | | | |
|---|---|---|---|---|
| Business inventories, billions $ | Dec. | 701.87 | r696.42 | 652.62 |
| Domestic crude oil, thousands bbls | Mar. 4 | 341,033 | 338,917 | 329,515 |
| Gasoline, thousands bbls | Mar. 4 | 237,503 | 238,876 | 251,327 |
| Factory Inventories, billions $ | Jan. | 336.34 | r333.66 | 320.69 |
| Newsprint, U.S. & Can., thousands metric tons | Jan. | 1,252 | r1,135 | 1,208 |

| New Orders Received | | | | |
|---|---|---|---|---|
| New factory orders, billions $ | Jan. | 212.57 | r213.82 | 186.63 |
| Durable goods, billions $ | Jan. | 113.86 | r115.62 | 95.54 |
| Non-durable goods, billions $ | Jan. | 98.71 | r98.20 | 91.09 |
| Machine tools, millions $ | Jan. | 298.5 | r241.4 | 146.7 |

| Unfilled Orders | | | | |
|---|---|---|---|---|
| Factory orders backlog | Jan. | 408.38 | r403.50 | 370.53 |

| Failures (D. & B.) | | | | |
|---|---|---|---|---|
| Business Failures | Feb. 19 | 943 | 1,278 | 1,179 |

| Business Incorporations (D.& B.) | | | | |
|---|---|---|---|---|
| New Incorporations | Dec. | 56,436 | 50,532 | 68,845 |

| Purchasing Power | | | | |
|---|---|---|---|---|
| Leading Indicators Composite Index a | Jan. | 190.2 | r191.3 | 185.8 |
| Consumer Price Index a | Jan. | 115.7 | a115.4 | 111.7 |
| Producer Price Index Finished Goods b | Feb. | 105.9 | 106.2 | 104.1 |
| Inventory-to-sales ratio | Dec. | 1.50 | 1.51 | 1.47 |
| Gross National Product Deflator | 4th qtr. | 118.7 | r117.9 | 114.9 |

| Employment | | | | |
|---|---|---|---|---|
| Civil labor force, thousands | Feb. | 121,300 | 121,200 | 119,349 |
| Employed, thousands | Feb. | 114,400 | 114,100 | 111,382 |
| Unemployed, thousands | Feb. | 6,900 | 7,000 | 7,967 |
| Unemployment Rate, % | Feb. | 5.7 | 5.8 | 6.7 |

| Construction | | | | |
|---|---|---|---|---|
| Advance planning (ENR), millions $ | Feb. 29 | 7,019.4 | 9,254.4 | 6,058.0 |
| Building contracts (Dodge), billions $ | Jan. | 228.0 | 250.3 | 226.10 |
| Construction spending, billions $ | Jan. | 395.2 | r406.8 | 384.7 |
| Residential spending, billions $ | Jan. | 191.3 | r196.5 | 187.8 |
| Non-residential spending, billions $ | Jan. | 90.9 | r92.9 | 85.1 |
| Public spending, billions $ | Jan. | 74.3 | r78.1 | 74.5 |
| Lumber production, millions board ft | Nov. | 3,458 | r3,942 | 3,496 |
| Lumber shipments, millions board ft | Nov. | 3,470 | r4,034 | 3,480 |
| New housing starts, thousands units | Jan. | 1,377 | r1,404 | 1,816 |

a-1982-1984 equals 100. b-1982 equals 100.
e-Estimate. p-Preliminary. r-Revised.

Source: Reprinted by courtesy of *Barron's National Business and Financial Weekly*, March 14, 1988.

and other reports. Excellent current summaries and discussions of economic conditions are available in *Business Week* and, biweekly, in *Fortune.*

### Survey of Current Business
Issued monthly by the Department of Commerce, this publication is among the best sources of information about the gross national product, production, labor statistics, interest rates, foreign trade, and general economic developments.

### Federal Reserve Bulletin
This monthly publication covers monetary aggregates, interest rates, credit conditions, Federal Reserve open market transactions, member bank reserves, and international finance.

### Business Conditions Digest
This monthly publication of the Department of Commerce contains charts and tables on the economic time series, including leading, coincident, and lagging indicators.

### Economic Indicators
A compact monthly publication prepared by the Council of Economic Advisors with a wide variety of data on spending, income, industrial and agricultural output, money supply, interest rates, trade, and related matters.

### Economic Report of the President
This report is prepared each January by the Office of the President for transmission to Congress. It contains a detailed discussion of developments during the previous year with extensive statistical tables.

### Monthly Labor Review
A Department of Labor publication with statistics on employment, unemployment, earnings, prices, and cost of living indexes.

For historical background material, the following may be helpful:

*Statistical Abstracts of the United States*
This Department of Commerce annual volume serves as a convenient statistical reference to a wide range of data. The end of the book also contains a number of references to sources of statistical information.

*Daily Report for Executives* (Bureau of National Affairs, Inc., Washington, DC)
An excellent daily series of reports on Washington and economic news that affects all aspects of business operations.

## INDUSTRY FINANCIAL RATIOS AND PERFORMANCE DATA

Financial ratios of companies of comparable size in the same industry are often used for evaluation analysis. Among the quantities commonly used for this purpose are company and industry price-earnings, price-sales, and price–book value ratios. (Ratio comparison techniques are discussed in Chapter 6.) Financial ratios for various industries can be found in the following:

L. Troy, *Almanac of Business and Industrial Financial Ratios* (Prentice-Hall, Englewood Cliffs, NJ)
(See Figure 2–4.)

*Annual Statement Studies* (Robert Morris Associates, Philadelphia, PA)
This an annual publication contains operation and financial ratios for over 345 lines of business. (See Figure 2–5).

# Figure 2-4.

## 2298 MANUFACTURING: TEXTILE MILL PRODUCTS:
## Other textile mill products

| Item Description For Accounting Period 7/83 Through 6/84 | A Total | B Zero Assets | C Under 100 | D 100 to 250 | E 250 to 500 | F 500 to 1,000 | G 1000 to 5,000 | H 5,000 to 10,000 | I 10,000 to 25,000 | J 25,000 to 50,000 | K 50,000 to 100,000 | L 100,000 to 250,000 | M 250,000 and over |
|---|---|---|---|---|---|---|---|---|---|---|---|---|---|
| | | | | | | SIZE OF ASSETS IN THOUSANDS OF DOLLARS (000 OMITTED) | | | | | | | |
| 1. Number of Enterprises | 2210 | 17 | 539 | 257 | 405 | 257 | 444 | 131 | 97 | 28 | 19 | 10 | 6 |
| 2. Total receipts (in millions of dollars) | 20934.7 | 197.5 | 159.1 | 83.6 | 351.4 | 594.6 | 2635.5 | 2211.6 | 2790.1 | 1938.1 | 2407.5 | 2405.1 | 5160.6 |
| **Selected Operating Factors in Percent of Net Sales** | | | | | | | | | | | | | |
| 3. Cost of operations | 76.4 | 86.7 | 80.3 | 62.1 | 78.3 | 77.6 | 78.9 | 77.2 | 78.5 | 75.3 | 72.7 | 76.8 | 75.2 |
| 4. Compensation of officers | 1.4 | 2.3 | 0.4 | 2.9 | 3.1 | 4.6 | 3.6 | 1.7 | 1.5 | 0.9 | 1.0 | 0.6 | 0.4 |
| 5. Repairs | 0.5 | - | 0.7 | 3.0 | 0.6 | - | 0.3 | 0.2 | 0.2 | 0.6 | 0.7 | 1.0 | 0.5 |
| 6. Bad debts | 0.2 | 1.2 | 1.6 | 0.2 | 0.1 | 0.1 | 0.2 | 0.2 | 0.3 | 0.2 | 0.2 | 0.3 | 0.1 |
| 7. Rent on business property | 0.8 | 0.3 | 2.0 | 3.2 | 1.3 | 1.2 | 0.6 | 0.6 | 0.6 | 0.5 | 0.6 | 0.6 | 1.4 |
| 8. Taxes (excl Federal tax) | 2.2 | 1.4 | 1.3 | 6.6 | 2.4 | 1.9 | 1.7 | 1.8 | 1.8 | 1.9 | 2.1 | 2.0 | 3.1 |
| 9. Interest | 2.3 | 3.2 | 4.1 | 0.3 | 0.8 | 1.0 | 1.3 | 2.0 | 1.9 | 1.3 | 1.7 | 2.7 | 3.7 |
| 10. Deprec/Deplet/Amortiz† | 3.4 | 2.9 | 1.2 | 6.6 | 1.5 | 1.2 | 2.0 | 2.5 | 2.5 | 2.5 | 3.4 | 3.5 | 5.6 |
| 11. Advertising | 0.6 | 0.1 | - | 0.1 | 0.5 | 0.3 | 0.2 | 0.4 | 0.4 | 0.9 | 0.5 | 0.7 | 1.1 |
| 12. Pensions & other benef plans | 1.2 | 0.7 | 0.7 | 0.3 | 0.8 | 0.8 | 1.1 | 1.0 | 1.2 | 1.2 | 1.0 | 0.9 | 1.7 |
| 13. Other expenses | 9.7 | 8.8 | 20.7 | 6.2 | 11.3 | 9.6 | 8.9 | 9.4 | 9.2 | 10.6 | 12.3 | 8.1 | 9.2 |
| 14. Net profit before tax | 1.3 | * | * | 8.5 | * | 1.7 | 1.2 | 3.0 | 1.9 | 4.1 | 3.8 | 2.8 | * |
| **Selected Financial Ratios (number of times ratio is to one)** | | | | | | | | | | | | | |
| 15. Current ratio | 1.7 | - | - | 2.3 | 2.1 | 1.6 | 1.6 | 2.0 | 2.0 | 2.2 | 2.4 | 1.6 | 1.3 |
| 16. Quick ratio | 0.9 | - | - | 1.8 | 1.0 | 1.0 | 0.8 | 0.9 | 1.0 | 1.1 | 1.1 | 0.7 | 0.7 |
| 17. Net sls to net wkg capital | 7.9 | - | - | 7.1 | 6.0 | 10.8 | 11.2 | 6.7 | 5.6 | 5.7 | 5.1 | 8.6 | 13.6 |
| 18. Coverage Ratio | 2.4 | - | - | - | 0.7 | 3.4 | 2.9 | 3.0 | 2.6 | 4.9 | 4.6 | 2.6 | 1.6 |
| 19. Asset turnover | 1.6 | - | - | 2.1 | 2.1 | - | - | 2.2 | 1.9 | 2.0 | 1.7 | 1.6 | 0.9 |
| 20. Total liab to net worth | 1.1 | - | - | 0.8 | 1.4 | 1.6 | 1.6 | 1.4 | 1.2 | 1.0 | 1.0 | 1.6 | 0.9 |
| **Selected Financial Factors in Percentages** | | | | | | | | | | | | | |
| 21. Debt Ratio | 53.3 | - | - | 43.4 | 58.7 | 60.9 | 62.1 | 58.8 | 54.8 | 50.0 | 50.3 | 62.1 | 48.2 |
| 22. Return on assets | 5.0 | - | - | 17.6 | - | 7.3 | 6.7 | 8.5 | 5.8 | 10.1 | 10.6 | 6.6 | 1.9 |
| 23. Return on equity | 5.8 | - | - | 23.8 | - | 14.9 | 11.6 | 12.4 | 6.2 | 12.2 | 11.7 | 10.0 | 1.8 |
| 24. Retained earn to net inc | 61.2 | - | - | 100.0 | 100.0 | 100.0 | 86.2 | 80.9 | 84.6 | 88.2 | 72.9 | 83.8 | - |

†Depreciation largest factor

Source: Leo Troy, Ph.D., *Almanac of Business and Industrial Financial Ratios* (Prentice-Hall, Inc., Englewood Cliffs, NJ, 1987).

# Figure 2-5.

**RETAILERS - HOUSEHOLD APPLIANCES** SIC# 5722

| Current Data | | | | | Type of Statement | Comparative Historical Data | | | | |
|---|---|---|---|---|---|---|---|---|---|---|
| 8 | 8 | 7 | 1 | 24 | Unqualified | | | 25 | 17 | 24 |
|  | 1 |  |  | 1 | Qualified | | |  | 2 | 1 |
| 11 | 13 | 1 |  | 25 | Reviewed | DATA NOT | AVAILABLE | 34 | 34 | 25 |
| 57 | 17 | 2 |  | 76 | Compiled | | | 64 | 63 | 76 |
| 13 | 3 | 3 |  | 19 | Other | | | 21 | 34 | 19 |
| 76(6/30-9/30/86) | | | 69(10/1/86-3/31/87) | | | | | 34 | | 19 |

| 0-1MM | 1-10MM | 10-50MM | 50-100MM | ALL | | 6/30/82-3/31/83 | 6/30/83-3/31/84 | 6/30/84-3/31/85 | 6/30/85-3/31/86 | 6/30/86-3/31/87 |
|---|---|---|---|---|---|---|---|---|---|---|
| 89 | 42 | 13 | 1 | 145 | NUMBER OF STATEMENTS | ALL 130 | ALL 133 | ALL 144 | ALL 150 | ALL 145 |
| % | % | % | % | % | **ASSETS** | % | % | % | % | % |
| 9.6 | 7.4 | 11.5 | | 9.1 | Cash & Equivalents | 8.8 | 8.4 | 9.8 | 9.3 | 9.1 |
| 16.0 | 26.1 | 17.9 | | 19.0 | Trade Receivables - (net) | 17.5 | 17.5 | 18.8 | 16.4 | 19.0 |
| 48.2 | 47.0 | 42.8 | | 47.5 | Inventory | 51.7 | 49.8 | 50.0 | 52.3 | 47.5 |
| 2.0 | 1.6 | 2.2 | | 1.9 | All Other Current | 1.9 | 2.0 | 1.3 | 1.7 | 1.9 |
| 75.7 | 82.1 | 74.4 | | 77.5 | Total Current | 79.9 | 77.6 | 79.9 | 79.7 | 77.5 |
| 15.0 | 11.2 | 16.5 | | 14.1 | Fixed Assets (net) | 14.6 | 16.2 | 14.7 | 13.9 | 14.1 |
| .5 | .9 | .6 | | .6 | Intangibles (net) | .5 | .8 | .4 | .6 | .6 |
| 8.8 | 5.7 | 8.5 | | 7.8 | All Other Non-Current | 5.0 | 5.5 | 5.0 | 5.9 | 7.8 |
| 100.0 | 100.0 | 100.0 | | 100.0 | Total | 100.0 | 100.0 | 100.0 | 100.0 | 100.0 |
| | | | | | **LIABILITIES** | | | | | |
| 18.9 | 16.6 | 7.6 | | 17.1 | Notes Payable-Short Term | 16.3 | 15.8 | 17.0 | 19.7 | 17.1 |
| 3.4 | 2.5 | 1.2 | | 3.0 | Cur. Mat.-L/T/D | 3.9 | 3.7 | 2.3 | 2.9 | 3.0 |
| 20.6 | 28.9 | 22.2 | | 23.3 | Trade Payables | 25.9 | 24.9 | 23.7 | 22.8 | 23.3 |
| .5 | .6 | .9 | | .6 | Income Taxes Payable | – | – | .9 | .8 | .6 |
| 8.3 | 10.4 | 8.0 | | 9.0 | All Other Current | 9.4 | 10.6 | 11.7 | 9.7 | 9.0 |
| 51.6 | 58.9 | 39.9 | | 53.0 | Total Current | 55.5 | 55.0 | 55.7 | 55.9 | 53.0 |
| 9.9 | 8.9 | 11.2 | | 9.7 | Long Term Debt | 10.8 | 11.5 | 11.5 | 10.1 | 9.7 |
| .3 | .3 | 2.3 | | .5 | Deferred Taxes | – | – | .3 | .2 | .5 |
| 3.3 | 2.3 | 2.9 | | 3.0 | All Other Non-Current | 2.5 | 3.2 | 2.5 | 1.9 | 3.0 |
| 34.9 | 29.5 | 43.8 | | 33.9 | Net Worth | 31.2 | 30.3 | 30.0 | 31.9 | 33.9 |
| 100.0 | 100.0 | 100.0 | | 100.0 | Total Liabilities & Net Worth | 100.0 | 100.0 | 100.0 | 100.0 | 100.0 |
| | | | | | **INCOME DATA** | | | | | |
| 100.0 | 100.0 | 100.0 | | 100.0 | Net Sales | 100.0 | 100.0 | 100.0 | 100.0 | 100.0 |
| 33.2 | 25.8 | 31.1 | | 30.8 | Gross Profit | 29.3 | 28.4 | 28.4 | 29.3 | 30.8 |
| 30.6 | 23.6 | 27.4 | | 28.2 | Operating Expenses | 27.1 | 26.3 | 25.1 | 25.7 | 28.2 |
| 2.6 | 2.2 | 3.7 | | 2.6 | Operating Profit | 2.2 | 2.1 | 3.4 | 3.6 | 2.6 |
| .5 | .3 | .4 | | .4 | All Other Expenses (net) | .2 | -.2 | .4 | .4 | .4 |
| 2.1 | 1.9 | 3.4 | | 2.2 | Profit Before Taxes | 2.0 | 2.4 | 3.0 | 3.2 | 2.2 |
| | | | | | **RATIOS** | | | | | |
| 2.1 | 1.9 | 4.5 | | 2.1 | Current | 1.9 | 2.0 | 2.0 | 1.9 | 2.1 |
| 1.4 | 1.3 | 1.8 | | 1.4 | | 1.4 | 1.4 | 1.5 | 1.4 | 1.4 |
| 1.2 | 1.2 | 1.2 | | 1.2 | | 1.1 | 1.1 | 1.1 | 1.1 | 1.2 |
| .9 | 1.0 | 2.6 | | .9 | Quick | .8 | .8 | .9 | .8 | .9 |
| .5 | .5 | .6 | | .5 | | .4 | .5 | .5 (149) | .4 | .5 |
| .2 | .3 | .3 | | .3 | | .2 | .2 | .2 | .2 | .3 |
| 6 60.3 | 15 24.6 | 4 102.5 | | 7 50.3 | Sales/Receivables | 8 45.3 | 9 42.4 | 8 43.3 | 7 51.4 | 7 50.7 |
| 14 26.3 | 25 14.5 | 16 23.3 | | 18 20.8 | | 16 23.2 | 18 19.9 | 17 21.3 | 16 23.3 | 18 20.8 |
| 29 12.5 | 54 6.7 | 76 4.8 | | 39 9.4 | | 34 10.8 | 33 10.9 | 37 9.8 | 30 12.0 | 39 9.4 |
| 52 7.0 | 52 7.0 | 79 4.6 | | 54 6.7 | Cost of Sales/Inventory | 68 5.4 | 63 5.8 | 54 6.7 | 56 6.5 | 54 6.7 |
| 91 4.0 | 74 4.9 | 91 4.0 | | 83 4.4 | | 94 3.9 | 96 3.8 | 83 4.4 | 87 4.2 | 83 4.4 |
| 130 2.8 | 104 3.5 | 130 2.8 | | 130 2.8 | | 130 2.8 | 135 2.7 | 118 3.1 | 122 3.0 | 130 2.8 |
| 7 50.7 | 26 13.8 | 28 13.1 | | 13 29.0 | Cost of Sales/Payables | 14 25.6 | 18 20.6 | 16 23.0 | 12 29.5 | 13 29.0 |
| 26 13.8 | 45 8.1 | 54 6.7 | | 36 10.2 | | 41 8.8 | 42 8.6 | 34 10.6 | 29 12.6 | 36 10.2 |
| 63 5.8 | 73 5.0 | 73 5.0 | | 68 5.4 | | 65 5.6 | 69 5.3 | 64 5.7 | 58 6.3 | 68 5.4 |
| 7.5 | 8.0 | 2.1 | | 7.5 | Sales/Working Capital | 6.8 | 5.7 | 6.6 | 7.2 | 7.5 |
| 13.7 | 18.0 | 9.0 | | 13.9 | | 11.8 | 13.4 | 11.8 | 14.5 | 13.9 |
| 33.0 | 31.2 | 71.3 | | 32.4 | | 46.9 | 40.1 | 27.0 | 34.9 | 32.4 |
| 5.3 | 7.4 | 9.2 | | 7.2 | EBIT/Interest | 3.9 | 5.4 | 6.6 | 8.2 | 7.2 |
| (79) 2.1 | (39) 3.1 | (11) 3.4 | | (130) 2.5 | | (115) 1.8 | (116) 2.9 | (123) 3.2 | (134) 3.3 | (130) 2.5 |
| 1.2 | 1.2 | 2.2 | | 1.2 | | .8 | 1.4 | 1.5 | 1.5 | 1.2 |
| 11.8 | 7.6 | | | 9.9 | Net Profit + Depr., Dep., Amort./Cur. Mat. L/T/D | 6.3 | 7.7 | 11.8 | 7.9 | 9.9 |
| (30) 2.2 | (25) 4.2 | | | (65) 3.2 | | (46) 1.4 | (57) 2.3 | (54) 3.8 | (58) 2.4 | (65) 3.2 |
| 1.1 | .5 | | | .8 | | .4 | 1.1 | 1.3 | 1.1 | .8 |
| .1 | .2 | .1 | | .2 | Fixed/Worth | .2 | .2 | .2 | .2 | .2 |
| .3 | .3 | .5 | | .3 | | .4 | .4 | .4 | .4 | .3 |
| .7 | .7 | .8 | | .7 | | 1.0 | 1.1 | 1.0 | .8 | .7 |
| 1.0 | 1.6 | .7 | | 1.0 | Debt/Worth | 1.1 | 1.2 | 1.2 | 1.2 | 1.0 |
| 2.0 | 3.2 | 1.7 | | 2.2 | | 2.5 | 2.3 | 2.3 | 2.8 | 2.2 |
| 4.8 | 5.0 | 2.5 | | 4.8 | | 9.0 | 6.4 | 5.8 | 6.1 | 4.8 |
| 36.8 | 41.8 | 36.1 | | 37.3 | % Profit Before Taxes/Tangible Net Worth | 35.7 | 43.7 | 55.4 | 48.2 | 37.3 |
| (85) 14.5 | (41) 17.3 | 21.6 | | (140) 17.5 | | (122) 11.4 | (121) 20.0 | (135) 21.6 | (139) 25.2 | (140) 17.5 |
| 1.7 | 4.0 | 3.2 | | 3.2 | | -1.5 | 7.5 | 9.7 | 8.0 | 3.2 |
| 9.7 | 10.2 | 15.2 | | 10.0 | % Profit Before Taxes/Total Assets | 9.4 | 11.2 | 12.6 | 14.7 | 10.0 |
| 4.5 | 5.2 | 4.6 | | 4.8 | | 3.1 | 6.2 | 6.8 | 6.3 | 4.8 |
| .7 | .5 | 1.5 | | .7 | | -1.5 | 1.9 | 2.4 | 1.9 | .7 |
| 67.1 | 62.0 | 26.3 | | 61.7 | Sales/Net Fixed Assets | 79.8 | 58.8 | 56.0 | 81.1 | 61.7 |
| 43.2 | 38.0 | 15.8 | | 38.4 | | 34.0 | 30.3 | 29.9 | 41.0 | 38.4 |
| 15.7 | 16.2 | 9.7 | | 14.3 | | 12.2 | 11.3 | 13.7 | 16.1 | 14.3 |
| 3.8 | 3.9 | 2.9 | | 3.7 | Sales/Total Assets | 3.6 | 3.4 | 3.7 | 3.9 | 3.7 |
| 3.0 | 3.1 | 2.3 | | 2.9 | | 2.9 | 2.7 | 2.9 | 3.0 | 2.9 |
| 2.2 | 2.4 | 1.1 | | 2.2 | | 2.1 | 2.1 | 2.3 | 2.3 | 2.2 |
| .7 | .6 | .5 | | .6 | % Depr., Dep., Amort./Sales | .5 | .5 | .5 | .5 | .6 |
| (75) 1.0 | (40) .9 | (12) 1.2 | | (128) 1.0 | | (118) .9 | (114) .9 | (133) 1.0 | (135) .9 | (128) 1.0 |
| 1.9 | 1.1 | 1.6 | | 1.5 | | 1.3 | 1.4 | 1.5 | 1.3 | 1.5 |
| 2.2 | 1.9 | | | 2.2 | % Officers' Comp/Sales | 2.3 | 1.7 | 2.0 | 1.6 | 2.2 |
| (49) 4.5 | (11) 2.3 | | | (64) 3.7 | | (70) 3.6 | (67) 3.2 | (67) 4.2 | (71) 3.7 | (64) 3.7 |
| 6.7 | 3.7 | | | 6.1 | | 6.1 | 6.1 | | | 6.1 |
| 122077M | 309957M | 639001M | 103786M | 1174821M | Net Sales ($) | 862862M | 891570M | 1488053M | 984125M | 1174821M |
| 40089M | 99985M | 289010M | 57273M | 486357M | Total Assets ($) | 311457M | 356613M | 529478M | 342208M | 486357M |

M = $thousand   MM = $million

*Interpretation of Statement Studies Figures:* RMA cautions that the studies be regarded only as a general guideline and not as an absolute industry norm. This is due to limited samples within categories, the categorization of companies by their primary Standard Industrial Classification (SIC) number only, and different methods of operations by companies within the same industry. For these reasons, RMA recommends that the figures be used only as general guidelines in addition to other methods of financial analysis.

Source: Reprinted with permission. Copyright 1987 Robert Morris Associates.

*Quarterly Financial Reports for Manufacturing, Mining and Trade Corporations* (U.S. Bureau of the Census, Washington, DC)

This quarterly contains balance sheets, income statements, and selected ratios.

*Media General IndustriScope* (Media General Financial Services, Richmond, VA)

This monthly tabloid provides financial ratios and stock market data on over 3,000 publicly traded companies grouped by industry (see Figure 2–6). This same publisher also issues the *Media General Financial Weekly,* which provides current industry and market data.

## ONLINE DATABASES

Of the many database vendors, two are of particular value for the purposes of acquisition planning and analysis: *DIALOG* and Dow Jones News Retrieval. Most needed information can be found in the many databases offered by these two vendors. A general description of these vendors is given here and a more detailed listing is provided in the appendixes to this chapter.

*DIALOG* is the largest vendor of databases, with 280 currently listed and more added each year. *DIALOG* also provides a number of useful services. For those who have no idea which databases to search, *DIALOG* provides a special database, *Dialindex,* which is helpful in selecting the best databases for the information needed. Another feature, *OneSearch,* permits searching up to 20 databases at the same time. These features can be used together. Once the appropriate databases have been identified through *Dialindex,* these can be simultaneously searched via *OneSearch* with a substantial savings in time.

A particularly valuable database available through *DIALOG* and other vendors is the *PTS PROMT* file. This file, used for industry, company, and product research, includes:

- Market Size/Shares/Trends
- Capital Expenditures/R&D/New Plants
- Mergers and Acquisitions

# Figure 2-6.

## Stocks by Industry -- Price and Volume

### January 29, 1988

| Company and Market | Price Change Trading Mo % | 3 Mo % | 6 Mo % | 12 Mo % | YTD % | vs S&P Trading Mo % | 3 Mo % | 6 Mo % | 12 Mo % | YTD % | Last Close $ | 52-Wk High $ | 52-Wk Low $ | 5-Yr High $ | 5-Yr Low $ | P/E Curr | P/E 5-Yr Hi | P/E 5-Yr Lo | % Of Market | Price to Common Equity | % Of Mkt Norm | % Of Ind Norm | Beta Up | Beta Down | Vol Shares 000 | Dollars $Mil | %Shrs Outstg | Liq Ratio $000 | On Bal Index |
|---|---|---|---|---|---|---|---|---|---|---|---|---|---|---|---|---|---|---|---|---|---|---|---|---|---|---|---|---|---|
| **241 Sport Vehicles** | | | | | | | | | | | | | | | | | | | | | | | | | | | | | |
| Ind Group | 2.6 | 8.3 | -34.4 | -31.1 | 2.6 | 99 | 94 | 83 | 74 | 99 | 9.03 | 16.34 | 6.82 | 11.04 | 2.79 | 10.6 | 23.7 | 10.3 | 129 | 183 | 75 | 94 | .61 | 1.04 | 1,732 | 17.5 | 1.91 | 87 | 32 |
| Coachmen Ind — N | -1.8 | -21.4 | -38.9 | -52.2 | -1.8 | 94 | 76 | 76 | 51 | 94 | 6.88 | 14.88 | 6.63 | 39.63 | 6.63 | 40.4 | 30.9 | 12.0 | 126 | 66 | 92 | 104 | .03 | 1.47 | 206 | 1.5 | 2.60 | 34 | 42 |
| DeTomaso Ind — N | 9.5 | 15.0 | -52.1 | -56.6 | 9.5 | 105 | 113 | 59 | 46 | 105 | 5.75 | 16.75 | 4.00 | 25.00 | 5.75 | 1.5 | NC | NC | NC | 72 | 0 | 0 | .03 | 1.08 | 19 | .1 | .92 | 1 | 15 |
| E B Marine Inc — O | .0 | -19.4 | -16.7 | -26.5 | .0 | 96 | 78 | 78 | 78 | 96 | 6.25 | 12.00 | 5.75 | NC | NC | NE | NC | NC | NC | 118 | 0 | 0 | -.15 | .45 | 44 | .3 | 2.21 | 4 | 4 |
| ElDorado Motor — O | .0 | -6.7 | -50.0 | -63.2 | .0 | 96 | 91 | 63 | 39 | 96 | 1.75 | 5.00 | 1.50 | 5.75 | NC | NE | NC | NC | NC | 81 | 0 | 0 | .60 | 1.48* | 30 | .0 | 1.13 | 1 | 25 |
| Genmar Ind — O | 10.6 | 65.9 | -27.7 | -19.8 | 10.6 | 106 | 162 | 90 | 86 | 106 | 9.13 | 13.75 | 5.38 | 13.75 | NC | 8.2 | NC | NC | NC | 232 | 0 | 0 | .39 | .59 | 355 | 3.0 | 1.21 | 110 | 16 |
| Harley David — N | -5.8 | -19.0 | 47.9 | 18.1 | -5.8 | 90 | 78 | 65 | 127 | 90 | 12.25 | 26.50 | 9.25 | NC | NC | 5.3 | NC | NC | NC | 323 | NA | NA | 1.54 | 1.30 | 377 | 5.0 | 5.46 | 111 | 24 |
| Kit Mfg — A | .0 | 12.5 | -25.0 | -4.5 | .0 | 96 | 110 | 94 | 102 | 96 | 7.88 | 11.25 | 5.88 | 12.25 | 3.50 | 6.3 | 16.8 | 9.6 | 77 | 155 | NA | NA | 1.11 | 1.01 | 10 | .1 | .68 | 4 | 18 |
| Polaris Ind — A | 1.6 | -3.7 | NC | NC | 1.6 | 97 | 94 | NC | 69 | 97 | 16.25 | 21.75 | 14.13 | 21.75 | NC | 6.3 | NA | NA | NA | 63 | NA | NA | NC | | 205 | 3.5 | 3.28 | 84 | 54 |
| Thor Inds — N | -2.2 | -17.0 | -48.8 | -35.8 | -2.2 | 93 | 81 | 64 | 69 | 93 | 11.00 | 24.13 | 10.00 | NC | NC | 7.6 | NC | NC | NC | 228 | 0 | 0 | .94 | 1.58 | 75 | .8 | 1.49 | 21 | 80 |
| Westerbeke Cp — N | .0 | 8.3 | -59.4 | -65.8 | .0 | 96 | 106 | 50 | 37 | 96 | 1.63 | 5.25 | .88 | 5.25 | NC | NE | NC | NC | NC | 99 | 0 | 0 | .06 | .80* | 18 | .0 | 1.40 | 0 | 7 |
| Winnebago Ind — N | .0 | 3.1 | -27.5 | -41.1 | .0 | 96 | 101 | 90 | 62 | 96 | 8.25 | 15.88 | 7.00 | 23.88 | 7.00 | 14.0 | 25.7 | 11.3 | 109 | 135 | 70 | 91 | .93 | 1.76 | 393 | 3.2 | 1.53 | 83 | 27 |
| **243 Photo Equipment, Supplies** | | | | | | | | | | | | | | | | | | | | | | | | | | | | | |
| Ind Group | -6.5 | -6.3 | -17.4 | -2.4 | -6.5 | 90 | 92 | 92 | 104 | 90 | 36.68 | 52.34 | 28.23 | 52.92 | 15.82 | 22.0 | 30.1 | 18.1 | 183 | 244 | 2 | 137 | 1.33 | 1.13 | 58,588 | 2161.1 | 7.36 | 27,839 | 116 |
| Authenticolor — O | -14.3 | .0 | .0 | .0 | -14.3 | 82 | 98 | 115 | 108 | 82 | 1.50 | 1.88 | 1.25 | 2.13 | 1.00 | NE | NM | NM | 43 | 64 | 0 | 0 | .60* | .38* | 3 | .0 | .50 | 0 | 0 |
| Bell & Howell — □ | 1.7 | 18.0 | 7.5 | 47.7 | 1.7 | 97 | 115 | 134 | 158 | 97 | 60.75 | 75.25 | 40.75 | 75.25 | 12.81 | 27.1 | 16.0 | 8.8 | 51 | 210 | 149 | 113 | .55* | .37 | 602 | 36.4 | 6.42 | 4,867 | 30 |
| Berkey Photo — O | 28.6 | 38.6 | -38.6 | -32.5 | 28.6 | 123 | 106 | 76 | 72 | 123 | 3.38 | 7.13 | 2.13 | 9.00 | 2.13 | NE | 50.3 | 21.4 | 324 | 59 | 0 | 0 | .93 | .73 | 266 | .8 | 5.70 | 11 | 84 |
| Eastman Kodak — ◇★N | -11.2 | -22.0 | -30.5 | -16.1 | -11.2 | 85 | 76 | 86 | 89 | 85 | 43.50 | 70.69 | 41.94 | 70.69 | 26.81 | 14.5 | 32.3 | 21.4 | 111 | 231 | 128 | 126 | 1.93 | 1.27 | 38,424 | 1807.1 | 11.34 | 32,714 | 115 |
| Fuji Photo Film — O | -3.3 | 20.3 | 11.8 | 37.9 | -3.3 | 92 | 118 | 139 | 147 | 92 | 61.38 | 67.63 | 33.00 | 67.63 | 11.75 | 57.9 | 33.3 | 16.4 | 103 | 324 | 194 | 160 | .84* | .95 | 347 | 21.9 | .19 | 950 | 71 |
| Horizons Research — O | 20.0 | .0 | .0 | 17.6 | 20.0 | 115 | 98 | 126 | 126 | 115 | 3.75 | 4.00 | 2.13 | 6.13 | 1.50 | 41.7 | 19.7 | 10.4 | 62 | 114 | 71 | 97 | .61 | .85* | 4 | .1 | .39 | 0 | 86 |
| Innovex Inc — O | 20.0 | -28.0 | -59.1 | -64.0 | 20.0 | 115 | 71 | 50 | 39 | 115 | 4.50 | 14.25 | 3.50 | 14.25 | 3.19 | 14.5 | 10.5 | 3.0 | 52 | 123 | 0 | 0 | .41 | 2.34* | 398 | 1.8 | 9.30 | 28 | 112 |
| Keystone Cam — A | 27.3 | -41.7 | -68.2 | -74.1 | 27.3 | 122 | 57 | 39 | 27 | 122 | 1.75 | 9.00 | .75 | 26.25 | .75 | NE | NM | NM | 28 | 63 | 0 | 0 | 1.10 | 1.70* | 81 | .1 | 1.35 | 1 | 16 |
| Nashua Corp — N | 1.4 | 2.8 | -23.0 | -.9 | 1.4 | 97 | 120 | 95 | 108 | 97 | 27.13 | 40.38 | 21.25 | 40.38 | 4.94 | 11.2 | 42.7 | 24.6 | 50 | 150 | 0 | 0 | .41 | 1.80 | 397 | 11.0 | 4.12 | 425 | 58 |
| Nimslo Intl Ltd — O | 33.3 | 60.0 | 166.7 | NC | 33.3 | 128 | 157 | 286 | | 128 | .25 | .28 | .09 | 2.03 | .06 | NE | NM | NM | NC | 4563 | 0 | 0 | -.20 | -2.10 | 798 | .2 | .73 | 3 | 81 |
| Photo Control — O | -5.4 | -30.0 | .0 | .0 | -5.4 | 90 | 92 | 88 | 108 | 90 | 4.38 | 6.75 | 4.00 | 8.50 | 3.41 | 13.7 | 83.8 | NM | NM | 80 | 70 | 103 | .42 | 1.11* | 17 | .1 | 1.19 | 1 | 33 |
| Polaroid Corp — ★N | 13.2 | 15.1 | -19.5 | -32.7 | 13.2 | 109 | 101 | 100 | 72 | 109 | 26.75 | 42.75 | 16.50 | 42.75 | 12.13 | 14.4 | 24.6 | NM | 139 | 167 | 104 | 91 | 1.14 | 1.25 | 8,706 | 216.2 | 14.06 | 3,643 | 107 |
| Realist Inc — O | 6.9 | 3.3 | -20.5 | 14.8 | 6.9 | 102 | 101 | 99 | 123 | 102 | 7.75 | 10.75 | 6.00 | 11.25 | 6.00 | 9.5 | NM | NM | NM | 68 | 0 | 0 | .65 | .45 | 14 | .1 | 2.27 | 8 | 96 |
| Seal Inc — O | 4.1 | 22.6 | -36.7 | 24.6 | 4.1 | 100 | 120 | 79 | 133 | 100 | 9.50 | 16.50 | 6.00 | 16.50 | 2.00 | 8.1 | 20.3 | 7.3 | 57 | 341 | 0 | 0 | 1.58 | .37 | 53 | .5 | 2.42 | 10 | 41 |
| Southwall Tech — O | 5.0 | -4.5 | -33.3 | NC | 5.0 | 101 | 93 | 58 | NC | 101 | 5.25 | 12.00 | 4.25 | 12.00 | NC | 40.4 | NM | NM | NC | 64 | 0 | 0 | NC | NC | 251 | .1 | 11.67 | 18 | 49 |
| Sterndig Inds — O | 3.7 | -26.3 | -37.8 | -45.1 | 3.7 | 99 | 72 | 78 | 58 | 99 | 7.00 | 13.75 | 6.00 | 14.59 | 1.41 | 17.5 | 11.8 | 5.0 | 36 | 91 | 75 | 35 | .38 | 1.01 | 10 | .1 | .68 | 4 | 6 |
| Stocker & Yale — O | 5.4 | -13.2 | -28.0 | -43.3 | 5.4 | 101 | 84 | 89 | 60 | 101 | 7.38 | 13.75 | 6.75 | 17.38 | 3.19 | 14.5 | 10.9 | 5.5 | 34 | 147 | 0 | 107 | -.36 | .88 | 16 | .1 | .59 | 0 | 24 |
| View-Master Ideal — O | 27.1 | 15.1 | -31.5 | -53.3 | 27.1 | 122 | 113 | 85 | 49 | 122 | 7.63 | 19.00 | 4.25 | 19.00 | 3.78 | NE | NM | NM | NC | 152 | 0 | 0 | .66 | 1.40 | 2,991 | 26.1 | 64.25 | 253 | 582 |
| WR Cp — O | 1.4 | -5.3 | -34.9 | -7.8 | 1.4 | 97 | 92 | 81 | 99 | 97 | 17.75 | 28.00 | 17.38 | 28.00 | NC | 12.0 | NC | NC | NC | 151 | 0 | 0 | 1.42 | .61 | 172 | 3.2 | 3.08 | 78 | 76 |
| X Rite — O | 16.1 | 33.3 | 28.6 | 42.6 | 16.1 | 112 | 130 | 160 | 153 | 112 | 18.00 | 18.75 | 10.63 | 18.75 | NC | 17.0 | NC | NC | NC | 433 | 0 | 0 | .95 | 1.47 | 55 | .9 | 2.12 | 19 | 162 |
| Xidex Corp — O | -1.9 | -15.0 | -51.9 | -52.8 | -1.9 | 94 | 83 | 83 | 60 | 94 | 6.38 | 16.00 | 5.75 | 25.75 | 5.75 | NE | 26.3 | 13.2 | 82 | 88 | 0 | 0 | .95 | 1.47 | 4,983 | 33.2 | 12.01 | 716 | 36 |

## Figure 2-6 cont'd.

# Stocks by Industry -- Fundamental Data

**January 29, 1988**

| Company | Rev Last Qtr % | Rev FY to Date % | Rev Last 12 Mos % | Earn Last 12 Mos $Mil | Per Sh Last 12 Mos $ | Per Sh Last Qtr % | Pct Chg FY to Date % | Pct Chg Last 12 Mos % | 5-Yr Grth Rate % | Par Grth Rate % | Date of Report | Div Current Rate Amt $ | Yield % | Div 5-Yr Grth Rate % | Payout Last FY % | Payout Last 5 Yrs % | Last X-Dvd Date | Profit Margin | Asset Turn-over | Return Total Assets | Lever-Ratio | Return on Equity | Debt to Equity % | Curr-ent Ratio | Market Value $Mil | Latest Shares Out-stndg 000 | Held by Banks Funds 000 | Insider Net Trad-ing 000 | Short Int-erest Ratio Days | Fiscal Year Ends Mo |
|---|---|---|---|---|---|---|---|---|---|---|---|---|---|---|---|---|---|---|---|---|---|---|---|---|---|---|---|---|---|---|
| **Ind. Group** ********* | 34.8 | 40.5 | 24.7 | 79.1 | .86 | -1.6 | 41.5 | 38.3 | 22 | 11 | -- | 31 | 3.4 | 0 | 16 | 14 | -- | 3.3 | 1.79 | 5.9 | 3.00 | 17.7 | 81 | 1.9 | 819 | 90,685 | 14,010 | +0 | 3.8 | -- |
| *241 Sport Vehicles* | | | | | | | | | | | | | | | | | | | | | | | | | | | | | | |
| Coachmen Ind | 13.1 | 4.5 | 5.8 | 1.4n | .17 | -100.0 | -65.5 | -22.7 | -24 | -2 | 09-87 | .40 | 5.8 | 0 | 75 | 24 | 11-09-87 | 5.3 | .70 | 3.7 | 18.14 | 67.1 | 9 | 1.1 | 55 | 7,934 | 3,852 | 0 | 38.5 | 12 |
| DeTomaso Ind | .7 | -7.7 | -5.0 | 11.0n | 3.87 | NE | NE | NE | NC | 67 | 09-87 | .00 | | 0 | 0 | 0 | 00-00-00 | | 1.75 | | | | | | 12 | 2,057 | 57 | 0 | 0.0 | 12 |
| E B Marine Inc | 2.6 | 5.9 | 13.5 | -4.6n | -2.26 | -100.0 | -100.0 | -100.0 | NC | 44 | 09-87 | .00 | | 0 | 0 | 0 | 00-00-00 | -5.5 | 1.75 | -9.6 | 4.56 | -43.8 | 193 | 1.6 | 12 | 1,998 | 302 | 0 | 0.0 | 12 |
| ElDorado Motor | 15.5 | 15.5 | 13.0 | -.2n | -.08 | -50.0 | -50.0 | -100.0 | -4 | 09-87 | .00 | | 0 | 0 | 0 | 00-00-00 | -.3 | 2.67 | -.8 | 4.38 | -3.5 | 47 | 1.2 | 5 | 2,650 | 0 | 0 | 0.0 | 06 | |
| Gemmer Ind | 42.4 | 28.7 | 26.5 | 32.9n | 1.11 | 66.7 | 55.7 | 46.1 | NC | 20 | 11-05-87 | .32 | 3.5 | 0 | 0 | 0 | 11-05-87 | 7.9 | 1.81 | 14.3 | 1.99 | 28.4 | 64 | 4.4 | 269 | 29,432 | 1,766 | 0 | 0.0 | 12 |
| Harley David | 150.6 | 132.3 | 98.9 | 14.6n | 2.32 | NC | 254.2 | 110.9 | 56 | NC | 09-87 | .00 | | 0 | 0 | 0 | 00-00-00 | 2.5 | 1.80 | 4.5 | 12.38 | 55.7 | 731 | 1.9 | 85 | 6,910 | 2,340 | 0 | 0.0 | 12 |
| Kit Mfg | 32.9 | 29.7 | 28.3 | 1.8n | 1.25 | 33.3 | 52.4 | 52.4 | NC | NC | 10-87 | .00 | | 0 | 0 | 0 | 00-00-00 | 2.6 | 5.31 | 13.8 | 1.74 | 24.0 | 1 | 1.9 | 12 | 1,472 | 44 | 0 | 3.1 | 10 |
| Polaris Ind | NA | NA | NA | NA | NA | NA | NA | NA | NA | NA | 00-00 | .75 | 4.6 | NA | NA | NA | 12-09-87 | NA | NA | NA | NC | NA | NA | NA | 102 | 6,250 | 42 | 0 | NA | NA |
| Thor Inds | -4.8 | -4.8 | 14.7 | 7.3q | 1.44 | -5.6 | -5.6 | 18.0 | NC | 29 | 10-87 | .06 | .5 | 0 | 0 | 0 | 12-14-87 | 4.5 | 3.91 | 17.6 | 1.70 | 30.0 | 114 | 2.1 | 55 | 5,036 | 1,389 | 0 | 0.0 | 07 |
| Westrotek Co | 51.4 | 41.3 | 28.5 | -.4n | -.28 | -100.0 | -100.0 | NC | NC | -19 | 07-87 | .00 | | 0 | NA | NA | 00-00-00 | NA | 2.14 | -4.7 | 4.04 | -19.0 | 0 | 2.0 | 5 | 1,284 | 142 | 0 | 0.0 | 10 |
| Winnebago Ind | 8.3 | 8.3 | 6.7 | 15.3q | .59 | -100.0 | -100.0 | -30.6 | 10 | 3 | 11-87 | .40 | 4.8 | 0 | 38 | 23 | 11-30-87 | 3.7 | 1.78 | 6.6 | 1.48 | 9.8 | 1 | 2.3 | 212 | 25,672 | 4,076 | +0 | 0.2 | 08 |
| **Ind. Group** ********* | 13.8 | 16.6 | 17.2 | 1,523.7 | 1.57 | 12.3 | 114.2 | 198.3 | -1 | 6 | -- | 86 | 2.4 | 0 | 86 | 62 | -- | 6.7 | 1.00 | 6.7 | 1.90 | 12.7 | 13 | 1.8 | 29,214 | 796,355 | 255,330 | -21 | .4 | -- |
| *243 Photo Equipment, Supplies* | | | | | | | | | | | | | | | | | | | | | | | | | | | | | | |
| Authenticolor | 20.0 | 12.7 | 25.0 | .08 | -.03 | -33.3 | 15.4 | -100.0 | NC | 6 | 07-87 | .00 | | 0 | 0 | 0 | 00-00-00 | | 1.00 | NC | NC | .0 | 7 | 1.3 | 1 | 597 | | 0 | 0.0 | 01 |
| Bell & Howell | -12.1 | -14.9 | -7.6 | 23.9n | .32 | -15.6 | -36.8 | -28.7 | NC | 6 | 09-87 | .82 | 1.0 | 6 | 20 | 19 | 02-01-88 | 3.1 | 1.00 | 3.1 | 2.84 | 8.8 | 63 | 1.4 | 570 | 9,375 | 5,399 | 0 | 1.6 | 12 |
| Berkey Photo | -11.9 | -16.8 | -18.3 | -8.4n | -1.83 | NE | NE | NE | NC | -31 | 09-87 | .00 | | 0 | 0 | 0 | 00-00-00 | -5.7 | 1.60 | -9.1 | 3.43 | -31.2 | 48 | 1.3 | 16 | 4,665 | 660 | -9 | 0.8 | 12 |
| Eastman Kodak | 12.4 | 14.7 | 12.8 | 1010.6n | 2.99 | 51.3 | 211.2 | 83.4 | -10 | 6 | 09-87 | 1.80 | 4.1 | 2 | 157 | 88 | 11-24-87 | 7.9 | .99 | 7.8 | 2.03 | 15.8 | 14 | 1.5 | 14,742 | 338,907 | 172,790 | +3 | 1.5 | 12 |
| Fuji Photo Film | 28.4 | 28.4 | 28.4 | 393.5f | 1.06 | -61.2 | 19.1 | 19.1 | NC | 6 | 10-86 | .14 | .2 | 2 | 10 | 5 | 10-13-87 | 8.2 | .80 | 6.6 | 1.70 | 11.2 | 6 | | 11,387 | 185,538 | 148 | 0 | 0.0 | 10 |
| Horizons Research | .0 | -2.9 | .0 | .00 | .09 | -28.6 | -13.3 | -40.0 | -18 | 0 | 09-87 | .00 | | 0 | 0 | 0 | 09-87 | | .0 | .0 | NC | .0 | 15 | 2.5 | 4 | 1,034 | 38 | 0 | 0.0 | 12 |
| Innovex Inc | 52.4 | 12.6 | 16.6 | .1.3f | .31 | .0 | -35.4 | -35.4 | NC | -17 | 09-87 | .00 | | 0 | 0 | 0 | 03-24-86 | 6.2 | 1.33 | 6.8 | 1.22 | 8.3 | 1 | 4.6 | 19 | 4,278 | 727 | 0 | 0.0 | 09 |
| Keystone Cam | 44.9 | 60.1 | 68.7 | -2.8n | -.28 | NE | NE | NE | NC | NC | 09-87 | .00 | | 0 | 0 | 0 | 00-00-00 | -5.2 | .88 | -4.6 | 3.65 | -16.8 | 115 | 1.5 | 11 | 6,008 | 856 | 0 | 1.9 | 12 |
| Nashua Corp | 23.3 | 21.0 | 17.9 | 23.6n | 2.42 | 83.3 | 17.1 | 5.7 | 12 | 12 | 09-87 | .28 | 1.0 | 0 | 18 | 23 | 12-10-87 | 3.9 | 2.52 | 7.3 | 1.85 | 13.5 | 15 | 1.8 | 282 | 9,642 | 6,437 | 0 | 0.0 | 12 |
| Nimslo Intl Ltd | -94.0 | -94.3 | -93.9 | -.12f | -.01 | NC | NC | NE | NC | 12 | 12-86 | .00 | | 0 | 0 | 0 | 00-00-00 | -60.0 | | -12.1 | | NM | 1200 | .00 | 27 | 109,503 | 270 | 0 | 0.0 | 12 |
| Photo Control | 15.6 | 7.6 | 25.0 | .5n | .32 | NE | -11.1 | NC | -29 | 6 | 12-87 | .00 | | 0 | 0 | 0 | 00-00-00 | 3.8 | 1.15 | 3.8 | 1.49 | 6.4 | 32 | 3.0 | 6 | 1,427 | 29 | 0 | 0.0 | 06 |
| Polaroid Corp | 7.5 | 12.2 | 14.2 | 115.7n | 1.86 | .0 | 18.3 | 27.4 | 32 | 8 | 09-87 | .60 | 2.2 | 0 | 30 | 65 | 11-30-87 | 6.6 | 1.18 | 7.8 | 1.49 | 11.6 | 0 | 2.3 | 1,656 | 61,918 | 33,830 | 0 | 1.7 | 12 |
| Realist Inc | 12.9 | 14.0 | 16.6 | .5n | .82 | NE | NE | NE | NC | 7 | 07-87 | .05 | .6 | 0 | NE | NE | 10-29-87 | 3.6 | 1.60 | 7.1 | 1.42 | 7.1 | 20 | 5.4 | 5 | 618 | 109 | -14 | 0.0 | 12 |
| Seal Inc | 48.2 | 57.2 | 50.0 | 2.6n | 1.18 | 12.0 | 145.7 | 55.3 | 43 | 43 | 07-87 | .00 | | 0 | 0 | 0 | 02-08-88 | 8.7 | 1.30 | 11.3 | 3.77 | 42.6 | 138 | 1.4 | 21 | 2,188 | 96 | 0 | 0.0 | 10 |
| Southwell Tech | 26.7 | 21.1 | 27.2 | .7n | .13 | .0 | 22.2 | 22.2 | NC | 4 | 09-87 | .00 | | 0 | 0 | 0 | 00-00-00 | 5.0 | .66 | 3.3 | 1.21 | 4.0 | 10 | 6.0 | 11 | 2,151 | 1,089 | 0 | 0.0 | 12 |
| Stendig Inds | 14.8 | 14.8 | 27.5 | .5n | .40 | -65.4 | -65.4 | NE | NE | 7 | 10-87 | .00 | | 0 | 0 | 0 | 12-31-85 | 1.0 | 1.40 | 1.4 | 3.14 | 4.4 | 137 | 3.6 | 10 | 1,463 | 180 | 0 | 0.0 | 07 |
| Stocker & Yale | -18.4 | -2.7 | -6.2 | .1.2n | .51 | -26.2 | -26.2 | -54.1 | -7 | 7 | 09-87 | .00 | | 0 | 0 | 0 | 01-15-88 | 8.0 | .88 | 7.0 | 1.26 | 8.8 | 0 | 7.4 | 20 | 2,728 | 420 | 0 | 0.0 | 12 |
| View-Master Ideal | 16.6 | 27.8 | 76.8 | -.7n | -.14 | -66.7 | -100.0 | -100.0 | -8 | -3 | 09-87 | .00 | | 0 | 13 | 11 | 03-10-87 | -.6 | 1.33 | -.8 | 3.75 | -3.0 | 152 | 2.8 | 35 | 4,655 | 2,189 | 0 | 0.0 | 12 |
| WMR Cp | 18.9 | 20.1 | 296.6 | 8.3n | 1.48 | -71.1 | -49.0 | -37.8 | NC | 24 | 11-87 | .80 | 4.5 | 0 | 18 | 12 | 02-08-88 | 1.5 | 3.73 | 5.6 | 2.25 | 12.6 | 40 | 2.4 | 99 | 5,588 | 1,083 | 0 | 0.0 | 02 |
| X Rite | 34.2 | 25.7 | 21.4 | 7.0n | .13 | .0 | 43.6 | 30.9 | NC | 0 | 09-87 | .00 | | 0 | 0 | 0 | 01-11-88 | 8.2 | 1.33 | 22.0 | 1.18 | 25.9 | 0 | 5.4 | 47 | 2,598 | 215 | 0 | 0.0 | 12 |
| Xidex Corp | 4.3 | 9.6 | 12.5 | -48.9s | -1.11 | 28.6 | -27.6 | -100.0 | NC | -13 | 12-87 | .00 | | 0 | 0 | 0 | 08-09-83 | -8.2 | .88 | -7.2 | 1.75 | -12.6 | 31 | 3.1 | 264 | 41,474 | 28,775 | -1 | 0.0 | 06 |

Source: *Media General IndustriScope.* Published by Media General Financial Services, Inc., Richmond, VA.

- New Products and Technologies
- Product Sales and Consumption
- Financial Reporting and Analysis
- Management Procedures
- Market Plans Strategies

A sample *PTS PROMT* abstract is shown in Figure 2–2. Another helpful database in *DIALOG* is *Mergers and Acquisitions.* This file contains detailed abstracts of every merger and acquisition document issued by the SEC since 1985. Other acquisition online databases are discussed in Chapters 3 and 7.

Dow Jones News Retrieval service (DJNews) online service is an excellent source of industry, product, and financial information. The convenience of using DJ News is enhanced by its capability of simultaneously searching a number of files. For example, *TEXT* permits simultaneous searches of the following files:

- *The Wall Street Journal*
- *Barron's*
- *Washington Post*
- *PR Newswire* (new product releases)
- Texts of 13 major U.S. and Canadian newspapers
- Major news and business journals (*Forbes, Fortune, Financial World,* and others)
- Texts of 140 U.S. and Canadian regional business magazines and newspapers

Another convenient service available on DJ News is *Quick* which offers detailed reports on public companies obtained from eight databases, including *The Wall Street Journal, Media General,* Standard & Poor's, *Disclosure* (SEC filings), *Zacks Earnings Projections, Insider Trading Reports,* and *Investext* (financial institution reports on companies and industries). A separate database, Dun's *Financial Records,* provides comprehensive financial data, business ratios, industry comparisons, and background on over 750,000 private and public U.S. companies.

# APPENDIX 2-A:
## *Introduction to Online Databases\**

Familiarity with online information services is an important part of the analyst's equipment. Assessing, analyzing, and distributing the incredible flood of information can most effectively be achieved by electronic means, that is, computerized database systems.

The latter may be defined as organized collections of data stored in a central computer which are retrievable via remote terminals or computers. The primary benefit provided by a computerized database is the capability of rapidly searching millions of pieces of information and organizing the selected data in accordance with the interests of the user. Moreover, electronically stored data can be manipulated by means of spreadsheets and other software.

The type of information provided by databases may be statistical, bibliographic, or full text. Statistical databases provide numerical data. Bibliographic bases contain only citations to published works. Citations usually include source, title, author, publication date, key words, or abstracts. Full-text databases provide the entire text of an article.

Literally hundreds of online databases are available, and new ones are constantly being added. A number of directories and newsletters are available to help keep users abreast of developments. These are listed in Appendix 2–B.

* Source: *The Financial Analyst's Handbook,* second edition, edited by Sumner N. Levine, ©Dow Jones–Irwin, 1975 and 1988.

# THE ONLINE INDUSTRY

The "manufacturing" segments of the online industry are referred to as *producers.* A producer is an individual or organization that takes raw data, such as company annual reports, SEC filings, investment opinions, or original work, and packages it electronically into a database.

This electronic package is then delivered via a provider (vendor). Providers such as *DIALOG, CompuServe,* and others lease space on their computers to producers. These vendors are in actuality a delivery system for the finished product. However, the distinction between the database producers and the vendor is not always clear-cut. Dow Jones News Retrieval, for example, is a producer of the databases derived from *The Wall Street Journal* and *Barron's* and also a vendor for the *Disclosure* and Standard & Poor's databases. With McGraw-Hill's *Data Resources, Inc.,* producer and vendor are the same.

Producers may make their databases available to several vendors. Disclosure databases, for example, are available from Dow Jones News Retrieval, *CompuServe, DIALOG,* and other vendors. The value added of the providers is that they have all the necessary facilities for delivering the information, such as telecommunications networks, billing systems, and the retrieval software.

The revenue structure of the industry is twofold. Producers charge a fee for using their information—no different than any research firm. Fees can be measured in connect time (the amount of time that the user is connected to the system), a subscription or registration fee, and access charges based on the amount of information. The vendor's bill includes the cost of running its computer system, telecommunications networks, and the like, as well as its profit margin. In all but the rarest circumstances, it is the vendor that tracks all usage and bills the user for all fees. Pricing structures are confusing and should be examined carefully because it is often possible to get the same information from two different vendors, each of which has a different price.

## ACCESS METHODS

Three essentials are required to go online:

1. a dumb terminal or, alternatively, a computer
2. a modem, that is, a piece of hardware which interfaces the terminal (computer) with a telephone line
3. communication software that enables the computer (terminal) to interact with the modem

Vendors may communicate with user terminals through their own telecommunication switching networks or may employ one or more commercial networks such as Telenet, Tymnet, or Uninet. *CompuServe,* for example, has its own network and also utilizes Tymnet and Telenet. The latter two permit access to locations not served by the *CompuServe* network.

The technical aspects of accessing a database are actually quite simple. The dumb terminal (given its name because it does not have any processing power) or personal computer (PC) are connected to a modem which allows the devices to communicate via telephone lines.

With a dumb terminal you are limited to viewing the information on the screen or to printing out the information if a printer is connected to the terminal.

Modems receive or transmit information at specific speeds measured in bits per second (bps). Common speeds with commercial databases are 300 bps, 1,200 bps, and 2,400 bps. Generally, the higher rates are more cost efficient. It should be mentioned that baud rate is often used for bps, but the two concepts are not the same.

With a personal computer, any number of communication software packages can be used to automatically log on, retrieve information, or save data in a disk file for use later in a spreadsheet or database program. In the case of specialized software, such as stock market analysis programs, the information can be fed into the computer and automatically analyzed.

## GATEWAY SERVICES

The conventional procedure for accessing a database requires an account with each producer/vendor you want to access as well as mastery of the commands peculiar to each database and vendor.

Gateways remove these limitations by allowing you to connect with several vendors. By using a gateway you can enter your queries in the same language or format for all the online systems accessible through that particular gateway. If, for example, you did not use a gateway and you needed to access *CompuServe* and *DIALOG* and entered the same query for the current profits for Allied Stores, you would have to rephrase your query for each system. The use of a gateway circumvents this by translating your query into a language understandable by both *CompuServe* and *DIALOG.*

Additionally, by using a gateway you can generally save a considerable amount of money by not having to maintain individual accounts with several producers/providers. Because of the volume of its purchasing, the gateway can often charge one fee which is less than if you went directly to the producer/ provider.

Western Union's *Infomaster System,* which provides access to some eight vendors, is an example of a useful gateway service. It is available via Western Union's *EasyLink System.*

Another example is Business Computer Network (BCN) of San Antonio, Texas, which provides one-call access to BRS, *CompuServe, DIALOG, EasyLink System,* Newsnet, Orbit, Dow Jones News Retrieval, Mead Data Central Nexis, and *VuText.* A similar service is *EasyNet* offered by Telebase Systems, Inc. of Narberth, Pennsylvania. *EasyNet* also provides a series of menus to help select the appropriate database to retrieve the required information. With BCN, in comparison, once you are connected to a vendor you are on your own.

# APPENDIX 2-B:
## DIALOG and Dow Jones News Retrieval Databases*

---

### DIALOG

**Dialog Information Services**
**3460 Hillview Avenue**
**Palo Alto, CA 04304**

Introduced in 1972, Dialog is one of the largest database vendors currently offering over 250 databases covering a wide scope of disciplines. Listed below are the on-line databases of particular interest to financial analysts.

*ABI/INFORM*®.   Extensive summaries of articles from top business and management journals—business practices, corporate strategies, and trends.

*ADTRACK*™.   Descriptions of advertisements from 150 U.S. consumer magazines—competitive tracking and product announcements.

*ARTHUR D. LITTLE/ONLINE.*   Management summaries from A.D. Little's market research reports—planning and industry research.

*BIOBUSINESS.*   Summaries of business-oriented articles in agriculture, biotechnology, food and beverage industry, and pharmaceuticals—locate areas of biological research with high potential for commercial growth.

*BLS CONSUMER PRICE INDEX.*   Time series of consumer price indexes calculated by the U.S. Bureau of Labor Statistics—economic analysis.

*BLS EMPLOYMENT, HOURS, AND EARNINGS.* Time series on employment, hours of work, and earnings for the United States by industry—economic trends and analysis.

*BLS PRODUCER PRICE INDEX.* Time series of producer price indexes, formerly Wholesale Price Indexes, for over 2,800 commodities—economic analysis.

*CENDATA™.* News releases from the U.S. Bureau of the Census with textual and tabular information covering Census surveys in business, agriculture, population, and more—tracking current economic and demographic trends.

*CHEMICAL INDUSTRY NOTES.* Extracts from articles in worldwide business-oriented periodicals for chemical-processing industries—chemical industry news and tracking.

*COMMERCE BUSINESS DAILY.* Definitive source of notices from U.S. Dept. of Commerce for government procurement invitations, contract awards, surplus sales, R&D requests—competitive tracking, purchasing, and sales leads.

*COMPARE PRODUCTS.* Information on computer-related manufacturing and distributing companies and products from display ads in 100+ U.S. business and computer publications—product/market research and sales planning.

*D&B—DUN'S MARKET IDENTIFIERS®.* Directory of over 1 million public and private companies with 10 or more employees, listing address, products, sales executives—corporate organization, subsidiaries, industry information, sales prospects.

*D&B—INTERNATIONAL DUN'S MARKET IDENTIFIERS®.* Directory listings, sales volume, corporate data, and references to companies for non-U.S. private and public companies from 133 companies—international trade and industry prospects.

*D&B—MILLION DOLLAR DIRECTORY®.* Privately held and public companies with net worths over $500,000, includes data on sales, type of organization, address, employees, key executives—corporate analysis and information.

*DISCLOSURE™ II.* Detailed financials for over 9,000 publicly held companies, based on reports filed with the U.S. SEC—sales, profit, corporate organization, key personnel.

*DISCLOSURE™/SPECTRUM OWNERSHIP.* Detailed ownership information for thousands of U.S. public companies—investment analysis.

*ECONOMIC LITERATURE INDEX.* Index to articles from economic journals and books—economic research and teaching.

*ECONOMICS ABSTRACTS INTERNATIONAL.* Summaries of literature in all areas of international economic sciences—determining industries, distribution channels.

*ELECTRONIC YELLOW PAGES.* Unparalleled number of listings of U.S. businesses, retail, services, manufacturers, wholesalers, etc. Over 9 million listings with name, location, line of business—sales prospecting and location tool.

FIND/SVP REPORTS AND STUDIES INDEX. Summaries of industry and market research reports, surveys from U.S. and international sources—market, industry, and company analyses.

*FINIS: FINANCIAL INDUSTRY INFORMATION SERVICE.* Marketing information for financial services industry and their products and services—development of marketing strategies.

*FOREIGN TRADERS INDEX.* Directory of manufacturers, services, representatives, wholesalers, etc. in 130 non-U.S. countries—direct marketing and sales outside the United States (available in United States only).

*HARVARD BUSINESS REVIEW.* Text of *Harvard Business Review*, covering the range of strategic management subjects—management practices and strategies.

*ICC BRITISH COMPANY DIRECTORY* and *ICC BRITISH COMPANY FINANCIAL DATABASE.* Listing of detailed financial information and ratios for nearly 1 million British companies as filed with the Companies Registry of Companies House—identification of U.K. companies and financial analysis.

*INDUSTRY DATA SOURCES*™. Descriptions of sources for financial and marketing data in major industries worldwide, including market research, investment banking studies, forecasts, etc.—industry tracking and analysis.

*INSURANCE ABSTRACTS.* Brief summaries of articles from life, property, and liability insurance journals—tracking insurance industry trends and practices.

*INTERNATIONAL LISTING SERVICE.* Directory of worldwide business opportunities—buying, selling, and financing for businesses.

*INVESTEXT*ᵉ. The complete text of prestigious Wall Street and selected European analysts' financial and research reports on over 3,000 companies and industries—corporate and industry analysis plus financial and market research.

*MANAGEMENT CONTENTS®.* Informative briefs on a variety of business and management related topics from business journals, proceedings, transactions, etc.—management, finance, operations decision making.

*MEDIA GENERAL DATABANK.* Trading information with detailed financial information on 4,000 publicly held companies over a seven-year period—charting market and financial performance.

*MERGERS.* Contains abstracts of every merger and acquisition document released by the SEC since early 1985.

*MOODY'S³ CORPORATE NEWS—INTERNATIONAL* and *MOODY'S³ CORPORATE NEWS—U.S.* Business news and financial information on 3,900+ international and 13,000+ U.S. corporations from annual reports, proxy statements, journals, and reports—competitive analysis, merger and acquisition activities, new product information.

*MOODY'S³ CORPORATE PROFILES.* Equity database with financial data and business descriptions of publicly held U.S. companies, with five-year histories, ratios, and analyses on companies with high investor interest—assess investment opportunities.

*P/E NEWS.* Current political, social, and economic information related to energy industries—monitor news, new technology, and legislation.

*PHARMACEUTICAL NEWS INDEX.* References to major report publications, covering drugs, cosmetics, health regulations, research, financial news—drug and cosmetic industry developments and regulation.

*PTS ANNUAL REPORTS ABSTRACTS.* Detailed statistical, financial, product, and corporate summaries from annual and 10-K reports for publicly held U.S. corporations and selected international companies—product, industry, company identification, and strategic planning.

*PTS DEFENSE MARKETS AND TECHNOLOGY.* Summaries of major articles and reports from defense sources, includes contracts, the industry, and more—defense industry contracting and tracking.

*PTS F&S INDEXES (Funk & Scott).* Brief descriptive annotations of articles and publications covering U.S. and international company, product, and industry information—company and industry tracking.

*PTS INTERNATIONAL FORECASTS.* Summaries of published forecasts with historical data for the world, excluding the United

States, covering general economics, all industries, products, end-use data—strategic planning for international development.

*PTS INTERNATIONAL TIME SERIES.* Forecast time series containing 50 key series for each of 50 major countries, excluding United States, and projected to 1990, as well as annual data from 1957 to date—international economic analysis.

*PTS PROMT.* Primary source of information on product introductions, market share, corporate directions and ventures, and companies in every industry, containing detailed summaries of articles from trade and industry sources—market and strategic planning, tracking new technologies and products.

*PTS U.S. FORECASTS.* Summaries of published forecasts for United States from trade journals, business and financial publications, key newspapers, government reports, and special studies—short- and long-term forecasting.

*PTS U.S. TIME SERIES.* 500 time series for United States from 1957 and projected to 1990 and annual data from 1957 to date on production, consumption, prices, international trade, manufacturing, etc.—tracking economic and industry trends.

*STANDARD & POOR'S CORPORATE DESCRIPTIONS.* In-depth corporate descriptions of over 7,800 publicly held U.S. companies with background, income account and balance sheet figures, and stock and bond data—competitive and financial analysis of companies and products.

*STANDARD & POOR'S NEWS.* Late-breaking financial news on U.S. public companies, including earnings, mergers and acquisitions, joint ventures, management and corporate changes and structure—current awareness of corporate activities.

*STANDARD & POOR'S REGISTER—BIOGRAPHICAL.* Personal and professional data on key executives in public and private companies with sales over $1 million—locate and profile U.S. and non-U.S. corporate leadership.

*STANDARD & POOR'S REGISTER—CORPORATE.* Company records and business facts on 45,000+ public and private corporations, primarily in the United States including financial and marketing information—market research and development, identification of business connections.

*THOMAS REGISTER ONLINE™.* Digest of 123,000 U.S. manufacturers, 50,000+ classes of products, and 102,000+ trade and brand names. Listing for over 1 million product and service sources—sales planning, market research, product line tracking.

*TRADE & INDUSTRY ASAP™*.  Indexing and complete text of articles from 85 industry trade journals and general business publications—current awareness and industry tracking.

*TRADE & INDUSTRY INDEX™*.  Index with selected summaries of major trade and industry journals and the complete text of press releases from PR Newswire—industry and company information and news.

*TRADE OPPORTUNITIES*.  Purchase requests by the international market for U.S. goods and services, describing specific products or services in demand by over 120 countries—leads to export opportunities, sales, and representation opportunities.

*TRINET COMPANY DATABASE*.  Directory information on U.S. and non-U.S. company headquarters with aggregate data from establishments, including sales by SIC code—headquarter analysis and industry sales.

*TRINET ESTABLISHMENT DATABASE*.  Directory of U.S. corporate establishments with address, sales, market share, employees, and headquarters information—corporate and market analysis.

---

## DOW JONES NEWS RETRIEVAL

### P.O. Box 300
### Princeton, NJ 08540

This database, started in 1974, originally provided only stock market information. It was expanded in 1977 to include news appearing in *The Wall Street Journal* and *Barron's*. Since then the service has been substantially expanded again to include the following databases:

*BUSINESS   The Business and Finance Report*
- Continuously updated business and financial news culled from *The Wall Street Journal*, The Dow Jones News Service, and other news wires.
- The latest news on domestic and international economies.
- Cross references to related information.

*DB   Dun's Financial Records*
- Consists of over 750,000 U.S. public and private companies.

*DEFINE   Words of Wall Street*<sup>SM</sup>
- Definitions of over 2,000 business and financial terms used by professional investors.

*DJNEWS  Dow Jones$^{SM}$ News*
- Stories from *The Wall Street Journal, Barron's,* and Dow Jones News Service.
- Stories as recent as 90 seconds, as far back as 90 days.

*DSCLO  Disclosure® Online*
- 10-K extracts, company profiles and other detailed data on over 10,000 publicly held companies from reports filed with the SEC.

*EPS  Corporate Earnings Estimator$^{SM}$*
- Timely earnings forecasts for more than 3,000 of the most widely followed companies compiled by Zacks Investment Research, Inc.

*INSIDER  Insider Trading Monitor*
- Insider trading information on over 6,500 publicly held companies. Reports on trades made by nearly 60,000 individuals (corporate directors, officers, or shareholders with more than 10 percent ownership).

*INVEST  Investext®*
- Provides full texts of more than 13,000 research reports from top brokers, investment bankers, and other analysts.
- Includes more than 3,000 U.S. and Canadian companies and 50 industries.
- Historical, current, and forecasted marketing and financial information.

*KYODO  Japan Economic Daily®*
- Same-day coverage of major business, financial, and political news from Japan's Kyodo News International, Inc.

*MG  Media General Financial Services*
- Detailed corporate financial information on 4,300 companies and 170 industries.
- Major categories include: revenue, earnings, dividends, volume, ratio, shareholdings, and price changes.
- Compare two different companies or company versus industry data on the same screen.

*MMS  Economic and Foreign Exchange Survey$^{SM}$*
- Weekly survey of U.S. money market and foreign exchange trends.
- Median forecasts of monetary and economic indicators.

*QUICK  Dow Jones$^{SM}$ QuickSearch*
- Corporate report drawing information from multiple news/ retrieval sources, searchable with one command.

*SP  Standard & Poor's Online®*
- Concise profiles of 4,600 companies containing earnings, dividend, and market figures for the current year and the past four years.

- Corporate overviews plus S&P earnings estimates for most major companies.

*TEXT    Text-Search Services*[SM]

- *The Wall Street Journal*: Full Text Version. All articles that appeared or were scheduled to appear in *The Wall Street Journal* since January 1984.
- Dow Jones News. News service articles and selected stories from *Barron's* and *The Wall Street Journal* since June 1979.
- *The Washington Post*: Full Text Version. Articles that appeared in *The Washington Post* since January 1984.
- The Business Library. Selected articles from *Forbes*, *Financial World*, and the full text of the PR newswire since January 1985.

*TRACK    Tracking Service*

- Create and track up to five profiles containing as many as 25 companies each.
- Track current quotes (minimum 15 minute delay) and the latest news stories and headlines automatically on the companies in your profiles.

*WSW    Wall $treet Week*[SM]

- Four most recent transcripts of the popular PBS television program "Wall $treet Week."

## Quotes and Market Averages

*CQE    Enhanced Current Quotes* (Minimum 15-minute delay during market hours)

- Common and preferred stocks and bonds.
- Mutual funds, U.S. Treasury issues, and options.
- News alert.

*DJA    Historical Dow Jones Averages*[SM]

- Daily high, low, close, and volume available for the last trading year for industrials, transportation, utilities, and 65 stock composites.

*FUTURES    Futures Quotes*

- Current quotes (10–30 minute delay) for more than 80 contracts from the major North American exchanges updated continuously during market hours.
- Daily open, high, low, last, and settlement prices.
- Daily volume and open interest, lifetime high and low.

HQ   *Historical Quotes*
- Daily volume, high, low, and close for stock quotes and composites.
- Monthly stock quote summaries back to 1979; quarterly summaries back to 1978.

RTQ   *Real-Time Quotes*
- Stock prices with no delay from the major exchanges, including composites.
- NASD National Market System prices.
- News alert.

# APPENDIX 2-C:
# Online Database Information Sources

## Information Sources

1. *Annual Directory of the Information Industry Association*, Information Industry Association, Washington, D.C.
2. *Directory of Online Data Bases*, Cuadra/Elsevier, New York, New York.
3. *North American Online Directory*, R. R. Bowker and Co., New York, New York.
4. *Encyclopedia of Information Systems and Services*, Gale Research Co., Detroit, Michigan.
5. *Data Base Directory*, Knowledge Industry Publications, White Plains, New York.
6. *DataPro Directory of Online Services*, DataPro Research Corporation, Delran, New Jersey.
7. "Online and Data Base" (newsletter), Online, Inc., Weston, Connecticut.
8. "Data Base Alert" (newsletter), Knowledge Industry Publications, White Plains, New York.
9. *Wall Street Computer Review*, a monthly magazine published by Dealers Digests, New York, New York.

* Source: *The Financial Analyst's Handbook*, second edition, edited by Sumner N. Levine, ©Dow Jones–Irwin, 1975 and 1988.

# Chapter 3

# *Identifying Acquisition Candidates*

*Sumner N. Levine*

After formulating acquisition criteria as discussed in Chapter 1, the next step is to identify acquisition candidates that meet the criteria. The intensity of the search and, hence, the rate of progress depend partially on the buyer's degree of commitment and the resources available. Although a high degree of commitment certainly helps, success depends on chance also. Even under the best of circumstances a deal is unlikely to be consummated in less than six months. Occasionally, the process may drag on for several years. A sense of realism is necessary in these matters because the ideal company may not be available—if indeed it exists at all. Compromise is often required. Consequently, setting priorities among the acquisition criteria, that is, deciding which criteria are essential and which can be relaxed, can greatly facilitate the search process.

A highly committed buyer may employ both in-house personnel and outside intermediaries for the search. The latter include investment bankers, brokers, accounting firms, legal firms, and direct industry contacts. In-house talent has the advantages that it has a better grasp of the firm's needs, can devote more time to the quest than can intermediaries, and often costs less. Outside professionals, on the other hand, have more experience with acquisitions and often have access to deals not otherwise available. Moreover, outside professionals associated with prestigious firms may give credibility to lesser-known buyers, thereby facilitating access to more target companies.

## OVERVIEW OF INTERMEDIARIES

We present here a brief discussion of the different types of intermediaries. A helpful general guide is the *Directory of Intermediaries* (Business Publications, San Diego, CA), which provides detailed information on over 350 selected firms involved in M&A and is also available on a floppy disk for use in personal computers.

### Investment Bankers and Other Financial Institutions

Included in this category are investment banks as well as the M&A departments of commercial banks and brokerage houses. These organizations are among the best sources of leads but have little interest in small deals. An annual directory is published in the periodical *Institutional Investor* (New York, NY). U.S. institutions, as well as the U.S. divisions of foreign financial institutions, are included in the listing.

The institutional firms not only act as finders but also provide introductions, make evaluations, participate in negotiations, and arrange financing. The more prestigious organizations often have unique access to attractive situations. Fees, although negotiable, are often based on the Lehman formula of 5 percent on the first million, 4 percent on the second, 3 percent on the third, 2 percent on the fourth, and 1 percent on the amount paid over $4 million.

### Brokers and Finders

Brokers and finders are more accessible to smaller firms. The distinction usually made between brokers and finders is that finders merely introduce the parties while brokers may also assist in the negotiations. A good broker can help screen candidates and prevent the negotiations from breaking down.

Because there are no licensing requirements, anyone is free

to act as a business broker or finder. However, if substantial real estate is involved, many states require that a business broker be licensed as a real estate broker.

There is a wide variety of business brokers. Some specialize in specific industries, such as retailing, high technology, restaurants, and motels while others specialize in geographic locations. In addition to small independent firms, nationally franchised brokers are also active. Broker listings are available in the previously mentioned *Directory of Intermediaries,* as well as in financial and trade publications. Also available is a helpful newsletter, the *Business Broker* (Business Broker Press, Concord, MA).

It is difficult to locate a business broker who is both knowledgeable and ethical. In addition to checking out references, it is helpful to obtain answers to the following questions before making a choice:

- How long has the broker been in business?
- How many deals similar to yours have been transacted by the broker in the last three years or so? Who were the parties involved? Where can they be contacted?
- Will the broker provide written confirmation that he or she is authorized to represent the sellers whose names are submitted?
- What are the broker's arrangements with respect to the finder's fee?

Although brokers generally represent the seller (who pays the fee), occasionally the buyer may assume responsibility for the fee. A representative buyer agreement is given in Appendix 3–B. To avoid any misunderstanding in dealing with brokers, many companies require the broker to sign an agreement such as that shown in Appendix 3–A.

### Legal and Accounting Firms

Attorneys and accountants frequently have access to acquisition opportunities. The larger firms have a substantial number of industrial and commercial clients and contacts. Most of the larger accounting firms such as the Big Eight now have merger and acquisition departments. Members of the legal profession who specialize in acquisitions can be found in the *Martindale-Hubbell Law Directory.*

In addition to merger and acquisition specialists, bank-ruptcy and estate lawyers are often helpful in identifying privately held opportunities. Similarly, the trust departments of banks as executors of estates may seek to sell businesses. Often, the merger and acquisition department of the bank is also aware of such situations.

## DEVELOPING THE PROSPECT LIST

In order to supplement the outside sources mentioned above, the buyer should tap all other available resources, including:

- basic company directories
- trade shows (see Chapter 2)
- trade publications (see Chapter 2)
- suppliers
- industry observers
- retailer/wholesalers

### Basic Company Directories

The major directories, such as those published by Dun and Bradstreet, Standard & Poor's, and Ward's, are useful for making a "first cut" of acquisition possibilities. Both privately and publicly held companies are included. These directories permit searches by industry SIC numbers, sales and asset size, private or public ownership, years in business, and location.

*Million Dollar Directory* (Dun and Bradstreet, New York, NY) contains information on over 160,000 public and private U.S. businesses with a net worth of over $500,000. Information

**Figure 3–1.** *Format of entries in Dun and Bradstreet* Million Dollar Directory.

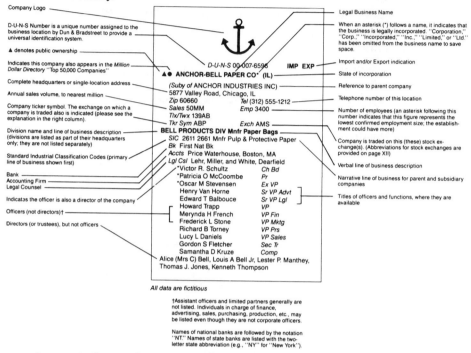

Company Logo

D-U-N-S Number is a unique number assigned to the business location by Dun & Bradstreet to provide a universal identification system.

▲ denotes public ownership

Indicates this company also appears in the *Million Dollar Directory* "Top 50,000 Companies"

Complete headquarters or single-location address

Annual sales volume, to nearest million

Company ticker symbol. The exchange on which a company is traded also is indicated (please see the explanation in the right column).

Division name and line of business description (divisions are listed as part of their headquarters only; they are not listed separately)

Standard Industrial Classification Codes (primary line of business shown first)

Bank
Accounting Firm
Legal Counsel

Indicates the officer is also a director of the company

Officers (not directors)†

Directors (or trustees), but not officers

Legal Business Name

When an asterisk (*) follows a name, it indicates that the business is legally incorporated. "Corporation," "Corp.," "Incorporated," "Inc.," "Limited," or "Ltd." has been omitted from the business name to save space.

Import and/or Export indication

State of incorporation

Reference to parent company

Telephone number of this location

Number of employees (an asterisk following this number indicates that this figure represents the lowest confirmed employment size; the establishment could have more)

Company is traded on this (these) stock exchange(s). (Abbreviations for stock exchanges are provided on page XII)

Verbal line of business description

Narrative line of business for parent and subsidiary companies

Titles of officers and functions, where they are available

*D-U-N-S 00-007-6596*    **IMP EXP**
▲● **ANCHOR-BELL PAPER CO\*** (IL)
*(Suby of* ANCHOR INDUSTRIES INC)
5877 Valley Road, Chicago, IL
Zip 60660                    *Tel* (312) 555-1212
*Sales* 50MM              *Emp* 3400
*Tlx/Twx* 139AB
*Tkr Sym* ABP            *Exch* AMS
**BELL PRODUCTS DIV Mnfr Paper Bags**
  *SIC* 2611 2661 Mnfr Pulp & Protective Paper
  *Bk* First Nat Bk
  *Accts* Price Waterhouse, Boston, MA
  *Lgl Csl* Lehr, Miller, and White, Dearfield
  \*Victor R. Schultz          *Ch Bd*
  \*Patricia O McCoombe       *Pr*
  \*Oscar M Stevenson         *Ex VP*
   Henry Van Horne           *Sr VP Advt*
   Edward T Balbouce         *Sr VP Lgl*
   Howard Trapp              *VP*
   Merynda H French          *VP Fin*
   Frederick L Stone         *VP Mktg*
   Richard B Torney          *VP Prs*
   Lucy L Daniels            *VP Sales*
   Gordon S Fletcher         *Sec Tr*
   Samantha D Kruze          *Comp*
  Alice (Mrs C) Bell, Louis A Bell Jr, Lester P. Manthey,
  Thomas J. Jones, Kenneth Thompson

*All data are fictitious*

†Assistant officers and limited partners generally are not listed. Individuals in charge of finance, advertising, sales, purchasing, production, etc., may be listed even though they are not corporate officers.

Names of national banks are followed by the notation "NT." Names of state banks are listed with the two-letter state abbreviation (e.g., "NY" for "New York").

Source: *Million Dollar Directory,* Dun's Marketing Services, Inc., a company of Dun and Bradstreet Corporation, Parsippany, NJ 07054.

provided includes names of top executives, industry SIC, sales size, number of employees, year founded, division names, principal banks, accounting, and legal firms (see Figure 3–1). Comparable information on Canadian and European firms is also available from D&B in other directories. The data can also be searched through *DIALOG.*

*Standard & Poor's Register of Corporations, Directors and Executives* (Standard & Poor's Corporation, New York, NY) provides information on over 45,000 public and private companies similar to that given in the *Million Dollar Directory.* A second volume provides brief data on executives. The information is also available online through *DIALOG.*

*Ward's Business Directory* gives data on over 90,000 public and private U.S. companies. Many of the 80,000 private companies are claimed to be unique to this directory. A helpful feature is the ranking by sales size within each SIC group. Information is provided on SIC classification sales volume, number of employees, name of chief executive, and year founded. Subsidiary/parent relationships are clearly indicated. A representative format is shown in Figure 3–2. Although not available online at this writing, the data is also provided on floppy disks.

## Screening Services

Several useful services are available for scanning databases for acquisition prospects.

*DunQuest* provided by Dun and Bradstreet, both online and hard copy by mail, helps identify candidates according to preselected criteria. The D&B database of 1.3 million companies can be screened by industry, sales, asset size, net worth, and location. The service also provides balance sheet data, financial ratios, and comparisons of company performance with the industry (see Figure 3–3). A similar service is available for foreign companies. Keep in mind, however, that the data provided to D&B is often based on unverified reports submitted by the companies.

*Deal Base* (available from Business Publications, San Diego, CA) provides information on periodically updated floppy disks on hundreds of companies available for acquisition. The software permits searching the database for such parameters as industry type, company size, earnings, location, management preference (stay, consult, leave), leveraged buyout opportunities, and other criteria. For example, the database will search all of the companies in plastics manufacturing located in the southwestern United States with sales in excess of $10 million and pretax profits of at least $700,000, with management willing to stay.

Two other widely used services are provided by Interactive Data Corp. (New York, NY) and FactSet Data Systems, Inc. (New York, NY). Both utilize the extensive financial data from 7,000 U.S. publicly traded companies on *Compustat*. The *Compustat* data is supplemented with earnings estimates provided by I/B/E/S (Lynch, Jones, Ryan of New York, NY), *Zacks Investment Research, Inc.* (Chicago, IL), and Value Line (New York, NY). Data on over 4,000 foreign companies, supplied by Exstat, is also available.

**Figure 3–2.** *Volume 3: U.S. private and public companies ranked by industry.*

Private & Public Companies, Subsidiaries, Divisions, etc; Ranked in Respective ***S.I.C. Industries*** by Sales Size; Subsidiaries, Divisions linked to Parent Cos. **S.I.C. 367-369**

| Rank | Company Name | Address | City | St | Zip | Chief Executive | Phone | S.I.C. | Alpha Description | Sales | Empl. | I. | E. | Yr.Fd. |
|---|---|---|---|---|---|---|---|---|---|---|---|---|---|---|
| 1347 | CRV Electronics Corp | 913 N Front St | Mchenry | IL | 60050 | CR Vyduna | 815-385-4900 | 3679 | Elec Compo,Nec | 1* | <.1 | | | 1967 |
| 1348 | Custom Electrnic Srvs | 2024 Bering Dr | San Jose | CA | 95131 | R Jacobs Jr | 408-298-3238 | 3679 | Elec Compo,Nec | 1 | <.1 | | | 1977 |
| 1349 | Douglas Electronics | 718 Marina Blvd | San Leandro | CA | 94577 | C Pennebaker | 415-483-8770 | 3679 | Elec Compo,Nec | 1 | <.1 | | | 1964 |
| 1350 | ECM Inc | 1515 W 259th St | Harbor City | CA | 90710 | WL Kirchoff | 213-530-3456 | 3679 | Elec Compo,Nec | 1 | <.1 | | | 1970 |
| 1351 | Electron Vision Corp | 9747 Bus Pk Ave | San Diego | CA | 92131 | WR Livesay | 619-566-0852 | 3674 | Semiconductors | 1 | | | | 1975 |
| 1352 | # Emstar | 1851 Reynolds | Irvine | CA | 92714 | JT Sandberg | 714-261-9478 | 3679 | Elec Compo,Nec | 1 | .1 | Y | | 1971 |
| 1353 | Electronic Tech Lab Inc | Po Drawer 111 | Vermillion | SD | 57069 | CC Woodman | 605-624-4054 | 3679 | Elec Compo,Nec | 1* | <.1 | | | |
| 1354 | Electrostatics Inc | 7718 Clairemont | San Diego | CA | 92111 | RD Mccartney | 619-279-1414 | 3679 | Elec Compo,Nec | 1 | <.1 | Y | Y | 1965 |
| 1355 | Production Resources | 1815 S E 7th | Portland | OR | 97214 | CR Englen | 503-231-0246 | 3679 | Elec Compo,Nec | 1 | <.1 | | | 1974 |
| 1356 | Hertz Filter Corp | 3 Aerial Way | Syosset | NY | 11791 | G Starr | 516-822-4770 | 3677 | Ele Coil,Trnsf | 1 | <.1 | | | 1970 |
| 1357 | Interswitch | 770 Airport Blv | Burlingame | CA | 94010 | WJ Purdy Jr | 415-347-8217 | 3679 | Elec Compo,Nec | 1 | <.1 | Y | | 1966 |
| 1358 | KR Electronics Inc | 91 Avenel St | Avenel | NJ | 07001 | C Kiall | 201-636-1900 | 3677 | Ele Coil,Trnsf | 1* | <.1 | | | 1973 |
| 1359 | Amer Radar Components | 39 Front St | Denville | NJ | 07834 | J Maluk Jr | 201-627-5530 | 3679 | Elec Compo,Nec | 1 | <.1 | | Y | 1953 |
| 1360 | Microplex Inc | 1977 S Stat Clg | Anaheim | CA | 92806 | C Kucenas | 714-634-1535 | 3676 | Resistors-Elec | 1 | <.1 | | | 1971 |
| 1361 | Microwave Systems Inc | 6505 Collamer | E Syracuse | NY | 13057 | MP Busse | 315-437-9951 | 3679 | Elec Compo,Nec | 1 | <.1 | | Y | 1963 |
| 1362 | Mills Resistor Co | 3840 Catalina | Ls Alamitos | CA | 90720 | BT Mills | 213-598-2454 | 3676 | Resistors-Elec | 1 | .1 | Y | Y | 1968 |
| 1363 | Electronics & Mtls Inds | Po Box 669 | Cedar Park | TX | 78613 | PR Davis | 512-837-8506 | 3679 | Elec Compo,Nec | 1 | <.1 | | | 1972 |
| 1364 | ■ Omynee Inds Inc | 5111 Argosy Ave | Huntngtn Bh | CA | 92649 | JF Northway | 714-898-3436 | 3679 | Elec Compo,Nec | 1 | <.1 | | | 1956 |
| | ■ Motors Products-Owoss | 201 S Delaney | Owosso | MI | 48867 | WL Rohm | 517-725-5151 | 3621 | Motor&Generatr | 13 | .2 | | | 1970 |
| | ★ Goodrich B F Co | 3925 Embassy Pk | Akron | OH | 44318 | JD Ong | 216-374-3985 | 2821 | Plastics Matrl | 2553 | 11.9 | Y | Y | 1870 |
| 1365 | Precision Inc | 3415 48th Ave N | Minneapolis | MN | 55429 | DR Head | 612-537-9340 | 3676 | Resistors-Elec | 1 | <.1 | | Y | 1965 |
| 1366 | Precisioneering Inc | 701 Leesburg Rd | Fort Wayne | IN | 46808 | OA Drake | 219-432-5511 | 3679 | Elec Compo,Nec | 1 | <.1 | | | 1970 |
| 1367 | PTC Transformers | Po Box 397 | Bordentown | NJ | 08505 | C Kafalas | 609-298-8200 | 3677 | Ele Coil,Trnsf | 1 | <.1 | | Y | 1955 |
| 1368 | Assoctd Craftsmen Inc | 171 Atlantic St | Hackensack | NJ | 07601 | D Imbert | 201-342-5739 | 3679 | Elec Compo,Nec | 1 | .1 | | | |
| 1369 | Reichenbach Engineering | 6887 Farmdle Av | N Hollywood | CA | 91605 | BL Johnson | 818-765-6040 | 3677 | Ele Coil,Trnsf | 1 | <.1 | | Y | 1964 |
| 1370 | Relational Memry Sys | Po Box 6719 | San Jose | CA | 95150 | JM Kelly | 408-729-3011 | 3679 | Elec Compo,Nec | 1* | <.1 | | Y | 1976 |
| 1371 | S & E I Manufacturing | Po Box 832 | Northridge | CA | 91324 | KP Ellenberger | 818-349-4111 | 3679 | Elec Compo,Nec | 1 | <.1 | | Y | 1963 |
| 1372 | Sloan Co The | 7704 Sn Frnando | Sun Valley | CA | 91353 | CS Sloan | 213-875-1123 | 3679 | Elec Compo,Nec | 1 | <.1 | Y | Y | 1957 |
| 1373 | Sound City Inc | 15456 Cabrito | Van Nuys | CA | 91406 | J Gottfried | 818-787-3722 | 3679 | Elec Compo,Nec | 1 | <.1 | | Y | 1969 |
| 1374 | Subminiature Instrumnts | 3147 Durahart | Riverside | CA | 92507 | DF Hazelman | 714-684-7133 | 3679 | Elec Compo,Nec | 1 | <.1 | Y | Y | 1958 |
| 1375 | Techni Data Labs | 1123 J Dominque | Carson | CA | 90746 | TF Boblak | 213-631-6111 | 3679 | Elec Compo,Nec | 1 | <.1 | | Y | 1962 |
| 1376 | Transducer Products Inc | Rt 63 | Goshen | CT | 06756 | C Thompson | 203-491-3251 | 3679 | Elec Compo,Nec | 1* | <.1 | | | |
| 1377 | Assembly Specialists | 914 Main St | Acton | MA | 01720 | GL Boyden | 617-263-9100 | 3679 | Elec Compo,Nec | 1* | <.1 | | | 1968 |
| 1378 | ★ Micro Display Systems | Po Box 455 | Hastings | MN | 55033 | JO Hildebrandt | 612-437-2233 | 3672 | Cathode Ray Tv | 1 | <.1 | | | 1983 |
| | | RL Zylstra, V-M | | | | LD Mcgregor, V-R | MK Hildebrandt, VP | | | MJ O'loughlin, SEC | | | | |
| 1379 | ★ Telenetics Corp | 895 E Yorba Lin | Placentia | CA | 92670 | H Dohmae | 714-524-5770 | 3674 | Semiconductors | 1 | <.1 | | | 1984 |
| | | W Kosoff, V-M | | | | K Nagarasan, V-R | | | | | | | | |
| 1380 | ★ Cryodynamics Inc | 191 Mill Lane | Mountainsid | NJ | 07092 | SF Malaker | 201-654-7700 | 3679 | Elec Compo,Nec | 1 | <.1 | | | 1982 |
| | | JJ Torre Jr, TR | | | | HR Cardoni, SEC | | | | | | | | |
| 1381 | ★ Cyber Digital Inc | 20 Floyds Run | Bohemia | NY | 11716 | JC Chatpar | 516-567-2900 | 3674 | Semiconductors | 1 | <.1 | | | 1983 |
| | | D Moroz, TR | | | | GT Geris, V-M | A Kobran, V-R | | | BS Surana, VP | | | | |
| 1382 | Masden Industries Inc | 20 Elm St | Rockaway | NJ | 07866 | C Fabend | 201-625-3500 | 3679 | Elec Compo,Nec | 1* | <.1 | | | 1950 |
| | TOTALS FOR SIC 367 | | | | | | | | | 66789 | 909.5 | | | |

**369 MISCELLANEOUS ELECTRICAL MACHINERY EQUIPMENT & SUPPLIES**

| Rank | Company Name | Address | City | St | Zip | Chief Executive | Phone | S.I.C. | Alpha Description | Sales | Empl. | I. | E. | Yr.Fd. |
|---|---|---|---|---|---|---|---|---|---|---|---|---|---|---|
| 1 | ■ Delco Electronics Corp | 700 E Firman St | Kokomo | IN | 46902 | RB Smith | 317-457-8461 | 3694 | Elec Eq-Engine | 3500 | 21.0 | | | |
| | ■ GM Hughes Electronics | 3044 W Grand Bl | Detroit | MI | 48202 | DJ Atwood | 313-556-5000 | 3662 | Radio&Tv Trans | 10440 | 102.0 | | | |
| | ★ Genl Motors Corp | 3044 W Grand Bl | Detroit | MI | 48202 | RB Smith | 313-556-5000 | 3711 | Motor Vehicles | 102814 | 876.0 | Y | Y | 1916 |
| 2 | # Delco Electrncs-Kokomo | 700 E Firmin St | Kokomo | IN | 46902 | DJ Almquist | 317-457-8461 | 3694 | Elec Eq-Engine | 1800* | 11.0 | Y | Y | 1936 |
| | ■ Delco Electronics Cor | 700 E Firman St | Kokomo | IN | 46902 | RB Smith | 317-457-8461 | 3694 | Elec Eq-Engine | 3500 | 21.0 | | | |
| | ■ GM Hughes Electroni | 3044 W Grand Bl | Detroit | MI | 48202 | DJ Atwood | 313-556-5000 | 3662 | Radio&Tv Trans | 10440 | 102.0 | | | |
| 3 | # Ford Mtr Electrcl & Elc | Mckean & Textil | Ypsilanti | MI | 48197 | FE Macher | 313-484-8400 | 3694 | Elec Eq-Engine | 1600* | 20.0 | | | 1975 |
| | ★ Ford Motor Co | Po Box 1899 | Dearborn | MI | 48121 | DE Peterson | 313-322-3000 | 3711 | Motor Vehicles | 62716 | 382.3 | Y | Y | 1919 |
| 4 | # Du Pont Biomedical Prdt | 1007 Market St | Wilmington | DE | 19898 | DD Mooberry | 302-774-1000 | 3693 | X-Ray Apparatu | 1150 | | | | |
| | ★ Du Pont E I De Nemour | 1007 Market St | Wilmington | DE | 19898 | RE Hecker | 302-774-1000 | 3981 | Divers,Conglom | 27148 | 141.3 | Y | Y | 1802 |
| 5 | # Genl Mtrs A C Spark Plg | 1300 N Dort Hwy | Flint | MI | 48556 | JR Wilson | 313-766-5000 | 3694 | Elec Eq-Engine | 1100* | 15.0 | Y | Y | 1908 |
| | ★ Genl Motors Corp | 3044 W Grand Bl | Detroit | MI | 48202 | RB Smith | 313-556-5000 | 3711 | Motor Vehicles | 102814 | 876.0 | Y | Y | 1916 |
| 6 | ■ Duracell Inc | Berkshire Indus | Bethel | CT | 06801 | CR Kidder | 203-796-4000 | 3691 | Storage Battry | 963 | 9.5 | | | |
| | ★ Kraft Inc | Kraft Court | Glenview | IL | 60025 | JM Richman | 312-998-2000 | 2022 | Cheese,Nat&Pro | 8742 | 51.3 | | Y | 1902 |
| 7 | ★ Echlin Inc | 100 Double Bch | Branford | CT | 06405 | FJ Mancheski | 203-481-5751 | 3694 | Elec Eq-Engine | 902 | 13.2 | Y | Y | 1959 |
| | | RB Patterson, V-F | | | | CJ Matti, V-P | RF Tobey, VP | | | MJ Makoski, VP | | | | |
| 8 | ★ Champion Spark Plug Co | 900 Upton Ave | Toledo | OH | 43661 | OL Henry | 419-535-2567 | 3694 | Elec Eq-Engine | 884 | 12.4 | Y | Y | 1910 |
| | | RA Stranahan Jr, CB | | | | JG Zimmerman, TR | RD Kudner, V-M | | | RL Black, V-R | | | | |
| 9 | ■ Ford Electrncs & Ref Pa | Church Rd | Lansdale | PA | 19446 | GA Lutz | 215-362-3013 | 3694 | Elec Eq-Engine | 520* | 2.9 | | Y | 1960 |
| | # Ford Electrncs & Ref | 3001 Miller Rd | Dearborn | MI | 48121 | PE Benton | 313-322-3000 | 3585 | Air Cond&Heatg | | | | | |
| | ★ Ford Motor Co | Po Box 1899 | Dearborn | MI | 48121 | DE Peterson | 313-322-3000 | 3711 | Motor Vehicles | 62716 | 382.3 | Y | Y | 1919 |
| 10 | # Ford Mtr Electrical-Mi | 128 Factory | Ypsilanti | MI | 48197 | F Macher | 313-484-8000 | 3694 | Elec Eq-Engine | 500 | 2.0 | | | 1932 |
| | # Ford Mtr Electrcl & E | Mckean & Textil | Ypsilanti | MI | 48197 | FE Macher | 313-484-8400 | 3694 | Elec Eq-Engine | 1600* | 20.0 | | | 1975 |
| | ★ Ford Motor Co | Po Box 1899 | Dearborn | MI | 48121 | DE Peterson | 313-322-3000 | 3711 | Motor Vehicles | 62716 | 382.3 | Y | Y | 1919 |
| 11 | ★ Medtronic Inc | 7000 Centrl N E | Minneapolis | MN | 55432 | WR Wallin | 612-574-4000 | 3693 | X-Ray Apparatu | 403 | 4.9 | Y | Y | 1949 |
| | | GD Nelson, EVP | | | | GC Planchon, EVP | | | | | | | | |
| 12 | GNB Inc | Po Box 64100 | St Paul | MN | 55164 | S Gaines | 612-681-5000 | 3691 | Storage Battry | 350 | 3.0 | | Y | 1983 |
| 13 | Exide Corp | 101 Gibraltar | Horsham | PA | 19044 | A Hawkins | 215-674-9500 | 3692 | Primary Battry | 300 | 2.0 | | | 1888 |
| 14 | ■ Genl Battery Corp | Po Box 14205 | Reading | PA | 19612 | JW Horton | 215-378-0500 | 3691 | Storage Battry | 300 | 3.5 | | | 1931 |
| | Farley Industries Inc | 233 S Wacker Dr | Chicago | IL | 60606 | WF Farley | 312-876-1724 | 2322 | Underwear-Male | 1200* | 25.0 | Y | Y | 1977 |
| 15 | ★ Std Motor Products | 37-18 Northern | Long Isl Cy | NY | 11101 | L Sills | 718-392-0200 | 3694 | Elec Eq-Engine | 286 | 3.2 | | Y | 1919 |
| | | NL Sills, CB | | | | B Fife, CB | MS Chanko, V-F | | | S Brown, V-M | | | | |
| 16 | # Genl Elec-Medical Sys | Po Box 414 | Milwaukee | WI | 53201 | J Trani | 414-544-3011 | 3693 | X-Ray Apparatu | 260* | 4.5 | Y | Y | 1973 |
| | ★ Genl Electric Co | 3135 Easton Tpk | Fairfield | CT | 06431 | JF Welch Jr | 203-373-2431 | 3621 | Motor&Generatr | 35211 | 359.0 | Y | Y | 1883 |
| 17 | ■ Eveready Battery Co | Checkerboard Sq | St Louis | MO | 63164 | JP Mulcahy | 314-982-1000 | 3691 | Storage Battry | 246 | | | | |
| | ★ Ralston Purina Co | Checkerboard Sq | St Louis | MO | 63164 | WP Stiritz | 314-982-1000 | 2048 | Anml Feed,Nec. | 5515 | 62.5 | Y | Y | 1894 |
| 18 | ■ Wickes Manufacturing Co | 26261 Evergreen | Southfield | MI | 48075 | NJ Feloa | 313-355-8000 | 3694 | Elec Eq-Engine | 215 | 5.4 | Y | Y | 1961 |
| | ★ Wickes Companies Inc | Po Box 4056 | Santa Monic | CA | 90405 | SC Sigoloff | 213-452-0161 | 5211 | Lumber&Mtrl De | 2806 | 57.4 | | Y | 1854 |
| 19 | Coulter Electronics Inc | 600 W 20th St | Hialeah | FL | 33010 | JR Coulter Jr | 305-885-0131 | 3693 | X-Ray Apparatu | 205* | 2.9 | Y | Y | 1959 |
| 20 | Rayovac Corp | 601 Rayovac Dr | Madison | WI | 53711 | TF Pyle | 608-275-3340 | 3692 | Primary Battry | 200 | 2.1 | | Y | 1906 |
| 21 | ★ Intermedics Inc | 4000 Technology | Angleton | TX | 77515 | RA Gilleland | 409-848-4000 | 3693 | X-Ray Apparatu | 178 | 1.6 | | Y | 1973 |
| | | JA Kenton, V-F | | | | RO Martin, VP | PG Dorflinger, VP | | | JS Fraser, VP | | | | |
| 22 | # Eagle-Picher Inds-Elect | Po Box 47 | Joplin | MO | 64802 | P Eddy | 417-623-8000 | 3692 | Primary Battry | 175 | 1.5 | Y | Y | 1843 |
| | ★ Eagle-Picher Industri | 580 Walnut St | Cincinnati | OH | 45202 | TE Petry | 513-721-7010 | 3981 | Divers,Conglom | 648 | 7.9 | Y | Y | 1843 |
| 23 | ■ Gates Energy Prdts-Fl | Po Box 114 | Gainesville | FL | 32602 | RH Shiley | 904-462-3911 | 3692 | Primary Battry | 175 | 3.0 | Y | Y | |
| | Gates Corp | Po Box 5887 | Denver | CO | 80217 | D Miller | 303-744-1911 | 3041 | Rub&Pla Hos&Bt | 1085* | 13.0 | | Y | 1911 |
| 24 | # Eaton Controls-Schiller | 9655 Soreng Ave | Schiller Pk | IL | 60176 | R Phillips | 312-678-4150 | 3699 | Elec Ma Eq,Nec | 165* | 5.0 | Y | Y | 1926 |
| | ★ Eaton Corp | Eaton Center | Cleveland | OH | 44114 | JR Stover | 216-523-5000 | 3714 | Vehicle Parts. | 3812 | 43.4 | Y | Y | 1911 |
| 25 | Rea Magnet Wire Co | Po Box 6128 | Fort Wayne | IN | 46896 | J Vann | 219-424-4252 | 3694 | Elec Eq-Engine | 150 | .7 | | | 1933 |
| 26 | ■ Philips Medical Sys Inc | 710 Bridgport | Shelton | CT | 06484 | DM Protomastor | 203-926-7674 | 3693 | X-Ray Apparatu | 137 | 2.0 | Y | Y | 1934 |
| | ■ No American Philips | 100 E 42nd St | New York | NY | 10017 | C Bruynes | 212-697-3600 | 3651 | Radio&Tv Recei | 4532 | 50.4 | Y | Y | 1954 |
| | ★ Philips Gloeilampen | Groenewoudseweg | Eindhoven | | 5621 | W Dekker | 31-40-783496 | 3573 | Elec Comp Equi | | | | | |
| 27 | Astronautics Corp/Amer | Po Box 523 | Milwaukee | WI | 53201 | NK Zelazo | 414-447-8200 | 3699 | Elec Ma Eq,Nec | 120 | 1.5 | Y | Y | 1959 |
| 28 | East Penn Mfg Co | Deka Rd | Lyon Sta | PA | 19536 | D Breidegam Jr | 215-682-6361 | 3691 | Storage Battry | 116 | 1.3 | Y | Y | 1946 |
| 29 | # Allied-Signal Autolite | 1600 N Union St | Fostoria | OH | 44830 | MW Semeyn | 419-435-6655 | 3694 | Elec Eq-Engine | 105 | 1.5 | Y | Y | 1927 |
| | ★ Allied-Signal Inc | Po Box 2245r | Morristown | NJ | 07960 | EL Hennessy Jr | 201-455-2000 | 3981 | Divers,Conglom | 11794 | 137.2 | Y | Y | 1920 |
| 30 | ★ Arrow Automotive Inds | 5 Speen St | Framingham | MA | 01701 | HA Holzwasser | 617-872-3711 | 3694 | Elec Eq-Engine | 100 | 1.6 | Y | Y | 1929 |
| | | DL Koontz, EVP | | | | JF Fagan, V-F | JD Holzwasser, V-M | | | RA Holzwasser, V-R | | | | |
| 31 | ■ Pac Chloride Inc | 1200 Brookstone | Columbus | GA | 31904 | B Brumback | 404-322-7337 | 3691 | Storage Battry | 100 | .8 | | | |
| | ★ Pac Dunlop Limited | 500 Bourke Stre | Melbourne | | 3000 | JB Gough | 61-3-602-424 | 3011 | Tire&Innr Tube | | | | | |
| 32 | # Duracell U S A-Tn | Po Box 3390 | Cleveland | TN | 37311 | E Battocchio | 615-476-7503 | 3691 | Storage Battry | 100 | .6 | | | 1961 |
| | ■ Duracell Inc | Berkshire Indus | Bethel | CT | 06801 | CR Kidder | 203-796-4000 | 3691 | Storage Battry | 963 | 9.5 | | | |
| | ★ Kraft Inc | Kraft Court | Glenview | IL | 60025 | JM Richman | 312-998-2000 | 2022 | Cheese,Nat&Pro | 8742 | 51.3 | | Y | 1902 |
| 33 | ■ Siemens Gammasonics Inc | 2000 Nuclear Dr | Des Plaines | IL | 60018 | G Barone | 312-635-3100 | 3693 | X-Ray Apparatu | 100 | .8 | | Y | 1955 |
| | ★ Siemens Ag | Postfach 103 Wi | Munich 2 | | D-800 | K Kaske | 49-89-234-1 | 3661 | Telephone&Telg | | | | | |
| 34 | C & D Power Systems Inc | 3043 Walton Rd | Plymth Mtg | PA | 19462 | D Murdoch | 215-828-9000 | 3692 | Primary Battry | 95* | 1.4 | | | 1906 |
| 35 | # Electronic Components | John St | Hudson Fls | NY | 12839 | P Mezey | 518-761-7578 | 3699 | Elec Ma Eq,Nec | 95* | 1.2 | Y | Y | |
| | ★ Genl Electric Co | 3135 Easton Tpk | Fairfield | CT | 06431 | JF Welch Jr | 203-373-2431 | 3621 | Motor&Generatr | 35211 | 359.0 | Y | Y | 1883 |
| 36 | # Bendix Engine Products | 7575 Baymeadows | Jacksonvll | FL | 32216 | JA Chrzan | 904-739-4000 | 3694 | Elec Eq-Engine | 92 | .7 | | | 1911 |
| | # Aircraft-Engine Sys | 1000 Wilson Blv | Arlington | VA | 22209 | FD Geldert | 703-527-0447 | 3724 | Aircraft Engin | | | | | |
| | ■ Aircraft Systems Co | 1000 Wilson Blv | Arlington | VA | 22209 | FM Adams | 703-276-2000 | 3662 | Radio&Tv Trans | | | | | |
| 37 | # Bendix Electric Power | 118 Rt 35 | Eatontown | NJ | 07724 | WH Graham | 201-542-2000 | 3694 | Elec Eq-Engine | 75 | 1.0 | | | |
| | ★ Allied-Signal Inc | Po Box 2245r | Morristown | NJ | 07960 | EL Hennessy Jr | 201-455-2000 | 3981 | Divers,Conglom | 11794 | 137.2 | Y | Y | 1920 |
| 38 | # Arrow Automotive-Sc | Po Box 1748 | Spartanburg | SC | 29304 | LG Szuhy | 803-583-7281 | 3694 | Elec Eq-Engine | 75 | .9 | Y | Y | 1952 |
| | ★ Arrow Automotive Inds | 5 Speen St | Framingham | MA | 01701 | HA Holzwasser | 617-872-3711 | 3694 | Elec Eq-Engine | 100 | 1.6 | Y | Y | 1929 |
| 39 | # Exide Corp-Sumter | Po Box 1797 | Sumter | SC | 29150 | AP Bracalente | 803-481-8511 | 3691 | Storage Battry | 70 | .5 | | | |
| | Exide Corp | 101 Gibraltar | Horsham | PA | 19044 | A Hawkins | 215-674-9500 | 3692 | Primary Battry | 300 | 2.0 | | | 1888 |
| 40 | # SAFT Amer Inc | Po Box 1886 | Valdosta | GA | 31601 | EL Nargi | 912-247-2331 | 3692 | Primary Battry | 70 | 1.1 | Y | Y | 1975 |
| | ■ SAFT | 156 Avenue De M | Romainville | | 93230 | GC Chazot | 33-1-48-43-9 | 3691 | Storage Battry | | | | | |
| | Electricite Cie Gen | 54 Rue La Boeti | Paris | | 75008 | G Pebereau | 33-1-4563141 | 3743 | Railroad Equip | | | | | |
| 41 | ■ Duracell U S A | Po Box 500 | Lancaster | SC | 29720 | D Byrd | 803-285-8401 | 3692 | Primary Battry | 68 | .8 | Y | Y | 1976 |
| | ★ Kraft Inc | Kraft Court | Glenview | IL | 60025 | JM Richman | 312-998-2000 | 2022 | Cheese,Nat&Pro | 8742 | 51.3 | | Y | 1902 |
| 42 | ★ Datascope Corp | Po Box 5 | Paramus | NJ | 07653 | L Saper | 201-265-8800 | 3693 | X-Ray Apparatu | 67 | .8 | | Y | |
| | | M Pitkowsky, V-F | | | | G Buis, V-M | G Heller, SRV | | | E Janzen, SRV | | | | |
| 43 | Ashley Products Inc | Rural Route 1 | Ashley | IN | 46705 | P Zimmerman | 219-587-9116 | 3699 | Elec Ma Eq,Nec | 65* | .7 | | Y | 1970 |
| 44 | ★ SL Industries Inc | 3 Greentree Cen | Marlton | NJ | 08053 | JC Instone | 609-596-7800 | 3694 | Elec Eq-Engine | 62 | .9 | | Y | 1956 |
| | | B Litschgi, CB | | | | CA Shipley, V-F | RT Cross, VP | | | GC Mason, VP | | | | |
| 45 | ■ Wells Manufacturing | Po Box 70 | Fond Du Lac | WI | 54935 | WE Allen | 414-922-5900 | 3694 | Elec Eq-Engine | 60 | .6 | Y | Y | 1903 |
| | UIS Inc | 600 5th Ave | New York | NY | 10020 | H Lebensfeld | 212-581-7660 | 3714 | Vehicle Parts. | 470 | 6.0 | Y | Y | 1944 |
| 46 | # Prestolite Electric-Al | Po Box 2205 | Decatur | AL | 35602 | S Florio | 205-353-8385 | 3694 | Elec Eq-Engine | 60 | .5 | | | 1960 |
| 47 | Jabil Circuit Co | 32275 Mally Rd | Madison Hts | MI | 48071 | W Morean | 313-589-3500 | 3694 | Elec Eq-Engine | 57 | .4 | | Y | 1965 |
| 48 | # IPM Co-Des Plaines | Po Box 5033 | Des Plaines | IL | 60017 | JR Schmelzer | 312-635-8080 | 3694 | Elec Eq-Engine | 55 | .2 | Y | Y | 1936 |
| | ★ Kearney-Natl Inc | 1701 Golf Rd | Rolling Mdw | IL | 60008 | RR Dyson | 312-593-6046 | 3621 | Motor&Generatr | 149 | 2.5 | | | 1843 |
| 49 | Electrochem Industries | 10000 Wehrle Dr | Clarence | NY | 14031 | W Graceville | 716-759-2828 | 3691 | Storage Battry | 52* | .5 | | | 1979 |
| 50 | # GNB Inc-Industl Battery | 2010 Cabot W #1 | Langhorne | PA | 19047 | AC Richards | 215-750-2600 | 3691 | Storage Battry | 50 | 1.0 | | | 1898 |
| | GNB Inc | Po Box 64100 | St Paul | MN | 55164 | S Gaines | 612-681-5000 | 3691 | Storage Battry | 350 | 3.0 | | Y | 1983 |
| 51 | ■ Gates Energy Prdts-Co | 1050 S Broadway | Denver | CO | 80217 | RH Shiley | 303-744-4806 | 3691 | Storage Battry | 50 | .9 | | | 1972 |
| | Gates Corp | Po Box 5887 | Denver | CO | 80217 | D Miller | 303-744-1911 | 3041 | Rub&Pla Hos&Bt | 1085* | 13.0 | | Y | 1911 |
| 52 | # Hewlett-Packard Mcmnnvl | 1700 S Baker St | Mcminnville | OR | 97128 | KM Patton | 503-472-5101 | 3693 | X-Ray Apparatu | 50 | .3 | | Y | |
| | ★ Hewlett-Packard Co | 3000 Hanover St | Palo Alto | CA | 94304 | JA Young | 415-857-1501 | 3573 | Elec Comp Equi | 7102 | 82.0 | Y | Y | 1939 |
| 53 | # Johnson Controls-Garlnd | Po Box 461729 | Garland | TX | 75046 | JG Lawrence | 214-494-2461 | 3691 | Storage Battry | 50 | .3 | | | 1935 |
| | ★ Johnson Controls Inc | Po Box 591 | Milwaukee | WI | 53201 | FL Brengel | 414-228-1200 | 3822 | Auto Controls. | 2639 | 26.9 | Y | Y | 1885 |
| 54 | ■ Automotive Controls | Echlin Rd | Branford | CT | 06405 | DS Carboni | 203-481-5771 | 3694 | Elec Eq-Engine | 50 | .2 | Y | Y | |
| | ★ Echlin Inc | 100 Double Bch | Branford | CT | 06405 | FJ Mancheski | 203-481-5751 | 3694 | Elec Eq-Engine | 902 | 13.2 | Y | Y | 1959 |
| 55 | ★ E-Z-Em Inc | 7 Portland Ave | Westbury | NY | 11590 | HS Stern | 516-333-8230 | 3693 | X-Ray Apparatu | 48 | .6 | | Y | 1962 |
| | | DJ Curtin, V-F | | | | ED Cohen, V-M | GP Carden, SRV | | | FR Greene, SRV | | | | |
| 56 | F & B Manufacturing Co | 5480 W Northwst | Chicago | IL | 60630 | MF Anderson | 312-774-6300 | 3694 | Elec Eq-Engine | 45 | .5 | | | |
| 57 | # Emerson Elec-Motor Div | Po Box 307 | Independnce | KS | 67301 | RC Boggs | 316-331-6650 | 3694 | Elec Eq-Engine | 42* | .8 | | | |
| | ★ Emerson Electric Co | 8000 W Florissa | St Louis | MO | 63136 | CF Knight | 314-553-2000 | 3621 | Motor&Generatr | 4953 | 60.7 | Y | Y | 1890 |
| 58 | # Boeing Electrncs-Dallas | Po Box 2707 | Irving | TX | 75061 | RD Riedasch | 214-659-2600 | 3694 | Elec Eq-Engine | 42* | .8 | | | 1979 |
| | ★ Boeing Co | 7755 E Marginal | Seattle | WA | 98108 | F Shrontz | 206-655-2121 | 3721 | Aircraft. | 16341 | 125.0 | | Y | 1934 |
| 59 | ■ Marathon Power Techngly | Po Box 8233 | Waco | TX | 76714 | RW Cowan | 817-776-0650 | 3691 | Storage Battry | 42* | .8 | Y | Y | 1971 |
| | ■ Marathon Manufacturin | 600 Jefferson | Houston | TX | 77002 | R Seegmeller | 713-659-7444 | 3533 | Oil Field Mach | 400 | 7.0 | Y | Y | 1969 |
| | ★ Penn Central Corp | 500 W Putnam | Greenwich | CT | 06836 | AW Martinelli | 203-629-5000 | 3674 | Semiconductors | 2388 | 24.3 | | | 1847 |
| 60 | ■ Power Conversion Inc | 495 Boulevard | Elmwood Pk | NJ | 07407 | B Jagid | 201-796-4800 | 3692 | Primary Battry | 40* | .8 | | Y | 1970 |
| | ★ Hawker Siddeley Group | 18 St James Squ | London | | SW1Y | P Baxendell | 44-1-930-617 | 3621 | Motor&Generatr | | | | | |
| 61 | # Exide Corp-Logansport | Po Box 30 | Logansport | IN | 46947 | G Durksen | 219-753-3177 | 3692 | Primary Battry | 40 | .3 | | | |
| | Exide Corp | 101 Gibraltar | Horsham | PA | 19044 | A Hawkins | 215-674-9500 | 3692 | Primary Battry | 300 | 2.0 | | | 1888 |
| 62 | Generac Corp | Po Box 8 | Waukesha | WI | 53187 | RD Kern | 414-544-4811 | 3694 | Elec Eq-Engine | 40 | .4 | Y | Y | 1959 |
| 63 | Phelon R E Co Inc | 70 Maple St | E Longmeadw | MA | 01028 | RD Phelon | 413-525-6471 | 3694 | Elec Eq-Engine | 38 | .8 | Y | Y | 1946 |

All figures in $ millions, except employees in 1000's. Type of Company: No code Private; ★ Public; # Division; ■ Subsidiary; * Affiliate; ¡ Joint Venture; △ Group; I. Import; E. Export; Yr.fd. Year Founded; * Ward's Estimate; < less than. Indented Companies are Parents of Divs., Subs., Etc. For other codes, abbrevs., see page at front.

Source: *1988 Ward's Business Directory*™. Published by Information Access Company, 362 Lakeside Drive, Foster City, CA 94404. Telephone numbers: 415-378-5300, 800-227-8431.

**Figure 3–3.** *Dun's Financial Records: Financials.*

| 12/31/85 Interim Financials | Company | % Change | Company % | Industry Norm % |
|---|---|---|---|---|
| Cash . . . . . . . . . . . . . . . . . . . . . . . . . . . . . . | 54,440 | 516.1 | 4.8 | 6.9 |
| Accounts Receivable . . . . . . . . . . . . . | 539,502 | 126.2 | 47.6 | 19.1 |
| Notes Receivable . . . . . . . . . . . . . . . . . | — | — | — | 0.1 |
| Inventory . . . . . . . . . . . . . . . . . . . . . . . | 364,396 | ( 11.4) | 32.1 | 18.6 |
| Other Current Assets . . . . . . . . . . . . . | 5,293 | ( 30.6) | 0.4 | 6.3 |
| **Total Current Assets** . . . . . . . . . . . . . . | 963,631 | 44.6 | 85.0 | 51.0 |
| Fixed Assets . . . . . . . . . . . . . . . . . . . . . | — | — | — | 25.7 |
| Other Non-current Assets . . . . . . . . . | 169,763 | 6.4 | 14.9 | 23.3 |
| **Total Assets** . . . . . . . . . . . . . . . . . . . . | 1,133,394 | 37.2 | 100.0 | 100.0 |
| Accounts Payable . . . . . . . . . . . . . . . . | 84,120 | 45.2 | 7.4 | 9.6 |
| Bank Loans . . . . . . . . . . . . . . . . . . . . . . | — | — | — | 1.3 |
| Notes Payable . . . . . . . . . . . . . . . . . . . | — | — | — | 3.6 |
| Other Current Liabilities . . . . . . . . . . | 584,971 | 804.9 | 51.6 | 15.4 |
| **Total Current Liabilities** . . . . . . . . . . . | 668,991 | 50.7 | 59.0 | 29.9 |
| Other Long Term Liabilities . . . . . . . . | 219,883 | ( 13.6) | 19.4 | 21.7 |
| Deferred Credits . . . . . . . . . . . . . . . . . | — | — | — | 0.3 |
| Net Worth . . . . . . . . . . . . . . . . . . . . . . | 244,520 | 92.0 | 21.5 | 48.1 |
| **Total Liabilities & Worth** . . . . . . . . . . . | 1,133,394 | 37.2 | 100.0 | 100.0 |
| Net Sales . . . . . . . . . . . . . . . . . . . . . . . | 1,392,686 | 7.1 | 100.0 | 100.0 |
| Gross Profit . . . . . . . . . . . . . . . . . . . . . | 497,170 | 17.1 | 35.6 | 32.6 |
| Net Profit After Tax . . . . . . . . . . . . . . | 117,181 | 101,181 | 8.4 | 6.9 |
| Dividends/Withdrawals . . . . . . . . . . | — | — | — | 1.8 |
| Working Capital . . . . . . . . . . . . . . . . . | 294,640 | 32.4 | — | — |

| Ratios | Company | % Change | Upper | Median | Lower |
|---|---|---|---|---|---|
| **Solvency** | | | | | |
| Quick Ratio . . . . . . . . . . . . . . . . . . . . . . | 0.9 | 50.0 | 1.4 | 1.0 | 0.5 |
| Current Ratio . . . . . . . . . . . . . . . . . . . . . | 1.4 | ( 6.6) | 2.7 | 1.8 | 1.3 |
| Current Liability to Net Worth (%) . . . . . | 273.6 | ( 21.5) | 32.3 | 61.8 | 121.0 |
| Current Liability to Inventory (%) . . . . . | 183.6 | 70.1 | 104.0 | 157.8 | 240.9 |
| Total Liability to Net Worth . . . . . . . . . . | 363.5 | ( 33.7) | 47.4 | 120.4 | 217.1 |
| Fixed Assets to Net Worth . . . . . . . . . . . | — | — | 48.3 | 93.2 | 126.1 |
| **Efficiency** | | | | | |
| Collection Period (days) . . . . . . . . . . . . | 141.2 | 78.2 | 37.9 | 48.5 | 70.3 |
| Sales to Inventory . . . . . . . . . . . . . . . . . | 3.8 | 40.7 | 14.3 | 7.2 | 4.2 |
| Assets to Sales (%) . . . . . . . . . . . . . . . . | 81.4 | 7.9 | 60.0 | 70.9 | 98.4 |
| Sales to Net Working Capital . . . . . . . . | 4.7 | ( 4.0) | 10.1 | 5.2 | 3.6 |
| Accounts Payable to Sales (%) . . . . . . . | 6.0 | 13.2 | 3.6 | 6.7 | 9.6 |
| **Profitability** | | | | | |
| Return on Sales (%) . . . . . . . . . . . . . . . | 8.4 | 133.3 | 9.0 | 5.4 | 2.7 |
| Return on Assets (%) . . . . . . . . . . . . . . . | — | — | 9.9 | 6.4 | 3.5 |
| Return on Net Worth (%) . . . . . . . . . . . . | — | — | 31.2 | 15.8 | 7.4 |
| Industry norms based on 92 firms. | | | | | |

**Dun's Financial Records** can provide financial statement information for up to three years (when available). Unshaded areas in the sample above indicate searchable fields.    *All illustrative data are fictitious.*

Source: *DunQuest.*

A representative screening available on the PC Screening Program of Interactive Data Corp. is shown in Figure 3–4. Here, the initial screening criteria are for a company in a specified industry with sales less than $30 million, net income in the 0- to $8-million range, a price-earnings ratio between 0 and 10, and a return on investment between 17 percent and 21 percent.

**Figure 3–4.** *Online searching with Interactive Data's "PC Screen."* ™

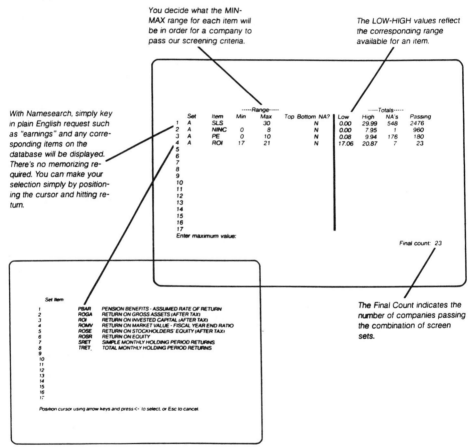

You decide what the MIN-MAX range for each item will be in order for a company to pass our screening criteria.

The LOW-HIGH values reflect the corresponding range available for an item.

With Namesearch, simply key in plain English request such as "earnings" and any corresponding items on the database will be displayed. There's no memorizing required. You can make your selection simply by positioning the cursor and hitting return.

| | Set | Item | ------Range----- Min | Max | Top | Bottom | NA? | Low | -----Totals----- High | NA's | Passing |
|---|---|---|---|---|---|---|---|---|---|---|---|
| 1 | A | SLS | | 30 | | | N | 0.00 | 29.99 | 548 | 2476 |
| 2 | A | NINC | 0 | 8 | | | N | 0.00 | 7.95 | 1 | 960 |
| 3 | A | PE | 0 | 10 | | | N | 0.08 | 9.94 | 176 | 180 |
| 4 | A | ROI | 17 | 21 | | | N | 17.06 | 20.87 | 7 | 23 |
| 5 | | | | | | | | | | | |
| 6 | | | | | | | | | | | |
| 7 | | | | | | | | | | | |
| 8 | | | | | | | | | | | |
| 9 | | | | | | | | | | | |
| 10 | | | | | | | | | | | |
| 11 | | | | | | | | | | | |
| 12 | | | | | | | | | | | |
| 13 | | | | | | | | | | | |
| 14 | | | | | | | | | | | |
| 15 | | | | | | | | | | | |
| 16 | | | | | | | | | | | |
| 17 | | | | | | | | | | | |

Enter maximum value:

Final count: 23

The Final Count indicates the number of companies passing the combination of screen sets.

| Set Item | | |
|---|---|---|
| 1 | PBAR | PENSION BENEFITS - ASSUMED RATE OF RETURN |
| 2 | ROGA | RETURN ON GROSS ASSETS (AFTER TAX) |
| 3 | ROI | RETURN ON INVESTED CAPITAL (AFTER TAX) |
| 4 | ROMV | RETURN ON MARKET VALUE - FISCAL YEAR END RATIO |
| 5 | ROSE | RETURN ON STOCKHOLDERS' EQUITY (AFTER TAX) |
| 6 | ROSR | RETURN ON EQUITY |
| 7 | SRET | SIMPLE MONTHLY HOLDING PERIOD RETURNS |
| 8 | TRET | TOTAL MONTHLY HOLDING PERIOD RETURNS |
| 9 | | |
| 10 | | |
| 11 | | |
| 12 | | |
| 13 | | |
| 14 | | |
| 15 | | |
| 16 | | |
| 17 | | |

Position cursor using arrow keys and press <- to select, or Esc to cancel

Let's say you're looking for a small company with sales less than $30 million, net income less than $8 million, but greater than 0, a price/earnings ratio between 0 and 10 and an acceptable return on investment. Twenty-three companies pass all the screening criteria.

By placing the cursor on any data item and hitting a single key, you can instantly display a histogram of the distribution of data values for the companies meeting your criteria.

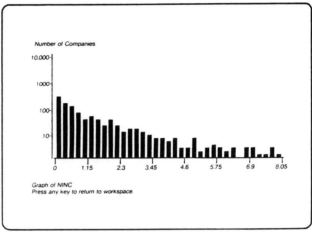

Hitting only one key, you can display a bar chart representing the distribution of the 960 companies passing your net income requirement.

At any point during a session the slash (/) key brings up the command list. You can change the screen by inserting or deleting a line, report results, or export the data to a 1-2-3 or Symphony spreadsheet.

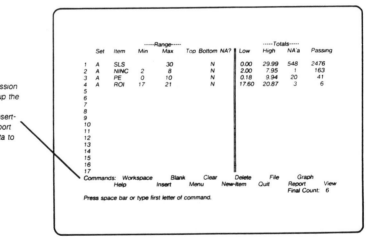

After seeing the graph, you decide to eliminate the outlying companies by modifying the net income to a range of $2 to $8 million. This narrows the final count to six companies.

Source: Interactive Data, Lexington, MA.

*FactSet* also provides extensive screening capabilities including provision for including custom-made variables. Both screening services provide considerable in-depth industry and company data. An analysis of a company by business sectors by *FactSet* is shown in Figure 3–6 and a comparative analysis (for example, drugs) of selected companies in an industry is shown in Figure 3–5.

**Figure 3–5.** *Illustrative screening data from FactSet: comparative analysis of companies within an industry (drugs).*

COMPARATIVE ANALYSIS

|  | ABT | BMY | MRK | LLY | PFE | SQB | UPJ |
|---|---|---|---|---|---|---|---|
| **VALUATION** | | | | | | | |
| Price ( 8/24/87) | 64.250 | 52.000 | 205.500 | 99.875 | 72.375 | 96.500 | 51.875 |
| Dividend | 1.00 | 1.40 | 2.20 | 2.00 | 1.80 | 1.20 | 0.60 |
| Yield | 1.6 | 2.7 | 1.1 | 2.0 | 2.5 | 1.2 | 1.2 |
| EPS | 2.52 | 2.31 | 5.69 | 4.29 | 4.14 | 2.94 | 1.52 |
| Sales/Shr | 17.74 | 17.93 | 33.22 | 28.22 | 27.31 | 18.61 | 12.93 |
| Book Value/Shr | 8.05 | 10.51 | 20.97 | 21.26 | 21.66 | 13.41 | 8.19 |
| P/E | 25.5 | 22.5 | 36.1 | 23.3 | 17.5 | 32.8 | 34.2 |
| Prc/Sls | 3.6 | 2.9 | 6.2 | 3.5 | 2.6 | 5.2 | 4.0 |
| Prc/Book | 8.0 | 4.9 | 9.8 | 4.7 | 3.3 | 7.2 | 6.3 |
| **GROWTH** | | | | | | | |
| Sales Growth | | | | | | | |
| 12 Mo. | 17.8 | 9.6 | 25.3 | 13.4 | 10.2 | 29.1 | 13.1 |
| 3 Yr | 10.5 | 5.5 | 9.7 | 9.5 | 4.8 | 0.2 | 2.5 |
| 5 Yr | 10.8 | 5.5 | 8.0 | 7.4 | 4.0 | 2.7 | 3.1 |
| EPS Growth | | | | | | | |
| 12 Mo. | 18.6 | 23.5 | 33.4 | 9.7 | 12.8 | 34.9 | 26.4 |
| 3 Yr | 17.4 | 11.3 | 16.3 | 9.4 | 12.5 | 14.0 | 15.4 |
| 5 Yr | 18.1 | 13.0 | 12.0 | 10.4 | 16.6 | 33.0 | 8.6 |
| R&D Expense | 284.9 | 311.1 | 479.8 | 427.0 | 335.5 | 163.0 | 314.1 |
| As % of Sales | 7.5 | 6.4 | 11.6 | 11.5 | 7.5 | 9.1 | 13.7 |
| Capital Expenditures | 383.4 | 221.9 | 210.6 | 322.6 | 196.1 | 95.1 | 201.9 |
| As % Beg. Gr Plant | 18.5 | 15.0 | 7.0 | 14.3 | 8.5 | 10.0 | 15.3 |
| **SIZE** | | | | | | | |
| Total Assets | 4069.4 | 4394.7 | 5473.6 | 4818.4 | 5715.6 | 2433.9 | 2853.3 |
| Net Sales (12 Mo) | 4067.5 | 5131.8 | 4563.2 | 3929.4 | 4672.7 | 1976.5 | 2422.7 |
| Net Income (12 Mo) | 580.0 | 661.0 | 781.0 | 615.4 | 702.8 | 311.7 | 284.4 |
| Market Value | 14658.3 | 14935.0 | 28131.3 | 13919.5 | 11947.2 | 10020.0 | 9730.5 |
| **PROFITABILITY** | | | | | | | |
| LATEST 12 MONTHS | | | | | | | |
| Asset Turnover | 1.04 | 1.22 | 0.85 | 0.81 | 0.89 | 0.73 | 0.90 |
| x Pretax Margin | 21.4 | 20.2 | 27.6 | 24.1 | 21.7 | 21.2 | 16.7 |
| = Pretax ROA | 22.3 | 24.7 | 23.5 | 19.6 | 19.4 | 15.5 | 15.0 |
| X 100-Tax Rate | 0.7 | 0.6 | 0.6 | 0.6 | 0.7 | 0.7 | 0.7 |
| = Net ROA | 14.9 | 15.7 | 14.6 | 12.6 | 13.4 | 11.4 | 10.6 |
| x Equity Leverage | 2.1 | 1.5 | 1.9 | 1.7 | 1.6 | 1.7 | 1.8 |
| = Net ROE | 31.5 | 23.3 | 27.3 | 21.0 | 20.8 | 19.8 | 19.1 |
| 5-YEAR AVERAGE | | | | | | | |
| Asset Turnover | 1.04 | 1.31 | 0.81 | 0.90 | 0.95 | 0.85 | 0.92 |
| x Pretax Margin | 20.2 | 18.4 | 22.7 | 24.1 | 19.8 | 16.3 | 12.5 |
| = Pretax ROA | 21.1 | 24.1 | 18.5 | 21.8 | 18.8 | 13.9 | 11.6 |
| X 100-Tax Rate | 0.6 | 0.6 | 0.6 | 0.6 | 0.6 | 0.7 | 0.7 |
| = Net ROA | 13.4 | 14.5 | 11.9 | 13.6 | 12.1 | 9.4 | 8.1 |
| x Equity Leverage | 2.0 | 1.5 | 1.8 | 1.6 | 1.7 | 1.7 | 2.0 |
| = Net ROE | 26.4 | 22.5 | 21.2 | 21.9 | 20.7 | 15.9 | 15.9 |

Source: FactSet Data Systems, Inc., New York, NY.

**Figure 3–6.** *Illustrative screening data from FactSet: company analysis.*

MRK   58933110   MERCK & CO

| | 12/86 | 12/85 | 12/84 | 12/83 | 12/82 | 12/81 | 12/80 | GROWTH RATE OR MEAN VALUES * 3 YEARS | 5 YEARS |
|---|---|---|---|---|---|---|---|---|---|
| HUMAN & ANIMAL HEALTH PRODS | (2834, | 2833) | | | | | | | |
| NET SALES | 3770.0 | 3097.1 | 2917.8 | 2640.5 | 2419.4 | 2265.8 | NA | 11.9 | 10.2 |
| COGS & SGA | 2624.5 | 2161.2 | 2068.7 | 1862.1 | 1778.8 | 1676.6 | NA | 11.3 | 8.7 |
| DEPRECIATION & AMORT. | 150.0 | 141.7 | 124.9 | 110.5 | 97.4 | 83.2 | NA | 11.0 | 12.7 |
| OPERATING PROFITS | 995.5 | 794.2 | 724.2 | 667.9 | 543.2 | 506.0 | NA | 13.8 | 14.1 |
| OPERATING CASH FLOW | 1145.5 | 935.9 | 849.1 | 778.4 | 640.6 | 589.2 | NA | 13.4 | 13.9 |
| CAPITAL EXPENDITURES | 196.8 | 219.2 | 243.0 | 222.7 | 237.0 | 296.0 | NA | -4.6 | -6.1 |
| IDENTIFIABLE ASSETS | 3253.6 | 3168.6 | 2953.4 | 2982.4 | 2478.3 | 2221.7 | NA | 3.4 | 7.8 |
| ANTIHYPERTENSIVES | 962.0 | 740.0 | 721.0 | 689.0 | 656.0 | 643.0 | NA | | |
| ANTI-INFLAMMATORIES | 630.0 | 546.0 | 591.0 | 591.0 | 586.0 | 570.0 | NA | | |
| ANTIBIOTIC-OPHTHAL | 886.0 | 713.0 | 585.0 | 219.0 | 202.0 | 206.0 | NA | | |
| OTHER-ANIMAL MEDIC | 1292.0 | 1092.0 | 1021.0 | 1142.0 | 975.0 | 847.0 | NA | | |
| % CHANGE ANALYSIS | | | | | | | | | |
| NET SALES | 21.7 | 6.1 | 10.5 | 9.1 | 6.8 | 0.0 | | | |
| OPERATING PROFITS | 25.3 | 9.7 | 8.4 | 23.0 | 7.4 | 0.0 | | | |
| PROFITABILITY ANALYSIS | | | | | | | | | |
| ASSET TURNOVER | 1.17 | 1.01 | .98 | .97 | 1.03 | NA | | * 1.06 | 1.03 |
| X OPERATING MARGIN | 26.4 | 25.6 | 24.8 | 25.3 | 22.5 | 22.3 | NA | * 25.6 | 24.9 |
| = OPERATING ROA | 31.0 | 25.9 | 24.4 | 24.5 | 23.1 | NA | | * 27.1 | 25.8 |
| OPERATING CASH ROA | 35.7 | 30.6 | 28.6 | 28.5 | 27.3 | NA | | * 31.6 | 30.1 |
| SPEC CHEMICAL-ENVIRONMENTAL | (2819, | 2899) | | | | | | | |
| NET SALES | 358.9 | 450.4 | 641.9 | 605.6 | 643.6 | 663.7 | NA | -17.5 | -11.0 |
| COGS & SGA | 291.7 | 370.1 | 537.1 | 528.6 | 559.9 | 568.6 | NA | -19.4 | -12.2 |
| DEPRECIATION & AMORT. | 17.2 | 21.9 | 26.7 | 24.7 | 23.7 | 21.8 | NA | -12.0 | -3.8 |
| OPERATING PROFITS | 50.0 | 58.4 | 78.1 | 52.3 | 60.0 | 73.3 | NA | -4.2 | -4.4 |
| OPERATING CASH FLOW | 67.2 | 80.3 | 104.8 | 77.0 | 83.7 | 95.1 | NA | -6.5 | -4.3 |
| CAPITAL EXPENDITURES | 13.8 | 18.4 | 31.4 | 50.1 | 58.1 | 26.8 | NA | -35.6 | -18.7 |
| IDENTIFIABLE ASSETS | 430.6 | 369.2 | 596.0 | 591.9 | 565.5 | 547.3 | NA | -13.4 | -6.8 |
| % CHANGE ANALYSIS | | | | | | | | | |
| NET SALES | -20.3 | -29.8 | 6.0 | -5.9 | -3.0 | 0.0 | | | |
| OPERATING PROFITS | -14.4 | -25.2 | 49.3 | -12.8 | -18.1 | 0.0 | | | |
| PROFITABILITY ANALYSIS | | | | | | | | | |
| ASSET TURNOVER | .90 | .93 | 1.08 | 1.05 | 1.16 | NA | | * .97 | 1.02 |
| X OPERATING MARGIN | 13.9 | 13.0 | 12.2 | 8.6 | 9.3 | 11.0 | NA | * 13.0 | 11.4 |
| = OPERATING ROA | 12.5 | 12.1 | 13.1 | 9.0 | 10.8 | NA | | * 12.6 | 11.5 |
| OPERATING CASH ROA | 16.8 | 16.6 | 17.6 | 13.3 | 15.0 | NA | | * 17.0 | 15.9 |
| COMPANY TOTALS | | | | | | | | | |
| NET SALES | 4128.9 | 3547.5 | 3559.7 | 3246.1 | 3063.0 | 2929.5 | .0 | 7.4 | 6.6 |
| COGS & SGA | 2916.2 | 2531.3 | 2605.8 | 2390.7 | 2338.7 | 2245.2 | .0 | 5.8 | 4.8 |
| DEPRECIATION & AMORT. | 167.2 | 163.6 | 151.6 | 135.2 | 121.1 | 105.0 | .0 | 7.4 | 10.0 |
| OPERATING PROFITS | 1045.5 | 852.6 | 802.3 | 720.2 | 603.2 | 579.3 | .0 | 12.5 | 12.4 |
| OPERATING CASH FLOW | 1212.7 | 1016.2 | 953.9 | 855.4 | 724.3 | 684.3 | .0 | 11.7 | 12.1 |
| CAPITAL EXPENDITURES | 210.6 | 237.6 | 274.4 | 272.8 | 295.1 | 322.8 | .0 | -8.8 | -7.6 |
| IDENTIFIABLE ASSETS | 3684.2 | 3537.8 | 3549.4 | 3574.3 | 3043.8 | 2769.0 | .0 | .9 | 5.5 |
| % CHANGE ANALYSIS | | | | | | | | | |
| NET SALES | 16.4 | -0.3 | 9.7 | 6.0 | 4.6 | 0.0 | | | |
| OPERATING PROFITS | 22.6 | 6.3 | 11.4 | 19.4 | 4.1 | 0.0 | | | |
| PROFITABILITY ANALYSIS | | | | | | | | | |
| ASSET TURNOVER | 1.14 | 1.00 | 1.00 | .98 | 1.05 | 2.12 | | * 1.05 | 1.04 |
| X OPERATING MARGIN | 25.3 | 24.0 | 22.5 | 22.2 | 19.7 | 19.8 | NA | * 24.0 | 22.8 |
| = OPERATING ROA | 29.0 | 24.1 | 22.5 | 21.8 | 20.8 | 41.8 | | * 25.2 | 23.6 |
| OPERATING CASH ROA | 33.6 | 28.7 | 26.8 | 25.9 | 24.9 | 49.4 | | * 29.7 | 28.0 |
| NET SALES | | | | | | | | | |
| HUMAN & ANIMAL HEALTH PRODS | 91.3 | 87.3 | 82.0 | 81.3 | 79.0 | 77.3 | NA | | |
| SPEC CHEMICAL-ENVIRONMENTAL | 8.7 | 12.7 | 18.0 | 18.7 | 21.0 | 22.7 | NA | | |
| OPERATING PROFITS | | | | | | | | | |
| HUMAN & ANIMAL HEALTH PRODS | 95.2 | 93.2 | 90.3 | 92.7 | 90.1 | 87.3 | NA | | |
| SPEC CHEMICAL-ENVIRONMENTAL | 4.8 | 6.8 | 9.7 | 7.3 | 9.9 | 12.7 | NA | | |
| CAPITAL EXPENDITURES | | | | | | | | | |
| HUMAN & ANIMAL HEALTH PRODS | 93.4 | 92.3 | 88.6 | 81.6 | 80.3 | 91.7 | NA | | |
| SPEC CHEMICAL-ENVIRONMENTAL | 6.6 | 7.7 | 11.4 | 18.4 | 19.7 | 8.3 | NA | | |
| IDENTIFIABLE ASSETS | | | | | | | | | |
| HUMAN & ANIMAL HEALTH PRODS | 88.3 | 89.6 | 83.2 | 83.4 | 81.4 | 80.2 | NA | | |
| SPEC CHEMICAL-ENVIRONMENTAL | 11.7 | 10.4 | 16.8 | 16.6 | 18.6 | 19.8 | NA | | |

(C) 1986, 1987, FACTSET DATA SYSTEMS

Source: FactSet Data Systems, Inc., New York, NY.

### *Where to Find More Detailed Information*

In-depth background information on publicly traded companies is available from the following:

*Moody's Manuals* (Moody's Investors Service, New York, NY). This annual seven-volume service has semiweekly or weekly updates. The titles of the manuals are:

- *Moody's Bank and Finance Manual*
- *Moody's Industrial Manual*
- *Moody's International Manual*
- *Moody's Municipal and Government Manual*
- *Moody's OTC Industrial Manual*
- *Moody's Public Utility Manual*
- *Moody's Transportation Manual*

Online access to the Moody's database is available through *DIALOG*.

*Standard & Poor's Corporate Descriptions* is another detailed compendium of information on publicly traded U.S. companies, similar in content to Moody's. Of the two services, Moody's tends to be more detailed. The S&P service is updated bimonthly and is also available on *DIALOG*.

*Disclosure* (Disclosure, Inc., Bethesda, MD) is a service that provides all reports filed with the SEC. Complete filings are available from 1968 to the present on microfiche, paper, and online through *DIALOG* or Dow Jones News Retrieval. *Disclosure* also provides a corporate profile service that includes a description of the business, information on shares and the number of shareholders, two-year balance sheets, three-year income statements, quarterly income statements, five-year summaries, names and remuneration of officers and directors, and information on labor contracts, pension plans, and so forth. Descriptions of all SEC filings are given in Appendix 3–C.

Detailed information concerning many nonpublic companies is available from the *Dun and Bradstreet PRO Reports.*

These reports provide in a narrative format an in-depth financial analysis, including a description of the business, the industry, and an analysis of operating results, assets, and liabilities. A companion *Financial Profile Report* provides a detailed spreadsheet of a company's financial statements, business ratios, and year-to-year changes in the data. Reports are available on paper or online through Dun and Bradstreet.

Credit information is also available from TRW Business Credit Service (Orange, CA) both online and through the mail. The *TRW* database includes over 8 million establishments. Data given includes a general description of the company, payment practices, date of last sale, detailed aging data on delinquent accounts, and banking information.

## Suppliers

Suppliers may provide a source of acquisition leads. A helpful guide to this source is *Thomas Register of American Manufacturers* (Thomas Publishing Company, New York, NY), available in hard copy and online through *DIALOG.*

If *Thomas Register* does not serve the need, then more specialized directories may be consulted using the various guides to directories listed in Chapter 2 or by contacting leading trade or professional organizations also described in Chapter 2.

When contacting suppliers, the best individuals to speak to are the sales personnel because they often have established relationships with their clients and hence may be aware of companies up for acquisition. Offering an incentive of some kind for sales personnel to come up with the names of attractive targets helps to ensure cooperation.

### Industry Observers

Industry observers are sometimes useful in providing industry information and leads to acquisitions. Included in this group are consultants, financial analysts, government experts, trade journal editors, and market researchers. Directories of different types of observers are listed below:

*Bradford's Directory of Market Research Agencies and Management Consultants in the United States and the World* (Bradford's Directory of Research Agencies, Fairfax, VA)

This reference provides information on over 500 agencies and consultants in marketing research.

*Consultants and Consultant Organizations* (Gale Research Co., Detroit, MI)

This comprehensive listing and description of over 12,000 consultants by industry is available online.

*Directory of Research Services* (Marketing Research Associates, Chicago, IL)

Gives over 400 market research organizations in the United States and Canada.

*Directory of Marketing Research Houses and Services* (American Marketing Association, New York, NY)

*Directory of Wall Street Research* (Nelson Publications, Rye, NY)

Useful for identifying financial analysts covering specific companies and industries.

*Guide to Washington Experts* (Washington Researchers Publications, Washington, DC)

Lists over 12,000 experts in U.S. government departments and agencies by area of interest.

*U.S. Industrial Outlook* (Government Printing Office, Washington, DC)

U.S. government experts with their telephone numbers are listed at the end of each review article.

### Regional and Local Press

Information relating to smaller companies is often reported

in the local press. Many of these publications can be accessed via the Dow Jones News Retrieval database, which covers some 140 U.S. and Canadian regional business magazines and newspapers. Perhaps the best online source of U.S. and Canadian local and regional news is *VuText* (VuText Information Services, Philadelphia, PA). Additional information can often be obtained by calling the author of a relevant article or the newspaper editor. Newspapers and regional business journals included in *VuText* are listed in Appendix 3–D.

## *Information on Labor Contracts and Litigations*

To obtain information on a target's labor contract, contact the public affairs or research department of the relevant labor union and request a copy of the contract. Labor union addresses are listed in the *Encyclopedia of Associations* (Gale Research Co., Detroit, MI) and the *Directory of U.S. Labor Organizations* (Bureau of National Affairs, Washington, DC). The Bureau of Labor Statistics in Washington provides data on employment and wages in the nonagricultural industries.

Researching federal and state court records can reveal information that is unavailable from other sources. A search of federal and state court records by company name on *Lexis* (Mead Data Central, Dayton, OH) or *Westlaw* (West Publishing Company, St. Paul, MN) online services is usually the most convenient approach. However, because all cases are not reported by these services, a more complete search requires examining courthouse records in the same county (for state cases) or federal court jurisdiction as the company of interest. The court clerk is the person to contact for information and transcripts.

## *Information on Patents and Trademarks*

Obtaining ownership to patents or trademarks is sometimes an important consideration in seeking an acquisition. Information on intellectual property owned by a firm can be obtained from the following sources.

*Claims* is an online database available on *DIALOG* listing all U.S. patents that have been assigned to a company. Another *DIALOG* database, *World Patent Index,* contains data on millions of patents filed in 30 countries.

*Patent Intelligence and Technology Report* (IFF/Plenum Data Corp., Alexandria, VA) is also helpful in identifying technological areas where particular companies have been awarded patents over the last five years.

Extensive information on trademarks is available on *Trademarkscan* provided online by *DIALOG.*

## APPENDIX 3-A:
## Conditions for Submission of Companies by Broker to Buyer*

Buyers will accept only those submissions that conform to the following conditions:

a) Buyers will be presented with a written agreement between seller and broker indicating that the broker represents the seller and the effective period of the agreement.

b) Broker will present the buyer with a statement of who is responsible for the payment of the broker's fee and how the fee will be determined.

c) The buyer assumes no obligation to do more than consider each submission and to indicate to the broker his or her interest, if any, in further pursuing the proposed acquisition.

d) The buyer will treat each submission and any related information with discretion and will instruct those employees and others involved in the decision-making process as to the need for confidentiality. However, the buyer will not assume any responsibility for any disclosure of the information by such employees and others involved in the decision process.

Signed this _____ day of _____ 19 ____

_____        _____
Signature of Broker                Signature of Buyer

*The above and all other forms are illustrative only. Service of a competent professional should be sought when preparing a document.

# APPENDIX 3-B:
## Sample Buyer-to-Pay-Broker Letter

                                              Date

Mr. Bill Broker
266 Washington Street
Boston, Massachusetts 11111

Dear Mr. Broker:

We agree that if XYZ Corporation (Company) acquired the
stock or assets of a firm as the result of any submission
or introduction made by you within two (2) years following
such submission or introduction, the Company will pay you
at the closing a fee based on the aggregate considerations
paid according to the following schedule:

On the first million dollars of consideration
                    or part thereof . . . . . 5% fee
On the second million dollars of consideration
                    or part thereof . . . . . 4% fee
On the third million dollars of consideration
                    or part thereof . . . . . 3% fee
On the fourth million dollars of consideration
                    or part thereof . . . . . 2% fee
On the fifth million dollars of consideration
or part thereof and all greater amounts . . . 1% fee

The aggregate considerations will be determined as follows:

(1) The total proceeds paid at the completion of the sale (including installment payments) inclusive of cash, stock, notes, consulting agreements, liabilities assumed, and agreements not to compete.

(2) If the considerations include contingent payments, then 30% of the maximum amount of such payments are to be included in the aggregate considerations.

(3) If the aggregate consideration includes publicly traded securities, then the price of each security will be determined by averaging the closing price over a two-week period prior to the closing. If no public market exists, the price shall be taken as the fair market value agreed to by buyer and seller.

If you are in agreement, please so indicate by signing and returning the enclosed duplicate of this letter.

Sincerely,

by _____ for the Company
        Mr. Buyer

Date _____

Accepted and Agreed to:

_____
        Broker

_____
        Date

## APPENDIX 3-C:
## Information Available in SEC Filings*

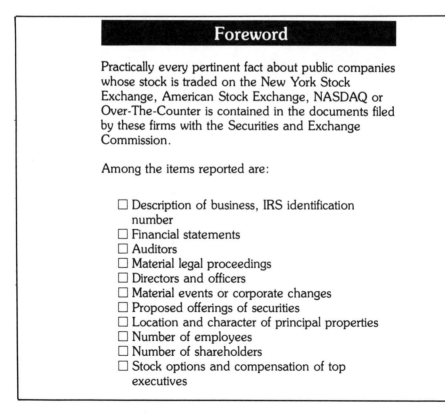

### Foreword

Practically every pertinent fact about public companies whose stock is traded on the New York Stock Exchange, American Stock Exchange, NASDAQ or Over-The-Counter is contained in the documents filed by these firms with the Securities and Exchange Commission.

Among the items reported are:

☐ Description of business, IRS identification number
☐ Financial statements
☐ Auditors
☐ Material legal proceedings
☐ Directors and officers
☐ Material events or corporate changes
☐ Proposed offerings of securities
☐ Location and character of principal properties
☐ Number of employees
☐ Number of shareholders
☐ Stock options and compensation of top executives

☐ Material agreements such as employment, financing, option and benefit plans, leases, etc.

This booklet explains the information that is contained in these reports and how often they are filed.

In addition, there is a reference chart to help you quickly pinpoint the filings that are of interest.

## Disclosure Statute

The purpose of the Federal securities laws is to provide disclosure of material financial and other information on companies seeking to raise capital through the public offering of their securities, as well as companies whose securities are already publicly held. This enables investors to evaluate the securities of these companies on an informed and realistic basis.

The Securities Act of 1933 is a *disclosure* statute. It generally requires that, before securities may be offered to the public, a registration statement must be filed with the Commission disclosing prescribed categories of information. Before the sale of securities can begin, the registration statement must become "effective," and investors must be furnished a prospectus containing the most significant information in the registration statement.

The Securities Act of 1934 deals in large part with securities already outstanding and requires the registration of securities listed on a national securities exchange, as well as Over-The-Counter securities in which there is a substantial public interest. Issuers of registered securities must file annual and other periodic reports designed to provide a public file of current material information. The Exchange Act also requires disclosure of material information to holders of registered securities in solicitations of proxies for the election of directors or approval of corporate action at a shareholders meeting, or in attempts to acquire control of a company through a tender offer or other planned stock acquisitions. It provides that insiders of companies whose equity securities are registered must report their holdings and transactions in all equity securities of their companies.

# 10-K

This report provides a comprehensive overview of the registrant. The report must be filed within 90 days after close of company's fiscal year and contains the following items of disclosure:

## ITEMS REPORTED
## PART I

**1. Business.** Identifies principal products and services of the company, principal markets and methods of distribution and, if "material," competitive factors, backlog and expectation of fulfillment, availability of raw materials, importance of patents, licenses, and franchises, estimated cost of research, number of employees, and effects of compliance with ecological laws.

If there is more than one line of business, a statement is included for each of the last three years. The statement includes total sales and net income for each line which during either of the last two fiscal years accounted for 10 percent or more of total sales or pretax income.

**2. Properties.** Location and character of principal plants, mines, and other important properties and if held in fee or leased.

**3. Legal Proceedings.** Brief description of material legal proceedings pending.

**4. Submission of Matters to a Vote of Security Holders.** Information relating to the convening of a meeting of shareholders, whether annual or special, and the matters voted upon.

## PART II

**5. Market for the Registrant's Common Stock and Related Security Holder Matters.** Includes principal market in which voting securities are traded with high and low sales prices (in the absence thereof, the range of bid and asked quotations for each quarterly period during the past two years) and the dividends paid during the past two years. In addition to the frequency and amount of dividends paid, this item contains a discussion concerning future dividends.

6. **Selected Financial Data.** These are five-year selected data including net sales and operating revenue; income or loss from continuing operations, both total and per common share; total assets; long-term obligations including redeemable preferred stock; cash dividend declared per common share. This data also includes additional items that could enhance understanding of trends in financial condition and results of operations. Further, the effects of inflation and changing prices should be reflected in the five-year summary.

7. **Management's Discussion and Analysis of Financial Condition and Results of Operations.** Under broad guidelines, this includes: liquidity, capital resources and results of operations; trends that are favorable or unfavorable as well as significant events or uncertainties; causes of any material changes in the financial statements as a whole; limited data concerning subsidiaries; discussion of effects of inflation and changing prices.

8. **Financial Statements and Supplementary Data.** Two-year audited balance sheets as well as three-year audited statements of income and changes in financial condition.

9. **Disagreements on Accounting and Financial Disclosure.**

## PART III

10. **Directors and Executive Officers of the Registrant.** Name, office, term of office and specific background data on each.

11. **Remuneration of Directors and Officers.** List of each director and three highest paid officers with

aggregate annual remuneration exceeding $40,000. Also includes total paid all officers and directors.

**12. Security Ownership of Beneficial Owners and Management.** Identification of owners of 5 percent or more of registrant's stock in addition to listing the amount and percent of each class of stock held by officers and directors.

**13. Certain Relationships and Related Transactions.**

## PART IV

**14. Exhibits, Financial Statement Schedules and Reports on Form 8-K.** Complete, audited annual financial information and a list of exhibits filed. Also, any unscheduled material events or corporate changes filed in an 8-K during the year.

## FORM 10-K SCHEDULES

    I. Investments other than investments in affiliates
    II. Receivables from related parties and underwriters, promoters and employees other than affiliates
    III. Condensed financial information
    IV. Indebtedness of affiliates (not current)
    V. Property, plant and equipment
    VI. Accumulated depreciation, depletion, and amortization of property, plant and equipment
    VII. Guarantees of securities of other issuers
    VIII. Valuation and qualifying accounts
    IX. Short-term borrowings
    X. Supplementary income statement information
    XI. Supplementary profit and loss information
    XII. Income from dividends (equity in net profit and loss of affiliates)

## 20-F

Annual Registration/statement filed by certain foreign issuers of securities trading in the United States. The

20-F report must be filed 6 months after close of fiscal year.

## PART I

Item 1 Business
Item 2 Description of Property
Item 3 Material Legal Proceedings
Item 4 Control of Registrant
Item 5 Nature of Trading Market
Item 6 Exchange Controls and Other Limitations
Affecting Security Holders
Item 7 Taxation
Item 8 Selected Financial Data
Item 9 Management Discussion and Analysis
Item 10 Directors and Officers
Item 11 Compensation
Item 12 Options to Purchase Securities from
Registrant or Subsidiaries
Item 13 Interests of Management in Certain
Transactions

## PART II

Item 14 Description of Securities

## PART III

Item 15 Defaults upon Senior Securities
Item 16 Changes in Securities and Changes in
Security for Registered Securities

## PART IV

Item 17 Financial Statements and Exhibits

## 10-Q

This is the quarterly financial report filed by most companies, which, although unaudited, provides a continuing view of a company's financial position during the year. The 10-Q report must be filed 45 days after close of fiscal quarter.

## ITEMS REPORTED

## PART I

### Financial Statements

1. Financial Statements
2. Management Discussion
3. Statement of Source and Application of Funds
4. A narrative analysis of material changes in the amount of revenue and expense items in relation to previous quarters, including the effect of any changes in accounting principles

## PART II

1. **Legal Proceedings.** Brief description of material legal proceedings pending; when civil rights or ecological statutes are involved, proceedings must be disclosed.
2. **Changes in Securities.** Material changes in the rights of holders of any class of registered security.
3. **Defaults upon Senior Securities.** Material defaults in the payment if principal, interest, sinking fund or purchase fund installment, dividend, or other material default not cured within 30 days.
4. **Submission of Matters to a Vote of Security Holders.** Information relating to the convening of a meeting of shareholders, whether annual or special, and the matters voted upon, with particular emphasis on the election of directors.
5. **Other Materially Important Events.** Information on any other item of interest to shareholders not already provided for in this form.
6. **Exhibits and Reports on Form 8-K.** Any unscheduled material events or corporate changes filed on an 8-K during the prior quarter.

## 8-K

This is a report of unscheduled material events or corporate changes deemed of importance to the shareholders or to the SEC. Corporate changes must be filed 15 days after the event, except for Other Materially Important Events which has no mandatory filing time.

1. Changes in Control of Registrant
2. Acquisition or Disposition of Assets
3. Bankruptcy or Receivership
4. Changes in Registrant's Certifying Accountant
5. Other Materially Important Events
6. Resignations of Registrant's Directors
7. Financial Statements and Exhibits

## 10-C

Over-The-Counter companies use this form to report changes in name or amount of NASDAQ-listed securities. It is similar in purpose to the 8-K and must be filed 10 days after change.

## 13-F

A quarterly report of equity holdings required of all institutions with equity assets of $100 million or more. This includes banks, insurance companies, investment companies, investment advisors and large internally managed endowments, foundations and pension funds. The report must be filed 45 days after close of fiscal quarter.

## Proxy Statement

A proxy statement provides official notification to designated classes of shareholders of matters to be brought to a vote at a shareholders meeting. Proxy votes may be solicited for changing the company officers, or many other matters. Disclosures normally made via a proxy statement may in some cases be made using Form 10-K (Part III).

## Registration Statements

Registration statements are of two principal types: (1)

"offering" registrations filed under the 1933 Securities Act, and (2) "trading" registrations filed under the 1934 Securities Exchange Act.

"Offering" registrations are used to register securities before they may be offered to investors. Part I of the registration, a preliminary prospectus or "red herring," is promotional in tone; it carries all the sales features that will be contained in the final prospectus. Part II of the registration contains detailed information about marketing agreements, expenses of issuance and distribution, relationship of the company with experts named in the registration, sales to special parties, recent sales of unregistered securities, subsidiaries of registrant, franchises and concessions, indemnification of directors and officers, treatment of proceeds from stock being registered, and financial statements and exhibits.

"Offering" registration statements vary in purpose and content according to the type of organization issuing stock:

**S-1**      Companies reporting under the 1934 Act for less than 3 years. Permits no incorporation by reference and requires complete disclosure in the prospectus.

**S-2**      Companies reporting under the 1934 Act for 3 years or more but not meeting the minimum voting stock requirement. Reference of 1934 Act reports permits incorporation and presentation of financial information in the prospectus or in an annual report to shareholders delivered with the prospectus.

**S-3**      Companies reporting under the 1934 Act for 3 or more years and having at least $150 million of voting stock held by non-affiliates, or as an alternative test, $100 million of voting stock coupled with an annual trading volume of 3 million shares. Allows minimal disclosure in the prospectus and maximum incorporation by reference of 1934 Act reports.

**S-4**      Registration used in certain business combinations or reorganization. Replaces S-14, S-15, 7/85.

**N-1A** Filed by open-end management investment companies other than separate accounts of insurance companies.

**N-2** Filed by closed-end management investment companies.

**N-5** Registration of small business investment companies.

**N-SAR** Annual statement of management investment companies.

**S-6** Filed by unit investment trusts registered under the Investment Act of 1940 on Form N-8B-2.

**S-8** Registration used to register securities to be offered to employees under stock option and various other employee benefit plans.

**S-11** Filed by real estate companies, primarily limited partnerships and investment trusts.

**S-18** Short form initial registration up to $7.5 million.

**SE** Non-electronically filed exhibits made by registrants filing with the EDGAR PILOT PROJECT.

**F-1** Registration of securities by foreign private issuers eligible to use form 20-F, for which no other form is prescribed.

**F-2** Registration of securities of foreign private issuers meeting certain 1934 Act filing requirements.

**F-3** Registration of securities of foreign private issuers offered pursuant to certain types of transactions, subject to the 1934 Act filing requirements for the preceding three years.

## Quick Reference Chart to Contents of SEC Filings

| REPORT CONTENTS | 10-K | 20-F | 10-Q | 8-K | 10-C | 6-K | Proxy Statements | Prospectus | F-10 8-A 8-B ('34 Act) | '33 Act "S" Type | ARS | Listing Application | N-SAR |
|---|---|---|---|---|---|---|---|---|---|---|---|---|---|
| **Auditor** | | | | | | | | | | | | | |
| ☐ Name | | | | | | | | | | | | | |
| ☐ Opinion | | | | | | | | | | | | | |
| ☐ Changes | | | | | | | | | | | | | |
| **Compensation Plans** | | | | | | | | | | | | | |
| ☐ Equity | | | | | | | | | | | | | |
| ☐ Monetary | | | | | | | | | | | | | |
| **Company Information** | | | | | | | | | | | | | |
| ☐ Nature of Business | | | | | | | | | | | | | |
| ☐ History | | | | | | | | | | | | | |
| ☐ Organization and Change | | | | | | | | | | | | | |
| **Debt Structure** | | | | | | | | | | | | | |
| **Depreciation & Other Schedules** | | | | | | | | | | | | | |
| **Dilution Factors** | | | | | | | | | | | | | |
| **Directors, Officers, Insiders** | | | | | | | | | | | | | |
| ☐ Identification | | | | | | | | | | | | | |
| ☐ Background | | | | | | | | | | | | | |
| ☐ Holdings | | | | | | | | | | | | | |
| ☐ Compensation | | | | | | | | | | | | | |
| **Earnings Per Share** | | | | | | | | | | | | | |
| **Financial Information** | | | | | | | | | | | | | |
| ☐ Annual Audited | | | | | | | | | | | | | |
| ☐ Interim Audited | | | | | | | | | | | | | |
| ☐ Interim Unaudited | | | | | | | | | | | | | |
| **Foreign Operations** | | | | | | | | | | | | | |
| **Labor Contracts** | | | | | | | | | | | | | |
| **Legal Agreements** | | | | | | | | | | | | | |
| **Legal Counsel** | | | | | | | | | | | | | |
| **Loan Agreements** | | | | | | | | | | | | | |
| **Plants and Properties** | | | | | | | | | | | | | |
| **Portfolio Operations** | | | | | | | | | | | | | |
| ☐ Content (Listing of Securities) | | | | | | | | | | | | | |
| ☐ Management | | | | | | | | | | | | | |
| **Product-Line Breakout** | | | | | | | | | | | | | |
| **Securities Structure** | | | | | | | | | | | | | |
| **Subsidiaries** | | | | | | | | | | | | | |
| **Underwriting** | | | | | | | | | | | | | |
| **Unregistered Securities** | | | | | | | | | | | | | |
| **Block Movements** | | | | | | | | | | | | | |

**Legend**

■ always included

▨ frequently included

▨ special circumstances

| TENDER OFFER/ACQUISITION REPORTS | 13D | 13G | 14D-1 | 14D-9 | 13E-3 | 13E-4 |
|---|---|---|---|---|---|---|
| Name of Issuer (Subject Company) | | | | | | |
| Filing Person (or Company) | | | | | | |
| Amount of Shares Owned | | | | | | |
| Percent of Class Outstanding | | | | | | |
| Financial Statements of Bidder | | | | | | |
| Purpose of Tender Offer | | | | | | |
| Source and Amount of Funds | | | | | | |
| Identity and Background Information | | | | | | |
| Persons Retained, Employed or to be Compensated | | | | | | |
| Exhibits | | | | | | |

F-6     Registration of depositary shares evidenced by the American Depositary Receipts (ADRs).

"Trading" registrations are filed to permit trading among investors on a securities exchange or in the Over-The-Counter market. Registration statements which serve to register securities for trading fall into three categories:

1. **Form 10** is used by companies during the first two years they are subject to the 1934 Act filing requirements. It is a combination registration statement and annual report with information content similar to that of SEC required 10-Ks.

2. **Form 8-A** is used by 1934 Act registrants wishing to register *additional* securities or classes thereof.

3. **Form 8-B** is used by "successor issuers" (usually companies which have changed their name or state of incorporation) as notification that previously registered securities are to be traded under a new corporate identification.

## Prospectus

When the sale of securities as proposed in an "offering" registration statement is approved by the SEC, any changes required by the SEC are incorporated into the prospectus. This document must be made available to investors before the sale of the security is initiated. It also contains the actual offering price, which may have been changed after the registration statement was approved.

## Annual Report to Shareholders

The Annual Report is the principal document used by most major companies to communicate directly with shareholders. Since it is not a required, official SEC filing, companies have considerable discretion in determining what types of information this report will contain and how it is to be presented.

In addition to financial information, the Annual Report to Shareholders often provides non-financial details of the business which are not reported elsewhere. These may include marketing plans and forecasts of future programs and plans.

## Form 8 (Amendment)

Form 8 is used to amend or supplement any 1934 Act report previously submitted. 1933 Act registration statements are amended by filing an amended registration statement (pre-effective amendment) or by the prospectus itself, as previously noted.

## Listing Application

Like the ARS, a listing application is not an official SEC filing. It is filed by the company with the NYSE, AMEX or other stock exchange to document proposed new listings. Usually a Form 8-A registration is filed with the SEC at about the same time.

## N-SAR

This form serves as either the annual or semiannual report for every registered investment company and as the annual report form for registered unit investment trusts. It is filed 60 days after the end of the appropriate period.

# TENDER OFFERS/ ACQUISITION REPORTS

## 13-G

An annual filing which must be filed by all reporting persons (primarily institutions) meeting the 5 percent equity ownership rule within 45 days after the end of each calendar year.

1. Name of issuer
2. Name of person filing
3. 13D-1 or 13D-2 applicability
4. Amount of shares beneficially owned:
   ☐ Percent of class outstanding
   ☐ Sole or shared power to vote
   ☐ Sole or shared power to dispose
5. Ownership of 5 percent or less of a class of stock
6. Ownership of more than 5 percent on behalf of another person
7. Identification of subsidiary which acquired the security being reported on by the parent holding company (if applicable)
8. Identification and classification of members of the group (if applicable)
9. Notice of dissolution of group (if applicable)
10. Certification

## 13-D

Filing required by 5 percent (or more) equity owners within 10 days of acquisition event.

1. Security and issuer
2. Identity and background of person filing the statement
3. Source and amount of funds or other consideration
4. Purpose of the transaction
5. Interest in securities of the issuer
6. Contracts, arrangements or relationships with respect to securities of the issuer
7. Material to be filed as exhibits which may include but are not limited to:
   ☐ Letter agreements between the parties
   ☐ Formal offer to purchase

## 14D-1

Tender offer filing made with the SEC at the time the offer is made to holders of equity securities of the target company, if acceptance of the offer would give the offerer over 5 percent ownership of the subject securities.

1. Security and subject company
2. Identity and background information
3. Past contacts, transactions or negotiations with subject company
4. Source and amount of funds or other consideration
5. Purpose of the tender offer and plans or proposals of the bidder
6. Interest in securities of the subject company
7. Contracts, arrangements or relationships with respect to the subject company's securities
8. Persons retained, employed or to be compensated
9. Financial statements of certain bidders
10. Additional information
11. Material to be filed as exhibits which may include but is not limited to:
    - ☐ The actual offer to purchase
    - ☐ The letter to shareholders
    - ☐ The letter of transmittal with notice of guaranteed delivery
    - ☐ The press release
    - ☐ The summary publication in business newspapers or magazines
    - ☐ The summary advertisement to appear in business newspapers or magazines

## 14D-9

A solicitation/recommendation statement that must be submitted to equity holders and filed with the SEC by the management of a company subject to a tender offer within 10 days of the making of the tender offer.

1. Security and subject company
2. Tender offer of the bidder
3. Identity and background
4. The solicitation or recommendation
5. Persons retained, employed or to be compensated
6. Recent transactions and intent with respect to securities
7. Certain negotiations and transactions by the subject company

8. Additional information
9. Material to be filed as exhibits

## 13E-4

Issuer tender offer statement pursuant to the Securities Exchange Act of 1934.

1. Security and issuer
2. Source and amount of funds
3. Purpose of the tender offer and plans or proposals of the issuer or affiliates
4. Interest in securities of the issuer
5. Contracts, arrangements or relationships with respect to the issuer's securities
6. Persons retained, employed or to be compensated
7. Financial information
8. Additional information
9. Material to be filed as exhibits which may include but is not limited to the offer to purchase which is being sent to the shareholders to whom the tender offer is being made

## 13E-3

Transaction statement pursuant to the Securities Exchange Act of 1934 with respect to a public company or affiliate going private.

1. Issuer and class of security subject to the transaction
2. Identity and background of the individuals
3. Past contacts, transactions or negotiations
4. Terms of the transaction
5. Plans or proposals of the issuer or affiliate
6. Source and amount of funds or other considerations
7. Purpose, alternatives, reasons and effects
8. Fairness of the transaction
9. Reports, opinions, appraisals and certain

negotiations
10. Interest in securities of the issuer
11. Contracts, arrangements or relationships with respect to the issuer's securities
12. Present intention and recommendation of certain persons with regard to the transaction
13. Other provisions of the transaction
14. Financial information
15. Persons and assets employed, retained or utilized
16. Additional information
17. Material to be filed as exhibits

*Source: *A Guide to SEC Corporate Filings,* Disclosure Incorporated, Bethesda, MD.

*Appendix 3-D*
*Representative Local Publications*
*Available on VuText*

| STATE | PUBLICATION | DATABASE | CITY PUBLISHED IN |
|---|---|---|---|
| ALABAMA | Alabama Business Review | BDL | (Montgomery) |
| | Birmingham Business Journal | BDL | (Birmingham) |
| | Birmingham News | PTS | (Birmingham) |
| | Business Alabama | PTS | (Birmingham) |
| ALASKA | Alaska Business Monthly | BDL | (Anchorage) |
| | Alaska Journal of Commerce | BDL | (Anchorage) |
| | Anchorage Daily News | N, PTS | (Anchorage) |
| ARKANSAS | Arkansas Business | BDL, PTS | (Little Rock) |
| | Arkansas Gazette | PTS | (Little Rock) |
| ARIZONA | Arizona Business Gazette | N, BDL,PTS | (Phoenix) |
| | Arizona Republic, The | N, PTS | (Phoenix) |
| | Arizona Trend | BDL | (Phoenix) |
| | The Business Journal-Phoenix and The Valley of the Sun | BDL, PTS | (Phoenix) |
| | Phoenix Gazette, The | N | (Phoenix) |
| | *Tucson Business Digest | BDL | (Tucson) |
| CALIFORNIA | Bakersfield Californian | PTS | (Bakersfield) |
| | Business Journal-Sacramento, The | BDL | (Sacramento) |
| | Business Journal-San Jose, The | BDL | (San Jose) |
| | *Business News-San Diego | BDL | (San Diego) |
| | California Business | PTS | (Los Angeles) |
| | California Executive, The | BDL | (Los Angeles) |
| | Daily News, Los Angeles | N | (Los Angeles) |
| | Executive, The | PTS | (Costa Mesa) |
| | Fresno Bee | N | (Fresno) |
| | Los Angeles Business Journal | BDL, PTS | (Los Angeles) |
| | Los Angeles Times | N, PTS | (Los Angeles) |
| | Orange County Business Journal | BDL, PTS | (Santa Ana) |
| | Orange County Register | PTS | (Santa Ana) |
| | Sacramento Bee | N. PTS | (Sacramento) |
| | San Diego Business Journal | BDL, PTS | (San Diego) |
| | San Diego Union | PTS | (San Diego) |
| | *San Francisco Business Journal | BDL, PTS | (San Francisco) |
| | San Francisco Business Magazine | BDL | (San Francisco) |
| | San Francisco Business Times | BDL,PTS | (San Francisco) |
| | San Francisco Chronicle | PTS | (San Francisco) |
| | San Francisco Examiner | PTS | (San Francisco) |
| | San Jose Business Journal | PTS | (San Jose) |
| | San Jose Mercury News | N, PTS | (San Jose) |
| | *Santa Clara County Business | BDL | (San Jose) |
| | *Santa Cruz County Business | BDL | (San Jose) |
| | *Silicon Valley | BDL | (Sunnyvale) |
| | Southern California Business | BDL, PTS | (Los Angeles) |
| DELAWARE | Morning News | PTS | (Wilmington) |
| | News Journal | PTS | (Wilmington) |
| FLORIDA | Business Journal-Jacksonville | BDL | (Jacksonville) |
| | Business View | BDL | (Naples) |
| | El Miami Herald | N | (Miami) |
| | Florida Business-Tampa Bay | BDL | (Tampa Bay) |
| | Florida Times-Union, The | PTS | (Jacksonville) |
| | Jacksonville Journal | PTS | (Jacksonville) |
| | Florida Trend | BDL, PTS | (St Petersburg) |
| | Fort Lauderdale News/ Sun-Sentinel | N, PTS | (Ft Lauderdale) |
| | Miami Herald, The | N, PTS | (Miami) |
| | Miami Review | PTS | (Miami) |
| | New Business | BDL | (Sarasota) |
| | Orlando Business Journal | PTS | (Orlando) |
| | Orlando Sentinel, The | N, PTS | (Orlando) |
| | South Florida Business Journal | BDL, PTS | (Miami) |
| | St Petersburg Times | PTS | (St Petersburg) |
| | Tampa Bay Business Journal | PTS | (Tampa) |
| | Tampa Tribune and Times | PTS | (Tampa) |
| | Tampa Tribune | PTS | (Tampa) |
| GEORGIA | Atlanta Business Chronicle | BDL, PTS | (Atlanta) |
| | Atlanta Constitution | PTS | (Atlanta) |
| | Atlanta Journal/Atlanta Constitution Weekend | PTS | (Atlanta) |
| | Business Atlanta | BDL,PTS | (Atlanta) |
| | Georgia Trend | BDL | (Atlanta) |
| HAWAII | Hawaii Business Magazine | BDL, PTS | (Honolulu) |
| | Pacific Business News | BDL, PTS | (Honolulu) |
| IDAHO | Idaho Statesman | PTS | (Boise) |
| ILLINOIS | Business News | BDL | (Winfield) |
| | Chicago Sun-Times | PTS | (Chicago) |
| | Chicago Tribune | N, PTS | (Chicago) |
| | Crains Chicago Business | BDL, PTS | (Chicago) |
| | *Crains Illinois Business | BDL | (Chicago) |
| | Tompkins Central Illinois Business | BDL | (Clinton) |
| INDIANA | Indiana Business Magazine | BDL, PTS | (Indianapolis) |
| | Indianapolis Business Journal | BDL, PTS | (Indianapolis) |
| | Indianapolis Star | PTS | (Indianapolis) |
| | Post-Tribune | N | (Gary) |
| IOWA | Business Record | BDL, PTS | (Des Moines) |
| | Des Moines Register | PTS | (Des Moines) |
| KANSAS | Kansas Business News | BDL | (Lindsborg) |
| | Wichita Business | BDL | (Wichita) |
| | Wichita Business Journal | BDL | (Wichita) |
| | Wichita Eagle-Beacon, The | N, PTS | (Wichita) |

| Publication | Database | Location |
| --- | --- | --- |
| Times Tribune | PTS | (Palo Alto) |
| Tribune | PTS | (Oakland) |

**CANADA**

| Publication | Database | Location |
| --- | --- | --- |
| Alberta Business | BDL, PTS | (Calgary) |
| Asia Pacific Business | BDL | (Vancouver) |
| Atlantic Business | BDL | (Halifax) |
| BC Business | BDL, PTS | (Vancouver) |
| Canadian Business Magazine | PTS | (Toronto) |
| Edmonton Journal | PTS | (Edmonton) |
| Financial Post | PTS | (Toronto) |
| Gazette | PTS | (Montreal) |
| Globe & Mail | PTS | (Toronto) |
| London Business Monthly Magazine (formerly Western Ontario Business) | BDL | (London) |
| Manitoba Business | BDL, PTS | (Winnipeg) |
| Metropolitan Toronto Business Journal | BDL | (Toronto) |
| Northern Ontario Business | BDL, PTS | (Sudbury) |
| Saskatchewan Business | BDL, PTS | (Regina) |
| Vancouver Sun | PTS | (Vancouver) |

**COLORADO**

| Publication | Database | Location |
| --- | --- | --- |
| Boulder County Business Report | BDL | (Boulder) |
| Colorado Business | BDL, PTS | (Littleton) |
| Denver Business | BDL, PTS | (Denver) |
| Denver Business Journal, The | BDL, PTS | (Denver) |
| Denver Post | PTS | (Denver) |
| *Rocky Mountain Business Journal | BDL, PTS | (Denver) |

**CONNECTICUT**

| Publication | Database | Location |
| --- | --- | --- |
| Business Journal Serving Hartford and New Haven | PTS | (Hartford) |
| Business Times, The | BDL | (East Hartford) |
| Connecticut Business Journal | PTS | (Ft Washington, PA) |
| Hartford Courant | PTS | (Hartford) |
| Intercorp | BDL, PTS | (Hartford) |
| Southern Connecticut Business Journal | PTS | (Stamford) |

**DC**

| Publication | Database | Location |
| --- | --- | --- |
| *Business Review | BDL, PTS | (Vienna, VA) |
| Washington Business Journal | BDL, PTS | (McLean, VA) |
| *Washington Dossier | BDL | (Washington, DC) |
| Washington Post | N, PTS | (Washington, DC) |

**KENTUCKY**

| Publication | Database | Location |
| --- | --- | --- |
| Business First-Louisville | BDL, PTS | (Louisville) |
| Courier-Journal, The | PTS | (Louisville) |
| *Kentucky Business Ledger | BDL, PTS | (Louisville) |
| Lexington Herald-Leader | N | (Lexington) |
| Louisville | BDL | (Louisville) |

**LOUISIANA**

| Publication | Database | Location |
| --- | --- | --- |
| Greater Baton Rouge Business Report, The | BDL, PTS | (Baton Rouge) |
| *New Orleans Business | BDL, PTS | (Gretna) |
| New Orleans CityBusiness | BDL, PTS | (Metairie) |
| *SHREVEPORT | BDL | (Shreveport) |
| *Shreveport Business | BDL | (Shreveport) |
| Times-Picayune | PTS | (New Orleans) |

**MAINE**

| Publication | Database | Location |
| --- | --- | --- |
| New England Business | BDL, PTS | (Boston, MA) |
| Southern Maine Business Digest | BDL | (South Portland) |

**MASSACHUSETTS**

| Publication | Database | Location |
| --- | --- | --- |
| Boston Business | BDL, PTS | (Boston) |
| Boston Business Journal | BDL, PTS | (Boston) |
| Boston Globe, The | N, PTS | (Boston) |
| Business Worcester | BDL, PTS | (Worcester) |
| New England Business | BDL, PTS | (Boston) |
| Western Massachusetts Business Journal | PTS | (Springfield) |

**MARYLAND**

| Publication | Database | Location |
| --- | --- | --- |
| Baltimore Business Journal | BDL, PTS | (Baltimore) |
| Capital, The | N | (Annapolis) |
| *Maryland Business & Living | BDL | (Baltimore) |
| Sun, The | PTS | (Baltimore) |
| Warfield's | PTS | (Baltimore) |

**MICHIGAN**

| Publication | Database | Location |
| --- | --- | --- |
| Crains Detroit Business | BDL, PTS | (Detroit) |
| Detroiter | PTS | (Detroit) |
| Detroit Free Press | N | (Detroit) |
| Detroit News | PTS | (Detroit) |
| Grand Rapids Business Journal | BDL | (Grand Rapids) |
| Grand Rapids Press | PTS | (Grand Rapids) |
| Michigan Business | BDL, PTS | (Southfield) |
| Oakland Business | BDL | (Union Lake) |

**MINNESOTA**

| Publication | Database | Location |
| --- | --- | --- |
| *Business Minnesota | BDL | (Minneapolis) |
| Business Today | BDL | (Rochester) |
| Corporate Report, Minnesota | BDL, PTS | (Minneapolis) |
| Minneapolis Star & Tribune | PTS | (Minneapolis) |
| Minneapolis-St Paul CityBusiness | BDL, PTS | (Minneapolis) |
| *Minnesota Business Journal | BDL | (Minneapolis) |
| St Paul Pioneer Press | PTS | (St Paul) |

**MISSISSIPPI**

| Publication | Database | Location |
| --- | --- | --- |
| Clarion-Ledger, The | PTS | (Jackson) |
| Clarion Ledger-Jackson Daily News | PTS | (Jackson) |
| Jackson Journal of Business | BDL, PTS | (Jackson) |
| Mississippi Business Journal | BDL, PTS | (Jackson) |

DATABASE KEY:

N - Full text of these newspapers and business publications is available on VU/TEXT, in separate databases.

BDL - Full text of selected articles from these business journals is available on VU/TEXT through the Business Dateline database.

PTS - Article summaries of these daily newspapers and business journals are available on VU/TEXT through the Predicasts PROMT database.

To search the Business Dateline, PROMT, and various newspaper databases, refer to the blue pages for their respective database descriptions.

PENNSYLVANIA

| Publication | Code | City |
|---|---|---|
| Lehigh Valley Business Digest | BDL, PTS | (Bethlehem) |
| Morning Call, The | N | (Allentown) |
| Philadelphia Business Journal | BDL, PTS | (Philadelphia) |
| Philadelphia Daily News | N | (Philadelphia) |
| Philadelphia Inquirer, The | N, PTS | (Philadelphia) |
| Pittsburgh Business Times & Journal | BDL, PTS | (Pittsburgh) |
| Pittsburgh Press | PTS | (Pittsburgh) |
| Woman of the Times | BDL | (Pittsburgh) |
| York-Harrisburg Business Digest | BDL | (York) |

PUERTO RICO

| Publication | Code | City |
|---|---|---|
| Caribbean Business | PTS | (Santurce) |

RHODE ISLAND

| Publication | Code | City |
|---|---|---|
| Ocean State Business | BDL | (Providence) |
| Providence Journal | PTS | (Providence) |
| Providence Journal-Bulletin | PTS | (Providence) |
| Providence Sunday Journal | PTS | (Providence) |

SOUTH CAROLINA

| Publication | Code | City |
|---|---|---|
| Greenville News | PTS | (Greenville) |
| South Carolina Business | BDL, PTS | (Columbia) |

SOUTH DAKOTA

| Publication | Code | City |
|---|---|---|
| *Western Business | BDL | (Billings, MT) |

TENNESSEE

| Publication | Code | City |
|---|---|---|
| Advantage | BDL, PTS | (Nashville) |
| Commercial Appeal | PTS | (Memphis) |
| Memphis Business Journal | BDL, PTS | (Memphis) |
| Nashville Business Journal | BDL | (Nashville) |
| Tennessean | PTS | (Nashville) |

TEXAS

| Publication | Code | City |
|---|---|---|
| Austin American-Statesman | PTS | (Austin) |
| Austin Business Journal | BDL, PTS | (Austin) |
| Dallas | PTS | (Dallas) |
| *Dallas Business Courier | BDL | (Dallas) |
| Dallas-Fort Worth Business Journal | BDL, PTS | (Dallas) |
| DALLAS Magazine | BDL | (Dallas) |
| Dallas Morning News | PTS | (Dallas) |
| Express News | PTS | (San Antonio) |
| FortWorth Magazine | BDL | (Fort Worth) |
| Fort Worth Star-Telegram | PTS | (Fort Worth) |
| Houston Business Journal | BDL, PTS | (Houston) |
| Houston Chronicle | PTS | (Houston) |
| *Houston Magazine | BDL, PTS | (Houston) |
| Houston Post, The | N | (Houston) |
| San Antonio Business Journal | BDL | (San Antonio) |
| *San Antonio Executive | BDL | (San Antonio) |
| West Texas Business Journal | BDL | (San Angelo) |

UTAH

| Publication | Code | City |
|---|---|---|
| Salt Lake City Tribune | PTS | (Salt Lake City) |

VERMONT

| Publication | Code | City |
|---|---|---|
| Vermont Business Magazine | BDL, PTS | (Brattleboro) |

MISSOURI

| Publication | Code | City |
|---|---|---|
| Corporate Report-Kansas City, The | BDL | (Kansas City) |
| Kansas City Business Journal | N, BDL, PTS | (Kansas City) |
| Kansas City Star | PTS | (Kansas City) |
| Kansas City Times | PTS | (Kansas City) |
| Springfield Business Journal | BDL | (Springfield) |
| St Louis Business Journal | BDL, PTS | (St Louis) |
| St Louis Commerce | PTS | (St Louis) |
| St Louis Post-Dispatch | PTS | (St Louis) |
| Woman, Inc. | BDL | (St Louis) |

MONTANA

| Publication | Code | City |
|---|---|---|
| Billings Business Journal | BDL | (Billings) |
| *Western Business | BDL | (Billings) |

NEBRASKA

| Publication | Code | City |
|---|---|---|
| Omaha World Herald | PTS | (Omaha) |
| Sunday World Herald | PTS | (Omaha) |

NEW HAMPSHIRE

| Publication | Code | City |
|---|---|---|
| Business New Hampshire | BDL, PTS | (Manchester) |
| New Hampshire Business Review | BDL, PTS | (Manchester) |
| Seacoast New Hampshire Business Digest | PTS | (Portsmouth) |

NEW JERSEY

| Publication | Code | City |
|---|---|---|
| Business Journal of New Jersey | BDL, PTS | (Morganville) |
| Mercer Business | BDL | (Trenton) |
| New Jersey Success | BDL, PTS | (Hillside) |
| Record | PTS | (Hackensack) |
| Southern New Jersey Business Digest | BDL, PTS | (Lawrence) |
| Star-Ledger | PTS | (Newark) |
| Sunday Record | PTS | (Hackensack) |

NEW MEXICO

| Publication | Code | City |
|---|---|---|
| Albuquerque Journal | PTS | (Albuquerque) |
| New Mexico Business Journal | BDL, PTS | (Albuquerque) |

NEVADA

| Publication | Code | City |
|---|---|---|
| Las Vegas Business Press | BDL | (Las Vegas) |

NEW YORK

| Publication | Code | City |
|---|---|---|
| Buffalo News | PTS | (Buffalo) |
| Business First-Buffalo | BDL | (Buffalo) |
| Capital District Business Review | BDL, PTS | (Albany) |
| Central New York Business Journal | BDL | (Dewitt) |
| Crains New York Business | BDL, PTS | (New York) |
| Democrat & Chronicle | PTS | (Rochester) |
| Journal of Commerce, The | N | (New York) |
| Knickerbocker News, The | N | (Albany) |
| Long Island Business | PTS | (Long Island) |
| Newsday | BDL | (Huntington) |
| *New York CityBusiness | PTS | (New York) |
| New York Times-national edition | PTS | (New York) |
| Reporter Dispatch | PTS | (White Plains) |
| Rochester Business Journal | BDL | (Rochester) |
| *Syracuse & Central New York Business Review | BDL | (Syracuse) |

| | | |
|---|---|---|
| Syracuse Business | BDL | (Syracuse) |
| Syracuse Herald-American | PTS | (Syracuse) |
| Post-Standard and Herald-Journal | N | |
| Times-Union | | (Albany) |
| Westchester Business Journal | BDL | (Port Chester) |

**NORTH CAROLINA**

| | | |
|---|---|---|
| Business-North Carolina | BDL, PTS | (Charlotte) |
| Charlotte Observer, The | N, PTS | (Charlotte) |
| Greensboro News & Record | PTS | (Greensboro) |
| News & Observer | PTS | (Raleigh) |

**NORTH DAKOTA**

| | | |
|---|---|---|
| *Western Business | BDL | (Billings, MT) |

**OHIO**

| | | |
|---|---|---|
| Akron Beacon Journal | N, PTS | (Akron) |
| Blade, The | PTS | (Toledo) |
| Business First-Columbus | BDL, PTS | (Columbus) |
| Cincinnati Business Courier | BDL, PTS | (Cincinnati) |
| *Cincinnati Business Journal | BDL, PTS | (Cincinnati) |
| Cincinnati Enquirer | PTS | (Cincinnati) |
| Columbus Business Journal | BDL | (Columbus) |
| Columbus Dispatch, The | N, PTS | (Columbus) |
| Crains Cleveland Business | BDL, PTS | (Cleveland) |
| *Dayton Business Journal | BDL | (Dayton) |
| Dayton-Springfield Business Life | BDL | (Centerville) |
| Ohio | BDL | (Columbus) |
| Ohio Business | BDL, PTS | (Cleveland) |
| Plain Dealer | PTS | (Cleveland) |
| Toledo Business Journal | BDL | (Toledo) |

**OKLAHOMA**

| | | |
|---|---|---|
| Daily Oklahoman, The | PTS | (Oklahoma City) |
| Journal Record | PTS | (Oklahoma City) |
| Oklahoma Business | PTS | (Oklahoma City) |
| Sunday Oklahoman | PTS | (Oklahoma City) |
| Tulsa Business Chronicle | BDL, PTS | (Tulsa) |
| Tulsa World | PTS | (Tulsa) |

**OREGON**

| | | |
|---|---|---|
| Business Journal-Portland | BDL, PTS | (Portland) |
| Oregon Business | BDL, PTS | (Portland) |
| Oregonian | PTS | (Portland) |

**PENNSYLVANIA**

| | | |
|---|---|---|
| Delaware Valley Business Digest | BDL, PTS | (Bala Cynwyd) |
| Executive Report | BDL | (Pittsburgh) |
| Focus | BDL, PTS | (Philadelphia) |
| Lancaster-Reading Business Digest (formerly Central Pennsylvania Business Digest) | BDL | (Bala Cynwyd) |

**VIRGINIA**

| | | |
|---|---|---|
| Business Journal-Richmond, The | BDL | (Richmond) |
| Richmond News Leader, The | N | (Richmond) |
| Richmond Times-Dispatch, The | N, PTS | (Richmond) |
| Tidewater Virginian | PTS | (Norfolk) |
| Virginia Business | N, PTS | (Norfolk) |
| Virginian-Pilot | PTS | (Norfolk) |
| Virginian-Pilot & Ledger-Star | PTS | (Norfolk) |

**WASHINGTON**

| | | |
|---|---|---|
| Pacific Northwest Executive | BDL | (Seattle) |
| Puget Sound Business Journal | BDL, PTS | (Seattle) |
| Seattle Business | BDL, PTS | (Seattle) |
| Seattle Post-Intelligencer | N | (Seattle) |
| Seattle Times | PTS | (Seattle) |
| Seattle Times Post-Intelligencer Sunday | PTS | (Seattle) |

**WEST VIRGINIA**

| | | |
|---|---|---|
| Sunday Gazette-Mail | PTS | (Charleston) |

**WISCONSIN**

| | | |
|---|---|---|
| Business Journal-Milwaukee, The | BDL, PTS | (Milwaukee) |
| *LaCrosse CityBusiness | BDL | (La Crosse) |
| Milwaukee Journal | PTS | (Milwaukee) |

**WYOMING**

| | | |
|---|---|---|
| *Western Business | BDL | (Billings, MT) |

* NO LONGER PUBLISHED OR COVERED, BUT BACK ISSUES ARE AVAILABLE ON VU/TEXT

Publications appearing in the Business Dateline and PROMT databases are subject to change due to the periodic acquisition/merger or closing of regional publications.

1/88

Source: VuText Information Services, Inc., Philadelphia, PA.

# Chapter 4

# *The Acquisition Campaign*

*Sumner N. Levine*

After the buyer has developed a list of prospects that meet the company's acquisition criteria, the next step is to initiate contact with the principals of the target companies. A key objective is to ascertain the feasibility of making the acquisition should the target prove desirable on further investigation. The following discussion assumes that the acquisition will be done on a negotiated, that is, friendly, basis. Initial contacts should be arranged with the individuals who are in a position to make the decision to sell the company. Meeting with other parties is often a waste of time, unless such parties can exert influence on the controlling individuals.

If the prospect has been identified by an intermediary, the latter usually initiates contact. When a buyer has identified the target through its own efforts, it is best for the buyer to initiate contact. Mutual acquaintances of the buyer and the prospect can be helpful, but should be employed only if they are tactful and discreet. Expectations concerning the possible payment of a fee for the introduction should be clarified beforehand.

Generally, it is recommended that buyers initiate their own contacts. This can be done by letter or telephone. The latter is probably the better choice because letters are often set aside for future action which, alas, may never be implemented. A phone call from the buyer's CEO to the seller's counterpart is generally effective in getting things started. The tone of the conversation should be congenial but straightforward. After stating his or her name, title, and affiliation, the buyer should refer to the target in a complimentary manner, such as "We have been very impressed with your company," and state an interest in meeting with the prospect to explore the possibility of being considered as a purchaser if the company becomes available for sale at any future time. Stating the matter this way is nonthreatening and does not force the prospect to take an immediate position concerning his or her own interest in selling the company.

The primary objective of the initial phone call is to arrange for a meeting. A meeting date within two weeks—generally the sooner the better—is desirable, as a date set too far into the future tends to be further delayed by unexpected events. If possible, it is best to meet the prospect at the seller's site because this arrangement provides an opportunity to gather direct impressions of the company—the condition of the physical facility, employee efficiency and morale, and the like. Some buyers prefer to arrive early so that they can drive around the prospect's site to obtain additional impressions of the physical layout.

The arrangements made on the phone should, of course, be confirmed with a follow-up letter. If the buyer's company has impressive promotional literature, this might be sent along to the prospect prior to the meeting.

## A REPRESENTATIVE PHONE INTRODUCTION

Following the introductory remarks, a typical phone conversation might proceed as follows:

**Buyer:** Mr. Jones, we have been very impressed with your organization. Your exhibit at the last trade show was excellent.

**Prospect:** Thank you. I'm sure our marketing people would be pleased to hear that.

**Buyer:** My reason for calling is that while we have no idea whether you or your shareholders have any intention of selling your company, we would like to be considered as a possible purchaser should you decide to sell at a future date.

**Prospect:** Well, we do not have any plans to sell (or similar denials).

**Buyer:** I understand. However, I would appreciate meeting with you in order to tell you about us so that you will be familiar with our firm in case there is a chance you would consider selling at a future date.

Occasionally, it can be difficult to get past a secretary who insists on knowing the call's purpose before putting it through. This impediment can sometimes be overcome by stating frankly that the call involves confidential business matters that can only be discussed directly with Mr. or Ms. CEO. If the target CEO is not free at the time of the call, then request a time when you might call back. Leave your own phone number and request the secretary's name. Often a callback with a friendly (but not too friendly) salutation using the secretary's name can be effective in getting through the blockade.

## WHERE TO FIND INFORMATION ABOUT THE TARGET'S EXECUTIVES

In addition to the research described in Chapter 3, it is also helpful to obtain, prior to the meeting, background information on the prospect's CEO and key decision makers. Among the published sources of executive information are the following:

*Reference Book of Corporate Management* (Dun and Bradstreet, New York, NY)

*Standard & Poor's Register of Corporation Directors and Executives* (Standard & Poor's Corporation, New York, NY)

*Who's Who In America* (Marquis Who's Who, Chicago, IL)

Marquis also publishes regional and other specialized types of "Who's Who," such as:

- *Who's Who in the East*
- *Who's Who in the Midwest*
- *Who's Who in the South*
- *Who's Who in the Southwest*
- *Who's Who in the West*
- *Who's Who in Finance and Industry*

Other sources include college alumni organizations, the files of local newspapers covering the region in which the company is located, and trade and professional organizations, since the latter often keep bibliographic material on prominent members.

Local chambers of commerce and industry organizations often have biographical information on local businesspeople. A good guide to chambers of commerce is *Johnson's Worldwide Chamber of Commerce Directory* (Johnson Publications, Loveland, CO).

The *Biography Master Index* database on *DIALOG* is particularly useful. It contains biographical information on nearly three million individuals found in more than 700 source publications. The records include the names of the source publications that have the information on the person listed. Also available online from *DIALOG* is the *Standard & Poor's Biographical Register* and Marquis *Who's Who*. The latter corresponds to *Who's Who In America* and *Who's Who in Science and Technology.*

Familiarity with the backgrounds of the prospect's key personnel is helpful in building personnel rapport. The importance of establishing a congenial relationship in the negotiation process should not be underestimated.


## THE INITIAL MEETING

Among the main objectives of the initial meeting are identifying the prospect's key decision makers and gauging the prospect's degree of interest in selling. The meeting also provides the buyer with an opportunity to present a case for why the target company would benefit from the acquisition. However, it is advisable to avoid high pressure sales tactics.

After the initial pleasantries, the buyer should briefly describe his or her organization and why the prospect seems to meet the firm's acquisition objectives. The discussion should then turn to the ways that the target company would benefit from the acquisition, emphasizing the positive aspects of what would happen after a deal is made—what the budget might be, how the company would be managed, and so forth.

Any questions about the prospect should be tactfully interwoven into the conversation during the course of the meeting. A list of questions based on the preliminary research should be prepared prior to the meeting. Assigning priorities to the questions is advisable because time limitations may preclude covering all of them. Notes should be made in writing—or better still on a tape recorder—immediately following the meeting. The use of concealed and unannounced miniature tape recorders during the meeting is, of course, unethical.

## THE FOLLOW-UP MEETING

A date for a second meeting is usually proposed in a follow-up letter unless it becomes evident during the initial meeting that the acquisition is not possible or that the situation no longer appears attractive. In the latter case, a letter should be sent promptly, thanking the prospect and indicating that there has been a change of plans with respect to an acquisition at this time.

A prospect's agreement to a second meeting usually indicates a substantial degree of interest in being acquired. At this point the buyer's objective is to keep the prospect sold and to develop further the personal relationship with the seller. Constructive personal relationships facilitate communication and may provide the buyer with further insight into the prospect's motivation for selling. These insights can be helpful in structuring the negotiations.

If a definite interest in selling develops, the buyer should inform the prospect of its procedures for evaluating the seller's firm. An outline of the formal evaluation procedures, the so-called due diligence process, is given in Chapter 5. The buyer should request the seller's financial statements covering the latest five-year period. Generally, a seller's willingness to provide the latter indicates a strong interest in selling.

## THE MATTER OF PRICING

Whenever possible, it is best for the buyer to avoid taking a position on a purchase price—at least until the financial statements have been examined. These, together with the other background information acquired, generally provide the basis for a preliminary offer which would, of course, be contingent on the results of the formal investigation. Techniques for setting a reasonable price range are discussed in Chapter 7.

However, it is to the purchaser's advantage to know before making an offer what price the seller has in mind, as it may be less than what the buyer is prepared to offer. The problem with raising the question of price is that the seller may offer a highly inflated figure that may be difficult to retreat from without losing credibility. Perhaps the best way to handle the situation is to treat the matter somewhat casually, saying, for example, "We appreciate your stating a price estimate. We'll take a hard look at the figures and see what can be arranged." At this stage it is important to avoid pressing the seller into defending a price and thereby digging a psychological hole it may be difficult to climb out of.

Of course, many factors other than purchase price are important, such as the form the price is to be paid in (cash, stocks, seller financing, consulting agreements, and so forth) and the schedule of payments. In many instances the terms of the financing are more important than the price. Other important matters relate to whether the target company's key people intend to remain, to leave shortly after the acquisition, or to serve in a consulting capacity. If the acquiring company has little or no managerial capability in the target's business, retaining management—at least until new experienced people can be put in place—is a matter of vital importance. Often providing a few perks and attractive bonus arrangements are sufficient to clinch a deal and ensure that the target's management remains after the acquisition.

## THE LETTER OF INTENT

After the parties have reached an agreement in principle concerning the aforementioned matters, it is customary to summarize the key terms in a nonbinding letter of intent (sometimes called an *agreement in principle*). The letter, issued by the buyer, usually states that the terms are subject to the results of the formal investigation and to approval by the boards of directors of both companies (assuming that corporations are involved). The letter of intent typically spells out whether the prospect's assets or stock will be acquired, the amount and type of considerations to be paid, and the arrangements with the target's key employees.

Some have questioned the need for a letter of intent, arguing that the time and effort are better spent on moving ahead with the acquisition contract. However, structuring the contract can be a lengthy process. In the meantime, the letter of intent represents a moral commitment to move ahead with the deal and provides a summary of the key terms agreed on. This summary may reduce future misunderstandings. A representative letter of intent is shown in Appendix 4–A.

When the acquisition involves public companies, it is necessary to announce by a press release that an agreement in principle has been reached. The intent here is to minimize the information advantage of the insiders over the trading public.

## SOME NEGOTIATION TIPS

1. Negotiate only with parties who can make the acquisition decision.
2. Maintain an outward demeanor of optimism and enthusiasm and an inner attitude of caution.

3. Do your homework. Always have a backup compromise to prevent the breakdown of a negotiation.

4. Never lose control of your emotions.

5. Be prepared for your next move. What will you do if the prospect agrees to a merger?

6. Try to project the favorable consequences to the prospect that will result when the deal is made.

7. Use each meeting to sell your position.

8. Keep control of the meeting dates.

9. Remember: A good deal has to be fair to both parties.

10. Be persistent. It pays.

## *REFERENCES*

Some particularly helpful references dealing with the initiation of contracts and related matters are the following:

Gordon Bing, *Corporate Acquisitions* (Gulf Publishing Co., Houston, TX, 1980)

James C. Freund, *Anatomy of a Merger* (Law Journal Press, New York, NY, 1985)

Arnold S. Goldstein, *The Complete Guide to Buying and Selling a Business* (New American Library, New York, NY, 1986)

# APPENDIX 4-A:
## Letter of Intent*

Mr. James Jones
Seller
1 Main Street
Cleveland, Ohio 11111

Dear Mr. Jones:

In accordance with our discussions, it seems that it would be of benefit to both parties to consider an exchange of common stock of Buyer for all (100%) of the outstanding stock of Seller in accordance with the following:

1. Buyer will set aside 10,000 shares of its common stock to be used in exchange for 100% of outstanding common stock of the Seller currently amounting to 5,000 shares.

2. At the closing the Buyer will transfer to the stockholders of the Seller two (2) shares of the Buyer's common for each outstanding share of the Seller.

3. The Seller agrees not to issue any additional shares of stock, stock options, or any securities convertible to stock.

* This is only illustrative. Service of a competent professional should be sought when preparing such a document.

4. All shares issued by the Buyer will be held by the Seller stockholder for a period of at least _____ years after the closing. The Seller stockholder will sign a letter provided by the Buyer confirming this understanding.

5. Simultaneously with the closing any loans outstanding between Seller and its stockholders will be paid in full by the Seller.

6. The Buyer will continue the Seller's present Retirement Plan after the closing.

7. For a period of two (2) years after the closing, the day-to-day management of the Seller shall continue to be under the control of _____ and _____ .

8. During the period indicated in paragraph 7, Buyer shall not require that the Seller's firm enter into any new business.

9. The Seller agrees to pay at closing all brokerage or finder's fees payable to _____ . Both parties represent that there are no other brokers or finders.

10. Seller agrees to make available to the Buyer's auditors, legal counsel, and other analysts all records and access needed for a full and independent investigation. All investigations will be conducted at the Buyer's expense.

11. Seller understands that this letter of intent is subject to the results of the independent investigation of the Buyer and thereafter to final approval by the Buyer's Board of Directors.

12. This letter of intent is not intended as a contract but as a statement of the present intention of the parties. The terms and provisions governing the acquisition are to be contained in a Purchase Contract subject to the approval of both parties. Such terms and provisions include the customary warranties, representations, and indemnities with respect to breach of warranties, and representations. The terms of the Purchase Contract shall be binding when such a Contract has been executed by both parties.

If you are in agreement with the above, please indicate by having all stockholders of the Seller sign and return two copies of this letter.

Sincerely,

_____
BUYER

Accepted by          No. of Shares          Date

_____      _____      _____

_____      _____      _____

_____      _____      _____

Note:
    In the instance of a cash deal, the letter of intent
would be modified by replacing paragraph 1 with the following:

    1. Buyer shall pay the stockholders of the Seller
$ _____ . in cash per share at closing.

    In the case of an <u>earn-out</u> type of arrangement, a par-
agraph such as the following is introduced:

    1. During the period from _____to _____ten percent
(10%) of the Seller's after-tax net earnings in excess of
$ _____ . shall be distributed to the Seller's stockholders
as cash. Of the above, each shareholder shall receive an
amount proportional to the fraction of the total shares which
the shareholders surrendered at closing. Each payment will
be made within _____ months following the end of the fiscal
year. However, the maximum amount payable each year shall
not exceed $ _____ .

    Net earnings for the purposes of the above will be de-
termined by the Buyer's independent accountants in accordance with generally accepted accounting principles. It is
understood that the Seller's business will be operated in
the ordinary manner during the earn-out period.

# The Formal Investigation

*Sumner N. Levine*

The formal investigation (due diligence) involves a detailed review of the seller's business and verification of the seller's representations. Generally, the due diligence process is started after an agreement in principle has been reached.

As may be surmised from the outline given in this chapter, the formal investigation requires a substantial commitment of time and resources, both of which are limited. Therefore, the extent to which any particular item should be pursued is related to its importance to the future viability of the business.

During the investigation a number of troublesome facts may, and often do, emerge. When such unexpected matters arise, it is necessary for the buyer to resist becoming overly critical of the prospect. After all, most businesses have problems. Of course, if the difficulties encountered place the economic viability of the deal in doubt and if no solution can be found, then the buyer has little alternative but to withdraw.

All important items shown in the following checklist should be verified by direct inspection. For example, with a manufacturing company, inventories of both raw and finished goods should be sampled and evaluated with respect to amount, condition, and extent of obsolesence. Plant and equipment should be similarly evaluated by technically competent individuals.

Copies of all legal and financial documents should be provided to the buyer's counsel and accountants. These include:

1. corporate charters and by-laws (or partnership agreement)
2. list of stockholders
3. list of the members of the board of directors
4. list of all locations, both domestic and foreign, at which seller conducts business
5. five years of audited financial statements
6. five years of income tax returns
7. a listing (with locations) of all major assets owned by the seller
8. list of all short-term, long-term, and contingent liabilities
9. all contracts, including license agreements, leases, realty arrangements, and the like
10. list of seller's patents, trademarks, copyrights
11. all insurance policies
12. list of all past, ongoing, and pending litigation
13. product literature
14. list of all major customers
15. list of major suppliers

## DUE DILIGENCE SCHEDULE

In order to coordinate and expedite the formal investigation, a schedule should be set up indicating who does what and when. A typical format is indicated below:

| Date | Activity | Who Has Responsibility | Location |
| --- | --- | --- | --- |

Both the tentative starting and completion dates for each activity should be indicated. The specific activities to be listed depend on the kind of deal under consideration. For example, some activities for investigation of a private corporation might be as follows:

1. assembling and verifying seller's legal and financial documents
2. inspection of seller's plant, equipment, inventories, and so forth (set completion date for due diligence report)
3. board of directors meeting of buyer to approve purchase
4. board of directors meeting of seller to approve purchase
5. press release
6. meeting of counsel for buyer and seller to review terms and conditions and allocate responsibilities for drafting contract
7. first draft of contract due (apply for IRS rulings)
8. meeting of buyer and seller to revise contract
9. drafting proxy for seller stockholder meeting
10. approval of contract by buyer and seller
11. calling meeting of seller's stockholders to approve acquisition
12. signing of acquisition of contract
13. closing

## COMMON PROBLEM AREAS

Some critical areas that buyers should look for when examining the state of the business and financial statements are the following:

1. dressing up of financial statements by the seller before the sale by reducing temporary expenses or deferrable expenses such as maintenance, R&D, inventories, advertising, and the like
2. weak relationship between sales and earnings
3. the loss of favorable leases, suppliers, or customer contracts after the acquisition

4. existence of favorable intercorporate arrangements that will not be available after the sale

5. reliance on a limited number of customers, some of whom may be lost after the acquisition

6. tax liabilities and contingencies

7. unrecorded liabilities such as warranties, pension liabilities, vacation pay, sales returns, and the like

8. overvaluation of inventories due to discontinued or obsolescent products

9. receivables that cannot be collected at the amounts recorded

10. pending litigations

11. repeated drops in insurance coverage or significantly increased insurance rates

12. increasing ratio of insurance expense to fixed assets

13. high employee turnover or history of labor militancy

14. a significant percentage of earnings obtained from problem business segments (such as sales from declining products, unstable foreign markets, short-term government contracts, and the like)

# BUSINESS INVESTIGATION CHECKLIST*

| ITEM | ASSIGNED TO | COMMENTS |
|------|-------------|----------|

I.   CORPORATE BACKGROUND

  A. Original name and purpose.

  B. Date of founding.

  C. Subsequent changes in corporate name or purpose.

  D. Brief description of present business.

  E. Classes of stocks or other securities.

  F. Concentration of ownership.

  G. Activity of shares and price ranges.

  H. Subsidiaries and operating investments.

  I. States in which qualified to do business.

  J. Legal location of all facilities and branches.

  K. Review of minutes of meeting of stockholders, board of directors and committees.

| *ITEM* | *ASSIGNED TO* | *COMMENTS* |
|---|---|---|

II.   BASIS OF PROPOSED
      ACQUISITION

    A. Highlights of agreement.

    B. Methods for evaluation.

III.  FINANCIAL

    A. General

        1. Source and authenticity
            of financial data.

    B. Financial Status

        1. Statement of condition
            (balance sheet).

        2. Analysis of assets.

           (a) Cash position
                (monthly for two
                years).

           (b) Projection of cash
                activity next six
                months.

           (c) Receivables
                (condition, turnover,
                bad debt experience,
                and reserve).

           (d) Inventories

               (1) Amount and
                    balance in raw
                    materials and
                    finished goods
                    inventories in
                    relation to
                    production
                    and sales
                    requirements
                    (turnover).

| *ITEM* | *ASSIGNED TO* | *COMMENTS* |
| --- | --- | --- |
| (2) Policy and extent of forward commitments on raw materials. | | |
| (3) Extent of vulnerability of business due to rapid price change of materials and time element in manufacture. | | |
| (4) Condition and obsolescence. | | |
| (e) Working capital position (monthly for two years). | | |
| (f) Investments (kinds, condition, and basis for evaluation). | | |
| (g) Officers and employees loans (amounts and situations). | | |
| (h) Analysis of prepaid expenses. | | |
| (i) Analysis of deferred charges. | | |
| (j) Properties | | |
| (1) Operating and nonoperating. | | |
| (2) Extent depreciated and rates. | | |

| ITEM | ASSIGNED TO | COMMENTS |
|---|---|---|
| (3) Net value related to sales volume. | | |
| (4) Insurance coverage. | | |
| (k) Goodwill (basis of valuation). | | |
| 3. Analysis of liabilities | | |
| (a) Bank loans (amount, dates, sources and rates over past two years). | | |
| (b) Accounts payable (policy on discounts). | | |
| (c) Special reserves. | | |
| (d) Contingent liabilities | | |
| (1) Existing and threatened law suits. | | |
| (2) Notes and obligations guaranteed. | | |
| (3) Liability under large purchase contracts. | | |
| (4) Funding pension liabilities (actuary's report). | | |

| ITEM | ASSIGNED TO | COMMENTS |
| --- | --- | --- |
|     (5) Other commitments. | | |
|   (e) Status of income taxes (federal, state, and local). | | |
|   (f) Trend and status of real estate and personal property taxes. | | |
| C. Financial Operations | | |
|   1. Statement of operations (profit and loss statement). | | |
|   2. Analysis of sales and income | | |
|     (a) Sales by product by year over last ten years. | | |
|     (b) Sales by product by month over last two years. | | |
|     (c) Present backlog by product. | | |
|     (d) Other income. | | |
|   3. Internal control system | | |
|   4. Analysis of manufacturing costs and gross profits. | | |

| ITEM | ASSIGNED TO | COMMENTS |
|---|---|---|
| (a)  Amounts and relative proportion of labor, material and manufacturing overhead. | | |
| (b)  Important items and trends of raw material costs. | | |
| (c)  Important items and trends of labor costs. | | |
| (d)  Analysis of items and trends of manufacturing overhead costs. | | |
| (e)  Separation of fixed and variable manufacturing costs. | | |
| (f)  Factory profit and gross margins by product. | | |
| (g)  Factory profit and gross margins on popular and/or representative makes or models. | | |
| (h)  Possible economies. | | |
| (i)  Possible future cost increases. | | |
| (j)  Possible purchased material price increases. | | |

| ITEM | ASSIGNED TO | COMMENTS |
|------|-------------|----------|
| 5. Analysis of expenses (amount, trends, and principal items). | | |
| (a) Selling expenses. | | |
| (b) Administrative expenses. | | |
| (c) General expenses. | | |
| (d) Possible economies in all expenses. | | |
| (e) Royalties received and paid. | | |
| 6. Analysis of profit from operations. | | |
| (a) Profits by branches, divisions, etc. | | |
| (b) Profits by trade classes. | | |
| (c) Deductions. | | |
| (d) Final surplus net profit. | | |
| 7. Analysis of surplus net profit. | | |
| (a) Profits from operations. | | |
| (b) Details of profits from other sources. | | |
| (c) Deductions. | | |

| *ITEM* | *ASSIGNED TO* | *COMMENTS* |
|---|---|---|
| (d) Final surplus net profit. | | |
| 8. Earnings record for ten-year period. | | |
| (a) Cash gains or losses from operations. | | |
| (b) Total gains or losses from operations. | | |
| (c) Earnings in percent of sales. | | |
| (d) Earnings in percent of invested capital. | | |
| ⁝ Dividend record for ten-year period. | | |
| (a) Kind and amount of dividends paid. | | |
| (b) Percent of earnings paid out in dividends by years. | | |
| (c) Dividends in arrears. | | |
| IV. PRODUCTS | | |
| A. Major classifications and relative Importance | | |
| B. Analysis of Major Products | | |
| 1. Catalogs and sales literature on products. | | |
| 2. Description and application of products. | | |

| ITEM | ASSIGNED TO | COMMENTS |
|---|---|---|
| 3. Competition | | |
|    (a) Names and grading of principal competitors. | | |
|    (b) Ranking in industry—past and present. | | |
|    (c) Relative qualities and prices of product. | | |
|    (d) Market share of national and regional business obtained by each competitor. | | |
| 4. Trend of market acceptance. | | |
| 5. Brand, trademark, or trade name practices and value. | | |
| 6. Styling and packaging— status and importance. | | |
| 7. Completeness of lines. | | |
| 8. Seasonal sales patterns. | | |
| C. Markets and Prices | | |
|   1. Statistical. | | |
|    (a) Location. | | |
|    (b) Market shares, national and regional. | | |

| *ITEM* | *ASSIGNED TO* | *COMMENTS* |
|---|---|---|
| (c) Trend. | | |
| (d) Price leadership. | | |
| 2. Characteristics. | | |
| (a) Seasonal characteristics. | | |
| (b) Economic factors influencing it. | | |
| (c) Stability. | | |
| (d) Susceptibility. | | |
| 3. Competitive practices. | | |
| (a) Competitive and trade practices. | | |
| (b) Extent of other cooperation. | | |
| (c) Imports, tariffs, and quotas. | | |
| 4. Price situation. | | |
| (a) Fair trade policies. | | |
| (b) Stability of price structure. | | |
| (c) Factors influencing. | | |
| (d) Trend of unit prices. | | |
| (e) Future outlook. | | |

| ITEM | ASSIGNED TO | COMMENTS |
|---|---|---|
| 5. Product Safety. | | |
|    (a) Product components, design and manufacture. | | |
|    (b) Product literature and hazard warnings. | | |
|    (c) Existing claims. | | |
|    (d) Product liability insurance coverage and cost. | | |
| 6. Supplies. | | |
|    (a) Identify critical components and raw materials. | | |
|    (b) Identify suppliers and ultimate sources. | | |
|    (c) Identify existing and potential shortages and quality problems. | | |
|    (d) Identify substitutes. | | |
|    (e) Intra-company pricing of components and raw materials produced internally. | | |
|    (f) Review supplier contracts. | | |

| *ITEM* | *ASSIGNED TO* | *COMMENTS* |
| --- | --- | --- |

D. Government Business

   1. Description of product.

   2. Status of supply
      contracts—prime and
      sub.

   3. Status of facilities
      contracts.

   4. Methods of pricing
      and payment.

   5. Present competitive
      situation.

   6. Future business outlook.

   7. Status of government
      appropriations to fund
      the contract.

   8. Possible termination for
      convenience of
      government.

   9. Security status.

  10. Patent and technology
      limits, if applicable.

  11. Government property
      among seller's assets.

  12. Equal employment
      opportunity and
      other contract
      compliance.

| ITEM | ASSIGNED TO | COMMENTS |
|---|---|---|
| V.   SALES | | |
|   A. Distribution | | |
|     1. Types of distribution used. | | |
|     2. Methods of securing and franchising distributors and agents. | | |
|     3. Geographical distribution and coverage of market (domestic and foreign). | | |
|     4. Lists and ratings of principal customers. | | |
|     5. Present competitive situation. | | |
|     6. Extent of use of private brand. | | |
|     7. Distributor's or customer's attitude toward company. | | |
|     8. Trade class distribution. | | |
|     9. Concentration of sales among important accounts. | | |
|    10. Backlog and/or turnover date. | | |
|    11. Product mix profitability data. | | |

| ITEM | ASSIGNED TO | COMMENTS |
|------|-------------|----------|

B. Sales Organization
1. Organization.

2. Sales methods employed.

3. Compensation of
sales staff, salary or
commission.

4. Branch offices.

C. Sales Policies
1. Prices.

2. Discounts.

3. Service and returns.

4. Consignment sales,
if any.

D. Sales Planning
1. Objectives.

2. Extent of sales
forecasting.

3. Extent of market
research activities.

4. Contingent sales, if any

E. Advertising and Promotion
1. Internal activities.

2. Agency activities

3. Current program—costs,
media.

| ITEM | ASSIGNED TO | COMMENTS |
|---|---|---|

4. Advertising budgets.

5. Public relations.

VI. MANAGEMENT AND
INDUSTRIAL RELATIONS

A. General Organization

  1. Organization chart.

  2. Number and type of
employees by
departments.

  3. Directors, officers,
committees, and their
duties.

  4. Data on key employees.

  5. Balance and alignment of
organization.

  6. Definiteness of duties
and responsibilities.

  7. Employment contracts.

  8. Consultants and outside
services used.

B. Management and Office
Personnel

  1. Adequacy of leadership.

  2. Adequacy of office
staff.

| *ITEM* | *ASSIGNED TO* | *COMMENTS* |
|---|---|---|

3. Rating and evaluation of all people with managerial responsibility.

4. Lines of succession— backing of key positions.

5. Will management stay if merged?

6. Methods and rates of compensation.

7. Key employee insurance.

8. Planned retirements.

9. Morale and points of friction, if any.

10. Physical arrangement and adequacy of offices.

C. Shop Labor

   1. Union contract status.

   2. Past difficulties.

   3. Present labor situation.

   4. Pending problems, if any.

   5. Methods of hiring and discharging.

| ITEM | ASSIGNED TO | COMMENTS |
|---|---|---|

6. Job classification and rates.

7. Methods of payment.

8. Working conditions.

9. Morale and productivity.

10. Safety records and workers' compensation claims.

D. Personnel Policies and Practices

    1. Personnel office and operating methods.

    2. Working rules and regulations.

    3. Hiring and promotion practices.

    4. Compliance with equal employment opportunity laws.

    5. Stock option arrangements.

    6. Bonus arrangements.

    7. Profit sharing.

    8. Pension program.

    9. Medical plan.

| ITEM | ASSIGNED TO | COMMENTS |
|------|-------------|----------|

10. Other employee benefit programs.

11. Vacation and holiday program.

12. Employee purchases.

VII.  FACILITIES

A. Land and Buildings

1.  Location, legal description, and ownership.

2.  Appraisals, if available.

3.  Surveys and plant area layouts.

4.  Possibility of sale and leaseback.

5.  Insurability—explosion, fire, flood, and police protection.

6.  Condition of buildings and repairs needed.

7.  Housekeeping.

8.  On-site waste treatment and disposal facilities.

B. Equipment

1.  Description, age and value of major items of machinery.

| *ITEM* | *ASSIGNED TO* | *COMMENTS* |
|---|---|---|

2. Special processing equipment— specifications.

3. Flexibility and adaptability to other products.

4. Condition and ownership of equipment.

C. Service and Utilities
    1. Transportation.

    2. Loading and unloading facilities.

    3. Electricity—capacity and ownership of transformers, etc.

    4. Lighting.

    5. Heat and air conditioning.

    6. Air, gas, water, fuel oil, and alternate fuels.

    7. Sanitary facilities.

    8. Air, water, waste and other pollution control permits and equipment.

    9. Maintenance.

D. Adequacy and Future Needs

| ITEM | ASSIGNED TO | COMMENTS |
|------|-------------|----------|

1. Location with respect to material, labor and markets.

2. Present utilization of facilities.

3. Expansion possibilities and plans.

VIII. PRODUCTION METHODS AND PROCESSES

    A. Component Fabrication Methods

    B. Assembly Methods

    C. Processing Operations

        1. Finishing operations.

        2. Other.

    D. Quality Control and Inspection

    E. Salvage Control

    F. Material Handling

        1. Conveyors.

        2. On-site transportation.

    G. Methods and Operation Sheets

    H. Tool Design, Procurement, and Repair

    I. Storage and Warehousing

| ITEM | ASSIGNED TO | COMMENTS |
|---|---|---|
| J. Transportation and distribution | | |
| K. Safety—insurer, OSHA and internal reports including chronic and imminent hazard | | |
| L. Efficiency of Production Operations | | |
| M. Adequacy of Facilities— Bottlenecks | | |
| N. Methods for disposal of hazardous waste, past and present | | |
| IX. ENGINEERING, TECHNICAL SERVICE, AND RESEARCH | | |
| A. Engineering Personnel | | |
| B. Facilities | | |
| C. Importance to Product | | |
| D. Adequacy of Product and Process Engineering | | |
| E. Technical Service | | |
| F. Research and Development | | |
| G. Relations with Manufacturing and Sales | | |
| H. Patents | | |
| 1. List of patents, trademarks, copyrights and applications. | | |

| ITEM | ASSIGNED TO | COMMENTS |
|------|-------------|----------|

2. Importance to product
   and processes.

3. Patent policies, pools,
   and licensing
   arrangements.

4. Patent agreements with
   employees.

I. Trade secrets

   1. Importance to
   products and
   processes.

   2. Secrecy agreements
   and other protective
   procedures.

X.   CONTROLS

  A. Financial Controls

     1. Budgets of sales,
      production costs,
      profits, cash
      requirements, etc.

     2. Kind of cost system
      employed.

     3. Method of sales,
      administrative and
      general.

     4. Method of controlling
      production costs.

     5. Status of operating
      procedures.

| ITEM | ASSIGNED TO | COMMENTS |
| --- | --- | --- |
| 6. Adequacy of internal checks. | | |
| 7. List of control reports issued. | | |
| 8. Methods of controlling capital expenditures. | | |
| 9. Accounting methods employed. | | |
| 10. Use of office machines. | | |
| 11. Internal audit reports. | | |
| B. Production Planning and Controls | | |
| 1. Master schedules—how set. | | |
| 2. Coordination between sales and production. | | |
| 3. Adequacy of product specifications. | | |
| 4. Production scheduling and machine loads. | | |
| 5. Purchasing methods and lead times. | | |
| 6. Material and inventory control. | | |
| 7. Cost estimating procedure. | | |

| *ITEM* | *ASSIGNED TO* | *COMMENTS* |
| --- | --- | --- |
| 8. Time study. | | |
| 9. Intra-plant coordination. | | |
| XI. OUTLOOK FOR BUYER | | |
| A. Earnings Prospects per Buyer Share | | |
| B. Return on Capital Required to Buy and Operate Seller | | |
| C. Cash-Flow Projections | | |

# LEGAL INVESTIGATION CHECKLIST*

Not every item appearing on a legal investigation checklist must be checked out in each acquisition. Emphasis on the areas requiring thorough investigation will vary with the type of acquisition involved. For example, as already mentioned, greater emphasis may be placed upon investigating a seller's stock books and minute books in a stock transaction than in an asset transaction, whereas local bulk sales laws will be given greater consideration in asset transactions. As in the case of the business investigation checklist, the legal investigation checklist can help keep the lawyer from overlooking possible legal complications which require solutions to close the particular acquisition.

### LEGAL INVESTIGATION CHECKLIST

| ITEM | ASSIGNED TO | COMMENTS |
|---|---|---|
| I.  STATE LAWS | | |
| A. State Corporation Statutes | | |
| 1. States of incorporation (seller and all subsidiaries). | | |
| 2. Preemptive rights of shareholders. | | |

| ITEM | ASSIGNED TO | COMMENTS |
|------|-------------|----------|

**(I)**

    3. Shareholder notice requirements.

    4. Vote of shares required to sell assets.

    5. Rights of dissenting shareholders.

    6. Statutory merger procedures.

    7. Restrictions on mergers with foreign corporations.

    8. Restrictions on mergers involving corporations in different business.

    9. Procedure of board of directors in either sale of assets or mergers.

    10. States and countries in which qualified to do business (seller and all subsidiaries).

    11. Withdrawals or additional qualifications indicated (seller and all subsidiaries).

**B.** State "Blue Sky" Laws

    1. Permits required prior to negotiating agreement.

    2. Registration requirements and exemptions.

| ITEM | ASSIGNED TO | COMMENTS |
|------|-------------|----------|

(I)

    3. Notice requirements
      and exemptions.

  C. Bulk Sales Laws

    1. Requirements to
      comply.

    2. Effect of
      noncompliance.

    3. Possible escrow of
      portion of purchase
      price.

  D. Assumption of Liabilities

    1. In an assets transaction,
      possible assumption of
      liabilities through
      operation of law.

II.   **SELLER'S CORPORATE
ORGANIZATION, POWERS
AND COMMITMENTS
(SELLER AND ALL
SUBSIDIARIES)**

  A. Corporate Charters

    1. **Review all original
      charters and all
      amendments.**

    2. **Authorized capital
      structure, including
      description of classes
      of common, preferred,
      preemptive rights.**

    3. **Variance of stockholder
      vote requirements from
      statutory requirements.**

    4. **Restrictions on sale of
      stock, and other
      restrictions.**

| *ITEM* | *ASSIGNED TO* | *COMMENTS* |
|---|---|---|

(II)

    5. If stock is being
       acquired, recommended
       amendments to charters.

  B. Bylaws

    1. Review for any unusual
       provisions, including
       powers of officers,
       notice provisions, etc.

    2. If stock is being
       acquired, recommend
       amendments to bylaws.

  C. Minute Books

    1. Stock validly issued,
       fully paid and non-
       assessable.

    2. Outstanding stock
       options.

    3. Restrictions on transfers
       of shares in charter,
       bylaws or buy-sell
       agreement.

    4. Warrants or other rights
       to purchase stock.

    5. Employment agreements.

    6. Bonus plans.

    7. Employee retirement
       payments.

    8. Profit-sharing plans.

    9. Pension plans, and other
       fringe benefit plans such
       as life insurance, Blue
       Cross, etc.

| *ITEM* | *ASSIGNED TO* | *COMMENTS* |
|---|---|---|

(II)

    10. Union contracts.

    11. Any major or long-term commitments.

    12. Any other operating details of importance such as the grant of exclusive licenses, franchises, state qualifications, etc.

  D. Stock Books

    1. Outstanding shares.

    2. Number of shareholders.

    3. Names and numbers of shares held by controlling shareholders.

    4. Shares held in the treasury.

    5. Payment of original issue and transfer taxes.

    6. Legality of any unusual transfers, such as transfers from estates and trusts.

    7. Missing certificates.

    8. Restrictive legends.

III.  ASSETS (SELLER AND SUBSIDIARIES)

  A. Real Property

    1. Locations.

    2. Descriptions.

| ITEM | ASSIGNED TO | COMMENTS |
|---|---|---|

(III)

    3. Title abstracts.

    4. Title opinions.

    5. Title insurance.

    6. Surveys

    7. Encumbrances, liens or charges, including tax liens, mortgages, rights of way and easements, restrictions, reversions, zoning laws and local ordinances.

  B. Real Property Leases

    1. Name of other party.

    2. Location, description and use.

    3. Date, term and termination rights.

    4. Rent per month.

    5. Net lease, or not.

    6. Guaranties.

    7. Defaults or breaches.

    8. Assignability.

  C. Personal Property

    1. Lists of machinery and equipment and miscellaneous such as airplanes, trucks, cars, etc.

| ITEM | ASSIGNED TO | COMMENTS |
|---|---|---|

(III)

    2. Search records of Secretary of State and County recorder for existence of any leases chattel mortgages, conditional sales contracts, or tax and other liens.

    3. Where government contracts are involved are any assets the property of the U.S. government.

  D. Intangibles

    1. Patents, inventions and know-how.

      a. List patents.

      b. Patent search.

      c. Appraisal of strength of patent position.

      d. Review of patent license agreements.

      e. Determine approach to invention disclosures.

      f. Employee patent, trade secret and nondisclosure agreements.

    2. Review of trademarks, tradenames, and copyrights.

    3. Industry organization and customer approvals (UL, ASTM, etc.).

| ITEM | ASSIGNED TO | COMMENTS |
|------|-------------|----------|

(III)

    4. Permits, registrations
       and approvals of
       government agencies
       for business activities,
       pollution control
       facilities, etc.

IV.   CONTRACTS

    A. Contracts Should Be Listed
       in Categories such as:

       1. Franchise and
          distributorship
          agreements.

       2. License agreements.

       3. Union contracts.

       4. Government contracts.

       5. Contracts with
          customers.

       6. Contracts with suppliers.

       7. Consulting contracts.

    B. All Major Contracts Should
       Be Reviewed To Check the
       Following:

       1. Assignability.

       2. Possible antitrust
          violations.

          a.  Relationship as
              customer or supplier
              of buyer.

          b.  Requirement
              contracts.

          c.  Robinson-Patman
              pricing problems—
              discounts, rebates,
              or allowances.

| ITEM | ASSIGNED TO | COMMENTS |
| --- | --- | --- |

**(IV)**

    d.  Exclusive dealings, etc.

   3. Enforceability.

   4. Breaches or defaults.

   5. Redetermination clauses.

   6. Escalation clauses.

V.   **LIABILITIES**

  A. Loan Agreements, Bonds, and Debentures

    1. Check restrictive covenants to determine conflict with buyer's loan agreements, bonds and debentures, and limitation on buyer's conduct of business after acquisition.

  B. Contingent liabilities for sale of defective products, disposal of hazardous waste, etc.

VI.  **ANTITRUST CONSIDERATIONS**

  A. Check for Existing Violations

    1. Sherman Act and Robinson-Patman violations, etc.

    2. Consent decrees.

    3. Federal Trade Commission proceedings and Justice Department complaints.

| *ITEM* | *ASSIGNED TO* | *COMMENTS* |
| --- | --- | --- |

(VI)

    4. Past and present anti-
       trust litigation and
       claims generally.

  B. Status of Acquisition under
    §7 of Clayton Act and
    Sherman Act

    1. Are buyer and seller
       competitors?

    2. Are the buyer and seller
       related to each other as
       customers or suppliers?

    3. Study of the products,
       geographical areas of
       business, percentages
       of markets, etc.

  C. Conduct of Business after
    Acquisition

    1. How does buyer intend
       to integrate business?

    2. Will integration result
       in ultimate problems?

VII. TAXES

  A. Income Taxes

    1. Tax-free acquisition.

      a. Are the requirements
         of Section 368(a)
         (1) (A) of the
         Internal Revenue
         Code met?

      b. Section 368(a) (1)
         (B)?

      c. Section 368(a) (1)
         (C)?

| ITEM | ASSIGNED TO | COMMENTS |
|---|---|---|

(VII)

    d.  Effect of basis, loss and all other carry-over provisions on buyer and seller.

    e.  Effect of depreciation and investment credit recapture provisions.

  2.  Taxable acquisition.

    a.  Allocation of purchase price.

        i.  real estate.

       ii.  buildings.

      iii.  leasehold interests.

      iv.  tools, dies and jigs.

       v.  inventory.

      vi.  patents.

     vii.  customer contracts.

    viii.  trademarks, tradenames.

      ix.  goodwill.

    b.  Effect of depreciation and investment credit recapture provisions.

| ITEM | ASSIGNED TO | COMMENTS |
|------|-------------|----------|

(VII)

    c. Will requirements of Section 337 or 338 of the Internal Revenue Code be met?

    d. Will appraisal of assets be obtained?

  3. Miscellaneous.

    a. Sales and use taxes and exemptions.

    b. Have seller's past taxes been paid and reviewed by taxing authorities?

    c. Will buyer be subject to transferee liability?

    d. Social Security taxes —transfer of experience rating.

    e. Excise taxes.

    f. Real estate taxes.

VIII. BROKERAGE

  A. Is a Broker Involved?

    1. Name and proof of authority to act.

    2. Whose agent is the broker?

| ITEM | ASSIGNED TO | COMMENTS |
|------|-------------|----------|

(VIII)

    3. Who is to pay the commission—buyer, seller, or seller's stockholders?

    4. Has written brokerage agreement specifying all terms been signed with broker?

    5. Will the parties indemnify one another against brokerage claims?

IX. SECURITIES AND EXCHANGE COMMISSION

  A. Registration of Buyer's Stock

    1. Does nonpublic offering exemption apply?

    2. Investment letters.

    3. Restrictive legend.

    4. Rule 144 effects.

X. STOCK EXCHANGE REQUIREMENTS

  A. Special Circumstances Requiring Special Action Not Otherwise Required by Law or Charter

    1. Stockholder vote required if:

      a. Buyer's directors, or officers have an interest in seller.

| ITEM | ASSIGNED TO | COMMENTS |
| --- | --- | --- |

(X)

    b.  Stock to be issued
        by buyer represents
        an increase in
        outstanding shares
        of 18.5 percent of
        more.

In summary, although the investigation of the seller's business should proceed in the three separate areas of (1) business, (2) law, and (3) accounting, the results of these investigations should be coordinated. The business team, the lawyer and the accountant should each be kept abreast of the results of the investigation of the other two. Since the lawyer has the ultimate responsibility for incorporating in the acquisition contract all of the provisions necessitated by the facts and problems developed in the course of the investigation, the business team and the accountant should transmit to the lawyer all information developed in their respective investigations. The procedure to be followed in a negotiation is dictated by the personalities involved, but, early in the negotiations, the lawyers should have an opportunity to consider possible initial legal problems and to shape the transaction. Basically, the buyer and often the seller should, as a major objective, attempt to determine the *real* objective of the other party in buying or selling. Where deemed important, the parties should take all possible precautions to keep the negotiations secret. Finally, timetables and checklists similar to those printed in this chapter may be helpful to both the buyer and seller involved in an acquisition.

*Source: From the book *Acquisitions, Mergers, Sales, Buyouts and Takeovers* by Charles A. Scharf, Edward E. Shea, George C. Beck © 1985. Used by permission of the publisher, Prentice-Hall, Inc., Englewood Cliffs, NJ.

# How to Understand and Analyze Financial Statements*

*Fred B. Renwick*
New York University
New York, New York

Analyzing financial statements in corporate annual reports can be easy, fun, and rewarding, if you know what to look for. This short essay explains in a nutshell what to look for and how to analyze financial statements.

Only four statements are important to understand and analyze, namely:

- the *balance sheet,* which states the financial condition of the corporation as of one particular date: the date posted at the top of the statement
- the *income statement,* which shows the amount of earnings for the year currently ending, and conveys information regarding the efficiency and profitability of the business
- the *statement of retained earnings,* which gives further information regarding one of the lines on the balance sheet, and also shows the division of net income for the year between dividend payout to stockholders and earnings retained and reinvested in the business

*Source: Fred B. Renwick, "How to Read Financial Statements" as it appears in *The Dow Jones–Irwin Business and Investment Almanac,* edited by Sumner N. Levine, Dow Jones–Irwin © 1988, pp. 313–327.

- the *statement of sources and uses of funds,* which gives further information regarding total current assets and total current liabilities as stated on the balance sheet, and shows the net changes during the year in working capital

Additionally, corporate annual reports usually contain supplementary information which expands upon items in the four basic statements, and includes:

1. a letter or report of independent accountants and auditors addressed to stockholders and directors of the company certifying and validating the figures in the four statements
2. notes which report material information regarding line items in each statement
3. segment information which summarizes selected information by industry and geographic segments
4. restatement pursuant to Financial Accounting Standards Board (FASB) *Statement of Financial Accounting Standards No. 33* to account for effects of inflation and changing prices on items in the four primary statements
5. a long-term (5- or 10-year) summary of selected items from the four primary statements

The following section explains each statement in detail; Section II explains how to analyze the statements; Section III explains notes and supplementary information.

## FOUR FINANCIAL STATEMENTS: WHAT TO LOOK FOR

### Balance Sheets

Table 6–1 shows a balance sheet for Universal Manufacturing Corporation (UMC), a hypothetical company that produces and distributes goods and services in the health industry. Universal's single line of business is divided into two industry segments: human and animal health products, and environmental health products and services.

**Table 6–1.**

## UNIVERSAL MANUFACTURING CORPORATION
### Balance Sheet
### December 31, 1983

| Assets | 1983 | 1982 |
|---|---|---|
| **Current assets** | | |
| Cash . . . . . . . . . . . . . . . . . . . . . . . . . . . . . . . . . . . . . . . . . | $ 350,000 | $ 250,000 |
| Marketable securities at cost (market value: 1983, $2,980,000; 1982, $1,900,000) | 2,850,000 | 1,830,000 |
| Accounts receivable | | |
| Less: Allowance for bad debt: 1983, $24,000; 1982, $21,000 . . . . . . . . . . . . . . . . . . . . . . . . . . . . . . . . . . . | 4,800,000 | 4,370,000 |
| Inventories . . . . . . . . . . . . . . . . . . . . . . . . . . . . . . . . . . . | 5,600,000 | 4,950,000 |
| Total current assets . . . . . . . . . . . . . . . . . . . . . . . | $13,600,000 | $11,400,000 |
| **Fixed assets (property, plant, and equipment)** | | |
| Land . . . . . . . . . . . . . . . . . . . . . . . . . . . . . . . . . . . . . . . . | $ 734,000 | $ 661,000 |
| Building . . . . . . . . . . . . . . . . . . . . . . . . . . . . . . . . . . . . . | 5,762,000 | 5,258,000 |
| Machinery. . . . . . . . . . . . . . . . . . . . . . . . . . . . . . . . . . . . | 11,435,000 | 10,011,000 |
| Office equipment . . . . . . . . . . . . . . . . . . . . . . . . . . . . . . | 614,000 | 561,000 |
| | 18,545,000 | 16,491,000 |
| Less: Accumulated depreciation . . . . . . . . . . . . . . . . . | 6,435,000 | 5,671,000 |
| Net fixed assets . . . . . . . . . . . . . . . . . . . . . . . . . . | 12,110,000 | 10,820,000 |
| Prepayments and deferred charges . . . . . . . . . . . . . . . . | 90,000 | 61,600 |
| Intangibles (goodwill, patent, trademarks) . . . . . . . . . . | 200,000 | 200,000 |
| Total assets . . . . . . . . . . . . . . . . . . . . . . . . . . . . . | $26,000,000 | $22,481,600 |

| Liabilities | 1983 | 1982 |
|---|---|---|
| **Current liabilities**. . . . . . . . . . . . . . . . . . . . . . . . . . . . . . | | |
| Accounts payable. . . . . . . . . . . . . . . . . . . . . . . . . . . . . . . | $ 2,910,000 | $ 2,300,000 |
| Notes payable . . . . . . . . . . . . . . . . . . . . . . . . . . . . . . . . | 1,420,000 | 730,000 |
| Accrued expenses payable . . . . . . . . . . . . . . . . . . . . . . . | 430,000 | 350,000 |
| Federal income taxes payable . . . . . . . . . . . . . . . . . . . . | 1,240,000 | 1,320,000 |
| Total current liabilities . . . . . . . . . . . . . . . . . . . . . | $ 6,000,000 | $ 4,700,000 |
| **Long-term liabilities** | | |
| First mortgage bonds, 8% interest, due 2003 . . . . . | $ 2,000,000 | $ 2,000,000 |
| Total liabilities . . . . . . . . . . . . . . . . . . . . . . . . . . | $ 8,000,000 | $ 6,700,000 |

| Stockholders' Equity | | |
|---|---|---|
| **Capital stock** | | |
| Preferred stock, 6% cumulative, $100 par value each; authorized, issued, and outstanding 13,600 shares . . | 1,360,000 | 1,360,000 |
| Common stock, 30 cents par value each; authorized, issued, and outstanding 760,000 shares . . . . . . . . . . | 228,000 | 228,000 |
| Capital surplus. . . . . . . . . . . . . . . . . . . . . . . . . . . . . . . . | 1,112,000 | 1,112,000 |
| Accumulated retained earnings . . . . . . . . . . . . . . . . . . . | 15,300,000 | 13,081,600 |
| Total stockholders' equity . . . . . . . . . . . . . . . . . . | $18,000,000 | $15,781,600 |
| Total liabilities and stockholders' equity . . . | $26,000,000 | $22,481,600 |

Observe the format of Universal's balance sheet, the *report form,* where total assets, $26 million, are itemized first and total financing (total liabilities and stockholders' equity), $26 million, are itemized below the asset section. Some corporations prefer to use the *account form,* where assets are listed on the left side of the form and liabilities and owners' equity sections are listed to the right of the asset section. UMC is using the *report form.*

The balance sheet shows the ownership of total corporate assets as of the date of the statement. For example, the following calculation implies that if UMC's tangible assets were liquidated as of the date posted at the top of the balance sheet, $17.8 million would be available for distribution among the preferred and common stockholders.

| | |
|---|---:|
| Total assets owned by UMC .................... | $26,000,000 |
| Less: Intangibles ............................. | 200,000 |
| Total tangible assets owned by UMC ............. | $25,800,000 |
| Amount required to pay total liabilities ........... | 8,000,000 |
| Amount remaining for the stockholders ........... | $17,800,000 |

Further, the above example illustrates a critical point: the difference between *current market value* (the amount UMC's assets would really bring if sold) versus the *accounting book value* (the $17.8 million). Relationships exist between market and book values, but accounting statements (except for FASB *No. 33*) are factual reports of *book,* not *market,* values of corporate assets.

The following paragraphs explain each line entry on balance sheets.

Starting at the top of the balance sheet, after the name of the corporation, title, and date of the statement, total assets are itemized, with current assets (total, $13.6 million) always first.

*Current assets* consist of:

1. *Cash,* $350,000, which is what you would expect, namely pocket-book currency and coins in the treasurer's office, plus demand deposits at a commercial bank. Cash is synonymous with liquidity.

2. *Marketable securities,* $2.85 million, which usually are cash equivalents or highly liquid securities such as Treasury bills of the federal government or negotiable certificates of deposit (CDs), or demand notes issued by large corporations.

3. *Accounts receivable,* $4.8 million, which consist of payments due from customers who purchased UMC's goods and services on credit and have not paid yet but are scheduled to pay within the next few months. Since a small fraction of customers might never pay (because of death, financial disaster, flood, or other catastrophe), an allowance is made, $24,000, pursuant to good accounting practices for bad debts.

4. *Inventories,* $5.6 million, which consist of *(a)* finished goods in stock and ready for sale or shipment, *(b)* work and merchandise in process, and *(c)* supplies and raw materials inventories, and are priced on the balance sheet at the lower of cost or market on either a first-in-first-out (FIFO) or last-in-first-out (LIFO) basis. Pricing policy is usually stated in a note.

*Total current assets,* $13.6 million, are the sum of the four aforecited figures and usually are earmarked for use within the coming 12 months. In other words, *current* means within the next 12 months.

*Fixed assets* (property, plant and equipment) are the permanent tangible capital owned by the business, and are listed *at cost* (original purchase price) next on the balance sheet, and consist of:

1. *Land,* $734,000, or ground upon which buildings or other assets such as forests, air or water rights, and the like are built

2. *Building,* $5.762 million, which are structures such as offices, warehouses, and the like where business is conducted

3. *Machinery,* $11.435 million, which is mechanical apparatuses for increasing productivity and economic efficiency

4. *Office equipment,* $614,000, which is what you would expect, namely desks, typewriters, copiers, and the like

*Accumulated depreciation,* $6.435 million, is the total depreciation (deterioration of property, plant, and equipment due to physical wear and tear) accumulated to date for accounting purposes against UMC's assets. It is important to know about three concepts of depreciation, namely:

1. depreciation calculated for tax purposes which is figured pursuant to the Tax Code to benefit from allowable accelerated rates of depreciation
2. accounting depreciation, which can be either straight-line or accelerated and is usually explained in a note
3. economic depreciation, which comes from technological obsolescence and deterioration in ability to continue generating future income at current rates due to changes in demand and markets for the goods and services produced by UMC

The balance sheet states only number two, accounting depreciation.

*Net fixed assets,* $12,110,000, are the sum of the four aforementioned figures, minus accounting depreciation, and are used by the business to generate future (beyond the coming 12 months) income.

*Prepayments and deferred charges,* $90,000, state total amounts paid in advance for assets not yet obtained (such as paid-up premiums on a fire insurance policy covering the next five years, or rental paid on computers for the next three years), and for benefits to be received in future years for expenditures already made (such as for research and development, moving the business to a new location, or expenses incurred in bringing a new product to market).

*Intangibles,* $200,000, are assets such as goodwill, trademarks, franchises, patents, copyrights, and the like which have no physical existence, yet are valuable in producing business income.

*Total assets,* $26 million, are current, plus fixed, plus prepayments and deferred charges, plus intangibles, and state the size of the business and are the total property owned by the business.

Look next at the lower part of the balance sheet, which

concerns the financing of the business. Financing must come from either borrowing (liabilities) or ownership equity.

Underneath the asset section of the balance sheet (or on the right side if the company uses the account form), total current liabilities, $6 million, are always itemized next, then long-term liabilities, $2 million, then finally stockholders' equity of $18 million.

*Total current liabilities* consist of bills due and payable by UMC within the next 12 months, all of which fall into one of four categories:

1. *Accounts payable,* $2.91 million, which are bills currently owed and due to creditors
2. *Notes payable,* $1.42 million, which are current obligations owed to a bank or other short-term lender
3. *Accrued expenses payable,* $430,000, include wages due employees, fees to attorneys, current pension or retirement obligations, and the like
4. *Federal income taxes payable,* $1.24 million, is the current tax payable to the Internal Revenue Service, and is sufficiently important to merit a line of its own on the corporate balance sheet

*Long-term liabilities,* $2 million for UMC, can include straight debt (like UMC's which pays 8 percent interest and matures in 2003), convertible bonds (bonds which pay interest like straight bonds but are convertible upon demand of the bond owner into a stated number of shares of common stock), or "other" long-term debt (like pollution control and industrial revenue bonds or sinking-fund debentures). UMC has only straight debt outstanding.

*Total liabilities,* $8 million, are the sum of current and long-term liabilities and constitute the total financing obtained from borrowings.

*Stockholders' equity,* $18 million, consists of:

1. *Capital stock,* $1.588 million, which includes both preferred stock and common stock but no convertible preferred stock

and no warrants or rights to purchase either bonds or common stock

2. *Capital surplus,* $1.112 million, which is the amount paid in by shareholders over the par or legal value of 30 cents for each common share

3. *Accumulated retained earnings,* $15.3 million, which are earnings not paid out in dividends but retained and reinvested in the business. Further information regarding accumulated retained earnings since inception of the business is set forth below in the *statement of retained earnings*

*Capital stock* represents proprietary interest in the company, is represented by stock certificates authorized and issued by the company, and can belong to either of several classes, including:

1. *Preferred stock,* which has preference or takes priority over other shares regarding dividend payout (6 percent in UMC's case), and which can be cumulative, which means that if the company fails to pay dividends for whatever reason for any year, then the 6 percent of $100 or $6 per preferred share accumulates on the books and must be paid before common stockholders can receive future dividends. Total preferred stock authorized and issued by UMC is $100 per share times 13,600 shares or $1.36 million.

2. *Common stock,* which represents the remaining ownership of the company and is entitled to receive a dividend along with fluctuations in value of the stock. Par value is the legal stated value of each common share; so the par value (30 cents per share times 760,000 shares or $228,000) plus the additional amount or capital surplus ($1.112 million) together state the amount UMC received upon issuing 760,000 shares, namely $1.34 million divided by 760,000 or $1.76 per share.

The bottom line, *total liabilities and stockholders' equity,* states the financing of the corporation, and shows where UMC obtained the $26 million to buy the total assets itemized at the top of the balance sheet.

We turn next to income statements.

### Income Statements

Table 6–2 shows UMC's income statement, where the important items to look for, after the name of the company, the title, and date of the statement at the heading, are:

1. *Net sales,* which is where most of the business revenue comes from for most businesses, except rental and leasing companies, $23,850,000.
2. *Net operating income* (NOI) or profit before interest and taxes, which states profit from business operations, without regard to financing, $5,878,000.
3. *Total income* before interest and taxes, which states the return on total capital available to the business during the year, $6,220,000.
4. *Less:* provision for federal income tax, $2,240,000.
5. *Total income,* after tax but before interest deduction, which states the after-tax profitability of the corporation and is widely used in computing cost of capital for a business enterprise, $3,980,000.
6. *Net income* (NI) or profit for the year, which states earnings after taxes and after all fixed charges. The net profit for the year is available for (a) dividend payout to preferred stockholders, (b) dividend payout to common stockholders, and (c) retention and reinvestment in the business, $3,820,000.
7. *Net earnings per share* (EPS), which equals total earnings available for distribution to common stockholders ($3.82 million minus 6 percent dividend owed on 13,600 shares of $100 par value preferred stock, or $3,738,400), divided by 760,000 common shares outstanding, $4.92.

$$\$3,820,000 - 0.06\,(13,600)\,(\$100) = \$3,738,400$$

$$\$3,738,400/760,000 = \$4.92 \text{ per share}$$

Cost of sales and operating expenses falls into one of three categories:

1. *Cost of goods sold,* which states the amount of labor, material, and other expenses in producing the items sold, $8,940,000
2. *Depreciation expense,* which states the amount of capital (producer's durables) consumed in producing the goods and services sold and which must be replaced or restored to its original capacity, $800,000
3. *Selling and administrating expenses,* which include office expenses, executives' salaries, salespersons' salaries, advertising and promotion expenses, and the like, $8,232,000

**Table 6–2.**

### UNIVERSAL MANUFACTURING CORPORATION
Consolidated Income Statement
December 31, 1983 and 1982

|  | 1983 | 1982 |
|---|---|---|
| Net sales | $23,850,000 | $19,810,000 |
| Cost of sales and operating expenses |  |  |
| Cost of goods sold | 8,940,000 | 7,209,000 |
| Depreciation | 800,000 | 750,000 |
| Selling and administrating expenses | 8,232,000 | 6,814,000 |
| Operating profit | $ 5,878,000 | $ 5,037,000 |
| Other income |  |  |
| Dividends and interest | 342,000 | 183,000 |
| **Total income** | $ 6,220,000 | $ 5,220,000 |
| Less: Interest on bonds | 160,000 | 160,000 |
| Income before provisions for federal income tax | $ 6,060,000 | $ 5,060,000 |
| Provision for federal income tax | 2,240,000 | 1,980,000 |
| **Net profit for year** | $ 3,820,000 | $ 3,080,000 |
| Common shares outstanding | 760,000 | 760,000 |
| Net earnings per share | $ 4.92 | $ 3.95 |

### Statement of Accumulated Retained Earnings

|  | 1983 | 1982 |
|---|---|---|
| Balance January 1 | $13,081,600 | $11,413,200 |
| Net profit for year | 3,820,000 | 3,080,000 |
| **Total** | $16,901,600 | $14,493,200 |
| Less: Dividends paid on |  |  |
| Preferred stock | 81,600 | 81,600 |
| Common stock | 1,520,000 | 1,330,000 |
| **Balance December 31** | $15,300,000 | $13,081,600 |

*Operating profit,* also called net operating income, $5.878 million, is the income from business operations, and is an important indicator of how efficiently the fixed assets were employed during the year.

*Other income,* $342,000, is from UMC's marketable securities of $1.83 million at cost as of one year ago.

*Total income,* $6.22 million, is the sum of operating profit from the business and income from other sources.

*Interest on bonds,* $160,000 (8 percent of $2 million), is itemized next on the income statement, followed by:

| | |
|---|---|
| *Income* after *interest,* before *tax* ................ | $6,060,000 |
| *Provision for federal income tax*................. | 2,240,000 |
| *Net profit for one year*........................ | 3,820,000 |
| *Net earnings per share*........................ | $4.92 |

We turn next to statements of accumulated retained earnings.

### Statements of Accumulated Retained Earnings

The bottom part of Table 6–2 contains the accumulated retained earnings statement for UMC, and shows at the beginning of the balance, since the starting date of the business to January 1 of the current year, $13,081,600—to which is added the net profit for the year, $3,820,000, to get total accumulated retained earnings of $16,901,600.

*Dividends paid* to stockholders are itemized next:

| | |
|---|---|
| *Preferred stock* dividend: 6 percent of $1,360,000 ... | $   81,600 |
| *Common stock* dividend: $2.00 per share declared times 760,000 shares................. | 1,520,000 |
| Total dividends paid ................. | $1,601,600 |

*Balance,* December 31 ($15.3 million), equals the difference between the total available ($16,901,600) and total dividends paid. Retained earnings are an important source of finance of corporate capital assets.

We turn next to statements of sources and uses of funds.

### Statements of Source and Application of Funds

Table 6–3 is a statement of source and application or use of funds for UMC. Ordinarily, *funds* imply cash; but in a broader sense, *funds* include cash equivalents and substitutes for cash, such as short-term credit, notes, and accounts payable and accrued liabilities to meet the short-term financing needs of the

**Table 6–3.**

UNIVERSAL MANUFACTURING CORPORATION
Statement of Source and Application of Funds
December 31, 1983

|  | 1983 |  |
|---|---|---|
| Funds were provided by |  |  |
| Net income | $3,820,000 |  |
| Depreciation | 800,000 |  |
| **Total** |  | $4,620,000 |
| Funds were used for |  |  |
| Dividends on preferred stock | $ 81,600 |  |
| Dividends on common stock | 1,520,000 |  |
| Plant and equipment | 1,720,300 |  |
| Sundry assets | 398,100 |  |
| **Total** |  | $3,720,000 |
| **Increase in working capital** |  | $ 900,000 |
| **Analysis of changes in working capital—1983** |  |  |
| Changes in current assets |  |  |
| Cash | $ 100,000 |  |
| Marketable securities | 1,020,000 |  |
| Accounts receivable | 430,000 |  |
| Inventories | 650,000 |  |
| **Total** |  | $2,200,000 |
| Changes in current liabilities |  |  |
| Accounts payable | $ 610,000 |  |
| Notes payable | 690,000 |  |
| Accrued expenses payable | 80,000 |  |
| Federal income tax payable | (80,000) |  |
| **Total** |  | $1,300,000 |

business. So *funds* in the broader sense imply net *working capital,* which is the difference between current assets and current liabilities.

Sources of funds in general include transactions which increase the amount of working capital, such as:

1. net profit from operations
2. sale or consumption of noncurrent assets
3. long-term borrowing
4. issuing additional shares of capital stock
5. annual depreciation

Uses of funds in general include transactions which decrease working capital, such as:

1. declaring cash dividends
2. repaying long-term debt
3. buying noncurrent assets
4. repurchasing outstanding capital stock

In the case of UMC and Table 6–3, funds were provided by net income, $3.82 million, and current depreciation expense, $800,000. Some analysts worry that depreciation is not cash; depreciation is a bookkeeping entry. But the capital was consumed in the process of producing the goods and services sold; so the business pays the cash to itself to ultimately replace the consumed capital. Depreciation expense is a source of funds.

*Total funds* provided for UMC are $4,620,000.

*Uses of funds* are itemized next, where all uses fall into one of four categories:

| | |
|---|---:|
| Dividends on preferred stock . . . . . . . . . . . . . . . . . . . | $    81,600 |
| Dividends on common stock . . . . . . . . . . . . . . . . . . | 1,520,000 |
| Plant and equipment . . . . . . . . . . . . . . . . . . . . . . . . . | 1,720,300 |
| Sundry assets. . . . . . . . . . . . . . . . . . . . . . . . . . . . . . . . | 398,100 |
| *Total uses* or application of funds . . . . . . . . . . . | $3,720,000 |

*Increase in working capital,* $900,000, is the difference between the total funds provided, $4.62 million, and the total funds used, $3.72 million.

An *analysis of changes in working capital* for the year is included in the statement of source and application of funds, and gives further information regarding the $900,000 increase in working capital, which is explained by analyzing changes in current assets together with changes in current liabilities.

*Changes in current assets* total $2.2 million, itemized as follows:

1. *Cash* increased from $250,000 to $350,000, giving a net change of $100,000
2. *Marketable securities* increased from $1.83 million to $2.85 million, giving a net change of $1.02 million
3. *Accounts receivable* increased from $4.37 million to $4.8 million, giving a net change of $430,000
4. *Inventories* increased from $4.95 million to $5.6 million, giving a net change of $650,000

*Changes in current liabilities* total $1.3 million, itemized as follows:

1. *Accounts payable* increased from $2.3 million to $2.91 million, giving a net change of $610,000
2. *Notes payable* increased from $730,000 to $1.42 million, giving a net change of $690,000
3. *Accrued expenses payable* increased from $350,000 to $430,000, giving a net change of $80,000
4. *Federal income taxes payable* decreased from $1.32 million to $1.24 million, giving a net change of ($80,000)

The difference between the changes in current assets ($2.2 million) and changes in current liabilities ($1.3 million) equals the $900,000 increase in working capital.

We turn next to understanding more regarding how to analyze financial statements.

## *ANALYZING FINANCIAL STATEMENTS*

The analysis of all four statements consists primarily of calculating ratios, but other methods including the time trend of the ratio, information theory, and flow-of-funds analysis are sometimes used. We shall limit our analysis to using ratios.

In general, financial analysts, investors, creditors, and others look for two kinds of information regarding business enterprises:

1. *risk,* including financial, business, market, and country or political risks
2. *return,* including productivity, efficiency, and profitability of corporate capital investments

A third factor, *growth rate,* is important too, primarily because high steady growth is usually worth more than low or no growth.

### *Balance Sheet Ratios*

Balance sheet ratios belong to one of the three following categories:

1. *liquidity and turnover ratios,* which indicate the ability of the corporation to pay current liabilities
2. *capitalization,* also called *leverage,* or *debt ratios,* which is the amount of borrowing relative to other factors such as total capitalization, total assets, or total equity
3. *net asset ratios,* which indicate the amount of assets backing each class of outstanding securities

*Liquidity ratios* are calculated to judge whether the corporation owns sufficient cash and cash-equivalents or substitutes to comfortably pay short-term obligations, and include:

1. *current liquidity,* the ability to pay current liabilities from current assets:

*Current ratio:*

$$\frac{\text{Current assets}}{\text{Current liabilities}} = \frac{\$13,600,000}{\$6,000,000} = 2.3 \text{ to } 1$$

In total dollar amounts, the numerator in the current ratio, minus the denominator, states *net working capital,* where

| | |
|---|---:|
| Total current assets......................... | $13,600,000 |
| Less: Total current liabilities ............... | 6,000,000 |
| Working capital ........................ | $ 7,600,000 |

2. *quick asset* (sometimes called *acid test*) *ratio:*

$$\frac{\text{Quick assets}}{\text{Current liabilities}} = \frac{\$8,000,000}{\$6,000,000} = 1.33$$

where quick assets are total assets minus inventories, because inventories usually are less liquid than either cash, marketable securities, or accounts receivable:

| | | |
|---|---:|---:|
| Total current assets ............. | $13,600,000 | |
| Less: Inventories .............. | 5,600,000 | |
| Quick assets..................... | | $8,000,000 |
| Less: Total current liabilities .... | | 6,000,000 |
| Net quick assets ............... | | $2,000,000 |

3. the *cash plus marketable securities ratio* indicates the firm's ability to pay current liabilities without relying on either inventories or accounts receivable:

$$\frac{\text{Cash plus marketable securities}}{\text{Total current liabilities}} = \frac{\$3,200,000}{\$6,000,000} = 0.53$$

*Liquidity and turnover of inventories ratios* indicate how closely inventories approximate true liquidity through total sales, and are the three following figures:

1. *inventory as a percentage of total current assets:*

$$\frac{\text{Inventory}}{\text{Total current assets}} = \frac{\$5,600,000}{\$13,600,000} = 41.18 \text{ percent}$$

2. *cost of goods sold,* including depreciation and capital consumption, *to average inventory ratio:*

$$\frac{\text{Cost of goods sold plus depreciation}}{\text{Inventory}} = \frac{\$9,740,000}{\$5,600,000} = 1.74$$

3. *inventory turnover ratio:*

$$\frac{\text{Net sales}}{\text{Inventory}} = \frac{\$23,850,000}{\$5,600,000} = 4.26 \text{ times}$$

*Liquidity of receivables ratios* indicate how closely accounts receivable approximate true liquidity through total sales, and are the two following figures:

1. Average collection period ratio, which indicates the number of day's sales in accounts receivables:

$$\frac{\text{Receivables} \times \text{Days in year}}{\text{Annual sales}} = \frac{\$4,800,000 \times 360}{\$23,850,000} = 72.45$$

2. Accounts receivable turnover ratio:

$$\frac{\text{Annual sales}}{\text{Accounts receivable}} = \frac{\$23,850,000}{\$4,800,000} = 4.97$$

*Liquidity and turnover of tangible and fixed asset ratios* indicate relationships between total sales and total assets, and are given by the following two figures:

1. Fixed asset turnover ratio:

$$\frac{\text{Sales}}{\text{Net fixed assets}} = \frac{\$23,850,000}{\$12,110,000} = 1.97$$

2. Total asset turnover ratio:

$$\frac{\text{Net sales}}{\text{Average total tangible assets}} = \frac{\$23,850,000}{\$25,800,000} = 0.9244$$

*Capitalization ratios* include:

1. Debt ratio:

$$\frac{\text{Total liabilities}}{\text{Total assets}} = \frac{\$8,000,000}{\$26,000,000} = 30.77 \text{ percent}$$

2. Current liabilities as a percentage of total liabilities:

$$\frac{\text{Current liabilities}}{\text{Total liabilities}} = \frac{\$6,000,000}{\$8,000,000} = 75 \text{ percent}$$

3. Debt-to-net-worth ratio:

$$\frac{\text{Total liabilities}}{\text{Net worth}} = \frac{\$8,000,000}{\$18,000,000} = 0.4444$$

4. Long-term debt capitalization ratio:

$$\frac{\text{Long-term debt}}{\text{Total capitalization}} = \frac{\$2,000,000}{\$19,800,000} = 10.10 \text{ percent}$$

5. Preferred stock ratio:

$$\frac{\text{Preferred stock}}{\text{Total capitalization}} = \frac{\$1,360,000}{\$19,800,000} = 6.87 \text{ percent}$$

6. Common stock ratio:

$$\frac{\text{Common stock plus accumulated earnings}}{\text{Total capitalization}} = \frac{\$16,440,000}{\$19,800,000} = 83.03 \text{ percent}$$

7. Summary:

| | | |
|---|---:|---:|
| Total assets . . . . . . . . . . . . . . . . . . . . . . | $26,000,000 | |
| Less: Intangibles . . . . . . . . . . . . . . . . | 200,000 | |
| Less: Total current liabilities . . . . . . . | 6,000,000 | |
| Total capitalization . . . . . . . . . . . . . . . . | $19,800,000 | 100.00% |
| Bonds (long-term debt) . . . . . . . . . . . | 2,000,000 | 10.10 |
| Preferred stock . . . . . . . . . . . . . . . . . | 1,360,000 | 6.87 |
| Common stock (including capital surplus and retained earnings) . . . | 16,440,000 | 83.03 |

8. Long-term debt as a percentage of total liabilities:

$$\frac{\text{Long-term debt}}{\text{Total liabilities}} = \frac{\$2,000,000}{\$8,000,000} = 25.00 \text{ percent}$$

*Net asset value ratios* include:

1. Net asset value per $1,000 bond; $9,900 per bond

$$\frac{\substack{\text{Net tangible assets available} \\ \text{to meet bondholders' claims}}}{\substack{\text{Number of \$1,000} \\ \text{bonds outstanding}}} = \frac{\$19,800,000}{2,000,000}$$

where the numerator is calculated as follows:

| | |
|---|---:|
| Total assets . . . . . . . . . . . . . . . . . . . . . . . . . . . . . | $26,000,000 |
| Less: Intangibles . . . . . . . . . . . . . . . . . . . . . . . . | 200,000 |
| Total tangible assets . . . . . . . . . . . . . . . . . . . . . | $25,800,000 |
| Less: Current liabilities . . . . . . . . . . . . . . . . . . . | 6,000,000 |
| Net tangible assets available to meet bondholders' claims . . . . . . . . . . . . . . . . . . . . . . . . . . . . . | $19,800,000 |

2. Net asset value per share of preferred stock: $1,308.82

$$\frac{\text{Net assets backing the preferred stock}}{\substack{\text{Number of shares of} \\ \text{preferred stock outstanding}}} = \frac{\$17,800,000}{13,600}$$

where the numerator is calculated as follows:

| | |
|---|---:|
| Total assets .............................. | $26,000,000 |
| Less: Intangibles .......................... | 200,000 |
| Total tangible assets ....................... | $25,800,000 |
| Less: Current liabilities.................... | 6,000,000 |
| Less: Long-term liabilities ................. | 2,000,000 |
| Net assets backing the preferred stock.......... | $17,800,000 |

3. Net book value per share of common stock: $21.63

$$\frac{\substack{\text{Net assets available} \\ \text{for the common stock}}}{\text{Total number of shares outstanding}} = \frac{\$16,440,000}{760,000} = \$21.63$$

where the numerator is calculated as follows:

| | |
|---|---:|
| Total assets .............................. | $26,000,000 |
| Less: Intangibles .......................... | 200,000 |
| Total tangible assets ....................... | $25,800,000 |
| Less: Current liabilities.................... | 6,000,000 |
| Less: Long-term liabilities ................. | 2,000,000 |
| Less: Preferred stock....................... | 1,360,000 |
| Net assets available for the common stock ..... | $16,440,000 |

Finally, estimate the youngest average plant age by dividing the current (1983) depreciation expense accrual ($800,000 from the statement of source and application of funds) into accumulated depreciation ($6,435,000 from the balance sheet) to get 8.04 years. Because some plants and pieces of equipment may have been fully written off over time, we can say that UMC's fixed assets, on average, are over 8 years old.

### Income Statement Ratios

Income statement ratios belong to one of the two following categories:

1. *coverage,* which analyzes financial risk by relating the financial charges of a corporation to its ability to service them

2. *productivity* or *capital efficiency ratios,* which relate income to total sales and to investment

*Coverage ratios* include:

1. Interest coverage ratio: 38.875

$$\frac{\text{Net operating income before interest and taxes}}{\text{Interest charges on bonds}} = \frac{\$6,220,000}{\$160,000} = 38.875$$

2. Cash flow coverage ratio, which indicates the firm's ability to service debt, which is related to both interest and principal payments and is not met out of earnings per se, but out of cash: 19.5 times

$$\frac{\text{Annual cash flow before interest and taxes}}{\text{Interest on bonds plus principal repayments}/(1 - T)} = \frac{\$7,020,000}{\$360,000} = 19.5$$

where:

---

Net operating income before interest and
   taxes............................... $6,220,000

Plus annual depreciation expense ....... <u>800,000</u>

Annual cash flow before interest and
   taxes............................... $7,020,000

   Face value 20-year 8% bonds due 2003 $2,000,000

   Annual repayment rate after taxes
     $2,000,000 divided by 20 years ..... 100,000

   Before-tax annual bond repayment rate
     $100,000 divided by 1 minus the
     effective tax rate, say 50%........ $200,000

Plus: 8% interest on $2,000,000 ........ <u>160,000</u>

Interest plus principal repayments ...... $360,000

---

Since interest payments are made before taxes, the adjustment is necessary to convert principal repayments which are made after taxes to before-tax equivalents.

3. Preferred dividend coverage ratio: 46.81

$$\frac{\text{Income available for paying preferred dividends}}{\text{Total dividends to preferred shareholders}} = \frac{\$3,820,000}{\$81,600} = 46.81$$

4. Earnings per common share: $4.92

$$\frac{\text{Earnings available for distribution to common shareholders}}{\text{Total number of common shares outstanding}} = \frac{\$3,738,400}{760,000} = \$4.92$$

where:

| Net profit for the year ....................... | $3,820,000 |
| Less: Dividend requirements on preferred stock | 81,600 |
| Earnings available for common stock ........... | $3,738,400 |

5. Primary earnings for the year: $4.94

$$\frac{\text{Earnings for the year}}{\text{Common stock plus stock equivalents}} = \frac{\$3,820,000}{773,500} = \$4.94$$

assuming the 13,600 preferred shares had been convertible and converted, on a share-for-share basis, into common stock.

13,600 + 760,000 = 773,600 common shares after conversion

6. Fully diluted earnings per share: $4.79

$$\frac{\text{Adjusted earnings}}{\text{Adjusted shares outstanding}} = \frac{\$3,900,000}{813,600} = \$4.79$$

where:

| Earnings for the year........................ | $3,820,000 |
| Plus: Interest on convertible bonds ........... | $ 160,000 |
| Less: Income tax applicable to interest deduction ................................ | 80,000 |
| Adjusted earnings for the year................ | $3,900,000 |
| Common shares outstanding ................... | 760,000 |
| Preferred convertible stock equivalent common shares...................................... | 13,600 |
| Twenty common shares per $1,000 convertible bond (2,000) outstanding........................ | 40,000 |
| Adjusted shares outstanding................... | 813,600 |

7. Summary:

| | |
|---|---|
| Earnings per share . . . . . . | $4.92 |
| Primary earnings . . . . . . . | 4.94 |
| Fully diluted earnings . . . | 4.79 |

8. Price-earnings ratio: Approximately 15 times

$$\frac{\text{Market price of stock}}{\text{Earnings per share}} = \frac{\$72.25}{\$4.92} = 14.69$$

*Productivity or capital efficiency* ratios include:

1. Operating margin of profit: 24.65%.

$$\frac{\text{Operating profit}}{\text{Sales}} = \frac{\$5,878,000}{\$23,850,000} = 24.65\%$$

Previous year:

$$= \frac{\$5,037,000}{\$19,810,000} = 25.43\%$$

2. Operating cost ratio: 75.35%.

| | Amount | Ratio |
|---|---|---|
| Net sales . . . . . . . . . . . . . . . . . . . . . . . . | $23,850,000 | 100.00% |
| Operating costs . . . . . . . . . . . . . . . . . . . | 17,972,000 | 75.35 |
| Operating profit . . . . . . . . . . . . . . . . . . | $ 5,878,000 | 24.65% |

3. Net profit ratio: 16.02%.

$$\frac{\text{Net profit for the year}}{\text{Net sales}} = \frac{\$3,820,000}{\$23,850,000} = 16.02\%$$

Previous year: 15.55%

$$= \frac{\$3,080,000}{\$19,810,000} = 15.55\%$$

### Ratios from Statements of Accumulated Retained Earnings

Retained earnings statements ratios belong to one of the two following categories:

1. dividend payout ratio

2. earnings retention ratio

The dividend payout ratio for UMC is 40.66%.

$$\frac{\text{Dividends paid to common stockholders}}{\text{Income available for common stockholders}} = \frac{\$1,520,000}{\$3,738,400} = 40.66\%$$

where:

| | |
|---|---:|
| Net profit for the year . . . . . . . . . . . . . . . . . . . . . . . . . . | $3,820,000 |
| Dividends on preferred stock . . . . . . . . . . . . . . . . . . . . . | 81,600 |
| Earnings available for common . . . . . . . . . . . . . . . . . . | $3,738,400 |

The earnings retention ratio for UMC is 59.34%.

$$\frac{\text{Earnings retained}}{\text{Earnings available for payout}} = \frac{\$2,218,400}{\$3,738,400} = 59.34\%$$

where:

| | |
|---|---:|
| Net profit for the year . . . . . . . . . . . . . . . . . . . . . . . . . | $3,820,000 |
| Less: Dividends paid on preferred stock . . . . . . . . . . | $    81,600 |
| Less: Dividends paid on common stock . . . . . . . . . . | 1,520,000 |
| Earnings retained . . . . . . . . . . . . . . . . . . . . . . . . . . . . | $2,218,400 |

Summary:

| | | |
|---|---|---|
| Dividend payout ratio .... | 40.66% |
| Earnings retention ratio ... | 59.34 |
| Earnings available ........ | 100.00% |

Dividends per share: $2.00.

$$\frac{\text{Total dividends paid to common shareholders}}{\text{Number of common shares outstanding}} = \frac{\$1,520,000}{760,000} = \$2.00$$

Balance December 31: $15,300,000.

### *Ratios from Statements of Source and Application of Funds*

Since an analysis was stated directly on the statement of source and use of funds in Table 6–3, that part of the analysis is completed; however, we still need to calculate profitability ratios which belong to one of the two following categories:

1. return on assets
2. return on equity

*Return on assets ratios* include:

*Return on total assets:* 27.67%.

$$\frac{\text{Total income}}{\text{Last year's total assets}} = \frac{\$6,220,000}{\$22,481,600} = 27.67\%$$

*After-tax return on total assets:* 17.70%.

$$\frac{\text{Total income after tax but before interest}}{\text{Last year's total assets}} = \frac{\$3,980,000}{\$22,481,600} = 17.70\%$$

where:

| | |
|---|---|
| Total income . . . . . . . . . . . . . . . . . . . . . . . . . . . . . . . . . . | $6,220,000 |
| Less: Provision for total taxes . . . . . . . . . . . . . . . . . . | 2,240,000 |
| After-tax total income . . . . . . . . . . . . . . . . . . . . . . . . . . | $3,980,000 |

*Return on equity* ratio: 25.92%.

$$\frac{\substack{\text{Income available for}\\\text{distribution to common stockholders}}}{\substack{\text{Last year's total equity}\\\text{of common stockholders}}} = \frac{\$3,738,400}{\$14,421,600} = 25.92\%$$

where:

| | |
|---|---|
| Last year's total stockholders' equity . . . . . . . . . . . . . . | $15,781,600 |
| Less: Preferred stock value . . . . . . . . . . . . . . . . . . . . | 1,360,000 |
| Last year's common stock equity . . . . . . . . . . . . . . . . | $14,421,600 |

We turn next to further discussion of notes and supplemental information.

## NOTES AND SUPPLEMENTAL INFORMATION

As explained in the introduction, financial statements in corporate annual reports usually are accompanied by:

- a *report of independent accountants and auditors* certifying the statements conform to generally accepted accounting principles and that generally accepted auditing standards and procedures were used
- *notes* which further explain details and disclose relevant information regarding line items on all four statements
- *segment information,* which summarizes selected items by business, industry, and geographic segment

- a *restatement* of almost everything in current (in contrast with the traditional historical original purchase) prices, accounting for the effects of inflation on items reported in the standard statements
- *long-term record* summarizing selected items over a five- or ten-year time span

### *Report of Independent Accountants*

A typical report of independent accountants is addressed to the stockholders and board of directors of the corporation and will read as follows:

> In our opinion, the accompanying consolidated financial statements, appearing on pages — through — , present fairly the financial position of Universal Manufacturing Corporation and its subsidiary companies at December 31, 1983 and 1982, and the results of their operations and changes in financial position for the years then ended, in conformity with generally accepted accounting principles consistently applied. Also, in our opinion, the five-year comparative consolidated summary of operations presents fairly the financial information included therein. Our examinations of these statements were made in accordance with generally accepted auditing standards and accordingly included such tests of the accounting records and such other auditing procedures as we considered necessary in the circumstances.

The report will be signed with the name and address of the accounting firm and dated.

### *Notes to Financial Statements*

Notes disclose additional information regarding entries in all four primary statements, and usually are considered an integral part of the statements, included in and covered by the auditor's certification. Some corporations include in the notes the next three items to be discussed: segment information, effects of inflation, and long-term comparative summary of operations.

If included in some place other than in the notes, then look for whether the statement was excluded from the auditor's audit.

### Segment Information

Notes disclosing geographic area and industry segment information usually summarize selected items such as net sales, operating income, total assets, depreciation and amortization, and capital expenditures for industry segments (business segments or product groups) and foreign operations.

Table 6-4 shows the segment information for UMC's two segments.

As you can see from Table 6-4, industry segment number one, Human and Animal Health Products, accounts for 84 percent ($20,044,000 divided by $23,850,000) of total sales, and 92 percent ($5,435,000 divided by $5,878,000) of UMC's operating income; all supported by 83.46 percent ($21,700,000 divided by $26,000,000) of total assets. Eleven percent ($234,100 divided by $2,118,400) of total capital expenditures were made in industry segment number two, Environmental Health Products and Services, for the treatment of water and air pollution.

Table 6-4 also shows, based on the following ratios, that UMC's business is roughly 60 percent domestic United States; 40 percent nondomestic:

Net sales:

$$\frac{\text{United States}}{\text{Total company}} = \frac{\$14,818,000}{\$23,850,000} = 62.13\%$$

Operating income:

$$\frac{\text{United States}}{\text{Total company}} = \frac{\$3,690,000}{\$5,037,000} = 62.78\%$$

Total assets:

$$\frac{\text{United States}}{\text{Total company}} = \frac{\$16,549,000}{\$26,000,000} = 63.65\%$$

**Table 6–4.** Segment reporting and foreign operations.

| | Industry Segments | | | Geographic Segments | | | | |
| | Segment No. 1 | Segment No. 2 | Consolidated | Domestic | Foreign OECD | Foreign Other | Eliminations | Consolidated |
|---|---|---|---|---|---|---|---|---|
| **1983** | | | | | | | | |
| Sales, unaffiliated customers | $20,044,000 | $3,806,000 | $23,850,000 | $12,647,000 | $ 9,029,000 | $2,175,000 | | $23,850,000 |
| Sales, intersegment | | | | 2,171,000 | 346,000 | 21,000 | ($2,539,000) | |
| Total sales | $20,044,000 | $3,806,000 | $23,850,000 | $14,818,000 | $ 9,375,000 | $2,196,000 | ($2,539,000) | 23,850,000 |
| Pretax operating income | 5,435,000 | 443,000 | 5,878,000 | 3,690,000 | 1,820,000 | 211,000 | 157,000 | 5,878,000 |
| Identifiable assets at December 31 | 21,700,000 | 4,300,000 | 26,000,000 | 16,549,000 | 10,168,000 | 2,353,000 | ( 3,070,000) | 26,000,000 |
| Depreciation expense | 666,000 | 134,000 | 800,000 | | | | | |
| Capital spending | 1,884,300 | 234,100 | 2,118,400 | | | | | |
| **1982** | | | | | | | | |
| Sales, unaffiliated customers | $16,629,000 | $3,181,000 | $19,810,000 | $10,519,000 | $ 7,511,000 | $1,780,000 | | $19,810,000 |
| Sales, intersegment | | | | 2,614,000 | 246,000 | 14,000 | ($2,878,000) | |
| Total sales | $16,629,000 | $3,181,000 | $19,810,000 | $13,133,000 | $ 7,757,000 | $1,794,000 | ($2,878,000) | 19,810,000 |
| Pretax operating income | 4,627,000 | 410,000 | 5,037,000 | 3,512,000 | 1,449,000 | 126,000 | ( 50,000) | 5,037,000 |
| Identifiable assets at December 31 | 19,027,000 | 3,473,000 | 22,500,000 | 14,728,000 | 8,660,000 | 2,005,000 | ( 2,893,000) | 22,500,000 |
| Depreciation expense | 611,000 | 127,000 | 738,000 | | | | | |
| Capital spending | 1,751,000 | 190,000 | | | | | | |
| **1981** | | | | | | | | |
| Sales, unaffiliated customers | $14,461,000 | $2,779,000 | $17,240,000 | $ 9,504,000 | $ 6,152,000 | $1,584,000 | | $17,240,000 |
| Sales, intersegment | | | | 2,677,000 | 155,000 | 3,000 | ($2,835,000) | |
| Total sales | $14,461,000 | $2,779,000 | $17,240,000 | $12,181,000 | $ 6,307,000 | $1,587,000 | ($2,835,000) | 17,240,000 |
| Pretax operating income | 4,163,000 | 378,000 | 4,541,000 | 3,552,000 | 1,234,000 | 119,000 | ( 364,000) | 4,541,000 |
| Identifiable assets at December 31 | 16,614,000 | 3,341,000 | 19,955,000 | 13,627,000 | 7,818,000 | 1,590,000 | ( 3,179,000) | 19,955,000 |
| Depreciation expense | 551,000 | 102,000 | 653,000 | | | | | |
| Capital spending | 1,969,000 | 238,000 | 2,207,000 | | | | | |

## Supplemental Information on Inflation Accounting

Pursuant to Financial Accounting Standards Board (FASB) *Statement of Financial Accounting Standards No. 33*, public enterprises that have either

1. inventories and property, plant, and equipment (before deducting accumulated depreciation) amounting to more than $125 million or
2. total assets amounting to more than $1 billion (after deducting accumulated depreciation)

are required to report supplementary information in addition to the primary financial statements. FASB *Standards No. 33* are:

For fiscal years ended on or after December 25, 1979, enterprises are required to report:

1. income from continuing operations adjusted for the effects of general inflation
2. the purchasing power gain or loss on net monetary items

For fiscal years ended on or after December 25, 1979, enterprises are also required to report:

1. income from continuing operations on a current cost basis
2. the current cost amounts of inventory and property, plant, and equipment at the end of the fiscal year
3. increases or decreases in current cost amounts of inventory and property, plant, and equipment, net of inflation

Enterprises are required to present a five-year summary of selected financial data, including information on income, sales and other operating revenues, net assets, dividends per common share, and market price per share. In the computation of net assets, only inventory and property, plant, and equipment need be adjusted for the effects of changing prices.

# Table 6–5.

## UNIVERSAL MANUFACTURING CORPORATION
### Schedule of Income from Continuing Operations and Other Changes in Shareholders' Equity Adjusted for Effects of Changing Prices
### For the Year Ended December 31, 1983

|  | As Reported (historical cost) | Adjusted for General Inflation (constant 1983 $) | Adjusted for Specific (current) Costs |
|---|---|---|---|
| Income from continuing operations............. |  |  |  |
| Net sales ............................ | $23,850,000 |  |  |
| Other income.......................... | 342,000 |  |  |
| **Total revenue from continuing operations** |  | $24,192,000 | $24,192,000 | $24,192,000 |
| Costs and other deductions |  |  |  |
| Depreciation expenses..................... |  | 800,000 | 1,076,000 | 1,115,000 |
| Other costs and expenses ................. |  | 17,172,000 | 17,699,000 | 17,273,000 |
| Interest expense........................ |  | 160,000 | 160,000 | 160,000 |
| Federal and foreign income taxes............. |  | 2,240,000 | 2,240,000 | 2,240,000 |
| **Total costs and other deductions** ...... |  | $20,372,000 | $21,175,000 | $20,788,000 |
| Net income from continuing operations ......... |  | 3,820,000 | 3,017,000 | 3,404,000 |
| Purchasing power gain on net monetary liabilities (net amounts owed) ...................... |  |  | 1,000 | 1,000 |
| Increase in current cost of inventories and property, plant and equipment during 1983 ............ |  |  |  | 1,911,000 |
| Less: Effect of increase in general price level during 1983 ..................... |  |  |  | 2,788,000 |
| Excess of increase in specific prices over increase in the general price level .................. |  |  |  | ($ 877,000) |
| **Net income** ............................ |  | $ 3,820,000 |  |  |
| **Adjusted net income** ....................... |  |  | $ 3,018,000 |  |
| **Net change in shareholders' equity from above**.... |  | $ 3,820,000 | $ 3,018,000 | $ 2,528,000 |

## Summarized Balance Sheet
## Adjusted for Changing Prices
## At December 31, 1983

| | As Reported | Adjusted for General Inflation (constant 1983 $) | Adjusted for Specific (current) Costs |
|---|---|---|---|
| Assets | | | |
| Inventories | $ 5,600,000 | $ 6,175,000 | $ 5,670,000 |
| Property, plant and equipment | 12,110,000 | 13,354,000 | 16,327,000 |
| All other assets | 8,290,000 | 9,141,000 | 7,506,000 |
| Total assets | $26,000,000 | $28,670,000 | $29,503,000 |
| Total liabilities | 8,000,000 | 7,600,000 | 7,600,000 |
| Shareholders' equity | $18,000,000 | $21,070,000 | $21,903,000 |

## Supplementary Financial Data
## Five-Year Comparison of Selected Data
## Adjusted for Changing Prices

| | Years Ended December 31 | | | | |
|---|---|---|---|---|---|
| | 1979 | 1980 | 1981 | 1982 | 1983 |
| Sales | | | | | |
| As reported | $14,020,000 | $15,610,000 | $17,240,000 | $19,810,000 | $23,850,000 |
| 1983 constant dollars | 19,543,000 | 20,211,000 | 20,063,000 | 20,970,000 | 23,850,000 |
| Net income | | | | | |
| As reported | | | | | $ 3,820,000 |
| 1983 constant dollars | | | | | 3,017,000 |
| Current costs | | | | | 3,404,000 |
| Earnings per share | | | | | |
| As reported | | | | | $4.92 |
| 1983 constant dollars | | | | | 3.86 |
| Current costs | | | | | 4.37 |
| Common stock dividends declared per share | | | | | |
| As reported | $1.40 | $1.43 | $1.55 | $1.75 | $2.00 |
| 1983 constant dollars | 1.95 | 1.85 | 1.80 | 1.85 | 2.00 |
| Net assets at year end | | | | | |
| As reported | | | | | $18,000,000 |
| 1983 constant dollars | | | | | 21,070,000 |
| Current costs | | | | | 21,903,000 |
| Purchasing power gain on net monetary liabilities | | | | | 1,000 |
| Market price per common share at year end | | | | | |
| Actual | $69.25 | $68.13 | $55.50 | $67.63 | $72.25 |
| 1983 constant dollars | 90.50 | 84.95 | 64.80 | 72.45 | 68.50 |
| Average consumer price index* | 181.5 | 195.4 | 217.4 | 239.0 | 253.0 |

* Hypothetical, for illustrative purposes only.

UMC, because of its "small company" asset size, would be exempt from FASB *No. 33's* reporting requirement. However, Table 6–5 restates UMC's statement of income from continuing operations, restated for changing prices, for the year ending December 31, 1983, and UMC's five-year comparison of selected data adjusted for changing prices.

A final note on Notes: Feel free to speak with your friendly auditor, or sleuth on your own, regarding additional information which might remain undisclosed and could pertain to:

1. liabilities arising out of company pension plans (e.g., ERISA)
2. contractual obligations (e.g., the capitalized value of lease payments)
3. legal judgments currently enforceable
4. contingent liabilities (e.g., pending lawsuits or possible income tax assessment)

### Ten-Year Financial Summary

Long-term performance of UMC is summarized and reported on the ten-year financial summary statement, Table 6–6.

The long-term view is used for detecting trends and changes in trends in important factors such as net sales, total assets, net operating income, earnings per share, and dividends per share. On balance, the trends for UMC look pretty good: upward.

## Table 6-6.

## UNIVERSAL MANUFACTURING CORPORATION
### Ten-Year Financial Summary

| | 1983 | 1982 | 1981 | 1980 | 1979 | 1978 | 1977 | 1976 | 1975 | 1974 |
|---|---|---|---|---|---|---|---|---|---|---|
| Net sales | $23,850,000 | $19,810,000 | $17,240,000 | $15,610,000 | $14,020,000 | $12,604,000 | $11,040,000 | $9,426,000 | $8,324,000 | $7,611,000 |
| Total income before tax | 6,060,000 | 5,060,000 | 4,535,000 | 4,164,000 | 3,783,000 | 3,619,000 | 3,195,000 | 2,747,000 | 2,521,000 | 2,286,000 |
| Net profit for the year | 3,820,000 | 3,080,000 | 2,775,000 | 2,555,000 | 2,288,000 | 2,105,000 | 1,827,000 | 1,512,000 | 1,314,000 | 1,179,000 |
| Earnings per share | 4.92 | 3.95 | 3.56 | 3.28 | 2.94 | 2.71 | 2.36 | 1.95 | 1.70 | 1.53 |
| | | | | | | | | | | |
| Dividends per share | 2.00 | 1.75 | 1.55 | 1.43 | 1.40 | 1.40 | 1.24 | 1.12 | 1.10 | 1.03 |
| Net working capital | 7,600,000 | 6,700,000 | 6,300,000 | 5,500,000 | 5,023,000 | 3,596,000 | 3,424,000 | 2,964,000 | 2,604,000 | 2,261,000 |
| Total assets | 26,000,000 | 22,481,600 | 19,934,000 | 17,594,000 | 15,390,000 | 12,433,000 | 9,890,000 | 8,348,000 | 7,365,000 | 6,643,000 |
| Net plant and equipment | 12,110,000 | 10,820,000 | 9,918,000 | 8,747,000 | 6,743,000 | 4,740,000 | 3,635,000 | 3,150,000 | 2,830,000 | 2,479,000 |
| Long-term debt | 2,000,000 | 2,000,000 | 2,000,000 | 2,000,000 | 2,000,000 | 2,000,000 | 2,000,000 | 1,000,000 | 1,000,000 | 1,000,000 |
| | | | | | | | | | | |
| Preferred stock | 1,360,000 | 1,360,000 | 1,360,000 | 1,360,000 | 1,360,000 | 1,360,000 | 1,360,000 | 1,360,000 | 1,360,000 | 1,360,000 |
| Common stock and surplus | 1,340,000 | 1,340,000 | 1,340,000 | 1,340,000 | 1,340,000 | 1,340,000 | 1,340,000 | 1,340,000 | 1,340,000 | 1,340,000 |
| Book value per share | 21.63 | | | | | | | | | |

Chapter **6,** PART **II**

# Determining the Cost of Capital*

*Erich A. Helfert*
Helfert Associates
San Mateo, California

The cost of capital plays an important role in the discounted cash flow valuation method discussed in Chapters 7 and 12. The following material describes various techniques for determining the cost of debt and equity capital.

## COST OF LONG-TERM DEBT

Most companies employ at least some type of long-term debt obligations to support part of their permanent financing needs arising from major capital outlays, growth of operations, or replacement of other types of capital. This type of debt, exemplified by bonds of various types issued by a company and traded in the financial markets, or long-term borrowing arrangements with banks and other financial institutions, becomes *integral to the capital structure* of the company. Management must make well-planned decisions, weighing the *cost, risk,* and *debt service* involved in relation to the prospective uses of the funds. Commitments to long-term debt by their very nature have a much more lasting impact on a company's situation

* Source: Erich A. Helfert, *Techniques of Financial Analysis,* © Richard D. Irwin, Inc., Chicago, IL, 1987.

than do short-term working capital financing or intermediate-term loans.

The *specific cost* of long-term debt is expressed in the stated annual interest rate of the financial instrument involved. Thus, for example, a 9 percent "debenture" bond, which is an unsecured (no specific assets are pledged) general debt obligation of the company, has a specific cost of:

$$9\% \times (1 - .46) = 4.86\%$$

if we assume that the company is able to take advantage of the interest deductibility. An incremental tax rate of 46 percent was used. In addition, we will assume that the bond had been sold at a price that *nets* the company its **par value** (face value). The *stated annual interest rate* (**coupon rate**) of a bond is based on the par value, or 100 percent of the principal due at a specified future date, regardless of the *actual proceeds* received by the issuing company. Proceeds vary because marketable debt securities are generally sold at the best possible price obtainable in the market through underwriters who take some or all of the risk of marketing the issue for a small percentage of the gross receipts. Legal and registration expenses are also borne by the company. Therefore, depending on the *issue price,* which is related to prevailing interest yields and to the quality of the company's credit rating, the company may actually receive net proceeds *below* par value, or it may receive a small *premium* over par.

In either case, the specific cost has to be *adjusted* to allow for the actual proceeds. If we assume that instead of 100 percent of par value the company received 95 percent for its debentures after all expenses and commissions, the *effective cost* with a 9 percent *coupon rate* is as follows:

$$.09 \, (1 - .46) \times \frac{1}{.95} = 5.12\%$$

Apart from the specific cost of interest, long-term debt also involves repayment of the principal. There are many types of repayment provisions, generally structured to fit the nature of the company and the type of risks the debtholder visualizes. Periodic repayment requirements may be met through a **sinking fund** set aside for that purpose. Partial or full principal payments due at the end of the lending period are called **balloon payments.** The point to remember, however, is that debt instruments, even if long term, must in some form and at some time be *repaid.* The cost of this repayment is implicit in the need to carefully plan future cash flows, and also to consider the company's ability to achieve future refinancing if the funds needs are likely to continue or even grow.

Another implicit cost of long-term debt involves the nature and degree of *restrictions* normally embodied in the debt agreement (**indenture**). Such provisions may limit management's ability to use other forms of credit, e.g., leasing; or may specify *minimum levels* of some financial ratios, e.g., working capital proportions or debt service coverage; or they may *limit* the amount of dividends that can be paid to shareholders. At times, specific assets may have to be *pledged* as security. Any set of such provisions carries an *implicit cost* in the form of limiting management's freedom of choice in making decisions. The greater the perceived risk of the indebtedness, the greater the restrictions are likely to be. Not to be overlooked is the introduction of *financial leverage* into the capital structure. The implicit cost of this condition depends on the degree of risk exposure caused by specific company and industry conditions.

## COST OF OWNERS' EQUITY

### Preferred Stock

This form of equity ownership is conceptually at the midway point between debt and common stock. Although subordinated to claims of the various creditors of the corporation, the holder of preferred shares has a claim on corporate *earnings* that ranks *ahead* of that of the holders of common shares up to the amount of the stated preferred dividend. In liquidation, the preferred shareholders' claims are satisfied prior to the residual claims of the holders of common stock. The *specific cost* of preferred stock is normally higher than that of debt with a similar quality rating, however.

Because of the near-equity status of preferred stock, preferred dividends are not tax deductible for the issuing corporation and are therefore an outflow of *aftertax* funds. For instance, a 10 percent preferred stock, issued at par (net of expenses) costs the corporation 10 percent after taxes. For each dollar of dividends to be paid on this preferred stock, the corporation must therefore earn, before taxes:

$$\$1.00 \times \frac{1}{1 - .46} = \$1.85$$

as compared to $1 for every dollar of interest paid on a long-term debt obligation. Where the 9 percent bond in the previous section had an aftertax cost of 4.86 percent, the 10 percent preferred has an aftertax cost of 10 percent. The stated dividend rate of a preferred stock is therefore directly comparable to the *tax-adjusted* stated interest rate of a bond.

We can easily compare the cost to the company of long-term debt and preferred stock if we assume that they were issued at prices which result in proceeds exactly equal to the par (face) value. When proceeds do *not* equal par value, as often happens because of market conditions, the *effective* cost, discussed above, must be based on the *proceeds.*

The additional *implicit* cost of preferred stock lies in the fact that it is a security *senior* to common stock, and the dividend claims of its holders rank *ahead* of the dividend claims of holders of common shares. In addition, the essentially *fixed* nature of preferred dividends (they can be omitted only under serious circumstances) introduces a degree of *financial leverage* with varying earnings levels. Preferred stock being, in effect, closer to owners' equity than to debt, however, makes the implicit costs of its encumbrances far less serious than those of debt.

### Common Equity

The holder of common shares is the *residual* owner of the corporation (the claims of common stock extend to all assets and earnings not subject to *prior* claims), and provides long-term funds expecting to be rewarded with an increase in the economic value of the shares. This value accretion is composed of the interlocking effects of, hopefully, growing *earnings* and growing *dividends* received on the market *valuation* of the shares, which in turn is affected by the *risks* specific to the industry and to the individual company. In other words, we are dealing with more variables, while at the same time there are no *contractual* provisions for compensation, such as coupon interest or the stated preferred dividend rate. As a result, the *specific cost* of common equity calls for a more complex evaluation than was the case with debt or preferred stock.

In the case of common equity, *cost* has to be viewed in an *opportunity framework.* The investor has provided funds to the corporation expecting to receive the *combined* economic return of dividends declared by the board of directors and future appreciation in market value. The investment was made—presumably on a logical basis—because the type of *risk* embodied in the company and its business reasonably matched the investor's *own risk preference* and because *expectations* about earnings, dividends, and market appreciation are satisfactory. The investor made this choice by *foregoing* other investment opportunities, however. The investment was made under conditions of uncertainty about *future* results, in that the only hard data available to the new investor are *past* performance statistics. The challenge of measuring the cost of the shareholder's funds to the corporation arises from the need to meet the investor's expectations about the risk/reward trade-off involved in investing in this opportunity. In other words, the company must compensate the shareholder with the economic return *implicit* in its past performance and future outlook.

Several approaches to measuring the cost of common equity are used in practice; all involve many assumptions and a great deal of judgment. The greatest difficulty lies in finding a specific link with the *risk versus value* judgments made in the securities markets, which affect the market value of the common shares. We will discuss three major methods: an **earnings** approach, a **dividend** approach, and a **risk assessment** approach based on the **capital asset pricing model.** The earnings and dividend approaches are fairly straightforward; in effect they value future streams of earnings or dividends. But they also use highly simplifying assumptions and thus are very *limited* in effectiveness. The third method, in contrast, approximates shareholder return expectations by adding to a *"normalized" rate of return* on securities, in general a calculated numerical *risk premium* that is *company* specific. As we will see, it is the only approach that arrives at an economic return for the *specific* security *relative* to average yields experienced in the securities markets.

*Earnings Approach to Cost of Common Equity.* The *price/ earnings ratio* is a rough indicator of market valuation. This relationship is the simplest way of approximating the cost of common equity. Because we are interested in a measure of the opportunity cost of common equity, we will use *projected* earnings per share as related to the *current* market price of the stock:

$$\text{Cost of equity} = \frac{\text{Projected earnings per share}}{\text{Current market price per share}}$$

$$k_e = \frac{eps}{P}$$

or

$$\text{Cost of equity} = \frac{1}{\text{Price/earnings ratio}}$$

$$k_e = \frac{1}{P/E}$$

This result is based on the implicit assumption that *all* of the earnings of the company will be paid out to the shareholders, which is *not realistic.* At the same time, the measure does not allow for the effect of any *reinvested* earnings creating further value for the shareholders. Finally, the result is static in that future *growth* in earnings is *ignored.* If the first assumption about a 100 percent payout holds, an alternative way of estimating the cost of equity would be to project, year by year, the expected earnings pattern and to find the discount rate that would equate these aftertax earnings with the current market value, adjusted for a terminal value at the time the analysis is cut off. Clearly, the number of assumptions we must make for the analysis to be valid multiplies rapidly under these conditions. This simple measure therefore is at best a rough approximation.

*Dividend Approach to Cost of Common Equity.* A more direct way of dealing with at least one of the direct benefits obtained by the shareholder is to use annual dividends to estimate the cost of common equity. Yet the measure also suffers from the liability of serious oversimplification, because companies vary greatly in their rate of dividend payout, and the effect of reinvestment of retained earnings is again ignored.

$$\text{Cost of common equity} = \frac{\text{Projected dividend per share}}{\text{Current market price per share}}$$

$$k_e = \frac{dps}{P}$$

Introducing *growth* in dividends into the formula is an improvement that partially adjusts for the *reinvestment* portion of the value received by shareholders. The assumption here is that successful reinvestment of retained earnings will lead to growing earnings and thus growing dividends. The mathematics of the formula allow us to simply add the *assumed rate of growth in dividends* to the equation shown above. We again begin with the dividend yield and add a *stable percentage* rate of dividend growth ($g$) to simulate the economic expectations of the shareholders:

$$k_e = \frac{dps}{P} + g$$

The difficulty, however, lies in determining the growth rate, which must be based on our best assumptions about future performance, tempered by past experience. Many estimating processes can be used. The concept of *sustainable growth* (given stable investment, payout, and financing policies) may yield clues to the growth rate that can be applied with the dividend approach, but a great deal of judgment must be exercised in projecting expected *future* policies. If significant changes in policies are forecast, the analyst may want to modify the approach, making a series of year-by-year assumptions and in effect, calculating a composite of future dividend growth patterns from these yearly forecasts.

A word about *taxes* is necessary here. In both the earnings and the dividend approaches we are dealing with *aftertax values* from the point of view of the company. Earnings per share are stated after taxes, while common dividends, like preferred dividends, are *not* deductible and are paid out of aftertax earnings. No adjustment is therefore necessary in the results to make them comparable with the aftertax cost of debt and preferred stock. The *investor* likewise is judging the opportunity to earn an economic return in these terms. However, interest and dividends *received* are taxable income to the individual. Therefore, because personal tax conditions vary greatly, one more adjustment is necessary to assess the investment options objectively from the *investor's point of view.* Yet the business analyst cannot perform this precise calculation without knowledge of the individual's tax status. Consequently, the only working assumption we can make in this context is that *most investors* are subject to *some taxation;* we can arrive at financial results that are consistent *up to the point* at which the individual investor must calculate his or her personal tax impact.

*Risk Assessment Approach to Cost of Common Equity.* As we said earlier, the risk assessment method does not rely on specific estimations of present and future earnings or dividends. Instead, a *normal market return* is developed from published data on financial returns and yields, which is adjusted by a *company-specific risk premium* or *discount.* The rationale is the assumption that a company's cost of equity in terms of shareholder return expectations is related to the *relative riskiness* of its common stock. The greater this relative risk, the greater the premium—in the form of an additional economic return over and above a normalized return—that should be expected by an investor. This approach makes intuitive sense and can also be demonstrated statistically. At any time, the securities markets yield a *spread* of rates of return ranging from those on essentially *risk-free* government securities at the low end of the scale to the sizable returns from *highly speculative* securities. The risk/ return trade-off inherent in the many classes of security investments is reflected in this spread. *Risk* is defined for this purpose as the *variability of returns* inherent in the type of security, while *return* is defined as the *total economic return* obtained from it, including both interest or dividends and changes in market value.

A number of specific methods have been developed over the years to express the *risk premium* concept of return on common equity—which reflects the *cost* of common equity to the corporation—as a methodology both theoretically acceptable and practically usable. While no individual method is totally satisfactory in these terms, the most widely accepted is the **capital asset pricing model (CAPM).** We will discuss some of its salient features here, but the conceptual and theoretical underpinnings are extensive and far beyond the scope of this book. The reader is encouraged to study the references at the end of the chapter for more exhaustive treatments of the evolution, theory, and validation of the CAPM.

Three elements are required in applying the capital asset pricing model approach, and each must be carefully estimated. The first is an expression of the level of return from a *risk-free security*. The purpose is to find the *lowest part* of the range of yields currently experienced in the security markets as the starting point from which to build up the higher, risk-adjusted return specific to the particular common stock. Long-term U.S. government obligations are commonly used as a surrogate for such a risk-free return. The yields on U.S. government obligations are widely quoted and accessible, both for the present and for historical periods. For purposes of analysis, *current* yields, possibly adjusted for expected changes during the next several years, can be used. Precision is not possible here, and reasonable approximations supported by the analyst's judgment are quite sufficient.

The second element is an estimate of the return from a comparable type of security of *average risk*. This is needed because the CAPM method develops a specific adjustment for the *relative* riskiness of the particular security *as compared to* an average or baseline. For our common equity problem, we can use an estimate of the total expected return for the Standard & Poor's 500 Index, a broad-based measure of the price levels of the common stocks of 500 widely traded companies. Such projections of the *total return—both* dividends and market appreciation—expected from the companies represented in the index, are frequently made by securities analysts and published by financial services and in newsletters. While the S&P 500 index provides a broad estimate of return, more specific indexes could be chosen. Again, the analyst must exercise judgment in using projections of future economic returns. The main point is to obtain a reasonable approximation of the *average return* from *average investments* of the type being evaluated.

The third element required is an expression of relative risk, which is based on the *variability of returns* of the particular security being analyzed. The definition of risk is *very specific* in the CAPM, and this has caused some controversy. Risk is *not* defined as *total variability* of returns, but rather, as the *covariance* of the particular stock's returns with those of assets of *average* risk. The assumption here is that an investor does not focus on the *total variability* of return experienced with each *individual* security, but rather on how each security affects the variability of the *total return* from the *portfolio* held. Thus, risk is a *very relative* concept in the CAPM, an assumption that may not be acceptable to everyone. We will ignore the arguments pro and con about this risk definition in our discussion and concentrate instead on *how* it is used in the CAPM to arrive at a company-specific return. The risk measure, in the form of the covariance of an individual stock's returns with that of the portfolio of stocks of average risk, is called "beta" ($\beta$). It is found by linear regression of *past* monthly total returns of the *particular* security against a *baseline* such as the S&P 500 Index. Services like Value Line provide the beta for publicly traded securities as a matter of course.

How are the three elements combined to arrive at the

expected return and, thus, the company's *cost of capital* for a particular equity security? The CAPM method defines the cost of common equity as the combination of the *risk-free return* and a *risk premium* that has been adjusted for the *specific company risk.*

The CAPM formula appears as follows:

$$k_e = R_f + \beta \, (R_m - R_f)$$

where $k_e$ is the cost of capital,

  $R_f$ is the risk-free return,

  $\beta$ is the company's covariance of returns against the portfolio,

  $R_m$ is the average returns on common stock.

$\beta$ is expressed as a simple factor which is used to multiply the *difference* between the expected return on the average portfolio and the expected risk-free return. This difference, of course, is the risk premium inherent in the *portfolio.* The $\beta$ factor *adjusts* this *average* risk premium to reflect the *individual* stock's higher or lower relative riskiness. $\beta$ goes above 1.0 as the relative risk of the stock exceeds the average, and drops below 1.0 when the relative risk is below average.

The calculation itself is quite simple, while deriving the *inputs* is not, as we observed. To illustrate, we will arbitrarily choose a risk-free rate of return of 9 percent, an S&P 500 return estimate of 13.5 percent, and a company with a fairly "risky" $\beta$ of 1.4. The cost of equity in this hypothetical example would be

$$k_e = 9.0 + 1.4 \, (13.5 - 9.0) = 15.3\%$$

composed of the risk-free return of 9 percent plus the calculated company-specific risk premium of 6.3 percent, for a total of 15.3 percent.

There are a large number of issues that surface when the CAPM or related measures are used to derive the cost of securities. One of these, already mentioned, is the estimate of both the risk-free return and of the average return on a portfolio of common stocks. While the return on long-term U.S. government securities is a reasonable surrogate for the former, estimating an average portfolio return is fraught with conceptual problems. If β is the indicator of relative risk, the nature of the portfolio against which covariance is measured is clearly important. Broad averages such as the S&P 500 may or may not be appropriate under the circumstances. Also, there is the problem of using *past* data, particularly for *variability* of returns, in estimating the *future* relationships that indicate shareholder expectations. Consequently, the results of these calculations, as with most types of financial analysis, should be used with caution and a great deal of commonsense judgment.

*Inflation.* We have been talking about costs of capital so far without reference to the impact of inflation. This is permissible because *no* adjustment is, in fact, needed. The risk-free return on a government bond *implicitly allows* for the expected level of inflation, inasmuch as expectations about future inflationary conditions *affect the yield* from such securities. When inflation abates, the yields decline—as has been dramatically occurring in the mid-1980s. When inflation expectations rise, so do bond yields. The same is true of the yields from other financial instruments. If no inflation existed, risk-free returns would probably be in the range of 3 to 4 percent. In fact, not just the CAPM but all of the measures of cost of capital we have been discussing include expected inflationary effects in that estimates of future returns take these expectations into account. The spectrum of returns ranging from risk-free bonds to those on speculative securities is also consistent in reflecting the effects of inflation.

*To summarize,* it should be obvious by now that the cost of common equity, apart from the specific method of calculation, is generally *higher* than the cost of interest-bearing securities or preferred stocks. As we said at the beginning of this section, the residual claim represented by common shares involves the *highest risk/reward trade-off.* Thus, returns expected from common shares are higher, which, in turn, must translate into the *highest cost of capital* from the corporation's standpoint.

## *WEIGHTED COST OF CAPITAL*

Having determined the specific costs of the various types of capital, we now have the cost input needed to make some of the *funding decisions* listed earlier. But judging the attractiveness of capital investments involves another step. Because most companies use more than one form of long-term capital in funding investments and operations, and because over time, the mix of sources used for long-term financing may change, it is necessary to examine the cost of the company's *capital structure* as a whole. The result we are looking for is a cost of capital that is *weighted* to reflect the differences in the various sources used. It encompasses the cost of compensating long-term creditors and preferred shareholders in terms of the specific provisions applicable to them, and the holders of common stock in terms of the expected risk-adjusted return.

Several issues have to be resolved in determining an overall corporate cost of capital. The first is generating appropriate *costs* for the different types of long-term capital employed, which we have already done conceptually. The second is a decision about the weights, or *proportions* of each type of capital in the structure to be analyzed. The third is the question of whether to apply *market values* versus *book values* of the various categories of capital in arriving at the weighting. It is only then that we can *calculate* a weighted cost of capital that is meaningful for the intended purpose.

### *Cost*

First to be resolved is the question of whether it is relevant to consider the *past* costs of existing securities in a company's capital structure, or alternatively, the *incremental* costs involved in adding newly issued securities. Quite often the *debt and preferred stock* section of the balance sheet lists an array of past issues, with interest or dividend rates that differ significantly from current experience. Obligations that are 10, 15, or 20 years old likely carry stated costs that are no longer relevant today. At the same time, the various methods of arriving at the cost of *common equity* are based on *future* expectations, which are not necessarily consistent with the costs of debt or preferred shares issued in the past. To solve this dilemma, remember that the *purpose* of the analysis determines the choice of data and methodology.

Normally, the key purpose of calculating a weighted cost of capital is for use in making decisions about capital investments which are judged against a standard of return that will adequately compensate all providers of capital. Unless a company undergoes significant restructuring, the funds for new capital commitments are likely to come from current internal cash flow, augmented by new debt or new equity or both. This is an *incremental* condition in that the choices for *adding* investments are still being made. Past decisions on investment and financing are *sunk costs.* Consequently, the cost of capital measure most appropriate here is based on the *incremental costs* of the various forms of capital employed by the company.

## *Weighting*

As we mentioned, we are deriving a weighted cost that reflects the *proportions* of the different types of capital in a company's capital structure. Again, significant issues arise. The current capital structure as reflected on the balance sheet is the result of *past* management decisions concerning funding both investments and operations. The question to be asked here is whether the types and proportions of capital in this capital structure are likely to hold in the *future,* i.e., whether they match the strategic plans of management. The intended capital budget supporting the company's future strategy, particularly when calling for sizable outlays, may indeed cause significant changes in the long-term financing pattern of a company. Also, management may choose to make gradual modifications in its financial policies which, over time, can cause sizable shifts in the capital structure.

In other cases, management may well be satisfied with the current proportions of the company's capital structure as a long-term objective. Yet raising the incremental capital required from time to time is normally done in *blocks* limited to *one* form of security, that is, debt, preferred stock, or common equity.

Therefore, in the near term, any type of capital may be emphasized *more* than the *long-term proportions* desired would suggest. Capital must be raised in response to *market conditions,* and the choice of which type is appropriate at any given point is based on a series of considerations.

The analyst has to resolve the dilemma caused by such divergences *judgmentally*. Given the fact that a company is never static in the long run, the choice of proportions has to be a compromise intended to approximate the conditions relevant for purposes of analysis, and precision becomes secondary to common sense. Current proportions are a starting point, but are modified by specific assumptions about the future direction of the company's long-term financing. It may also be useful to generate a range of assumptions to bracket the findings.

### Market Versus Book Values

The weights to be assigned to different types of capital are clearly going to be *different* if we choose to apply current market values as contrasted with the stated values on the right-hand side of the balance sheet. Again we must be guided by the *purpose* of the analysis in deciding which value is relevant. If we are deriving a criterion against which to judge expected returns from *future* investments, we should use the *current market values* of the various types of capital employed by the company, because these values reflect the expectations of *both* creditors and shareholders. The latter certainly did not invest in the *book* value of common equity, which may differ significantly from the share value in the market. Further, the obligation of management is to meet the expectations of the shareholder in terms of the future *economic value* to be created by investments and operations, and to compensate creditors with future earnings. Stated book values, as we observed before, are static and not responsive to changing performance. The choice of market values also complements the use of *incremental* funding in that both are expressed in current market terms. The market value of common equity automatically (and implicitly) includes *retained earnings* as reported on the balance sheet. Although many people feel that retained earnings bear no cost, this is a misconception. In fact, retained earnings represent part of the residual claim of the shareholders, even if they are imperfectly valued on the balance sheet because of accounting conventions.

### Calculation of Weighted Cost of Capital

Let us now turn to a simplified example of calculating a weighted cost of capital for a hypothetical company. This will allow us to demonstrate the mechanics of what we now understand to be a process that involves a great deal of judgment. We will use the condensed balance sheet of ABC Corporation (Table 6–7), augmented by some additional data and assumptions. The company has three types of long-term capital. We assume that it could issue new bonds at an effective cost of 9 percent, and new preferred stock at an effective cost of 10 percent, based on proceeds from expected pricing in the market and after applicable underwriting and legal expenses. Note that these current costs are *below* the rates the company has been paying on its long-term capital as stated in the balance sheet. ABC's common stock is currently trading between $63 and $67, and most recent earnings per share were $4.72. Dividends per share last year were $2.50. The company's $\beta$, as calculated by security analysts, is 1.1, a fairly average risk factor. We further assume that the estimated risk-free return is 7.5 percent, and the best available forecast for the total return from the S&P 500 is 12.5 percent.

**Table 6–7.**

ABC CORPORATION
Condensed Balance Sheet
($000)

| Assets | | Liabilities and Net Worth | |
|---|---|---|---|
| Current assets . . . . . . . | $27,500 | Current liabilities . . . . . . . . . . . . . . | $ 9,500 |
| Fixed assets (net) . . . . | 35,000 | Bonds (12%) . . . . . . . . . . . . . . . . . . | 12,000 |
| Other assets . . . . . . . . . | 1,500 | Preferred stock (13%) . . . . . . . . . . . | 6,000 |
| Total assets . . . . . . . . . | $64,000 | Common stock (1.0 million shares) | 10,000 |
| | | Retained earnings . . . . . . . . . . . . . . | 26,500 |
| | | Total liabilities and net worth . . . . | $64,000 |

Overall company prospects are assumed to be satisfactory, and securities analysts are forecasting normal growth in earnings at about 6 percent. Given this background, it is possible to calculate a weighted cost of capital. As we proceed, the choices to be made will be highlighted.

The respective *costs* of the three types of capital employed can be derived as shown below. Note that we are employing the *incremental* cost of funds in each case, rather than the *past* costs as reflected in the balance sheet, where outstanding bonds carry a rate of 12 percent and preferred stock a dividend rate of 13 percent. The calculations for each type of capital appear as follows, using the methods discussed earlier:

Long-term debt: $k_d = 9.0 \times (1 - .46) = 4.86\%$ after taxes

Preferred stock: $k_p = 10.0\%$ after taxes

Common equity: $k_e = 7.5 + 1.1(12.5 - 7.5)$
$$= 13.0\% \text{ after taxes}$$

The cost of debt was based on the effective cost of 9 percent, adjusted for taxes, while the effective cost of preferred stock required no tax adjustment. The CAPM was used for the common equity calculation.

The result for common equity can be compared to the less satisfactory results obtained using the earnings or dividend approaches. The *earnings approach* provides the following cost of common equity when we employ the average current market price of $65 (½($63 + $67)):

$$\text{Common equity: } k_e = \frac{1}{\$65/\$4.72} = 7.3\% \text{ after taxes}$$

If we were to modify the formula to include expected growth in earnings ($g$), in this case, where $g = 6$ percent, the result would come close to the cost derived using the CAPM:

$$\text{Common equity: } k_e = 7.3\% + 6.0\% = 13.3\% \text{ after taxes}$$

The *dividend approach* provides an alternative result, which is a function of the dividend rate and the expected growth rate:

$$\text{Common equity: } k_e = \frac{\$2.50}{\$65} + 6.0\% = 9.8\% \text{ after taxes}$$

It is not uncommon to find that the three approaches to determining the cost of equity provide rather *different results,* as the data and assumptions going into the calculations are not the same. We highlighted the most significant issues when we discussed each measure earlier.

The *weights* to be used in calculating the corporate cost of capital depend both on the relative stability of the current capital structure and on the relevance of market values to the results. Let us assume that management is satisfied with the current capital structure and over time, is likely to raise funds in the same proportions. Let us also assume that the bonds of the company are currently trading at 123 (that is, a $1,000 face value bond with a coupon rate of 12 percent is worth a premium price of $1,230), while the preferred stock with a $13 dividend rate is trading at 119 (each share with a nominal value of $100 is currently worth $119). Table 6–8 shows the proportions that result when we list both book value and market value for each type of capital.

**Table 6–8.** *Capital structure of ABC Corporation.*

|  | Book Value | Proportion | Market Value | Proportion |
|---|---|---|---|---|
| Bonds . . . . . . . . . . . . . . . | $12,000 | 22.0% | $14,760 | 17.0% |
| Preferred stock . . . . . . . . . | 6,000 | 11.0 | 7,140 | 8.2 |
| Common equity . . . . . . . . | 36,500 | 67.0 | 65,000 | 74.8 |
| Totals . . . . . . . . . . | $54,500 | 100.0% | $86,900 | 100.0% |

Depending on the way management assesses its future needs, the proportions could remain as shown in the table, or they could be altogether different. Assuming that no significant change is foreseen, we can calculate the weighted cost of capital for *both* the market and book value, as shown in Table 6–9.

The results in this case do not differ materially. Significant differences would have amounted to one or more percentage points. Given that the assumptions and choices needed to make the calculations all involved a margin of error, the results should be liberally rounded off before the measure is used as a decision

**Table 6–9.** *Weighted cost of capital for ABC Corporation.*

|  | Book Value Weighting | | | Market Value Weighting | | |
|---|---|---|---|---|---|---|
|  | Cost | Weight | Composite | Cost | Weight | Composite |
| Bonds ............... | 4.86% | .22 | 1.07% | 4.86% | .17 | 0.83% |
| Preferred stock ......... | 10.00 | .11 | 1.10 | 10.00 | .08 | 0.80 |
| Common equity ........ | 13.00 | .67 | 8.71 | 13.00 | .75 | 9.75 |
| Totals ........... |  | 1.00 | 10.88% |  | 1.00 | 11.38% |

criterion. We can say that in the case of ABC Corporation, under the stipulated conditions, the weighted cost of incremental capital is *approximately* 11 percent. If the measure is used to judge the expected return from new investments, it would represent a minimum standard of return from investments with *comparable risk characteristics.* Under these conditions, the weighted cost of capital could be used as the discount rate to determine net present values.

## COST OF CAPITAL AND RETURN STANDARDS

We stated all along that the basic purpose of deriving a weighted cost of capital was to find a reasonable *criterion* for measuring new investments by establishing a level of return high enough to compensate all providers of funds according to their expectations. By implication, projects considered acceptable when their cash flows are *discounted* at this return standard would create *economic value* for the shareholder in the form of growing dividends and market appreciation. However, using a weighted cost of capital for this purpose warrants further discussion. In this section we will examine more closely the notion of this measure as a **cutoff rate,** and then discuss the question of projects in different **risk categories.** We will also review the problem of the **multibusiness firm** in which a *variety* of *business risks* are combined. Finally, we will touch on the issue of modified standards using **multiple discount rates.** In all of these areas a balance has to be found between the theoretically desirable and the practically feasible.

## Cost of Capital as a Cutoff Rate

In a *single-business company* with fairly definable risk characteristics, the weighted cost of capital as we have calculated it can well serve as a cutoff rate in assessing capital investment projects ranked in declining order of economic desirability. If *consistent* analytical methods and judgments are applied to projecting the cash flows, and if the *risks* inherent in the projects are *similar* and have been consistently estimated and tested through sensitivity analysis, this minimum return standard can be used to accept or reject the project. We are assuming that the company can finance all of the projects being considered at the same incremental cost of capital and without significantly changing its capital structure.

The weighted cost of capital works well in this ideal condition because the risk premium built into the measure, the proportions of the sources of new funds, and the range of risks embodied in the projects are all *consistent* with each other and with the business risk inherent in the company. When some of these conditions *change,* however, managerial judgment must be exercised to modify the cost of capital and its application.

One common problem even in the single-business firm is the real possibility that the *amount* of potential capital spending will *exceed* the readily available financing to some degree. If the list of projects contains many that just meet or are somewhat above the standard, they may be attractive enough for management to *modify* the company's capital structure to accommodate them. Then the weighted cost of capital will likely change. Increasing leverage may introduce *additional risk,* thus exerting upward pressure on the cost of both debt and equity. Increasing the equity base significantly will result in near-term *dilution* of earnings per share, thus affecting the market value of the stock and possibly the β of the company's common stock as judged by securities analysts. While the changes may be manageable, the point is that the process of business investment and the selection of appropriate standards is never a static exercise.

Another practical issue is management's attitude toward taking *business risks.* Knowing that the analyses underlying capital investment projects entail many uncertainties, management may wish to set the cutoff rate arbitrarily *higher* than the weighted cost of capital, to allow for *estimating error* and even for *deliberate bias* in the preparation of the estimates—not at all uncommon in most organizations as managers compete for funds—and also to play it a little safer in view of the degree of reliability of the *return standard itself.* From a theoretical standpoint, this approach may cause opportunity losses in that potentially worthwhile projects are likely to be rejected. From a practical standpoint, however, it may be deemed prudent to leave a margin for error. It is still possible, of course, to reach *below* the higher standard if a project entails many other strategic or operational advantages that mitigate the effects of marginal economic performance.

Finally, we must reiterate that capital budgeting and project selection are *not merely numerical processes.* Even in the most tightly focused single-product company, where all levels of management have firsthand knowledge about the business setting, the decision process is always a *combination of judgments* affected by personal preferences, group dynamics, and the pressures of organizational realities.

### Risk Categories

By definition, the weighted cost of capital represents a company's unique relative risk and particular capital structure. Yet in a sense, this is misleading because even in the single-business company, different capital investment projects will involve different *degrees of risk.* Normally, a company encounters a variety of classes of investments ranging from *replacement* of equipment and facilities to *expansion* in existing markets, and beyond that to potential *ventures* into new products or services and new markets. The degrees of risk inherent in these classes of investments will differ, sometimes materially, even though the products and services involved are within the scope of a *single industry* with a definable overall risk. Replacement of physical assets to continue serving a proven market where the company holds a strong position clearly is far less risky and permits more reliable estimates of cash flow benefits than is entering a new domestic or international market.

A common way of handling such divergences is to set a *higher discount standard* for projects that are perceived to be riskier. A hierarchy of minimum rates of return can be established, somewhat arbitrarily, that ranges upward from the weighted cost of capital cutoff point. For example, if the weighted cost of capital is, say, 15 percent, that standard may be applied to ordinary replacements and expansion in markets where the company has a position. A standard of 16 or 17 percent may be applied to entering related markets, while a new venture may be measured at a premium standard of 20 percent or even higher. As we demonstrated earlier in discussing the power of discounting, particularly at the higher rates, the chances of riskier projects being acceptable will be severely tested under such conditions. Yet such a demanding risk/reward trade-off standard may be appropriate if management's risk preferences are modest.

On the other hand, it is often argued, particularly in a single-business company, that the weighted cost of capital *implicitly embodies* the whole range of risks normally encountered while participating and growing in that business. Consequently, the idea has been utilized that the range of discount standards should be grouped *around* the weighted cost of capital. In effect, this allows the less risky projects to be discounted at a return standard *below* the weighted cost of capital, while riskier ones would be tested at or above that level. When all projects are combined, the result should be an *average* return at or above the weighted cost of capital. This would require, however, that the proportions of projects being approved in the various risk classes be carefully monitored to ensure that, over time, the overall average will achieve the desired result. Otherwise the company could encounter significant deviations from expected performance.

An additional practical issue tends to support *raising the return standards* for different classes of capital projects. Every company faces a certain percentage of capital expenditures that yield *no definable* cash flow benefits. Among these are mandated outlays for environmental protection, investments for improved infrastructure of facilities, expenditures for office space and equipment, etc. A strong argument can be made that funds required for these purposes must, in fact, be economically "carried" by the expected cash flow benefits from all other productive investments. By definition, therefore, the *total* amount of capital invested should provide a return sufficient to meet or exceed the weighted cost of capital. If some *part* of the capital budget is economically *neutral,* the returns from the economically positive projects will have to be *higher* to make up for such "nonproductive" investments. If management chooses to adjust its return standards for this condition, the modification will likely involve a fair degree of subjective judgment.

Our discussion has gone beyond the purely analytical aspects of the subject, and we have pointed out many *practical* issues involved in choosing and using economic measures for business decisions, of which discount standards are only one form. It is important to remember that the actual procedures employed by a company are likely to allow for a fair degree of *judgmental override* of the quantitative results of any financial analysis. This includes the *specific* return standards for capital investments, which are likely to be modified from time to time, to assist not only in *project-specific* economic assessment, but also in shifting the strategic emphasis *between classes* of investments. Senior management must, of course, continuously monitor and guide the pattern of investments they wish to undertake so that shareholder expectations are met. The pattern of investments suggested by the economic analyses and the return standards can and should be modified to fit the changing strategic direction of a company.

### Cost of Capital in Multibusiness Companies

The issues involved in setting appropriate return standards become even more complex when a company has several divisions or subsidiaries engaged in rather *different businesses* and *markets* that vary greatly in their risk characteristics. While it is possible to calculate an overall cost of capital for the company, with the help of a $\beta$ that reflects the company's covariance of *consolidated* returns with the market, it is far more difficult to derive equivalent cost of capital standards for the *individual* operating divisions. Most commonly a multibusiness company has a single capital structure that supplies funds for the various businesses. Therefore, capital cannot be apportioned to the different risk categories on the basis of individual cost of capital standards that employ specific *betas* and debt ratings. These would be available only if the divisions were *autonomous* companies whose shares are traded in the securities markets.

The approach often used under such conditions is to estimate *surrogate* costs of capital based on costs for comparable *independent* companies, if this is possible. In this way, modified by judgment, a series of standards can be developed for the multibusiness company that are similar to the array of risk categories in a single-business company. Obviously, the apportionment of capital in a multibusiness setting is also complicated by the practical issues of dealing with members of management who are competing for limited funds while having to meet *different* standards. Senior management must be very careful first to establish *broad allocations* of funds to the various operating divisions that match the desired corporate strategic emphasis. Then projects can be ranked *within* those individual blocks of allocated funds according to the different discount rates, and decisions can be made to accept or reject specific investments. A predictable consequence of such an approach, however, is the dilemma of having to refuse specific higher return (and higher risk) opportunities in one division, whose overall allocation is exhausted, in favor of lower return opportunities (and lower risk) in another division. This dilemma has to be resolved at the top management level, keeping in mind the strategic direction of the *total* company. The main point to remember is that senior management needs to shape the company's overall capital investment portfolio in line with shareholder expectations, so that the sum of the parts can be expected to meet or exceed the corporate weighted cost of capital standard.

### Multiple Rate Analysis

One additional *technical* observation should be made here. Some practitioners argue for applying *different* discount rates to different *portions* of the cash flow pattern of a *single project* when calculating the measures of economic desirability, in order to reflect the relative riskiness of the various elements of the project. In effect, this is one more risk adjustment beyond the risk premium already *inherent* in a particular discount standard. There are many variations of this approach, although it is not widely used in practice.

It should be apparent that the uncertainties inherent in project analysis and the complexities involved in establishing the standards for multiple rate analysis may not be warranted in most *normal* business investment situations. At the same time, they may indeed be necessary in assessing *special* projects, such as real estate investments, complex leasing proposals, and other uniquely structured cash flow proposals. In such instances, some of the financial contracts *integral* to the projects may warrant discounting their portion of the cash flows at lower rates that reflect their *contractual* nature, as compared with other parts of the cash flow pattern that are subject to the uncertainties of *operating* in the business environment. These analytical refinements are too specific to be covered here, but are dealt with in the reference materials listed at the end of the chapter.

## KEY ISSUES

The following is a recap of the key issues raised directly or indirectly in this chapter. They are enumerated here to help the reader keep the analysis techniques discussed within the perspective of financial theory and business practice:

1. The specific costs to a company of indebtedness and pre- ferred securities are readily apparent in their tax-adjusted cash obligations, but it is difficult to measure the secondary costs implicit in debt service, credit-rating effects and market assessment.

2. Determining the cost of equity capital is inextricably linked to the risk/reward expectations of the financial markets, because the cost must be expressed in terms of an expected economic return for the shareholder of the company.

3. Simple surrogates for the cost of equity capital, such as earnings and dividend models, suffer from both variability

of underlying conditions, which can distort their results, and from conceptual shortcomings.

4. The link established by modern financial theory between general financial market expectations and the value of an individual company's equity securities remains an approximation based on a series of simplifying assumptions.

5. The use of a company-specific risk factor ($\beta$) to adjust average return expectations is a valid theoretical concept, but both definition and measurement of this factor remain open to disagreement and continue to pose practical problems.

6. The development of a weighted cost of capital raises significant questions regarding not only the elements comprising the various costs, but also regarding the weights to be used and the concept of measuring incremental funding.

7. The use of weighted cost of capital in setting capital investment return standards is conceptually useful for projects within a company's normal range of risk, but the measure may need modification for business investments of dissimilar risk.

8. The theory of finance continues to evolve, but as concepts generated are introduced and refined in the decision-making process, careful linkages to both data sources and to the organization have to be established in order to make practical application both understandable and feasible.

9. Objective analytical approaches to capital investment assessment are only one important input in the choices management must make. Individual and group attitudes, preferences, and judgments exert significant influences over interpretation and decision processes in the areas of investment, operations, and financing.

10. The precision implied in the calculations of economic measures like cost of capital or net present value must be tempered by the knowledge that the data and assumptions underlying them are potentially subject to a wide range of error.

## SUMMARY

In this chapter we have sketched out the rationale for determining the **costs** of various forms of financing as an input in making different types of financial decisions. We found that the specific **cost of debt,** both short term and long term, was relatively easy to calculate, given the nature of the contracts underlying it in most cases. The same was true for **preferred stock.** We also found that the fixed nature of the obligations incurred with debt and preferred stock raised a host of secondary considerations that exact an **economic cost** from the company in terms of debt service and restrictive covenants. Establishing the **cost of common equity** was particularly challenging because of the residual claim holders of common shares have on the company, and because of their risk/reward expectations which are reflected in the market's valuation of the shares.

Once we discussed techniques for calculating the respective costs of the three basic types of financing, and pointed out the theoretical and practical caveats, we developed the **weighted cost of capital** as an input in investment analysis. Here we found that the application of the weighted cost of capital as a **minimum standard** for discounting investment cash flows is affected by the way project and business risks are interpreted within the corporate portfolio, and by the attitudes of corporate decision makers. At the same time, we found the approximate weighted cost of capital to be a conceptually appropriate **target** around which to build a series of return standards befitting a particular company's range of businesses and the investments and risks connected with them.

## SELECTED REFERENCES

Richard Brealey and Stewart Myers, *Principles of Corporate Finance,* second edition (McGraw-Hill, New York, NY, 1984)

Diana R. Harrington, *Modern Portfolio Theory. The Capital Asset Pricing Model and Arbitrage Pricing Theory: A User's Guide,* second edition (Prentice-Hall, Englewood Cliffs, NJ, 1986)

David W. Mullins, Jr., "Does the Capital Asset Pricing Model Work?," *Harvard Business Review,* January–February 1982, pp. 105–114

Ezra Solomon and John J. Pringle, *An Introduction to Financial Management,* second edition (Goodyear, Santa Monica, CA, 1980)

James C. Van Horne, *Financial Management and Policy,* seventh edition (Prentice-Hall, Englewood Cliffs, NJ, 1986)

Fred J. Weston and Thomas E. Copeland, *Managerial Finance,* eighth edition (Dryden Press, Chicago, IL, 1986)

# APPENDIX 6-A:
## Key Business Ratios and Their Meanings

### Solvency Ratios

**Quick Ratio** $= \dfrac{\text{Cash} + \text{Accounts Receivable}}{\text{Total Current Liabilities}}$

Shows the dollars of liquid assets available to cover each dollar of current debt.

**Current Ratio** $= \dfrac{\text{Total Current Assets}}{\text{Total Current Liabilities}}$

Measures the margin of safety present to cover any possible reduction of current assets.

**Current Liabilities to Net Worth** $= \dfrac{\text{Total Current Liabilities}}{\text{Net Worth}}$

Contrasts the amounts due creditors within a year with the funds permanently invested by the owners. The smaller the Net Worth and the larger the Liabilities, the greater the risk.

**Current Liabilities to Inventory** $= \dfrac{\text{Total Current Liabilities}}{\text{Inventory}}$

Tells you how much a firm relies on funds from disposal of unsold inventories to meet debt.

**Total Liabilities to Net Worth** $= \dfrac{\text{Total Liabilities}}{\text{Net Worth}}$

Compares the company's total indebtedness to the venture capital invested by the owners.

**Fixed Assets to Net Worth** $= \dfrac{\text{Fixed Assets}}{\text{Net Worth}}$

Reflects the portion of net worth that consists of fixed assets. Generally, a smaller ratio is desirable.

### Efficiency Ratios

**Collection Period** $= \dfrac{\text{Accounts Receivable}}{\text{Sales}} \times 365 \text{ Days}$

Reflects the average number of days it takes to collect receivables. Quality of receivables can be determined when compared with selling terms.

**Inventory Turnover** $= \dfrac{\text{Sales}}{\text{Inventory}}$

Determines the rate at which merchandise is being moved and the effect on the flow of funds into a business.

**Assets to Sales** $= \dfrac{\text{Total Assets}}{\text{Sales}}$

This rate ties in sales and the total investment in assets that is used to generate those sales.

**Sales to Net Working Capital** $= \dfrac{\text{Sales}}{\text{Net Working Capital}}$

*(Net Working Capital* $= Current\ Assets - Current\ Liabilities)$

Measures the efficiency of management to use its short term assets and liabilities to generate revenues.

**Accounts Payable to Sales** $= \dfrac{\text{Accounts Payable}}{\text{Sales}}$

Measures the extent to which the supplier's money is being used to generate sales. When this ratio is multiplied by 365 days, it reflects the average number of days it takes the company to repay its suppliers.

### Profitability Ratios

**Return on Sales (Profit Margin)** $= \dfrac{\text{Net Profit after Taxes}}{\text{Sales}}$

Reveals profits earned per dollar of sales and measures the efficiency of the operation.

**Return on Assets** $= \dfrac{\text{Net Profit after Taxes}}{\text{Total Assets}}$

This is the key indicator of profitability for a firm. It matches operating profits with the assets available to earn a return.

**Return on Net Worth (Return on Equity)** $= \dfrac{\text{Net Profit after Taxes}}{\text{Net Worth}}$

Analyzes the ability of the firm's management to realize an adequate return on the capital invested by the owners of the firm.

Source: Dun and Bradstreet Credit Services, Dun and Bradstreet, Inc.

# Valuation and Pricing of Acquisitions

*Patrick F. Dolan*
Peat Marwick Main & Co.
New York, New York

This chapter describes commonly used methods for valuing private companies, and divisions and subsidiaries of public companies, which are being considered for sale or acquisition. We have tried to be as practical as possible in providing the reader with guidelines for performing a valuation analysis and penetrating the mystique of the valuation process. All of the discussion and examples here are based on our work. We present no theories, concepts, or ideas that we ourselves do not commonly use. Accordingly, you may wish to refer to this chapter when presented with a valuation challenge, or when critiquing the work performed by others.

Under some circumstances, the valuation methods described in this chapter may be used to value publicly traded companies for sale or acquisition. We have, however, focused our analysis on the valuation of nonpublic entities because:

- a greater number of deals are done in the private sector than in the public sector

- we expect most of our readers to be more interested in pricing nonpublic transactions

- valuing a nonpublic entity is more challenging and subjective

Unlike a publicly traded company, a nonpublic entity has no current public market for its shares; its financial statements may not reflect its true economic performance because some owners tend to manage their companies to minimize income tax and/ or maximize their personal well-being; and the nonpublic entity may not have audited financial statements.

## REASONS FOR PERFORMING A VALUATION ANALYSIS

The price at which property (tangible and intangible) is exchanged determines, in many instances, whether a deal is successful. The price and the terms are the reasons cited most often when a deal does not go through and negotiations are discontinued. Once an owner decides to sell his or her business or a potential buyer becomes genuinely interested in the seller's business, price becomes particularly important.

A thorough valuation analysis can help sellers:

- determine a range of possible values based on today's market conditions
- ensure that they do not underprice or overprice the business
- establish reasonable price expectations and build consensus among owners
- provide feedback for decisions to sell, hold, go public, or liquidate the company
- strengthen sale negotiations by using information developed during the valuation

A thorough valuation analysis can help buyers:

- determine a range of possible values based on today's market conditions
- ensure that they do not overpay for the company
- determine the available methods of financing based on expected purchase price and internal cash flows

- consider the impact that alternative growth scenarios may have on the attractiveness of a deal
- strengthen purchase negotiations by using information developed during the valuation analysis
- appreciate the tax ramifications of the transaction
- improve their knowledge of the industry and the competitive position of the subject company

A valuation analysis can help the boards of both the selling and buying companies fulfill their fiduciary duty to their respective shareholders.

## METHODS OF VALUING A COMPANY

All property can be valued using one (or more) of three approaches:

- market
- income
- cost

A business enterprise, as one form of property, can also be valued using these three methods. Of course, these three generic approaches have several variations.

The market approach relies on prices paid for similar securities as a basis for valuing the subject company. Three different markets providing reported prices are: prices paid for publicly traded shares, prices paid in reported acquisitions, and prices paid in initial public offerings. The valuation methods that rely on these prices are commonly referred to as the *market comparison methods*. The primary focus of these methods is on transactions that have recently taken place in the public marketplace.

The income approach relies on the forecasted profits and surplus cash flows of the subject company as a basis for valuing the subject company. The method is commonly referred to as the *discounted cash flow* (DCF) *method.* Its primary focus is on the future financial performance of the subject company.

The cost approach relies on the current values of the subject company's assets (tangible and intangible) and liabilities as a basis for its valuation. This method is referred to as the *restated balance sheet method,* the *net asset value method,* or the *adjusted book value method.* Its primary focus is on the individual assets (tangible and intangible) of the subject company.

### Analysis Used to Evaluate the Owner's Alternatives

Every business owner has at least four theoretical alternatives at any point in time: sell, go public, hold, or liquidate. Each of the three valuation approaches provides input to the owner on one or more of these alternatives.

- The market comparison methods give the owner a range of prices at which the business could be sold to a buyer/investor, as well as the price the owner could expect to receive through an initial public offering.

- The discounted cash flow method gives the owner a price at which the business could be sold, that is, the DCF value. This method also shows the owner the future benefits (surplus cash flows) of holding the business and not selling.

- The restated balance sheet method shows the owner how much could be received as a result of liquidating the business in an orderly manner.

The valuation methods described in this chapter are applicable to most types of businesses, ranging from basic manufacturing to banking and personal service businesses. Certain methods, of course, may be more appropriate in certain situations.

## STUDY THE SUBJECT COMPANY

The first and most important step in determining the value of a company is to analyze and understand the company's operations, finances, and markets. We, therefore, stress the need to perform a thorough study of the subject company and its industry before performing other steps of the valuation analysis.

Your initial study of the subject company enables you to form an opinion on the viability of the company and its future prospects, which in turn influences every aspect of your subsequent valuation analysis. You can begin to answer the question, "Does the company deserve to be valued at, above, or below current industry valuation benchmarks?" The study may also uncover special items that may alter your valuation approaches. A side benefit of this study may be that both parties to a proposed deal can improve its structure in a mutually beneficial manner.

### Focus of Study

In analyzing the company and its industry you should focus on the following:

*For the Company:* Recent history, ownership history, current owners and ownership interests, owner's compensation and management philosophy, changes in business and current lines of business and main products or services, customers, suppliers, financial performance (historical and prospective), nonrecurring and discretionary items, management and personnel, facilities, business plans and objectives, organization charts, and level of past and ongoing investment requirements to conduct the business.

*For the Industry:* Definition of industry and market served, competitors, recent acquisitions of competitors, size and nature of market, growth of market (historical and prospective), regulatory environment, elements of competition (such as price, quality, service, or reputation), barriers to entry, and factors influencing demand such as sensitivity to general business cycles and sensitivity to foreign competition, market and submarket trends, demographics. The purpose here is to assess how industry conditions impact the company and its prospects.

*For the Company Within Its Industry:* Company's market share, its competitive advantage(s) and disadvantage(s), growth strategy, geographic concentration, methods of distribution and methods of sale, latent or unaccommodated opportunities, the company's financial performance and prospective performance relative to its industry.

## Sources of Company Information

Some of the most important sources of information on the subject company are the audited financial statements,[1] internal business plans and other company documents, interviews with management and advisors, review of major facilities, and articles in trade journals and newspapers. One way to make sure you don't overlook any important information is to develop a standard checklist.

Sometimes management has prepared financial projections. Review these projections after you understand the company and its industry so that you can determine whether the projections and underlying assumptions are realistic. The audited financial statements often provide clues to any unusual features of the subject company; interviews with management may provide others. In general, your access to detailed company data depends heavily on whether you represent the buyer or the seller. A seller and his or her advisors should have access to all relevant company data, and company management can "educate" the seller's advisors on the company's business and its industry. The buyer and his or her advisors, on the other hand, have to rely on the cooperation of the seller and on their own knowledge of the business and its markets.

## Sources of Industry Information

The following sources, among others, provide useful industry information and indicate major companies in each industry: *Standard & Poor's Industry Surveys, The Value Line*

---

[1] Audited financial statements are crucial to both prospective buyers and sellers. Without audited financial statements the buyer will not be confident in the performance of the company as presented in the fi..ancial statements and the seller will have difficulty reassuring the buyer that "the numbers are good." Accordingly, many valuation experts will not express a valuation opinion if the company does not have audited financial statements.

*Investment Survey, The Wall Street Transcript, U.S. Industrial Outlook,*[2] research by wall street firms,[3] and industry and trade sources. These and other information sources are described more fully in Chapter 2.

In practice, access to information is rarely perfect; valuations depend on a mix of judgment and hard facts. Imperfect access to company and industry information need not prevent you from approximating the value of a company.

### Adjustments to Company's Financial Statements

In the process of studying the company, it may be appropriate to adjust the historical financial statements which will be used in your valuation analysis. Normally, financial statements are adjusted to better reflect the ongoing or recurring profitability of the company or to place the company on a more comparable basis for comparison with selected public companies. Financial statements are often adjusted for the following items:

- extraordinary or nonrecurring items
- methods for depreciation, inventory accounting, or other accounting practices
- unrecorded liabilities (for example, lawsuits)
- commitments (for example, to sell a key asset)
- owner's compensation
- special tax characteristics
- nonoperating assets and liabilities such as surplus cash and cash equivalents, unused land in the case of assets, and a loan for unused land in the case of liabilities
- borrowings at nonmarket rates

---

[2] *U.S. Industrial Outlook* is published by the U.S. Department of Commerce, International Trade Administration, and is available from the U.S. Government Printing Office, Washington, DC 20402.

[3] *Nelson's Directory of Investment Research,* Rye, NY, provides a list of firms and analysts by industry. Old wall street reports can also be obtained on line from the *NEXIS* database.

In essence, you must strip away whatever layers necessary to get to the core businesses. In addition, you should make these adjustments at the beginning of the financial analysis of the subject company and before you apply the specific valuation methods.

### Company Financial Analysis

As the first step in the financial analysis process, reread in detail the financial statements of the company and the notes to those financial statements. The financial analysis may cover the following:

- income statement financial history
- income statement items as a percentage of operating revenues
- income statement comparative growth trends in revenues and expenses
- balance sheet financial history
- balance sheet items as a percentage of total assets
- balance sheet trends
- balance sheet liquidity ratios such as quick asset ratio, current ratio, working capital ratio, accounts receivable turnover, and inventory turnover
- leverage ratios such as debt-equity ratio, total assets to stockholders' equity ratio, and interest and fixed change coverage ratio
- percentage analysis of income statement data (operating revenues, gross profit, operating income, net income, and so forth) to year end or average assets and common stockholders' equity
- statement of changes in financial position history including capital expenditures, depreciation and amortization, working capital, and dividend history

Pay particular attention to the financial information that most influences investors' perceptions of value. This may include:

- historical surplus cash flow[4]
- capital spending forecasts
- forecasted surplus cash flow
- estimated weighted average cost of capital
- "normalized" net income or EBIT (earnings before interest and taxes)
- tangible book value
- long- and short-term debt
- total assets
- nonoperating assets
- industry-specific data, for example, number of beds for a hospital, number of subscribers for cable TV

If you are comfortable using a financial analysis software package, you can capture on a few pages the financial history and performance of the company including the adjustments. An example of an analysis using a software package is given in Chapter 12.

A model may also show important financial characteristics of the subject company alongside the same information for the public companies *(market comparison methods),* making comparison easy. You can then use the public entities that are most financially similar for further analysis.

### Company Risk Analysis

In the course of studying the company, you will consider the company's competitive position, its strengths and shortcomings and, in particular, the unique risks to which it is subject. Any major risks will negatively influence investors' perceptions of fair market value. For descriptive purposes, risks may be either: qualitative or quantitative.

---

[4] Cash flow can be defined in different ways depending on the valuation method used. We define the term *cash flow* as used in each specific approach.

The following qualitative risks are common across industries:

- dependency on one or a few key customers for a major percentage of revenues
- dependency on one or a few key inputs (for example, skilled labor or a raw material)
- dependency on a key owner and manager
- reliance on a small market share in a nonfragmented industry, in a fragmented industry that is in the process of consolidation, or in a multinational/global industry with limited geographic impediments to trade

Although these risks are qualitative, it may be possible to quantify the reduction in fair market value that the risk represents.

The following quantitative risks are common across industries:

- a break-even point higher than historical and/or industry norms
- higher fixed costs than industry average
- operating revenues as a percentage of total assets lower than industry average
- highly leveraged relative to competitors

You should consider these risks throughout the valuation analysis and take appropriate discounts at the end of the valuation to reflect the weaker position of the subject company. See Appendix 7–C for an example of how subject company weaknesses (relative to selected public companies) can be reflected in the valuation analysis.

After you have completed a study of the company, its business, financial performance, and relative position in its industry and after making appropriate adjustments to the financial statements, you are ready to apply specific valuation techniques. The best known methods are the *market comparison methods.*

# MARKET COMPARISON METHODS

The market comparison methods are based on the premise that the value of a private company can be estimated by analyzing the prices paid for minority or total ownership interests in similar companies. Prices paid for ownership interests in similar companies can be obtained from three different markets which provide reported prices:

- prices paid for publicly traded shares (that is, prices paid by investors in the secondary market for very small ownership interests in publicly traded companies)
- prices paid in reported acquisitions (that is, prices paid by purchasers of ownership interests in reported acquisitions)
- prices paid in initial public offerings (IPOs) (that is, prices paid by investors for very small ownership interests in a company when its common stock is first issued to the public)

Select companies for comparison to the subject company that, as a group, have characteristics similar to the subject company. Ideally, the selected companies should have operational, financial, and size characteristics similar to those of the subject company. In practice it is rare to find companies that are both operationally and financially similar to the subject company. Sometimes you will be forced to select a mixture of companies in which some are only financially comparable and others are only operationally comparable. For example, we recently valued a small lease advisory/brokerage firm with no similar public companies. We used two groups of companies— larger brokerage firms in different industries and small service firms of similar size and performance to the subject company.

## How to Apply the Market Comparison Methods

The market comparison methods have four distinct steps:

1. determine market price multiples
2. apply market price multiples derived from (1) above to subject company data

3. weight resulting indicated values to obtain one overall value

4. apply discounts and/or premiums

Market price multiples are obtained by dividing the market price of the common stock by important performance characteristics that contribute to its market value such as earnings, cash flow, and book value to obtain market price multiples (or ratios); for example, price-earnings, price–cash flow, and price–book value.

These multiples are then applied to the adjusted financial data of the subject company, resulting in a separate estimate of fair market value for each multiple applied. For example, a price-earnings multiple, a price–cash flow multiple, and a price–book value multiple would result in three separate estimates of value. The closer together these values are, the more confidence you should have in them. For example, of the nine multiples used in Table 7–1, five multiples resulted in very similar values. (See column four of Table 7–1.)

An overall estimate of value is calculated by attributing weights (such as one-third, one-third, and one-third) to the separate estimates of value. The weights are normally judgmental, based on which performance characteristics are most important in driving market value, but can also be influenced statistically by the consistency of the multiples derived from the public companies.

Finally, discounts, premiums, or other adjustments may be made to the estimated value of the subject company to reflect differences between the private company and the group of public entities from which the value was estimated.

### Types of Market Price Multiples

Market price multiples can be developed based on the market value of the equity (equity multiples) or the market value of the equity and the debt, commonly referred to as the total capital (total capital multiples). The market value of the equity is calculated by multiplying the per-share price of the common shares by the total number of common shares outstanding. The market value of the equity and the debt is calculated by adding the long-term and short-term debt outstanding (obtained from a recent balance sheet) to the market value of the equity. Long-term debt includes capitalized lease obligations and normal borrowings. Short-term debt includes notes payable to financial institutions and current portion of long-term debt. Market price multiples can be calculated in aggregate or on a per-share basis.

Applying equity multiples gives you the estimated fair market value of the stockholders' equity of the subject company. Applying total capital multiples gives you the estimated fair market value of the total capital (equity plus debt) of the subject company. You should subtract the long-term debt and short-term debt of the subject company from the estimated value of its total capital to determine the value of the equity alone.

The total capital multiples tend to provide more consistent estimates of value when either the subject company or the selected public companies are highly leveraged or when the capital structures of the selected public companies and the subject company vary significantly. See Table 7–1 for the application of total capital multiples of selected public companies in the valuation of a specialty chemicals manufacturer. Specific market price multiples, both equity and total capital, are described in Appendixes 7–A and 7–B.

## PRICES PAID FOR PUBLICLY TRADED SHARES

This approach is based on the premise that the value of a private company can be estimated by analyzing the prices paid by investors in the secondary market for minority ownership interests in publicly traded companies. There are approximately 13,000 publicly traded companies in the United States with complete information from which to choose publicly traded companies comparable to the subject company. Standard & Poor's maintains current information on approximately 5,000 of the most actively traded public companies. Some of this data, including recent stock prices, is published monthly in the S&P *Stock Guide*. Publicly traded companies file with the SEC annually and quarterly. These public documents provide detailed descriptive and financial information on each company. (By

**Table 7-1.**

## SPECIALTY CHEMICALS, INC.
### Application of Capital Multiples of Selected Public Companies

| Description of Multiple[1] | Market Multiple[2] | SCI Component of Value[3] | Value of Equity and Debt[4] | Weight[5] | Weighted Amount[6] |
|---|---|---|---|---|---|
| Total Capital/ Current 12 Months' EBIT | 8.2 | $ 15,220,000 | $ 124,804,000 | 15% | $ 18,700,000 |
| Total Capital/ Recent Fiscal Year EBIT | 8.3 | 14,758,000 | 122,491,400 | 15% | 18,400,000 |
| Total Capital/ 3 Years' Average EBIT | 10.0 | 11,739,000 | 117,390,000 | 8% | 9,400,000 |
| Total Capital/ 5 Years' Average EBIT | 10.8 | 9,948,000 | 107,438,400 | 8% | 8,600,000 |
| Total Capital/ Current 12 Months' EBIT Cash Flow | 6.5 | 18,435,000 | 119,827,500 | 15% | 18,000,000 |
| Total Capital/ Recent Fiscal Year EBIT Cash Flow | 6.9 | 17,722,000 | 122,281,800 | 15% | 18,300,000 |
| Total Capital/ 3 Years' Average EBIT Cash Flow | 8.0 | 12,958,000 | 103,664,000 | 8% | 8,300,000 |
| Total Capital/ 5 Years' Average EBIT Cash Flow | 8.2 | 10,746,000 | 88,117,200 | 8% | 7,000,000 |
| Total Capital/ Total Assets | 1.2 | 65,886,000 | 79,063,200 | 8% | 6,300,000 |
| Total Value of Equity and Debt | | | | 100% | $ 113,000,000 |
| Less: Outstanding Debt at June 30, 1988[7] | | | | | (29,900,000) |
| Estimated Value of Equity If Publicly Traded | | | | | 83,100,000 |
| Less: 10% Illiquidity Discount[8] | | | | | (8,300,000) |
| | | | | | 74,800,000 |
| Add: 20% Control Premium[8] | | | | | 15,000,000 |
| Estimated Value of Equity Based on Selected Public Companies[9] | | | | | $ 89,800,000 |

[1] See Appendix 7-B for description of multiples.
[2] See Table 7-2 for market multiples of selected companies.
[3] From adjusted figures of SCI.
[4] The value of equity and debt is the product of the market multiple and the component of value.
[5] The weights are based on our judgment of the relative importance of each component of value.
[6] The weighted amount is the product of the value of equity and debt and the corresponding weight.
[7] From SCI June 30, 1988 Balance Sheet.
[8] See Appendix 7-C for discussion.
[9] See Table 7-12 for use in overall estimate of value.

contrast, a lack of detailed financial information may prevent you from using the reported acquisitions approach. Lack of data and lack of confidence in published data often complicate the reported acquisitions approach.)

### The Search for "Comparable" Companies

Although there are approximately 13,000 public companies in the United States, it is seldom possible to identify a public company that is identical to the subject company. Realizing that finding an exact match is unlikely, you should define comparability in broad terms. Remember that you are searching for public companies with characteristics similar to the subject company; they do not necessarily have to be *operationally* similar. The goal is to find companies which, *as a group,* can be viewed by rational investors as having similar investment characteristics.

The first step in this search process is to define the business of the subject company in general economic terms. For example, the company might be a metals processor, or a professional services firm, or a wholesaler of consumer nondurables. You should identify the subject company's main line of business by a four-digit (primary) Standard Industrial Classification (SIC) Code, using the *Standard Industrial Classification Manual 1987* (most recent edition). (This government publication is prepared by the Office of Management and Budget.) You should also identify other SIC Codes under which public companies similar to the subject company may be classified. You are then ready to conduct a search for comparable companies.

*Sources of Names.* The following listing describes certain secondary sources of data on publicly traded companies.

**Standard & Poor's Report.** Standard and Poor's (S&P) has grouped 4,689 public companies (January 26, 1988) by its own four-digit industry code classifications.[5] These public companies

---

[5] S&P's classifications appear to be much more relevant in today's economy than the *Standard Industrial Classification Manual* codes.

are grouped under 241 categories and listed by name with other information in a 113-page report. They are also listed in alphabetical order in another report. S&P maintains detailed information on each company and updates the information daily. (The same companies appear monthly in the S&P *Stock Guide.*) You can request a custom report[6] with whatever data elements you desire. One may obtain our custom reports showing by industry and alphabetically: four-digit code, company name, principal business, exchange, stock rating, sales (in millions), net income (in millions with one decimal place), equity (in millions), price-earnings, price-revenues, and price-equity.

**Ward's Business Directory.** Volume 3 of *Ward's Business Directory* lists U.S. private and public companies by industry. Companies are ranked by sales under a four-digit SIC Code. Each company has the following data elements: rank, public or private, name, address, city, state, zip, chief executive, phone, SIC Code, industry description, sales (in millions), employees (in thousands), and year founded.

**Disclosure Incorporated (Disclosure).** Disclosure maintains data on public companies which are classified by a four-digit primary SIC Code and also by secondary SIC Code(s). You can obtain from Disclosure limited information such as a list of public companies under a given primary SIC Code or extensive data such as five years of sales and net income data, three years of detailed financial information, recent quarterly 10Q data, three years of ratio analysis, and a brief description of the business. This extensive information is equivalent to the data provided by Standard & Poor's in its *Standard Stock Reports* (NYSE, ASE, and OTC), which are commonly referred to as *tear sheets.*

**Standard & Poor's Compustat Services, Inc.** Compustat Services, Inc. maintains annual and quarterly data on over 6,800 public companies, classified by a four-digit SIC Code. A sub-

---

[6] Both reports can be obtained for $300, which is a great value relative to other data sources. The S&P *Report* can be obtained from Standard & Poor's Corporation, 25 Broadway, New York, NY 10004. You may request our custom report mentioned above: Custom Report No. 504 (Peat Marwick).

scriber can get a list of names by SIC Code and a brief description of the business segment. You can extract detailed financial information and calculate various financial ratios based on the extracted financial information.

*Moody's OTC Industrial Manual.* This manual is a reference source for over-the-counter industrial firms in the United States, covering over 3,200 companies that are not listed on national or regional stock exchanges. In the "Special Features" section (blue pages), company names are classified by business activity under approximately 170 categories. The manual provides brief data on each company including name, history, business, subsidiaries, and summary financial information.

*Moody's Industrial Manual.* This manual is a reference source of companies listed on the New York and American Stock Exchanges as well as companies listed on regional American exchanges. In the "Special Features" section (blue pages) in Volume 1, company names are classified by business activity.

*The Corporate Finance Bluebook.*[7] Section 4 of Volumes I and II groups public and private firms into 865 different industries by four-digit SIC Codes.

*Directory of Companies Required to File Annual Reports with the SEC.*[8] This directory groups the names of all public companies under four-digit SIC Codes. It is a tedious source to use, however, because more than 100 names may be listed under one SIC Code. You would have to review Standard & Poor's *Standard Stock Reports* (tear sheets) for each company and many would not be comparable after closer inspection.

[7] *The Corporate Finance Bluebook* is produced by The Zehring Company, Wilmette, IL, a subsidiary of National Register Publishing Company, and published by National Register Publishing Co.

[8] *Directory of Companies Required to File Annual Reports with the SEC* is published by U.S. Securities and Exchange Commission and sold by the Superintendent of Documents, U.S. Government Printing Office, Washington, DC 20402.

*The Unlisted Market Guide.*[9] This guide has a two-page descriptive and financial summary on each company. *The Unlisted Market Guide* maintains data on about 450 smaller public companies, which are grouped under 24 major categories in the industry index. The index shows under each industry category the following information: company name, bid price, P/E, book value per share, 12 months' earnings per share, and revenue.

*Keefe Bankbook 1988.*[10] This publication lists approximately 310 banks by state. They are also grouped by total asset size and ranked by return on assets for 1987, 1986, and 1985. The banks are also ranked by return on equity and equity generation rate for the same three years. For example, 45 banking companies with total assets under $750 million are listed and ranked by return on assets, return on equity, and equity generation rate for 1987, 1986, and 1985.

*Moody's Bank & Finance Manual.* Published in three volumes, this manual covers the field of finance represented by banks, insurance companies, investment companies, unit investment trusts, and miscellaneous financial enterprises. We use this source only for descriptive and financial information after names have been identified from another source.

*List of Potential Comparables.* After reviewing some of these sources, you will have developed a list of possible comparable companies. This list might have as few as ten names or more than 100 names. The number of names depends on the industry, your interpretation of what might be considered comparable, and the time constraints for completing the valuation analysis. You will also have found additional information on certain names, but not enough to select a group of public companies for further analysis. The next step is to obtain sufficient descriptive and financial information to make a decision on whether a company should be considered comparable.

[9] *The Unlisted Market Guide* is published by The Unlisted Market Service Corporation, P.O. Box 160, Glen Head, NY 11545.

[10] *Keefe Bankbook 1988,* published by Keefe Bruyette & Woods, Inc., New York, NY, is the most recent publication.

*The Preliminary Selection.* Standard & Poor's *Standard Stock Reports* (tear sheets) provide the best information upon which to make a preliminary decision based on the list of names. Tear sheets are filed by exchange in three separate categories (NYSE, ASE, and OTC). If there is no tear sheet for a particular company, you should refer to *The Unlisted Market Guide,*[9] which maintains data on about 450 smaller public companies. If both sources fail to provide further information on a company, you should refer to detailed financial and descriptive information provided by Disclosure Incorporated.

During the process of your preliminary selection of comparable companies, you may consider breaking the names into yes, maybe, and no categories. Remember, you are searching for publicly traded companies with business and investment characteristics similar to those of the subject company. Appropriate business characteristics may vary from similar business activity (distributor of similarly priced products) to similar economic characteristics (same or related markets). Appropriate investment characteristics may include consistent profitability[11] (as measured by return on revenues and return on assets), similar earnings before interest and tax (EBIT) and similar EBIT plus depreciation expressed as a percentage of revenues and total assets, and similar size (as measured by revenues, EBIT, equity, and total assets). The public companies included in your preliminary selection should not be "in play," that is, their current market prices should not be influenced by public announcements of a potential sale.

*Original Source Documents.* You should obtain recent SEC 10K and 10Q filings for companies considered to be potentially comparable. 10Ks include a company's annual audited financial statements for the current and prior years and a detailed description of its business. Read the business description, audited financial statements, and notes to the audited financial statements. 10Qs include unaudited financial statements for the current quarter and cumulative period year to date. You must use these original source documents to compute market price multiples.

---

[11] Profitability excludes extraordinary and nonrecurring items.

*The Final Selection.* Make a final selection of the group of comparable companies after reviewing their recent 10Ks and 10Qs. You can then use the financial data in these documents to compute selected multiples. If you use a computer model to compare relevant financial performance of the selected public companies with the subject company, you should make your final selection after reviewing a printout of the comparative financial data. Select those companies that have a financial history most similar to the financial history of the subject company.

### Market Price Multiples

Market price multiples (or ratios) are based on a current share price and one or more financial attributes of the company. It is wise to rely on audited financial information obtained from original source data when calculating market price multiples. The value you derive for a company is especially sensitive to the price multiples, so it is especially important to use correct information and to calculate the multiples correctly.

As discussed earlier, you can use equity multiples or total capital multiples. The total capital approach lets you consider the effect of debt on the value of the company. It is the approach we tend to prefer.

Commonly used equity multiples include price-earnings, price–3-year average earnings, price–5-year average earnings, and price–tangible book value. Commonly used total capital multiples include total capital–earnings before interest and taxes (EBIT), total capital–3-year average EBIT, total capital–5-year average EBIT, and total capital–tangible book value plus debt. See Appendixes 7–A and 7–B for a definition of commonly used equity multiples and total capital multiples.

The actual multiples used depend on the industry and on the financial characteristics of the subject company. For example, price-revenues may be a more important indicator of the value of a service business such as an insurance brokerage firm than of a manufacturing company. Conversely, a price–tangible book value multiple may be a better indicator of the value of a manufacturing business than of an insurance brokerage company. See Table 7–2 for total capital multiples of selected public

# Table 7-2.

## SPECIALTY CHEMICAL, INC.
### Capital Multiples of Selected Public Companies[1]

| Company | Total Capital/ Current 12 Months' EBIT | Total Capital/ Recent Fiscal Year EBIT | Total Capital/ 3 Years' Average EBIT | Total Capital/ 5 Years' Average EBIT | Total Capital/ Current 12 Months' Cash Flow | Total Capital/ Recent Fiscal Year Cash Flow | Total Capital/ 3 Years' Average Cash Flow | Total Capital/ 5 Years' Average Cash Flow | Total Capital/ Total Assets |
|---|---|---|---|---|---|---|---|---|---|
| Lawter International, Inc. | 8.9 | 9.7 | 11.9 | 11.4 | 7.9 | 8.5 | 10.3 | 10.0 | 2.0 |
| The Valspar Corp. | 8.4 | 8.5 | 10.1 | 11.7 | 6.4 | 6.5 | 8.0 | 9.5 | 1.3 |
| Guardsman Products, Inc. | 7.2 | 7.5 | 8.1 | 9.7 | 5.8 | 6.0 | 6.5 | 7.7 | 1.2 |
| Aceto Corporation | 7.0 | 7.3 | 6.0 | 6.2 | 6.6 | 6.8 | 5.7 | 5.9 | 0.8 |
| Lilly Industrial Coatings, Inc. | 8.0 | 8.1 | 9.0 | 9.2 | 6.9 | 7.1 | 7.9 | 8.2 | 1.7 |
| MacDermid, Inc. | 8.6 | 9.6 | 11.5 | 10.1 | 6.3 | 6.9 | 8.5 | 8.1 | 1.2 |
| Crompton & Knowles Corp. | 9.6 | 11.0 | 13.4 | 14.2 | 3.2 | 9.3 | 11.1 | 11.6 | 1.2 |
| Stepan Co. | 7.2 | 7.8 | 9.9 | 11.6 | 4.6 | 4.9 | 6.0 | 6.8 | 1.0 |
| Selected Multiples[2] | 8.2 | 8.3 | 10.0 | 10.8 | 6.5 | 6.9 | 8.0 | 8.2 | 1.2 |

[1] See Appendix 7–B for definition of total capital multiples.
[2] See Table 7–1 for application of selected multiples. Selected multiples are based on the medians.

companies used for the valuation of a specialty chemicals manufacturer. If the subject company has had a history of recent
losses, an investor should place greater emphasis on the
price–tangible book value multiple than if the company has
had a history of profitability.

*Sources of Price Data.* Market prices can be obtained from
the following publications: S&P *Stock Guide* (month-end price
only), *Daily Stock Price Record, The National Monthly Stock
Summary, The New York Times, The Wall Street Journal,* and
*Investor's Daily.*

### Control Premium and Illiquidity Discount

After applying the appropriate market price multiples and
weighting the resulting values to obtain one overall estimate of
value, you must consider adjusting this value amount to reflect
valuation differences between owning 100 percent (or at least
a large holding) of a private company and owning a small
minority position in a public company.[12] Remember, by relying
on multiples at which the public values traded firms, you are
actually relying on prices paid for small numbers of shares
rather than for the whole firm. Two valuation differences exist
if you are valuing a controlling interest in a private company
and using multiples developed from prices paid for publicly
traded shares.

*Control Premium.* Prices paid for publicly traded shares
normally represent a small (noncontrolling) ownership interest,
and market multiples based on such prices reflect a minority
interest in a public company. However, the purchaser of a
controlling interest in a public company would have to pay
more than the per-share price currently being paid for a minute
ownership interest in the company. This difference in price is
known as a control premium. A control premium, then, represents the difference in price per share between ownership of
100 percent of the common stock (or at least a controlling

[12] See section on "How to Apply the Market Comparison Methods."

interest) and ownership of a partial (noncontrolling) interest in the company. The control premium represents the additional price you must pay to have significant influence over or control of the company. An investor with control of a company has the power to change the nature of the business, its cost structure, its management, its policies on dividends, capital investments, and capital structure. An investor with control also has the power to sell or liquidate the company or any part of it, or to go public. Generally, a holder of a minority interest has none of these powers.

The W.T. Grimm & Co. *MergerStat Review*[13] is a good source of data on control premiums.

*Illiquidity Discount.* Prices paid for publicly traded shares represent a liquid investment that can be sold at any time and exchanged for cash at the then-current price. Ownership of a private company, however, represents an illiquid investment. The value of a privately held company determined by the market comparison method, using prices paid for publicly traded shares, should be reduced by an appropriate discount. This difference in price is known as an illiquidity or nonmarketability discount.

See Appendix 7–C for an example of the development of a control premium and an illiquidity discount for a specialty chemicals manufacturer. *Note:* An illiquidity discount for a minority block of stock is normally computed as the difference in price per share between ownership of a marketable security and an otherwise identical restricted security in the same company.

### Other Premiums and Discounts

You should adjust the value obtained from the market comparison methods if differences exist between the subject company and the group of public companies that affect the value of the subject company. For example, the subject company may have a performance history and prospects better than the

[13] *MergerStat Review,* The W.T. Grimm & Co., 135 South Lasalle Street, Chicago, IL 60603.

group of public companies. Accordingly, the value of the subject company may have to be adjusted upward (if its superior prospects were not already reflected through an adjustment in the market multiples). Such upward adjustments are frequently referred to as premiums. Frequently, however, the value of the subject company is adjusted downward because of the subject company's weaker position relative to the selected public companies. Such adjustments are commonly referred to as discounts. Commonly applied discounts include: key person discount, key customer discount, and key supplier discount. These discounts are applied because the subject company may depend on one or a few key people to manage the company, or on one or a few customers or suppliers for a significant percentage of business, while the public companies are not similarly dependent. Discounts may also be appropriate if the subject company depends on one product or service or one geographic region for its business and the selected public companies do not or if the subject company is substantially smaller than those public companies.

### *Advantages of the Publicly Traded Shares Method*

The market comparison method, using prices paid for publicly traded shares, is probably the best known and most widely used valuation approach for valuing both private companies and divisions of public companies. This method has many positive features:

- It uses the actual prices that others have freely paid for small ownership interests in similar public companies.
- There are 13,000 publicly traded companies in the United States with current prices and a complete financial history to choose from. Standard & Poor's maintains current information on 5,000 of the most actively traded firms.
- You can have confidence in the data used to develop the market multiples, because the financial statements of the public companies are audited and publicly available and their stock prices and shares outstanding are also known publicly.
- You can develop many multiples (price–financial data ratios) using this method because the financial history of the public

company is available. Because the data is available, it is wise to apply as many multiples as possible and then select the multiples you believe contribute most to the subject company's fair market value. The more multiples that result in similar values, the more confident you can be in these values.

- If you cannot find public companies that are operationally comparable, you can broaden your search to companies that are financially comparable.
- Most of the public information used in the valuation analysis can be found in a good business library, and 10Ks and 10Qs can be obtained from Disclosure Incorporated.[14] Similar financial information may be obtained for Canadian and U.K. public companies from Micromedia Limited[15] and Extel Financial Limited,[16] respectively.

### Limitations of the Publicly Traded Shares Method

Although the market comparison method, using prices paid for publicly traded shares, has many attractive features, it requires experience to apply it correctly:

- You must be highly skilled to correctly apply this approach and obtain a transaction price that is reasonable relative to the market. Unskilled people could obtain vastly different opinions of value while applying this approach.
- Control premiums and illiquidity discounts represent significant percentages of value. And, to some extent, the estimated amounts of control premiums and illiquidity discounts are subjective. It is a common mistake to overvalue a private company by either overstating the control premium or understating the illiquidity discount.
- You may understate hidden values or future opportunities that are specific to the subject company.

[14] Disclosure Incorporated, 5161 River Road, Bethesda, MD 20816.

[15] Micromedia Limited, Business Information Centre, 158 Pearl Street, Toronto, Ontario M5H 1L3.

[16] Extel Financial Limited, Fitzroy House, 13–17 Epworth Street, London EC2A 4DL.

# PRICES PAID IN REPORTED ACQUISITIONS

This approach is based on the premise that the value of a private or public company can be estimated by analyzing the prices paid by purchasers of ownership interests in reported acquisitions. There are approximately 5,000 reported acquisitions on average per year in the United States that provide some financial history on the seller. You can use financial information from these transactions to develop appropriate acquisition price multiples, which you can use to value the subject company. Similar transactions may be identified through secondary sources that specialize in collecting merger and acquisition transaction data. However, to develop acquisition price multiples you can rely only on original source documents describing the transaction.

Most reported acquisitions are of public companies or divisions of public companies, or the buyer is a public company. Transaction details involving two private companies tend not to be reported. And even if the transaction price were reported, you could not compute the acquisition price multiples without financial information on the seller.

### The Search for "Comparable" Acquisitions

Although in the United States, thousands of transactions that provide some financial history on the seller are reported each year, seldom do you find a recent transaction that will be operationally and financially similar to the subject company. You may have to define comparability in terms at least as broad as you did during your search for comparable companies. At this point you should reread our comments on "The Search for 'Comparable' Companies," because they apply here as well.

*Sources of Merger and Acquisition Transaction Data.* The following listing describes certain secondary sources of data on publicly reported merger and acquisition transactions.

*The W.T. Grimm & Co. MergerStat Review.*[13] W.T. Grimm & Co. maintains data on between 2,000 and 3,000 merger, acquisition, and divestiture transactions per year. Each transaction is classified into one of 50 industry categories. For each transaction Grimm identifies the buyer and the seller, relevant dates, annual sales of target, price paid, method of payment (cash/stock/debt), price-earnings paid, price–book value, and premiums paid over market. You can also calculate the price-revenue multiple from the data provided.

Grimm's *MergerStat Review* offers a host of useful statistical data, including percent premium paid over market by industry, by year; median price-earnings paid, public versus private, over a seven-year period; price-earnings ratios, percent paid over S&P 500 over a 20-year period; and price-earnings paid, by industry classifications, over a five-year period. Grimm's *MergerStat Review* is published annually.

*Mergers & Acquisitions.*[17] This bimonthly journal has current articles and a roster of recent mergers, acquisitions, divestitures, leveraged buyouts, and tender offers. The "Roster" section lists information on the buyer or investor group, the selling entity, the terms including price, the revenues and net income of the seller, and the fiscal year of the reported revenues and net income. Transactions are categorized under a two-digit SIC Code. The information contained in the Roster section is extracted quarterly from the *M&A Data Base,*[18] which contains information on more than 20,000 transactions valued at $1 million or more involving both public and private companies from 1979 to the present. It is a computer-accessible historical database on announced M&A transactions involving U.S. companies.

*The Merger Yearbook.*[19] This publication covers 6,300 transactions announced in 1987, down from 7,100 transactions in 1986. The types of transactions reported include negotiations, offers to acquire, letters of intent, agreements in principle,

---

[17] *Mergers & Acquisitions* (ISSN 0026–0010). *The Journal of Corporate Venture* is published bimonthly by MLR Publishing Company, 229S 18th St., Philadelphia, PA 19103.

[18] For information on regular online access to the *M&A Data Base,* contact ADP Network Services.

[19] *The Merger Yearbook* is published by Cambridge Corporation, P.O. Box 670, Ipswich, MA 01938.

definitive agreements, tender offers, minority stock purchases, and completed acquisitions. The transactions are classified by a two-digit SIC Code and a description of the industry. The data elements include the buyer and the seller, a description of the seller's business, transaction price, and the sales and earnings of the seller.

*Mergers and Corporate Policy.*[20] This biweekly supplement for *The Merger Yearbook* includes recent transactions, giving the same data as the yearbook gives. It is written as a newsletter and also contains brief articles. It should be used in conjunction with *The Merger Yearbook.*

*The Acquisition/Divestiture Weekly Report.*[21] This weekly report has current newsworthy items and current transactions. It includes the following information: a description of the seller (company name, four-digit SIC Code, type of business, sales and net income for the most recent three years, book value, book value per share, and earnings per share) and of the buyer (purchase price, price-earnings, price-revenues, and price–book value of the seller), plus a description of the transaction and the key individuals and entities.

*Securities Data Company, Inc.*[22] Securities Data Company, Inc., maintains data on mergers, acquisitions, partial acquisitions, tender offers, self-tender offers, divestitures, and repurchases of stock. The mergers and acquisitions database provides immediate access to approximately 35,000 transactions reported since January 1, 1980; it lists approximately 4,000 domestic transactions per year and 1,000 foreign transactions per year. Of course you should search for recent transactions because they represent deals done at current prices. A typical report shows the seller's

---

[20] *Mergers and Corporate Policy* is published biweekly by Cambridge Corporation Publishers, P.O. Box 670, 145 Argilla Road, Ipswich, MA 01938–9989.

[21] *The Acquisition/Divestiture Weekly Report* is published by Quality Services Co., 5290 Overpass Road, Santa Barbara, CA 93111.

[22] Securities Data Company, Inc., 62 William Street, New York, NY 10005.

name, business, and four-digit SIC Code; name of buyer; date of announcement; revenues; net income; stockholders' equity and total assets of the target; transaction price; book value per share; date of financials; shares outstanding; and status and description of transaction. From this data source, you can calculate common acquisition multiples such as price-revenues, price-earnings, price–book value, and price–total assets. Use this database to identify similar acquisitions in terms of business, SIC Code, general size, and date of announcement. You should use original source documents to calculate acquisition multiples.

*IDD Information Services, Inc.*[23] This company maintains data on U.S. and U.K. mergers and acquisitions. The U.S. database covers U.S. domestic and major international transactions since 1984. It contains over 24,000 deals with approximately 175 data items per deal. Information is maintained on both the target company and the acquiring company. The U.K. database covers U.K. domestic transactions only since 1986. It contains over 2,200 deals with approximately 175 data items per deal. Information is maintained on the target company only. Both databases are updated daily. The U.K. database is maintained by IDD Information Services, Inc. and Extel Financial Limited.[16] You may request on-line service with IDD Information Services, Inc. or you may request a specific search and pay on a per-project basis.

*Standard & Poor's Standard Stock Reports.* The *Standard Stock Reports* (tear sheets) are concise, two-page descriptive and financial summaries on publicly traded companies. You should frequently refer to these tear sheets when conducting a search for comparable public companies. Each tear sheet has a section on important developments that discusses mergers, acquisitions, and divestitures. During the market comparison method, using prices paid for publicly traded shares, you should also make note of reported acquisition and divestiture activity on the tear sheets to be included in the reported acquisition analysis. The

---

[23] IDD Information Services, Inc., Two World Trade Center, New York, NY 10048.

tear sheets are often a rewarding source of relevant acquisitions. Standard & Poor's also provides a special tear sheet when it stops covering a company and gives the reason for this change, for example, if the company was acquired.

*The NEXIS Service.*[24] This service is a full-text research and information retrieval service having as its core the *NEXIS* library, a database of general, business, and news information. The *NEXIS* library comprises more than 145 files of information from U.S. and overseas newspapers, magazines, journals, newsletters, wire services, and broadcast transcripts.

You may find this data source useful for identifying acquisitions by well-known companies within an industry. For example, you may wish to identify names and other details of real estate brokerage firms acquired by Grubb & Ellis in the past three years. With such details, you could then search for original source documents.

You should now reread the following sections: "List of Potential Comparables" and paragraph two of "The Preliminary Selection" under "Prices Paid for Publicly Traded Shares."

*Original Source Documents.* You must obtain relevant 8Ks, proxy statements, and 10Ks or 14D1 filings with the SEC for those transactions considered to be comparable. 8Ks contain information mostly on important developments such as a completed sale or a purchase of a business. Proxy statements provide descriptive and financial information on the transaction. Sometimes the 10Ks contain a reference to the transaction in the notes to the financial statements. The 14D1 document is a formal offer to purchase, including relevant information on the target and the transaction price. Within ten days of a formal offer, a company must respond with a 14D9 document. Frequently, you may be unable to find original source documents for a transaction identified in a secondary source because the acquisition is small relative to the size of the buyer, or the buyer is not a public company, or the buyer and seller are both

[24] *The NEXIS Service* is provided by Mead Data Central, 200 Park Avenue, New York, NY 10166.

private companies. See Appendix 7–D for an example of a search for comparable companies that were recently acquired and a description of the selected acquisitions.

### Market Price Multiples

You should calculate as many market price multiples as the financial information provided in the original source documents allows. Frequently, the financial information in source documents is scant and you will be lucky to compute four or five multiples. See Table 7–5 for capital multiples of comparable acquisitions in the specialty chemicals industry. See Table 7–3 for application of capital multiples of comparable acquisitions. See Table 7–4 for application of capital multiples of the most comparable acquisition.

### Premiums and Discounts

A control premium is already reflected in the prices paid in an acquisition of a private or public company. In the reported acquisitions method you have to consider applying an illiquidity discount and other premiums and discounts. In Tables 7–3 and 7–4, for example, an illiquidity discount was not applied because three of four acquisitions used to estimate the value of SCI were of privately held firms. Accordingly, the prices paid in these acquisitions already reflected both a control premium and an illiquidity discount. You should reread the sections on "Control Premium and Illiquidity Discount" and "Other Premiums and Discounts."

### Advantages of the Reported Acquisitions Method

The market comparison method, using prices paid in reported acquisitions, is a recognized valuation approach for pricing acquisition candidates. This method is used by both buyers and sellers, and in theory it has many advantages:

- It uses the actual prices that buyers have freely paid for the ownership of similar companies.

**Table 7–3.**

## SPECIALTY CHEMICAL, INC.
### Application of Capital Multiples of Comparable Acquisitions

| Description of Multiple[1] | Market Multiple[2] | SCI Component of Value[3] | Value of Equity Plus Debt[4] | Weight[5] | Weighted Value[6] |
|---|---|---|---|---|---|
| Total Capital/Recent Fiscal Year Revenue | 1.05 | $ 100,072,000 | $ 105,075,600 | 20% | $ 21,000,000 |
| Total Capital/Recent Fiscal Year EBIT | 8.6 | 14,758,000[3] | 126,918,800 | 25% | 31,700,000 |
| Total Capital/Recent Fiscal EBIT Cash Flow | 7.9 | 17,722,000[3] | 140,003,800 | 25% | 35,000,000 |
| Total Capital/Tangible Book Value Plus Debt | 2.3 | 33,152,000[7] | 76,249,600 | 15% | 11,400,000 |
| Total Capital/Total Assets | 1.6 | 65,886,000[7] | 105,417,600 | 15% | 15,800,000 |
| Total Value of Equity Plus Debt | | | | 100% | 114,900,000 |
| Less: Debt at June 30, 1988[7] | | | | | (29,900,000) |
| Estimated Value of Equity Based on Comparable Acquisitions[8] | | | | | $ 85,000,000 |

[1] See Appendix 7–B for definition of total market multiple.
[2] See Table 7–5 for capital multiples of comparable acquisitions.
[3] From adjusted figures of SCI.
[4] The value of total capital (equity plus debt) is the product of the market multiple and the component of value.
[5] The weights are based on our judgment of the relative importance of each component of value.
[6] The weighted value is the product of the value of total capital (equity plus debt) and its corresponding weight.
[7] From SCI Balance Sheet at June 30, 1988.
[8] See Table 7–12 for use in overall determination of value.

**Table 7-4.**

## SPECIALTY CHEMICAL, INC.
### Application of Capital Multiples of the Most Comparable Acquisition

| Description of Multiple[1] | Market Multiple[2] | SCI Component of Value[3] | Value of Equity Plus Debt[4] | Weight[5] | Weighted Value[6] |
|---|---|---|---|---|---|
| Total Capital/ Recent Year Revenue | 1.26 | $ 100,072,000 | $ 126,090,720 | 25% | $ 31,500,000 |
| Total Capital/ Recent Year EBIT | 8.9 | 14,758,000[3] | 131,346,200 | 25% | 32,800,000 |
| Total Capital/ Recent Year EBIT Cash Flow | 8.7 | 17,722,000[3] | 154,181,400 | 25% | 38,500,000 |
| Total Capital/ Tangible Book Value Plus Debt | 3.4 | 33,152,000[7] | 112,716,800 | 25% | 28,200,000 |
| Value of Equity and Debt | | | | | 131,000,000 |
| Less: Debt at June 30, 1988[7] | | | | | (29,900,000) |
| Estimated Value of Equity Based on Most Comparable Acquisition[8] | | | | | $ 101,100,000 |

[1] See Appendix 7–B for definition of multiples.
[2] See Table 7–5 for capital multiples for Pentech Chemicals, Inc.
[3] From adjusted figures of SCI.
[4] The value of total capital (equity plus debt) is the product of the market multiple and the component of value.
[5] The weights are based on our judgment of the relative importance of each component of value.
[6] The weighted value is the product of the value of total capital (equity plus debt) and its corresponding weight.
[7] From SCI Balance Sheet at June 30, 1988.
[8] See Table 7–12 for use in overall determination of value.

**Table 7-5.**

## SPECIALTY CHEMICAL, INC.
### Capital Multiples of Comparable Acquisitions[1]

| Company[2] | Purchase Price/ Recent Year Revenue | Purchase Price/ Recent Year EBIT | Purchase Price/ Recent Year EBIT Cash Flow | Purchase Price/ Tangible Book Value Plus Debt | Purchase Price/ Total Assets |
|---|---|---|---|---|---|
| Omnicron Holdings, Inc. | 0.82 | 6.7 | 4.8 | 1.6 | 1.0 |
| Uniroyal Chemical Co. | 1.28 | 8.3 | 7.0 | 2.2 | 1.7 |
| Pentech Corp.[3] | 1.26 | 8.9 | 8.7 | 3.4 | 2.3(NM)[4] |
| Reichhold Chemicals, Inc. | 0.84 | 14.9 | 9.9 | 2.3 | 1.4 |
| Selected Multiples[5] | 1.05 | 8.6 | 7.9 | 2.3 | 1.6 |

[1] See Appendix 7–B for description of multiples.
[2] See Appendix 7–D for description of selected comparable acquisitions.
[3] See Table 7–4 for application of multiples. This transaction is the most comparable of the four acquisitions.
[4] Not meaningful. Assets of Pentech Corp. are significantly understated due to a bargain purchase adjustment from a prior acquisition.
[5] Selected multiples are based on median values. See Table 7–3 for application of selected multiples.

**Table 7–6.**

SPECIALTY CHEMICAL, INC.
Application of Capital Multiples of Pending Acquisition ($000)

> The target company manufactures flush and dry colors for printing inks, carbon paper, and artists' colors. The target company's revenues were similar to SCI with a gross margin of 20% and adjusted net earnings of roughly 9% of revenue. The target company is currently considering a tender offer for 100% ownership of the company. We derived capital multiples based on the current negotiated price and unaudited financial data provided to us and applied it to SCI to estimate the company's value.

| | |
|---|---|
| SCI recent year EBIT | $ 14,758 |
| EBIT multiple of acquisition target[1] | × 8.6 |
| Estimated value of debt plus equity based on EBIT value | $126,919 |
| | |
| SCI recent year EBIT Cash Flow | $ 17,722 |
| EBIT Cash Flow multiple of target[1] | × 6.8 |
| Estimated value based on EBIT Cash Flow | $120,510 |
| | |
| Midpoint of values | 123,715 |
| | |
| Less: Debt outstanding at June 30, 1988[2] | (29,900) |
| Estimated value of equity based on pending acquisition[3] | $ 93,815 |

[1] See Appendix 7–B for description of multiples.
[2] From SCI June 30, 1988 Balance Sheet.
[3] See Table 7–12 for use in overall estimate of value.

- The control premium is already included in the prices paid.
- An illiquidity discount may also be included in the price paid if you use acquisitions of privately held companies.
- You can easily calculate the illiquidity discount to be applied to a private firm if you use prices paid in acquisitions of publicly traded companies and assume that the appropriate

illiquidity discount for a private firm is the difference between the multiples paid for public and private companies.

- You can use many good secondary sources of data to identify similar acquisitions.

### Limitations of the Reported Acquisitions Method

The market comparison method, using prices paid in reported acquisitions, appears to be the most useful to a prospective buyer or seller of a business. But, in reality, this approach has many pitfalls:

- It is rare to find similar transactions in terms of business activity, financial performance, and size that have occurred in the recent past.

- It is difficult to obtain from original source documents sufficient financial data on the seller to compute an adequate array of acquisition price multiples. Compiling a financial history on the target from original source documents can be expensive and time consuming.

- You cannot rely on the accuracy of financial information from secondary sources for purposes of computing acquisition price multiples.

- The prices paid in reported acquisitions may include a "synergistic premium," which the buyer anticipated would develop as a result of the acquisition and for which he or she was willing to pay a premium over the stand-alone value of the target. The transaction that you are considering may not have a synergistic benefit, and even if it does, the buyer may not want to pay for it because (a) it may not materialize and (b) the buyer is providing the synergistic potential, not the seller. The buyer may contend that the subject company should be valued as a stand-alone entity.

- The acquisition price multiples are computed using the acquisition price and the financial performance of the seller. However, the acquisition price may have been based on an expectation of the seller's greatly improved performance after acquisition, not on the seller's historical performance. Accordingly, you could easily overvalue the subject company using such multiples.

- Sometimes there are unknown variables, for example, seller duress.

## PRICES PAID IN INITIAL PUBLIC OFFERINGS (IPOs)

This approach is based on the premise that the value of a private company can be estimated by analyzing the prices paid by investors for partial ownership interests in a company when its common stock is first issued to the public. Each year hundreds of private companies go public in order to raise capital for further growth and to allow current investors (including venture capitalists and owners) as well as debt holders to "cash in" their investments. *The IPO Reporter* listed approximately 550 companies that went public with a firm commitment offering during 1987. Many companies that seek capital through an initial public offering are relatively new and frequently do not have a track record of profitability. In such cases, you can compute few useful market multiples.

The IPO market offers equity financing for young businesses with prospects. This market is cyclical in terms of volume and volatile in terms of price. For example, the aftermarket for 1987 performed poorly as measured by the change from the initial price to the closing price on December 31, 1987.

An owner of a young growing business may find (depending on market conditions) that there are better prospects of "getting out" through a public offering than through the sale of the business. An owner may also use the IPO as a means of "cashing out" part of his or her investment, while still controlling the fortunes of the company. Prospective sellers of more mature businesses naturally wish to compare their company's range of possible IPO prices with a range of possible sale prices.

### The Search for "Comparable" IPOs

In a search for IPOs you should define comparability in broad terms, as we described in the section on "The Search for 'Comparable' Companies." You should use secondary sources of data to screen for initial public offerings, but rely only on data from original sources to compute IPO price multiples. Of course, you may develop multiples using secondary source data to get a sense of the market. If you are to act on the resulting value, however, you should recompute these multiples along with others, using original source data.

*Sources of IPO Data.* The following listing describes certain secondary sources of data on initial public offerings.

*Going Public, The IPO Reporter.*[25] This publication has descriptive and financial information on new offerings and tracks their price performance in the aftermarket. For each expected offering, it shows company name and address, expected date, manager, revenues, net income, common equity, pro forma book value, price-earnings, percentage offered to the public, and total market valuation. You can identify possible comparable offerings from the descriptive and financial information provided. From this data you can calculate price-earnings, price-revenues, and price–pro forma book value. Many of these new issues are startups and development companies. A quick review of *The IPO Reporter* gives you an idea of the quality of certain companies that have raised equity capital through initial public offerings.

*IDD Information Services, Inc.*[23] IDD Information Services, Inc. maintains comprehensive information on all initial public offerings. You can screen data by SIC Code and any number of other search criteria. Some of the most important data elements are offer date, issuer, dollar amount issued, fully diluted price-earnings multiple, market value after offer, market value–book multiple after offer, market value–revenues multiple after offer,

---

[25] *Going Public, The IPO Reporter* is a publication of the Dealer's Digest, Inc., 150 Broadway, New York, NY 10038.

five-year financial summary, and a description of the business.

You can use these two secondary sources in conjunction to identify comparable initial public offerings for which you may wish to request original source documents for further analysis.

*Original Source Documents.* You must obtain the original documents filed with the SEC, the most common of which is called an S1, to compute market price multiples. Other filing forms and references are S2, S18, and N2. You may obtain copies of these documents from Disclosure Incorporated.[14] The initial public offering documents give you a description of the company, its history, detailed financials, a postoffering balance sheet, and details on the current offering. Use this information to decide whether the company may be considered comparable, and, if so, compute multiples using the financial data reported in the S1 or other SEC filings.

### Market Price Multiples

Table 7–7 provides an example of a price-earnings multiple developed from IPOs.

### Control Premium and Illiquidity Discount

You would have to consider applying both a control premium and an illiquidity discount in valuing a privately held company for acquisition or divestiture, using prices paid in initial public offerings. (See the section "Control Premium and Illiquidity Discount" under "Prices Paid for Publicly Traded Shares" and Appendix 7–C for further discussion.)

### Other Premiums and Discounts

You should adjust the value obtained from the initial public offering method if differences exist between the subject company and the group of IPOs that affect the value of the subject company. For further details, reread the section "Other Premiums and Discounts" under "Prices Paid for Publicly Traded Shares."

# Table 7-7.

## PHYSICIAN CARE CENTER, INC.
### Initial Public Offerings of Similar or Related Type Businesses[1]

| Reported Date | Company Name | Revenues ($000) | Earnings ($000) | Offering Amount ($000) | Price/ Earnings | Line of Business |
|---|---|---|---|---|---|---|
| 6/6/85 | Pacific Care Health Systems, Inc. | 76,499 | 4,815 | 24,300 | 18.6 | Owns and operates health maintenance organizations |
| 5/30/85 | Ameri Care Health Corporation | 87,316 | 4,628 | 25,625 | 16.0 | Owns and operates health maintenance organizations |
| 5/9/85 | Sierra Health Services, Inc. | 27,920 | 797 | 18,750 | 62.5[3] | Operates health maintenance organizations |
| 4/25/85 | Occupational Medical Corporation of America, Inc.[2] | 3,629 | 350 | 4,750 | 22.7 | Operates medical care units for work-related illnesses |
| 2/14/85 | American MedCenters, Inc. | 12,719 | 1,588 | 11,200 | 19.0 | Develops and manages health maintenance organizations |
| 9/20/84 | Women's Care Corporation | 164 | (27) | 800 | d | Operates a health clinic |
| 6/21/84 | Health Mark Centers, Inc. | 4 | (50) | 1,775 | d | Operates health care centers |
| 5/31/84 | Occupational-Urgent Care Health Systems, Inc. | 287 | (15) | 1,950 | d | Manages medical centers |
| 5/10/84 | U.S. Medical Enterprises, Inc.[2] | 4,741 | 571 | 11,000 | 25.0 | Operates industrial medical centers |
| 4/12/84 | Minor Emergency Centers, Inc. | 71 | (3) | 3,000 | d | Will operate immediate medical care centers |
| 3/8/84 | Pri Med, Inc. | 98 | 9 | 2,400 | NM | Establishes and manages ambulatory treatment centers |
| 1/19/84 | UCI Medical Affiliates, Inc. | 0 | 0 | 8,250 | NM | Will acquire medical centers |
| 1/12/84 | Life Concerns | 994[4] | 124[4] | 4,400 | 200.0[3] | Manages walk-in health clinics |
| | Average (of 5 multiples) | | | | 20.3 | |

[1] From *The IPO Reporter* 1984 and 1985.
[2] Company appears to be very similar to Physician Care Center, Inc. in line of business, revenues, and earnings potential.
[3] Have excluded price-earnings multiple from average calculation.

### Advantages of the Initial Public Offering Method

The market comparison method, using prices paid in initial public offerings, is a valuation method commonly used when considering bringing a company public. It is less often used in the domain of acquisitions. Nevertheless, it does have uses and benefits within this context:

- It uses the actual prices that others have freely paid for small ownership interests in similar companies when they are first issued to the public.

- In theory, going public is an alternative for every owner. As such, an owner can contrast the benefits of going public at the estimated IPO price against the other strategic alternatives of hold, sell, or liquidate.

- You may uncover a comparable new issue that may not have been found during the publicly traded shares method.

- If you cannot use this method because there are too few comparable IPOs, these few can be added to the publicly traded shares method.

- Information on IPOs is easy to obtain.

### Limitations of the Initial Public Offering Method

- Comparable initial public offerings are rare.

- Many of the firms going public are either concepts (with no history), development companies, or unprofitable companies, and so the usefulness of price multiples is limited.

- The IPO market is cyclical in terms of volume of new issues and volatile in terms of price. For example, 1987 was a bad year for investors in IPO stock. Many issues lost more than 50 percent of the offer price between the offer date and December 31, 1987.

- The IPO market appears to be more speculative than the secondary market.

## DISCOUNTED CASH FLOW METHOD

The discounted cash flow (DCF) method is based on the premise that the value of a private or public company can be estimated today by forecasting the future financial performance of the business and identifying the surplus cash (cash flow) that the business generates. Surplus cash flow for all future years is then discounted by a risk-adjusted cost of capital back to the present to obtain the net present value of those future cash flows. The net present value is defined as the market value of the company. Accordingly, the DCF method views a business purely in cash terms. The more cash flow the business generates, the more valuable the company.

The mechanics of the DCF method force you to focus internally on the subject company and forward in time. To apply the DCF methods, you must have a good understanding of the business and its past performance along with a good sense of the company's growth prospects. Some further aspects of the DCF method are given in Chapter 12.

### How to Apply the DCF Method

The discounted cash flow method has six steps:

1. develop a debt-free forecast of the subject company's financial performance and condition for five or more years
2. identify the surplus cash (cash flow)—negative or positive—that you expect the business to generate in each forecasted fiscal year
3. estimate the value of the company at the end of the forecast period (terminal value)
4. estimate the subject company's risk-adjusted cost of capital
5. discount the forecasted cash flows and the terminal value amounts by the cost of capital
6. subtract today's borrowings (long-term and short-term) to estimate the value of the business to its owners

*Forecast the Subject Company's Financial Performance and Condition.* To develop a realistic financial forecast for the business, you should have already performed a study of the subject company as outlined earlier (see the section "Study the Subject Company"). You should have a good understanding of the company, its industry, the company's position within its industry, the current phase of the business cycle, and prospects for growth.

The forecast is normally developed in the following order: sales, costs, asset turns, assets, and liabilities.

The statement of changes in financial position provides a bridge between the balance sheet and the income statement. All three statements—income statement, statement of changes, and balance sheet—should be developed because errors will come to your attention if the statements do not tie together. If you project only the income statement and the balance sheet, you may miss many errors and may fail to understand fully the economics of the business you are valuing.

Ideally, you should use a simple forecast model to develop the financial forecast. A model lets you test assumptions and perform a sensitivity analysis. Good DCF valuation models provide you with a list of assumptions and the required inputs and relationships and allow you to observe the impact on value of a change in an assumption.

*Identify the Surplus Cash (Cash Flow).* We define cash flow as the surplus cash that the business generates from operations. In theory, surplus cash could be taken out of the business each year without impairing the company's current performance or growth potential. To avoid distortions in value caused by historical borrowings, cash flows are calculated as if the company were debt free throughout the forecast period. In financial terms cash flow is defined as operating cash receipts minus all operating cash disbursements, whether recorded on the income statement or balance sheet. Cash flow excludes the costs of debt financing, such as interest expense, debt repayments, and new debt financing.

You can use accounting data to approximate cash flows, as follows:

Operating earnings before interest and taxes (EBIT) and other nonoperating, noncash expenses such as goodwill amortization (adjusted EBIT)

<u>Less:</u>  Provision for income taxes on EBIT or adjusted EBIT
<u>Add:</u>   Depreciation
<u>Less:</u>  Capital expenditures
<u>Less:</u>  Changes in noncash working capital

You can obtain depreciation and capital expenditures directly from the statement of changes in financial position, along with changes in working capital.

See Table 7–8 for an example of a cash flow forecast.

*Estimate the Terminal Value of the Subject Company.* In the DCF method, financial statements are normally forecasted for five years, although some people project financial statements for ten years. Most DCF valuation models can carry at least ten years of forecasted data. In theory, you should forecast as many years as it takes for the subject company to "bump up against" a mature marketplace, so that no further value can be created for shareholders.

At the end of the fifth or tenth year, you will still have an operating company (hopefully) with value at that point in time. This terminal value often represents a significant percentage of the company's net present value. Accordingly, the terminal value must be estimated and reflected in the DCF analysis. So how do you estimate what the value will be five to ten years from now? Essentially, you can make a terminal value assumption, the most common of which is known as the perpetuity assumption.

The perpetuity method assumes that the operating cash flows in the last forecasted period will remain constant forever. The perpetuity method is based on the concept that competitors will enter the business and drive down the returns of the subject company until the value of the company cannot be increased by additional investment. There are also variations on the perpetuity method, such as assuming that the expected cash flows in the last forecast period will grow at a certain rate forever.

**Table 7-8.** *Summary of forecasted cash flows[1] by year: example.*

| | | | | | Years | | | | | |
|---|---|---|---|---|---|---|---|---|---|---|
| | 1 | 2 | 3 | 4 | 5 | 6 | 7 | 8 | 9 | 10 |
| Sales | $ 21,000 | $ 22,000 | $ 23,000 | $ 24,000 | $ 26,000 | $ 28,000 | $ 30,000 | $ 33,000 | $ 36,000 | $ 39,000 |
| Earnings Before Interest and Taxes (EBIT)[2] | 1,400 | 1,500 | 1,600 | 1,700 | 1,900 | 2,100 | 2,300 | 2,600 | 2,900 | 3,200 |
| Income Taxes on EBIT[3] | (600) | (500) | (600) | (600) | (600) | (700) | (800) | (900) | (1,000) | (1,000) |
| "Debt-Free" Earnings After Taxes[4] | 800 | 1,000 | 1,000 | 1,100 | 1,300 | 1,400 | 1,500 | 1,700 | 1,900 | 2,100 |
| *Add:* Depreciation[5] | 300 | 300 | 300 | 400 | 400 | 400 | 500 | 500 | 500 | 600 |
| *Less:* Capital Expenditures[5] | (400) | (400) | (400) | (500) | (500) | (500) | (600) | (600) | (600) | (700) |
| *Less:* Increase in Working Capital[5,6] | (200) | (200) | (200) | (200) | (400) | (400) | (400) | (600) | (600) | (600) |
| Cash Flow[7] | $ 500 | $ 700 | $ 700 | $ 800 | $ 800 | $ 900 | $ 1,000 | $ 1,000 | $ 1,200 | $ 1,400 |

[1] Cash flow can be approximated from accounting data as follows:
Operating earnings before interest and taxes (EBIT) and other nonoperating, noncash expenses such as goodwill amortization (adjusted EBIT)
  *Less:* Provision for income taxes on EBIT or adjusted EBIT
  *Add:* Depreciation
  *Less:* Capital expenditures
  *Less:* Changes in noncash working capital

[2] Represents the operating profits of the company.
[3] Income tax is calculated based on EBIT even if the company has an interest expense.
[4] Represents after-tax profits of a "debt-free" company.
[5] Obtain from statement of changes in financial position.
[6] Represents the additional cash investment in items such as receivables and inventories, net of current payables and accruals, required by the expanding level of business.
[7] See Table 7-9 for use in the discounted cash flow method.

255

Another way to estimate the terminal value of the company is to apply multiples to certain financial attributes of the subject company estimated for the last year of the forecast period, such as price-EBIT, price–EBIT plus depreciation, price-earnings, and price–book value. In other words, you could use the forecasted financial statements and certain market price multiples to value the company as if you were following one of the market comparison methods. You would then discount this terminal value amount back to the present, using the company's estimated risk-adjusted cost of capital.

It is wise to calculate the terminal value in more than one way because if two or more assumptions provide similar values, you increase your level of confidence in the terminal value amount. Likewise, you should assess the reasonableness of the estimated terminal value, however determined, by comparing that amount to the forecasted book value of the subject company at the end of the forecast period. It is important to calculate a realistic terminal value because this amount often contributes 50 percent or more to the net present value amount when you use a five-year forecast period.

*Estimate the Subject Company's Risk-Adjusted Cost of Capital.* At this point in the DCF analysis you have identified the cash flows for each year of the forecast period, and you have also estimated the value of the subject company at the end of the forecast period. You must now combine these separate pieces of value to arrive at one total value as of today using a discount rate. The discount rate should reflect the business and financial risk of an investment in the subject company. The discount rate can also be adjusted upward to reflect the likelihood that the forecasted cash flow levels may not be achieved. Remember, a higher discount rate means a lower value; conversely, a lower discount rate means a higher value. So investors' perceptions of what the discount rate should be affect the value of the business, if all other valuation variables are held constant. The discount rate most often used for DCF analysis is the blended cost of equity and debt capital, because it is assumed that an owner will choose to borrow. Even if a company is "debt free," it is assumed to have the ability to borrow, thereby changing its overall blended cost of capital and its DCF value.

*Cost of Equity Capital.* The cost of equity capital represents the expected after-tax returns to investors in the subject company, to compensate them for both the business and the financial risk inherent in the subject company. The cost of equity capital of a private company can be expressed by the formula:

$$\text{COEC} = R_f + \beta(R_p)$$

where COEC is the cost of equity capital, $R_f$ is the "riskless" rate of return, $\beta$ is the beta on the stock, and $R_p$ is the equity risk premium.

The *"riskless" rate of return* is the yield you can get on an investment considered to be risk free, such as a government security. *Beta* measures the price volatility of the stock relative to the price volatility of the overall stock market. The *equity risk premium* is the additional total returns that an investment in the stock market would have provided over and above the yields of a "riskless" security such as a government bond.

For example, a few years ago we calculated the cost of equity capital for a privately held firm in a stable industry as follows:

COEC = 8.1% (intermediate-term Treasury rate) plus 1.07 (beta of stock) × 7.3 (equity risk premium)

   = 8.1 + 1.07 (7.3)

   = 15.9%

A government security is normally selected as the "riskless" rate of return. The duration of the security is normally selected to match the forecast period. The beta of 1.07 was based on the betas of the public companies selected in the market comparison method, using prices paid for publicly traded shares. The equity risk premium is the difference between common stock total returns and intermediate-term government bond yields.[26]

[26] From *Stocks, Bonds, Bills and Inflation, 1988 Year Book Market Results 1926–1987,* Ibbotson Associates, Chicago, IL.

*Cost of Debt Capital.* The cost of debt capital represents the after-tax interest cost to the subject company of borrowing longer-term funds. The cost of debt capital can be expressed by the formula:

$$\text{CODC} = i\,(1 - TD)$$

where CODC is the cost of debt capital, $i$ is the borrowing rate, and $TD$ is the corporate income tax rate. In the valuation mentioned above, we estimated the after-tax cost of debt capital at 9.7 percent (interest rates were relatively high). Of course, the benefit of debt financing is offset in incremental steps by the additional financial risk that the subject company assumes as it increases its debt as a percentage of total capital. Such financial risk drives up marginal borrowing costs.

*Weighted Average Cost of Capital.* The *weighted average cost of capital* (WACC) is the blended cost of equity and debt capital for the subject company. The weighting is based on the expected capital structure of equity and debt at their market, not book, values. In the valuation mentioned above we calculated the WACC as follows:

|                                   | Cost  | Weight | Weighted Amounts |
|-----------------------------------|-------|--------|------------------|
| Equity capital                    | 15.9% | 1/2    | 7.95%            |
| Debt capital                      | 9.7%  | 1/2    | 4.85%            |
| Weighted average cost of capital  |       |        | 12.80%           |

We weighted the components of the capital structure equally because we estimated that each had an equal market value. We assumed that the acquired company would have a debt-equity ratio of 2 to 1, and we estimated that the market value of the equity would be two times book (based on a market comparison method), whereas the market value of the debt would be its stated balance sheet value.

The WACC is usually used as the discount rate in the DCF analysis, because it represents the average cost of funds for the subject company. The WACC assumes that the capital structure includes debt and that the proportion of debt relative to equity at market values can be determined.

*Discount the Forecasted Cash Flows.* At this stage of the DCF analysis, you have identified the cash flows by year during the forecast period, estimated the terminal value of the subject company, and estimated the weighted average cost of capital. To arrive at the net present value of the subject company's total capital (debt and equity), you should now discount the cash flows and terminal value by the weighted average cost of capital. In our example, we used a discount rate of 13 percent. The discount factors are calculated as follows:

| Year | Formula | | Discount Factor |
|------|---------|---|-----------------|
| 1 | $1/1.13$ | $=$ | 0.885 |
| 2 | $1/(1.13)^2$ | $=$ | 0.783 |
| 3 | $1/(1.13)^3$ | $=$ | 0.693 |
| 4 | $1/(1.13)^4$ | $=$ | 0.613 |
| | (et cetera) | | |

You apply the discount factors to the appropriate cash flows and terminal value amount to obtain the present value of each annual cash flow. The net present value is the sum of the present values by period. In this example, for simplicity, we assume that cash would be received at year end. In practice, you should assume that cash flows are received throughout the year, so that on average the cash is received mid-year.

*Subtract Today's Borrowings.* The net present value of the cash flows and the terminal value amount represent the market value of the subject company's total capital (debt and equity). Since most businesses have some level of debt, you should subtract this debt to arrive at the value of the company to its owners. This is necessary because the claims of debtholders represent a stake in the value of the company that must be settled, in theory, before the owners can obtain value for their stake. The recorded amount of borrowings may approximate market value if the interest rate on debt represents current market rates. If the interest rate is not a market rate, the market value of the debt may differ from the recorded amount. (See Table 7–9 for an example of a DCF analysis).

### Nonoperating Assets

The DCF method allows you to estimate the value of the operating company based on its expected cash generating performance. The DCF method values only the operating entity. Assets that are not used in the operating entity accordingly are not valued through the DCF approach. Such assets provide additional value to the subject company above the DCF value. (Conversely, nonoperating liabilities detract from value.) Therefore, you should identify all nonoperating assets such as cash, marketable securities, unused land, buildings, plant and machinery, or an investment in another business not generating income. You should appraise these nonoperating assets and estimate their value. Add the cumulative amount to the DCF value to arrive at the value of the operating entity and the nonoperating assets.

As an aside, you should pay particular attention to businesses with significant real estate holdings.

### Advantages of the DCF Method

People normally buy goods, services, and property (tangible and intangible) for a future use or benefit (short-term or long-term) that they hope to derive. The value of the item is the amount we are willing to pay today for the future use of a product, service, or item of property. The DCF method values a company based on its future economic benefit to its owner. The owner of a business has at least four theoretical alternatives at any point in time: sell, hold, go public, or liquidate. The DCF method shows the seller the benefits (present value of surplus cash flows) of holding the company. Since a rational

**Table 7–9.** *Summary of discounted cash flow method: example (assume a 13% discount rate).[1]*

| Year | Cash Flow[2] | Discount Factor[3] | Present Value[4] | Cumulative Present Value |
|------|------|------|------|------|
| 1 | $ 500 | 0.885 | $ 442 | $ 442 |
| 2 | 700 | 0.783 | 548 | 990 |
| 3 | 700 | 0.693 | 485 | 1,475 |
| 4 | 800 | 0.613 | 491 | 1,966 |
| 5 | 800 | 0.543 | 434 | 2,400 |
| 6 | 900 | 0.480 | 432 | 2,832 |
| 7 | 1,000 | 0.425 | 425 | 3,257 |
| 8 | 1,000 | 0.376 | 376 | 3,633 |
| 9 | 1,200 | 0.333 | 399 | 4,032 |
| 10 | 1,400 | 0.295 | 412 | 4,444 |
| Residual Value | 10,800[5] | 0.295 | 3,181 | 7,625[6] |
| Less: Present Value of Debt Assumed[7] | | | | (1,000) |
| Add: Assets Not Required for Operations[8] | | | | 1,100 |
| Value of Equity | | | | $ 7,725 |

[1] See text page 258 for calculation of weighted average cost of capital.
[2] See Table 7–8 for summary of forecasted cash flows.
[3] This discount factor is based on the discount rate and the cash flow year. See text page 259 for calculation of discount factor. These numbers are rounded.
[4] The present value is the cash flow amount multiplied by the discount factor.
[5] We assume that the Year 10 cash flow will continue at that level forever. The present value of a perpetuity is the cash flow amount divided by the discount rate. In our example, the perpetuity is calculated as follows:

$$\frac{\$\ 1{,}400}{.13} = 10{,}800 \text{ (rounded)}$$

This amount represents the value of the business at the end of Year 10. We discount this amount by the Year 10 discount factor to obtain its present value as of today.
[6] This amount represents the value of the firm's total capital (equity and debt) based on its operating cash flows.
[7] See text page 259 for explanation.
[8] Additional value in business entity not reflected by the DCF value.

prospective purchaser can be expected to perform a similar analysis, the DCF method also helps the seller predict the approximate amount at which he or she can sell the company.

There are several reasons why the DCF method is used so frequently:

- The DCF method forces you to translate the future benefits from a business into hard dollars. Assurances of "strategic value" don't hold much weight unless such strategic value can be quantified. Corporate bidders must heed this point or they will surely overpay.

- The DCF value depends more on an understanding of the subject company than on swings in market conditions.

- Market methods often force the user to rely on market myopia—the tendency of the market to ignore distant horizons. The DCF method forces you to focus squarely on the future.

- You can consider the impact of the business cycle on the subject company's business and reflect the expected future stage of the business cycle in the DCF analysis.

- To develop realistic forecasts of the future you must thoroughly understand the business. This discipline can avoid casual bidding and the uncomfortable aftermath.

- The DCF method allows you to identify the expected surplus cash that may be used to service debt. In an age of leveraged buyouts, this is crucial.

- The DCF analysis may be used by both the buyer and the seller in their negotiations, as an effective way of resolving their differences and developing a deal structure that bridges the gap.

### Limitations of the DCF Method

- The DCF method is technically complex. Quick and dirty valuations are difficult.

- It is difficult to forecast with any degree of accuracy (economists who have spent their lives studying the present and past in order to predict the future have not had much success). Forecast accuracy is not a prerequisite to performing a DCF analysis, however. One can develop different operating scenarios and measure their impact on value.

- Certain key assumptions, such as the discount rate, the forecast growth rate, and capital requirements, can wildly alter DCF values. Forecast assumptions should be compared with past performances as a reasonableness check.

- Terminal values, when discounted back to the present, often contribute more than 50 percent of the total net present value. The terminal value represents the expected value of the business at the end of the forecast period. It is ironic that, in order to perform a DCF analysis, you must pretend that you can predict the value of the company five or ten years in the future!

- There is a subtle danger to the DCF method, especially for a purchaser who aggressively factors synergies into forecasts. If such a purchaser pays the DCF value, there is no further room for value creation. The DCF value, including synergies, should be thought of as the *maximum* price.

If you apply the DCF method with common sense and correctly use the DCF techniques, you will obtain insight into the company and its value.

## *RESTATED BALANCE SHEET METHOD*

The restated balance sheet method is also referred to as the net asset value method or the adjusted book value method. According to this method, the value of an operating business depends on its assets, less its liabilities, where each asset and liability is appraised at fair market value. The value of the subject company is assumed to be the sum of the individual assets restated to fair market value less the sum of the individual liabilities restated to fair market value.

The restated balance sheet method is important in many acquisitions because future depreciation expenses are estimated using the market values of the tangible and intangible assets as of the transaction date. The estimated depreciation expenses are used in the DCF method.

The restated balance sheet method can be pursued on a going-concern premise or a liquidation premise. In the going-concern premise, each asset is valued as part of a going concern on a continuing use basis, using a cost, income, and/or market approach. In a liquidation premise, each asset is valued as if it were to be sold today or in an orderly manner over a short period of time. The earning performance and viability of the subject company may determine which premise makes more sense. For example, if the company is consistently unprofitable, a liquidation premise looks more relevant in most cases. Our discussions focus on a going-concern premise.

This valuation method is particularly relevant for businesses where the market value or replacement value of certain significant assets differs from their stated balance sheet values. For example, a restated balance sheet method is relevant for a holding company with only a portfolio of marketable securities, a real estate partnership or S corporation, or a fleet of tugs and barges. Also, companies that rely on resources in the ground, or that have liquid, fast-turning assets, are often valued by using the restated balance sheet method.

### How to Apply the Restated Balance Sheet Method

The restated balance sheet method is simple in theory. You value each tangible and intangible asset separately and each liability separately. The difference between the assets (restated to market value) and liabilities (restated to market value) is deemed to be the value of the subject company. Valuing each asset and liability, however, can be cumbersome. You must value each asset and each liability at its fair market value using a cost, income, and/or market approach.

Table 7–10 shows a very simple example of a restated balance sheet for a residential apartment complex. Land and buildings, net of depreciation, represent 98 percent of the total assets recorded on the restated balance sheet. Land and buildings were appraised using replacement cost and income approaches.

**Table 7–10.**

GARDEN APARTMENTS, INC.
Restatement of Assets and Liabilities to Fair Market Value

| | Balance Sheet at December 31, 1988[1] | Adjustment to Reflect Appraised Value[2] | Adjusted Balance Sheet at December 31, 1988 |
|---|---|---|---|
| *Assets* | | | |
| Current Assets: | | | |
| Cash in Bank | $ 22,000 | | $ 22,000 |
| Fixed Assets: | | | |
| Land | $ 160,000 | | |
| Building | 1,470,000 | | |
| Total | 1,630,000 | | |
| Less: Accumulated Depreciation | 520,000 | | |
| Total Fixed Assets | 1,110,000 | 3,000,000 | 4,110,000[2] |
| Other Assets: | | | |
| Loan—Officers and Affiliates | 60,000 | | |
| Other Investments | 8,000 | | |
| Total Other Assets | 68,000 | | 68,000 |
| TOTAL ASSETS | $1,200,000 | | $4,200,000 |
| *Liabilities and Stockholders' Equity* | | | |
| Current Liabilities: | | | |
| Mortgage Payable | $ 45,000 | | |
| Taxes Payable | 1,000 | | 46,000 |
| Total Current Liabilities | 46,000 | | |
| Long-Term Liabilities: | | | |
| Mortgage Payable | 1,050,000 | | |
| Tenant Security | 84,000 | | |
| Total Long-Term Liabilities | 1,134,000 | | 1,134,000 |
| Stockholders' Equity: | | | |
| Capital Stock | 20,000 | | |
| Retained Earnings | 0 | | |
| Total Stockholders' Equity | 20,000 | 3,000,000 | 3,020,000[3] |
| TOTAL LIABILITIES AND STOCKHOLDERS' EQUITY | $1,200,000 | | $4,200,000 |

[1] From financial statements.
[2] From appraised report.
[3] Adjusted net asset value.

Cash and other assets represent the remaining 2 percent of adjusted assets. The mortgage on the property was deemed to be at market rates and terms, so that no restatement of liabilities was necessary. Accordingly, the adjustment of land and building to fair market value and the corresponding change in stockholders' equity were the only changes required to create a restated balance sheet. The example in Table 7–10 represents the simplest restated balance sheet scenario since the business had only one major asset, that is, real estate.

A more comprehensive example using a ready-mix concrete company is shown in Table 7–11. Assets are grouped under current assets, noncurrent assets, and property, plant, and equipment. Liabilities are grouped under current liabilities and long-term liabilities.

### Estimated Fair Market Value of Tangible Assets

Typically, current assets include cash, marketable securities, accounts and notes receivable, inventories, and prepaid expenses. We mention frequently used valuation methods for each tangible asset category below.

*Cash.* Cash is usually stated at fair market value on the books, so there are usually no adjustments needed.

*Marketable Securities.* These are valued at prices quoted on the valuation date. Sometimes this requires adjustments to recorded values on the books.

*Certificates of Deposit.* CDs, or equivalent instruments, are normally valued at their face value, less any penalties for early liquidation.

*Accounts and Notes Receivable.* The value of accounts and notes receivable is the present value of the expected collections. You must project the amounts and timing of the expected collections and discount this future stream of cash flows back to the present. The appraiser usually relies on past collection history and on an aged trial balance to project the collection cash flows. The discount rate should reflect the time value of money and the risk of noncollection. Accordingly, it would be appropriate to increase progressively the discount rate for older receivables.

*Inventories.* For a ready-mix concrete company, inventories include sand, gravel, and cement, as well as the ready-mix concrete and other supplies. Inventories should be valued at current replacement cost because it represents the cost of replacing the inventory today, which in turn represents its value today. However, there should be little difference between the replacement cost and historical cost of inventories (in the ready-mix example) when these inventories turn quickly. Inventory not used in business operations is often valued at scrap or liquidation value. An alternate way to value inventory is to compute the present value of the cash generated by selling today's inventory at rates consistent with historical inventory turns.

*Prepaid Expenses.* These expenses represent payments for services to be rendered in a future period, for example, prepaid rent, prepaid insurance, and prepaid utilities. For going concerns, prepaid expenses are normally valued at historical cost because it is a good indication of current value. If liquidation is assumed, prepaid expenses would not usually be valued at historical cost but at a much lesser amount, sometimes zero.

*Life Insurance Policy.* The policy is normally valued at its current cash surrender value because that is the amount which, in theory, could be obtained by the company if the policy were liquidated.

*Notes Receivable.* A discounted cash flow approach is often used to value notes receivable. If the note bears a market rate of interest, its recorded value on the books is usually a good indication of its fair market value.

*Land.* Undeveloped land is normally appraised using a market approach. This method compares the subject property to recent sales of similar properties. You express the price paid in similar transactions as a standard unit of measure, such as price per square foot, price per square meter, or price per acre. You then apply the market price per square foot or per square meter to the area of the subject property. Finally, adjustments are made to reflect the unique aspects of the subject property, such as zoning or demographics. In the example shown in Table 7–11, the current fair market value of the land was dramatically higher than its historical cost because the land was bought 20 years ago, and it has since become a suburb of a major residential area. The land is valued at its highest and best use.

*Buildings.* Buildings and improvements may be valued using a cost, income, and/or market approach. The cost approach, however, is often more appropriate when the building functions as an integral part of a business that is being valued under the premise of a going concern. Using the cost approach, all improved land is first appraised under the assumption that it is unimproved and vacant. Second, the improvements are appraised separately based on replacement cost estimates. Third, this combined value is reduced to reflect physical deterioration, functional obsolescence, technological obsolescence, and economic obsolescence.

*Machinery and Equipment.* These assets may be valued using a cost, income, and/or market approach. Again, because these assets usually serve as an integral part of the business being valued, the going-concern premise and the replacement cost approach are the most commonly used approaches.

First, estimates are made of the cost to replace all owned productive machinery and equipment. Second, the estimated replacement cost of each item of productive equipment is reduced by an allowance for physical deterioration, functional obsolescence, technological obsolescence, and economic obsolescence. The replacement cost of transportation equipment is appraised in a similar manner.

*Furniture and Fixtures.* These, too, may be valued using a cost, income, and/or market approach. The cost approach is the most commonly used. The first step requires an estimate

**Table 7–11.**

## READY MIX COMPANY
### Restatement of Assets and Liabilities to Fair Market Value

| | Balance Sheet at December 31, 1988[1] | Adjusted Balance Sheet at December 31, 1988[2] |
|---|---|---|
| *Assets* | | |
| Current assets: | | |
| Cash and marketable securities | $ 1,150,000 | $ 1,100,000 |
| Accounts and notes receivable | 4,070,000 | 3,600,000 |
| Inventories | 400,000 | 400,000 |
| Prepaid expenses | 200,000 | 200,000 |
| Total current assets | 5,820,000 | 5,300,000 |
| Cash surrender value of life insurance policy | 310,000 | 310,000 |
| Notes receivable, net of current portion | 200,000 | 200,000 |
| Property, plant, and equipment: | | |
| Land | 170,000 | 2,900,000 |
| Buildings | 570,000 | 1,400,000 |
| Machinery and equipment | 2,640,000 | 1,700,000 |
| Transportation equipment | 3,950,000 | 1,800,000 |
| Furniture and fixtures | 390,000 | 340,000 |
| Laboratory equipment | 20,000 | 20,000 |
| Fence | 30,000 | 30,000 |
| | 7,770,000 | |
| Less: accumulated depreciation and amortization | 5,000,000 | — |
| Total property, plant, and equipment | 2,770,000 | 8,190,000 |
| TOTAL ASSETS | $ 9,100,000 | $14,000,000 |
| *Liabilities and Stockholders' Equity* | | |
| Current liabilities: | | |
| Notes payable | $ 700,000 | $ 700,000 |
| Current installments of long-term debt | 300,000 | 300,000 |
| Accounts payable | 3,240,000 | 3,240,000 |
| Accrued expenses | 570,000 | 570,000 |
| Total current liabilities | 4,810,000 | 4,810,000 |
| Long-term debt, excluding current installments | 2,250,000 | 2,250,000 |
| Deferred income taxes | 1,040,000 | 700,000 |
| Total long-term liabilities | 3,290,000 | 2,950,000 |
| Stockholders' equity | 1,000,000 | 6,240,000[3] |
| TOTAL LIABILITIES AND STOCKHOLDERS' EQUITY | $ 9,100,000 | $14,000,000 |

[1] From audited financial statements of subject company.
[2] All assets and liabilities were appraised at fair market value.
[3] Adjusted stockholders' equity increased by $5,240,000 due to (a) a $520,000 reduction in current assets, (b) a $5,420,000 increase in property, plant, and equipment, and (c) a $340,000 reduction in deferred income taxes.

of the cost to replace office furniture, fixtures, computers, and other office equipment. Second, an allowance is deducted for all forms of obsolescence, including functional and technological.

### Estimated Fair Market Value of Intangible Assets

Typical intangible assets of a ready-mix concrete company include contracts in progress, client proposals outstanding, a trade name, a trained and assembled work force, management employment contracts, favorable supply contracts, going-concern value, and goodwill. Intangible assets often represent a sizable percentage of total net assets values and should be valued with care. We mention frequently used valuation methods for the following intangible asset categories.

*Contracts in Progress.* Client contracts are normally valued by discounting the expected incremental cash flow (surplus cash flows after all related expenditures) from each unfinished contract by a market risk-adjusted discount rate. The incremental cash flow from a contract is normally better (in percentage terms) than the average cash flows from the same project because most of the expenditures have already been incurred.

*Client Proposals Outstanding.* Client proposals represent bids for new work that has not been started. Some proposals may have been accepted by the client; most may be still in the client review process. Proposals are also valued using a DCF approach with the added complication that the appraiser must value each proposal as if it were a firm contract and then attach probabilities to each proposal based on the likelihood of its being accepted as a firm contract. For each proposal, you should consider the expected revenues from the contract and costs of the contract, the timing of revenues and costs, and an estimate of the probability of being awarded the contract.

*Trade Name or Trademark.* A firm may get business specifically because it has a recognized name in a market. Name recognition was probably developed over many years through promotions, advertising, and by consistently providing a quality product or service. Name recognition has an economic benefit that can be quantified. Many methods may be used to value a trade name or trademark. A common method is the "relief from royalty" approach. The value of a trade name or trademark using this method is the net present value of royalties avoided. The appraiser has to determine a royalty rate and a discount rate. Royalty rates are normally established as a percentage of the subject companies' revenues. The discount rate often used is the weighted average cost of capital. (See DCF method for discussion.) Another less used approach would be to estimate the cost to reproduce the current level of market awareness. To use this method, you would summarize promotional and advertising expenditures by year, going back for a number of years. This approach is more subjective than the "relief from royalty" approach.

*Assembled Work Force.* An assembled work force includes all full-time employees of the company. A trained work force of a profitable business is an intangible asset that should be valued. An assembled work force is often valued based on the cost to recruit and train a replacement work force of comparable quality and experience. In practice, it is necessary to review each employee's salary records and estimate the costs (recruiting, training, and the like) to replace that person. The costs could range upwards from 10 percent of the employee's annual salary.

*Management Employment Contracts.* Senior members of management are typically given employment contracts. One valuation method deems the fair market value of the employment contracts to be the difference between the current salary level and a "market" salary level over the remaining life of the employment contract. Another common valuation method is to estimate the replacement cost of this employee and value the employment contract as the benefit from deferring the cost of replacing the employee.

*Favorable Supply Contracts.* This term indicates that the company has supply terms (either in price or terms) better than the "market." Favorable supply contracts are frequently valued using a DCF method. The future economic benefits during the remaining contract period are discounted by a market, risk-adjusted rate of return. The DCF value is deemed to be the value of the supply contracts.

*Going-Concern Value.* This value represents the difference in price between buying an operating business with a history of profitability and starting the same business from scratch. In estimating the going-concern value, you must be careful not to include the costs and cash flows associated with other intangible assets such as trade names, client contracts and proposals, and assembled work force. The income approach is commonly used to estimate the going-concern value of a business. This approach has five steps:

1. Estimate the time and cash flows (negative and positive) associated with a hypothetical startup of the same business.
2. Discount those start-up cash flows during the estimated start-up period.
3. Identify the cash flows from the operating business for the same time period as the estimated startup.
4. Deduct a reasonable return for the tangible and other intangible assets used in the business and already valued.
5. Discount the cash flows of the operating entity after deducting a reasonable return for the other assets used in the business.

The going-concern value is the difference (over the start-up period) between the net present value of the cash flows from the operating entity and the net present value of the cash flows from the hypothetical startup.

*Goodwill.* Goodwill is an intangible asset not accounted for elsewhere. In a purchase price allocation, it is the difference between the acquisition price and the sum of the net tangible and intangible assets stated at current market values. Goodwill usually exists because a firm is highly profitable. To use this method, first value all other assets—tangible and intangible—

then subtract the sum from the acquisition price. The difference is goodwill.

### Estimated Fair Market Value of Liabilities

At this point you have restated all the company's assets to fair market value. The next step is to restate all liabilities to fair market value.

The fair market of a liability is the amount of money the debt issuer would have to pay to the debtholders today in order for the debtholders to terminate the liability immediately (instead of holding the paper until maturity). Remember, there may be prepayment penalties associated with prepayment of debt.

In our example of a restated balance sheet for a ready-mix concrete company, we grouped liabilities into current and long-term liabilities. The current liabilities include notes payable, current installments of long-term debt, accounts payable, and accrued expenses. You should determine the current value of each of these liability accounts. If these liabilities are payable in less than one year it would be reasonable to value them at their historical amounts, less some discount to reflect that certain of these accounts need not lead to cash outflows at once.

The non-interest-bearing liabilities due in less than one year would have a fair market value lower than historical amounts because the time value of money is working in the company's favor. For example, a liability due one year from now has a lower value than the same liability due today. Conversely, if the interest rate on the notes payable and the current installments of long-term debt is above comparable market rates, then the fair market value of these two liabilities would be higher than the principal outstanding. In practice, however, current liabilities are normally valued at their historical amounts.

*Long-Term Debt.* The current value of long-term debt is calculated by discounting the future cash flows from the payment of interest and the repayment of principal by a risk-adjusted rate, often determined by reference to market rates. If the interest rate (annual percentage rate) on the debt is lower than a market interest rate (based on similar risk and maturity), the fair market value of the debt is lower than the principal outstanding. The converse is also true.

*Deferred Income Taxes.* Such taxes represent obligations to pay taxes in the future that have already been recognized as an expense. The fair market value of deferred income taxes is calculated by discounting the expected payment of these taxes by a market rate of interest. Because deferred income obligations don't bear interest and may not be paid until some distant future time, their current market value will normally be much lower than the historical liability. Furthermore, the premise of the valuation (for example, liquidation vs. going concern) can dramatically affect how deferred taxes are both estimated and valued.

### Fair Market Value of Business

The fair market value of the equity ownership is the difference between the total assets (restated to fair market value) and total liabilities (restated to fair market value). This method assumes that the buyer purchases an entire ownership interest.

### Advantages of the Restated Balance Sheet Method

The advantages of the restated balance sheet method are the following:

- The restated balance sheet method is frequently chosen to value certain businesses such as a portfolio of marketable securities, a venture capital fund, a real estate partnership or S corporation, and broadcast properties (although the actual stations would be valued using a market and DCF approach, and these market values would then replace the recorded amounts of broadcast properties on the balance sheet).

- Asset-based lenders lean toward this method. A borrower is able to obtain cheaper financing on that part of the borrowing that is collateralized by tangible assets. A balance sheet stated at current market values facilitates the lender's decision on how much to lend based on the assets of the company and how much should be based on cash flow.

- The restated balance sheet method serves to allocate the purchase price for a business among its tangible and intangible assets and to support the allocation on economic grounds. This can be crucial for tax purposes. The depreciation expense based on the new asset values may be used in the DCF method.

- The tangible net asset value of a company (obtained through the restated balance sheet approach) shows a prospective buyer the level of downside risk.

- The owner of a business has at least four theoretical alternatives: sell, hold, go public, or liquidate. The restated balance sheet method, using a liquidation premise, can provide an estimate of the liquidation value of the company. In a liquidation scenario the intangible assets may have no value, receivables, inventories, and other tangible asset values may be less than book value. Liquidation expenses may also be incurred such as employee severance pay, selling expenses, transfer taxes, and other taxes. The appraiser would also have to consider the time value of money in the valuation because the liquidation would normally take place over a period of time.

### Limitations of the Restated Balance Sheet Method

- The restated balance sheet method has limited application because no consideration is given to the effect of total business profits or cash flow on business value.

- The method is cumbersome because different asset groups require vastly different methods of analysis.

- The net asset value of many service businesses is largely intangible. People assets, name recognition, and the like are often much harder to value than the assets shown on the balance sheet. In fact, the existence of intangibles in most businesses greatly complicates calculating net asset value.

## COMBINING VALUATION METHODS AND RESULTS

As was indicated earlier, it is a good idea to estimate the fair market value of a company in more than one way. After applying all the relevant valuation methods, you must decide how to combine all the results to obtain one value for the subject company. Weigh the resulting values based on your judgment as to which method (in this particular situation) provides the most reliable estimate of value. It would be nice if all valuation methods used resulted in similar values, but this does not happen frequently. Try to determine why you are obtaining disparate values, and in the process you will likely understand which method is a more reliable indication of value. See Table 7–12 for an example of a rational approach to selecting one valuation method over another.

**Table 7–12.**

SPECIALTY CHEMICALS, INC.

Summary of Values of Specialty Chemicals, Inc. at September 23, 1988

| | |
|---|---|
| Estimated value based on selected public companies[1] | $ 89,800,000 |
| Estimated value based on selected acquisitions[2] | $ 85,000,000 |
| Estimated value based on most comparable acquisition[3] | $101,100,000 |
| Estimated value based on pending acquisition[4] | $ 93,800,000 |
| Estimated range of values[5]: $85,000,000 to $95,000,000 | |

---

[1] See Table 7–1 for determination of value.
[2] See Table 7–3 for determination of value.
[3] See Table 7–4 for determination of value.
[4] See Table 7–6 for determination of value.
[5] In developing our overall opinion of value, we have placed most emphasis on the value derived from the selected public companies because: (a) we relied on eight public companies, as a group, to develop value (not one or four), (b) we applied nine different capital multiples (not four or five) which resulted in very similar values, (c) we used public market prices as of September 23, 1988 to calculate capital multiples (not prices in 1986 and 1987), (d) we selected public companies in the specialty chemical business with consistent profitability, (e) we applied a control premium lower than the industry average which reflected our opinion that Specialty Chemicals, Inc. has less value enhancement opportunities than the average public company being acquired in its industry.

In general, the market comparison method, using prices paid for publicly traded shares, and the discounted cash flow (DCF) method are relevant in nearly every situation. As a buyer, you may wish to place more emphasis on the DCF method if it yields a lower value than the market approach, because it suggests that the subject company's surplus cash flows are expected to grow at a slower rate than those of the public companies (or the market approach overvalues the company). Therefore, the subject company should not be valued at the same multiples as the public companies.

The other market comparison methods, using prices paid in reported acquisitions and in IPOs, are normally weighted less heavily than the methods mentioned above. The restated balance sheet method is relevant only in special situations (such as a portfolio of marketable securities, a venture capital fund, a real estate partnership or S corporation, resource companies, and companies with liquid, fast-turning assets).

While the market comparison method, using prices paid for publicly traded shares, and the DCF method may be used in most cases, certain situations may make one method more relevant than another. For example, the market comparison method would be more relevant if the subject company had little or no surplus cash flow in the business. The DCF method would be key if the prospective buyer was going to borrow heavily based on the cash flows and assets of the subject company.

The reported acquisitions method would be more relevant if comparable transactions existed and if other methods were not available. The IPO method would be relevant if comparables existed and you intended to use the valuation analysis to develop an estimated IPO price for the subject company.

Each of the three approaches (market, income, and cost) is not as separate and distinct as described in this chapter. In practice, information from one approach is frequently used in another. For example, the restated balance sheet method effectively provides a postacquisition balance sheet from which depreciation expenditures can be accurately projected and used in the DCF method. Likewise, the DCF method may use certain market multiples to estimate the residual value of the firm at the end of the forecast period. A hypothetical leveraged buyout price may also be estimated using the criteria applied by certain LBO lenders and the financial information developed in the restated balance sheet method and the DCF method.

## *POSTSCRIPT*

The fair market value of a company is constantly changing. Consider, for instance, the recent history of the stock market. Between 1982 and 1987 the Dow Jones Industrial Average (Dow) exploded from 800 to an all-time high of 2,722 in August 1987. The great bull market of the 1980s ended five years after it had started. On October 19, 1987, the Dow closed at 1,739 having lost 508 points in one day. On February 7, 1989, the Dow closed at 2,347, a new post-crash high as of the date of this writing, regaining all the lost ground of the October 19, 1987 crash. Stock market history nevertheless suggests that the crash of 1987 is the first stage of a severe bear market.

# APPENDIX 7-A:
## Definition of Equity Multiples

We list and define 15 equity multiples that you may consider in performing a valuation analysis. In each multiple, price or market value is defined as price per share multiplied by the total number of common shares outstanding. However, if you intend to rely on more than the current 12 months' performance (as we suggest) as a determinant of value and if the number of shares outstanding has changed during the past five years, multiples should be calculated on a per-share basis instead of an aggregate basis. Per-share calculations in prior years should be based on the average number of shares outstanding during the year as reported on the 10K. This procedure eliminates the distortion resulting from dividing the market value of a company's current equity capital by reported earnings of five years ago perhaps generated by half the current equity capital. In short, if the common shares outstanding of a selected publicly traded company have substantially increased during the past five years, the three-year and five-year price multiples calculated in aggregate based on current price and shares outstanding will be erroneously overstated. Accordingly, you should develop three-year and five-year price multiples based on per-share data. The 15 equity multiples are defined below:

1. Price-Revenues = Price per share divided by most recent 12 months' revenues per share. The total number of shares outstanding may be obtained from the first page of the 10K or 10Q, or from the S&P *Stock Guide.* The stock price should be a recent quotation. This multiple can also be calculated using aggregate data if the number of shares outstanding has not changed during the last 12 months.

2. Price–Current 12 months' earnings = Price per share divided by most recent 12 months' earnings (after tax) per share. Earnings should exclude extraordinary and nonrecurring items. Earnings should also be adjusted if the company paid below or above normal tax rates. This multiple can also be calculated using aggregate data if the number of shares outstanding has not changed during the last 12 months.

3. Price–Recent fiscal year earnings = Price per share divided by latest fiscal year earnings (after tax) per share. Earnings per share should be calculated using the average number of common shares outstanding during the latest fiscal year. Earnings should exclude extraordinary and nonrecurring items and be adjusted for below or above normal tax rates.

4. Price–3-year average earnings = Price per share divided by average earnings (after tax) per share for the past three fiscal years. Earnings per share should be calculated on a fiscal year basis using the average number of common shares outstanding during a particular fiscal year. Earnings should exclude extraordinary and nonrecurring

items and be adjusted for below or above normal tax rates.

5. Price–5-year average earnings

= Price per share divided by average earnings (after tax) per share for the past five fiscal years. Earnings per share should be calculated on a fiscal year basis as described above. Earnings should exclude extraordinary and nonrecurring items and be adjusted for below or above normal tax rates.

6. Price–Current 12 months' pretax cash flow

= Price per share divided by the sum of (a) pretax earnings per share and (b) depreciation and amortization per share, for the most recent 12 months. Earnings should exclude extraordinary and nonrecurring items. This multiple can also be calculated using aggregate data. Depreciation and amortization should be obtained from the statement of changes in financial position.

7. Price–Recent fiscal year pretax cash flow

= Price per share divided by the sum of (a) pretax earnings per share and (b) depreciation and amortization per share, for the latest fiscal year. Earnings per share should be calculated using the average number of common shares outstanding during the latest fiscal year. Earnings should exclude extraordinary and nonrecurring items. Depreciation and amortization should be obtained from the statement of changes in financial position.

8. Price–3-year average pretax cash flow

= Price per share divided by average pretax cash flow (as defined above) per share for the past three fiscal years. Cash flow per share should be calculated on a fiscal year basis using the average number of common shares outstanding during a particular fiscal year. Cash flow should exclude extraordinary and nonrecurring items.

9. Price–5-year average pretax cash flow

= Price per share divided by average pretax cash flow (as defined above) per share for the past five fiscal years. Cash flow per share should be calculated on a fiscal year basis as described above.

10. Price–Current 12 months' posttax cash flow

= Price per share divided by the sum of (a) earnings (after tax) per share and (b) depreciation and amortization per share, for the most recent 12 months. Earnings should exclude extraordinary and non-recurring items. Depreciation and amor-tization should be obtained from the statement of changes in financial posi-tion. This multiple can also be calcu-lated using aggregate data.

11. Price–Recent fiscal year posttax cash flow

= Price per share divided by the sum of (a) earnings (after tax) per share and (b) depreciation and amortization per share, for the latest fiscal year. Earnings per share should be calculated using the av-erage number of common shares out-standing during the latest fiscal year. Earnings should exclude extraordinary and nonrecurring items. Depreciation and amortization should be obtained from the statement of changes in finan-cial position.

12. Price–3-year average posttax cash flow

= Price per share divided by average post-tax cash flow (as defined above) per share, for the past three fiscal years. Cash flow per share should be calculated on a fiscal year basis using the average number of common shares outstanding during a particular fiscal year. Cash flow should exclude extraordinary and non-recurring items.

13. Price–5-year average posttax cash flow

= Price per share divided by average post-tax cash flow (as defined above) per share, for the past five fiscal years. Cash flow per share should be calculated on a fiscal year basis using the average number of common shares outstanding during a particular fiscal year. Cash flow should exclude extraordinary and non-recurring items.

14. Price–Tangible book value

= Price per share divided by tangible book value per share. Tangible book value excludes intangible assets such as goodwill. The book value amount should be obtained from the most recent balance sheet. This multiple can also be calculated using aggregate data.

15. Price–Tangible total assets

= Price per share divided by tangible total assets per share. Total assets should be obtained from the most recent balance sheet. This multiple can also be calculated using aggregate data.

# APPENDIX 7–B:
## Definition of Total Capital Multiples

We list and define 11 total capital multiples that you may consider in performing a valuation analysis:

1. Total capital–
   Revenues
   = Price per share plus long-term debt and short-term debt per share, divided by most recent 12 months' revenues per share. This multiple can also be calculated using aggregate data. The total number of shares outstanding may be obtained from the first page of the 10K or 10Q, or from the S&P *Stock Guide.* The stock price should be a recent quotation. Long-term debt and short-term debt should be obtained from the most recent balance sheet.

2. Total capital–
   Current
   12 months'
   EBIT
   = Price per share plus long-term debt and short-term debt per share, divided by most recent 12 months' earnings before interest and taxes (EBIT) per share. EBIT should exclude extraordinary and non-recurring items. This multiple can also be calculated using aggregate data. Long-

term debt and short-term debt should be obtained from the most recent balance sheet.

3. Total capital–
Recent
fiscal year
EBIT

= Price per share plus long-term debt and short-term debt per share, divided by latest fiscal year earnings before interest and taxes (EBIT) per share. EBIT should exclude extraordinary and nonrecurring items. This multiple can also be calculated using aggregate data. Long-term debt and short-term debt should be obtained from the most recent balance sheet.

4. Total capital–
3-year average
EBIT

= Price per share plus long-term debt and short-term debt per share, divided by average earnings before interest and taxes (EBIT) per share for the past three fiscal years. EBIT per share should be calculated on a fiscal year basis using the average number of common shares outstanding during a particular fiscal year. EBIT should exclude extraordinary and nonrecurring items. Long-term debt and short-term debt should be obtained from the most recent balance sheet.

5. Total capital–
5-year average
EBIT

= Price per share plus long-term debt and short-term debt per share, divided by average earnings before interest and taxes (EBIT) per share for the past five fiscal years. EBIT per share should be calculated on a fiscal year basis using the average number of common shares outstanding during a particular fiscal year. EBIT should exclude extraordinary and nonrecurring items. Long-term debt and short-term debt should be obtained from the most recent balance sheet.

6. Total capital–    = Price per share plus long-term debt and
   Current             short-term debt per share, divided by
   12 months'          the sum of (a) earnings before interest
   EBIT Cash           and taxes (EBIT) per share and (b) de-
   Flow                preciation and amortization per share,
                       for the most recent 12 months. This
                       multiple can also be calculated using
                       aggregate data. Depreciation and amor-
                       tization should be obtained from the
                       statement of changes in financial posi-
                       tion. EBIT should exclude extraordinary
                       and nonrecurring items. Long-term debt
                       and short-term debt should be obtained
                       from the most recent balance sheet.

7. Total capital–    = Price per share plus long-term debt and
   Recent fiscal       short-term debt per share divided by the
   year EBIT           sum of (a) earnings before interest and
   Cash Flow           taxes (EBIT) per share, and (b) depre-
                       ciation and amortization per share, for
                       the latest fiscal year. This multiple can
                       also be calculated using aggregate data.
                       Depreciation and amortization should
                       be obtained from the statement of
                       changes in financial position. EBIT
                       should exclude extraordinary and non-
                       recurring items. Long-term debt and
                       short-term debt should be obtained from
                       the most recent balance sheet.

8. Total capital–    = Price per share plus long-term debt and
   3-year average      short-term debt per share divided by
   EBIT Cash           average cash flow (as defined above) per
   Flow                share, for the past three fiscal years. Cash
                       flow per share should be calculated on
                       a fiscal year basis using the average num-
                       ber of common shares outstanding dur-
                       ing a particular fiscal year. Cash flow
                       should exclude extraordinary and non-
                       recurring items. Long-term debt and

short-term debt should be obtained from the most recent balance sheet.

9. Total capital– 5-year average EBIT Cash Flow

= Price per share plus long-term debt and short-term debt per share divided by average cash flow (as defined above) per share, for the past five fiscal years. Cash flow per share should be calculated on a fiscal year basis using the average number of common shares outstanding during a particular fiscal year. Cash flow should exclude extraordinary and non-recurring items. Long-term debt and short-term debt should be obtained from the most recent balance sheet.

10. Total capital– Tangible book value plus debt

= Price per share plus long-term debt and short-term debt per share divided by the sum of (a) tangible book value per share and (b) long-term debt and short-term debt per share. Long-term debt and short-term debt should be obtained from the most recent balance sheet. This multiple can also be calculated using aggregate data. Tangible book value excludes intangible assets such as goodwill.

11. Total capital– Tangible total assets

= Price per share plus long-term debt and short-term debt per share divided by tangible total assets per share. This multiple can also be calculated using aggregate data. Long-term debt and short-term debt should be obtained from the most recent balance sheet.

# APPENDIX 7-C:
## Specialty Chemical, Inc.
## Control Premium and Illiquidity Discount

After applying the appropriate total capital multiples to SCI and weighting the resulting values to obtain an overall estimate of value, we adjusted our estimate to reflect differences between owning 100 percent of a private company and owning a minority position in a public company. By determining a value based on multiples derived from stock prices of publicly traded firms, the value relies on prices paid for small numbers of shares rather than for the whole firm. There are two valuation differences between valuing a controlling interest in a private company and using multiples developed from prices paid for publicly traded shares: control premium and illiquidity discount.

## CONTROL PREMIUM

A control premium represents the difference in price per share between ownership of 100 percent of the common stock and ownership of a minority (noncontrolling) interest in the company. The control premium represents the additional price one must pay to control the company. An owner of a company has the power to change the nature of the business, its cost structure, its management, its policy on dividends, capital in-

vestments, and capital structure. The owner also has the power to sell or liquidate the company or any part of it, or to go public. Generally, a holder of a minority interest has none of these powers.

According to W.T. Grimm & Co., a recognized source of statistical data on merger and acquisition transactions, the average premium paid over market price during 1987 was consistent with the range of the past several years, an average of 38.3 percent and a median of 30.8 percent, based on 237 transactions in which price was disclosed and premiums were paid.

Grimm correctly points out, however, that premiums are skewed by a lack of distinction between the three quarters prior to the stock market crash and the one quarter subsequent to the crash. As prices declined after the crash, premiums rose significantly, but the higher fourth-quarter premiums were offset by relatively lower premiums during the first three quarters— especially in the third quarter.

For 1987, Grimm reported an average percent premium paid over market of 28.6 percent for the chemicals, paints, and coatings industry based on two transactions with reported premiums. For the six months ended June 30, 1988, Grimm maintains that the premium was 26.6 percent for the same industry based on six transactions with reported premiums. Premiums for all transactions during the first six months of 1988 were 43.3 percent based on 206 transactions with reported premiums.

Many improvements have been made to SCI since its acquisition. Operating expenses are generally lower and changes have been made to reduce corporate expense as well. The company has also been restructured.

Based on our understanding of SCI with respect to its operations and in relation to other companies and the current economic situation, we applied a 20-percent control premium. This premium is lower than the market median both for the industry and the market as a whole. We believe that many of the efficiency and restructuring opportunities that can be applied to a newly acquired company, and which are intrinsic in the control premium, have already been reflected in the 1987 and

12 months ended June 30, 1988 financial statements, although not in the prior four years (1983–1986). Thus, SCI has fewer enhancement opportunities than most public companies that are currently being acquired.

Also reflected in the control premium is our understanding that SCI's expected financial performance from fiscal 1988 may be similar to fiscal 1987, while industry analysts project 11-percent growth in net earnings for the industry for fiscal 1988 over 1987.

## ILLIQUIDITY DISCOUNT

As we have stated, the main difference between SCI and the selected public company is that SCI is not public. Many of the public firms are of similar size and, like SCI, have been consistently profitable. However, their equity bases are different.

Equity shares in a privately held company are not as marketable and are worth less than if those shares were publicly traded. Therefore, we have applied an illiquidity discount to the value derived based on prices paid for comparable companies whose shares are publicly traded.

We have estimated that SCI could go public through an initial public offering at a cost of 10 percent of the offering price. Accordingly, we have reflected a 10-percent illiquidity discount in our valuation analysis to account for the value differential between SCI and the selected public companies. An illiquidity discount can also be viewed as the cost (transaction cost and return foregone) to turn assets (tangible and intangible) into cash.

# APPENDIX 7-D:
## Specialty Chemical, Inc.
### Description of Comparable Acquired Companies and the Selection Process

We conducted a search for comparable companies with a specialty chemical orientation with similar earnings and growth trends that were recently acquired.

Our search involved reviewing publicly available financial and operational information of comparable companies whose acquisitions were reported in one of five recognized sources of merger and acquisition data. These sources and the periods for which the search was performed are listed below:

- *Securities Data M&A Database* (for previous 18 months)
  —SIC Codes:
    - —2851    Paints, Varnishes, Lacquers, Enamels, and Allied Products
    - —2893    Printing Ink
    - —2895    Carbon Black
    - —2899    Chemicals and Chemical Preparations Not Elsewhere Classified

- The 1987 and 1988 *Yearbooks on Corporate Mergers, Joint Ventures and Corporate Policy*
  —Section:
    - —28    Chemicals, Pharmaceuticals

- *Mergers and Corporate Policy,* 1986
  —Section:
    —28      Chemicals, Pharmaceuticals
- *Mergers & Acquisitions,* 1986–1988
  —Section:
    —28      Chemicals, Pharmaceuticals
- W.T. Grimm, 1986 and 1987

From these sources we identified eight acquisitions for our review. After preliminary analysis we identified four companies with similar financial characteristics. One company, Pentech Corp. (Pentech), had marked similarities to SCI and we applied the multiples of Pentech to SCI as a separate analysis (Table 7–4). The four companies and their acquisitions are described below.

### Omnicron Holdings, Inc. (Omnicron)

On December 23, 1986 PD Carbon Co., a wholly owned subsidiary of Phelps Dodge Corp., acquired all the outstanding capital stock of Omnicron for approximately $250 million.

Omnicron's primary asset is a 100-percent interest in Columbian Chemicals Co. (CCC). CCC owns and operates, either directly or indirectly, 11 carbon black and two iron oxide plants in the United States and abroad.

CCC's earnings from operations for the nine months ending September 30, 1986 were $14,529,000 on revenues of $230,025,000. Stockholders' equity, long-term debt (including current portion), and total assets were $138,607,000, $19,350,000, and $241,330,000, respectively. For financial data of Omnicron see Appendix 7–E. Both companies are headquartered in New York, NY.

### Pentech Corporation (Pentech)

On December 30, 1986 Pentech sold all of the shares of Pentech Chemicals, Inc. and QO Chemicals, Inc. (the Companies) to Great Lakes Chemical Corporation for $121 million plus debt assumed of $25 million. The Companies manufacture furfural (an aldehyde) from agricultural waste materials, which is then used as a base to manufacture furfuryl alcohol and other specialty products. The Companies employ approximately 440 people.

Earnings for the year ended March 31, 1986 were $11,053,000 on revenue of $107,972,000. Total assets, stockholders' equity, and long-term debt (including the current portion) at December 31, 1986 were $63,955,000, $18,172,000, and $25,261,000, respectively. For financial data of Pentech see Appendix 7–E.

The Pentech Corporation's headquarters are located in Oak Brook, IL. Great Lakes Chemical Corp. is headquartered in West Lafayette, IN.

### Reichhold Chemicals, Inc. (Reichhold)

On June 25, 1987 DIC Holdings Corp., a wholly owned subsidiary of Dainippon Ink and Chemicals, Inc., commenced a successful tender offer for all outstanding stock of Reichhold for approximately $532 million plus debt assumed of $109 million.

Reichhold manufactures adhesives and polymers primarily for the adhesives, paper chemicals, coatings, and plastics market. The company operates 59 plants internationally.

For the year ended December 31, 1986 net earnings were $15,859,000 on revenues of $765,588,000. Total assets, stockholders' equity, and long-term debt (including the current portion) were $458,446,000, $196,087,000, and $98,127,000, respectively. For further financial information see Appendix 7–E.

Reichhold's headquarters are in White Plains, NY. Dainippon Ink and Chemicals, Inc. is headquartered in Tokyo, Japan.

### Uniroyal Chemical Co. (Uniroyal)

On October 30, 1986 Avery, Inc., through several holding companies, acquired from Uniroyal, Inc., all issued and outstanding shares of Uniroyal for $710,000,000, plus debt assumed of $12 million.

Uniroyal is in the business of manufacturing specialty chemicals and polymers.

Earnings for the 12 months ended September 30, 1986 were $44,855,000 on revenues of $562,315,000. Total assets, stockholders' equity, and long-term debt (including the current portion) were $424,052,000, $322,359,000, and $5,216,000, respectively. For further financial data see Appendix 7–E.

Uniroyal's headquarters are in Middlebury, CT. Avery, Inc.'s headquarters are in New York, NY.

# APPENDIX 7-E

## SPECIALTY CHEMICAL, INC.
### Financial Data of Comparable Acquisitions ($000)

| Financial Data | Omnicron Holdings, Inc. | Pentech Corp.[8] | Reichhold Chemicals, Inc. | Uniroyal Chemical, Inc. |
|---|---|---|---|---|
| Operating Income Before Taxes | $ 34,351[1] | $ 12,285 | $ 28,831 | $ 84,746 |
| Other Income | | 1,795 | | |
| Less: Taxes | 14,979[1] | 3,027 | 12,972 | 39,891 |
| After Tax Income | 19,372[1] | 11,053 | 15,859 | 44,855 |
| Interest Expense | 3,148[1] | 2,370 | 14,314 | 1,737 |
| EBIT[7] | 37,499[1] | 16,450 | 43,145 | 86,483 |
| Depreciation | 14,645[1] | 416 | 21,517 | 17,184[5] |
| Cash Flow (Before Int. and Tax) | 52,144[1] | 16,866 | 64,662 | 103,667 |
| Revenue | 306,700[1] | 115,863 | 765,588 | 562,315 |
| Total Assets | 241,330 | 63,955 | 458,446 | 424,052 |
| Stockholders' Equity | 138,607 | 18,172 | 196,087 | 322,359 |
| Long-Term Debt | 14,540 | 25,261 | 92,942 | 3,732 |
| Short-Term Debt | 4,810 | — | 16,356 | 8,116 |
| Tangible Book Value | 138,607 | 18,172 | 163,942 | 322,359 |
| Total Capital | 157,957 | 43,433 | 305,385 | 334,207 |
| Purchase Price (Equity and Debt) | 250,000[2] | 146,261[3] | 641,692[4] | 721,848[6] |

[1] Represents annualized amount based on nine months ended December 31, 1986.
[2] $60mm cash; $180 million note, $10 million of assumed debt.
[3] $121mm in cash plus debt of 25.261 million.
[4] $532,394 in cash plus debt of $109,298.
[5] Annualized amount based on depreciation for nine months ended 9/28/86.
[6] $710mm in cash plus assumption of debt of $11,848.
[7] EBIT is the sum of operating and other income before taxes and interest expense.
[8] For Pentech we used data from the year ended March 31, 1986 for earnings data and information from the year ended December 31, 1986 for the revenue and balance sheet purposes. We believe that these numbers are most indicative of continuing operations.

Chapter **8**

# Tax Aspects of Acquisitions

*Paul Broderick*
Christian, Barton, Epps, Brent & Chappell
Richmond, Virginia

The business community is now adjusting to Congress' major overhaul of the rules under which businesses are acquired and disposed of. It is important to remember that Congress had no intention and made no attempt to stop the way companies do business. The Congress changed the rules primarily to impose additional taxes on regular corporations as well as to limit transactions undertaken solely for tax avoidance purposes. Tax revenue slippage was what Congress was trying to change, not the form of transactions. In general, the forms of acquisitions and dispositions with which businesspeople are familiar remain the same. The tax treatment, however, can vary significantly from the tax treatment of earlier transactions.

## HOW THE 1986 TAX REFORM ACT (TRA)* AFFECTED MERGERS AND ACQUISITIONS

### General Utilities

Throughout discussions on the TRA, the term *General Utilities* has become a household word. *General Utilities* was the name of a case decided by the U.S. Supreme Court, which

---

*As modified by the Technical and Miscellaneous Revenue Act of 1988 (TAMRA).

held that a corporation recognizes no gain or loss when it distributes appreciated assets. Congress later added the *General Utilities* doctrine to the Internal Revenue Code (the Code). Congress went beyond *General Utilities,* however, by adopting separate rules for corporations that distributed their assets to either corporate or noncorporate shareholders.

Absent special liquidation treatment, a corporation would have recognized gain on appreciated property that it either sold or distributed to its shareholders, just as if it sold the property. Thus, prior to the 1986 TRA, no gain or loss was recognized by the liquidating corporation on the distribution of appreciated property (Section 336). This rule applied to sales of property in the case of a 12-month liquidation (Section 337), as well as to distributions to shareholders or noncorporate entities in special one-month liquidations (Section 333). The shareholders, however, generally had to recognize gain on the difference between their cost (tax basis) in the stock and the fair market value (FMV) of property or amount of cash that they received in exchange for their stock.

The tax treatment of liquidating corporations has now been changed. Corporations must now recognize gain or loss on the distribution of inventory, capital goods, or investment property to shareholders in complete liquidation just as if the assets were sold for FMV. The amount of gain recognized may be even more if the amount of liabilities assumed by the shareholder, or to which the distributed assets are subject, exceeds the FMV of the distributed assets. With the expiration in 1988 of virtually all of the "Transitional Rules," a corporation must now recognize gain or loss regardless of its size and regardless of whether it distributes the property in kind or sells it and distributes the proceeds.

With one exception, the shareholders are treated the same as under prior law. Under the old regime, despite nonrecognition of gain or loss at the corporate level, the shareholders were subject to gain or loss when the assets were distributed. Regardless of whether the shareholders actually paid tax, they received the distributed property with a stepped-up or fair-market-value tax basis. The result of a stepped-up basis was larger individual income tax deductions for depreciation and depletion and a higher basis for recognition of gain if later sold

by the distributee. A distribution in liquidation was distinguishable under prior law from a post–1986 TRA distribution by
the fact that the shareholder receiving a liquidating distribution
under prior law was generally taxed at favorable capital gains
rates. Although the capital gains mechanism remains, that distinction has now been eliminated with the abolition of the
preferential tax rates for capital gains.

*Stock and Asset Acquisitions Affected.* Also gone with the
TRA are some familiar techniques for maximizing the nonrecognition rules. One familiar technique was the 12-month liquidation. Under those rules, a corporation that sold its assets
after adopting a plan of liquidation recognized no gain or loss
on the sale of its assets and the distribution of the proceeds,
so long as the distribution occurred within a 12-month period.
At the shareholder level, the proceeds were taxed at capital
gains rates. As with other types of liquidations, the shareholders
received any unsold assets with a stepped-up basis.

The 1982 amendments to the Code brought Section 338
with them. Section 338 made famous a type of liquidation that
had essentially been in the Code for years. A Section 338
purchase is well known as an acquisition technique. Under the
technique, if a corporation purchased at least 80 percent of the
stock of another corporation and made a timely election, the
effect was to step up the basis of the assets of the acquired
corporation. The step-up could be accomplished without liquidating the acquired corporation. Section 338 was based on a
fictional transaction under which the acquired corporation was
deemed to have sold its assets to itself in a 12-month liquidation,
thus recognizing no gain or loss on the hypothetical sale. The
only cost to the acquired corporation was in the form of
depreciation and other types of recapture. Net operating loss
carryforwards (NOLs) of the acquired corporation could be used
to offset the income on the deemed liquidation. Any remaining
NOLs or other tax attributes were lost. The effect which the
*General Utilities* repeal had on Section 338 purchases was that
the deemed sale of assets of the target corporation was no longer
eligible for tax-free treatment due to the repeal of the 12-month

liquidation rules. As a result, the usefulness of the Section 338 purchase technique has been severely limited.

Another type of liquidation that was eliminated by the *General Utilities* repeal was the one-month liquidation. Corporations and shareholders can no longer escape gain recognition through the distribution of corporate assets within one calendar month. This technique had been extremely useful for corporations with appreciated property whose shareholders wished to eliminate the corporate structure. For example, real estate held in a corporation, which could formerly be transferred tax free to a partnership, will now be taxed as if sold by the corporation.

One type of liquidation which has generally retained its tax-free status is the complete liquidation of subsidiary corporations (Section 332). Generally, if a corporation distributes all of its assets to its 100-percent corporate shareholder, the distributing corporation continues to recognize no gain or loss on the distribution. On the other side of the equation, the parent corporation receives the assets with the same tax basis (carryover basis) that the liquidating subsidiary had. Gain is not recognized until the distributed property is sold to an outsider. In order for the tax-free liquidation of a subsidiary rule to apply, the distributee corporate shareholder must own stock representing at least 80 percent of the total voting power and 80 percent of the total value of the stock of the liquidating corporation.

The rules are different for distributions to less-than-100% shareholders in liquidation. So long as assets are distributed to an 80-percent corporate shareholder, the distributing corporation recognizes no gain or loss on those assets and the 80-percent corporate shareholder takes them with a carryover basis. Gain or loss is recognized, however, to the distributing corporation on the assets going to less-than-80% shareholders who take those assets with a stepped-up basis.

A special rule applies when the 80-percent shareholder is a tax-exempt organization. The nonrecognition rule does not apply if the organization uses the assets in an activity which is not subject to tax. Congress' intent was to allow tax-free treatment where the tax-exempt organization uses the distributed property in an activity that is subject to unrelated business income tax. An entity that begins to use the distributed assets in an unrelated business and then converts their use to an exemption function is subject to tax at that time. Also, the tax exemption for liquidation of 80%-or-more subsidiaries does not apply when the 80%-or-more corporate shareholder is a foreign corporation. In order to avoid inequity in the case of a distribution to a foreign corporation in a taxable liquidation, TAMRA has a provision which gives the foreign parent corporation a stepped-up basis in the former subsidiary's assets.

Although distributions to 80%-or-more corporate shareholders exempt the distributing corporation from gain or loss recognition, a distribution in liquidation by a less-than-100% subsidiary results in nonrecognition of gain or loss only on the property actually distributed to the 80-percent corporate shareholder. Assume, for example, that an 80-percent subsidiary has two assets, one with a value of $8,000 and a tax basis of $7,000, and another asset with a value of $2,000 and a basis of $1. If it distributes the first asset to its 80-percent corporate shareholder and the smaller asset to the minority shareholder in liquidation, it avoids the $1,000 gain on the distribution of the larger asset but recognizes in full gain of $1,999 on the distribution of the smaller asset. No losses are ever allowed to be recognized in a liquidation where the corporate shareholder acquires the assets with a carryover basis.

As noted, the amount of gain to be recognized in a complete liquidation may be increased if a shareholder assumes a liability in liquidation or the corporation distributes property subject to a liability to the extent such liabilities exceed the FMV of the distributed assets. In addition, although built-in losses are generally permitted to offset built-in gains recognized on a liquidating distribution, losses are generally not available on certain distributions to related persons. The term *related person* includes an individual and a corporation, more than 50 percent of the stock of which is owned directly or indirectly (for example, through family ownership, a fiduciary of a trust or a beneficiary, a corporation, and a commonly owned partnership). Capital loss on corporate assets distributed to such shareholders can be disallowed if the distribution is not pro rata or the property distributed is disqualified property. That term includes property that was transferred to the distributing corporation within the preceding five years in a transaction in which the basis of the property was carried over to the corporation. This would occur on the transfer of property to an 80-percent controlled corporation (Section 351) or upon a contribution to capital. This limitation was intended to prevent threshold contributions of property, that would generate a loss if sold, made to circumvent the *General Utilities* repeal by taking advantage of such built-in loss.

A related rule prohibits the recognition of loss on any distribution of property that was acquired by the liquidating corporation as part of a plan to recognize a loss in the liquidation or sale. A prohibited plan is assumed under the Code if the property was acquired within two years of the adoption of the plan of liquidation. Exceptions are provided in the Code for property acquired within the first two years of the corporation's existence, and for assets that are related to the distributing corporation's business. One way the new law limits the amount of loss that can be utilized by the liquidating corporation is the requirement that the corporation's tax basis be reduced by the amount that the contributing shareholder's basis exceeds FMV. It is anticipated that the IRS will issue regulations requiring the inclusion in income of a built-in loss rather than the denial of the recognition of such loss.

### Liabilities and Losses

A special rule for using the NOLs of a selling corporation is available under Section 338 for corporations filing consolidated returns. Under an election (Section 338(h)(10)), the acquired corporation, which is otherwise not treated as a member of either the buying or selling group, can be treated as a member of the selling group. The effect of the special election is that a selling group recognizes no gain or loss on the sale of the stock; however, gain or loss on the deemed sale of assets does flow through the selling group's consolidated return. A similar election has now been added to the Code by the TRA for affiliated groups which do not file consolidated returns with the departing subsidiary. Under new Section 336(e), which becomes effective upon the publication of regulations, an election can be made in respect of a corporation which sells, exchanges, or distributes the stock of a controlled corporation to avoid gain or loss on the disposition of stock of such corporation as if such corporation were liquidated. The purpose of the new election is to conform the treatment currently provided to corporations filing a consolidated return to corporations not filing a consolidated return. In addition, it ensures that the controlled subsidiary's assets are stepped up just as they would be when a Section 338 election is made.

### *Transition Rules on Liquidations*

The repeal of *General Utilities* was generally effective for any distribution in complete liquidation or deemed sale of assets pursuant to Section 338 occurring after July 31, 1986, unless the corporation was completely liquidated before January 1, 1987. The other notable exception was for certain small corporations which completely liquidated prior to January 1, 1989. A small corporation qualified under the transitional rule if, as of August 1, 1986, and at all times thereafter before the corporation was completely liquidated, its value did not exceed $5,000,000, and more than 50 percent (by value) of the stock of such corporation had been held by ten or fewer "qualified" persons on such date. Individuals, estates, and some trusts constituted qualified persons. In determining stock ownership for this purpose, stock attribution rules were applied. Under the attribution rules, in determining whether stock was held by ten or fewer qualified persons, stock owned by members of the same family was treated as owned by a single person and stock owned by a corporation was treated as owned by the shareholder. Further, stock held by a corporation, trust, or partnership was treated as held proportionately by its shareholders, beneficiaries, or partners. No further discussion of the transitional rules is warranted except to illustrate that some liquidations thought to be taxable may, following a close review of the facts, be tax free afterall.

### Revised Code Provisions Require Recognition

In addition to the repeal of *General Utilities,* the 1986 TRA also repealed or modified various exceptions to recognition that permitted corporations to make nonliquidating distributions to shareholders. Prior to amendment, Section 311 permitted corporations to avoid recognition on the distribution of appreciated property to certain long-term noncorporate shareholders who owned at least 10 percent of the stock, on distributions to help pay estate tax, on redemptions of private foundation stock, and on redemption of regulated investment company stock on demand by a shareholder. Only the last of these exceptions from gain recognition survives. As in the case of liquidating distributions, the amount of gain to be recognized includes any liability assumed by the shareholder to whom the asset is distributed or any liability to which the distributed asset is subject.

The amendments to Section 311 of the Code remove the incentive to distribute appreciated property either as dividend distributions or as distributions in redemption. Since the new rules do not apply to distributions of a corporation's obligation, the use of debt or cash, or a combination, is likely to replace the use of appreciated property. Another alternative is to restructure a distribution of property as a tax-free spinoff of stock of a subsidiary. TAMRA makes it clear that Section 311 does not apply to nonliquidating distributions not characterized as a dividend.

## LEVERAGED BUYOUTS AND MIRROR TRANSACTIONS

A key feature of a leveraged buyout (LBO) is the sale of target assets to help pay for the acquisition. In order to avoid tax on the sale of the unwanted assets, the acquirer required a stepped-up basis in the assets to be sold. The use of mirror transactions was a way of solving the basis problem.

The goal of mirror transactions was to permit a corporation to acquire selected assets of a target corporation with a stepped-up basis in the purchased assets while the target corporation recognized no gain or loss on its liquidating distribution. Like the magician who uses a mirror to accomplish an illusion, mirror transactions were often carried out with newly formed subsidiaries of the acquiring corporation.

The Revenue Act of 1987 (1987 Act) virtually eliminated the mirror technique and further discussion is unwarranted except to note that if 80 percent or more of the stock of the target was acquired or subject to a binding contract or tender offer on December 15, 1987, the old rules will continue to apply to mirror transactions occurring prior to 1993.

## TAX-FREE ACQUISITIONS VIRTUALLY UNCHANGED BY TRA

Neither the 1986 TRA, the 1987 Act, nor TAMRA changed the basic structure of tax-free corporate reorganizations. A tax-free corporate reorganization differs from a sale or a liquidation of a corporation in one significant respect. In the case of a sale of stock or liquidation of a corporation, the historic shareholders have cashed in their investment and are subject to capital gains tax. Similarly, a corporation that sells its assets has generally always been subject to tax at the corporate level. Now that *General Utilities* has been repealed, there is no effective way to prevent tax from occurring at the corporate level. In the case of a reorganization, however, there is generally no tax at the corporate level on a transfer of assets because the Code recognizes that no change occurs. This tax-deferred treatment continues. The operative word in corporate reorganizations is continuity. The corporate business continues, possibly in an altered form, and the shareholders' investment continues.

### Tests for Tax-Free Reorganizations

The tax-free reorganization provisions of the Code are contained in Section 368. Section 368 and its subsections are purely definitional. A transaction which appears to fit into one of the subsections of Section 368 must pass several tests to determine whether it qualifies for tax-free treatment. If it meets that general test, a number of other Code sections come into play in determining the overall tax treatment of the transaction.

The regulations under Section 368 provide the following three general tests which must be satisfied if the transaction is to qualify for tax-free treatment.

1. *Continuity of shareholder interest* is the most widely known of the reorganization tests because it has been the subject of the most litigation. The continuity-of-shareholder-interest requirement is satisfied if the shareholders of the acquired corporation have a sufficient continuing interest through stock ownership in the acquiring corporation. The continuity-of-shareholder-interest test looks to the percentage of value of the acquired corporation that is represented by an equity interest in the acquiring corporation. It is not tied to the percentage of equity in the acquiring corporation held by the former shareholders of the acquired corporation. If that were the case, an acquisition by a very large corporation could never meet the continuity-of-shareholder-interest test. Although some courts have permitted a lesser percentage, the commonly accepted rule of thumb is the 50-percent continuing interest required by the Internal Revenue Service (the Service). The IRS test is met if the shareholders of the acquired corporation own stock in the acquiring corporation equal in value to at least 50 percent of the value of the stock of the acquired corporation which they held at the date of acquisition. The continuing interest must be an equity or stock interest. Debt instruments generally do not qualify although a combination of cash and debt does not necessarily disqualify a reorganization.

The continuity-of-shareholder-interest test goes beyond counting stock ownership on the date of the acquisition. The Service requires that the shareholders have a continuing interest. Accordingly, if a sufficiently large number of shareholders act on prearranged plans to sell stock received in a reorganization or fail to hold it long enough, it could result in disqualifying the reorganization. Because each shareholder is required on his, her, or its tax return to report the tax-free exchange of stock, the Service has notice that the transaction has occurred and has the opportunity to audit it.

2. *Continuity of business enterprise* is the second requirement for a successful corporation reorganization. While the case law is quite lenient on the issue of how much of the acquired corporation's assets must be retained, as well as on the issue of whether the acquired corporation's business must be continued at all, the regulations are more strict. The IRS regulations generally require that the acquiring corporation either continue the historic business of the acquired corporation or use a significant portion of the business assets of target in a business.

3. *Corporate business purpose* is the final requirement. A corporate business purpose is distinguishable from a shareholder motive for having a company acquired. This is by far the easiest standard to meet since the Service recognizes that corporate acquisitions and restructurings are not undertaken lightly.

### Types of Corporate Reorganizations

There are seven types of corporate reorganizations, including:

*Type A: The Versatile Merger* (Figure 8–1). The most commonly known reorganization type is the consolidation or statutory merger. This type of reorganization occurs when one

**Figure 8–1.** *Statutory merger.*

All of the assets of ABC pass to XYZ on the merger of ABC into XYZ. The corporate existence of ABC ceases and the ABC stock in the hands of the ABC shareholders automatically becomes a right to receive an equivalent number of shares of XYZ stock.

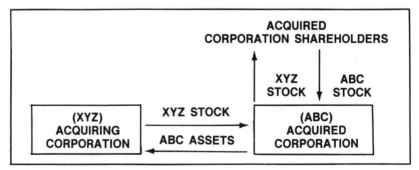

or more corporations "merge" into another corporation pursuant to the laws of the respective states of incorporation. In a merger, the legal existence of the transferor or acquired corporation ceases while the transferee or acquiring corporation continues to exist as an operating corporation. Whereas mergers typically involve a single transferor, consolidations involve the combination of two or more corporations into a newly created corporate entity in a transaction in which both of the transferor corporations go out of existence. The size of the combining corporation is unimportant. Thus, the term *reorganization* encompasses both the merger of a large corporation into a small corporation as well as the more typical merger of a small corporation into a larger corporation.

One of the appeals of a Type A reorganization for both acquirer and acquired is that it offers them a great deal of flexibility in structuring the direction of the transaction as well as in the type of consideration which the stockholders or security holders of the transferor corporation may receive. For example, the Code permits all or part of the assets of the acquired corporation to be transferred to a subsidiary of the acquiring corporation. (See Figure 8–2.) It is even permissible for the assets to be transferred directly to one or more subsidiaries of the acquiring corporation.

The type of stock to be issued to the shareholders of the acquired corporation may generally be common or preferred,

**Figure 8–2.**

The facts are the same as in Figure 8–1 except that XYZ drops (transfers) all or part of the ABC assets into controlled subsidiary of XYZ.

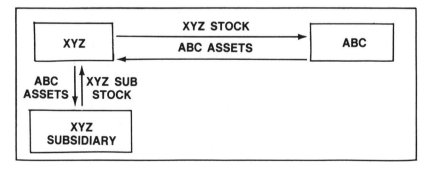

voting or nonvoting, depending on state merger statutes. The amount of nonstock consideration the shareholders receive in the transaction determines the degree of taxability of the transaction. For example, if the shareholders of a merging corporation receive common and preferred stock and other property or cash (boot) in a merger, the boot will subject the exchanging shareholder to tax. The same boot recognition rule now also applies to the transferor corporation as well as the target corporation.

A special rule applies to the acquisition by one corporation of stock of another corporation when both are owned by the same parties (Figure 8–3) and anything other than stock of the acquiring corporation is used to acquire the stock of the related corporation (Section 304). No problem occurs in either situation if the sole consideration issued is stock of the acquiring corporation. The application of Section 304 can result in an unpleasant surprise in the form of a dividend to the selling shareholder even in acquisitions that are not driven by tax avoidance.

## Figure 8–3.

If X acquires the Y stock held by A for X stock, the transaction will be tax free to A. If, however, all or part of the Y stock is acquired by X for other consideration, such as cash or other property, the transaction could be taxable to A as a dividend. There are exceptions to this general rule, such as where the "other property" is the assumption of acquisition debt incurred by A in the acquisition of the Y stock.

In testing for dividend treatment under the statutory rules of Section 304 of the IRC, the property transferred from X to A is treated as if distributed in redemption of X's stock. For this purpose, A is to be treated as a continuing owner of Y stock by A's ownership of X stock. Generally, a dividend is from earnings and profits of the distributing corporation only. However, for the purposes of determining whether a dividend has occurred in an acquisition of a related corporation, the earnings and profits of both X and Y are taken into consideration.

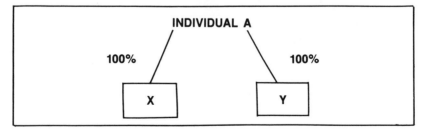

The best protection from Section 304 is full awareness whenever a corporation is to be acquired by a related corporation, even a subsidiary. Special exceptions apply to the formation of holding companies such as bank holding companies. A Section 338 election may also be possible where no dividend treatment is indicated.

The reorganization provisions often overlap with other provisions of the Code. Thus, a merger of an 80%-or-greater subsidiary into its parent corporation constitutes a Type A reorganization as well as a tax-free liquidation of the subsidiary corporation. No gain recognition is possible, however, despite the repeal of *General Utilities,* because no assets are to be distributed to the minority shareholder. In the case of a *downstream* merger (Figure 8–4) of a parent into a subsidiary, the reorganization rules apply.

A Type A reorganization also includes so-called subsidiary merger or *triangular merger* transactions. (See Figure 8–5.) The subsidiary merger technique is a variation of the transaction in which assets of the acquired corporation are dropped tax free into a subsidiary of the acquiring corporation. In a subsidiary

**Figure 8–4.**

XYZ could merge "downstream" following the acquisition of the ABC stock in a tax-free Type A reorganization. The fact that the ABC shareholders have no continuing interest does not affect the tax-free nature of the merger because the continuity rules apply to the acquired corporation only (XYZ).

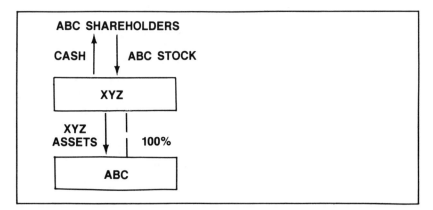

**Figure 8–5.** *Subsidiary merger.*

The assets of the acquired corporation are transferred directly to the subsidiary of the acquiring corporation (compare Figure 8–2) in exchange for stock of the acquiring corporation (XYZ).

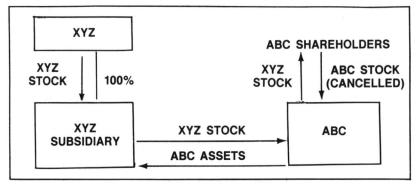

reorganization, the acquired corporation merges into a subsidiary of the controlling parent corporation and the shareholders of the acquired corporation receive stock of the parent corporation.

The triangular reorganization is used principally by corporations wishing to avoid obtaining shareholder approval for the acquisition of assets of another corporation. The *reverse triangular reorganization* occurs when the acquiring corporation causes its subsidiary to merge into the target corporation. (See Figure 8–6.) As a result of the transfer, the merging subsidiary (usually a newly formed corporation) goes out of existence and the target corporation becomes a wholly owned subsidiary of the acquiring parent corporation. In addition to the standard continuity-of-interest, continuity-of-business-enterprise, and business purpose requirements, triangular reorganizations have strict stock and asset rules which must be satisfied in order for the transaction to qualify as a Type A reorganization. Triangular transactions can also be used to purchase corporations in taxable acquisitions.

In some cases, a Type A reorganization is the last step in a series of steps designed to effect the acquisition of the acquired corporation's assets following the acquisition of all of its stock. The tax effect of so-called *creeping mergers* is dependent largely upon the independence of the steps. If all of the target's stock is acquired over a sufficiently long period of time for cash or

**Figure 8–6.** *Reverse triangular reorganization.*

Acquiring often forms a subsidiary (Newco) by transferring to Newco an amount of XYZ stock (or a combination of stock and other consideration) in exchange for 100% of the stock of Newco. When Newco merges into ABC, the Newco stock automatically converts into ABC stock. ABC retains all of its assets and becomes a wholly owned subsidiary of XYZ. This technique is also used to acquire corporations in taxable transactions (i.e. cash for stock) and to force out minority shareholders who will not agree to an acquisition. The latter is accomplished through the use of a triangular merger because in a merger a dissenter can be forced to accept the cash value of his or her shares.

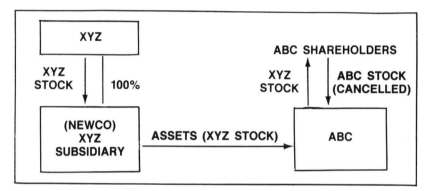

other nonstock consideration, the subsequent merger transaction will likely qualify as a tax-free reorganization. For example, if the purchase of all of the target corporation's stock is *old and cold,* the acquiring corporation will be deemed to be the historic shareholder for purposes of meeting the continuity-of-interest requirement on a subsequent merger or consolidation. Generally, the shorter the period between the purchase of stock and the reorganization, the more likely the IRS will be to challenge the reorganization on the ground that the continuity-of-shareholder-interest requirement has not been met. If at least 50 percent of the stock is acquired for stock of the acquiring corporation, however, the transaction will qualify.

Other appealing features of Type A reorganization include its many acceptable variations and liberal consideration requirements. Often a Type A reorganization may preserve tax-free treatment for a transaction that fails to qualify for tax-free treatment under another reorganization definition even though the steps of the transaction fit the pattern of the statutory requirement. For example, a reorganization that fails as a Type B reorganization because something other than voting stock was received by the target shareholders will generally qualify as a Type A reverse triangular reorganization so long as control is acquired solely for voting stock. This means that up to 20 percent of the stock may be acquired for nonstock consideration. Conversely, a Type A reorganization may also qualify as Type C, Type D, or Type F reorganizations, each of which has its own requirements and limitations.

*Type B: A Stock-for-Stock Acquisition Stressing Control* (see Figure 8–7). Not all reorganization transactions require the termination of the transferor corporation. The Type B reorganization, for example, does not. In this type of reorganization, the acquired corporation continues to exist: It becomes a subsidiary of the acquiring corporation, retaining all of its assets and tax attributes. The only change that occurs in a Type B reorganization is that the former shareholders of the acquired corporation become shareholders of the acquiring corporation, or a corporation in control of the acquiring corporation.

Because it stresses control, Section 368(a)(1)(B) of the Code includes in the definition of a reorganization the acquisition of

**Figure 8–7.**

Type B reorganization can also be effected through the use of a subsidiary of XYZ in the case where XYZ does not want to hold the ABC stock directly.

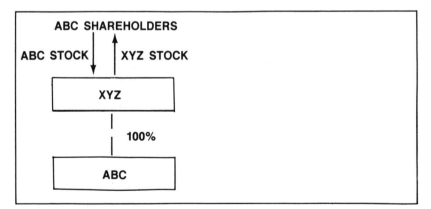

all of the stock of a corporation solely in exchange for voting stock of the acquiring corporation (or a corporation in control of the acquiring corporation) following which the acquiring corporation is in control of the acquired corporation. Section 368(c) defines control as the ownership of stock possessing at least 80 percent of the total combined voting power of all classes of stock entitled to vote and at least 80 percent of the total number of shares of all other classes of stock of the corporation.

A Type B reorganization leaves no leeway for any consideration other than voting stock. There is no mitigating de minimis rule. Any other consideration, including warrants, will cause the transaction to fail. There is no restriction, however, on issuing preferred stock, provided it is voting stock. In addition, although it is permissible to issue stock of the acquiring corporation or the parent of the acquiring corporation, a combination of the stock of both is not permitted.

It is not necessary that control be obtained in one transaction in order for it to qualify as a Type B reorganization. For that matter, control need not be acquired solely for voting stock. All that is required is that after the acquisition of stock, the acquiring corporation is in control of the acquired corporation. Accordingly, a Type B reorganization would include the acquisition of 1 percent of the stock of a corporation in which the acquiring corporation already owned a 79-percent interest. Similarly, a corporation that owned 99 percent of the stock of another corporation could acquire the last 1 percent solely for voting stock in a Type B reorganization. Some or all of the stock already owned by the acquiring corporation may have been acquired for cash or other nonstock consideration. The taxpayer must be able to prove that these prior purchases were not related to the present effort to qualify as a Type B reorganization. It is also possible to purge stock acquired in a manner which would disqualify a subsequent Type B reorganization.

The substantial amount of overlap among various types of tax-free transactions may create or eliminate problems depending upon the desired result. For example, suppose that an acquirer wishes to effect a Type B transaction, but a 2-percent shareholder of the target corporation refuses to accept the acquirer's voting stock, and that the acquirer does not wish to have minority shareholders owning stock in its new subsidiary. To get tax-free status, the acquiring corporation can create a wholly owned subsidiary and transfer to that subsidiary an amount of acquiring stock equal to the fair market value of all of the outstanding stock of the target corporation. They may then effect a statutory merger in which the newly formed subsidiary is merged with and into the target corporation. In the merger transaction, the exchanging shareholders of the target corporation receive solely voting stock of the acquiring corporation while dissenters are, in effect, bought out.

The transaction works as a Type B even though shareholders who do not wish to accept voting stock of the acquiring corporation receive payment from the target for their stock upon the exercise of their dissenters' rights. This payment to dissenters does not affect the solely-for-voting-stock requirement provided the cash comes only from the target. The corporate existence of the new subsidiary terminates and the target corporation becomes a wholly owned subsidiary of the acquiring corporation. The interim steps are ignored.

On the other hand, unintended treatment as a Type B reorganization can have undesirable effects, such as when preferred stock issued by a corporation in exchange for stock of a controlled corporation is deemed to be Section 306 stock because the transaction overlaps with a Type B reorganization. Section 306 stock is preferred stock, the sale or exchange of which will result in ordinary income to the shareholder no matter how long held and in what manner disposed of. Finally, the acquisition of all of the stock of a corporation followed by the prearranged liquidation of the acquired corporation into the acquiring corporation will qualify neither as a Type A nor Type B reorganization, but will likely qualify as a tax-free Type C reorganization.

*Type C: Substantially All Assets for Voting Common* (see Figure 8-8). A Type C reorganization is an acquisition by one corporation of substantially all of the properties of another corporation in exchange solely for all or a part of its voting stock.

As is the case with Type B reorganizations, it is permissible to issue either stock of the acquiring corporation, or stock of

**Figure 8–8.** *Type C.*

The acquired corporation must distribute all of the stock it receives plus its remaining assets.

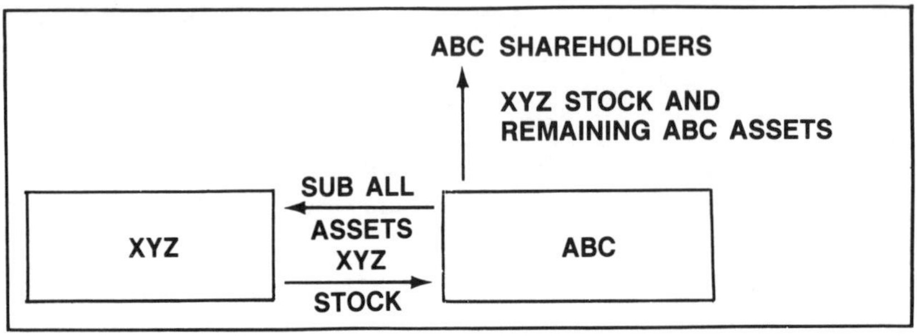

a corporation in control of the acquiring corporation, but not stock of both. The key requirement of a Type C reorganization is that substantially all (but not all) of the assets must be acquired solely for voting stock. Thus, a limited amount of money or other property may be used to acquire the assets of the target corporation. Target liabilities may also be assumed in the transaction.

If all of the assets are acquired, as is normally the case, establishing the existence of a Type C reorganization is not difficult. A problem arises, however, when less than all of the assets of the target corporation are acquired. In that case it is necessary to establish that "substantially all" of the assets have been acquired solely for voting stock. For advance ruling purposes, the IRS considers the term *substantially all* to mean at least 90 percent of the fair market value of the net assets and at least 70 percent of the fair market value of the gross assets of the transferor corporation, taking into consideration distributions which are part of a plan of reorganization. Any assets that are not transferred to the acquiring corporation must generally be distributed to the target shareholders in liquidation.

The Type C reorganization was created to grant tax-free treatment to reorganizations that could not qualify as statutory mergers. However, to prevent shortcutting the complex spinoff rules of Section 355, the Code provides that transactions which qualify as both Type C and Type D reorganizations are treated only as Type D reorganizations.

Overlap between a Type C and Type D reorganization can have two deleterious effects. First, a transaction that fully qualifies as a Type C reorganization may become taxable simply because it is also described as a Type D reorganization and all of the requirements of a Type D reorganization have not been met. For example, a Type D reorganization does not permit the dropdown of acquired assets to a subsidiary while a Type C does. To prevent Type C reorganizations with dropdowns from being recast as nonqualifying Type D reorganizations, the Service has announced a policy to permit such dropdowns in C/D overlap situations.

One way of ensuring the desired tax treatment is to obtain an advance ruling from the IRS. Another way is to ensure that the transaction cannot also be described as a Type D reorganization. One means of accomplishing this is to use a parenthetical Type C reorganization in which stock of a corporation in control of the acquiring corporation is distributed to the shareholders of the acquired corporation. This is because the Type C, like a Type B, permits the use of parent stock while Type D does not.

The second deleterious effect of the C/D overlap is that transactions which qualify as Type D reorganizations are subject to the requirements of Section 357(c) of the Code. That Section provides that, in the case of a Type D reorganization transfer, if the sum of the amount of liabilities assumed, plus the amount of liabilities to which the transferred assets are subject, exceeds the total of the adjusted tax basis of the property transferred, the excess will be considered as a taxable gain to the transferor. Section 357(c) also applies to transfers to controlled corporations in transactions that qualify under Section 351.

Although in determining whether a transaction qualifies as a Type C reorganization one may disregard the assumption of liabilities by the acquiring corporation or the acquisition of properties subject to liabilities, the assumption of an abnormal amount of liabilities may cause the transaction to fail as a tax-free reorganization. The definition of a Type C reorganization requires that substantially all of the properties of another corporation be acquired solely in exchange for voting stock of the acquiring corporation. The Code further provides that up to 20

percent of the assets can be acquired for cash or other property. The assumption of a liability is treated, for this purpose, as other property. If cash or other property is used, the acquiring corporation must acquire at least 80 percent of the fair market value of all of the property of the transferor corporation solely for voting stock.

For the purpose of determining whether 80 percent has been acquired solely for voting stock, the amount of any liabilities assumed by the acquiring corporation, as well as the amount of any liabilities to which the property acquired is subject, shall be treated as money paid for the property. For example, corporation Y has property valued at $100,000 which is subject to a liability of $17,000. Corporation X proposes to acquire all of the assets of corporation Y for a combination of corporation X voting stock and cash. Since corporation X will take the corporation Y assets subject to the liability, the liabilities will be treated as cash or other property. Therefore, at least 80 percent of the assets of corporation Y ($80,000) must be acquired for corporation X stock. The maximum amount of cash that can be paid is $3,000, because the liabilities of $17,000 are treated as cash or other property even though corporation X does not assume those liabilities.

*Type D: Transfer to Controlled Corporation* (see Figure 8–9). A Type D reorganization is a transfer by a corporation of all or part of its assets to a corporation controlled by the transferor corporation, but only if stock or securities of the controlled corporation are distributed in a transaction which qualifies under Section 354, 355, or 356 of the Code. To qualify under Section 354, the transferor or acquired corporation must transfer substantially all of its assets to the acquiring corporation. Although the IRS's definition of "substantially all" is the same for both Type C and Type D reorganizations, the judicial interpretation of "substantially all" is much more liberal than the IRS's advance ruling requirement. A Type D reorganization usually occurs where the assets transferred are sufficient to constitute an active trade or business even though the amount does not meet the IRS's definition of substantially all.

Section 368(a)(1)(D) of the Code provides for the transfer by a corporation of all or part of its assets to another corporation. The use of such language was intended to cover the two types of situations which occur in Type D reorganizations. The first is the Section 354 transaction where at least substantially all of the assets are transferred. The second is the Section 355 transaction in which a valid Type D reorganization occurs where only a part of the assets is transferred. However, in order to qualify as a Type D reorganization pursuant to Section 355 of the Code, the requirements of the latter section must be met. Section 355 provides an exception from dividend treatment for divisive-type transactions in which stock of a controlled corporation is distributed (spun off) to some or all of the shareholders of the distributing corporation.

As explained in the foregoing, Congress tried to prevent taxpayers from "end-running" the difficult divisive reorganization rules contained in Section 355 of the Code. The normal rule requiring a transfer of substantially all of the transferor's assets in a Type D reorganization is inapplicable if the stock of the transferee corporation is distributed pursuant to Section 355. Through this exception, Type D reorganization permits division of corporate business enterprises through separate corporations.

**Figure 8–9.** *Type D.*

Control may be established through the use of stock attribution rules. The IRS will often try to assert that a liquidation followed by a transfer of some of the liquidated assets to a new corporation controlled by the shareholder of the liquidating corporation is, in fact, a Type D reorganization. The issue is whether a distribution of assets is in liquidation (thus taking stock basis into consideration) or a dividend.

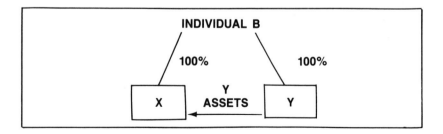

*Type E (Recapitalization): Restructuring a Single Firm.* A recapitalization is the readjustment of the financial structure of a single corporation. Unlike acquisitive reorganizations such as Type A, Type B, Type C, and Type D transactions, Type E recapitalizations affect only one corporation. Recapitalization exchanges are exempt from the continuity-of-shareholder-interest rules. Type E reorganizations are not, however, exempt from the limitation of net operating loss carryover rules which accompany a 50-percent change in ownership of a corporation. The only other tax impact of a recapitalization is on the shareholders of the recapitalized corporation. For example, a Type E used to squeeze out minority shareholders will result in a taxable sale to those shareholders.

There are three principal types of recapitalization transactions. The first and most common is the stock-for-stock exchange. Typically, older generation shareholders exchange old common stock for new preferred stock. This has the effect of providing the exchanging shareholder with guaranteed income and the nonexchanging shareholders with future capital growth. The value of the children's stock can be included in the parents' estate for federal estate tax purposes, however. The second is the bond-for-stock exchange in which a bondholder exchanges senior interest (bonds) for junior interest (stock) in the corporation. This is normally done to improve the balance sheet by eliminating debt. The third type of exchange is the bond-for-bond exchange which usually occurs in the wake of changes in interest rates, profitability, or creditworthiness of the debtor corporation.

One of the pitfalls of a Type E recapitalization is the classification of newly issued preferred stock as Section 306 stock. Section 306 stock arises most often in a recapitalization when the exchanging shareholder winds up with both common and preferred stock of the same corporation. Section 306 stock can also result from an otherwise innocent transaction which overlaps with a corporate reorganization. Fortunately, there are a number of ways of eliminating the Section 306 stock taint.

*Type F: A Mere Change in Form of a Single Corporation.* A Type F reorganization is defined in the Code as "a mere change in identity, form, or place of organization, of one corporation however effected." The principal differences between Type F reorganizations and other types of reorganizations lie in the way the tax attribute carryover and limitation rules apply to them. Section 381(a) of the Code provides for the carryover of various tax attributes to the acquiring corporation. In each instance, the taxable year of the transferor corporation ends and the acquiring corporation is not permitted to carry back a net operating loss to a taxable year of the transferor corporation. The exception to the rule is the Type F reorganization. The taxable year of the corporation which has undergone a Type F reorganization remains the same and it is free to carry back net operating losses to its prior taxable years. The reason for the exception is a congressional recognition that the reorganized corporation is, in substance, identical to the old corporation. The other exemption for Type F reorganizations is from the NOL limitation rules of Section 382.

It is important to note that a transaction that qualifies as both a Type C and a Type D reorganization may also qualify as a Type F reorganization. This overlap may have a favorable result for the taxpayer in the case of the transaction which qualifies as a Type C and a Type D reorganization. For example, Type F status prevents the application of the gain recognition rules of Section 357(c), which can apply in C/D overlap situations.

*Type G (Bankruptcy): Insolvency Reorganization.* The most recent addition to the reorganization provisions is the Type G reorganization enacted by Congress as part of the Bankruptcy Tax Act of 1980. The Type G reorganization provisions affect Title 11 bankruptcy reorganizations. The Type G reorganization is often similar to a Type D reorganization in form; however, in the case of overlaps the Type G has exclusive jurisdiction. Thus, a transfer of assets in exchange for stock or securities pursuant to a court-approved insolvency reorganization plan constitutes a tax-free Type G reorganization. No gain or loss will be recognized to the transferor corporation or to the exchanging shareholders and security holders. In addition, the tax attributes of the debtor corporation carry over to the transferee corporation subject to the NOL limitations of Section 382. The

Type G reorganization also permits triangular reorganizations as well as the postreorganization downstream transfers of assets to subsidiary corporations now allowable in other reorganizations.

The Code makes the new Type G reorganization the sole remedy for bankruptcy asset transfers by denying tax-free (Section 351) treatment for any transfer of property by a bankrupt debtor to a corporation to the extent that stock or securities received in exchange for property are used to satisfy the transferor's debts. A similar rule disqualifies transfers of unsecured debt by creditors to corporate debtors.

## SPECIAL PROBLEMS AND ISSUES AFFECTING TAX-FREE REORGANIZATIONS

### Alternative Minimum Tax (AMT)

The 1986 TRA added to the tax burden of corporate taxpayers by subjecting them to the same AMT that individuals have been subject to. Essentially, AMT is calculated by comparing book income with income reported for tax purposes. In doing so, items of preference income such as excess depreciation and depletion deductions, certain tax-exempt interest, gain on charitable gifts, and the like are added back to arrive at alternative minimum taxable income. If the AMT is higher than the regular tax, the taxpayer pays the higher tax.

The Code provides for the nonrecognition of gain or loss when a corporation transfers assets to another corporation in a tax-free reorganization. While that remains true as to the recognition of income, the transferor corporation realizes income to the extent it transfers appreciated property. That appreciation may be subject to AMT if included in book income.

### NOL Limitation Rules (Section 382)

One of the major changes of the 1986 TRA was its effect on carryover (built-in) NOLs of corporations that undergo ownership changes. An ownership change occurs when the percentage of stock owned by one or more new or existing 5-percent shareholders increases by more than 50 percentage points during a testing period. A testing period is generally three years but could be a shorter period. The change can occur through a purchase of stock, tax-free reorganization, redemption of stock, transfer to a controlled corporation, or a public offering of stock.

When an ownership change occurs, the carryover NOLs of the loss corporation that can be used each year in the future are limited to an amount which is the product of the value of the loss corporation immediately prior to the ownership change times the current federal long-term tax-exempt bond rate.

Stock rights and warrants issued by a corporation are generally to be treated as exercised if the exercise would result in an ownership change.

In determining the value of a loss corporation, the value is to be reduced by capital contributions that were motivated by tax avoidance purposes. Under the regulatory scheme, there is a rebuttable presumption that capital contributions to a corporation that were made within the two-year period preceding the ownership change had a tax avoidance motive.

One of the traps for the unwary under the Section 382 rules is that NOLs are lost unless the loss corporation continues substantially the same business for at least two years after the change in ownership. In other rules, so-called built-in gains on appreciated property owned by the loss corporation may increase the annual limit if these gains and losses exceed 25 percent of the value of the corporation's assets immediately before the ownership change. Under these special rules, built-in gains recognized within five years of the ownership change are fully sheltered by carryover NOLs, while built-in losses recognized during the period are treated as prechange losses. The use of NOLs is further limited in the case where at least one-third of the loss corporation's assets are passive assets. An exception is provided for both regulated investment companies and real estate investment trusts.

The rules limiting the use of NOLs following an ownership change call for special treatment of corporations and other entities that are under the jurisdiction of a court in a Title 11 (bankruptcy) or similar case. Generally, following a bankruptcy reorganization, if the shareholders and creditors of the loss corporation own at least 50 percent of the stock of the new loss corporation, the rules limiting the use of NOLs do not apply. A special rule also applies in the case of a financially troubled thrift institution which is acquired or converted to stock prior to January 1, 1990. In the case of a mutual savings and loan, for example, which has no capital stock, the old depositors are counted as equity owners of the acquiring or converted institution provided that they have a continuing interest through account deposits. If there was a second ownership change following the conversion of the financially troubled thrift and that second ownership change is unrelated to the supervisory change, the Section 382 NOL limitations apply. As an example of another trap for the unwary, if the size of the acquiring institution is so great that the percentage of equity deemed to be held by the old depositors is less than a minimum 20 percent of total value, the exception from the NOL limitation rules does not apply.

### Consolidated Return Issues

Other limitations on the use of NOLs arise from consolidated return regulations. An acquired entity that has safely avoided the shoals of the reorganization rules, Sections 269 and 382, may find itself confronted with SRLY or CRCO problems. SRLY and CRCO are acronyms for separate return limitation year and consolidated return change of ownership, respectively. SRLY refers only to losses generated during tax years in which the loss corporation was not a member of the consolidated group that wishes to use the loss corporation's NOLs. Unlike NOLs subject to the Section 382 limitations, SRLY losses can be used only against income of the loss member. Since Section 382 and the SRLY rules are unrelated, a corporation that, due to its high value, has a large annual limitation under Section 382 may still be prevented from using its losses due to the SRLY provisions.

A CRCO is a change in ownership that results from a more-than-50-percentage-point change due to a purchase or redemption of stock of a parent corporation. When a CRCO occurs, the losses of the purchased group of corporations become subject to the SRLY rules. It is important to note that the consolidated return regulations are extremely complex and contain numerous examples of additional situations in which the use of an acquired corporation's NOLs can be limited.

### *Corporate Separations (Section 355)*

Distributions that qualify under Section 355 represent an important exception from the general tax treatment of distributions to shareholders as dividends. Section 355 permits a corporation (Distributing) to distribute the stock of an 80-percent subsidiary (Controlled) to its own shareholders either pro rata or in exchange for stock of Distributing held by all or some of its shareholders. The statutory requirements of Section 355, which are voluminously supplemented by revenue rulings, are three: There must be a business purpose which is primarily related to the continuing operations of Distributing; there must be a distribution of stock of a corporation that is engaged in a trade or business that has been actively conducted for at least five years prior to the distribution while after the distribution both Distributing and Controlled must be so engaged; and there must also be a demonstrable absence of a device to distribute earnings and profits of Distributing or Controlled, or both. A corporation that can meet these tests can pass highly appreciated stock to its shareholders without the distribution being taxed as a dividend.

The five-year requirement for establishing an active trade or business was put into the law to prevent a profitable corporation from purchasing the stock of a corporation with its retained earnings and distributing the stock to shareholders as a tax-free distribution. Similarly, control of Controlled must not have been acquired in a taxable transaction within the five-year period preceding the date of distribution. The 1987 Act added an additional requirement that stock of Distributing not be acquired in a taxable purchase within the five-year period preceding the distribution. TAMRA has extended that prohibition to direct or indirect acquisitions of the controlled (distributed) corporation during a five-year period. Further, boot in a spinoff will now be subject to tax under Section 311.

Equally important to the active trade or business requirement is the corporate business purpose requirement. The business purpose may also direct the form of the transaction. Although the term commonly used for a Section 355 distribution is a spinoff, it also encompasses split-offs and split-ups. A spinoff is generally a pro rata distribution of stock to shareholders. A split-off occurs most often when the shareholders of a corporation have serious business disputes that can be resolved only by cutting the business in half, usually through the formation of a new subsidiary to be followed by the distribution of the stock of the new subsidiary to one of the shareholders in exchange for all of the stock of Distributing which that shareholder owns. A split-up could occur, for example, where each shareholder of a holding company takes the stock of a subsidiary upon the dissolution of the holding company.

### Corporate Stock Redemptions (Section 302)

Redemptions after the TRA (Section 302) are subject to the same general rules as before tax reform, with one exception. Prior to the TRA, the redemption provisions provided an important exception to dividend treatment when money, installment notes, or other property was distributed to shareholders in exchange for all or a part of their stock. In order to avoid dividend treatment, the taxpayer had to be able to establish that the distribution was in reality a sale of stock to the corporation and not a substitute for a dividend. On the first look, it appears relatively easy to prove that stock has actually been sold. The problem arises, however, when all of the shareholder's stock has been redeemed but stock in the corporation continues to be held by a spouse, child, or other related person. Under a mandatory application of stock attribution rules, the net result of the redemption could be that the redeeming shareholder's practical percentage of stock ownership remains the same.

In order to overcome the dividend presumption, two safe harbors can be relied upon. In the first, known as a disproportionate redemption, if the redeeming shareholder's resulting stock ownership is less than 80 percent of what that shareholder owned prior to redemption and represents less than 50 percent of the voting stock, and no stock is owned by a related person or entity, the redeeming shareholder is guaranteed redemption treatment. In the second, a shareholder who is completely redeemed can cut off attribution from a child or other related person, if such redeeming shareholder agrees not to reacquire any stock within a ten-year period and is not an officer or employee of the redeeming corporation.

Even though the capital gains exclusion has been repealed, the redemption rules remain intact. One general reason given for the retention of the redemption rules is the possible return of preferential capital gains tax rates.

### Foreign-Flavored Acquisitions

The tax-free-reorganization, formation, redemption, spinoff, and other rules generally apply to both foreign and domestic corporations. Transfers may also be inbound or outbound. The addition of the foreign status can significantly affect the tax treatment of the overall transaction, however. An inbound transfer of assets from a foreign corporation to a U.S. corporation could result in significant income recognition. Similarly, an outbound transfer could trigger significant "toll charges." As with any tax issues, awareness of the issue is the key to dealing with it or planning to avoid its impact.

### Troublesome Overlaps

It has been shown how liabilities in excess of asset basis can result in immediate gain recognition. This problem arises, for example, in a Type D reorganization that does not also qualify as a Type F reorganization. A difficult choice also arises after a stock purchase that qualifies under Section 338. The decision whether to elect to step up the basis of the acquired corporation's assets must be made only after ascertaining the immediate tax recapture cost and the longer-term tax benefits that flow from depreciation. The purchasing corporation that elects Section 338 knows that any NOLs of the target corporation left after recognizing recapture income are lost. This must be weighed against the future availability of losses that are subject to the Section 382 annual limitation if no Section 338 election is made. In other words, unless the target can use up its annual allotment of losses before they expire, the combination of the SRLY limits and the Section 382 limits may make the Section 338 election more attractive.

## TAXABLE TRANSACTIONS

As noted, many of the transactions described above can be accomplished in both tax-free and taxable transactions. For example, because the continuity-of-interest provisions apply only to the acquired corporation, it is possible to purchase the stock of a target corporation and maintain it as a subsidiary, make it the surviving corporation in a tax-free reorganization, or a combination of the two. Let us assume that X purchases 90 percent of the stock of Y for cash, but is unable to acquire the last 10 percent. If X does not wish to have a minority shareholder owning stock in Y it can do the following. X can form a new wholly owned subsidiary (Z), transfer an amount of cash to Z equal to the value of the Y stock which it could not purchase, and have Z merge into Y in a tax-free triangular reorganization. In the transaction, X's Z stock is converted into Y stock and the unyielding Y shareholders can be forced to accept cash for their Y shares. The only other alternative available to the Y shareholders is to claim their dissenters' rights under state law which generally limit their remedy to an amount of cash equal to the value of the Y stock.

In another example of how a taxable and nontaxable transaction can overlap, take the example of individual A who owns 20 percent of the stock of Target. Acquiring wants to purchase the stock of Target from the shareholders for cash. Eighty percent of Target shareholders are willing to accept cash while A is elderly and recognizes that he can totally avoid capital gains if he passes his Target stock to his heirs at death. Unlike the prior transaction, Acquiring wishes to accommodate A's wishes. Accordingly, Acquiring forms N and transfers to N an amount of cash equal to the value of 80 percent of Target's stock. In exchange, Acquiring receives all of the common stock of N. A also transfers his 20-percent stock interest in Target to N in exchange for preferred stock of N. Together, Acquiring and A control N; thus A's transfer to N is tax free under Section 351. Following the transfer, N forms Z Corporation by transferring to it all of the cash which it received from Acquiring. Following the formation of Z, Z is merged into Target in a tax-free reorganization. In the merger, the 80 percent shareholders of Target received cash, Z goes out of existence, and Target becomes a wholly owned subsidiary of N. A has succeeded in deferring the gain on the disposition of his Target stock while the other shareholders received cash in a taxable transaction.

It should be noted that taxable transactions require the same degree of precision as tax-free transactions. For example, if a target corporation which has significantly appreciated assets is to be acquired in a taxable reorganization, it makes a significant difference whether a new subsidiary is merged into Target or Target is merged into the new subsidiary. In the first transaction, Target is unaffected unless a Section 338 election is made; while in the second transaction Target is treated as having sold all of its assets. Since this result could be unintended and will be irreversible, extreme care must be taken. Further, if Acquiring plans to purchase stock of Target for Acquiring's debt and the acquisition is actually made by a subsidiary using Acquiring's debt, the acquiring subsidiary may be taxed on the difference between its basis in the debt (zero) and the fair market value of the Target stock. This problem can be solved easily by having Acquiring purchase the stock and drop it down or by having Subsidiary acquire the stock for its own debt which is guaranteed by Acquiring.

Finally, if a transaction meets the definition of a tax-free reorganization, no gain or loss will be recognized by the shareholders except to the extent of boot received. If the Target shareholders had a loss in their stock and wish to recognize that loss, a tax-free transaction can often be rendered taxable by an intentional failure to follow the tax-free requirements noted above. It should also be noted that many of the rules described above, such as the rules under Sections 269, 304, 311, and 382 and the consolidated return regulations limiting the use of NOLs, apply equally to taxable and tax-free transactions.

## *CONCLUSION*

The repeal of *General Utilities* is a step in an overall plan to review and revise the Code as it affects corporate restructuring. Congress is currently behind on its scheduled review of Subchapter C of the Code. Subchapter C generally encompasses all of the issues presented and discussed in this chapter. It is safe to say that tax reform in this area is ongoing. Accordingly, with change as a theme and with Treasury advice and guidance not yet fully implemented, careful tax planning is more important than ever. Often, the slightest plan change or failure to meet all requirements of a standard can make a difference. Given the complexity of the rules and the far-reaching impact of failure to plan properly, the advice of an acquisitions and dispositions expert is essential.

Chapter **9**

# *Accounting for an Acquisition**

*Joseph H. Marren*
Kidder, Peabody & Co., Inc.
New York, New York

## *INTRODUCTION*

As a general rule the author believes that the accounting treatment for an acquisition should not affect either the decision to acquire a target or the purchase price decision. Nevertheless, acquisition accounting is an important consideration in any transaction because the decision maker needs to understand the effect of the transaction on (1) the balance sheet of the acquiring company, (2) the acquiring company's earnings and earnings per share on a consolidated basis, and (3) the target's separate division or company results when they are actually reported. The second consideration is personally very key to the decision maker because the executive's future compensation is generally tied to the performance of the total company. The third consideration is important to the executive of the acquiring company who will be responsible for bringing in the results—assuming that the executive is presently employed by the acquiring company and involved somewhat in the negotiating process.

*Source: Joseph H. Marren, *Mergers and Acquisitions,* Dow Jones–Irwin, © 1985, pp. 199–213.

There are two accounting methods prescribed by the accounting profession for acquisitions: the Pooling of Interests Method and the Purchase Method.[1] The purpose of this chapter is to describe these mutually exclusive methods. It should be noted that the asset and liability values recorded for accounting purposes under either method typically differ from the values recorded for tax purposes. Furthermore, the decision on which method to apply is made without regard for either the legal form of the transaction or the tax nature of the contemplated transaction.

Generally, most acquisitions in the 1980s are accounted for using the Purchase Method. Therefore, the primary focus of this chapter will be on this method. The Pooling of Interests Method is rarely used because of the stringent conditions associated with it.

## PURCHASE METHOD OF ACCOUNTING

The Purchase Method of accounting is based on the theory that the accounting should follow the economic substance of the bargained transaction. Under the Purchase Method the assets and liabilities of the target company are recorded on the books of the acquiring company at their relative fair market values as of the acquisition date.

*Example A* ABC Corporation sells all of its assets and liabilities to XYZ Corporation in an Asset Acquisition for $1,700. What values would XYZ Corporation record for accounting purposes?

---

[1] See Accounting Principles Board Opinion No. 16, "Accounting for Business Combinations," American Institute of Certified Public Accountants, New York, NY, 1970.

|                                     | Asset and Liability Values Appearing on ABC's Books | Assumed Fair Market Values | Values Recorded on XYZ's Books |
| ----------------------------------- | ---------------------- | ---------------- | ---------------- |
| Accounts receivable                 | $100                   | $ 100            | $ 100            |
| Inventories                         | 300                    | 900              | 900              |
| Property, plant, and equipment      | 700                    | 1,100            | 1,100            |
| Accounts payable and accrued expenses | (400)                | (400)            | (400)            |
|                                     | $700                   | $1,700           | $1,700           |

In circumstances where the purchase price exceeds the net fair market value of the assets purchased and liabilities assumed, goodwill is recorded for accounting purposes. This "goodwill" figure is generally defined as an expectancy of earnings in excess of a normal return on the assets employed in a business. The expectancy of excess returns can come from any number of factors including location, trade secrets, brand names, reputation, or management skill. Any goodwill recorded must be amortized over its useful life which cannot exceed 40 years. Generally straight-line amortization is used, although another method may be employed if it is more appropriate.

*Example B* Same facts as Example A except that XYZ Corporation pays $2,000.

|                                     | Asset and Liability Values Appearing on ABC's Books | Assumed Fair Market Values | Values Recorded on XYZ's Books |
| ----------------------------------- | ---------------------- | ---------------- | ---------------- |
| Accounts receivable                 | $100                   | $ 100            | $ 100            |
| Inventories                         | 300                    | 900              | 900              |
| Property, plant, and equipment      | 700                    | 1,100            | 1,100            |
| Goodwill                            |                        |                  | 300*             |
| Accounts payable and accrued expenses | (400)                | (400)            | (400)            |
|                                     | $700                   | $1,700           | $2,000           |

* Purchase price less net fair market values of assets purchased and liabilities assumed ($2,000 − $1,700 = $300).

In cases where there is a bargain purchase (the purchase price is less than the net fair market value of the assets purchased and liabilities assumed), the values assigned to noncurrent assets (excluding long-term investments) are reduced by the difference between the purchase price and the net fair market value of the assets purchased and liabilities assumed.

*Example C* Same facts as Example A except that XYZ Corporation pays $1,500.

|  | Asset and Liability Values Appearing on ABC's Books | Assumed Fair Market Values | Values Recorded on XYZ's Books |
|---|---|---|---|
| Accounts receivable | $100 | $ 100 | $ 100 |
| Inventories | 300 | 900 | 900 |
| Property, plant, and equipment | 700 | 1,100 | 900* |
| Accounts payable and accrued expenses | (400) | (400) | (400) |
|  | $700 | $1,700 | $1,500 |

* Fair market value of property, plant, and equipment less the difference between the net fair market value of the assets purchased and liabilities assumed and the purchase price ($1,100 − ($1,700 − $1,500) = $900).

In special situations where the noncurrent assets have been reduced to zero value and a bargain purchase still remains, then a deferred credit for the excess of the value of identifiable assets over the cost of the target company should be recorded. This deferred credit is sometimes referred to as "negative goodwill." This deferred credit appears on the balance sheet between long-term debt and stockholders' equity and is amortized into income.

*Example D* Same facts as Example A except that XYZ Corporation pays $500.

| | Asset and Liability Values Appearing on ABC's Books | Assumed Fair Market Values | Values Recorded on XYZ's Books |
|---|---|---|---|
| Accounts receivable | $100 | $ 100 | $100 |
| Inventories | 300 | 900 | 900 |
| Property, plant, and equipment | 700 | 1,100 | 0* |
| Accounts payable and accrued expenses | (400) | (400) | (400) |
| Negative goodwill | | | (100)† |
| | $700 | $1,700 | $500 |

* Bargain purchase exists in amount greater than $1,100 so property, plant, and equipment reduced to $0.
† Bargain purchase remaining after reducing property, plant, and equipment to $0.

In the four preceding examples we have made two important assumptions: (1) that the cost of the acquisition and (2) the fair market values of all assets and liabilities were known.

The first assumption is valid if the acquiring company paid cash. But what if another consideration is used to effect the transaction? How is the cost of the acquisition determined in that situation for accounting purposes? The basic rule in such cases is that cost is determined either by the fair value of the consideration given or by the fair value of the property acquired, whichever is more clearly evident. The problem of allocating the purchase price is the subject of the following paragraph.

### Allocation of the Purchase Price

The problem of allocating the purchase price can be viewed as involving two questions:

1. How do we determine the fair value of specific assets and liabilities?
2. Having determined the assets' and liabilities' fair value, how do we allocate the purchase price among the acquired assets and liabilities?

*Valuing Specific Assets and Liabilities.* In valuing specific assets and liabilities, the following techniques are applied:

- *Cash*—valued dollar for dollar.

- *Marketable Securities*—valued at current net realizable values.

- *Receivables*—valued by discounting at appropriate current interest rates the amounts to be received less any necessary bad debt or collection costs.

- *Inventories*—Finished goods and work in process inventories are valued at estimated selling prices less the sum of
  (a) costs to complete
  (b) costs of disposal
  (c) a reasonable profit allowance for the completing and selling effort.
  Raw materials inventories are valued at current replacement cost.

- *Plant and Equipment*—For that portion of plant and equipment to be used by the acquiring company, a value should be recorded equal to the current replacement costs for similar capacity unless the expected use by the acquirer indicates a lower value. In most instances this will mean that an appraised value will be used. Current replacement cost may be determined from a used asset market or from the new asset market less an estimated amount for depreciation. Plant and equipment that are to be sold should be valued at current net realizable value.

- *Intangible Assets*—which can be identified should be valued at their appraised values.

- *Other Assets*—including land, natural resources, and non-marketable securities should be valued at appraised values.

- *Goodwill*—is valued as indicated in the section "Purchase Method of Accounting."

- *Liabilities*—All liabilities (except deferred taxes) are to be valued by discounting at appropriate current interest rates the amounts to be paid.

*General Allocation Rules.* The general rules to follow in allocating the purchase price among the assets acquired and liabilities assumed are:

1. Assign value to all tangible and identifiable intangible assets based on their fair market values.
2. Assign value to liabilities assumed based on the present value of those liabilities.
3. If necessary, assign a value to goodwill equal to the difference between the purchase price and the net fair market value of the assets acquired and liabilities assumed.
4. If necessary, reduce the values assigned to noncurrent assets by a proportionate share of the difference between the purchase price and the net fair market value of the assets purchased and liabilities assumed. In unusual circumstances where the noncurrent assets have been reduced to zero value and a bargain purchase still remains, then record a deferred credit on the balance sheet.
5. If necessary, adjust the value assigned to assets to reflect the fact that certain assets will produce greater or lesser cash flows to the company because their tax basis differs from the assets' fair market value. In circumstances where an asset will produce different cash flows over a number of years, these cash flows should be discounted at a reasonable rate.
6. Recompute the items described in (3) and (4) above.

In allocating the purchase price, Rule 5 above indicates that the effect of taxes should be considered. What does this mean? Basically whenever the tax basis of an asset differs from the asset's fair market value, the acquiring company will adjust the asset's fair market value for the present value of the tax benefit or detriment associated with the difference. However, it must be noted that a large number of acquisitions are recorded without adjustment for the effect of taxes.

*Example E* ABC Corporation sells all of its assets to XYZ Corporation in an Asset Acquisition. The assets sold include property, plant, and equipment with a fair market value of $170 and a tax basis to the acquiring company of $224. What should the book value of the property, plant, and equipment be assuming a 50 percent tax rate?

|  | Assumed Fair Market Value | Tax Basis | Difference |
|---|---|---|---|
| Property, plant, and equipment | $170 | $224 | $54 |

### Calculation of Present Value of Tax Benefit

| Year | 5-Year ACRS Depreciation Percentages | Difference | Depreciation Deductions | Taxes at 50 Percent | 10 Percent Discount Factor | PV of Taxes |
|---|---|---|---|---|---|---|
| 1 | .15 | $54 | $ 8.10 | $4.05 | .9091 | $ 3.68 |
| 2 | .22 | 54 | 11.88 | 5.94 | .8264 | 4.91 |
| 3 | .21 | 54 | 11.34 | 5.67 | .7513 | 4.26 |
| 4 | .21 | 54 | 11.34 | 5.67 | .6830 | 3.87 |
| 5 | .21 | 54 | 11.34 | 5.67 | .6209 | 3.52 |
|  |  |  | $54.00 |  |  | $20.24 |
|  |  |  | Present value of tax benefit, say | | | $20 |

### Calculation of Book Value of Property, Plant, and Equipment

| | |
|---|---|
| Fair market value | $170 |
| Plus: Present value of tax benefit from excess of tax basis over fair market value | 20 |
| Book value | $190 |

Based on the calculations above, XYZ Corporation will record property, plant, and equipment on its accounting books at $190.

*Example F* Same as Example E except that we analyze inventories that had a fair market value of $280 and a tax basis of $369.

|  | Fair Market Value | Tax Basis | Difference |
|---|---|---|---|
| Inventories | $280 | $369 | $89 |

Here the book value will equal $324 (($280 ÷ (89 × 50% tax rate)) because presumably the inventory will be sold within one year.

The examples above dealt with a situation where the tax basis of assets did not significantly differ from their fair market values. In acquisitions where a No Change in Basis Acquisition Method is employed, one could expect to see significant adjustments for tax effects.

### Differences Between Book and Tax Allocations

These techniques differ from those described above for allocating value to assets for accounting reasons using the Purchase Method of accounting. An obvious result is that the allocations of the purchase price for book and tax typically do not agree.

*Example G* ABC Corporation sells all of its assets to XYZ in an Asset Acquisition for $1,000. ABC's assets and their respective fair market values are listed below. What are their new tax basis and book values in the hands of XYZ? The tax basis of the assets in the hands of XYZ is $1,000. Since the purchase price exceeds the fair market value of ABC's assets a second tier, allocation must be performed. These calculations appear below.

### Calculation of Tax Basis of Assets

| Asset | (A) Fair Market Value | (B) Second Tier Allocation Calculation | (C) Allocation | (A) and (C) Tax Basis |
|---|---|---|---|---|
| Cash | $ 30 | | | $   30 |
| Receivables | 140* | | | 140 |
| Inventories | 280 | ($280/$630) × ($1,000 − $800) = $89 | | 369 |
| Property, plant, and equipment | 170 | ($170/$630) × ($1,000 − $800) = 54 | | 224 |
| Goodwill | 180† | ($180/$630) × ($1,000 − $800) = 57 | | 237 |
| | $800 | | | $1,000 |

\* Equals gross value.
† The fair market value of goodwill is estimated for tax purposes, but for accounting purposes goodwill is calculated as described in the section "Purchase Method of Accounting."

The fair market value of the tangible assets purchased is $620. We will assume that there are no identifiable intangible assets. If we also assume for the moment that the acquiring company has elected not to adjust asset values for any tax effects associated with a different tax basis for the assets (see the section "General Allocation Rules"), XYZ Corporation will record the following values on its books:

### Calculation of Book Values

| Asset | Fair Market Value | Book Value |
|---|---|---|
| Cash | $ 30 | $ 30 |
| Receivables | 140 | 140 |
| Inventories | 280 | 280 |
| Property, plant, and equipment | 170 | 170 |
| Total | $ 620 | |
| Purchase price | $1,000 | |
| Less total above | 620 | |
| Goodwill | $ 380 | 380 |
| | | $1,000 |

These book values are compared to the tax basis of the assets below.

### Comparison of Book Values and Tax Basis

| | Book Value | Tax Basis | Difference |
|---|---|---|---|
| Cash | $ 30 | $ 30 | |
| Receivables | 140 | 140 | |
| Inventories | 280 | 369 | $(89) |
| Property, plant, and equipment | 170 | 224 | (54) |
| Goodwill | 380 | 237 | 143 |
| Total | $1,000 | $1,000 | $ 0 |

If however the acquiring company elects to adjust asset values for the tax effects associated with the difference in the tax basis of the assets, XYZ will record different values for book purposes. These calculations appear below. Note that for book purposes, goodwill amounts to $316—the difference between the purchase price and the net fair market value of the assets acquired adjusted for tax effects.

## Calculation of Book Values

| Asset | Fair Market Value | Adjustments for Tax Effects | Book Value |
|---|---|---|---|
| Cash | $    30 | | $    30 |
| Receivables | 140 | | 140 |
| Inventories | 280 | $44* | 324 |
| Property, plant, and equipment | 170 | 20* | 190 |
| Total | $  620 | $64 | $  684 |
| Purchase price | $1,000 | | $1,000 |
| Less total above | 620 | | 684 |
| Goodwill | $  380 | | $  316 |

* See section "General Allocation Rules."

## Comparison of Book Values and Tax Basis

| | Book Value | Tax Basis | Difference |
|---|---|---|---|
| Cash | $    30 | $    30 | |
| Receivables | 140 | 140 | |
| Inventories | 324 | 369 | $(45) |
| Property, plant, and equipment | 190 | 224 | (34) |
| Goodwill | 316 | 237 | 79 |
| Total | $1,000 | $1,000 | $  0 |

*Example H* Same as Example G except the purchase price is $500. The tax basis of the assets in the hands of XYZ is $500. Since the purchase price is less than the fair market value of ABC's assets, a second tier allocation must be performed. The calculations are as follows:

## Calculation of Tax Basis of Assets

| Asset | (A) Fair Market Value | (B) Second Tier Allocation Calculations | (C) Allocation | (A) and (C) Tax Basis |
|---|---|---|---|---|
| Cash | $ 30 | | | $ 30 |
| Receivables | 140* | | | 140 |
| Inventories | 280 | ($280/$630) × ($500 − $800) = $(133) | | 147 |
| Property, plant, and equipment | 170 | ($170/$630) × ($500 − $800) = | (81) | 89 |
| Goodwill | 180 | ($180/$630) × ($500 − $800) = | (86) | 94 |
| | $800 | | | $500 |

* Equals gross value.

The fair market value of the tangible assets purchased is $620. We will assume that there are no identifiable intangible assets. If we also assume for the moment that the acquiring company has elected not to adjust asset values for any tax effects associated with a different tax basis for the assets (see the section "General Allocation Rules"), XYZ Corporation will record the following values on its books:

### Calculation of Book Values

| Asset | Fair Market Value | Adjustment for Negative Goodwill | Book Value |
|---|---|---|---|
| Cash | $ 30 | | $ 30 |
| Receivables | 140 | | 140 |
| Inventories | 280 | | 280 |
| Property, plant, and equipment | 170 | $(120) | 50 |
| Total | $ 620 | | |
| Purchase price | 500 | | |
| Less total above | 620 | | |
| Negative goodwill | $(120) | | $500 |

These book values are compared to the tax basis of the assets below.

### Comparison of Book Values and Tax Basis

| | Book Value | Tax Basis | Difference |
|---|---|---|---|
| Cash | $ 30 | $ 30 | |
| Receivables | 140 | 140 | |
| Inventories | 280 | 147 | $133 |
| Property, plant, and equipment | 50 | 89 | (39) |
| Goodwill | 0 | 94 | (94) |
| Total | $500 | $500 | $ 0 |

If, however, the acquiring company elects to adjust asset values for the tax effects associated with the difference in the tax basis of the assets, XYZ will record different values for book purposes. These calculations appear below. Note that for book purposes, negative goodwill amounts to $24—after adjusting for tax effects. Thus, property, plant, and equipment is reduced by that amount in determining book values.

## Calculation of Book Values

| Asset | Fair Market Value | Adjustment for Tax Effects | Sub-total | Adjustment for Negative Goodwill | Book Value |
|---|---|---|---|---|---|
| Cash | $ 30 | | $ 30 | | $ 30 |
| Receivables | 140 | | 140 | | 140 |
| Inventories | 280 | $(66)* | 214 | | 214 |
| Property, plant, and equipment | 170 | (30)† | 140 | $(24) | 116 |
| Total | $620 | $ 64 | $524 | | $500 |

* (Fair market value − Tax basis) × Tax rate. ($280 − $147) × 50% = $66.
† Assuming all property is five-year ACRS property, the proper adjustment is $30 calculated below.

| Year | ACRS Percent | Difference | Depreciation Deductions | Taxes at 50 Percent | 10 Percent Discount Factor | PV of Taxes |
|---|---|---|---|---|---|---|
| 1 | .15 | $81* | $12.15 | 6.08 | .9091 | $ 5.53 |
| 2 | .22 | 81 | 17.82 | 8.92 | .8264 | 7.33 |
| 3 | .21 | 81 | 17.01 | 8.50 | .7513 | 6.39 |
| 4 | .21 | 81 | 17.01 | 8.50 | .6830 | 5.81 |
| 5 | .21 | 81 | 17.01 | 8.50 | .6209 | 5.28 |
| | | | $81.00 | | | $30.38 |
| | | | | Present value of tax benefit, say, | | $30.00 |

* Fair market value of plant, property, and equipment less tax basis ($170 − $89 = $81).

The resulting book values and tax basis of the assets are compared below.

## Comparison of Book Values and Tax Basis

| | Book Value | Tax Basis | Difference |
|---|---|---|---|
| Cash | $ 30 | $ 30 | |
| Receivables | 140 | 140 | |
| Inventories | 214 | 147 | $ 67 |
| Property, plant, and equipment | 116 | 89 | 27 |
| Goodwill | 0 | 94 | (94) |
| Total | $500 | $500 | $ 0 |

Although the book and tax differences are substantial in the examples, they pale by comparison to the differences between book and tax values that result when one uses the Purchase Method of accounting in an acquisition where the transaction is effected using a No Change in Basis Acquisition Method. In acquisitions effected under those methods, the tax basis of the assets of the target does not change, yet the fair market values of the assets of the target are recorded on the books of the acquiring company; sometimes net of the tax benefits that are lost as a result of not being able to step up the tax basis of the assets of the target to their fair market values.

### Financial Statement Disclosure

If the Purchase Method of accounting is used to record an acquisition, the notes to the financial statements of the acquiring company must describe the target, the date it was acquired, the cost of the acquisition including the types of consideration exchanged, the amount of any goodwill resulting from the transaction, and any contingent payments, options, or commitments associated with the acquisition. Furthermore, the acquiring company must disclose the following results of operation on a pro forma basis: (1) operating results for the current period assuming the acquisition took place at the beginning of the period and (2) if comparative financial statements are presented, operating results for the immediately preceding period assuming the transaction had been effected at the beginning of that period. Pro forma presentation of the results of operations of any other prior periods is not permitted. The pro forma information disclosed must include revenue, income before extraordinary items, net income, and earnings per share.

## POOLING OF INTERESTS METHOD

The Pooling of Interests Method of accounting is based on the assumption that certain transactions are merely arrangements between stockholder groups to exchange equity securities. Therefore, the only accounting adjustment to record in these situations is a change in the ownership interests of the stockholders. This is effected by eliminating the capital stock of the target company and recording the new stock issued by the acquiring company to the target company's shareholders. Otherwise, the acquiring company and the target company merely combine assets and liabilities at their historical book values on the acquisition date.

*Example I* XYZ Corporation agrees to purchase ABC Corporation in a Type B reorganization. XYZ will exchange one share of its common stock for every share of ABC Corporation outstanding. We will assume that the transaction meets all the requirements for Pooling of Interests treatment and that the company's balance sheets before the transaction are as follows:

|                                                | Book Values | |
|------------------------------------------------|--------:|--------:|
|                                                | XYZ | ABC |
| Cash and accounts receivable                   | $ 500 | $ 100 |
| Inventories                                    | 700 | 300 |
| Property, plant, and equipment                 | 2,000 | 700 |
| Total assets                                   | $3,200 | $1,100 |
| Accounts payable and accrued expenses          | $ 700 | $ 400 |
| Common stock (par $1)                          | 250 | 70 |
| Contributed capital in excess of par value     | 1,250 | 530 |
| Retained earnings                              | 1,000 | 100 |
| Stockholders' equity                           | 2,500 | 700 |
| Total liabilities and stockholders' equity     | $3,200 | $1,100 |

The acquiring company would record the investment in ABC Corporation on its books on the date of the transaction in the amount of $700. The journal entry that XYZ would record is:

|                                      | Debit | Credit |
|--------------------------------------|:-----:|:------:|
| Investment in ABC Corporation        | 70 |    |
| Common Stock (par $1)                |    | 70 |

However, the consolidated balance sheet of the entities would eliminate this investment against ABC's stockholders' equity accounts.

## Consolidation Worksheet

| | Book Values | | Eliminations | | XYZ and ABC |
|---|---|---|---|---|---|
| | XYZ | ABC | Debit | Credit | Consolidated |
| Cash and accounts receivable | $ 500 | $ 100 | | | $ 600 |
| Inventories | 700 | 300 | | | 1,000 |
| Investment in ABC Corporation | 70 | | | $70 | |
| Property, plant, and equipment | 2,000 | 700 | | | 2,700 |
| Total assets | $3,270 | $1,100 | | | $4,300 |
| Accounts payable and accrued expenses | $ 700 | $ 400 | | | $1,100 |
| Common stock (par $1) | 320 | 70 | $ 70 | | 320 |
| Contributed capital in excess of par value | 1,250 | 530 | | | 1,780 |
| Retained earnings | 1,000 | 100 | 100 | | 1,000 |
| Stockholders' equity | 2,570 | 700 | | | 3,200 |
| Total liabilities and stockholders' equity | $3,270 | $1,100 | | | $4,300 |

### Criteria for Pooling

*Accounting Principles Board Opinion No. 16*, "Business Combinations," prescribes 12 specific criteria for a pooling. If any of the criteria are not met, the transaction must be accounted for using the Purchase Method. The criteria are classified into three categories:

(a) attributes of the combining companies

(b) manner of combining the interests

(c) absence of planned transactions

### Attributes of the Combining Companies

1. Each of the combining companies must be autonomous and must not have been a division or subsidiary of another corporation for two years prior to the initiation of the plan of combination. A new enterprise generally meets this re-

quirement unless it is a successor to part or all of an entity that does not meet the requirement.

2. The combining entities must be independent of the other combining entities. This means that a combining entity can hold no more than a 10-percent interest in the outstanding voting common stock of another combining entity.

*Manner of Combining the Interests*

3. The combination must be accomplished within one year according to a specific plan or by a single transaction.

4. The surviving corporation must issue only common stock with rights identical to those of the majority of its outstanding voting common stock in exchange for substantially all of the voting common stock of the other combining entities at the date the plan of combination is consummated. For purposes of this requirement, a class of stock that has voting control is the majority class. Furthermore, substantially all of the voting common stock means 90 percent or more.

5. None of the combining entities may change the equity interest of the voting common stock through exchanges, retirements, issuances, or distributions in contemplation of effecting the combination.

6. Any of the combining entities may reacquire shares of voting common stock, but only if the purpose is unrelated to the business combination. Furthermore, after the plan of combination is initiated, only a normal number of shares may be so acquired.

7. Each individual common shareholder who exchanges stock must receive a voting common stock interest exactly in proportion to its relative voting common stock interest before the transaction.

8. The voting rights of the stockholders of any of the combined entities cannot be deprived or restricted as part of the plan of combination.

9. The combination must be resolved at the date the plan of combination is consummated. No provision is allowed for the issuance of securities or other consideration.

### Absence of Planned Transactions

10. The combined entity cannot agree directly or indirectly to retire or reacquire any or part of the common stock issued to effect the combination.

11. The combined enterprise cannot enter into other financial arrangements for the benefit of the former stockholders of a combining enterprise, such as a guaranty of loans secured by stock issued in the combination, that in effect negates the exchange of equity securities.

12. The combined enterprise cannot intend or plan to dispose of a significant part of the assets of the combining enterprises within two years after the combination, other than disposals in the ordinary course of business of the formerly separate enterprises and to eliminate duplicate facilities or excess capacity.

**Financial Statement Disclosure**

Any company that applies the Pooling of Interests Method of accounting to a combination must report results of operations for the period in which the combination occurs as though the enterprises had been combined as of the beginning of the period. Furthermore, balance sheets and other financial information of the separate enterprises as of the beginning of the period must be presented as though the companies had been combined at that date. Any financial statements and financial information of the separate enterprises presented for prior years must also be restated on a combined basis to furnish comparative information. All restated financial statements and financial summaries must indicate clearly that financial data is on a combined basis.

The notes to the financial statements of a combined enterprise must disclose a description of the combined entities, detailed information (including, for example, revenue, extraordinary items, and net income) on the results of operations of the previously separate companies for the period before the combination that are included in current combined net income, and miscellaneous other information.

# REFERENCES

Accounting Principles Board Opinion No. 16, "Accounting for Business Combinations" (American Institute of Certified Public Accountants, New York, NY, 1970)

Accounting Principles Board Opinion No. 17, "Accounting for Intangibles" (American Institute of Certified Public Accountants, New York, NY, 1970)

Philip L. Defliese, Kenneth P. Johnson, Roderick K. MacLeod, *Montgomery's Auditing,* ninth edition (John Wiley & Sons, New York, NY, 1975, pp. 669–703)

*Interpretations of APB Opinion Nos. 16 and 17,* fifth edition (Arthur Anderson & Co., New York, NY, 1981)

Arnold J. Pahler and Joseph E. Mori, *Advanced Accounting: Concepts and Practice* (Harcourt Brace Jovanovich, Inc., New York, NY, 1981, pp. 37–234)

Paul J. Wendell, *Corporate Controller's Manual* (Warren, Gorham & Lamont, Inc., Boston, MA, 1981, chaps. 30–33)

# Financing Acquisitions

*John D. Carton*
MMG Patricof & Co., Inc.
New York, New York

This chapter outlines instruments used to fund corporate acquisitions, including smaller, private transactions, and explores some of the underlying considerations in choosing each type of instrument. The chapter also examines the range of sources that provide acquisition financing. References to rates and terms in this chapter reflect market conditions at the time of writing and may not be applicable at later dates.

In broad terms, the financial "currencies" for corporate acquisitions include:

- debt
- equity
- hybrid securities
- contingent payments
- other forms of financing
- cash

## DEBT

Assuming a buyer wishes to tap sources of outside financing rather than use retained internal capital, a wide range of financial securities are available to choose from. Debt financing is perhaps the most widely used and the most varied.

Generally, debt financing is arranged on a friendly, negotiated basis between borrowers and lenders. The borrower may choose to arrange to place different pieces of debt with different lenders, based on their particular lending interests. In this way, the borrower may be able to optimize the amount and terms for the acquisition funding.

Despite the number of debt instruments available to help finance acquisitions, all of them may be understood by reference to four factors:

- seniority (position relative to other obligations)
- pledge of assets (secured vs. unsecured)
- financial terms (rate, payment schedule)
- special factors

### Seniority

Seniority in the event of liquidation is one of the most basic desires of all lenders. Debt which is entitled to repayment ahead of other borrowings is called senior debt while debt with less priority is called junior or subordinated debt. Historically, banks, insurance companies, pension funds, and other lenders have tended to concentrate their lending efforts on only one type of debt, either senior or junior. On occasion, the degree of seniority may be negotiated with lenders. In addition, some institutions now have departments that offer financing ranging from senior to junior debt. More often, however, the borrower selects the appropriate lender(s) based on the type of debt sought.

### Security

A second factor that distinguishes various types of debt is the degree to which assets, if any, are pledged as collateral for the debt. Debt for which specific collateral is pledged is called secured debt while other borrowings that rely only on the general credit of the borrower are called unsecured debt. As in the case of seniority, lenders tend to specialize in either secured or unsecured debt.

Many types of collateral may be offered and the amount of secured debt that is financeable varies depending on which asset is pledged. Lenders have developed a number of guidelines to determine how much they will lend against each asset. Although a full discussion of these formulas is beyond the scope of this chapter, an overview is helpful for understanding of the potential amount of acquisition financing available from secured lenders. Generally, one can obtain financing for 70 to 100 percent of eligible receivables. *Eligible receivables* are defined broadly as less than 90 days old, net of reserves, and exclusive of accruals for partial completion of projects. Inventory financing is even more varied. Raw materials and finished goods can usually be financed for from 50 to 90 percent of their cost. Work in process, however, is not as marketable and, therefore, will support financing for only around 20 percent. The amount of secured debt that can be supported by property, plant, and equipment is usually based on a lender's assessment of the appraised fair market value of these assets under a forced sale or liquidation scenario (that is, the "knock-down" or "under-the-hammer" value).

Secured lenders may provide "strips" of debt secured by individual assets or they may provide wrap-around debt with a secured interest in *all* of the company's assets. However, the structure of a transaction sometimes makes it difficult, or impossible, to provide a direct security interest in specific assets. For example, the debt may be raised by a shell corporation whose only asset is the shares of the acquired company. In such situations, it is still possible to raise secured debt. Many secured lenders will accept a pledge of the acquired company's common stock as collateral. Additional collateral may take the form of a letter of credit from an unrelated third party (such as an institution with financial substance) or even a guarantee of payment from the buyer (assuming the buyer has some financial resources apart from the entity being acquired). Under these conditions, the secured lender may also require protective clauses or covenants in the loan indenture (the document that describes the contractual relationship between the borrower and the lender). The covenants can be positive (for example, maintaining assets in good order, maintaining certain financial ratios) or negative (for example, not paying dividends, not incurring additional indebtedness).

### Financial Terms

The financial terms associated with acquisition debt are influenced by the debt's seniority and the amount of collateral. Financial terms are also influenced by the lenders' perceptions of the quality of the underlying assets, the company's historical performance, its management, and the acquired company's prospective ability to generate cash adequate to service the acquisition debt. The basic financial terms include the interest rate and when the interest and principal are to be paid.

Interest rates can be variable or fixed for some or all of the life of the debt. Variable interest rates are generally indexed to the prime lending rate of a financial institution, the London Inter-Bank Offered Rate (LIBOR), the rate of publicly traded certificates of deposit, or other similar instruments. Lenders may set interest rates ranging from prime (or near prime) for investment grade borrowers to several percentage points over prime for riskier credits. Many average buyers of small and medium-sized businesses are charged rates in the range of 1½ to 2 percent over prime.

An additional premium is generally required for fixed rate debt, ranging from ½ percent to several percentage points depending on the term of the loan and qualitative factors such as seniority, security, and the history of the company. Even if an institution does not offer fixed rate loans, there are ways for a borrower to obtain protection against large interest rate swings. Some of the more common methods include interest rate swaps, collars, caps, and cash caps. In an *interest rate swap,* the borrower pays a one-time fee to the lender to couple the borrower's variable rate debt with a similar fixed rate debt of another borrower. The borrowers may not know each other's identity and the lenders (or other intermediaries in the swap) usually assume responsibility for interest payments even if one party defaults. Collars and caps are negotiated between the borrower and the lender in order to limit rate changes. In a *collar,* the lender agrees to limit the amount by which a variable rate may rise when interest rates go up and the borrower agrees to a floor, or minimum rate, to be paid when interest rates go down. In a *cap,* the lender agrees to limit the amount by which the rate for the particular loan may rise when interest rates go up.

Some institutions are willing to issue debt with performance incentives, which reduce the interest rate spread over prime if the borrower achieves certain financial performance goals (for example, debt-to-equity ratio stays below a certain level, cash-flow-to-interest ratio stays above a certain level).

Interest rates on acquisition debt are subject to usury laws, which vary from state to state and are based on the form of the borrower (that is, corporation, partnership, or individual).

Interest payments are generally made monthly, quarterly, or semiannually, dating from the time the loan is made, although some acquisition debt allows for a deferral of interest payments in the initial years.

Most acquisition debt calls for the amortization of principal over the life of the indebtedness. However, the rate of amortization can vary. Loans secured by specific assets are usually amortized in relation to the economic life of such assets. Loans that are general obligations of the borrower are amortized in a variety of ways. Many lenders allow principal repayments to be deferred in the initial years of the loan and some permit a large balloon payment upon the loan's maturity. It is not unusual to expect to repay at least 60 percent of a loan before the maturity. For such loans, maturity generally ranges from five to ten years.

### Special Factors

Factors that differentiate forms of debt include those that are tax motivated in response to federal, state, and municipal economic and social concerns. For example, tax authorities frequently offer tax preferences for loans associated with the preservation of jobs or the development of local or regional enterprises. Industrial revenue bonds, Small Business Administration loans, and loans to leveraged employee stock ownership plans (ESOPs) are examples of loans that are or have been tax advantaged to the lender or the borrower. Although a discussion of the intricacies of each of these factors is beyond the scope of this chapter, a brief overview of ESOPs, as an example, may give a sense of the potential impact of these factors on the terms for acquisition debt.

ESOPs are similar to other traditional employee retirement plans except for two key differences: ESOPs can borrow money and they use their funds to buy equity in the employer company rather than a diversified portfolio of securities. The Internal Revenue Code permits companies to make significant, tax-deductible contributions to qualified ESOPs (as much as 15 to 25 percent of total annual payroll under certain circumstances). Thus, a buyer who uses an ESOP to raise acquisition debt can use the tax-deductible contributions to retire acquisition debt that would otherwise be retired with after-tax earnings. Accordingly, the terms for the amortization of the acquisition debt can be set to reflect the higher (that is, pretax) cash flow available for debt service. In addition, the Internal Revenue Code allows lenders to avoid taxes on 50 percent of the interest they earn from loans to ESOPs. Accordingly, lenders to ESOPs may be able to charge lower interest rates and still realize the same after-tax profit on their loans.

### Senior and Secured Debt

Senior debt can take two forms: general corporate debt or asset-specific financing.

Senior general corporate borrowing is secured by a pledge of all tangible assets, the company's shares, or other collateral. Lenders provide senior acquisition debt based on a variety of standards, the foremost of which is the value and quality of the company's assets. However, lenders are strongly influenced by industry conditions, the company's market position, the company's track record, the adequacy of its management, geographic location, growth potential, the degree of diversification of the business, and the concentration of key customers and suppliers. As a result of these considerations, lenders may provide financing representing a relatively high multiple of the company's cash flow and which may even exceed the company's tangible book value, if the lender feels especially sanguine about the company's prospects. This aggressive lending is illustrated in radio, television, and cable acquisitions in which senior lenders have provided up to seven times cash flow with additional funding provided by subordinated lenders. The converse is illustrated in other industries, such as magazine publishing, in which senior lenders are sometimes hesitant to provide much more than two times cash flow.

Companies with substantial tangible assets may be candidates for financing of such assets. Some common types of specific asset financing include mortgages on real property, equipment leasing, and accounts receivable or inventory factoring.

### Mortgages

Real estate mortgages are generally based on the appraised fair market value of real estate assets, which can be substantially greater than their historical book value. In many corporations, the true value of real estate assets may not be fully reflected in the valuation of the company based on traditional multiples of earnings or book value. Hence, mortgage financing may be a means of realizing greater funding than that obtainable from cash flow or historical book value financing.

Real estate mortgages can also be attractive to borrowers because lenders generally look to have a security interest only in the underlying real estate, thus leaving the other assets unencumbered and available as collateral for additional financing.

Typically, mortgages are arranged through an institutional private placement. However, the borrower can access larger groups of lenders or the public market by issuing a mortgage bond. Such bonds can be especially valuable in acquiring a growing company because they can have "open-end" provisions that allow for the issuance of subsequent debt without having to obtain a new mortgage.

### Equipment Financing

Financing specific pieces of equipment in a business acquisition is generally accomplished through equipment leasing or via equipment trust certificates. In both instances, the fair market value of the equipment determines the amount of financing (usually on the order of 80 to 100 percent of fair market value). Generally, an independent appraiser is retained to help determine a range of values. These values may bear no relation to book value. For example, technologically obsolete or immovable items such as telephone systems may be appraised at a fraction of their book value, commodity-type items such as cars and trucks may be appraised at or near their depreciated book value, and certain unique equipment may be appraised at a significant premium to book value. Clearly, the potential hidden value in certain equipment can be a motivation in seeking specific equipment financing as part of an acquisition financing package.

As with mortgages, the lender's security interests can usually be satisfied by the value of the underlying equipment, thereby leaving the company's other assets free for other financing. However, most equipment has a shorter economic life than real estate. Institutions that finance equipment therefore require a repayment schedule reflecting the life of these assets. This may be a drawback for borrowers seeking long-term acquisition financing.

### Factoring

Financing accounts receivable and inventories (factoring) is another mechanism for securing debt collateralized by specific assets. Receivables and inventories turn over quickly. Most current assets in place at the time of an acquisition will probably be collected or sold soon after the transaction. Thus, financing associated with these assets is usually short term. In an ongoing business, current assets tend to renew themselves. Hence, a revolving loan may enable a borrower to use debt secured by current assets as part of the acquisition financing. However, the risk is that the collateral could diminish if the business shrinks, causing a premature demand for repayment. Thus, the use of factoring in financing an acquisition is somewhat limited.

### Junior and Subordinated Debt

Despite the attraction of financing discrete assets, the financing available through this type of debt may be insufficient to meet the buyer's needs. It may be necessary for the buyer to seek some unsecured, junior, or subordinated debt to complete its acquisition financing.

Subordinated lenders are influenced by the same qualitative factors that determine loan availability from senior lenders, and the amount of subordinated debt attainable varies widely among lenders. Depending on the circumstances, a subordinated lender may provide debt of two to three times cash flow. This financing would be *in addition to* any senior debt.

Interest rates for subordinated debt are typically higher than for senior debt, reflecting the higher financial risk associated with the junior position relative to other debt and the absence of a major secured interest in the company's assets. Subordinated debt that is very junior or very large relative to the company's cash flow *(mezzanine debt)* may command a rate of return to the lender close to the return required by an equity holder. As a consequence, it may be impractical to provide the full return in the form of interest alone. For this reason, some subordinated debt sometimes carries other "sweeteners" such as warrants or conversion rights (see "Hybrid Securities").

### Bridge Loans

Occasionally, an acquisition must be completed very quickly. The time may be too brief to complete the process of arranging suitable long-term debt financing. Rather than lose the chance to complete the deal, some buyers raise part of the capital necessary to complete the deal and seek the balance in the form of a bridge loan from a financial institution. Bridge loans are a specialized form of debt requiring a speedy commitment from a lender—sometimes before a traditional due diligence process can be completed. In consequence, only a few institutions regularly invest in this type of debt.

Typically, bridge financing is intended to remain outstanding for less than a year and is generally retired sooner with proceeds from "permanent" capital raised in the form of long-term debt and equity or from the sale of certain assets. As compensation for the higher degree of financial risk, bridge lenders usually receive interest and sweeteners similar to some subordinated and mezzanine lenders.

## EQUITY

Equity securities offer a buyer some attractive financing features. For example, equity investors look to achieve a return based on the long-term appreciation of their investment, rather than from current interest payments. In addition, equity holders do not have security interests in specific company assets—leaving these assets available as collateral for other debt financing. Another major attraction to financing a transaction with equity is that it enables the parties to effect a tax-free reorganization, if so desired.

The primary features distinguishing various types of equity securities include:

- seniority in liquidation
- redemption privileges (including puts and calls)
- voting rights
- dividends

The following discussion of some of the commonly used forms of equity illustrates these features.

### Preferred Stock

This class of equity receives preference over common stock in the payment of dividends and in any claims against the company's assets in the event of liquidation. However, all equity holders, including preferred stockholders, are usually subordinated to debtholders in the event of liquidation.

As with acquisition debt, the issuance of preferred stock is usually consummated through friendly negotiations. Thus the terms associated with preferred stock can be quite varied. It is fairly common for preferred stock to bear a dividend. However, this dividend may be cumulative, which means that the dividend will accrue but not be paid unless the company has sufficient operating earnings. Voting privileges generally are not given to preferred shareholders except under certain circumstances, some of them contractual such as failure to pay dividends for a certain number of quarters and some as a matter of state law such as in the event of merger or liquidation. Sometimes preferred stockholders have an option to convert their shares into common shares, which upon conversion gives the holders a right to vote. Preferred shareholders frequently have certain protective clauses that may call for early redemption in the event of a major corporate change such as a merger or liquidation.

### Common Stock

Common stock as a form of consideration is absolutely necessary if pooling accounting is to be used. Aside from this factor which mandates the use of common stock, there occasionally are strong financial motivations for using common stock. For example, if the buyer's stock carries a high price-earnings multiple it may be able to offer relatively few shares to complete the deal.

Common stock can be used in a number of ways. Most logically, it can be issued directly to the seller as consideration for the sale of the business. However, if circumstances dictate that the seller receive cash, common stock may be issued to institutional investors, whose cash will then be used to pay the seller. This mechanism is frequently used in a variety of leveraged buyout situations. If the buyer is a public company, a new issue in the public market or a rights offering to existing shareholders can be used to raise the cash.

Common stock typically has no maturity or redemption requirements and frequently carries no dividend in order to enable the company to use its resources to service and retire other financial obligations or to grow the business.

Most common stock investors are prepared to hold onto their shares for a relatively long time before recognizing the appreciation in their investment. Ultimately, though, common shareholders will require some way to recognize their gain. If the company is publicly traded, the public market provides the necessary mechanism (subject to holding period constraints under federal and state securities laws or by agreement with the company). However, if the company is privately held and there is no ready market for the shares, some other mechanisms can

be employed to ensure ultimate liquidity for the common shareholders:

- puts and calls
- demand registration
- demand sale

The right to "put" shares back to the company, that is, to
have the company buy out a particular shareholder's interest,
may provide the liquidity necessary to realize the shareholder's
gains. The value of the shares may be set by a predetermined
formula, for example, a fixed dollar amount or a multiple of
earnings, or it may be determined by an independent third-
party expert. Generally, the right to put stock back to the
company can be exercised only during a finite period so that
the company is not perpetually hampered by the threat of a
potentially massive call on its capital. Also, the company may
require reciprocal treatment, that is, if the shareholders have
the right to put stock back to the company, then the company
may also want the right to "call" their shares at its election,
generally at the same time and on the same terms as those
applicable to the put.

In lieu of puts and calls, a buyer may agree to the public
sale of its shares. If the company is private, the company may
grant holders the right to cause the company to try to go public
by a specific date, if by such date it has not already done so.
This is known as a demand registration right. In addition, the
company may grant holders the right to add their shares to
initial or later public offerings of the company or its shareholders,
the so-called piggyback right.

There may be important reasons, however, for the company
to remain private. If this is the case, the company would resist
giving shareholders demand registration rights. Generally, new
shareholders would have the right to sell their shares to other
investors in private transactions. However, in some circumstances they may be contractually constrained from doing so by
agreement with the existing shareholders. Also, if the ownership
interest is not substantial enough to exercise some control over

the company, it may be difficult to attract a buyer. In these situations, the company and its shareholders may give the new shareholders the right to cause a sale of the entire business to create liquidity both for themselves and the other shareholders. The exercise of this right may be sufficient to precipitate some other action by the company, such as buying the new shareholders' shares back, rather than risking a total change in control.

Because equity, whether preferred or common, is generally riskier than debt securities, it usually commands a higher rate of return. The equity holder bears the greatest risk in exchange for the prospect of the greatest return. As an indication of the expected return from equity investments, consider the growth in the Standard & Poor's composite index (500 stocks) as illustrated in Table 10–1.

**Table 10–1.** *Standard & Poor's composite index (500 stocks).*

|  | Compound Annual Growth |
|---|---|
| Five years ended December 1987 | 11.4% |
| Ten years ended December 1987 | 10.3% |
| Peak to peak June 1983 to August 1987 | 17.8% |
| Peak to peak November 1980 to August 1987 | 13.9% |

Source: Standard & Poor's Corporation.

The expected rate of return for equity investments in private companies may be even higher, given the lack of liquidity and greater potential risk for investors. Typically, institutional equity funds and venture capital pools seek an "average" 30- to 50-percent compound annual growth for their investments. In order to achieve this "average" rate of return, which reflects the failed investments as well as the successful ones, the fund managers may set their target rates of return as high as 50 to 100 percent (assuming the company achieves its financial goals and the equity appreciates correspondingly in value).

# HYBRID SECURITIES

## Debt with Equity Features

As discussed earlier in the section on debt financing, investors may perceive a greater degree of financial risk in junior or subordinated debt than in senior or secured debt. Thus, the target rate of return will be higher than for senior debt. Although one way of satisfying this requirement is to set a higher interest rate, the debt service may be overly burdensome for a newly acquired business.

Solutions to this problem include zero-coupon bonds (zeros) or payment-in-kind securities (PIKs). Zeros accrue interest to be paid at a later date or as part of the scheduled amortization of principal. PIKs pay interest currently, but in the form of additional securities rather than in cash. Both zeros and PIKs may solve the borrower's need to defer the payment of interest. Nonetheless, they may not be a totally attractive solution for certain lenders, since many lenders require some current income in order to pay dividends to their investors. Zeros and PIKs usually have no cash payments in the initial years. Also, they may create potential tax liabilities for the holder as a result of accrued interest. For these reasons, lenders may prefer another type of security to achieve the higher rate of return.

One method of achieving a higher rate of return is to sweeten the debt with equity features, thereby creating a hybrid security. The "sweetener" (also called a kicker) may take the form of warrants or options to purchase a specified number of shares of common stock at a given price. Alternatively, debt may be convertible into common stock at some time prior to its maturity.

The cost of subordinated debt financing depends on the degree of subordination to other obligations, the financial performance of the company, the investor's perception of the industry, the general creditworthiness of the company, the amount of tangible collateral in the business, and other variables. When the debt is junior to all other debt and is senior only to the company's equity, it is called *mezzanine debt*. In a private company, this kind of debt would require a 20- to 30-percent

annual return. In a comparable public company, the rate of return might be somewhat lower. Typically, interest of 12 to 16 percent would be paid on a current basis and equity features, when exercised, would provide the additional return to the debtholder. To illustrate, consider the case of a lender who has targeted a rate of return of 25 percent per year but is prepared to have current interest payments limited to 12 percent annually. In order to make up the shortfall in the rate of return, the lender negotiates to have the right to convert its debt into common stock at will. Carrying this example one step further, let's establish a few more facts regarding this hypothetical investment:

- The lender invests $1,000,000 which matures in five years.
- The company's pretax earnings have grown 30 percent per year for each of the last five years and totaled $500,000 in the most recent year.
- The company is being acquired for $5,000,000 or roughly ten times pretax earnings.
- The lender expects the company's earnings to continue to grow at 30 percent per year for the next five years—which would imply pretax earnings of $1,850,000 in the fifth year and suggest a potential future value for the business of $18,500,000 (that is, ten times future earnings assuming an exit P/E to be the same as the entrance P/E).

If the debt is convertible into 10 percent of the company's common stock and the lender converts at the end of the fifth year, the resulting rate of return would be:

$$\frac{10\% \times \$18,500,000}{\$1,000,000} = 13\% \text{ compounded annually}$$

Thus, the 12-percent current coupon plus the 13 percent implied by the conversion feature gives the lender an "all-in" rate of return of 25 percent.

### Equity with Contingent Elements

The return on equity securities can also be enhanced by hybridizing them with other securities.

This technique can be seen in the conversion and redemption rights of various types of preferred stock. As an example, preferred stock may have a PIK dividend payable in additional shares as well as a current cash dividend. Another hybrid feature involves conversion rights into common stock in lieu of redemption at face value. If the holder expects the company's value to appreciate (as in the example used for the mezzanine debt), the conversion feature will enhance the preferred shareholder's return.

Common stock can also be hybridized by adding warrants, which vest and become exercisable over time or based on performance.

## CONTINGENT PAYMENTS

Only rarely do buyers and sellers believe that the company is worth the same amount. This is especially true in private transactions. Generally, these differences are resolved during negotiations and the transaction proceeds at a mutually agreed-on price. However, occasionally buyers and sellers have irreconcilable differences of opinion regarding the value of the business, resulting from different perceptions of the company's future earnings potential. For example, the seller may feel that the company is postured to achieve significantly higher earnings in the future than it demonstrated in the past. Such improvements may be attributed to attractive growth prospects or to hidden earnings that may have been understated as a result of accounting or operating policies designed to minimize taxes. Accordingly, the seller wants to be compensated for this impending improvement in financial performance. On the other hand, the buyer's lack of familiarity with the business may cause him or her to be more circumspect. Thus, the buyer may resist paying for earnings that have not yet materialized.

One method for dealing with this roadblock is to "finance" the difference between the seller's price and the buyer's price with a contingent payment of the difference (or a portion thereof) when, or if, the company achieves higher operating results. These contingent payments are frequently called *earnouts*.

There are limitless ways to structure earnouts, in part because of the factors unique to each deal. Two of the more common strategies follow.

For illustration, consider an example in which the seller has the following characteristics:

| | |
|---|---|
| Sales | $10,000,000 |
| Net income | 500,000 |
| Seller's price | 6,500,000 (13 × P/E) |
| Buyer's price | 5,000,000 (10 × P/E) |
| Difference to be financed through an earnout | 1,500,000 |

In this situation the buyer may offer to pay $5,000,000 at closing *plus* an earnout at the end of five years based on the amount by which *average* earnings for the five-year period exceed a base level of earnings. In order to develop a meaningful formula to calculate the additional earnout payment, the buyer needs to know the financial projections upon which the seller is basing his or her price. The buyer and seller would then agree on an appropriate formula (for example, a multiple of net income), which would result in an earnout in the desired amount. In this example, assume that the seller expects to achieve earnings of $650,000, on average, during the next five years. Thus, a formula of ten times the amount by which future average earnings exceed the base earnings would produce the desired earnout (that is, $10 \times (650,000 - 500,000) = 1,500,000$). Table 10–2 illustrates the hypothetical future earnings of the company and the calculation of the earnout payment assuming earnings grow consistently over the next five years:

**Table 10-2.**

| (in thousands of dollars) | | | | | | |
|---|---|---|---|---|---|---|
| *Year 1* | *Year 2* | *Year 3* | *Year 4* | *Year 5* | *Total* | *Average* |
| $ 550 | $ 600 | $ 650 | $ 700 | $ 750 | $3,250 | $ 650 |
| | | | | | Base year | − 500 |
| | | | | | Earnout basis | 150 |
| | | | | | Multiple | × 10 |
| | | | | | Earnout amount | $1,500 |

Based on this example, the seller will get his or her full asking price if the company is successful in achieving the growth in earnings that the seller anticipates.

A common complaint by sellers, however, is that they have to wait a long time to receive any additional payments. One way around this problem is to pay a portion of the earnout annually based on the amount by which earnings in each year exceed the earnings from the year before. In this case, the earnout formula (that is, multiple) would have to be different because the base amount each year represents the *total* annual increase in earnings, rather than the *average* of the annual increases in earnings. For illustration, assume that the buyer and seller agree to a formula of six times the increase in earnings (see Table 10–3).

**Table 10-3.**

| | (in thousands of dollars) | | | | | |
|---|---|---|---|---|---|---|
| | *Year 1* | *Year 2* | *Year 3* | *Year 4* | *Year 5* | *Total* |
| Earnings | $ 550 | $ 600 | $ 650 | $ 700 | $ 750 | $3,250 |
| Prior year | 500 | 550 | 600 | 650 | 700 | |
| Earnout base | 50 | 50 | 50 | 50 | 50 | |
| Earnout formula | × 6 | × 6 | × 6 | × 6 | × 6 | |
| Earnout | $ 300 | $ 300 | $ 300 | $ 300 | $ 300 | $1,500 |

Based on this example, the seller would still get the desired earnout but starts to get it sooner, rather than waiting five years.

These simple examples illustrate how contingent payment formulas can be used to finance a portion of the acquisition price. Nonetheless, structuring a contingent payment formula often requires a great deal of imagination and compromise in order to satisfy legitimate but conflicting concerns among buyers and sellers.

*Buyers' Concerns.* Some frequent concerns voiced by buyers include:

- The buyer may be obligated to make a larger payment than anticipated if the acquired company has erratic earnings, or if it experiences some growth but then starts to decline, or if its earnings skyrocket in one year.
- The buyer will be obligated to pay the earnout even if earnings improve because of the buyer's hard work rather than because of any impending growth by the seller's company at the time of the acquisition.
- For accounting purposes, "potentially issuable" shares must be included in the calculation of fully diluted earnings per share—even if the earnout has not yet materialized.
- An earnout may make it impossible to account for an acquisition on a pooling basis.

Many of these concerns are addressable. For example, concerns about overpaying may be assuaged by agreeing to a cap or ceiling on the amount of the total earnout. Also, earnings that fall below the prior period could be penalized and there could be limits placed on the amount of any single payment.

Some concerns cannot be relieved. In these situations, the buyer must decide if the concerns warrant paying a higher fixed price rather than pursuing the alternative of an earnout in which the buyer pays only for earnings that materialize.

*Sellers' Concerns.* Some of the concerns that sellers frequently express include:

- The seller must wait before receiving the remaining portion of the sale price.

- It may be hard to achieve the projected earnings.

- The buyer may not manage the company in the same way as the seller. For example, the buyer may cut back on overhead, sales force, or capital improvements, thus compromising the company's ability to achieve the seller's projections for revenues or earnings.

- The seller may not believe that he or she will get a "good" accounting from the buyer. As an example, the seller may be concerned that there will be unreasonable allocations of parent company expenses (if the buyer is a corporation), which will depress future earnings and prejudice the calculation of the seller's earnout.

- The amount of the earnout may not be sufficient to make the uncertainty of an earnout worthwhile.

- An earnout may not be practical if the seller has a large shareholder group with diverse interests (for example, a public company).

Many of these concerns can be resolved in structuring the earnout formula. For instance, the concern about achieving projected earnings in later years may be circumvented by agreeing to a higher earnout multiple during the first few years following the sale of the business. Concerns associated with the seller's lack of control over the business subsequent to the sale may be relieved if the earnout is based on a simpler benchmark, such as revenues instead of earnings. However, an earnout based on revenues may be conditioned on the maintenance of designated profit margins in order to eliminate the incentive for the seller to develop profitless sales simply to achieve the earnout.

Nonetheless, not all concerns can be eliminated. At some point the seller must decide if the potential benefits of an earnout such as receiving his or her full asking price and deferring some tax liability (by electing to be taxed under the installment sale method) outweigh his or her concerns.

## OTHER FORMS OF FINANCING

Certain acquisitions lend themselves to nontraditional types of financing. Some nontraditional financing can be arranged through third-party institutions while the balance is the result of imaginative negotiations between buyer and seller.

### Sale-Leasebacks

Although one typically thinks of raising funds by issuing secured debt which is collateralized by the assets of the seller company, some assets may be financed more readily if sold to a financial institution and leased back by the company. Certain equipment, vehicles, buildings, and real estate are among the assets that frequently fall into this category.

### Assets Retained by the Seller

Some acquisitions are structured as a purchase of the shares of a company while others are structured as the purchase of operating assets and liabilities. If a transaction is structured as an asset purchase, the seller may agree to retain certain assets that are not essential to the business and, in exchange, reduce the purchase price for the value of the assets the seller keeps. Examples of these assets include:

- surplus cash and marketable securities

- accounts receivable (which can be collected on consignment by the buyer)

- obsolete inventories (which can be sold on consignment by the buyer)

- excess or superfluous machinery, buildings, or real estate

- assets used for private purposes by the seller, such as artwork, airplanes, automobiles, condominiums, memberships in clubs, paid-up life insurance

### *Assets Leased from the Seller*

The seller may also agree to keep certain assets that are used in the business and to lease these assets back to the company after its acquisition. This has the same effect as a sale-leaseback with an institution except that it avoids certain transaction costs as well as the need to find an institution interested in buying the particular assets in question.

The opportunity to retain certain assets sometimes may have special appeal to the seller. Real estate, for example, is commonly retained by sellers of smaller, private businesses. The potential for continued appreciation is attractive while long-term leases can be attractive for both parties. Other assets that often are leased to acquirers include computer equipment and software.

### *Service Contracts*

In some situations, the seller may agree to provide ongoing services to the buyer for a fee. Depending on the amount of the fee, the seller may agree to reduce the purchase price. Examples of the types of services include accounting, financial reporting, data processing, distributing certain products, and manufacturing certain components.

### *Employment Contracts*

Businesses in which the seller is also an employee provide an opportunity to negotiate ongoing employment contracts, if the seller plans to remain active in the business. Depending on the terms of the contract, the seller may agree to a reduction of the purchase price—in essence "financing" a portion of the price with compensation from an employment agreement. With capital gains and ordinary income tax rates now the same, this tactic, which previously had been resisted by many sellers, is likely to become more acceptable.

### Noncompetition Agreements

Selling shareholders who possess valuable knowledge may agree to accept a portion of the purchase price over time and to characterize those payments as noncompetition compensation. Such payments have tax consequences similar to those of employment contracts.

## CASH

Despite many financing alternatives available in today's markets, a number of circumstances may lead a buyer to consider using cash or other capital already retained in the company rather than seek external acquisition financing.

Many times, this decision is tax motivated. For instance, a mature company generating substantial cash from operations faces the question of whether or not to distribute dividends to its shareholders (which could result in a second tier of taxation at the shareholder level). As an alternative to raising new financing specifically for an acquisition, the company may elect to forego its shareholder distributions, accumulate cash in the company, and reinvest that cash in an acquisition.

In an effort to minimize the second tier of taxation, some companies give up dividend payments even before they identify a specific use for the retained funds. However, simply refraining from the distribution of dividends, over time, may not be sufficient to avoid taxation. Eventually, the accumulated cash could be subject to an involuntary tax imposed by the Internal Revenue Service on monies deemed to be excess retained earnings.[1] Thus, many buyers (including foreign corporations who have chosen not to repatriate monies earned in the United

---

[1] Sections 531–537 of the Internal Revenue Code call for a tax on accumulated earnings in excess of the "normal" requirements of a business, under the reasoning that such earnings would usually be distributed to the shareholders and taxed as dividends when received by the shareholders. However, "normal" business requirements may include working capital, capital additions, *and* business acquisitions.

States) are motivated to use cash to make acquisitions, rather than raise new financing to do so.

Another reason cash sometimes is chosen is that access to alternative sources of capital may be temporarily limited or undesirable. For example, foreign buyers may not have the same ready access to certain U.S. capital markets as U.S. companies. However, even U.S. companies sometimes have difficulty accessing markets in which they would normally raise funds for an acquisition. Immediately following the stock market crash of 1987, for example, a number of companies that traditionally received financing in the private institutional marketplace found it difficult to raise money there. This was due, in part, to displacement by larger corporate borrowers who resorted to private institutional markets for significant amounts of funding, which normally would have come from the public markets. Hence, the demands made on the private institutional marketplace diverted funds that otherwise might have been available for smaller acquisitions.

## SOURCES OF ACQUISITION FINANCING

Historically, smaller businesses (especially private ones) have had more limited funding alternatives than their larger counterparts. Smaller businesses needing financing to acquire other businesses could look to a limited number of sources:

- cash which had accumulated in the business of the buyer or the seller
- loans from the buyer's commercial lenders
- a guarantee or even a capital infusion from the owner of the buyer
- notes to the seller
- a funding of the acquisition partly out of the seller's future cash flows in consequence of contingent earnout payments

Funding available to larger and especially public companies via secondary offerings or institutional private placements were not viable alternatives for the smaller company.

In recent years, however, there has been significant growth in the financial markets, much of which relates to corporate acquisition financing. Thus, today funding opportunities for corporate acquisitions by smaller companies are more numerous. Employee retirement plans and pension funds, for example, have grown from roughly $239 billion in 1970 to nearly $2 trillion in 1986.[2] Although the vast majority of these monies are invested in government securities and investment-grade corporate securities, a growing percentage is targeted for investment in smaller businesses. Insurance companies are another major source of private capital. In 1986, the investment portfolios of life insurance companies were estimated to exceed $937 billion.[3] Roughly $433 billion, or 46 percent of the total insurance portfolios, was invested in corporate securities, a significant portion of which has been invested in private acquisitions, buyouts, and recapitalizations. Commercial banks have also grown both in terms of assets managed and in the range of financing they provide. In 1975, commercial banks had total assets of roughly $1.1 trillion. By 1986, total commercial banking assets had grown to nearly $2.9 trillion, of which $600 billion (21 percent) was earmarked for commercial and industrial loans.[4] The public securities markets have grown dramatically as well. In 1975 there were 5,090 issuers of publicly traded debt and equity securities with market value in excess of $1 trillion. By 1986 there were 6,943 issuers whose public securities had a market value in excess of $4 trillion.[5] Many of these issuers were relatively small and had issued securities as traditional as common equity or long-term debt and as diverse as high-yield "junk" bonds, equipment certificates, mortgage certificates, zero-coupon bonds, and payment-in-kind (PIK) obligations, to name but a few.

[2] U.S. Bureau of Census, *Statistical Abstract of the United States: 1988* (108th edition), Washington, DC, 1987, p. 345.

[3] Ibid., p. 488.

[4] Ibid., p. 473.

[5] Ibid., p. 487.

### *Private Placements Among Financial Institutions*

The major players in the institutional marketplace for corporate acquisitions of smaller businesses are commercial banks, insurance companies, pension funds, and venture capital and special-purpose investment funds. There are many directories that are helpful in identifying specific institutions. Some of these directories are listed in the appendix to this chapter. Also, various financial trade associations publish helpful lists of potential sources.

Many institutions focus on a narrow or well-defined range of investments. Some commercial banks, for example, concentrate on senior, secured loans and do not invest in subordinated debt or equity. Some venture capital funds, on the other hand, seek only equity investments. Some institutions limit their investments to certain industries. Knowing these interests can be helpful in selecting an institutional investor likely to be interested in investing in your business.

Other institutions have much broader investment interests. Many commercial banks, insurance companies, and pension funds invest in securities ranging from senior secured loans to subordinated mezzanine debt to equity. (The practice of investing in a variety of securities in a single company in the same private placement is known as strip financing.) However, the ability of certain institutions to participate in part or all of a private placement may be subject to legal and regulatory constraints.[6]

---

[6] Banks are constrained by legal lending limits that restrict the amount of their investment in a single situation to a percentage of the institution's total capital. Other bank restrictions also limit the amount of equity banks may hold (that is, less than five percent of the voting common stock and less than 25 percent of all classes of equity securities). Also, institutions that invest in secured loans and voting securities in the same company will be concerned about equitable subordination (Section 510(c) of the Federal Bankruptcy Code) and fraudulent conveyance statutes (arising out of Section 548 of the Federal Bankruptcy Code and now adopted in about half of the states in the United States). A determination of equitable subordination by a bankruptcy court could cause a "secured" lender to have its security interest in assets subordinated to the same level as all other equity holders' interests in those assets. The determination of equitable subordination could arise if a lender makes a substantial loan with equity features and thus potentially has control over the company (that is, the court may rule that

### Public Markets

Depending on general stock and bond market conditions at a given time, going public may or may not be a feasible acquisition financing alternative. Even when available, additional costs such as underwriting costs, selling expenses, additional legal expense for securities counsel, and public reporting costs (if the company is not already public) need to be weighed against the somewhat lower borrowing rates associated with publicly traded debt and the relatively large amounts that can be raised with publicly issued debt and equity.

### Sellers

Seller financing is not always done grudgingly. In fact, there are a number of benefits a seller can realize by participating in the financing. For instance, notes, bonds, or other debt financing assumed by the seller may enable him or her to elect installment sale treatment under the Internal Revenue Code and thereby defer a portion of tax liability. Equity may permit the seller to treat the sale as a tax-free exchange of securities. Earnouts and other nontraditional financing vehicles give the seller an opportunity to realize a higher price for the business than may be possible otherwise.

### Buyers

If the buyer has enough shareholders, there may be opportunities for it to raise funds through a rights offering of common stock. With a small group of shareholders, financing may be obtained from the buyer's shareholders by offering co-investment rights in the company that is being acquired.

---

the loan was veiled equity). Fraudulent conveyance has a similar thrust to equitable subordination. If an acquisition is financed heavily with debt and the borrower goes into bankruptcy, the bankruptcy court may conclude that in retrospect the debt burden was unreasonably large and in consequence the sale was predicated on a financing scheme that defrauded the company's other creditors. Such a holding could cause the transaction to be reversed, thereby giving the original creditors a preferential claim to the assets and leaving the lender with no easy way to get its investment back.

## *CHOOSING FINANCING*

The selection of financing for any acquisition generally requires a measure of strategic foresight but frequently reflects fortuitous circumstances as well. The controlling factors in the selection of financing involve:

- matching the type of financing with the nature of the company's assets and business
- managing the cost of capital and balancing the costs and constraints of various financing instruments
- recognizing periodic constraints or limitations in raising capital in various financial markets
- adapting the financing to certain constraints imposed by the seller

# APPENDIX 10-A:
## Recommended Directories of Financing Sources

*The Corporate Finance Sourcebook*

The Zehring Company
3004 Glenview Road
Wilmette, IL 60091
(312) 256-6067

*Merger & Acquisition Sourcebook*

Walter Jurek
Quality Services Company
Santa Barbara, CA

*Directory of Financing Sources*

Editor: J. Terrence Greve
Buyout Publications
San Diego, CA

*Directory of Pension Funds & Their Investment Managers*

Money Market Directories, Inc.
300 East Market Street
Charlottesville, VA 22901
(804) 977-1450

*Guide to Venture Capital Sources*

Stanley E. Pratt
Capital Publishing Corporation
Two Laurel Avenue, Box 348
Wellesley Hills, MA 02181
(617) 235-5405

Chapter 11

# Acquiring the Turnaround Candidate

Ronald G. Quintero
Gibbons, Quintero & Co.
New York, New York

Investing in turnarounds can be the most exciting, disheartening, exhilarating, discouraging, lucrative, capital intensive, and satisfying area of mergers and acquisitions. As our economy gears up for the twenty-first century, turnarounds are playing an increasingly important role in corporate management and acquisition strategy. This chapter describes the characteristics of turnaround candidates, and how they are analyzed and acquired. However, when the acquisition is consummated, the turnaround process has scarcely begun, and it is doomed to likely failure if not accompanied by a well-contemplated and well-executed turnaround strategy. Accordingly, this chapter also includes a discussion of how to achieve the turnaround.

## WHY ARE TURNAROUNDS IMPORTANT?

Any investor that is actively involved in mergers and acquisitions is periodically involved in turnarounds, either by choice or because the condition of an acquired company is declining. Some traditional rules of thumb indicate that of every five acquisitions that are completed, one is successful, two fall short of expectations, and two can be regarded as complete failures. Because business is a dynamic environment, it is inevitable that there will always be companies requiring turn-around assistance. For defensive purposes, corporate owners must be prepared to initiate remedial action mandated by the early warning signals of decline, or to accelerate divestiture activities before value deteriorates further. From an acquisition standpoint, investors need to recognize when they are looking at a turnaround candidate, in order to evaluate and structure an acquisition accordingly.

Many factors attributable to the evolution of corporate America during the 1980s have given rise to turnaround candidates as symptoms, victims, and beneficiaries of underlying economic, financial, and legal forces. The stage for what was to come was set in 1979 when Congress liberalized the bankruptcy laws to afford greater protection to debtors and to make it easier for bankruptcy professionals to collect fees for services rendered. The more favorable treatment of debtors enabled bankruptcy to become an important rehabilitative strategic alternative, rather than the desperate action of a moribund debtor. Several operationally healthy companies such as Johns Manville, A. H. Robins, and Texaco have used bankruptcy as a means of preserving shareholder value. The ability to generate and collect significant professional fees, legislated for the purpose of ensuring that a debtor's recovery is not impaired by an inability to engage capable professionals, has had the effect of attracting a number of talented individuals into an area that was hitherto regarded by many as the backwater of the professional community. Many leading law firms, accounting firms, and investment banks have staffed up to accommodate the substantial growth in turnarounds and insolvencies. The commitments of people and capital were both symptoms of and contributory factors to the heightened activity level in turnarounds.

The domestic economic landscape of the 1980s has been characterized by the longest period of uninterrupted economic expansion this century, a sustained bull market, relaxed interpretation and enforcement of antitrust regulations, low interest and inflation rates compared to the levels of the previous decade, and the emergence of high-yield "junk" bonds as an important financing vehicle. These factors led to record levels of acquisition activity, at hitherto unreached prices, often financed in large part by junk bonds. Many of the acquisitions were poorly conceived or poorly executed, overpriced, undercapitalized, or predicated upon growth or divestiture assumptions that did not materialize. The globalization of the U.S. economy, making domestic companies more susceptible to international competition, as well as the declining life cycle of new technologies, has generated significant corporate turmoil. Many companies have responded by downsizing and adopting more efficient cost structures. The preponderance of displaced executives seeking new opportunities and the lure of entrepreneurial ventures that accompanies any period of economic prosperity and low-cost capital led to a high rate of business formation, which, as the riskiest segment of corporate activity, preceded a large number of business failures. Disappointing acquisitions, companies struggling to meet competitive challenges, and fledgling business ventures collectively have made turnaround candidates abundantly present.

Turnaround candidates have the potential to be the most lucrative acquisition opportunities, often involving less risk than is commonly perceived. For starters, the entry costs can be quite modest. Many acquisitions of turnarounds require little or no initial outlay of capital, with nothing more than an agreement to assume debt or provide capital infusions into the company. The debt assumed may be restructured to provide more advantageous terms to the acquirer, including an extended payback period, reduced rates of interest, and the forgiveness of principal. The amount of capital truly at risk can be far less than the cost of launching and building a new business venture, or the downside risk of buying a profitable company at the multiples of earnings that have prevailed since the mid-1980s. Although comprehensive data has not been compiled to quantify precisely the comparative capital costs and risks of turnarounds, startups, and acquisitions of profitable companies, Figures 11-1 and 11-2 provide an indication of the comparative order of magnitude of each type of investment. Investing in turnarounds clearly has the potential to provide the most cost-effective method of buying or building companies. It can be compared with buying a handyman's special in the housing market. Furthermore, turnarounds can provide enormous returns on capital. Table 11-1

**Figure 11–1.** *Example of the comparative order of magnitude of the acquisition costs of turnarounds, venture capital investments, and M&A candidates.*

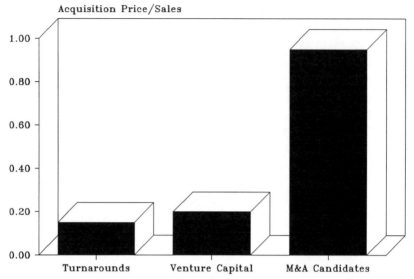

**Figure 11–2.** *Example of the comparative order of magnitude of the total capital investment for a "typical" turnaround, venture capital investment, and M&A candidate of equal annual sales potential.*

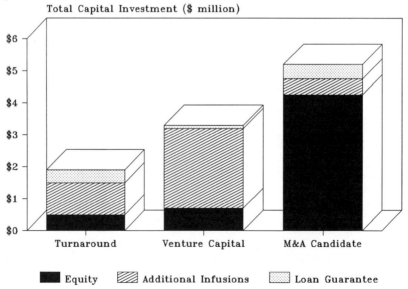

**Table 11-1.** *Changes in the aggregate stock market capitalization of the common equity of selected turnarounds.*

|  | Low Point | 1 Year Later | 2 Years Later | 5 Years Later | 10 Years Later |
|---|---|---|---|---|---|
| AM International | 1982 | 933% | 950% | 8370% | NA |
| Chrysler | 1981 | 284% | 1209% | 2228% | NA |
| Itel | 1981 | 825% | 2350% | 12043% | NA |
| Navistar | 1982 | 322% | 663% | 1512% | NA |
| Penn Central | 1976 | 35% | 4332% | 9729% | 24931% |
| Toys "R" Us | 1974 | 733% | 2567% | 28143% | 331161% |
| Wickes Companies | 1982 | 200% | 1199% | 2583% | NA |

reveals the appreciation in equity values of some of the better-known turnarounds in recent years. The attractiveness of these potential returns, the prevalence of turnaround candidates, and the need for companies to adapt to ever-increasing competitive challenges make turnarounds an important aspect of the present investment environment.

## CLASSIFICATIONS OF TURNAROUNDS

Nearly every company from time to time faces challenges, crises, and competitive threats that can impair profitability and require the implementation of turnaround procedures. This chapter, however, focuses on some characteristics unique to companies that are experiencing problems that potentially jeopardize viability. The most common causes (as opposed to the symptoms described in Figure 11-3) of the problems that they face include excessive use of financial leverage, an inadequate or inappropriate capital structure, poor management, and/or an inability to adapt to change. The problems are often exacerbated by the failure of the parties involved to recognize the problems and respond to them in an effective and timely manner.

### Overleveraged Companies

Low interest rates, lax credit standards, cooperative and aggressive lenders, a burgeoning market for junk bonds, leveraged buyouts, corporate recapitalizations, and optimistic com-

**Figure 11–3.** *Symptoms of financial distress.*

---

### EXTERNAL SYMPTOMS

- Competitors are known to be experiencing financial difficulties.
- Industry price structure has deteriorated; cost structure has increased.
- Industry has surplus capacity; too many competitors.
- Customers are suffering from a downturn or industry slowdown.
- Legislative or regulatory developments threaten key products or may significantly increase the cost structure.
- Competition from foreign competitors or substitute products and services is being felt.
- Technological changes requiring significant product innovations or capital expenditures are necessary.


### OPERATIONAL SYMPTOMS

- Turnover in senior management is occurring.
- Members of the board of directors have resigned.
- Board members insist on improved directors' liability insurance coverage.
- Poor financial systems and controls fail to give management information that is accurate, timely, and meaningful.
- Company has an inadequate planning process; financial projections are consistently inaccurate.
- Significant modifications to business extend beyond past experience of management, for example, acquisition, major product introduction, entry into a new market, adoption of new production methods.
- Staff reductions, wage freezes, spending cuts, and other indications of an austerity program are in evidence.
- Labor unrest impairs productivity and/or results in work stoppages.

- Prices have been reduced to generate additional sales.
- A major customer has been lost.
- Company utilizes an unnecessarily large number of vendors, perhaps to elicit additional credit or because of poor vendor relations.
- Vendors demand C.O.D. or payments in advance of delivering goods and services.
- Creditors that are also customers are increasing purchases, possibly to offset outstanding balances due from the company.
- Key elements of cost structure have increased significantly or are excessive for level of revenues.

## FINANCIAL SYMPTOMS

- Auditor is late at completing annual audit.
- Auditor is expanding the scope of the annual audit.
- Change of auditor may suggest the possibility of disagreements over accounting or auditing issues.
- Accounting methods that maximize earnings, such as capitalizing expenses, depreciating assets over extended time periods, and recognizing revenues before cash is collected, are being employed.
- Nontraditional financing methods, such as off–balance sheet financing, factoring, and offering unusual incentives for rapid payment of invoices, are being used.
- Indebtedness increases significantly.
- Company is shopping for new lenders.
- Debt is renegotiated at terms that are more onerous than those previously in place.
- Lenders request collateral, pledging of assets, and/or personal guarantees to keep loan in force.
- Bank is reluctant to engage in a candid conversation about the company, due to fear of lender liability in a potentially litigious environment.

- Lender has transferred loan to workout department.
- Average days outstanding of accounts receivable have grown, suggesting possible customer dissatisfaction with products or services, or the failure of the company to recognize a writeoff.
- Returns and allowances are increasing, suggesting a relaxing of quality control standards to reduce costs.
- Inventory turnover slows, suggesting a possible accumulation of slow-moving or unsalable goods.
- Accounts payable are being "stretched."
- Accounts payable are being converted to notes payable.
- Security interests in assets are being granted to certain key creditors.
- Deposits to trust funds, such as payroll taxes, are delinquent.
- Discretionary expenditures, such as capital purchases, product development, advertising, and maintenance, have been reduced.
- Dividends have been reduced or eliminated; shareholders have made loans to the company or provided capital infusions.
- Legal costs have increased, due to lawsuits in progress or the costs of opposing judgments.
- Purchase commitments are made at prices or terms in excess of those currently available.
- Long-term sale agreements are below current market prices.
- The company has large, unfunded pension liability.
- The company is liable for significant retiree medical costs.


## MISCELLANEOUS SYMPTOMS

- Company is being "shopped" to several potential buyers.
- Sellers express a sense of urgency regarding the closing of the transaction.

- Sellers resist information requests or a thorough due diligence review.
- Miscellaneous assets have been sold.
- Judgments have been awarded against the company for failure to comply with financial or contractual obligations.
- Company is under investigation for EPA violations.
- Insurance coverage is inadequate for potential liabilities from pending litigation and unasserted claims.
- Company has engaged bankruptcy counsel and/or other insolvency professionals.

pany forecasts have all contributed to an environment that has permitted many companies to become overleveraged. Relying on debt as a significant source of capital has become a way of life for many American companies. Employing leverage can be prudent up to a point, since the after-tax cost of debt capital is less than the cost of equity capital and it reduces the amount of equity that shareholders must commit. However, changed circumstances or faulty financial forecasts can cause leverage to become an unmanageable burden. Moreover, it is generally creditors who inflict the pain resulting from financial distress, sometimes resulting in forced divestitures, operational constraints, cutbacks, Chapter 11, and even liquidation.

### Undercapitalized Companies

Overleveraged companies are usually undercapitalized as well. However, insufficient equity or inappropriate capitalization can be unique problems unto themselves, often preceding the overabundance of leverage, which may develop as a response to the equity deficiency. Even a profitable company can grow beyond its capacity to finance operations. This capital deficiency frequently occurs because product and service expenses are borne up front, whereas sales and the eventual collection of accounts receivable can occur one to three months later. The deficiency can become more acute because of the need to invest in facilities, equipment, product development, marketing, and personnel. A failure to make adequate provisions for the ongoing capital requirements of a business is one of the most common causes of business failures.

Another variation of the same problem is an inappropriate capital structure. This might occur if long-term assets are financed by short-term debt, for example. The capital structure of a firm must be properly matched with the timing and amounts of cash flows and cash requirements.

### Poorly Managed Companies

An argument can be made (and is frequently proffered by disgruntled creditors) that financial distress is the result of bad management. Although this view may be too harsh, poor decision making, inadequate planning, and a failure to respond effectively to change clearly contribute significantly to financial distress. Often the management that built a company may be ill equipped to manage during a period of retrenchment. The optimism and vision required for growth may be at odds with the mind set required to cut back. A natural tendency is to persist with behavior and practices that resulted in past successes, rather than to adopt a plan designed for a new environment. Frequently, the entrepreneurial management that launched the enterprise may lack the professional discipline or administrative skills required to manage a larger, mature entity. The passing away of a founder or the departure of a strong leader may also leave a void that is not adequately filled.

Companies with capable managers may be debilitated by an ineffective management process. This occurs when communication within management and among the rank and file is poor, personality clashes inhibit cooperation and lower morale, responsibility and authority are inadequately delegated, excessive administrative management layers insulate senior executives from what's happening in their business, controls are ineffective, and/or accountability is lacking. Even though the individual ingredients for success may be present, they do not work in sync and the machine malfunctions.

## Industries or Markets in Transition

The last, and potentially most, challenging classification of turnarounds comprises companies whose industries or geographical markets are adversely impacted by change. The first three classifications of turnarounds reflect internal problems that are specific to the company. The state of an industry or market, however, is a macroeconomic phenomenon that a manager generally has limited ability to influence. An industry downturn can be a temporary condition, brought about by supply and demand imbalances or by weaknesses in the businesses of customers, or it can be the result of a permanent shift away from a product due to new technologies, more desirable alternative products, or the end of a product life cycle. Likewise, market weaknesses can be temporary or permanent. Companies susceptible to international competition may be significantly affected by fluctuations in the value of the dollar. This reality became evident in a positive way with the resurgence of basic manufacturing in the United States during the late 1980s due to a weak dollar, enabling many companies to enjoy cost advantages over foreign competitors. Also, the saturation of a market, as may be evident in an overbuilt real estate market, or legislation prohibiting a product, such as the prohibition of alcoholic beverages during the 1920s and early 1930s, can have a prolonged or permanent effect on a company dependent on that market.

## IDENTIFYING TURNAROUND CANDIDATES

More often than not, turnaround candidates are sold, rather than bought. The pressures accompanying financial distress, which management may be ill equipped and inadequately capitalized to contend with, can cause the turnaround expert to be perceived as the white knight. Creditors frequently welcome and even encourage new owners who offer prospects of capital and management acumen that may enable creditors to be repaid and the company, their customer, to survive. Management and shareholders may view any price received for the company's equity as a way of salvaging some value before any additional deterioration occurs, preferring the transfer of control to bankruptcy or liquidation. Employees are often receptive to a buyer that can stabilize the company and offer greater job security. Each major constituency may be strongly inspired to endorse the sale of the company. Yet to many would-be buyers, the universe of available turnaround candidates may appear to be restricted to the largest, most visible distress situations.

Why are such willing sellers not evident to a broader spectrum of potential suitors? In the early stages of financial decline everyone involved typically fails to recognize the existence and the severity of the problem. Deteriorating financial performance is regarded as a temporary aberration that will be ameliorated by external forces such as a market rebound or improved economic conditions, rather than by direct actions. Management believes that it does not require outside assistance, bankers sensitive to accusations of lender liability are reluctant to encourage a debtor to consider selling, and employees and trade creditors usually lack sufficient timely information to be aware of the scope of the problem. As a consequence, the effort to solicit a turnaround investor is usually not initiated until the financial problems have begun to approach crisis proportions. At that stage, the effort is often complicated by the severity of the problem, which discourages many prospective investors; the sense of urgency with which investors are requested to make a decision; and the difficulty of professionally soliciting prospective investors when constrained by a lack of funds, a deteriorating financial condition that may prevent the company from surviving long enough to be sold, and insufficient value to retain the attention and assistance of merger and acquisition intermediaries.

To be a successful turnaround investor, it is desirable to adopt a proactive approach to identifying turnaround candidates. Gaining early access to the turnaround candidate can enable prospective buyers to:

- have more time to conduct a thorough investigation and to negotiate the transaction
- preempt other buyers discouraged by the advanced stages of negotiations or inadequate time for decision making

- influence the turnaround candidate not to undertake irreversible actions such as divestitures or a bankruptcy filing, that would be in conflict with a buyer's plans
- prevent the deterioration from getting beyond the point of no return

The focus of the approach used to identify turnaround candidates is influenced by the acquisition criteria of the prospective investor. Because time is a finite resource constraining everyone, prospective acquirers should focus their efforts on the approaches most likely to be suitable according to predetermined acquisition criteria. For example, it would probably be unproductive for a company seeking acquisitions in the Northeast to spend time soliciting candidates from West-Coast bankers. Defining the acquisition criteria as explicitly as possible enables prospective buyers to make efficient use of time, to focus objectives, to provide a basis for evaluating candidates, to appear credible to third parties who may direct them to turnaround candidates, and to elicit their maximum cooperation. Figure 11–4 delineates some of the key considerations in formulating acquisition criteria.

**Figure 11–4.** *Key considerations in developing acquisition criteria.*

- Motive(s) for acquisition: increasing market share? entry into a specific industry? geographical diversification? industry diversification? bargain purchase price opportunity for turnarounds? turnaround expertise?
- Classification of turnaround deemed acceptable: overleveraged companies? undercapitalized companies? poorly managed companies? industries or markets in transition?
- Availability of resources: management? capital for acquisition? ongoing capital infusions? administrative support? surplus production capacity?
- Strengths and weaknesses of buyer: management? financial? industry expertise? marketing?
- Industry preferences
- Geographical location
- Size: revenues? purchase price? assets? indebtedness?

- Industry profile: one or a few major competitors? numerous competitors, with no decisive leaders? regional leaders? international competition?
- Industry life cycle: expansion? maturity? contraction?
- Basis for competition: price? quality? technological innovation? service? reputation? marketing? depth of product line? convenience? related products and services? scale of operations?
- Product or service profile: commodity? unique? end product? component or input? recurring purchase? occasional purchase? significant cost to customer? significant element of customer's end product?
- Capital investment: recurring requirements? machinery and equipment? facilities? research and development?
- Employees: skilled? unskilled? semiskilled? unionized?
- Scale of operations: one location? numerous locations? regional? domestic? international?
- Customer base: consumers? socioeconomic traits? large companies? small companies? specific industries? regional? domestic? international?
- Significance of regulatory environment
- Company's competitive position: leader? prominent company? nondominant position?
- Ownership: public versus private?
- Source(s) of financing to consummate purchase
- Structure of transaction: purchase of entire company? significant interest through capital infusion? buy assets? product line(s)? merger? claims of creditors in a bankruptcy? installment purchase? contingent payouts?
- Willingness to retain management? present availability of successor management?

An appropriate starting point and a worthwhile investment of time for investors serious about becoming active in turnarounds is to become acquainted with the members of the bankruptcy and insolvency community. A small but growing number of bankers, lawyers, accountants, consultants, and investment bankers are involved in the majority of bankruptcies of significant size. Listings of many of the firms and individuals that are prominently involved in bankruptcies are periodically published in a newsletter entitled *Turnarounds & Workouts.* Multidisciplinary professional organizations such as the American Bankruptcy Institute and the Turnaround Management Association provide additional means of getting to know the members of the bankruptcy community. Bankruptcy professionals and members of the workout departments of major banks may be receptive to investors who offer the prospect of capital and/or management that can be employed to salvage a financially distressed debtor. For investors with a regional or a local orientation, the insolvency professionals in the appropriate jurisdiction represent important allies. Besides being supportive by referring investment opportunities, as representatives of creditors, they can be obstructive by preventing investors from acquiring control. Therefore, it is worthwhile establishing satisfactory working relationships with them.

Another way to identify opportunities for buying bankrupt companies is to talk with the court clerk of the United States Bankruptcy Court in the circuit or district of interest. Although the court clerks do not necessarily have detailed knowledge of particular companies or cases, they may be able to identify some of the more prominent bankruptcy filings in the jurisdiction, as well as companies in a particular industry that have filed. Because bankruptcy filings are public proceedings, a wealth of information is normally available for review to determine whether a candidate is worth pursuing.

A number of individuals who are tangentially or unintentionally involved in turnarounds can also prove to be sources of investment opportunities. Such a list would include venture capitalists, asset-based lenders, underwriters of high-yield debt, owners of commercial real estate, and participants in leveraged buyouts. At present, a growing number of scavengers are beginning to track LBOs like vultures in the desert, waiting for them to become prey as a result of unrealized business plans, a rise in interest rates, and/or an economic downturn.

Online computerized databases such as *Compustat,* the *Standard & Poor's Stock Guide* database, *Dun & Bradstreet Credit Reports,* and the *Value Line* database provide electronic means of screening turnaround candidates. Statistical measures such as declines in revenues, profitability, and aggregate stock market valuation, as well as changes in debt-equity ratios, current ratios, and liquidity can highlight companies requiring turnaround assistance. News databases, such as *Dow Jones News/ Retrieval* or *NEXIS,* can provide nonquantitative means of identifying turnaround candidates. A supplement or alternative to electronic screening methodologies is to monitor corporate earnings releases reported in *The Wall Street Journal* or other business or trade publications for evidence of companies experiencing declines. More detailed investigations can be pursued by obtaining copies of a publicly held company's Forms 10K and 10Q filed with the SEC, as well as by reviewing information and publications compiled by Standard & Poor's, Moody's, Value Line, and Dun & Bradstreet. Numerous other sources of information on public and private companies are available and are covered in greater detail in Chapter 3.

Within a specific industry, turnaround candidates can be identified through conversations with industry executives, consultants, bankers, business brokers, customers, members of trade organizations, and editors of trade journals. Attendance at an industry trade show provides an excellent means of obtaining a rapid knowledge about an industry and about key developments, companies, and executives.

As in marriage, the likelihood of success is enhanced when prospects are thoroughly screened. The current environment contains many suitors, so those using creative, well-conceived screening programs enabling them to be first in line can enjoy a considerable advantage.

## DIAGNOSING THE CAUSES OF FINANCIAL DISTRESS

Once a turnaround candidate worthy of serious consideration has been identified, it should be subjected to a thorough diagnostic review. A diagnostic review constitutes an application

of due diligence procedures, the focus of which is on interpretation and action rather than information gathering. Such a review is vital for:

- evaluating the causes and extent of the company's problems
- assessing the viability of the candidate
- determining what actions are necessary to achieve a turnaround
- estimating the timing, cost, and potential upside attainable from a turnaround
- deciding whether or not to pursue the turnaround candidate

The diagnostic review provides the foundation for a turnaround and is a critical activity that should precede any investment in the company. Failing to conduct a thorough diagnostic review prior to making a commitment of funds is tantamount to walking blindfolded off a platform where the drop could be five inches or 500 feet.

The diagnostic review should be planned and executed by a team of individuals experienced at identifying and evaluating the types of problems likely to affect the turnaround candidate and in developing remedial actions. Members of the team must have an awareness of a broad range of business issues as well as specific knowledge of accounting, taxes, law, bankruptcy, and the specific industry of the turnaround candidate, and must also recognize the areas requiring guidance from independent experts. As the investigation progresses, the input of independent experts is likely to be significant. The cost of such experts is usually insignificant compared to the potential downside of an ill-advised or poorly executed turnaround, and nominal compared to the financial rewards of a successful turnaround.

All significant areas of the business should be subjected to diagnostic review procedures. These questions should recur throughout the review:

- What is the current status?
- What problems exist?
- How do they impact the rest of the business?

- What remedial actions can be taken?
- How much time, capital, and other resources are required before the remedial actions have their desired effect?
- Is the problem of such magnitude that individually, or in conjunction with the other problems identified, it warrants aborting the potential acquisition?


The tools required to implement a diagnostic review are both qualitative and quantitative. Qualitative tools revolve around questionnaires and checklists such as those included in Chapter 5. Quantitative measures are derived from the candidate's financial statements, subledgers, cost accounting systems, and various other forms of internal statistical data, as well as from external data on competitors' and the candidate's industry. (See Chapter 6.) Financial analyses conducted as of a specific date and revealing trends over a period of time can reveal a number of additional issues that require further investigation. Some of the symptoms of financial distress enumerated in Figure 11–3 may become evident during the conduct of the diagnostic review. However, the diagnostic review does not normally stop at the point of identifying the symptoms. Rather, it seeks an explanation for the presence of the symptoms, quantifies and interprets their significance, outlines potential remedial actions, and weighs their potential impact upon the viability of the company and the potential acquisition.

Figure 11–5 provides an example of a diagnostic review of accounts receivable. Clearly, the financial data alone provides significant insight into the condition of accounts receivable. For example, if the accounts receivable balance of a hypothetical acquisition candidate represented 40 days' sales, it would appear that receivables were reasonably current by way of comparison to prevailing norms in American business. The careful diagnostic review, however, does not stop at this single quantitative measurement. If the diagnostic review revealed that less than half of the dollar volume of sales was made on credit, then the receivable balances with an ostensible average age of 40 days would actually have an average age in excess of 80 days. If the standard terms of sale were 2%/10, net 30, the delinquent accounts receivable could highlight a serious problem in collections and possibly reflect customer dissatisfaction with products or services. The quantitative measures and qualitative issues contained in Figure 11-5 are useful guides for isolating and quantifying the problems. The potential remedial actions cited may provide a basis for relieving or lessening the impact of the problems. Nevertheless, certain types of problems pertaining to receivables (such as those listed in the figure) may be sufficiently momentous, either individually or in conjunction with others, as to raise the possibility of aborting the prospective acquisition.

Expanding Figure 11-5 to apply to the broad range of issues affecting most companies is beyond the scope of this chapter. Moreover, the risk of such an expanded listing is that it tends to oversimplify the diagnostic review process. Checklists are nothing more than guidelines or starting points for initiating an investigation. There is no substitute for experienced professionals capable of recognizing problems and modifying analytical approaches to suit the ever-evolving picture of the candidate.

The most broadly relevant observations emerging from a diagnostic review are those that may signal a need to consider aborting a prospective acquisition. The decision to abort is difficult to make, particularly if it is preceded by a significant investment of time and money, and if the prospective buyer has become enamored of the business and its apparent upside

**Figure 11-5.** *An example of diagnostic review procedures. Subject area: accounts receivable.*

---

### QUANTITATIVE MEASURES

- Aged accounts receivable, classified by:
  Customer
  Salesperson
  Geographical region
  Product classification

- Financial ratio analysis:
  Accounts receivable turnover
  Average collection period
  Days' sales outstanding
  Accounts receivable as a percentage of total assets

Percentage of sales on credit
Bad debt reserve as a percentage of accounts receivable
Bad debt expense as a percentage of sales
Cost of Credit Department per dollar of sales
Collection percentage on balances outstanding 30–60 days;
    61–90 days; more than 90 days
- Cost of accounts receivable:
Incremental costs of items or services sold on account
Credit Department
Interest
Auditing and control
Data processing

## QUALITATIVE ISSUES

- What systems and controls are in place?
- How are credit decisions made?
- Are credit standards too lenient? too restrictive?
- What are normal credit terms? How do they compare with those of the industry?
- How does the company's credit collection experience compare with that of competitors?
- When are customers billed?
- What procedures are in force to handle delinquent accounts?
- What criteria are used to make writeoffs and adjustments to accounts?
- What incentives does management have to overstate receivables? (for example, does the company have a credit line based on reported net receivables?)
- Are collection problems an indication of customer dissatisfaction with products or services? customer intentions to change vendors?
- Are customers experiencing financial difficulties that would impair collections?

## POTENTIAL REMEDIAL ACTIONS

- Improve accounts receivable management systems and procedures.
- Centralize/decentralize activity.
- Hire a new credit manager.
- Pay sales commissions only on collection of the account.
- Adjust sales commissions to timeliness of receivable collections.
- Expedite billing, especially on large invoices.
- Focus collection efforts on large accounts.
- Offer a one-time discount for immediate payment of delinquent balances.
- Use aggressive collection procedures, such as using a collection agency or taking back inventory.
- Set off balances due against balances owed to customers.
- Use an outside organization or a factor to manage receivables.
- Sell receivables to a third party.

## POSSIBLE SIGNALS TO ABORT PROSPECTIVE PURCHASE

- Fraud or gross misstatement of receivable balances is evident.
- Inadequate information casts doubt on information received in other areas.
- Customers are dissatisfied with product or service.
- Customer base has pervasive financial difficulties.
- Mismanagement provides evidence of pervasive management incompetence.
- Company lacks undisputed ownership of receivables.
- Value of receivables is unquantifiable or inadequate relative to minimum acquisition price.

potential. However, certain problems are formulas for disaster or accidents waiting to happen that can make previous expenditures pale in comparison to prospective costs and risks. Among these warning signals are:

- inadequate financial information that prevents the prospective buyer from reasonably evaluating the past and present financial condition of the acquisition candidate
- poor financial controls that could undermine the integrity of the financial information provided and conceal serious problems
- any indications of latent or pervasive fraud
- management's unwillingness to make full and complete disclosure of information that is vital to the evaluation of the company, due to the "confidential" nature of the information
- management's insistence that a due diligence program be unreasonably restricted because of its disruptiveness or because of some stated sense of urgency
- background checks of key shareholders or members of senior management that reveal a history of fraud, deception, or other legal misdeeds
- asset title searches disclosing information about ownership or encumbrances that conflicts with information in the company's financial records or with representations by management
- contingent liabilities that would jeopardize the financial welfare of the company
- a trend toward mounting losses that defies any probable reversal in the foreseeable future
- unmeasurable future capital commitments or estimated capital requirements that exceed what the investor is willing to commit to the turnaround candidate
- evidence of an impending bankruptcy filing or liquidity crisis that the prospective buyer is unprepared to contend with
- incompetent management that the prospective acquirer has no ability to assist or replace in the near term

- an industry, market, or customer base that is demonstrating protracted deterioration with no end in sight

One mark of successful investors is knowing their limitations and realizing when to cut their losses short. Numerous successful investors have attributed a significant portion of their wealth to bad investments that they were fortunate or smart enough to avoid. Since turnarounds tend to be both management and capital intensive, most investors are constrained by an inability to take on too many at a time. Consequently, it is important to have clear parameters for abandoning an acquisition project and moving on to the next one.

## STRUCTURING THE ACQUISITION OF A TURNAROUND

### Dynamics of the Acquisition Environment

As mentioned earlier, the acquisition environment for turnaround candidates is one in which investors provide badly needed capital and/or management expertise that can preserve the company and enable creditors to be repaid. Unlike individuals specializing in acquisitions of healthy companies, who are often denigrated as "raiders," successful turnaround artists such as Lee Iacocca or Victor Palmieri are heralded in business as saviors and admired executives. Even the uncomplimentary terms "scavengers" and "vultures" connote making use of what would otherwise be a waste product or a corpse.

Turnaround investors tend to enter the picture after management has lost credibility, financial performance has suffered for a prolonged period of time, creditors have become concerned about the likelihood of being repaid, and the value of equity has deteriorated or completely disappeared. More often than not, management attempts to remedy the situation without turning to outside investors until there is no other choice. People, especially those who have been successful in the past, have a natural reluctance to concede failure. Shareholders tend to resist seeking outside investors until a crisis emerges because they do not wish to sell equity at depressed values. It often requires an impending crisis to make management and shareholders receptive to a turnaround investor, and it is not until that point that creditors are in a position to influence the activities of the company.

Because most turnarounds are characterized by a sense of urgency, comparative unattactiveness, and a need for capital and turnaround expertise, there is a relatively select group of buyers for the increasingly growing number of turnaround candidates. This combination of factors can enable a turnaround investor to buy the candidate on quite advantageous terms.

### *Valuation Methods*

Each of the valuation methods described in Chapter 7 is relevant to the valuation of turnaround candidates. However, it is important to ensure that the factors unique to turnaround candidates are properly reflected in the valuation methods.

The asset-based valuation methods are profiled in Table 11–2. Book value is not a true valuation method, but rather, it indicates the adjusted historical costs of assets reflected in the company's financial statements, reduced by liabilities outstanding. The net amount may have no relationship to the value of the company or its assets.

Liquidation value is of relevance to sellers and creditors as they weigh the option of selling to the turnaround specialist as opposed to liquidating the company. Net liquidation value constitutes a floor value to the turnaround investor, or a measure of downside risk. If the turnaround proves unsuccessful, the investor could recoup the net liquidation value at a future date, probably reduced by any additional cash flow deficiencies that would be incurred until the liquidation is completed.

Net appraised value provides the investor with a measure of what the assets are worth, if realized at full value. The amounts may be useful for adjusting the book value of the assets for accounting and tax purposes, as well as for seeking financing and determining the appropriate level of insurance coverage. If reduced for the amount of any additional capital infusions that an investor would be required to make until the

**Table 11–2.**

SOS, LTD.
Examples of Asset-Based Valuation Methods
December 31, 1989

| | Book Value | Appraised Value | Liquidation Value |
|---|---|---|---|
| Cash | $ 250,000 | $ 250,000 | $ 250,000 |
| Accounts receivable | 6,000,000 | 5,400,000 | 4,200,000 |
| Inventory | 5,700,000 | 4,845,000 | 2,850,000 |
| Other current assets | 600,000 | 525,000 | 250,000 |
| Net fixed assets | 8,000,000 | 9,000,000 | 5,500,000 |
| Other assets | 900,000 | 650,000 | 175,000 |
| Current liabilities | (8,000,000) | (8,000,000) | (8,000,000) |
| Long-term debt | (6,800,000) | (6,800,000) | (6,800,000) |
| Required capital infusions | | (2,000,000) | |
| Liquidation costs | | | (529,000) |
| | $ 6,650,000 | $ 3,870,000 | $(2,104,000) |

cash flow of the business turned positive, net appraised value can provide a basis for developing a purchase price. Unfortunately, the methodology fails to take into consideration the fact that a business is more than an aggregation of assets and liabilities. The economic value of any business is derived from the prospective cash flows that the owner realizes.

The most theoretically sound method of establishing the value of a company is derived from discounted cash flow analysis. The methodology yields a value that exactly reflects the value of the projected cash flows to be realized by the investor, reduced by the amount of any necessary capital infusions, and discounted to a present value based on the cost of capital or required rate of return on the capital employed. (See Table 11–3.) Discounted cash flow analysis is useful because it can be directly related to the projected cash flow to be realized through the implementation of the investor's turnaround program. If achieved, this projected cash flow will enable the investor to realize the target rate of return built into the cost of capital.

## Table 11-3.

### SOS, LTD.

An Application of Discounted Cash Flow Analysis to Value the Equity of a Turnaround Candidate Based on Projections for the Seven Years Ended December 31, 1996 ($000)

| | 1990 | 1991 | 1992 | 1993 | 1994 | 1995 | 1996 | Present Value of Equity |
|---|---|---|---|---|---|---|---|---|
| *Projected Annual Cash Flow* | | | | | | | | |
| Receipts from product sales | $ 31,000 | 32,550 | 35,805 | 38,490 | 40,800 | 42,840 | 44,982 | |
| Production disbursements | (21,390) | (21,809) | (23,631) | (25,019) | (26,520) | (27,846) | (29,238) | |
| Cash flow from sales | 9,610 | 10,741 | 12,174 | 13,471 | 14,280 | 14,994 | 15,744 | |
| Operating disbursements | (8,370) | (8,463) | (8,951) | (9,623) | (10,200) | (10,710) | (11,245) | |
| Income tax refunds (payments) | 400 | 180 | 50 | (385) | (612) | (857) | (900) | |
| Operating cash flow | 1,640 | 2,458 | 3,273 | 3,463 | 3,468 | 3,427 | 3,599 | |
| Capital expenditures | (450) | (700) | (900) | (700) | (735) | (772) | (810) | |
| Other receipts and disbursements, net | (550) | (150) | 100 | 105 | 110 | 116 | 122 | |
| Cash flow before debt service | 640 | 1,608 | 2,473 | 2,868 | 2,843 | 2,771 | 2,911 | |
| Net debt service | (1,600) | (1,350) | (1,275) | (1,150) | (975) | (900) | (800) | |
| Cash flow available to shareholders | (960) | 258 | 1,198 | 1,718 | 1,868 | 1,871 | 2,111 | |
| Capital infusions | 1,500 | 500 | 0 | 0 | 0 | 0 | 0 | |
| Shareholder distributions | 0 | 0 | (1,078) | (1,547) | (1,681) | (1,684) | (1,899) | |
| Net change in cash | $ 540 | 758 | 120 | 171 | 187 | 187 | 212 | |

| *Residual Value* | | | | | | | | Present Value |
|---|---|---|---|---|---|---|---|---|
| Capitalization of 1996 operation cash flow at weighted cost of capital, 20%[1] | | | | | | | | 17,993 |
| Long-term debt | | | | | | | | (3,500) |
| Net residual value | | | | | | | | 14,493 |
| *Present Value of Equity, Discounted at 25%* | | | | | | | | |
| Capital infusions | (1,200) | (320) | 0 | 0 | 0 | 0 | 0 | (1,520) |
| Shareholder distributions | 0 | 0 | 552 | 634 | 551 | 441 | 398 | 2,576 |
| Net residual value | | | | | | | 3,039 | 3,039 |
| Net residual value | $ (1,200) | (320) | 552 | 634 | 551 | 441 | 3,437 | 4,095 |

[1] Reflects weighted cost of debt and equity.

Notwithstanding the merits of the output from discounted cash flow analysis, there is no assurance that the assumptions can be realized, so other corroborative valuation methods are frequently employed.

Capitalization multiples derived from publicly held companies ("comparable companies") and acquisitions of companies with investment characteristics resembling those of the acquisition candidate ("similar acquisitions") provide additional commonly employed valuation benchmarks. The multiples of these companies are applied to the earnings, cash flow, revenues, book value, and/or other financial attributes of the turnaround candidate, and are weighted and adjusted as shown in Tables 11–4 and 11–5, to provide another indication of value. These methodologies offer the following advantages: They are reasonably objective because they are based on capitalization multiples reflecting numerous independent transactions between buyers and sellers, they require no assumptions as to future financial performance, and they are indirectly based on future cash flow because this factor underlies and influences the capitalization multiples of the comparable companies and similar acquisitions. A shortcoming of these methods is the difficulty of identifying comparable companies or similar acquisitions that also display the same degree of financial deterioration and risk as the turnaround candidate. Usually the turnaround candidate has subsidized losses by taking on debt, which further reduces earnings because of interest costs and causes the capital structure to be heavily weighted in favor of debt. A means of accommodating the difference between the capital structure of the turnaround candidate and the comparable companies and similar investments is to calculate the multiples based on aggregate capitalized value (the sum of long-term debt plus the total value of equity). Comparing aggregate capitalized value to operating cash flow, operating earnings (before reductions for interest and debt service), and other financial variables can provide a more meaningful comparison among companies in the present era where recapitalization has caused them to take on quite divergent capital structures. The aggregate capitalized value mitigates the effects of varying capital structures. The capital structure employed does not influence the value of the business, only the allocation of value between debt and equity.

## Table 11-4.

### SOS, LTD.
### Example of the Comparable Company Valuation Method

| | Capitalized Value (CV)/ Revenues | CV/ Operating Income | CV/Operating Cash Flow (OCF) | CV Weighted[1] Average OCF | CV/ Capital Employed[2] | Total |
|---|---|---|---|---|---|---|
| Comparable company #1 | 0.58 | 10.1 | 6.8 | 7.8 | 1.39 | |
| Comparable company #2 | 0.49 | 8.8 | 5.9 | 7.1 | 1.24 | |
| Comparable company #3 | 0.61 | 11.4 | 7.7 | 8.2 | 1.51 | |
| Comparable company #4 | 0.39 | 8.6 | 5.8 | 6.6 | 1.19 | |
| Comparable company #5 | 0.56 | 10.3 | 7.0 | 9.1 | 1.40 | |
| Average | 0.53 | 9.8 | 6.6 | 7.8 | 1.35 | |
| | × | × | × | × | × | |
| SOS, Ltd.[3] | $29,500,000 | $ 950,000 | $1,400,000 | $ 2,100,000 | $10,670,000 | |
| | $15,517,000 | $9,348,000 | $9,296,000 | $16,296,000 | $14,361,820 | |
| Weighting | 10% | 20% | 20% | 25% | 25% | 100% |
| Weighted value | $ 1,551,700 | $1,869,600 | $1,859,200 | $ 4,074,000 | $ 3,590,455 | $ 12,944,955 |
| Control premium, 20%[4] | | | | | | $ 2,588,991 |
| Gross value | | | | | | $ 15,533,946 |
| Insolvency discount, 30%[5] | | | | | | $ (4,660,184) |
| | | | | | | $ 10,873,762 |
| Long-term debt | | | | | | $ (6,800,000) |
| Value of common equity | | | | | | $ 4,073,762 |

[1] Operating cash flows of a multiple-year period are weighted by applying a numerical weighting to the operating cash flows of each year and dividing the sum of the products of the weight times the cash flow of each year by the sum of the weights.

[2] Long-term debt plus equity, which also equals total assets less noncapital obligations.

[3] Revenues, operating income, operating cash flow, weighted average operating cash flow, and capital employed by SOS, Ltd. during financial reporting periods matching those of the comparable companies.

[4] The premium associated with owning the entire company rather than the fractional interest reflected in stock prices.

[5] Reflects a discount for the additional risk and inferior performance of SOS, Ltd. in comparison to the comparable companies.

**Table 11-5.**

## SOS, LTD.
## Example of the Similar Acquisitions Valuation Method

| | Capitalized Value (CV)/ Revenues | CV/ Operating Income | CV/Operating Cash Flow (OCF) | CV Weighted[1] Average OCF | CV/ Capital Employed[2] | Total |
|---|---|---|---|---|---|---|
| Similar acquisition #1 | 0.46 | 10.1 | 7.0 | 7.9 | 1.44 | |
| Similar acquisition #2 | 0.59 | 10.5 | 7.1 | 8.5 | 1.51 | |
| Similar acquisition #3 | 0.71 | 12.2 | 8.3 | 9.4 | 1.67 | |
| Similar acquisition #4 | 0.73 | 13.5 | 9.2 | 9.9 | 1.82 | |
| Average | 0.62 | 11.6 | 7.9 | 8.9 | 1.61 | |
| | × | × | × | × | × | |
| SOS, Ltd.[3] | $29,500,000 | $ 950,000 | $ 1,400,000 | $ 2,100,000 | $10,670,000 | |
| | $18,363,750 | $10,996,250 | $11,060,000 | $18,742,500 | $17,178,700 | |
| Weighting | 10% | 20% | 20% | 25% | 25% | 100% |
| Weighted value | $ 1,836,375 | $ 2,199,250 | $ 2,212,000 | $ 4,685,625 | $ 4,294,675 | $15,227,925 |
| Insolvency discount, 30%[4] | | | | | | $(4,568,378) |
| Gross value | | | | | | $10,659,548 |
| Long-term debt | | | | | | $(6,800,000) |
| Value of common equity | | | | | | $ 3,859,548 |

[1] Operating cash flows of a multiple-year period are weighted by applying a numerical weighting to the operating cash flows of each year and dividing the sum of the products of the weight times the cash flow of each year by the sum of the weights.

[2] Long-term debt plus equity, which also equals total assets less noncapital obligations.

[3] Revenues, operating income, operating cash flow, weighted average operating cash flow, and capital employed by SOS, Ltd. during financial reporting periods matching those of the comparable companies.

[4] Reflects a discount for the additional risk and inferior performance of SOS, Ltd. in comparison to the comparable companies.

No single valuation methodology is universally applicable. Other valuation methodologies specific to particular industries, as well as variations on the aforementioned valuation methodologies, may provide meaningful information. Often, several valuation methodologies are employed to develop a reasonable range of value. Ultimately, valuation methodologies provide analytical measures that can be used to support and substantiate acquisition negotiations and financing, and provide investors an indication of their potential return on an investment.

### Negotiating the Purchase Price

Despite the output of the valuation methodologies, in an unrestricted market, price is normally a result of negotiations between buyers and sellers, rather than the result of any intrinsic value that an asset has. The relative uniqueness of the acquisition candidate, the number of competing buyers, the negotiating skills and financial resources of prospective buyers, and the degree of urgency associated with the transaction exert significant influence on the negotiated purchase price.

Numerous factors may further reduce the price paid by the purchaser. Frequently, key shareholders and selected other individuals have personally guaranteed the indebtedness of the acquisition candidate. The desire to be relieved of the personal guarantees often outweighs any expectations of proceeds from the sale of equity. A willingness to assume personal guarantees, subject to cooperation from creditors, can enable the buyer to achieve a significant reduction in purchase price.

When creditors have a significant influence in the disposition of equity, they tend to be supportive of buyers that will enhance their prospects of being repaid and of preserving the company that has been their customer in the past. Any money that the buyer pays to existing shareholders is money that will not be paid to creditors. Therefore, creditors satisfied with the business acumen and creditworthiness of the prospective buyer can be allies in pressuring the seller to relinquish shares at an advantageous price.

An owner whose company is experiencing a serious decline and who is quickly running out of time and money often has a limited number of options. The alternatives can literally be a choice between salvaging some modest value or winding up with nothing or even a deficit, due to additional capital infusions that may be required and an obligation to honor personal guarantees. Furthermore, an emotional hardship is always associated with being obliged to experience a business failure, enduring the legal proceedings of a Chapter 11 or Chapter 7 filing, closing facilities, laying off employees, selling assets, telling friends and creditors that past promises and commitments will not be honored, and undertaking the other activities associated with a defensive retrenchment. These emotions run counter to all the instincts and activities that enabled management to build the business. Accepting a reduced value is often a price that shareholders will pay to see their creation survive or to be spared having to participate in dismantling it.

A method of resolving the difference between the value of the company at its nadir and the potential value that exists as a result of all that was previously achieved is to provide sellers with a combination of a modest down payment, augmented by contingent payments derived from future earnings. An example of a contingent payout or "earnout" would be paying shareholders 20 percent of profits for the five years subsequent to the transaction. Since the structure of the earnout is a negotiating point, considerable flexibility exists regarding the way that it is structured. The length of the measurement period can vary, as can the percentage of earnings paid, and a ceiling of a specified dollar amount can be applied. Besides relating the contingency to earnings, it can also be tied to cash flow, operating earnings, revenues, various forms of growth such as appreciation in market value, and a host of other carefully defined factors. A contingent arrangement is particularly useful as an incentive to selling shareholders if their involvement is crucial to achieving a turnaround. It is also a fair way of recognizing the inherent value of the company that exists, to the extent that it contributes to the potential future profitability of the company.

An alternative to a contingent payout is an installment purchase. The timing of the installments can be designed to minimize the cash flow burden in the early stages of a turnaround when cash must be devoted to the business and creditors.

If the installment payments are not secured by any assets other than those of the candidate, the payments can be viewed as having risks similar to a contingent payout, because the ongoing risk is associated with the prospective performance of the turnaround candidate.

### Form of the Business Combination

The basic forms by which acquisitions of turnarounds are executed include the same range of approaches used to acquire other companies, that is, acquisition of stock or assets, or a statutory merger. Prominent attributes of each classification are discussed in Chapters 8 and 9. Special considerations and nuances pertinent to turnarounds are reviewed in this section.

The acquisition of assets is the least risky form of business combination. It can enable the acquirer to cherrypick the most desired assets and lines of business, without assuming all of the existing and contingent liabilities. The acquirer also would appear to be insulated from the adverse impact of a Chapter 11 filing or other legal actions against the corporate entity. However, asset purchases are not always feasible because of creditors' liens, possible adverse tax consequences to sellers, bulk sales restrictions, and a reluctance of sellers to relinquish the most desirable operating assets of the company, while retaining a number of the actual and contingent liabilities. Furthermore, if the transaction were followed by a bankruptcy filing within 12 months, creditors may possibly initiate legal proceedings to attempt to void the transaction as a fraudulent transfer, on the theory that the consideration received was less than fair value and that the debtor was insolvent on the date of the transfer or as a result of the transfer.

An acquisition of stock is the more common way to gain control of turnaround candidates. A stock acquisition results in the transfer of ownership of all positive and negative attributes of the company. One of the greatest risks of this type of transaction is that the equity of a company can quickly become worthless to existing shareholders as a result of a bankruptcy filing. For this reason, a thorough due diligence and diagnostic review should include meetings with key creditors prior to completing the acquisition to ascertain that they are not on the verge of initiating any adverse legal actions.

Another consequence of a transaction in which the acquirer receives more than 50 percent of the voting stock of the target company is that under the Tax Reform Act of 1986 the amount of the company's existing net operating loss (NOL) carryforward that can be offset against income taxes is limited to a formula based on the value of the company's stock immediately before the transaction, multiplied by the long-term tax-exempt interest rate published by the U.S. Treasury Department. For example, if the value of the company's stock was $5 million prior to the transaction and the long-term tax-exempt rate stood at 6 percent, the maximum NOL that can be used that year is $300,000. If the value of the equity prior to the change of control was modest, then the ability to use the NOL can be severely restricted. The standard for evaluating a 50-percent ownership change considers common stock and voting preferred stock, newly issued equity, mergers, various convertible securities, and rights to equity. The Tax Code does not generally view stock issued by distressed corporations to creditors in satisfaction of claims as a change in control that would be subject to the aforementioned restrictions.

A statutory merger involving the exchange of stock for stock is an approach used less frequently in turnarounds, particularly by profitable, publicly held companies. The obligation of merged companies under generally accepted accounting principles to restate their historical financial statements so that they would appear to have always been merged can be onerous, because the restatement can significantly dilute or more than offset the historical earnings of the acquiring entity and create the appearance of a significantly debilitated financial condition. Also, there is a natural reluctance to merge the distressed entity into a healthier company because of the risk of jeopardizing the financial welfare of the healthier business concern. It is normal to isolate the risk associated with acquiring a turnaround to the investment in that company and, possibly, to selected other assets or financial guarantees.

A myriad of other alternatives exist for structuring acquisitions of financially troubled companies. An approach adopted from the venture capital community is to provide a capital infusion through a convertible debt instrument or convertible preferred stock. This form of financing provides the investor with a senior financial instrument in comparison to common stock, while the conversion privileges provide the appreciation potential of common stock. Despite the enhanced security, this form of investment should still be regarded as risk capital, because preferred shareholders and unsecured creditors often receive little, if any, of the value of a company in liquidation or emerging from a Chapter 11 reorganization.

Another method of acquiring control of a turnaround candidate is through options or warrants. This approach can be particularly useful when a prospective buyer needs additional time to determine whether to buy the company, or if the buyer wishes to see the outcome of an event, such as debt restructuring, prior to making a full capital commitment. The transaction may be structured in such a way that the prospective buyer makes a badly needed capital infusion directly into the company and, in some cases, is provided with a degree of influence over the activities of the company. The buyer employing this approach is able to lock in a fixed purchase price, while limiting the amount of potential loss. A problem with this type of transaction is that the buyer usually does not have control until the options or warrants are exercised, by which time it may be too late. Management and shareholders are often reluctant to entertain a transaction that does not constitute a definite commitment, yet still constrains their ability to seek other investors. A way to mitigate this constraint is to allow the distressed entity to repurchase the options or warrants at a specified premium over their issuance price.

In situations where the acquisition candidate requires an immediate capital infusion and there is insufficient time to complete a satisfactory due diligence investigation or to secure financing, a bridge loan may be a necessary prelude to concluding a purchase. This approach would be appropriate when creditors cannot be forestalled and when the prospective buyer is reasonably confident about both the ability and the desire to consummate the purchase. Such funds should be committed on a LIFO basis; because they are the last going into the company, they should be the first to be repaid. To achieve this may require the consent of certain creditors: The rationale for their agreeing to this arrangement would be that the capital is vital to the survival of the company and to preserving the integrity of their loans. Such capital would clearly be high-risk capital, infused at a time when lenders were unwilling to make the required infusion. If they are unwilling to make concessions, it raises a serious question about their perception of the turnaround prospects of the company and their willingness to be cooperative during a turnaround.

Any transaction structure employed has significant accounting, tax, and legal consequences. Relevant tax, statutory, and case law is constantly evolving. Certain elections have irreversible consequences. Also, as a practical matter, it can be difficult to modify the terms of a potential transaction after they have been favorably received by a prospective seller. For these reasons, it is important for the prospective acquirer to be well advised from the very early stages of the potential transaction.

### Exacting Concessions

As mentioned earlier, every constituency in a turnaround stands to gain from the capital and expertise of the turnaround investor: Shareholders salvage something from the value of their investment and are generally relieved of personal guarantees of indebtedness; employees have the prospect of retaining a job with a revitalized corporation; creditors have improved prospects of being repaid; trade creditors have a customer that can continue to give them business; and governmental entities retain an employer that will continue to pay taxes and provide jobs. The list of beneficiaries is almost as long as the list of individuals and entities doing business or planning to do business with the turnaround candidate. The difference between most of the aforementioned constituencies and the turnaround investor is that they are unwilling bearers of risk, whereas the turnaround investor is opting to reduce their risk by assuming risk. In consideration of the benefits that each constituency stands to enjoy,

**Table 11–6.** *Examples of potential concessions by various constituencies in a turnaround.*

| Constituency | Examples of Concessions |
|---|---|
| Lenders | Additional credit; extended repayment period; reduced fees and interest rates; debt forgiveness; release of collateral; less onerous financial or operating constraints; waiver of certain covenants; conversion of debt to equity; agreement to refrain from foreclosure or a Chapter 11 petition; application of assets against indebtedness at a favorable price |
| Trade creditors | Additional credit; willingness to provide goods or services, possibly on a C.O.D. basis; conversion of trade payables to notes payable or equity; satisfaction of debts by receipt of goods and services; forgiveness of debt; relief from onerous purchase commitments |
| Employees | Wage concessions; benefits reductions; elimination of restrictive work rules; acceptance of equity in lieu of some wages and benefits; longer hours at same aggregate compensation; fewer hours at same hourly rate |
| Taxing entities | Extended payment plan; reduction or elimination of penalties; reduced basis for real estate taxes |
| Lessors | Reduced rental rate; extend payment term on equipment leases; take back leased equipment as full satisfaction of outstanding indebtedness; permit sale or transfer of leases |
| Litigants | Drop litigation |
| Customers | If appropriate leverage exists: deposits or payment in advance; prompt payment of invoices; agree to long-term purchase commitment; renegotiate price or terms |
| Joint venture | Relief from onerous obligations; modify joint venture agreement; provide capital; buy out distressed company's share in joint venture |

it is appropriate for them to share some of the sacrifices prior to, or as a condition of, the investment.

Although each acquisition is unique, and careful legal guidance is required, it is generally preferable to begin to seek concessions, with the approval of management and shareholders, prior to consummating the transaction. It is precisely at this stage that the greatest leverage exists to exact concessions. In the time of greatest need, when there is concern about the viability of the entity, it is increasingly likely that the various constituencies will make concessions for self-serving reasons. After the crisis has subsided or the turnaround investor has made a commitment of funds and time, the incentive on the part of others to share in the pain may be reduced.

Examples of the nature of the concessions frequently sought are enumerated in Table 11–6. These concessions are not always attainable, and some require more time to obtain than is available prior to completing the acquisition agreement. Also, in some cases, sellers are unable or unwilling to initiate the dialogue to exact concessions, and they refuse to grant the prospective buyer permission to engage in such discussions. Engaging in discussions regarding concessions may even entail a legal risk in that, if the acquisition is not consummated, disgruntled shareholders may claim that their business was damaged as a result of the discussions entered into or encouraged by the prospective buyer. Nevertheless, with proper legal counsel, these risks can be reduced to a manageable level. To the extent that concessions are obtained prior to the completion of the acquisition, the accompanying risks are reduced and financing may be obtainable on more advantageous terms.

## BUYING A COMPANY IN CHAPTER 11

### Legal Environment of Chapter 11

Chapter 11 is an enlightened alternative to torturing and incarcerating debtors and liquidating their assets. It allows a company protection from actions by creditors so that obligations can be realigned in an equitable manner. The price paid to enjoy this protection is close scrutiny by the court and the creditors with their retinue of professionals, and a limitation on what actions management can undertake without obtaining court approval.

A Chapter 11 petition can be filed in a voluntary action by management, or as a result of an involuntary proceeding initiated by three or more creditors with delinquent obligations. Once the petition has been filed with the bankruptcy court, the assets of the company are protected through an automatic stay of the actions of creditors. The rights of creditors can be represented by one or more committees comprising creditors with various classifications of claims. Equity holders may have a committee and certain classifications of creditors such as banks or financial institutions may choose to unite without official committee status. Each party in interest is represented by legal counsel, as well as by other professionals such as accountants, management consultants, and investment bankers who may be required to safeguard the party's interests.

The judicial proceedings are presided over by a bankruptcy judge in the district where the bankruptcy petition is filed. The judge is supported by a U.S. Trustee, who handles a variety of the administrative matters of a Chapter 11 proceeding. A court-appointed trustee may assume control of the company in liquidations and in cases where management has resigned, or if an examiner or other responsible party has demonstrated substantial evidence of fraud, incompetence, or gross mismanagement.

For the duration of the Chapter 11 proceedings, management is not only relieved of the obligation of paying prepetition debts, it is prohibited from doing so without court approval. Most postpetition obligations must be paid as they become due. The company is generally besieged by professionals charged with the tasks of pursuing various legal matters and bankruptcy informational requirements, substantiating claims and interests, investigating the possibility of fraud or misapplication of funds, assessing management actions during the administration of the case, and formulating and evaluating a proposed liquidation or reorganization plan. All significant actions of a nonroutine nature such as selling assets subject to liens, creating secured obligations, or hiring professionals must be proposed to the court and the parties in interest, and be executed only after obtaining court approval.

Among the numerous challenges that management of a bankrupt company faces are:

- stabilizing the company, including retaining customers and key employees
- managing the company while being distracted by the administrative obligations and constraints of Chapter 11
- obtaining court approval for the use of cash collateral
- procuring funding and generating adequate cash flow to sustain the company
- gaining credit from the trade
- demonstrating financial viability and progress toward a reorganization to prevent creditors from pressing for the use of their collateral, additional collateral, the imposition of a trustee, replacement of management, or the conversion of the case to a liquidation in Chapter 11 or Chapter 7
- enhancing the operational efficiency of the business
- formulating and gaining confirmation of a plan of reorganization

### Buying a Company in Chapter 11

The transaction structures for acquiring a company in Chapter 11 resemble those enumerated in the previous section. The key distinction is the process by which approval for the sale is obtained.

Outside the umbrella of Chapter 11, the key parties to completing a transaction are the management and shareholders of the respective companies, as well as any regulatory organizations, financial institutions, or other entities that may have to provide their consent. In Chapter 11, all of the attributes of the company comprise the estate, in which shareholders, creditors, and other parties in interest have a financial interest. Any potential transactions of substance must be subjected to scrutiny and potential obstruction by this broadened range of parties. Court approval is required to complete a business combination and the mandatory public notice and disclosure expose the prospective acquirer to being preempted by higher and/or better offers.

The purchase of assets, with possible assumption of certain liabilities, is normally an easier transaction to effect than the acquisition of the company, because it can be accomplished without the confirmation of a plan of reorganization. Once the terms of sale have been agreed to, a request is made to the court for a hearing of a motion to grant an order authorizing the sale. At least 20 days before the scheduled hearing, a representative of the court sends a notice by mail to the debtor, the trustee, all creditors, and indenture trustees, announcing the hearing date and describing the assets to be sold, and the proposed terms and conditions. In some instances the court may supplement the mailing by publishing a public notice in various newspapers or other publications. Other parties are normally invited to review public documents available through the bankruptcy court for the purpose of submitting a higher and/or better offer. Any objections to the proposal must be received in writing by the court no less than five days before the hearing. Assuming the absence of valid objections or of a higher and/or better offer, the bankruptcy court issues at the hearing an order that authorizes the transaction.

Although this process circumvents many of the administrative and documentation requirements of a reorganization plan, it may require the same degree of consensus building among the various parties to the bankruptcy, particularly if the acquisition is of substantially all of the operating assets of the estate. In such an instance, acceptance of the sale normally precludes the potential for reorganization and constitutes the equivalent of a liquidation. Shareholders and creditors must compare the consideration they would receive as a result of the transaction to what they might be entitled to in a reorganization or as a result of a sale at a later date. If the sale is for cash or cash and debt only, the potential proceeds to be realized by shareholders and creditors of the company are limited to the price to be paid, with no prospects of additional consideration.

Often, it is the prospect of a recovery in the value of the company, some or all of which would inure to the benefit of creditors, that provides them with their only potential to be repaid in full. Different creditors are likely to have divergent views regarding the recovery prospects of the company and the degree to which they will individually benefit from the potential recovery. For this reason, it can be critical to negotiate individually with each major party in interest, convincing them that they will be treated at least as well, if not better, with a higher degree of certainty, than could be attained by any other alternative. To mollify any objections associated with the upside potential of the business, it may be desirable to offer to include a portion of the purchase price in the form of equity, warrants, or a profit-based contingent payout.

A second alternative is to acquire or merge with an entity in Chapter 11. This affords the buyer all of the attributes of the acquired company, including its negative attributes, plus whatever net operating loss carryforward survives the reorganization and change in control. Moreover, it may be the only type of transaction that shareholders and creditors are willing to accede to. Shareholders may view the transfer of equity as a means of being relieved of any further liabilities or impairments of the value of their stock. Creditors may regard the transaction as a means of achieving a solution to the indefinite deferral of their claims resulting from the bankruptcy filing. In order to accomplish the transaction and be relieved of the constraints of Chapter 11, it will be necessary to formulate and gain confirmation of a plan of reorganization.

The required contents of a reorganization plan are precisely defined in the U.S. Bankruptcy Code. The main features of a reorganization plan are a designation of each class of claims and interests and an indication of how they will be treated in the proposed reorganization. The plan must be equitable with regard to the legal rights of each class of creditors and shareholders, and their comparative claims to the assets of the estate. The total consideration provided should exceed what would be realized in liquidation. Moreover, the plan must be achievable and make adequate provision for the financial requirements of the reorganized company.

In order for the parties in interest to have a basis for evaluating the reorganization plan, they must receive a disclosure statement. Prior to its dissemination, the disclosure statement must be subjected to any objections or proposed modifications advanced by parties in interest, and be reviewed and approved by the court. The nature of descriptive information normally contained in a disclosure statement may include:

- the purpose of the disclosure statement
- the voting procedure to be followed
- a summary of the reorganization plan
- an overview of the company, including a discussion of significant prepetition and postpetition events
- historical financial statements
- a business plan, accompanied by financial projections detailing the sources and applications of funds
- a valuation of the company and its assets
- a liquidation analysis
- identity, experience, and compensation of senior management and directors
- a description of any new securities to be issued or funding to be received
- liabilities, litigation, and other factors that may impact the execution of the plan

The amount of time for voting on the reorganization plan and the date of the confirmation hearing are established by the court. The plan submitted may be modified as a result of objections or other developments and it may be challenged by one or more competing plans in certain situations. The votes of each class are tabulated separately. A class of creditors is deemed to have accepted the plan if a majority of those voting comprising at least two-thirds of the dollar amount of the claims represented by those casting a ballot approves the plan; approval is deemed to have been received from shareholders if two-thirds of the number of shares voted accept the plan, irrespective of the number of shareholders that they represent. Any classes that are not impaired are deemed by the court to have accepted the plan, whereas classes receiving nothing are deemed to have rejected it. All classes do not have to accept the plan for it to be confirmed. There are "cramdown" provisions and other legal remedies for contending with dissident classes. However, resolving as many differences as possible prior to the submission of the plan to a vote increases the likelihood that the reorganization plan will be confirmed.

The effects of confirmation are that the company emerges from Chapter 11, all parties affected by the plan are bound by its provisions, and the property of the estate is reorganized debtor free and clear of all claims of creditors and equity security holders, unless provided for in the plan or order of confirmation.

A prospective acquirer can buy the stock of the company prior to its emergence from Chapter 11. However, there is significant risk that the stock will be worth little, if anything, after a reorganization plan is consummated. A more common means of gaining control is by purchasing claims of the company in bankruptcy. For this approach to be effective, the claims need to be of sufficient dollar size and number to grant the acquirer significant influence in constructing and approving the plan of reorganization. Irrespective of whether or not equity or claims are acquired prior to the filing of the disclosure statement, the acquirer should have a significant influence in formulating the reorganization plan if funding the plan, rehabilitating the company, and repaying creditors are dependent on the acquirer's capital and expertise.

Emergence from Chapter 11 alters the tax attributes of the company. The net operating loss carryforward is reduced by 50 percent of all principal indebtedness forgiven by creditors receiving stock as part of the reorganization, 100 percent of all unpaid interest accrued within three years of the filing which was satisfied in the plan by issuance of stock, and 100 percent of all other indebtedness that was forgiven. If the acquirer fails to continue with the operations or assets of the turnaround candidate for a minimum of two years, or if an ownership change occurs during that period, the net operating loss carryforward will be lost in its entirety.

# IMPLEMENTING A TURNAROUND

No matter how difficult it may have been to execute the acquisition, particularly if it had to be achieved through gaining confirmation of a Chapter 11 reorganization plan, the biggest challenge occurs subsequent to gaining control. The acquirer must strive for success where others have met failure. A program must be put into place that reverses a downward trend which was probably a long time in developing. Some of the key ingredients of a turnaround are described as follows.

## Stages of a Turnaround

Turnarounds are seldom achieved overnight. If their problems were that simple, they probably would already have been corrected. The typical turnaround is characterized by three stages—crisis, stabilization, and rebuilding.

The urgent need for the initiation of a turnaround becomes blatantly obvious during a time of crisis. At this stage, the company is perilously short of funds, creditors are clamoring for payment, the company may be hemorrhaging from various and sundry cash drains, employee morale is low, and events occur on a daily basis that threaten the viability of the company. This is usually the point at which the turnaround investor is privileged to enter the scene.

The immediate challenge is to "stop the bleeding." This tends to be accomplished by decisive cost cutting (often perceived as ruthless), restricting all cash expenditures, seeking cash from whatever near-term sources are available, and convincing creditors to refrain from initiating legal actions while financial order is being restored. Many of these activities, such as selling assets, provide a one-time quick fix, but have little to do with restoring the operating viability of the business.

As the threat of immediate extinction subsides, management efforts are refocused to stabilizing the company to prevent a recurrence of the crisis. Management introduces measures that will enable the company to operate with greater efficiency, while redirecting the lines of business or product lines to those demonstrated to be profitable. Unprofitable operations are sold or

**Figure 11–6.** *Example of the potential equity appreciation at various stages of a turnaround.*

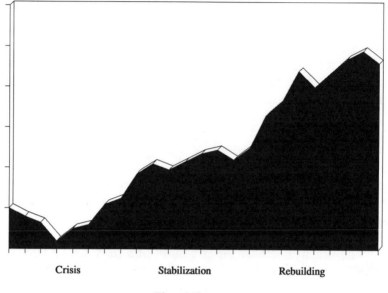

Equity Appreciation

Crisis      Stabilization      Rebuilding

Elapsed Time

closed. To the extent possible, debts are restructured and the capitalization of the firm is revamped so that the company is clearly self-sustaining, with some margin for error.

It is at this stage that the company is poised for growth and prepared to transcend the struggle for survival that characterized its recent past. The emphasis switches toward constructive activities such as product development, geographical expansion, carefully conceived acquisitions, and other strategies that will result in revenue growth and capital appreciation. The implications of each of these stages to the value of the turnaround investor's equity interest are represented in Figure 11–6.

## Building Blocks of the Turnaround

Turnaround campaigns are resource-intensive activities, placing heavy demands on the two most precious corporate resources—money and management. Any turnaround program deficient in either of these areas is susceptible to probable failure.

Clearly, management is the *sine qua non* of turnarounds. Turnarounds are accomplished by people, not by business plans and computer printouts. The best laid plans can be scuttled or poorly executed by inadequate management. Cash balances can be quickly dissipated if they are not safeguarded by a prudent custodian. Conversely, good management can cause a limited amount of cash to go a long way and can play a primary role in attracting additional capital from investors and financial institutions and in eliciting sacrifices from creditors and employees. Making provisions for equity, either directly or through options or warrants to be awarded to senior management based on performance, can be an inexpensive way of attracting, retaining, and motivating quality individuals who will play a critical role in the company's recovery.

Turnarounds make the heaviest demands on management's ability to plan, implement, and control. There is not the margin for error typically present in healthy companies. Management is constrained by a shortage of time and money. Planning is critical. The downside of venturing in the wrong direction is significant. Yet, at the same time, most turnarounds do not have the luxury of an abundance of time and people to study every angle of each issue. "Paralysis by analysis" can be fatal to the company. Management must be able to act prudently and decisively, yet be willing to change direction quickly if a plan of action is not producing the intended results.

In implementing a plan, management must adhere to it without apprehensions or excuses. It is inevitable that not everybody will agree with all aspects of a turnaround plan and, invariably, mistakes will be made along the way. Sometimes, the need to undertake an immediate action precludes conducting sufficient analysis to ensure making the right decision. Some short-term necessities may be at the expense of potential long-term opportunities. However, a failure of everybody to work as an undivided unit can jeopardize the success of a turnaround. Management must enlist the cooperation and participation of every employee in the company to implement the turnaround program and control the process to make sure that it is properly and effectively implemented.

It is a truism that money is an essential ingredient of a turnaround. Financial distress is all about not having enough money. A probable indication of a recovery is that money will no longer be desperately required.

To achieve a turnaround, it is crucial to have access to sufficient capital to meet immediate requirements and ongoing needs that will arise as the plan is implemented, as well as a reserve for the inevitable unanticipated shortfalls and emergencies that almost always arise during the road to recovery. A failure to make an adequate provision for prospective capital requirements increases the likelihood that the rescuer will have to be rescued.

## TURNAROUND STRATEGIES

There is no such thing as a standard turnaround strategy. A turnaround strategy must be tailored to the unique attributes of the turnaround candidate and modified as warranted by situations that arise. Any successful turnaround is the result of numerous independent and interdependent actions. Although their precise content may vary from one turnaround to another, they generally fall into the six categories enumerated below.

### Reducing Expenditures

The turnaround strategy likely to achieve the most immediate results is the reduction or elimination of nonessential cash disbursements. Included within the purview of this approach is literally every expense, obligation, or other payment that the company may have to make. The severity of the cutback depends upon the financial resources of the company. A company that is not anticipating a serious cash crisis may be content merely to reduce the level of spending, whereas a company in more desperate financial straits may have to undergo much more severe spending cuts while deferring obligations that are currently due.

Expense reduction programs are generally implemented in phases. In a cash crisis, a single decisive reduction of expenses may be followed by a more careful analysis that results in the restoration of certain expenses and a pruning of others. In a

less urgent environment, expense reductions occur in a more orderly fashion, after a close examination of alternatives and an evaluation of the consequences of each potential area of reduction.

The most common method of achieving expense reductions is to eliminate people and items that generate expenses. A normal consequence of this approach is a reduction in output, employee morale, and possibly a diminished standing in the business community. The most desirable, albeit uncertain, way to achieve cost reductions is through an increase in efficiency. This may include making more efficient use of existing resources while maintaining output levels, eliminating nonessential activities, or making an investment in equipment, systems, and/or procedures to achieve the expense reduction.

Deferring obligations is a temporary measure for conserving cash. Although it has no impact on increasing efficiency, it can represent a cash-starved company's only method for rationing funds. Careful attention should be given to determining which deferrals are made. For example, payroll taxes represent obligations for which senior management can be held personally liable and, as a consequence, are seldom deferred. Also, provisions may have to be made for payments to critical vendors threatening to withhold vital products or services, and to parties threatening to initiate disruptive legal proceedings. Eventually, deferred obligations must be dealt with, either through repayment, restructuring, forgiveness, or some other manner of treatment.

### Increasing Revenues

Another approach to increasing cash flow is to increase revenues. This can be accomplished by increasing prices, unit volume, and/or the breadth of products or services available to customers. At some stage, revenue growth needs to be an element of nearly every turnaround, since there is a limit to how much can be achieved by slicing away at costs.

A distinction between the turnaround strategies of increasing revenues and reducing expenditures is the timing and certainty associated with their implementation. If management elects to reduce costs, the financial impact will be immediate, whereas the ability to increase revenues requires the cooperation of market forces and the ability to fulfill any additional demand for products or services that may ensue from the new strategy. Price increases are not always attainable and sufficient demand may not exist to permit an increase in unit volume. The financial impact of such a strategy requires time for the market to respond to the change. Because most goods and services are sold on account, there is an additional time lag from the point at which revenues are generated until the cash is collected. This means that the initial impact of a revenue-growth strategy may actually be a reduction in cash flow, due to the incremental investment that may be required in inventory and receivables.

Successful implementation of a revenue-growth strategy requires an excellent understanding of the company's market environment. An acquirer with no previous experience in the particular market needs to exercise caution in implementing the revenue growth plan, taking care to ensure that the plan is consistent with the realities and constraints of the market and that there is sufficient capital available to accommodate the plan. A prerequisite to the plan is that the company have an adequate cost accounting system to ensure that any growth in unit volume is concentrated in products that will have the most pronounced beneficial impact upon cash flow.

### Altering Product or Business Mix

Most companies with multiple products, services, or lines of business achieve varying degrees of profitability and cash flow from each element of their business. Assuming that adequate financial information exists for decision making, one approach to achieving greater profitability is to expand the business in its profitable areas or, conversely, to deemphasize, discontinue, divest, or liquidate the unprofitable segments. The new focus can be enhanced by expanding the breadth, depth, or market coverage of the desirable products or services, which can result from internal growth or acquisitions.

Profitability can be evaluated from several different perspectives. A single product can have varying degrees of profitability, depending on the marketing methods employed, freight and delivery expense, service costs, geographical location of customers, quantity sold, production methods used, production costs, allocation of indirect costs, and the degree to which it is customized for a particular customer. Often, a modification of any of the aforementioned variables, as well as others that may be relevant, can have a profound effect on determining the optimal business mix.

### Enhancing Asset Utilization

Selling assets or reducing the net investment in assets can provide a one-time cash infusion or reduction in the financial requirements of the business. Asset sales provide a nonrecurring near-term source of cash, depending on the liquidity of the assets and the willingness to accept the offers that are generated. An important element of any turnaround is to determine which assets are not vital to the business and sell them as soon as is practical. Even important assets can constitute sources of cash via secured loans, sale-leasebacks, or an outright sale and subsequent lease or rental of a similar asset.

Reducing the investment in inventory, receivables, and other elements of working capital has the same financial impact as a capital infusion—the level of assets that must be funded by debt or equity is reduced. As inventory and receivables are converted into cash, the proceeds can be redeployed for other purposes. The reductions should be the result of improved inventory and receivable management procedures rather than policies that would impair sales or customer goodwill.

### Restructuring Debt

As mentioned earlier, creditors are involuntary stakeholders in the turnaround candidate, who can have a significant interest in a successful turnaround. Often, they have unwittingly provided the capital that has enabled the turnaround candidate to survive. If a turnaround can be demonstrated to be more desirable than liquidation, the potential exists to significantly modify the terms of indebtedness, including extending payment dates, reducing interest rates, obtaining forgiveness, and exchanging debt for equity. The restructuring can be achieved in bankruptcy, as was previously described, or through a voluntary out-of-court debt restructuring or composition agreement.

### Raising Capital

Many of the elements of a turnaround strategy require time to implement. However, the turnaround candidate may have urgent capital needs that have to be met. An immediate capital infusion is frequently required to buy time to establish, implement, and achieve the effects of a turnaround plan. The initial infusion by investors tends to take the form of equity or subordinated debt, whereas funding provided by lenders is generally secured debt.

As the turnaround plan is formalized and begins to show demonstrable evidence of achievability, it may be possible to raise capital in order to implement the plan or to impose a more suitable capital structure. The capital, consisting of equity and/or debt, may be raised in a single transaction, a series of simultaneous transactions, or in successive stages, as the need arises. New capital is often a critical ingredient to achieving a turnaround. The ability to raise the capital can be the external barometer of the confidence of outsiders in the progress and achievability of the turnaround.

## TOOLS REQUIRED TO IMPLEMENT A TURNAROUND

### Organization Structure

An effective organization structure is the instrument through which a turnaround plan is developed, communicated, implemented, and controlled. It should be designed to foster communication and pinpoint responsibility.

Starting at the top, a small nucleus of people, representing the key functional disciplines and lines of business, should lead the company and be actively involved in the management process. Turnarounds are not achieved by one or two people; they require that every employee be involved in the process so that they collectively function as a unit. The number of layers of management insulating senior management from what is happening in the business should be minimized to prevent information blockage. To ensure that policy and orders from the top are accurately conveyed, they should be translated through as few screens as possible. Feedback from the market-place or the shop floor should be readily accessible to senior management so they can respond to change in a timely manner.

The responsibility and authority of each individual within the organization should be unambiguous. Everyone must be personally responsible and accountable for specific tasks and actions to ensure that policies and actions mandated by senior management are properly executed in a timely fashion. There should be no potential for improper execution of a plan of action due to unclear directives or vague designation of re-sponsibility. The organization contemplated by this operating style is one that places a premium on maintaining an ongoing dialogue between senior management and rank-and-file em-ployees. The open environment tends to clarify goals and ob-jectives and induces employees to buy into a program in which they become major stakeholders.

### Business Plan

The business plan is the navigation chart used to guide the turnaround. As distinguished from an annual business plan developed by many companies for internal purposes or one designed for raising capital (both of which are one-time exercises resulting in an archival document), a business plan for a turn-around is a fluid document that is continuously updated to reflect management's responses to a changing environment.

A business plan is normally segregated by major lines of business, and then by functional areas. The topical breakdown of a manufacturer's business plan may include distinct sections on existing products, product development, marketing, manu-facturing, employees, facilities, and finance, with the salient points contained in an executive summary. Each section includes an introspective evaluation, explaining the current condition, absolute and comparative performance, as well as a prospective plan of discrete actions and their anticipated timing and results. The purpose of the introspective evaluation is to build a logical framework for the prospective plans of action.

The physical form of a business plan is of less significance than the quality of its contents and the process by which it is developed. Because the business plan deals with every significant activity of the business, it is important that it be assembled with input from each area. Action-oriented business plans are not developed by an analyst or consultant secluded in an office. They depend on input from a management that is expected to understand, embrace, and implement the plan. The business plan should be the product of a process whereby key members of management develop and submit information and plans relating to their particular areas of responsibility. This leads to an interactive process in which the collective information of management is accumulated, evaluated, challenged, and scrutinized for cross-organizational compatibility and documented in the form of a business plan. The resulting document should be reviewed, modified, and approved by senior management and/or the board of directors.

The core of the business plan is a specific series of actions, each involving an assignment of responsibilities to individuals, reasonable time frames for executing the tasks, expected time frames for witnessing results, and measurement criteria for evaluating success. The business plan must be simple enough that it is understood by everybody responsible for its implementation so that the time required to prepare and update it does not outweigh the benefits that it provides. On the other hand, it must be sufficiently detailed that it constitutes a well-contemplated plan of action on which the ultimate success of the business will depend.

The business plan provides a means of focusing the activities of senior management, evaluating their performance, placing their activities in the context of the broader plans of the company, and encouraging communication across functional and business boundaries. It reinforces the notion that management is working toward a common goal. Pertinent sections or abstracts of the business plan should be shared with middle management so that they understand what is expected of them and become integrated into the process.

A good business plan is a guide, rather than a millstone, which substantiates how goals will be attained. As conditions dictate, action plans must be modified, and the business plan updated to conform to the prevailing intentions of management. The ever-evolving business plan allows management to be responsive to a dynamic environment and to move forward in harmony, with a knowledge of their mission and the steps that will be taken to produce successful results.

### Financial Projections

A carefully conceived set of financial projections quantifies the financial consequences of the activities reflected in the business plan. Financial projections that are continuously updated and evaluated for variances between actual and projected performance are an indispensable tool for planning and monitoring a turnaround. They are the yardstick against which all plans will be evaluated and results judged. Financial projections are the basis for determining capital requirements and for estimating the potential financial rewards of a successful turnaround.

Traditional accrual-based financial statements are of limited usefulness in managing a turnaround. During the critical stages of the turnaround, cash and cash flow are of paramount importance. Accordingly, a projection of cash flow is required to manage and control the company.

Table 11–7 provides an example of a useful format for a statement of cash receipts and disbursements of a manufacturing company. It is segregated into five distinct classifications: product receipts and disbursements, operating costs, nonfinancial receipts and disbursements, debt financing, and shareholder receipts and disbursements. Each of the net amounts or subtotals has a distinct significance. Receipts from product sales constitute the recurring source of cash that must support the business. This amount is reduced by production costs and other operating costs. Nonfinancial receipts and disbursements consist of various items that do not result from the company's operations, some of which are nonrecurring or discretionary in nature. The net amount that remains determines the company's ability to service debt. If net debt financing is positive, it indicates that lenders are financing the company's cash requirements. Any remaining cash flow is available to distribute to shareholders or replenish cash balances.

The format in Table 11–7 pinpoints the sources and applications of funds on an aggregate basis, in a manner that is not contemplated by the statement of changes in financial position. Additional details are also provided in a format that is more meaningful to financially troubled companies than what is provided by the cash flow statement resulting from FASB Statement No. 95. When viewed in conjunction with a current and projected balance sheet, the statement of cash receipts and disbursements can provide a very accurate indication of what is actually happening in a business.

The financial projections should be the by-product of the same process undergone to develop the business plan, enlisting the input of the key people in the organization. Because critical business decisions will have to be made based on the financial projections, they should represent management's best estimate of prospective financial performance, rather than an optimistic goal or a pessimistic, yet eminently achievable, target that will be exceeded. To view the financial consequences of alternative scenarios, it is useful to perform a sensitivity analysis. Modifying certain key assumptions such as sales volume, unit prices, or costs can highlight the financial risks and opportunities in the business. A variance analysis such as that shown in Table 11–7 is useful for indicating areas where the projection assumptions may be defective.

The financial projections become a vital management tool when they are used to measure business performance and evaluate future decisions and financial needs. The financial projections should be continuously updated and monitored. Elements of the business plan that do not enhance cash flow within the desired time frame must be questioned as to their viability. In the end, cash flow is the only true arbiter of the success of a turnaround.

# Table 11-7.

## SOS, LTD.
### Projection of Cash Receipts and Disbursements for the 12 Months Ended December 31, 1989

| | Actual Thru Sep. | Oct. Projected | Oct. Actual | Variance | Nov. Projected | Dec. Projected | 1989 Projected |
|---|---|---|---|---|---|---|---|
| Product receipts and disbursements: | | | | | | | |
| Receipts from product sales | $ 23,100 | 2,500 | 2,150 | (350) | 2,300 | 2,000 | 29,550 |
| Production disbursements: | | | | | | | |
| Raw materials | (5,775) | (625) | (523) | 102 | (575) | (500) | (7,373) |
| Production labor | (6,930) | (750) | (725) | 25 | (690) | (550) | (8,895) |
| Overhead | (3,465) | (375) | (323) | 52 | (345) | (315) | (4,448) |
| Cash flow from sales | 6,930 | 750 | 579 | (171) | 690 | 635 | 8,834 |
| Operating costs: | | | | | | | |
| Selling disbursements | (2,310) | (250) | (215) | 35 | (230) | (210) | (2,965) |
| General and administrative disbursements | (3,465) | (375) | (360) | 15 | (345) | (300) | (4,470) |
| Income tax refunds (payments) | (350) | 0 | (10) | (10) | 0 | 0 | (360) |
| Operating cash flow | 805 | 125 | (6) | (131) | 115 | 125 | 1,039 |
| Other receipts and disbursements: | | | | | | | |
| Net proceeds from asset sales | 125 | 50 | 30 | (20) | 20 | 20 | 195 |
| Capital expenditures | (350) | (25) | 0 | 25 | (25) | (26) | (401) |
| Other receipts and disbursements, net | (250) | 40 | (30) | (70) | 10 | 10 | (260) |
| Cash flow before debt service | 330 | 190 | (6) | (196) | 120 | 129 | 573 |
| Debt service: | | | | | | | |
| Net loan proceeds | 250 | 0 | 0 | 0 | 0 | 0 | 250 |
| Principal payments | (650) | (100) | 0 | 100 | (100) | (250) | (1,000) |
| Interest payments | (500) | (60) | 0 | 60 | (59) | (58) | (617) |
| Cash flow available to shareholders | (570) | 30 | (6) | (36) | (39) | (179) | (794) |
| Shareholder receipts and disbursements: | | | | | | | |
| Common stock issued | 250 | 0 | 0 | 0 | 0 | 0 | 250 |
| Shareholder distributions | 0 | 0 | 0 | 0 | 0 | 0 | 0 |
| Net change in cash | (320) | 30 | (6) | (36) | (39) | (179) | (544) |
| Beginning cash | 575 | 255 | 255 | NA | 249 | 210 | 575 |
| Ending cash | $ 255 | 285 | 249 | (36) | 210 | 31 | 31 |

### *Organizational and Financial Controls*

Organizational and financial controls are fundamental to ensuring proper execution of the turnaround plan and to safeguarding the company's assets and resources. Often, the lack of adequate organizational and financial controls is a major contributory factor to the severity of a company's financial difficulties.

A system of organizational controls depends on the continuous, dynamic interaction between established objectives, actual performance, and management intervention. An illustration of this process appears as Figure 11–7. The foundation of a system of organizational control is a clear, understandable, and measurable set of goals, objectives, procedures, or plans, referred

**Figure 11–7.** *Interactive management control systems.*

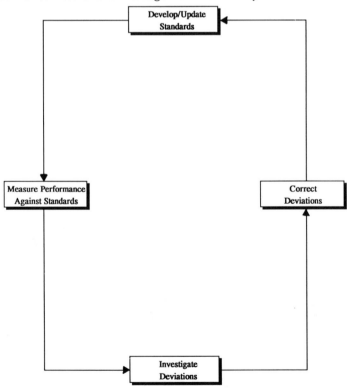

to here as standards. Actual performance must be compared to standards, with deviations being investigated and corrected where possible. In addition to scrutinizing performance, the standards should be under constant review to ensure that they are appropriate and consistent with the current objectives and constraints of the company. Examples of organizational controls include financial budgets, operating procedures, and employee performance reviews.

For a system of organizational controls to be effective, they must be tailored to the plans of the company, clearly communicated to and understood by the people responsible for their implementation, measurable on a timely basis by reasonably objective quantitative or qualitative standards, and cost effective to implement so that the cost of the system does not outweigh its benefits. In a financially troubled company constrained by a shortage of funds, personnel, and time, organizational controls tend to be focused on those areas most vital to the preservation of capital and emergence from the state of crisis. The means of measuring conformity to standards can include:

- statistical or financial data
- special reports and analyses of areas of particular interest
- operational audits of a department or a functional area
- personal observation

The benefits are derived from organizational controls when they are used as management tools, rather than as analytical tools. Their function is to influence corrective behavior that will improve prospective performance, rather than to provide an explanation of historical performance. The highest and best application of organizational controls is as a means of communicating management goals and objectives to influence employee behavior and provide catalysts for corrective action.

Financial controls are aimed at safeguarding the assets of the company and ensuring the integrity of financial information. A company cannot be managed effectively without financial information that is accurate, timely, and meaningful. A financially troubled company can be out of business before anyone realizes it without a reliable basis for monitoring financial performance.

The need for accurate financial information is without dispute. Its timeliness is imperative so that it can serve as a tool for appropriate action. The usefulness of the information is an issue which, although intuitively obvious, is often overlooked in practice. The tendency facilitated by advances in computer technology is to produce more reports than management can possibly deal with, often while failing to provide the information most vital to successful operation. The constraints and requirements of a financially troubled company can provide an impetus for revisiting financial information systems.

The output of the financial information system should be meaningful in the sense that it provides valuable information that will influence actions by management. The data should be in a format that is understood by users. Reports that are not being used should be discontinued, modified to suit the needs of users, or discussed with intended users so that their cooperation in using the reports can be enlisted or alternatives can be proposed. Whenever possible, reports with redundant information should be consolidated into a single report. All reports should be subjected to scrutiny to ensure that management is getting the right information on which to base decisions. This information should be appropriate for the resultant decision and should be predicated on meaningful assumptions. For example, to price a product, cost data should be available that distinguishes between direct costs, indirect costs, and allocated costs. Any allocations should be made on a meaningful basis, with inherent limitations clear to decision makers.

The integrity of the financial information and the security of assets depend on a reliable system of internal control. Fraud has been a major contributory cause to many notable bankruptcies. The ability to forestall a financial crisis is often inhibited by erroneous financial information. Deterrants to fraud and erroneous financial records are a reliable system of internal control which incorporates the following features:

- proper authorization of transactions and activities
- segregation of duties that reduces the opportunities to allow any person to be in a position to both perpetrate and conceal errors or irregularities

in the normal course of his duties—assigning different people the responsibilities of authorizing transactions, recording transactions, and maintaining custody of assets

- design and use of adequate documents and records to help ensure the proper recording of transactions and events, such as monitoring the use of prenumbered shipping documents

- adequate safeguards over access to and use of assets and records, such as secured facilities and authorization for access to computer programs and data files

- independent checks on performance and proper valuation of recorded amounts, such as clerical checks, reconciliations, comparison of assets with recorded accountability, computer-programmed controls, management review of reports that summarize the details of account balances (for example, an aged trial balance of accounts receivable), and user review of computer-generated reports

Source: AICPA Statement on Auditing Standards No. 55, pp. 6–7.

## TIMING REQUIRED TO ACHIEVE A TURNAROUND

If money and management are the vital ingredients to achieving a turnaround, patience and tolerance are crucial traits of any manager or investor desiring to get involved in turnarounds. Invariably, the old adage that things take more time, cost more, and earn less than expected is particularly well suited to turnarounds. Many detours and barricades tend to accompany the turnaround process. Usually, the problems contributing to a company's financial decline take several years to develop. Management, employee, creditor, customer, and vendor practices and attitudes don't change overnight. Contributory problems related to an industry, market, or the economy can take several months or even years to be reversed or adequately addressed. Unless the problem can be resolved by a one-time capital infusion or debt restructuring, the turnaround investor should be prepared to be a long-term investor in a project that may show limited financial rewards during the first year or two. Turnarounds are not generally suitable for speculators or investors with a limited attention span.

The amount of time required to achieve a turnaround is partially influenced by the severity of the problem. A company that is only slightly ill can be restored to health with a lesser dose of medicine.

The size of the company has less to do with the amount of time required to achieve the turnaround than with the probability of achieving the turnaround. Large companies may require more time and money to turn around; however, the potential turnaround has an enhanced probability of success because:

- More stakeholders have a large vested interest in the success of the turnaround.
- Large companies tend to have visibility and market share that is of value and garner the attention of participants in a prospective turnaround.
- Capable management and professional advisors are more readily obtainable.
- A large company has a greater potential for the existence of surplus assets that can be sold or for an excessive cost structure that can be reduced than does a small company that has been run by resource-constrained owners/operators.
- Capital can be more readily obtained.

The series of actions leading to a turnaround is executed on both a simultaneous and a sequential basis. For example, reducing costs does not preclude simultaneously endeavoring to sell surplus assets. However, raising capital may require that many of the results of a turnaround program already be in evidence, revealing an established trend of profitable results. Generally, the time frame required to stabilize a company can be measured in weeks or months, whereas the time required to achieve a full turnaround is measured in quarters or years. Some turnaround candidates never achieve a turnaround, but seem to survive in a continuing tenuous state or eventually are sold and absorbed into another entity or are liquidated.

The increase in the aggregate market capitalization of some rather notable turnarounds in recent years (shown in Table

11–1) provides an indication of the time frame required to reap the rewards of a turnaround. Although each turnaround was accomplished as a result of considerable effort, risk, time, and money, the payback achieved clearly rewarded those involved in the process.

## REFERENCES

*Chapter 11 Reporter* (Business Laws, Inc., Chesterland, OH)

*The Code of the Laws of the United States of America: Title 11 (Bankruptcy)*

Arnold S. Goldstein, *Corporate Comeback* (John Wiley & Sons, New York, NY, 1988)

*Internal Revenue Code*

Richard L. Leza and José F. Placencia, *Develop Your Business Plan* (Oasis Press, Sunnyvale, CA, 1982)

William Loscalzo, *Cash Flow Forecasting* (McGraw-Hill, New York, NY, 1982)

Michael E. Porter, *Competitive Strategy: Techniques for Analyzing Industries and Competitors* (The Free Press, New York, NY, 1980)

Donald Lee Rome, *Business Workouts Manual* (Warren, Gorham & Lamont, Boston, MA, 1985)

*Rules and Forms of Practice and Procedure in Bankruptcy*

*Turnarounds & Workouts* (Beard Group, Inc., Washington, DC)

Robert Willens, *Taxation of Corporate Transactions: A Guide for Corporate, Investment Banking and Tax Advisers* (John Wiley & Sons, New York, NY, 1984) (annual supplements reflect revisions to the Tax Code)

Interdisciplinary Organizations:
American Bankruptcy Institute, Washington, DC
Turnaround Management Association, Cary, NC

# Chapter 12

# *Acquisition Formulas and Calculations*

*Sumner N. Levine*

This chapter provides a summary of a number of helpful quantitative techniques for analyzing acquisitions.

## POSTACQUISITION EARNINGS

The simplest (and least accurate) estimate of the initial postmerger earnings $(I_c)$ of the acquiring firm is given by the sum of the premerger earnings of the acquiring $(I_b)$ and the acquired $(I_s)$ firms,

$$I_c = I_b + I_s$$

or                                                                              (1)

$$I_c = E_b N_b + E_s N_s$$

where $E_b$ and $E_s$ are the premerger earnings per share or the acquiring and acquired firms, respectively.

$N_b$ and $N_s$ are the number of shares outstanding of the acquiring and acquired firms, respectively.

A more realistic evaluation of the postmerger earnings requires consideration of operating synergies, interest payments on the acquisition debt, and tax effects. Taxes in turn depend on how the acquisition is structured.

With a straight asset-acquisition deal there may be a step-up in the cost basis of the acquired firm's assets (hence a corresponding increase in depreciation) and the recognition of goodwill. Consequently the postmerger earnings per share of the acquiring firm are given by

$$E_c = [S - (X + D + Q)] (1 - T) - G \qquad (2)$$

where, on a per-share basis,

$S$ = the postmerger sales including synergy effects
$X$ = postmerger operating costs before interest on acquisition debt, depreciation, and taxes
$D$ = depreciation
$Q$ = interest on the acquisition debt
$T$ = tax rate
$G$ = amortization of goodwill

In the above, any recapture has been neglected. Note that the amortization of goodwill decreases earnings but not taxes.

When the acquisition is structured as a straight stock purchase or reorganization, no change in the cost basis of the assets is recognized and goodwill is not created. However, with certain restrictions, operating losses of the acquired firm can be assumed by the acquiring firm. The earnings per share, postmerger, is then given by

$$E_c = [S - (X + D + Q + \text{NOL})] (1 - T) \qquad (3)$$

where NOL is the amortization per share of the assumed operating losses. The other symbols have their previous meanings.

## STOCK-FOR-STOCK TRANSACTIONS AND EXCHANGE RATES

With the stock-for-stock acquisition, the acquiring company purchases the target by exchanging its stock for that of the selling company. Often as an inducement to the selling company a *premium* (an amount in excess of the market price of the company) is offered to the seller. The premium (Z) is given by

$$Z = \frac{P' - P_s}{P_s}$$

where $P'$ = the price offered for the seller's stock
$\quad\;\; P_s$ = the market price of the seller's stock before an acquisition attempt is rumored or announced

The number of shares offered by the buying firm for the shares of the selling firm is given by

$$P_b \, N_p = P_s \, N_s \, (1 + Z) \tag{4}$$

where $N_p$ = the number of buyer shares offered for the shares of the selling firm
$\quad\;\; N_s$ = the shares outstanding of the selling firm
$\quad\;\; P_b$ = the market price of the buying firm's stock
$\quad\;\; P_s$ = the market price of the selling firm's stock

The *exchange* ratio, R, is given by

$$R = \frac{N_p}{N_s} = \frac{P_s \, (1 + Z)}{P_b} \tag{5}$$

The ratio gives the number of shares of the acquiring firm given in exchange for those of the selling firm. In recent years premiums have sometimes exceeded 100 percent.

## ACQUISITION WITH STOCK, CASH, AND OTHER CONSIDERATIONS

The foregoing discussion can be generalized to the case in which the acquiring firm employs a combination of stock, cash, and debt to purchase the target stock at a premium. The relationship is

$$P_b N_p + (\text{PVD} + C) N_s = N_s P_s (1 + Z) \tag{6}$$

On a *per-share* basis we define

PVD = present value of the interest payments and principal
$C$ = cash used in the purchase

All other symbols have the meanings defined earlier. From equation (6), the exchange ratio is found to be

$$R = \frac{N_p}{N_s} = \left[ (1 + Z) P_s - (\text{PVD} + C) \right] \frac{1}{P_b} \tag{7}$$

Using this formula it is possible to determine the shares of the acquiring company's stock required to purchase the target's stock whenever a specified amount of cash and notes are used in partial payment. Alternatively, equation (7) can be used to calculate the amount of payment in debt and/or cash given the "optimal" value of $R$ discussed in the following example.

*Example* ABC offers to purchase the shares of XYZ (the target) at a 30 percent premium over the market price of XYZ. The market price of XYZ (determined by taking a six-month average value) is $20 per share, while the average price of ABC over a corresponding interval is $30. XYZ has 1,000,000 shares outstanding and ABC has 5,000,000 shares outstanding.

In order to reduce the postmerger dilution of ABC earnings, ABC offers the following package to XYZ:

- 50 percent of the purchase price to be paid in ABC common
- 30 percent of the purchase price to be paid in cash
- 20 percent of the purchase price to be paid in 9-percent notes maturing in three years and paying interest semiannually

To find the exchange ratio and express the offer on a per-share basis of XYZ stock assume that the minimum acceptable rate of return for the XYZ shareholders is 12 percent.

*Solution* The total offering price for XYZ = (1.3) ($20) or $26/share.

The cash payment per share of XYZ = (.30) ($26) or $7.80/share.

The face value of notes offered per share of XYZ = (.2) ($26) or $5.20/share.

Because the notes are to be issued in multiples of $5 face value per share, the payment was rounded to $5 face value of notes per share of XYZ. At a 12-percent discount, the present value (PV) of the principal and six semiannual interest payments is $4.67 per share of XYZ.

The exchange ratio can now be calculated as

$$R = \frac{26 - (7.80 + 4.67)}{30} = .451$$

Hence, .451 shares of ABC per share of XYZ are to be included in the offering price. The market value of these ABC shares is (.451) ($30) = $13.53.

The total price offered per share of XYZ is

| | |
|---|---|
| Dollar value of ABC stock | $13.53 |
| Cash | 7.80 |
| PV of notes | 4.67 |
| | $26.00 |

After the merger the outstanding shares of ABC would be

$$5,000,000 + .451 (1,000,000) = 5,451,000$$

## POSTMERGER EARNINGS PER SHARE

A simple approximation to the postmerger earnings per share of the acquiring firm $E_c$ is obtained from equation (1) using the relation

$$I_c = E_c \, (N_b + N_p)$$

The result is

$$E_c = \frac{E_b \, N_b + E_s \, N_s}{N_b + N_p} \tag{8}$$

The postmerger earnings per share of the acquiring firm will be greater than the premerger earnings provided

$$E_c > E_b$$

From equation (8), the result is

$$E_s > E_b \, R$$

Introducing the expression for $R$ given by equation (5) gives

$$\frac{P_b}{E_b} > \frac{P_s}{E_s} (1 + Z) \tag{9}$$

Thus the per-share earnings of the acquiring firm benefits from the merger provided the premerger P/E ratio of the acquiring firm exceeds that of the acquired firm adjusted for the acquisition premium.

By similar arguments it is easy to see that postmerger earnings dilution of the acquiring company occurs when

$$E_s < E_b$$

Hence from equation (1)

$$E_s < E_b \, R$$

or

$$\frac{E_b \, N_p}{E_s \, N_s} > 1 \tag{9a}$$

## POSTMERGER EARNINGS GROWTH RATE

It is sometimes useful to estimate the postmerger earnings growth rate ($g_c$) of the acquiring firm given the premerger growth rates. The required relation follows from the expression

$$I_c (1 + g_c) = I_b (1 + g_b) + I_s (1 + g_s)$$

where $g_b$ and $g_s$ are the premerger growth rates of the acquiring and target firms, respectively.

Using the relation for the premerger and postmerger incomes of the firms,

$$I_c = I_b + I_s$$

it is easy to show that the required relation is

$$g_c = \frac{I_b \, g_b + I_s \, g_s}{I_b + I_s} \tag{10}$$

Thus the growth rate of the merged firm is the sum of the premerger growth rates weighted by relative contributions to the total earnings. As discussed earlier, the above result neglects the effects of postmerger synergies, taxes, and financing.

## BREAK-EVEN ANALYSIS

When an acquisition results in an initial dilution of earnings per share of the acquiring company, the question arises as to how long it will take for the postmerger earnings per share to equal the earnings per share if the merger had not occurred. This time is referred to as the break-even point ($T$) shown in Figure 12–1. At the break-even point, the per-share earnings of

**Figure 12–1.** *The earnings per share and break-even point are shown for the case in which the per-share earnings of the merged company are less than those of the company without the merger. Here the earnings growth rate of the acquired company is greater than that of the acquiring company.*

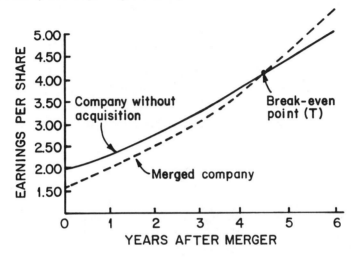

the merged firm equal those of the acquiring firm *premerger,* that is,

$$E_c = E_b \text{ at time } T$$

If once again the simplifying assumption is made that the earnings growth rates of both firms are the same, at break-even

$$\frac{E_b N_b (1 + g_b)^T + E_s N_s (1 + g_s)^T}{N_b + N_p} = E_b (1 + g_b)^T$$

Solving the above for $T$ results in

$$T = \frac{\log\left(\dfrac{E_b R}{E_s}\right)}{\log\left[\dfrac{(1 + g_s)}{(1 + g_b)}\right]} \tag{11}$$

or from equation (5), this can be written

$$T = \frac{\log\left[\dfrac{\left(\dfrac{P_s}{E_s}\right)\left(1+Z\right)}{\dfrac{P_b}{E_b}}\right]}{\log\left[\dfrac{1+g_s}{1+g_b}\right]} \tag{12}$$

When initial earnings dilution occurs, then from equation (9a)

$$\frac{E_b\, N_p}{E_s\, N_s} > 1 \tag{13}$$

In order for the break-even point to be positive (and hence financially meaningful), we must have

$$g_s > g_b$$

This is the case shown in Figure 12–1.

It is also instructive to consider the case in which the initial earnings dilution does not occur so that the initial earnings per share of the merged firm are greater than that premerger. The acquiring firm has, in effect, bought earnings. However, if the growth rate of the merged firm is less than that premerger, as shown in Figure 12–2, then after the break-even point the earnings per share will be less than that of the firm without the acquisition. In this all-too-common occurrence, the firm has bought initial earnings which vanish after the break-even point.

*Example* In a stock-for-stock transaction, ABC agrees to purchase XYZ at a premium of 10 percent. The market P/E of ABC is 10 while that of XYZ is 12 so that initial dilution of ABC earnings will occur. What is the break-even point if the growth rate of ABC is 8 percent and that of XYZ is 15 percent?

**Figure 12-2.** *The earnings per share and break-even point are shown for the case in which the per-share earnings of the merged company are more than those of the company without the merger. Here the earnings growth rate of the acquired company is less than that of the acquiring company.*

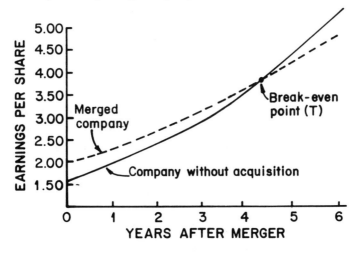

*Solution* From equation (12), we have, using the above data

$$T = \frac{\log\left[\dfrac{12\,(1.10)}{10}\right]}{\log\left(\dfrac{1.15}{1.08}\right)} = 4.4 \text{ years}$$

## OPTIMAL EXCHANGE RATIO

It is often of interest to the acquiring firm to determine the largest exchange ratio that will not result in a decrease in shareholder wealth (stock value) after the acquisition. The post-acquisition market price will depend on the postacquisition earnings and P/E ratio so that

$$P_c = E_c\,(P/E)_c \tag{14}$$

To preserve postacquisition shareholder wealth, we require

$$P_c \geq P_b$$

Since under the usual simplifying assumptions

$$E_c = \frac{N_b E_b + N_s E_s}{N_b + R N_s}$$

It is easily shown on introducing the expresssion for $E_c$ into the two previous expressions that the maximum exchange ratio for the acquiring company shareholders is given by

$$R_{max} = \left[ \left( \frac{E_b N_b + E_s N_s}{P_b} \right) (\text{P/E})_c - N_b \right] \frac{1}{N_s} \qquad (15)$$

When the exchange ratio exceeds $R_{max}$, then the per-share price of the stock will be less than the preacquisition value of the stock. The relationship between $R_{max}$ and $(\text{P/E})_c$ is shown in Figure 12–3.

The acquired firm's stockholders, on the other hand, benefit from a high exchange ratio. The minimum value of $R$ that preserves the share value for the acquired firm's stockholders, after their shares are exchanged for those of the acquiring firm, can be found from the condition

$$P_c N_p \geq P_s N_s$$

The expression on the left-hand side of this inequality is the wealth of the acquired firm's stockholders after merger while that on the right side is the wealth before merger.

Introducing equation (14) and the expression for $E_c$ we find on solving for the minimum exchange ratio ($R_{min}$) that

$$R_{min} = \frac{P_s N_b}{(N_s E_s + N_b E_b) (\text{P/E})_c - P_s N_s} \qquad (16)$$

The dependency of $R_{min}$ on the postmerger P/E ratio is shown in Figure 12–4. The various possibilities for both acquiring and acquired stockholders are shown in Figure 12–5. Of particular interest is Region 1 in which both groups of shareholders win.

## DISCOUNTED CASH FLOW CALCULATIONS

The discounted cash flow (DCF) evaluation of the maximum acceptable price for an acquisition is based on the premise that ownership is essentially a claim on the cash flow generated by a firm's assets. Otherwise stated, the current value of an operating asset is the present value of the cash flows generated by the asset. However, because nonessential or redundant assets are soon sold, these are valued at their estimated current market price which is added to the purchase price calculated by the DCF method. Also added to the DCF value are marketable securities (Treasury bills and the like) held by the target. Assumed liabilities of the acquired firm are subtracted from the DCF price.

It is important to recognize that the relevant qualities with this method are the *incremental* cash flows resulting from the acquisition. The *incremental cash flow* is defined as the cash flow that the acquired firm is expected to contribute (taking into account savings and synergies) less the expected cash flow of the acquiring firm without the acquisition. This view clearly makes sense because, if the incremental cash flow contributed by the target is zero, then the target has no value to the acquiring firm. It is important to take into account all the major synergies and savings made possible by the acquisition, such as

- increased sales
- reduction of wages and salaries resulting from the elimination of redundant positions
- savings resulting from the closing of less-efficient facilities
- reduction in unit selling and advertising costs

**Figure 12–3.** *The dependency of the wealth of the acquiring firm's shareholders on the exchange ratio and the postmerger P/E ratio.*

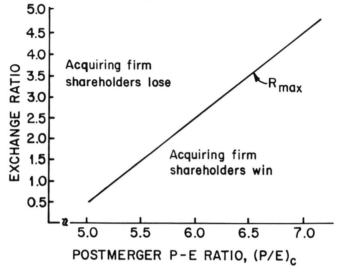

**Figure 12–4.** *The dependency of the acquired firm's shareholder wealth on the exchange ratio and the postmerger P/E ratio.*

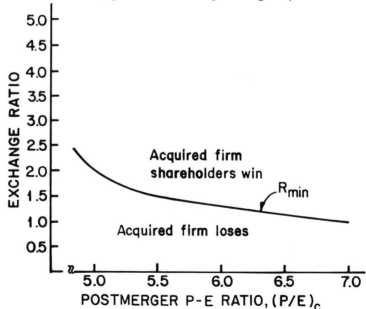

**Figure 12–5.** *The combination of Figures 12–3 and 12–4, showing all possible outcomes.*

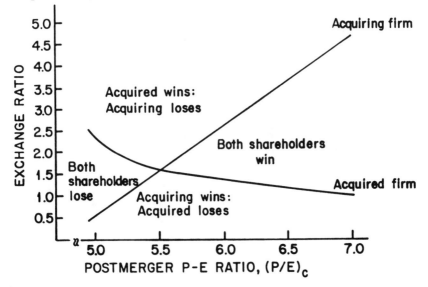

The discounted cash flow (DCF) of the incremental cash flow stream is given by the well-known expression

$$PV = \sum_{t=1}^{N} \frac{CF_t}{(1+r)^t} + \frac{1}{(1+r)^N}\left[\frac{CF_n(1+g_c)}{r-g_c}\right] \qquad (17)$$

The foregoing assumes that the cash flows continue to perpetuity. The first term on the right side of the equation is the year-to-year estimate of the cash flow (CF) obtained by using the expression given in equation (18). The weighted cost of capital for the acquired firm is designated by $r$. Because of the difficulties and uncertainties in making estimates of the projected cash flows, the year-to-year calculation is usually confined to a period of five years or so. This time interval is designated by $N$. The present value of the remaining cash flows (from years $N + 1$ to infinity) constitutes the second term in the above equation, the so-called *residual*. To calculate this term the simplifying assumption is made that the cash flow at year $N$ ($CF_n$) grows at a constant rate $g_c$. Generally $g_c$ is taken as zero.

The cash flows are estimated using the expression

$$CF_t = S_{t-1} (1 + g_t) P_t (1 - T_t) + D_t - (S_t - S_{t-1}) (f_t + w_t) \quad (18)$$

where subscript $t$ = the year end
$S$ = the incremental sales
$g$ = the expected growth in sales
$P$ = the expected operating profit margin after acquisition
$T$ = the marginal tax rate
$D$ = the incremental depreciation, depletion, goodwill, and other noncash charges
$f$ = the fixed investment required per dollar of increased sales
$w$ = the working capital required per dollar of increased sales

The DCF method as formulated above assumes that the acquisition is financed with cash on hand. Thus the DCF method gives the maximum acceptable cash price. In practice, different financing arrangements result in different cash flows. Introducing the consequences of the many different financing arrangements into the analysis greatly complicates the analysis and diverts attention from the basic operational considerations. By confining that analysis to cash financing, not only is the work simplified, but a uniform basis is provided for comparing different acquisition opportunities—since the acquisition decision is separated from financing decisions.

The tedium of doing a DCF analysis is considerably alleviated with the aid of available software packages such as that provided by the Alcar Group (Skokie, IL) and others.

# Chapter 13

# The Acquisition Contract*

David I. Karabell
O'Sullivan, Graev and Karabell
New York, New York

The following discusses the acquisition contract in the context of a hypothetical case involving the sale of a dog food company called Chomp-Chomp, a division of the Fabulous Corp. owned by Myron Rushmore. The buyer is the Ice Cold Doggie Company, whose principals are Finbar McQue and Willington Lafayette. —*Editor's Note*

## PREPARING THE ACQUISITION AGREEMENT

Preparing the first draft of an acquisition agreement is an activity in which the attorney often engages alone. Sometimes he will prepare the agreement without having met or spoken in detail with counsel for his opposite number and without having participated in the ebb and flow of initial negotiations and the activity surrounding execution of a preliminary agreement such as a letter of intent. Under such circumstances, thorough discussions with the client, review of documented facts, and a decent understanding of the business to be acquired are

*Source: *Handbook of Mergers, Acquisitions and Buyouts,* edited by Steven James Lee and Robert Douglas Colman ©1981. Used by permission of the publisher, Prentice-Hall, Inc., Englewood Cliffs, NJ.

essential preconditions to setting pen to paper. With the acquisition of Chomp-Chomp, I had been fortunate. Not only had I obtained background from the preliminary negotiations, but McQue and Lafayette were sophisticated deal-oriented clients, having the capacity to provide insights and guidance concerning the decisions to be made as the agreement was drafted.

Our firm's form file provided relevant documentary precedent for this transaction. Also relevant was data concerning Chomp-Chomp's business—including publicly available documents from its competitors—and specific information, including financial statements, delivered to our clients by Fabulous and its counsel. I assembled prior first drafts of asset acquisition agreements. These provided the benefit of a buyer's document undiluted by negotiations and eliminated the time which would have been required to re-do a fully negotiated form agreement.

## AN AGREEMENT OUTLINE

The draft agreement prepared contained the provisions outlined below.

1. A preamble identifying the parties, stating their relative roles, and the assets being sold;
2. Provision for transfer of the assets being sold, the price to be paid and the manner in which the price will be paid (in the event securities are being issued in payment of the purchase price, methods of valuing those securities might be appropriate in this section) and, in connection with transfer of assets, provision for the buyer's assumption of liabilities;
3. Representations and warranties of the seller;
4. Representations and warranties of the buyer;
5. A statement of the manner in which the seller will conduct the business prior to the closing;
6. Those conditions which are to precede the obligations of the buyer to be performed at the closing;

7. Those conditions which are to precede the obligations of the seller to be performed at the closing;

8. A summary of the closing itself, the mechanics thereof and the documents to be delivered at the closing;

9. Agreements and commitments relating to the relationship of the parties and the activities of the business sold after the closing;

10. Agreements relating to the survival of the representations and warranties of the parties and, importantly, the indemnification provisions to be provided by the seller and buyer;

11. For an asset transfer, provisions relating to bulk sales laws;

12. For a stock transfer, provisions relating to the securities laws and rights to resell securities issued pursuant to registration statements or otherwise;

13. A provision relating to brokers;

14. Provisions related to employee benefits; and

15. Miscellaneous provisions including notices, the completeness of the agreement, the law governing the interpretation of the agreement, whether or not the provisions of the agreement will be severable and other general provisions desired by the parties.

## THE ACQUISITION AGREEMENT IN DETAIL

The initial draft I prepared was a reasonable starting point for the agreement and had assembled in cohesive form the material from which it was derived. McQue had reviewed the document and had suggested changes which, in his belief, would present to our seller a reasonable document rather than a tough, one-sided initial draft. The latter would require haggling and, possibly, engender rancor in the process. McQue was not, however, undermining what he believed were his basic needs. He wanted firm representations concerning Chomp-Chomp and its business in the agreement without qualification as to "materiality" or the "best knowledge" of his seller. He also wanted a firm indemnity with no floor and no ceiling on the amounts which could be claimed thereunder. Since materiality, knowledge, and indemnities are three of the most common arguing points in acquisitions, he hadn't really conceded much at all.

### Preamble

The parties to the agreement were Fabulous, Chomp-Chomp and Ice Cold Doggie. Although Chomp-Chomp was the party transferring the assets owned by it, I believed it critical to insure that Fabulous was included and fully liable for representations, agreements and indemnities. Once the transaction had closed, the seller would be an empty shell, a funnel distributing proceeds to its stockholder, Fabulous. To insure that the buyer had a real party to deal with in the event of problems or losses arising out of breaches of the agreement, the presence of Fabulous was important.

### The Property Being Transferred; the Liabilities Assumed; Mechanics

In the acquisition of the assets of Chomp-Chomp, our initial paragraphs were straightforward. We detailed all of the items to be transferred which included the following:

1. real estate, machinery, equipment and other items of personal property either described or located at facilities of Chomp-Chomp;
2. work in process and inventories as well as containers and other material relating to the items being shipped either on hand or in transit;
3. rights of Chomp-Chomp to contractual commitments set forth in an exhibit or made in the ordinary course of business;
4. accounts and notes receivable;
5. business records of Chomp-Chomp;
6. sales data; and
7. trademarks, tradenames, etc. and rights to use them and the good will connected therewith.

We also provided for the transfer of other assets which were eliminated in the course of negotiations including cash, specified pre-paid expenses in cases where the buyer would not obtain the benefit thereof, deferred credits and insurance policies and insurance reserves. Exclusion of these items did not affect price since the price was to be adjusted at closing based upon a closing pro forma balance sheet.

Chomp-Chomp's insurance was in large part covered by the blanket insurance of Fabulous. At closing, Fabulous would terminate that aspect of its blanket insurance coverage related to the business of Chomp-Chomp and the buyer would be obligated to obtain its own coverage. Fabulous was also terminating its pension plan to the extent it related to the employees of Chomp-Chomp and would cover those employees separately to the extent of vested service. The buyer was, in turn, commencing a new profit-sharing plan in connection with its operation of Chomp-Chomp's business which would be less expensive and, in the buyer's opinion, would provide a better incentive to the employees of Chomp-Chomp to perform in the future. In determining whether or not to continue the pension plan of Fabulous to the extent it was applicable to Chomp-Chomp's employees, the buyer had engaged its own actuary to independently review the data relating to the pension plan.

This section of the agreement also described in broad brush strokes the kind of instruments to be utilized in the transfer of the assets and further provided that anything which needed to be done, in the reasonable opinion of the buyer, would be done to insure that the buyer received the benefit of all the assets transferred in connection with the buyer's operation of Chomp-Chomp's business.

We set up in the acquisition agreement a separate section relating to the liabilities and obligations of Chomp-Chomp to be assumed by the buyer. These included current liabilities and obligations reflected on a pro forma balance sheet to be attached to the acquisition agreement to the extent remaining unpaid as of the closing date, current liabilities and obligations for trade accounts payable incurred by Chomp-Chomp in the ordinary course of its business subsequent to the date of the balance sheet through the closing date, and liabilities and obligations of

Chomp-Chomp arising under agreements which were to be assigned to the buyer. The agreement specifically negated the buyer's assumption of other liabilities including tax liabilities, liabilities to customers for shortages and defects in goods and liabilities based on events occurring before the closing date or on products sold before the closing date.

### The Purchase Price

If the purchase price for the acquisition of Chomp-Chomp's assets had been all cash, the purchase price section of the agreement would have merely provided for a cash payment to the seller at the closing equal to book value of Chomp-Chomp plus $1,000,000 against delivery of all the documents required. I also would have argued for an escrow with a third party of a portion of the purchase price in order to protect the buyer against obligations for which Fabulous had indemnified the buyer.

Since McQue had successfully negotiated for deferral of part of the purchase price, the purchase price section of the agreement provided for a method of determining price (book value as shown on the pro forma balance sheet at closing plus $1,000,000), the payment of $300,000 of the price by delivery of a 5 year promissory note in the form attached to the agreement as an exhibit, $300,000 of the price by issuance of preferred stock in the form attached to the agreement as an exhibit and the balance in cash.

Exhibits designated in the purchase price section of the agreement included the following documents:

1. a purchase money promissory note to the seller;
2. a "non-recourse" guaranty by McQue and Lafayette of the promissory note;
3. a pledge agreement securing the guaranty;
4. a security agreement granting to the seller a second security interest in the assets being sold;
5. a second mortgage on Chomp-Chomp's realty;

6. an amendment to the Certificate of Incorporation of Ice Cold Doggie defining the relative rights of the preferred stock to be issued to the seller; and

7. a pro forma balance sheet.

In a subsection relating to the purchase price, we provided for preparation of a pro forma balance sheet of Chomp-Chomp at the closing date upon which the final price would be based. An adjustment would be made if the pro forma book value on the closing date exceeded or was less than the book value shown on the pro forma balance sheet attached to the agreement. A schedule to the agreement set out an allocation of the purchase price to the assets being transferred, much of which had been previously discussed with Myron and his counsel. Accounts receivable and inventory were to be purchased at the face amount thereof and the real estate and equipment were allocated with reasonable relationship to the appraisals obtained therefor.

The purchase price section of the agreement contained or referred to many "toothy" items upon which all parties to the transaction spent much time chewing. The section had expanded from what I had originally believed would be a simple statement of a cash payment to its present state since Fabulous was to be given purchase money security interests in assets.

### The Purchase Money Note and Security Therefor

Preparation of the exhibits to the purchase price section of the agreement opened a "Pandora's Box" of possible provisions which I examined. Although this chapter is not designed to deal with loan documents, loans are often a critical part of acquisitions and must be a standard number in the repertory of every acquisition attorney. The decisions reached in drafting the purchase money note and related documents involved many provisions, only a few of which are dealt with below.

The purchase money note was a two-edged sword. To protect the buyer, the note was to be subject to offset and non-negotiable, so that it could not be transferred to a good-faith purchaser, thereby cutting off defenses to payment which might be available to the buyer. The note was specifically subject to the provisions of the acquisition agreement including those provisions which might entitle the buyer to be paid by the seller.

The seller, of course, wanted the note to serve as an evidentiary basis for payment by the buyer of the amount of principal and interest agreed upon. However, the twists and turns of the transaction complicated that simple purpose. Not only was payment of the purchase money note subject to offset, but it was made subordinate to payment of the buyer's obligation to the bank. However, to benefit the seller the note was to be secured by a second security interest in the assets being sold and the course of negotiations had resulted in a commitment from Lafayette and McQue to further secure the note with all capital stock of the buyer. To make Lafayette and McQue parties to the arrangement, I provided for their guaranty to the seller of payment of the note with the guaranty secured by their pledge to the seller of the buyer's capital stock. The guaranty was without recourse personally against Lafayette and McQue. The remedy of the seller in the event the guaranty was drawn upon was solely against the capital stock securing the guaranty.

Since the seller would continue to be interested in the buyer and its performance until payment of the promissory note (and redemption of preferred stock to be issued to the seller), I had to consider the kind of negative and positive covenants of a continuing nature which would be provided by the buyer to Fabulous so long as the note remained outstanding. These covenants were built into the security agreement under which the buyer granted to the seller a second security interest in the buyer's assets. Ultimately, the covenants and agreements provided to Fabulous in the security agreement mirrored substantially those covenants and agreements provided by the buyer to Winston Largess's bank. In my initial draft of the security agreement, I specified in brackets under sections headed, respectively, "Affirmative Covenants" and "Negative Covenants" "[to be provided based, in part, on bank documents]."

Although the borrower under a security agreement will typically provide detailed representations and warranties to the secured party concerning its ownership rights and the condition of title to the assets serving as security, those were not present in my draft. In those transactions where the secured party is transferring the assets to the debtor and concurrently taking back a security interest, I believe that the secured party should not require the debtor's representations and warranties as to facts better known to the secured party than the debtor and it would be unwise for the debtor to assume those responsibilities. I was also reluctant to provide to Largess's bank representations and warranties from the buyer concerning title to the property. The solution to the bank's desire to be protected was an assignment to the bank of the buyer's rights against the seller and Fabulous in the event of breach of representations and warranties in the acquisition agreement. However, many banks will not accept such an assignment in lieu of a direct representation from the borrower. In that case, the borrower must weigh the business risks involved in providing full title representations and counsel must determine its ability to legally opine thereon.

The extent of subordination by the seller of its right to payment under the promissory note had to be determined as did the scope of the guaranty to be delivered. I focused upon issues such as these while I was drafting. Typically, it was the preparation and submission of documents which brought to the negotiating table these many issues not discussed by the parties.

### Preferred Stock

In the prolonged negotiation of preferred stock provisions with Myron, McQue had agreed upon a $300,000 liquidation preference, a dividend of 10 percent and a mandatory redemption of the stock within five years. Preferred stock has five basic elements: dividends, preference on liquidation, voting rights, redemption and conversion. Within these elements are diverse variations limited only by the imagination of the draftsman. Accounting treatment of the preferred stock on the balance sheet of the issuer is also an important element to be considered in determining provisions of that stock.

McQue, a man with a strong aversion to paying taxes, had reconsidered a 10 percent dividend in light of its non-deductibility as a corporate expense and had determined, with Myron, to provide an average 10 percent return on the $600,000 of the

purchase price for Chomp-Chomp which was being deferred—
14 percent under the purchase money note and 6 percent as a
dividend under the preferred stock. Myron acquiesced, notwithstanding better tax treatment available to a corporation
upon receipt of a dividend than upon receipt of interest, since
a large percentage of the dividend received is excluded from
taxation. My initial draft provided for a cumulative 6 percent
dividend payable semi-annually; a liquidation preference for
$300,000 plus accrued and unpaid dividends; voting rights to
elect one director (out of five) only in the event of failure to
pay dividends for two years or failure to redeem; redemption—
at the option of Ice Cold Doggie—in the fifth year for $300,000
plus accrued and unpaid dividends and no conversion.

The preferred stock finally agreed upon included sinking
fund provisions and mandatory conversion of the stock to a
demand promissory note if it had not been redeemed by the
sixth year after issuance.

Stock (whether preferred or common) is *not* equivalent to
a direct obligation to pay even after the stock may have been
transmogrified into a promise to pay. The payment of dividends
on stock and payment of a redemption price therefor are generally subject to the existence of a "surplus" (frequently defined
as the excess of net assets over liabilities), as defined by the
applicable corporation law. The payment may also require that
a corporation be "solvent" at the time it is made. Thus, a
corporation may have an absolute defense to payment under a
contract requiring that it redeem stock or under a promissory
note issued to redeem stock if the corporation does not meet
the corporate law tests at the time payment is to be made. The
jurisdiction in which Ice Cold Doggie was incorporated imposed
such restrictions on payment of dividends and payment in
connection with redemption.

### The Closing

Deciding the time and place for a closing requires delib-
eration. To be considered are sales and other transfer taxes, the
desires of any lender and the myriad number of considerations

affecting the business needs and convenience of the parties. Winston Largess's bank maintained a small "promotional" office in New York which Winston was willing to utilize to close the transaction. He had indicated his desire to preclose and execute loan documents in the Midwest so that he could reasonably apply local law to the interpretation of those documents. He would then wire funds directly to Fabulous's bank in New York when all the additional elements of the transaction had been completed to his satisfaction.

Since we had the option to close in New York, my agreement recited that the closing was to be held at our offices, a convenience which I deem the prerogative of the party preparing the agreement if all other elements permit a local closing.

### Representations and Warranties of the Seller

As we have stated before, the representations and warranties in the agreement are designed to disclose to the buyer all pertinent facts concerning the business of the seller, and to shift to the seller the risks from untrue statements concerning those facts. These provisions give the buyer basis for terminating the agreement or, possibly, renegotiating its terms. Subsequent to the closing, the representations and warranties provide a factual basis for utilization of indemnity provisions in the agreement.

In addition to general representations concerning Fabulous and Chomp-Chomp and their organization, corporate power and power to enter into the agreement and consummate the transactions provided for in the agreement, several business representations were necessary. In order to provide the buyer with an accurate snapshot of Chomp-Chomp's business at a given point in time, balance sheets and statements of income and changes in financial position as of the end of the fiscal year and as of the end of its most recent interim period were to be attached to the agreement. Often, financial statements of subsidiaries of public companies are not separately certified by accountants. However, Chomp-Chomp for many years had been separately certified by an accounting firm which did not audit the statements of Fabulous. If a separate certification is not available, the buyer might have to settle for non-audited financials (which should be carefully reviewed by buyer's accountants and accompanied by appropriate representations).

I requested that Chomp-Chomp represent with Fabulous that the certified financial statements, together with the notes, were complete and correct, presented fairly the financial condition and results of operation of the business of Chomp-Chomp at the dates and for the periods indicated, and were prepared in accordance with generally accepted accounting principles consistently applied. This reference to "GAAP" was a key to the financial protections which we desired. Accounting standards have been relatively solidified and to the extent generally accepted accounting principles are referred to, disputes can frequently be resolved by accounting firms. Even with application of generally accepted accounting principles, accountants (and lawyers and principals) can differ, but the utilization of this familiar terminology goes a long way toward solving potential problems. The pro forma balance sheet referred to in the purchase price section of the agreement consisted of the numbers on the "GAAP" balance sheet, adjusted based upon those assets and liabilities excluded from the transaction. That pro forma balance sheet would be used in the purchase price calculation at closing.

I provided that there were no liabilities not disclosed on the balance sheet and that all reserves established on the balance sheet were adequate. In addition, I provided that since the balance sheet date, the business of Chomp-Chomp had been operated in the ordinary course and that no material changes or damage or destruction had occurred. Provisions were added pursuant to which Chomp-Chomp and Fabulous represented that no labor trouble had occurred, no statutes had been adopted adversely affecting the business of Chomp-Chomp, no termination or waivers of rights had occurred and that no increase in compensation had occurred except as disclosed.

I also provided for representations concerning tax payments, notwithstanding the fact that in connection with this acquisition, the buyer was only assuming certain narrowly proscribed tax liabilities. The representations and warranties then referred to specific facets of the business of Chomp-Chomp and provided for the schedule to relate details concerning each of these.

The real estate of Chomp-Chomp was dealt with in detail including a legal description of the realty and representations concerning compliance with law, its title condition, zoning, etc. Leases and agreements were to be described in detail and the schedule was to completely itemize personal property, trademarks and tradenames, insurance, all contracts, including a list of specific contracts which were to be disclosed, and accounts receivable, including a firm representation as to collectability of those accounts which would later tie into the buyer's ability to "put" the accounts to the seller in the event they were not collected within a 90-day period. The schedule was to particularize information relating to litigation, laws and compliance with laws affecting the business of Chomp-Chomp and inventories including the usability and quantity thereof. The agreement also contemplated full information on the schedule concerning compensation of employees, pension plans, union arrangements and major customers and suppliers and arrangements, if any, between Chomp-Chomp and Fabulous.

Additional representations related to overall accuracy of the information supplied, the general business of Chomp-Chomp and the fact that the business would be operated in its normal course to the closing date and, importantly, that the assets being transferred to the buyer were sufficient for the buyer to operate the business of Chomp-Chomp in the ordinary course.

### Representations and Warranties of the Buyer

If the deal had been all cash, the buyer would provide to the seller only limited representations as to incorporation, authority, and compliance with law. The promissory note and preferred stock increased the complexity of the buyer's representations. However, I managed to convince the attorneys for Fabulous to permit many of the buyer's representations to appear, not in the acquisition agreement, but in the security agreement which would be executed at closing. This is not necessarily the best place for the seller to have the representations since the consequence of a breach is generally acceleration of the obligation secured rather than damages. Representations and warranties in the acquisition document, rather than the security agreement, might better protect a seller against losses for breach thereof.

Additional representations made by the buyer included those concerning the capitalization of the buyer, its commitment from a reputable financial institution for loans sufficient to finance the purchase price and, combined with other funds to be available, to operate the business of Chomp-Chomp after the closing, and honor its contracts and agreements. An assertion was made by the buyer that its ownership of the assets would be free and clear of liens and encumbrances (other than those of Largess's bank). Other items designed to make Fabulous comfortable with its legal claim to monies under the purchase note included maintenance by Ice Cold Doggie of its business in an agreed-upon financial state.

Substantial negotiation had occurred when the seller's counsel requested that McQue personally obligate himself for the representations and warranties in this agreement. McQue kicked and shrieked when the issue arose. His passion, and the logic with which it was presented, resulted in the issue being dropped. The compromise involved the nonrecourse guaranty secured by capital stock which McQue and Lafayette provided for the purchase note.

### The Hiatus Between Signing and Closing

We had provided in the seller's representations and warranties that the business of Chomp-Chomp would be operated in the ordinary course to the closing date. In addition, I provided for the following:

- Full access by the buyer's representatives to books, records and other data pertaining to the business of Chomp-Chomp to enable a complete investigation to occur;

- no diminution of the representations, warranties and agreements by reason of the investigation;

- best efforts to preserve relationships with customers, suppliers, etc.; and

- delivery of monthly interim financial and other data.

If stock or substantially all assets of a public company are being sold, this section must also set out and require compliance with regulatory mechanics prior to closing. This includes preparation and submission of proxy material to stockholders to permit them to vote on the transaction.

Seller's counsel may request that the representations and warranties exclude adverse information known to the buyer— in effect, that those representations and warranties diminish based upon the buyer's investigation. The seller doesn't want the buyer to close the transaction and then sue for a breach of representations and warranties which was known at closing. However, whether the buyer had knowledge of a fact is a difficult question to answer, and a seller has the ability to protect itself by carefully disclosing in schedules or exhibits all facts concerning the business to be sold.

### Conditions Precedent to the Obligations of the Parties

There are certain relatively standard conditions to closing contained in acquisition agreements. These conditions are designed to insure that the representations in the agreement remain accurate at closing and that the commitments in the agreement have been complied with by closing if compliance by closing is required. To nail down these conditions, most acquisition attorneys will provide for the delivery by the parties of certificates as to compliance with conditions and as to accuracy of representations and warranties.

As additional backup for the accuracy of representations and warranties, corporate proceedings reasonably satisfactory to counsel for each party were required to have been completed, and attorneys' opinions relating to matters of law contained in the representations and warranties were required to be delivered. I also requested a comfort letter from the accountants for Chomp-Chomp which would indicate to a date not later than five days prior to the closing that they had performed a review of the financial statements of Chomp-Chomp and would stand by the scheduled financial statements as disclosed in the comfort letter. An accountant's comfort letter would probably not have been available to the buyer if separately audited financial statements had not been prepared for Chomp-Chomp.

Letters from attorneys and accountants are very important to the preparers thereof. McQue scoffed at the concern of our firm and of counsel for Fabulous about the respective opinions we prepared. However, the opinions provided additional insurance to the recipient and placed at risk the providers of the opinions.

There were certain additional conditions which I believed were crucial to the buyer. These included confirmation from certain major customers of orders, appropriate title insurance on the real estate and appraisals for the real estate and equipment indicating a minimum value of $1,000,000. In fact, McQue was confident the appraisal would be made at $2,000,000 but we did not wish to include a number so large as to provide grounds for additional inquiry from Myron and his counsel. A five-year non-compete agreement from the seller and Fabulous was also provided for in this section and attached as an exhibit.

Because Fabulous wished to insure that the buyer obtained appropriate insurance relating to the business of Chomp-Chomp, including product liability insurance, I inserted a condition to the seller's obligations relating to the kind and nature of insurance to be obtained. I also provided for the consent of Chomp-Chomp's unions as a condition to the seller's obligations because of the seller's concern about its relationship with those unions in other businesses. Myron's request for the buyer to maintain such items as insurance and union relationships after closing was provided for in the security agreement.

### Closing Adjustments

I had not discussed with counsel for Fabulous those items which were to be adjusted at the closing and, as the drafter of the document, was in a position to exactly determine the cards I would initially place on the table. I assumed that subsequent meetings would result in additions and deletions to the agreement which would be satisfactory to all the parties.

The agreement provided for termination of utilities service at the closing date, a request by the seller for final bills to that date and the commencement of new service in the name of the buyer. These utilities included telephone, gas and electric. In order to help maintain the continuity of the business, the buyer and seller were to request that the same telephone numbers be used subsequent to the transfer of the business to the buyer.

Salaries, including fringe benefits and vacation accruals, were to be adjusted to the last shift on the closing date. Since Chomp-Chomp paid its employees in arrears, this item would require a rebate from the seller to the buyer once the specific amount of the adjustment had been determined. Taxes accruing on real estate and personal property were prorated. Special assessments relating to real estate which dealt with work commenced prior to the closing date would be paid by the seller and assessments, if any, for work commenced after the closing date were to be paid by the buyer. Certain miscellaneous items such as water, fuel, sewer expenses, license and permit fees, rentals on equipment and obligations under service contracts were to be apportioned to the close of business on the closing date. I also provided for the payment by the seller to the buyer of trade accounts payable in excess of the maximum number agreed upon.

Proration adjustments were to be paid within 30 days after the closing date based upon an adjusted amount to be agreed upon by buyer and seller after examination of the books and records of Chomp-Chomp. In case of a problem, I set up a method to resolve disputes in a later section of the agreement which contemplated utilizing the services of an arbitration association.

At closing, the buyer would deliver to the seller the purchase money note, preferred stock and cash based upon the pro forma balance sheet attached to the agreement. I wanted closing adjustments to be made quickly based upon McQue's estimate that, due to a seasonal shift in business, the closing pro forma balance sheet would result in a purchase price adjustment in favor of the buyer.

I had advised McQue that we should seek to maintain the purchase money note at $300,000 and provide that other adjustments be paid in cash when incurred. Offsets under the purchase note were not as good as cash since the note was due five years from the closing and only semi-annual interest thereon (at 14 percent) could be used for offset prior to that time.

Counsel for Fabulous wanted the principal amount of the purchase note to be adjusted six months from closing if adjustments were required in buyer's favor. By adjusting the note, Fabulous would obtain the maximum cash possible. Ultimately, after much effort and several concessions to Fabulous, we agreed that adjustments would be made in cash.

### After the Closing

In order to mechanically expedite adjustments, a closing pro forma balance sheet was to be prepared promptly after closing. A list of post-closing activity included insurance adjustments, purchase by the seller of accounts receivable unpaid within 90 days after the closing, adjustment of inventories which did not meet terms set forth in the representations and warranties provided by the seller, adjustments in connection with credits and adjustments for goods returned for credit or otherwise. I also provided for the seller's right of access to the business operated by the buyer after closing to deal with the items to be adjusted and for the seller's assumption of claims relating to product liability.

To help maintain continuity of the business of Chomp-Chomp, the agreement provided that Fabulous would continue to provide to the buyer computer servicing of certain accounting functions for up to 90 days after closing. Compensation for computer services was based upon the cost of those services to Fabulous.

A mechanism was provided to resolve disputes which might occur in connection with preparation of the closing pro forma balance sheet. Initially, that balance sheet was to be prepared by the accountants for the buyer and submitted to the accountants for the seller. The two accounting firms were to agree upon the pro forma balance sheet and if they did not agree, arbitration by a third accounting firm was provided for. The buyer and the seller were to split the costs relating to the preparation of the closing pro forma balance sheet.

The agreement also provided for the seller's payment of all its liabilities not assumed and for the change of the seller's name to something other than Chomp-Chomp. McQue wanted to continue using that trade name after closing for certain products. In acquiring all or substantially all assets of public companies, plans of liquidation should be required that will not only require payment of creditors, but also distribution of funds to stockholders and compliance with other conditions of proxy material relating to the transaction.

### Further Agreements of the Parties

The acquisition agreement included a series of commitments from the parties which were not representations and warranties, but which related to activities in which the parties were to engage in connection with the acquisition.

A series of meetings had occurred with counsel for Largess's bank in connection with the loan documents. The bank's counsel had arranged, prior to closing, to pre-file Uniform Commercial Code Financing Statements in order to perfect, upon execution of security agreements, the bank's security interest in inventory, accounts receivable and machinery and equipment. The first mortgage to the bank (and the second mortgage to the seller) had been fully negotiated and the title company engaged had indicated that it would issue at closing to the bank a firm title insurance policy based upon delivery to its representative of the executed mortgage and the deed to the property. No substantial mortgage tax was imposed in the jurisdiction in which Chomp-Chomp was located. This eliminated the high cost of mortgage tax which is encountered in jurisdictions such as New York. At the 1½ percent tax rate imposed in New York City, the tax on recording a $2,000,000 mortgage is substantial.

The seller's security interests did not require advance filing. However, the agreement did provide for the mechanics of preparing and filing the documents required to perfect the seller's security interests and impose its liens.

### Survival of Representations; Indemnification

My initial draft of the agreement simply provided for the survival of representations, warranties, and agreements subsequent to closing and the consummation of the transaction contemplated by the agreement. If that provision had stood, the buyer would have had a period of time equal to the appropriate statute of limitations within which to bring any actions under the acquisition agreement. In many states, that time period is six years.

To insure that the schedule and other attachments to the agreement would be included as part of the representations and warranties made in the agreement, I provided for their inclusion in this section of the document. I also provided that any material delivered by the seller to the buyer concerning the business and financial condition of Chomp-Chomp would be deemed a representation and warranty by Fabulous and the seller as to the contents thereof. Counsel for Fabulous said that was "cute" and we agreed to delete the line.

I assumed that Fabulous would request a limit upon survival of its representations and warranties. I hoped that our five-year promissory note might provide a reasonable basis for five (rather than six) years limitation within which claims could be asserted. However, a two-year limitation on enforcement of representations and warranties was, in the process of compromising issues, ultimately built into the agrrement at the urging of the seller and its counsel.

My initial indemnity provision was broad. I sought a full indemnity of the buyer by Fabulous and Chomp-Chomp against any liabilities not assumed and any damages or loss (including costs and expenses) which were incurred due to inaccuracy of representations, warranties or agreements. A mechanism was established to implement the indemnity provisions requiring that a party claiming indemnity provide specified written notice of those claims to the other party and permit the other party to assert defenses for such claims under stipulated circumstances. The party indemnified was granted the right to be represented by its own advisory professional help at the expense of the other side. The agreement provided for mutual access to all material relevant to the claim and that no claim would be settled without the written consent of the indemnified party. The indemnity provisions were designed to make the injured party whole if damages occurred, including giving effect to the tax consequences of the damage.

Indemnity provisions, along with opinions of counsel, are usually among the most hotly negotiated items in an agreement. Fabulous, in addition to hewing to a two-year period within which the buyer could enforce the agreement, was unwilling to provide a complete indemnity. Counsel for Fabulous was ultimately successful in negotiating a $100,000 "basket" as part of the trade-off for cash adjustments and no personal liability for the buyer's stockholders. Thus, if the aggregate claims for which the buyer wished to be indemnified did not exceed $100,000, no indemnity could be sought and the buyer would only be entitled to indemnification for amounts in excess of $100,000. If a "trigger" rather than a "basket" had been built into the indemnity, the "trigger" would provide that the buyer would not seek indemnity unless the aggregate amount for which it was to be indemnified exceeded the triggering amount, in this case $100,000. However, once the amount for which indemnity was sought did exceed $100,000, the buyer would have the right under the indemnity to recover from the seller all monies from the first dollar involved. The indemnity section clearly stated that any remedies available to either party were cumulative, that they could be exercised one on top of another, and that they could be exercised at any time.

Since the indemnity provisions were reciprocal, the seller also had the right to recover against the buyer for damages caused by buyer's breach of representations and warranties. However, since the seller was not exposed to the exigencies arising from operation of a "new" business and since the buyer made far fewer representations than the seller, I did not anticipate that the indemnity provisions would be meaningful to the extent that the buyer was the indemnifying party. They were provisions principally designed for the buyer's benefit.

### Employee Benefits

The complexities of employee benefits, particularly insofar as they are controlled by the Employee Retirement Security Act of 1974 ("ERISA") and its regulations, may often warrant separate provisions. The representations and warranties had referred to details pertaining to employee benefits in the schedule to the agreement, including actuarial reports. This particular section of the agreement was designed to insure that there were no violations of law in connection with any of the plans maintained by Fabulous for the employees of Chomp-Chomp and that all funding had occurred thereunder. Since the buyer would be employing the employees of Chomp-Chomp after the closing and would rely upon those employees in operating the business acquired, the agreement should insure that the benefits which had accrued to those employees during the period that the business was under the aegis of Fabulous were properly funded and available. Maintenance of good employee relations is critical in connection with any business acquisition and various sections of the acquisition agreement, including the representations and warranties, convenants, conditions to closing and special employee benefit sections, are relevant to those relations.

As facts developed, underfunding of the Fabulous pension and profit-sharing plan became a major problem in connection with this transaction and required not only a commitment for Fabulous to pay a portion of the cash proceeds from the sale of Chomp-Chomp to increase funding of the plan, but also an agreement from Fabulous to maintain contributions at specified levels over a period of time.

### Brokers

The agreement included cross-representations by the parties that none of them had dealt with any brokers or finders in a manner requiring payment of a fee in connection with the transaction and that each party would, to the extent a fee was payable because of their actions, pay the fee and indemnify the other party with respect thereto. Although both Fabulous and McQue had dealt with finders, neither was obligated to pay them fees in connection with the acquisition.

## Miscellaneous Provisions

Miscellaneous provisions are crucial. They may include an allocation of expenses, a reference to the parties in interest to the transaction, that the agreement is complete, provisions pertaining to the headings of the agreement and other items which may seem superficially to warrant the appellation of "boiler-plate," but which are important enough to require careful preparation.

Notices under the agreement require attention not only as to address, but as to the method to be used to give notice and the time within which notices are to be received. Since I expected that many of the notices would issue from the buyer and involve the making of claims or a request for data from the seller, as buyer's counsel I wanted easy and "loose" notice provisions: "notice will be given by personal delivery or by first-class mail, postage pre-paid, and will be deemed given when delivered or mailed at a post office box." The seller wanted a tighter procedure which would require that notices be deemed given only when actually received. Registered or certified mail or personal delivery were finally chosen as the methods for notifying parties and, for greater evidentiary certainty, notices were deemed to be delivered based upon the receipts provided by the post office or facts concerning delivery.

Other miscellaneous provisions in the agreement included a reference to consultation on publicity, the designation of governing law and reference to the fact that waivers would not be deemed continuing and that any waiver of a provision would not operate as a waiver of any other provision. Detailed arbitration procedures, referred to earlier, were also set forth under this section of the agreement.

### Bulk Sales Laws

The provisions of bulk sales laws are often waived in connection with the purchase of assets from a division or subsidiary of a large company. Buyers often believe that an indemnity will be sufficient to protect them if problems arise. In addition, since bulk sales laws are designed to protect buyers against claims of creditors of the seller affecting assets acquired, they may be less important in situations, like this one, which include the buyer's assumption of obligations to those creditors.

Largess's bank, notwithstanding what was typical, initially demanded full compliance by Chomp-Chomp with the Bulk Sales Law. Bank counsel believed that seller's creditors might, in this divisional acquisition case, have priority in a bankruptcy over the secured position of the bank. Compliance with bulk sales laws would have required that Fabulous notify all creditors of Chomp-Chomp in order to cut off claims which might affect the assets being acquired. This procedure is cumbersome and would have delayed closing. It also has the effect of putting suppliers on notice of the sale, enabling them to reassess relationships with the business being sold. However, the bank's lawyers finally agreed with our conclusion that failure to comply with bulk sales laws could be made without undue risk and the transaction proceeded without compliance.

## THE MECHANICAL CLOSING PROCESS

Finally, after four weeks of investigating the business of Chomp-Chomp, negotiating with Fabulous, Largess and their counsel and arranging for completion of all of the acts contemplated by the agreement, we set a closing date. The acquisition agreement had not yet been signed and, notwithstanding a contemplated delay between signing and closing, it was not, in fact, signed until the closing date. This is not a desirable state of facts for either buyer or seller, but is not an uncommon development in some mergers and acquisitions.

In the event that a transaction involves delay between signing and closing, a signing of the acquisition agreement would occur first. All exhibits and schedules to the agreement would be in final form and attached to the agreement. Subsequent to signing, documents related to the closing would be prepared, reviewed and negotiated by the parties, and delivered at the actual closing.

Prior to the concurrent signing and closing of the Chomp-Chomp transaction, I prepared closing memoranda for circulation, one for the acquisition of Chomp-Chomp and the second for the financing to be engaged in by the buyer. The memoranda contained detailed descriptions of the items to be delivered by each party at closing and a full list of all documents related to the transaction. The circulation list, which had expanded as negotiations proceeded, included three sets of lawyers (including bank counsel), two accountants, McQue, Lafayette, Myron and the Treasurer of Fabulous, the President and Treasurer of Chomp-Chomp, Largess and, with respect to limited documents, the title company—a total of 13 copies!

Once our final documents were circulated, I advised both McQue and Lafayette to warm their right arms in preparation for signing.

From the foregoing, it should be clear that the success of a merger or acquisition depends, in substantial part, upon the availability of talented support staff and the reliability of the automated office machinery which they operate. The mechanics of any transaction must be assiduously attended to in order to avoid a shift of focus from the substantive problems which often arise.

Some of the problems arising prior to closing have been mentioned in the description of the acquisition agreement itself. In addition to pension and profit-sharing plan difficulties, our title report indicated encroachments on the real estate of Chomp-Chomp which could potentially affect the salability thereof and which could not be removed without negotiating with an adjoining land owner. This real estate was, of course, critical to the buyer's financing requirements and the operation of the business. The negotiations with the adjoining land owner, in which Fabulous's counsel played the major role, resulted in an agreement which removed the encroachments, at a cost of approximately $75,000 to Fabulous. Thus, the encroachments, along with pension and profit-sharing requirements, decreased meaningfully the cash available to Fabulous from this transaction. By the time the additional dollars had to be expended, it was difficult to back out. Fabulous had agreed to firm representations in the agreement which were violated by the facts and, despite the failure of the parties to execute the agreement before closing, Fabulous adhered to its word.

The investigation of Chomp-Chomp's business preceding the closing process indicated that certain agreements should be reached with suppliers and three distributors to insure their continued relationship with the business after closing. In attempting to ferret out problems and facts, McQue also determined that two present employees of Chomp-Chomp were sufficiently important to warrant employment agreements. A condition for those agreements had been included in the acquisition agreement after negotiations with Fabulous and its counsel.

A Uniform Commercial Code search report was delivered prior to closing to reveal any security interests in the assets of Chomp-Chomp other than the interest of Fabulous's lender. That lender had provided to the buyer a written commitment to release its lien at closing, subject to payment of $1,000,000, and Largess had arranged to wire the payoff amount direct to that lender at closing.

Transfer documents relating to registered motor vehicles, along with documents creating liens on those vehicles, had been prepared prior to closing and reviewed by the bank.

In connection with the acquisition, I attempted to prepare all documents reflected in the closing memoranda as early as possible so that they could be fully reviewed by the various parties. Legal and accounting letters often undergo substantial negotiation and should be delivered sufficiently in advance of closing to permit study and negotiation and avoid the all-night sessions often required in order to finish transactions. Pre-closings prior to the time the principals are available for signing often help diminish the frequent problems which arise on a closing date and sometimes pre-signing of an agreement may be desirable.

The lawyers in our firm, along with counsel for Fabulous, had worked well into the night the day before a pre-closing was to occur in order to finalize all documents. At the pre-closing, additional changes were made as required and virtually a full day was spent correcting and organizing all documents in form for signing.

The buyer had pre-signed all of its documents with the lender at the request of Largess and those documents remained in escrow with the attorneys for the lender. At closing, the buyer would deliver to its lender the mortgage and title policy along with documents related to registered equipment. Based upon delivery of those documents (along with the deed for the real estate being transferred) and evidence of the closing of the asset acquisition, the lender was prepared to wire funds. Wires, however, often get lost. Notwithstanding my reluctance to wire funds, it was the only method seemingly available in this situation since Largess would not issue checks prior to the time all documents had been completed and delivered.

We planned to finish as early as possible on the day of closing in order to insure that wired funds might, with luck and constant attention, arrive prior to the close of business on that day. The principals of the buyer, the seller, Fabulous, the title closer and counsel for the parties arrived at our offices at 8:00 A.M. to commence signing the ten execution copies of documents. By 11:00 A.M. documents had been executed and instructions issued to wire funds. Acknowledgement of arrival of funds was not received until 2:45 P.M. when the transaction was finally completed.

## WHAT HAPPENED AFTER CLOSING

McQue had resigned from his current job two weeks before the closing occurred and on the day of closing immediately flew to the facility of Chomp-Chomp to commence running its business. The pro forma closing balance sheet was not prepared without many threats and, eventually, preparation by us of a summons and complaint against Chomp-Chomp and Fabulous. We never got together on arbitration. Final resolution, however, did occur. When last I heard from McQue, he was happily engaged in the dog food business and looking for another deal.

# APPENDIX 13-A*

## PURCHASE AGREEMENT

THIS AGREEMENT is made this ___ day of September, 19___ by and between _____ _____ an Ohio corporation (the "Seller"), and _____ an Ohio corporation (the "Buyer").

WHEREAS, Seller desires to sell and Buyer desires to purchase all of the assets of Seller's Tractor Division (the "Division") other than its cash, receivables and prepaid expenses upon the terms hereinafter set forth;

NOW, THEREFORE, in consideration of the premises and the mutual covenants herein contained, the parties hereto, intending to be legally bound hereby, agree as follows:

## I. BASIC TERMS OF TRANSACTION

1.1 Sale of Assets. Seller hereby agrees to sell, transfer, assign and deliver to Buyer on the Closing Date (as hereinafter defined), and Buyer hereby agrees to purchase from Seller, free and clear of all liens, security interests, charges and encumbrances, all of the Division's assets and business as a going concern, of every kind, nature and description and wherever stiuated, tangible and intangible, owned by Seller at the close of business on the Closing Date, including, but not limited to: the Division's land, plant facility and office space located at a legal description of which is attached hereto as Exhibit A, machinery and equipment (including, but not limited to, those items set forth on Exhibit B), furniture, office equipment, business machines, vehicles, inventory (including, but not limited to, the raw materials, work in process, finished goods and supplies set forth on Exhibit C), trade secrets, know-how, trade names, trademarks, logos, rights under contracts, tooling, patterns, dies, jigs, fixtures, patents, product designs and claims, rights, choses in action, operating data and records (including customer lists, credit information and correspondence), and all rights to use, to the exclusion of Seller, the names _____ and _____ either alone or in conjunction with other words, EXCEPT, however, for the following assets of the Division which shall not be included in the purchase and sale transaction herein contemplated:

    (a) the Division's accounts receivable existing on the Closing Date;

    (b) the Division's prepaid expenses existing on the Closing Date; and

    (c) the Division's cash and bank deposits existing on the Closing Date.

The assets of the Division being purchased and sold hereunder are hereinafter called the "Acquired Assets." Coincident with such sale, assignment and

---

*Source: From the book, *Handbook of Mergers, Acquisitions and Buyouts,* edited by Steven James Lee and Robert Douglas Colman ©1981. Used by permission of the publisher, Prentice-Hall, Inc., Englewood Cliffs, NJ.

transfer Seller shall place Buyer in effective possession and control of the Acquired Assets.

1.2 Purchase Price. Buyer agrees to pay Seller the following separately identifiable purchase price for the Acquired Assets:

(a) for the Division's inventory of finished goods, raw materials, supplies and work in process, a purchase price of _____ ($____ ); which shall be allocated among the items of inventory in the manner set forth in Exhibit C;

(b) for the Division's land, plant facility, and office space located at _____, a purchase price of _____ which shall be allocated $____ to the building comprising the office space and plant facility; and

(c) for all other Acquired Assets a purchase price of _____ ($____) which shall be allocated among the Acquired Assets in the manner set forth in Exhibit B attached hereto.

Seller shall, prior to the Closing Date, conduct a physical count of all inventory of the Division in the presence of a representative of Buyer, which shall be adjusted to the Closing Date for activity subsequent to said count. Said physical count, as so adjusted, shall be used as the basis for determining pursuant to Section 2.1 the increase or reduction (if any) in the purchase price of said inventory as stated above.

1.3 Assumed Liabilities. Buyer agrees to assume, perform and/or discharge the following obligations and liabilities of the Division (the "Assumed Liabilities"):

(a) all customers' orders relating to the purchase of the Division's products, accepted in the ordinary and usual course of business, which are on hand and unfilled or incomplete as of the Closing Date (all of which are set forth on Exhibit D) and all orders for the purchase by the Division of goods, materials and supplies, entered into in the ordinary and usual course of business, which are outstanding and unfilled or incomplete as of the Closing Date (all of which are set forth on Exhibit D);

## 2. PAYMENT OF PURCHASE PRICE

2.1 Inventory Purchase Price. The purchase price for the inventory of the Division, computed according to the provisions of Subsection 1.2(a) shall be paid by check at Closing in the amount of $____ subject to the reconciliation provided for below.

It is the intention of the parties that Buyer shall purchase all of the Divison's inventory but that Buyer be obligated to pay for hereunder only such inventory of Seller relating to the Division which is not defective, substandard, obsolete or slow moving in every case

where the same had remained in Seller's inventory of finished goods for and has not been sold during a period of one (1) year from the date it was manufactured. Subject to the foregoing standards, the purchase price for all the Division's inventory of raw material, work in process, finished goods and supplies shall be either reduced or increased dollar for dollar to the extent the Division's inventory on hand at Closing (valued at the lower of actual cost or net realizable value) is (a) either greater or less than _____ and (b) not defective, substandard, obsolete or slow moving. Said inventory shall be certified by an officer of the Company based upon inventory taken by Price Waterhouse & Co.

2.2 Other Acquired Assets Purchase Price. The purchase price for all the other Acquired Assets shall be paid at the Closing by check in the amount of $____ and by delivery of Buyer's Subordinated Promissory Note in the principal amount as set forth in Exhibit E.

## 3. ADDITIONAL COVENANTS AND UNDERTAKINGS

3.1 Bulk Sales Law. Buyer and Seller agree to waive compliance with any laws relating to the bulk sales and bulk transfers applicable to the transaction contemplated by this Agreement, and in consideration of such waiver Seller agrees to defend and indemnify Buyer against and hold it harmless from any and all loss, liability, damage or expense (including all reasonable costs and expenses, including attorneys' fees) arising out of or resulting from such noncompliance.

3.2 Change of Name. Promptly after the Closing, Seller shall cease to use the names _____ and _____ or any other trade name heretofore used in connection with the Division's business.

3.3 Pro-Ration of Labor Costs. Seller shall, as promptly as reasonably possible after the Closing or the date payable, if later, pay directly or reimburse Buyer for all compensation of employees of the Division (including FICA contributions) earned for services rendered prior to the Closing together with Seller's pro rata share of the cost of any and all fringe benefits of said employees for the period prior to the Closing including, but not limited to, life and disability insurance premiums, contributions to health and welfare or supplemental unemployment benefit plans and other fringe benefits set forth in the Labor Agreement. Seller's pro rata share of any such expense which is payable periodically for a period ending subsequent to the Closing shall be equal to such expense multiplied by the ratio that the number of days in such period occurring prior to Closing bears to the total number of days in the period. Notwithstanding anything herein to the contrary, Seller shall, within 10 days after the Closing, pay to Buyer in cash an amount equal to the full amount of all vacation pay and sick leave accrued or accruable as of the Closing for all employees of the Division.

3.4 Assignments. Seller agrees to obtain and deliver to Buyer at the Closing duly executed consents to the assignment and transfer by Seller to Buyer of all rights of the Division in and to all agreements, commitments, and other specific assets and properties to be assigned and transferred to Buyer hereunder in all instances in which the same may, in the opinion of Buyer's counsel, be necessary to vest in Buyer all of the Seller's right, title and interest therein and thereto.

Notwithstanding anything herein to the contrary, to the extent the assignment of any right to be assigned to Buyer pursuant to the provisions hereof shall require the consent of any other party, or shall be subject to any equity or option in any other person by virtue of a request for permission to assign or transfer, or by reason of or precedent to any transfer to Buyer, this Agreement shall not constitute a breach thereof or create rights in others not desired by Buyer. Seller shall use its best efforts to procure consent to any such assignment. If any such consent is not obtained, Seller shall cooperate with Buyer in any reasonable arrangement designed to provide for Buyer the benefit of any such right, including enforcement of any; and all rights of Seller against the other party to any contract arising out of the breach or cancellation thereof by such party or otherwise.

3.6 Purchase of Plant Facility. Simultaneous with the Closing Seller shall execute and deliver to Buyer a general warranty deal pursuant to which Seller will transfer and convey free and clear of all liens, encumbrances, charges and imperfections of title, all its right, title and interest in and to the real property comprising its plant and office facility located at a complete legal description of which is contained in Exhibit A.

3.7 Transfer and Sales Taxes. Seller shall pay directly, unless Buyer is required to tender payment in which case Seller shall promptly reimburse Buyer for, all sales or other transfer taxes, if any, applicable to the transaction contemplated by this Agreement.

3.8 Further Assurances and Assistance. Buyer and Seller agree that each will execute and deliver to the other any and all documents in addition to those expressly provided for herein that may be necessary or appropriate to effectuate the provisions of this Agreement, whether before, at or after the Closing. Seller further agrees that at any time and from time to time after the Closing, it will execute and deliver to Buyer such further assignments or other written assurances as Buyer may reasonably request to perfect and protect Buyer's title to the Acquired Assets.

The parties agree to cooperate with each other to any extent reasonably required in order to fully accomplish the transaction herein contemplated and put Buyer in possession and control of the Acquired Assets. The parties acknowledge that the customers of Seller and other third parties may not fully and immediately appreciate the consequences of the transaction herein contemplated, and Seller and Buyer each agree to remit promptly to the other any payments received by such party which are properly for the account of the other.

3.9 Employee Pension Benefit Plans. Seller shall take all necessary measures including, where applicable, adopting or causing to be adopted appropriate amendments to its relevant employee pension benefit plan (as such term is defined in Section 3 (2) of The Employee Retirement Income Security Act of 1974), to fully vest every person employed by the Division as of the Closing Date, in his accrued benefits, determined as of the Closing Date, under the relevant employee pension benefit plans, and, for all purposes of said employee pension benefit plans, to treat such employees as participants who have terminated their employment with the Division.

4. THE CLOSING

4.1 Time and Place of Closing. The transfers and deliveries to be made pursuant to this Agreement shall take place at the Closing at the offices of _____ at 10:00 A.M., local time, on _____, 1978, or such other place, time and/or date as Seller and Buyer agree upon in writing (the "Closing Date"), and shall be deemed to be effective as of the begining of business on the Closing Date.

4.2 Deliveries at the Closing. At the Closing, Buyer and Seller respectively shall deliver the following documents in substitution therefor as are satisfactory to the recipient:

   (a) Seller shall deliver to Buyer:
     (i)  an Incumbency Certificate with respect to the officers of Seller executing documents or instruments on behalf of Seller;
     (ii)  good standing certificates for Seller from the Secretary of State of Ohio dated not more than 10 days prior to the Closing Date;
     (iii)  certified copies of the proceedings of Seller's Board of Directors and Shareholders with respect to approval of this

Agreement and authorization of the consummation by Seller of the transaction herein contemplated;

(iv) the certificate specified in Subsection 9.1.1;

(v) such bills of sale, endorsements, assignments and other good and sufficient instruments of transfer as shall be deemed necessary or appropriate by counsel for Buyer to transfer and assign to Buyer good and marketable title to the Acquired Assets;

(vi) the general warranty deed described in Section 3.6;

(vii) an appropriate amendment to the Labor Agreement, in form and substance satisfactory to the parties and their respective counsel, substituting Buyer as the employer thereunder, properly executed by Seller and the union; and

(viii) an opinion of Seller's counsel in form and substance satisfactory to Buyer confirming Seller's representations and warranties set forth in Sections 5.1, 5.2, 5.9 (first sentence only), and 5.17.

(b) Buyer shall deliver to Seller:

(i) an Incumbency Certificate with respect to officers of Buyer executing documents or instruments on behalf of Buyer;

(ii) a good standing certificate for Buyer from the Secretary of State of Ohio dated not more than 10 days prior to the Closing Date;

(iii) certified copies of the proceedings of Buyer's Board of Directors with respect to approval of this Agreement and authorization of the consummation by Buyer of the transactions herein contemplated;

(iv) the certificate specified in Subsection 9.2.1;

(v) Buyer's check in the aggregate amount determined pursuant to Sections 2.1(a) and 2.2;

(vi) Buyer's Subordinated Promissory Note executed by Buyer in the form set forth in Exhibit E;

(vii) an instrument evidencing the assumption by Buyer of those obligations of Seller described in Section 1.3; and

(viii) the amendment referred to in Subsection 4.2(a) (vii), properly executed by Buyer.

5. REPRESENTATIONS AND WARRANTIES OF SELLER

As an inducement to Buyer to enter into this Agreement and consummate the transaction contemplated herein, Seller represents and warrants to Buyer as follows:

5.1 Organization; Corporate Power; Qualification. Seller (i) is a corporation duly organized, validly existing and in good standing under the laws of the State of Ohio; (ii) has all requisite corporate power and authority to own the Acquired Assets and to sell and transfer the Acquired Assets to Buyer; and (iii) has all requisite corporate power and authority to own, lease and operate the properties of the Division and carry on its business as and where such properties are now owned or leased and such business is presently being conducted. Seller is qualified to do business as a foreign corporation in the State of _____ and, to the best of Seller's knowledge and belief, the business and properties of the Division do not require that Seller be qualified as a foreign corporation in any other jurisdiction.

5.2 Title to Property. Seller has, and at the Closing, Buyer will be vested with good and marketable title to all of the Acquired Assets free and clear of any liens, security interests, claims, charges, restrictions, easements or other encumbrances.

5.3 Use of Premises. Seller has all necessary permits and licenses with respect to its operation of the business of the Division, all of which are valid and continuing. Seller's use of the factory and office facilities of the Division, including all machinery and equipment, conforms to all applicable environmental, safety, health, building, zoning or other laws, ordinances and regulations. Seller has received no notice of any zoning, health, safety or other violations or of any assessments, either general or special, relating to the operations or properties of the Division.

5.4 Contracts. Seller is not a party to or bound by, nor has it any rights under, any contract or commitment relating to the Division except for (i) the customer orders and purchase orders listed on Exhibit D all of which were entered into in the ordinary course of business, (ii) the Labor Agreement, and (iii) the *(names of all employee pension benefit plans)* to which Seller contributes with respect to employees of the Division. Seller has not defaulted, nor is there a valid basis to claim any such default on the part of Seller, under any of the customer orders or purchase orders listed on Exhibit D or under the Labor Agreement. None of the customer orders listed on Exhibit D nor any outstanding binding quotation with respect to the products or services of the Division involves the future sale and/or delivery of products or services of the Division at prices other than the Division's regular prices as in effect at the time of delivery.

5.5 <u>Compensation and Benefits</u>. Exhibit F sets forth a complete listing and description of all current compensation and benefits for each employee of the Division.

5.6 <u>Proprietary Rights</u>. With respect to the conduct of the business of the Division, Seller does not own or use any patents, inventions (whether or not patentable) trademarks, copyrights or service marks other than those set forth on Exhibit G attached hereto, and with respect thereto Seller has not received any notice or claim of conflict with the asserted rights of others. Seller is not required to pay any royalty, license fee or similar type of compensation in connection with the current or prior conduct of the business of the Division.

5.7 <u>Employment of Labor</u>. Seller has complied in all material respects with all applicable Federal and state laws and local ordinances relating to the employment of labor of the Division, including the provisions thereof relating to wages, hours, employee benefit plans (as defined in Section 3(3) of the U.S. Employee Retirement Income Security Act of 1974) and the payment of social security taxes, and is not liable for any arrearages of wages or any tax or penalties for failure to comply with any of the foregoing. There are no controversies pending or, to the knowledge of Seller threatened, between the Seller and any employees of the Division, nor have there been any such controversies within the past three years. Seller has complied with all Federal and state labor laws, if any, applicable to the transaction contemplated by the Agreement. In the event of any labor dispute arising after the Closing based upon acts arising prior to the Closing or as a result of this transaction, Seller agrees to cooperate with Buyer in the resolution of any such disputes and agrees to hold Buyer harmless from any costs and expenses including reasonable attorney fees incurred in connection therewith.

5.8 <u>Books and Records</u>. The books and records of Seller relating to the Division are in all material respects correct and complete, and have been maintained in accordance with sound business practices.

5.9 <u>Litigation</u>. There is no litigation, proceeding or governmental investigation existing or pending, or any order, injunction or decree outstanding, against Seller with respect to the Division or its assets or business, nor does Seller know or have reasonable grounds to know of any basis for any such litigation, proceeding or governmental investigation. Seller is not, with respect to the Division, acting, or suffering to exist a condition which is, in material contravention or violation of any applicable law, regulation, ordinance, order, injunction or decree, or any other requirement of

any governmental body or court, nor has Seller failed to remedy any such previously existing violation.

5.10 <u>Acquisition Balance Sheet</u>. The unaudited balance sheet for the Division for the period ending September 30 is set forth on Exhibit H (hereinafter the "Division Balance Sheet"). The Division Balance Sheet has been prepared in conformity with generally accepted accounting principles, consistently applied, and presents fairly the financial condition of the Division at the date stated.

5.11 <u>Real Property</u>. Exhibit A contains a description of the real property owned or used by the Division, the legal description thereof, and lists all the buildings and facilities pertaining to the operation of the Division as of the date hereof. Seller owns all such real property and has good and marketable title thereto, free and clear of all mortgages, hypothecs, liens, charges, pledges, security interests, encumbrances and other claims whatsoever except as disclosed in Exhibit I, none of which materially interfere with the operations of the business or the marketability of the premises. All buildings and other improvements to the real property are situated wholly within the limits of the real property and there are no encroachments on the real property of buildings or structures adjacent thereto. Seller's operations on and use of real property in connection with the operation of the Division conform to applicable zoning regulations, including use, set-back and area requirements, and other restrictions and covenants on the use of said real property. The real property and all improvements located thereon comply in all material respects with all other applicable municipal and other governmental law, by-laws, orders, regulations and restrictions including, without limitation, those with respect to building, safety, fire protection, access, parking, pollution, elevators and boilers. Seller has not received, nor does it have any knowledge of, any notice of violation or any zoning regulations, ordinance or other law, regulation or requirement applicable to the Division's real property nor has it received any notices of assessments, either general or special, relating to the Division's operations or its owned or leased properties for which an accrual has not been made on the Division Balance Sheet. There are not outstanding work orders relating to the real property described in Exhibit A from or required by any police or fire department, sanitation, health or factory authorities or from any other federal or municipal authority, or any matters under discussion with any such departments or authorities relating to work orders.

All licenses and permits required for the operation and use of the real property, buildings, fixtures and equipment have been obtained and are in full force and effect.

5.12 Products Liability. No claims based upon any theory of product liability have been made or threatened against Seller or the Division, which claims arose by reason of the manufacture, sale or use of any product of the Division. Neither Seller nor the Division has breached any product warranty or contract made by either of them to customers in connection with the business of the Division. No written or oral warranties or guarantees have been made or are being made by Seller and/or the Division in connection with the present or prior operations and products of the Division.

5.13 Accounts Receivable. The accounts receivable of the Division reflected in the Division Balance Sheet arose in the ordinary course of business of the Division and are good and enforceable in full, without any defenses, set-offs or other deductions. Seller has not received any notice or threat that merchandise previously shipped by the Division, or by Seller on behalf of the Division (payment for which has not yet been received) is to be returned to Seller for any reason other than returns made in the ordinary course of business and has no knowledge or reason to believe that unusual returns of merchandise will occur subsequent to the date hereof.

5.14 Taxes. Seller has filed all Federal, state, county and local tax returns presently required to be filed in connection with the operations of the Division, and all taxes owing by Seller in connection therewith have been paid when due, including all estimated corporate income tax payments due and payable through the date hereof.

5.15 Inventories. The Division's inventory of raw materials, work in process and finished goods reflected in the Division Balance Sheet is good and usable, and has been valued at the lower of actual cost or net realizable value consistent with prior practices and computation methods of the Division, and reasonably can be anticipated to be sold, use or consumed in the usual and ordinary course of business of the Division now conducted. The inventory of the Division has been maintained at levels consistent with past practice and prior periods and Seller has not caused the inventory of the Division to be increased or decreased except as was required in the ordinary course of its business. Items included in the Division's inventory have been paid for or the liability therefor recognized in the Division's Balance Sheet. Neither Seller nor the Division has received payment or downpayment from any vendor with respect to those items of inventory set forth in the Division Balance Sheet.

5.16 Supply of Raw Material. Seller is not aware of any shortage of raw materials from any source(s) which would materially adversely affect the operations of the Division as presently and heretofore conducted.

5.17 Customer Lists. Exhibit J contains a complete and accurate listing of all customers of the Division to which the Division has made sales and/or provided services in the ordinary course of its business operations.

5.18 Authorization of Agreement. This Agreement, the consummation of the transaction herein contemplated, and the performance, observance and fulfillment by Seller of all of the terms and conditions hereof on its parts to be performed, observed and fulfilled, have been approved and authorized by the Board of Directors and Sole Shareholder of Seller. This Agreement has been duly and validly executed and delivered by Seller and constitutes the valid, binding and enforceable obligation of Seller. Seller has the right, power, legal capacity and authority to enter into and perform its obligations under this Agreement, and no consent of any third party is necessary with respect thereto. The execution and delivery of this Agreement by Seller, the consummation of the transaction herein contemplated, and the performance of, fulfillment of and compliance with the terms and conditions hereof by Seller do not and will not (i) violate any provisions by any judicial or administrative order, award, judgment or decree applicable to Seller, (ii) conflict with any of the provisions of Seller's Articles of Incorporation or Code of Regulations, (iii) conflict with, or result in a breach of, or constitute a default under any agreement or instrument to which Seller is a party or by which it is bound, or (iv) result in the creation or imposition of any lien, charge or encumbrance against any of the Acquired Assets.

5.19 Continuing Accuracy. Each representation and warranty made by Seller in this Agreement or pursuant hereto shall continue to be true and correct at the time of the Closing as though such representation or warranty is being made again at and as of such time.

## 6. REPRESENTATIONS AND WARRANTIES OF BUYER

As an inducement to Seller to enter into this Agreement and consummate the transactions herein contemplated, Buyer hereby represents and warrants as follows:

6.1 Incorporation, Corporate Power. Buyer is a corporation duly organized, validly existing and in good standing under the laws of the State of Ohio and has all requisite corporate power and authority to enter into this Agreement and consummate the transactions herein contemplated.

6.2 Authorization of Agreement. This Agreement, the consummation of the transaction herein contemplated and the performance, observance and fulfillment by Buyer of all of the terms and conditions hereof on its part to be performed, observed and fulfilled, have all been approved and authorized by the Board of Directors of Buyer. This Agreement has been duly and validly executed and delivered by Buyer and constitutes the valid, binding and enforceable obligation of Buyer. The execution and delivery of this Agreement, the consummation of the transaction herein contemplated and the performance of, fulfillment of and compliance with the terms and conditions hereof by Buyer do not and will not (i) violate any provisions of any judicial or administrative order, award, judgment or decree applicable to Buyer, (ii) conflict with any of the provisions of the Articles of Incorporation or Code of Regulations of Buyer or (iii) conflict with, result in a breach of, or constitute a default under any agreement or instrument to which Buyer is a party or by which it is bound. Buyer has the right, power, legal capacity and authority to enter into and perform its obligations under this Agreement, and no consent of any third party is necessary with respect thereto.

6.3 Continuing Accuracy. Each representation and warranty made by Buyer in this Agreement or pursuant hereto shall continue to be true and correct at and as of the time of Closing as though such representation and warranty is being made again at and as of such time.

## 7. SURVIVAL OF REPRESENTATIONS AND WARRANTIES: INDEMNIFICATION

7.1 Survival. The parties hereto agree that the representations and warranties contained in this Agreement or in any document, certificate, instrument or Exhibit delivered in connection herewith shall survive the Closing and continue to be binding regardless of any investigation made at any time by the parties.

7.2 Indemnification. The seller shall indemnify Buyer against and hold it harmless from: (i) any and all taxes and other liabilities and obligations of Seller not expressly assumed by Buyer hereunder, including, without limitation, all liabilities of Seller and/or the Division arising from the Seller's or the Division's hiring, firing or employment of labor, all liabilities and obligations of Seller with respect to any product manufactured, sold or delivered prior to the Closing Date resulting from any and all claims (including the expense of defense and settlement thereof) for or relating to bodily injury, wrongful death or property damage allegedly caused by a defective or faulty product or based upon any theory of product liability (tort, abso-

lute or otherwise), resulting from any and all claims based upon any theory of product warranty; (ii) any and all liabilities, obligations, losses, damages and deficiencies resulting from or arising out of any inaccuracy in or breach of any representation or warranty made by Seller in this Agreement or pursuant hereto, or from any nonfulfillment or breach or default in the performance by Seller of any of the covenants made by Seller herein, and (iii) any and all costs and expenses (including reasonable legal and accounting fees) relating to the foregoing.

7.3 Notice of Claim; Defense of Action. In the event that any legal proceedings shall be instituted or that any claim or demand shall be asserted by any third party in respect of which the obligation to indemnify may arise under the provisions of Section 7.2, Buyer shall give or cause to be given to Seller written notice thereof, and Seller shall have the right, at its option and expense, to be represented by counsel of its choice in connection with the defense of any claim or proceeding, but not to control the defense or settlement thereof. The parties agree to cooperate with each other in connection with the defense of any such legal proceeding, claim or demand, provided, however, that Buyer shall be reimbursed for all direct and indirect payroll expenses, and Seller shall pay all living and travel expenses related to out-of-town assistance, with respect to employees of Buyer who are called upon to provide assistance in connection with such defense.

## 8. ADDITIONAL COVENANTS OF THE SELLER

8.1 Access to Information. During the period between the date hereof and the Closing Date (the "Interim Period"), Buyer and its representatives may make such investigation of the properties, assets and business of the Division as Buyer may reasonably request, and Seller shall give to Buyer and to its counsel, accountants and other representatives, full access during normal business hours throughout the Interim Period to all of the properties, books, contracts, commitments, records and files of the Division, and shall furnish to Buyer during the Interim Period all such documents and copies of documents (certified as true and complete if requested) and information concerning the business and affairs of the Division as Buyer may reasonably request.

8.2 Conduct of Business Pending the Closing. During the Interim Period, except as Buyer may consent in writing:

8.2.1 The business of the Division shall be conducted only in the ordinary course (which, without limitation, shall include the maintenance in force of all existing insurance policies) and in such a manner as to avoid any breach of any of the representations and warranties made by Seller in this Agreement; and

8.2.2 Seller shall use its best efforts to preserve the business organization of the Division intact, to keep available the services of the present employees of the Division and to preserve the goodwill of all those having business relations with it.

Seller will give Buyer advance written notice of its desire to, and without the advance written consent of Buyer will not, enter into any transaction in which Seller:

8.2.3 Transfers, leases or otherwise disposes of any material assets or properties of the Division, or causes the Division to acquire or lease any material assets or properties;

8.2.4 Cancels or compromises any debt or claim relating to the Division;

8.2.5 Waives or releases any rights of material value relating to the Division; or

8.2.6 Transfers or grants any material rights under the lease, licenses, agreements, patents, inventions, trademarks, trade names, service marks, copyrights or with respect to any know-how relating to the Division.

## 9. CONDITIONS PRECEDENT TO OBLIGATIONS TO CONSUMMATE THE TRANSACTIONS

9.1 Conditions Precedent to Obligations of Buyer. The obligations of Buyer to consummate the Closing as provided in Section 4 of this Agreement is subject to the fulfillment, at or prior to the Closing Date, of each of the following conditions:

9.1.1 All representations and warranties of Seller contained herein shall be true at and as of the Closing Date with the same effect as though such representations and warranties are made at and as of such time, Seller shall have performed and complied with all obligations, covenants and conditions required by this Agreement to be performed or complied with by it prior to or at the Closing Date, and Buyer shall have been furnished with a certificate executed by the President of Seller, in form and substance satisfactory to Buyer, certifying that (a) each of the foregoing conditions has been fulfilled and (b) that the value of the Division's inventory computed at the lower of actual cost or net realized value is reflected in the Division Balance Sheet.

9.1.2 Buyer shall not have learned of any fact or condition with respect to the business, properties, assets or earnings of the Division which is materially at variance with one or more of the representations or warranties of Seller set forth in this Agreement or which in Buyer's reasonable opinion materially and adversely affects such business, properties, assets or earnings, or the ownership, value or continuance thereof.

9.1.3 Seller shall have obtained all consents, approvals and discharges of lenders which may be necessary to complete the transaction contemplated herein.

9.1.4 There shall not be any actual or threatened action, proceeding or investigation which, in the reasonable judgment of Buyer, is directed toward challenging, restraining, prohibiting or invalidating the transaction contemplated herein or which, in the reasonable judgment of Buyer, may affect the right of Buyer to own, operate or control after the consummation of the transaction contemplated herein any of the Acquired Assets or business of the Division.

9.2 Conditions Precedent to the Obligations of Seller. The obligations of Seller to consummate the Closing as provided in Section 4 of this Agreement is subject to the fulfillment, at or prior to the Closing Date, of each of the following conditions:

9.2.1 All representations and warranties of Buyer shall be true at and as of the Closing Date with the same effect as though such representation and warranties are made at and as of such time, Buyer shall have performed and complied with all obligations, covenants and conditions required by this Agreement to be performed or complied with by it prior to or at the Closing Date, and Seller shall have been furnished with a certificate of an executive officer of Buyer in form and substance satisfactory to Seller, certifying to the fulfillment of the foregoing conditions.

## 10. MISCELLANEOUS

10.1 Finder's Fees.

10.2 Ratings and Deposits. Promptly after the Closing Seller will use its best efforts to make available to Buyer the unemployment and workmen's compensation ratings held by Seller and relating to the Division and to assign to Buyer any unrefundable deposits made by Seller with respect to such programs, to the extent permitted by law.

10.3 Expenses. Buyer shall bear and pay all of its own expenses incident to the transaction contemplated by this Agreement, and Seller shall bear and pay all of its own expenses incident to the transaction contemplated by this Agreement. Such expenses include, without limiting the generality thereof, legal fees, accounting fees, and costs of public document certificates.

10.4 Best Efforts to Meet Conditions. Each of the parties agrees to use its best efforts to fulfill as soon as practicable after the date hereof the conditions precedent to the Closing which are dependent upon such party's action or forbearance.

10.5 Amendment. At any time prior to the Closing, Seller and Buyer, with the authorization or consent of their respective Boards of Directors, may amend or modify this Agreement in such manner as they may mutually agree upon provided such amendment or modification is set forth in a writing executed by both parties with the same formality as this Agreement has been executed.

10.6 Waiver. Buyer may waive compliance by Seller with any of the conditions set forth in Section 9.1 of this Agreement, and Seller may waive compliance by Buyer with any of the conditions set forth in Section 9.2 of this Agreement, provided in each case that any such waiver shall be set forth in a writing executed, with the same formality as this Agreement has been executed, by the party granting such waiver.

10.7 Termination. This Agreement may be terminated at any time prior to Closing:

10.7.1 By the mutual agreement of Seller and Buyer with the authorization or consent of their respective Boards of Directors, provided such termination is set forth in writing executed by both parties with the same formality as this Agreement has been executed;

10.7.2 By Buyer, with the authorization or consent of its Board of Directors, if any of the conditions specified in Section 9.1 shall not have been timely met and shall not have been waived by Buyer pursuant to section 10.6; or

10.7.3 By Seller, with the authorization or consent of its Board of Directors, if any of the conditions set forth in Section 9.2 shall not have been timely met and shall not have been waived by Seller pursuant to Section 10.6.

Any termination pursuant to Subsection 10.7.2 or 10.7.3 above shall be effective immediately upon the giving of notice by the terminating party to the other party.

10.8 Notices. All notices and other communications made pursuant to this Agreement shall be in writing and shall be deemed to have been given if delivered by hand or mailed by registered or certified mail to the parties at the following addresses (or such

other address for a party as shall be specified by notice given pursuant hereto):

   (i) If to Buyer, to it in
       care of:
   (ii) If to Seller, to it in
       care of:

10.9 Headings. The headings in this Agreement are intended solely for convenience of reference and shall be given no effect in the construction or interpretation of this Agreement.

10.10 Exhibits. All Exhibits to this Agreement constitute an integral part of this Agreement as if fully rewritten herein.

10.11 Execution in Counterparts. This Agreement may be executed in two or more counterparts, each of which shall be deemed an original, but all of which together shall constitute one and the same document.

10.12 Entire Agreement. This Agreement and the documents to be delivered hereunder constitute the entire understanding and agreement between the parties hereto concerning the subject matter hereof. All negotiations between the parties hereto are merged into this Agreement, and there are no representations, warranties, covenants, understandings or agreements, oral or otherwise, in relation thereto between the parties other than those incorporated herein or to be delivered hereunder. Nothing expressed or implied in this Agreement is intended or shall be construed so as to grant or confer on any person, firm or corporation other than the parties hereto any rights or privileges hereunder.

10.13 Governing Law. This Agreement shall in all respects be interpreted and construed in accordance with and governed by the laws of the State of Ohio.

10.14 Binding Effect. This Agreement and all of the provisions hereof shall be binding upon and insure to the benefit of the parties hereto and their respective successors and assigns, provided, however, that neither party hereto may make any assignment of this Agreement or any interest herein without the prior written consent of the other party hereto.

IN WITNESS WHEREOF, the parties hereto have caused this Agreement to be executed by their duly authorized officers as of the date and year first above written.

Attest:

_____

By _____
Secretary

Attest:

_____  By _____
Secretary

# APPENDIX 13-B:
## *Acquisition Contract Checklist**

The following is a checklist of acquisition contract provisions. Not every item in the checklist will be included in a particular acquisition agreement. For example, where a buyer acquires assets the contract will normally not contain a representation or warranty of title to the seller's stock, and conversely, where the buyer acquires stock, the contract will normally not contain a "bulk-sales" act provision. The checklist should prove helpful in determining whether any particular item may have been omitted from a proposed form of acquisition contract before the contract is executed.

*Source: From *Acquisitions, Mergers, Sales, Buyouts and Takeovers* by Charles A. Scharf, Edward E. Shea, George C. Beck © 1985. Reprinted by permission of the publisher, Prentice-Hall, Inc., Englewood Cliffs, NJ.

## A CHECKLIST FOR ACQUISITION CONTRACTS

*General Statement of Agreement.*

1. Are assets being acquired?
2. Is stock being acquired?
3. Will payment be made in stock?
4. Will payment be made in cash?
5. Is the transaction tax-free?
6. Is the transaction taxable?
7. Is the transaction a statutory merger?

*ARTICLE I—Representations and Warranties of Seller.*
(Where a seller owns stock in subsidiary corporations, the seller's representations and warranties should also be made with respect to the subsidiaries.)

1.1 Seller's corporate status.
    (a) Proper organization of seller.
    (b) Capital structure of seller.
1.2 Seller's shareholders unencumbered title to their stock, and description of stock ownership.
1.3 Authority of seller's officers to act.
1.4 Seller's financial statements.
    (a) How many balance sheets are warranted?
    (b) Are profit and loss statements and statements of retained earnings warranted?
    (c) Are financial statements recent?
1.5 Necessary qualifications of seller to do business in foreign states.
1.6 Description of and title to property and assets.
1.7 Description of and condition of machinery and equipment.
1.8 Listing of patents, trademarks, tradenames and copyrights and infringement warranties.
1.9 Listing of contracts and suppliers.
1.10 Litigation
1.11 Representations as to actions not taken since latest financials:
    (a) No issuance of securities.
    (b) No distributions of stock.
    (c) No mortgages or encumbrances.
    (d) No sale of assets.
    (e) No extraordinary losses or obligations.
    (f) No catastrophes.
    (g) No salary increases.
1.12 Tax returns and accruals.
1.13 Tax withholdings.
1.14 Government contracts renegotiation status.

1.15 Accounts Receivable.
  (a) Do any offsets exist?
1.16 Insurance.
  (a) Sufficient in amount?
1.17 Inventories and Improvement Disclosures.
  (a) Do they belong to seller?
  (b) Where are they located?
  (c) Will patent applications be executed?
1.18 No defaults under contracts.
1.19 Compliance with federal and local laws.
1.20 No liabilities except as stated in contract.
1.21 Non-declaration of dividends.
1.22 Buyer's stock taken for investment purposes only.
1.23 Truth of representations and warranties and no omission of material facts.

*ARTICLE II—Representations and Warranties of Buyer.*

2.1 Buyer's corporate status.
  (a) Proper organization of buyer.
  (b) Buyer's capitalization.
2.2 Status of Buyer's stock.
  (a) Classes.
  (b) Properly issued.
  (c) Listed on stock exchange.
  (d) Registered
2.3 Authority of Buyer's officers to act.
2.4 Seller's stock taken for "investment purposes" only.
2.5 Buyer's financial condition.
2.6 Non-violation of buyer's loan agreements.
2.7 Truth of representations and warranties and no omission of material facts.

*ARTICLE III—Assets to Be Acquired by Buyer.*

3.1 All of seller's stock.
3.2 Substantially all of seller's assets.
3.3 Selected assets.
  (a) Clear definition of assets.
  (b) Exclusion of tax refunds.

*ARTICLE IV—Payment of Purchase Price.*

4.1 Tax-free acquisition
  (a) Payment solely in voting stock.
  (b) Assumption of liabilities.
  (c) Types of securities in statutory merger.
  (d) Formula price based on market value of stock.

(e)  Formula price based on future earnings.
(f)  Imputed interest.
(g)  Effect on price of dissenting shareholders.
(h)  Limitations on numbers of shares.
4.2  Taxable acquisition.
(a)  Allocation of purchase price.
(b)  Internal Revenue Code Section 1245 assets.
(c)  Internal Revenue Code Section 1250 assets.
(d)  Investment credit recapture.
(e)  Price stated as one lump sum.
(f)  Pricing of inventory.
(g)  Formula price based on future earnings.
(h)  Imputed interest.
(i)  Effect on price of dissenting shareholders.
(j)  Section 337 liquidation.
(k)  Section 338 election.

*ARTICLE V—Buyer's Assumption of Liabilities.*

5.1  Assumption of all liabilities, unknown, contingent or otherwise.
5.2  Assumption of specified liabilities only.
(a)  Those disclosed in seller's balance sheet.
(b)  Disclosed litigation.
(c)  Obligations under listed contracts and agreements.
(d)  Obligations incurred in ordinary course of business since balance sheet.
(e)  Other obligations specifically listed.

*ARTICLE VI—Seller's Indemnification of the Buyer.*

6.1  Indemnification against all but assumed obligations.
6.2  If seller is to be liquidated, indemnification by seller's principal shareholders.
6.3  Stock or cash placed in escrow to satisfy indemnification.
(a)  Amount of escrow.
(b)  Length of time of escrow.
(c)  Gradual reduction of escrow.

*ARTICLE VII—Seller's Conduct of the Business Pending the Closing.*

7.1  Positive covenant to conduct business only in ordinary course.
7.2  Negative covenants not to:
(a)  Issue securities.
(b)  Make distributions to shareholders.
(c)  Subject property to liens.
(d)  Sell capital assets.

(e) Make substantial capital expenditures.
(f) Increase compensation.
(g) Incur any liabilities, except current liabilities in ordinary course.

*ARTICLE VIII—Conditions Precedent to the Closing*

8.1 Buyer's conditions precedent:
(a) Seller's warranties and representations true at closing.
(b) Opinion of seller's counsel as to corporate organization, titles, etc.
(c) Certificate of seller's officer re: conduct of business since contract signing.
(d) Report of buyer's auditors.
(e) Seller's business not materially adversely affected by storm, etc.
(f) Seller's performance of all covenants.
(g) Tenders of resignation of seller's directors and officers.
(h) Delivery of secret processes.
(i) Delivery of invention and improvement disclosures.
(j) Employment contracts with key employees.
(k) Favorable opinion of Price Marwick &Co. on "pooling of interest," and letter from SEC concurring with such opinion.
(l) Securities and Exchange Commission "No Action Letter."
(m) Investment letters from principal stockholders.
(n) Delivery of escrowed shares.
(o) Limitation on percentage of dissenting shareholders.
(p) Internal Revenue Service Ruling.
(q) Justice Department Ruling.
(r) Certified resolutions of seller's directors and shareholders.
8.2 Seller's conditions precedent:
(a) Internal Revenue Service Rulings.
(b) Opinion of buyer's counsel as to buyer's corporate status, officer's authority, validity of stock delivery, etc.
(c) Truth of buyer's representations and warranties at closing.
(d) Certified resolutions of buyer.
(e) Certificate of officer of buyer that all action properly taken.
(f) Buyer's business not materially, adversely affected by storm, etc.

*ARTICLE IX—The Plan of Reorganization.*

9.1 Stock for stock:
(a) Delivery of seller's stock properly endorsed.
(b) Minimum percentage of seller's stock acceptable to buyer.
(c) Payment of stamp taxes.
(d) Delivery of buyer's stock—no fractional shares.
9.2 Stock for assets:
(a) Documents delivering title to seller's assets.

       (b) Certificate of amendment changing seller's name.

       (c) Delivery by buyer of its stock.

       (d) Retention of funds by seller to defray acquisition and liquidation expenses.

       (e) Deposit of buyer's shares with agent for seller's shareholders—to match fractional rights.

       (f) Assumption of liabilities by buyer.

       (g) Liquidation and dissolution of seller.

9.3  The Statutory merger:

       (a) Literal compliance with requirements of the state statutes involved.

*ARTICLE X—Brokerage.*

10.1  Payment of brokerage commissions.

       (a) Parties indemnification of each other against brokerage claims.

       (b) If broker involved, provision for party liable to pay.

       (c) Terms of any written brokerage agreement.

       (d) If broker involved, agreement should be reduced to writing.

*ARTICLE XI—General Provisions.*

11.1  Non-registration of shares of buyer's stock—or closing or post-closing registration of buyer's stock.

11.2  Access to investigate seller's business—buyer to keep information confidential.

11.3  Antitrust escape clause.

11.4  Bulk sales clause.

11.5  Sales and use tax clause.

11.6  Employment contracts.

11.7  Pension and profit-sharing plans.

11.8  Pensions of previously retired employees.

11.9  Employee stock option.

11.10  Other employee benefit plans.

11.11  Collective bargaining agreement.

11.12  Employee security clearances.

11.13  Delivery and retention of books, records and classified documents.

11.14  Avoidance of selling shareholders receiving double dividend.

11.15  Transfer of assets to buyer's subsidiary.

11.16  Bank accounts—information as to amounts and signatories.

11.17  Novation of customer contracts.

11.18  Covenant not to compete.

11.19  State "blue sky" laws.

11.20  Publicity.

11.21  Specific performance—a legal remedy.

11.22  Survival of representations and warranties.

11.23 Due diligence of parties.

11.24 Right to waive failures of other party and conditions.

11.25 Further assurances of execution of additional documents.

11.26 Entire agreement in contract.

11.27 Governing state law.

11.28 Third parties.

11.29 Transactions and documents subject to approval of counsel.

11.30 Assignability of contract.

11.31 Execution of additional counterparts.

11.32 Date, time, and place of closing.

11.33 Notices.

In addition to many of the clauses checklisted in Articles I through IX, above, most acquisition contracts will have miscellaneous exhibits or schedules attached. What exhibits or schedules are to be attached must be determined from the agreement itself. For example, if patents form an important part of a seller's business, the contract may have attached to it a complete list of seller's patents and patent application. Finally, the acquisition contract may provide for the execution by the parties of forms of supplementary agreements that are normally delivered at the closing.

A list of some usual exhibits or schedules as well as supplementary agreements follows:

### *Exhibits or Schedules*

A. Financial Statements.

B. Seller and Subsidiary and Affiliated Companies or Entities of Seller—Capital Structure and Jurisdictions in Which Qualified to Do Business.

C. Outstanding Warrants, Options, or Subscription to Capital Stock of Seller and Entities.

D. Real Estate Owned by Seller.

E. Properties Leased by Seller.

F. Patents and Trademarks of Seller.

G. General Contracts of Seller.

H. Major Suppliers and Customers of Seller.

I. Description of Litigation.

J. Lists of Significant Stockholders.

### *Supplementary Documents*

A. Indemnity Agreement.

B. Escrow Agreement.

C. Investment Letter.

D. Employment Contract.

# APPENDIX 1:
## Revenue Rulings

The following presents several key IRS rulings. Of particular importance in the valuation of private businesses is Revenue Ruling 59–60, which designates eight factors to be considered in arriving at a valuation:

1. the nature and history of the business
2. the economic outlook of the business
3. the earnings capacity of the company
4. the company's ability to pay dividends
5. the book value of the company and the general financial position of the business
6. whether or not the company has goodwill or other intangible values
7. the size of the block of stock to be valued
8. the market price of the stock of publicly traded companies engaged in similar lines of business

Revenue Ruling 65–193 is an update of Revenue Ruling 59–60. Revenue Ruling 68–609 makes 59–60 applicable to the valuation of all businesses. When the stocks of a private business are subject to restrictions, Revenue Ruling 77–287 is intended to provide valuation guidelines. Valuation of private company preferred stock in reorganizations is given in Revenue Ruling 83–120.

Readers who wish to keep current on IRS and court rulings concerning valuation and related matters pertaining to discounts for lack of marketability, minority interest, and other restrictions should consult J.A. Bishop and I.A. Howitt, *Federal Tax Valuation Digest* (Warren, Gorham and Lamont, Boston, MA).

# REVENUE RULING 59-60

## SECTION 2031.—DEFINITION OF GROSS ESTATE

26 CFR 20.2031-2: Valuation of stocks and        Rev. Rul. 59–60
bonds.
(Also Section 2512.)
(Also Part II, Sections 811 (k), 1005, Regulations
105, Section 81.10.)

> In valuing the stock of closely held corporations, or the stock of
> corporations where market quotations are not available, all other
> available financial data, as well as all relevant factors affecting the
> fair market value must be considered for estate tax and gift tax
> purposes. No general formula may be given that is applicable to
> the many different valuation situations arising in the valuation of
> such stock. However, the general approach, methods, and factors
> which must be considered in valuing such securities are outlined.
> Revenue Ruling 54–77, C.B. 1954–1, 187, superseded.

SECTION 1. PURPOSE.

The purpose of this Revenue Ruling is to outline and review in
general the approach, methods and factors to be considered in valuing
shares of the capital stock of closely held corporations for estate tax
and gift tax purposes. The methods discussed herein will apply likewise to the valuation of corporate stocks on which market quotations
are either unavailable or are of such scarcity that they do not reflect
the fair market value.

SEC. 2. BACKGROUND AND DEFINITIONS.

.01 All valuations must be made in accordance with the applicable
provisions of the Internal Revenue Code of 1954 and the Federal
Estate Tax and Gift Tax Regulations. Sections 2031(a), 2032 and
2512(a) of the 1954 Code (sections 811 and 1005 of the 1939 Code)
require that the property to be included in the gross estate, or made
the subject of a gift, shall be taxed on the basis of the value of the
property at the time of death of the decedent, the alternate date if
so elected, or the date of gift.

.02 Section 20.2031–1(b) of the Estate Tax Regulations (section
81.10 of the Estate Tax Regulations 105) and section 25.2512–1 of
the Gift Tax Regulations (section 86.19 of Gift Tax Regulations 108)
define fair market value, in effect, as the price at which the property
would change hands between a willing buyer and a willing seller
when the former is not under any compulsion to buy and the latter
is not under any compulsion to sell, both parties having reasonable
knowledge of relevant facts. Court decisions frequently state in addition that the hypothetical buyer and seller are assumed to be able,
as well as willing, to trade and to be well informed about the property
and concerning the market for such property.

.03 Closely held corporations are those corporations the shares of
which are owned by a relatively limited number of stockholders.
Often the entire stock issue is held by one family. The result of this

situation is that little, if any, trading in the shares takes place. There is, therefore, no established market for the stock and such sales as occur at irregular intervals seldom reflect all of the elements of a representative transaction as defined by the term "fair market value."

SEC. 3. APPROACH TO VALUATION.

.01 A determination of fair market value, being a question of fact, will depend upon the circumstances in each case. No formula can be devised that will be generally applicable to the multitude of different valuation issues arising in estate and gift tax cases. Often, an appraiser will find wide differences of opinion as to the fair market value of a particular stock. In resolving such differences, he should maintain a reasonable attitude in recognition of the fact that valuation is not an exact science. A sound valuation will be based upon all the relevant facts, but the elements of common sense, informed judgment and reasonableness must enter into the process of weighing those facts and determining their aggregate significance.

.02 The fair market value of specific shares of stock will vary as general economic conditions change from "normal" to "boom" or "depression," that is, according to the degree of optimism or pessimism with which the investing public regards the future at the required date of appraisal. Uncertainty as to the stability or continuity of the future income from a property decreases its value by increasing the risk of loss of earnings and value in the future. The value of shares of stock of a company with very uncertain future prospects is highly speculative. The appraiser must exercise his judgment as to the degree of risk attaching to the business of the corporation which issued the stock, but that judgment must be related to all of the other factors affecting value.

.03 Valuation of securities is, in essence, a prophesy as to the future and must be based on facts available at the required date of appraisal. As a generalization, the prices of stocks which are traded in volume in a free and active market by informed persons best reflect the consensus of the investing public as to what the future holds for the corporations and industries represented. When a stock is closely held, is traded infrequently, or is traded in an erratic market, some other measure of value must be used. In many instances, the next best measure may be found in the prices at which the stocks of companies engaged in the same or a similar line of business are selling in a free and open market.

SEC. 4. FACTORS TO CONSIDER.

.01 It is advisable to emphasize that in the valuation of the stock of closely held corporations or the stock of corporations where market quotations are either lacking or too scarce to be recognized, all available financial data, as well as all relevant factors affecting the fair market value, should be considered. The following factors, although not all-inclusive are fundamental and require careful analysis in each case:

(a) The nature of the business and the history of the enterprise from its inception.

(b) The economic outlook in general and the condition and outlook of the specific industry in particular.

(c) The book value of the stock and the financial condition of the business.

(d) The earning capacity of the company.

(e) The dividend-paying capacity.

(f) Whether or not the enterprise has goodwill or other intangible value.

(g) Sales of the stock and the size of the block of stock to be valued.

(h) The market price of stocks of corporations engaged in the same or a similar line of business having their stocks actively traded in a free and open market, either on an exchange or over-the-counter.

.02 The following is a brief discussion of each of the foregoing factors:

(a) The history of a corporate enterprise will show its past stability or instability, its growth or lack of growth, the diversity or lack of diversity of its operations, and other facts needed to form an opinion of the degree of risk involved in the business. For an enterprise which changed its form of organization but carried on the same or closely similar operations of its predecessor, the history of the former enterprise should be considered. The detail to be considered should increase with approach to the required date of appraisal, since recent events are of greatest help in predicting the future; but a study of gross and net income, and of dividends covering a long prior period, is highly desirable. The history to be studied should include, but need not be limited to, the nature of the business, its products or services, its operating and investment assets, capital structure, plant facilities, sales records and management, all of which should be considered as of the date of the appraisal, with due regard for recent significant changes. Events of the past that are unlikely to recur in the future should be discounted, since value has a close relation to future expectancy.

(b) A sound appraisal of a closely held stock must consider current and prospective economic conditions as of the date of appraisal, both in the national economy and in the industry or industries with which the corporation is allied. It is important to know that the company is more or less successful than its competitors in the same industry, or that it is maintaining a stable position with respect to competitors. Equal or even greater significance may attach to the ability of the industry with which the company is allied to compete with other industries. Prospective competition which has not been a factor in prior years should be given careful attention. For example, high profits due to the novelty of its product and the lack of competition often lead to increasing competition. The public's appraisal of the future prospects of competitive industries or of competitors within an industry may be indicated by price trends in the markets for commodities and for securities. The loss of the manager of a so-called "one-man" business may have a depressing effect upon the value of the stock of such business, particularly if there is a lack of trained person-

nel capable of succeeding to the management of the enterprise. In valuing the stock of this type of business, therefore, the effect of the loss of the manager on the future expectancy of the business, and the absence of management-succession potentialities are pertinent factors to be taken into consideration. On the other hand, there may be factors which offset, in whole or in part, the loss of the manager's services. For instance, the nature of the business and of its assets may be such that they will not be impaired by the loss of the manager. Furthermore, the loss may be adequately covered by life insurance, or competent management might be employed on the basis of the consideration paid for the former manager's services. These, or other offsetting factors, if found to exist, should be carefully weighed against the loss of the manager's services in valuing the stock of the enterprise.

(c) Balance sheets should be obtained, preferably in the form of comparative annual statements for two or more years immediately preceding the date of appraisal, together with a balance sheet at the end of the month preceding that date, if corporate accounting will permit. Any balance sheet descriptions that are not self-explanatory, and balance sheet items comprehending diverse assets or liabilities, should be clarified in essential detail by supporting supplemental schedules. These statements usually will disclose to the appraiser (1) liquid position (ratio of current assets to current liabilities); (2) gross and net book value of principal classes of fixed assets; (3) working capital; (4) long-term indebtedness; (5) capital structure; and (6) net worth. Consideration also should be given to any assets not essential to the operation of the business, such as investments in securities, real estate, etc. In general, such nonoperating assets will command a lower rate of return than do the operating assets, although in exceptional cases the reverse may be true. In computing the book value per share of stock, assets of the investment type should be revalued on the basis of their market price and the book value adjusted accordingly. Comparison of the company's balance sheets over several years may reveal, among other facts, such developments as the acquisition of additional production facilities or subsidiary companies, improvement in financial position, and details as to recapitalizations and other changes in the capital structure of the corporation. If the corporation has more than one class of stock outstanding, the charter or certificate of incorporation should be examined to ascertain the explicit rights and privileges of the various stock issues including: (1) voting powers, (2) preference as to dividends, and (3) preference as to assets in the event of liquidation.

(d) Detailed profit-and-loss statements should be obtained and considered for a representative period immediately prior to the required date of appraisal, preferably five or more years. Such statements should show (1) gross income by principal items; (2) principal deductions from gross income including major prior items of operating expenses, interest and other expense on each item of long-term debt, depreciation and depletion if such deductions are made, officers' salaries, in total if they appear to be reasonable or in detail if they seem to be excessive, contributions (whether or not deductible for tax purposes) that the nature of its business and its community position require the corporation to make, and taxes by principal items, including income and excess profits taxes; (3) net income available for dividends; (4) rates and amounts of dividends paid on each class of stock; (5) remaining amount carried to surplus; and (6) adjustments to, and reconciliation with, surplus as stated on the balance sheet. With profit and loss statements of this character available, the appraiser should be able to separate recurrent from nonrecurrent items of income and expense, to distinguish between operating income and investment income, and to ascertain whether or not any line of business in which the company is engaged is operated consistently at a loss and might be abandoned with benefit to the company. The percentage of earnings retained for business expansion should be noted when dividend-paying capacity is considered. Potential future income is a major factor in many valuations of closely-held stocks, and all information concerning past income which will be helpful in predicting the future should be secured. Prior earnings records usually are the most reliable guide as to the future expectancy, but resort to arbitrary five-or-ten-year averages without regard to current trends or future prospects will not produce a realistic valuation. If, for instance, a record of progressively increasing or decreasing net income is found, then greater weight may be accorded the most recent years' profits in estimating earning power. It will be helpful, in judging risk and the extent to which a business is a marginal operator, to consider deductions from income and net income in terms of percentage of sales. Major categories of cost and expense to be so analyzed include the consumption of raw materials and supplies in the case of manufacturers, processors and fabricators; the cost of purchased merchandise in the case of merchants; utility services; insurance; taxes; depletion or depreciation; and interest.

(e) Primary consideration should be given to the dividend-paying capacity of the company rather than to dividends actually paid in the past. Recognition must be given to the necessity of retaining a reasonable portion of profits in a company to meet competition. Dividend-paying capacity is a factor that must be considered in an appraisal, but dividends actually paid in the past may not have any relation to dividend-paying capacity. Specifically, the dividends paid by a closely held family company may be measured by the income needs of the stockholders or by their desire to avoid taxes on dividend receipts, instead of by the ability of the company to pay dividends. Where an actual or effective controlling interest in a corporation is to be valued, the dividend factor is not a material element, since the payment of such dividends is discretionary with the controlling stockholders. The individual or group in control can substitute salaries and bonuses for dividends, thus reducing net income and understating the dividend-paying capacity of the company. It follows, therefore, that dividends are less reliable criteria of fair market value than other applicable factors.

(f) In the final analysis, goodwill is based upon earning capacity. The presence of goodwill and its value, therefore, rests upon the excess of net earnings over and above a fair return on the net tangible assets. While the element of goodwill may be based primarily on earnings, such factors as the prestige and renown of the business, the ownership of a trade or brand name, and a record of successful operation over a prolonged period in a particular locality, also may furnish support for the inclusion of intangible value. In some instances it may not be possible to make a separate appraisal of the tangible and intangible assets of the business. The enterprise has a value as an entity. Whatever intangible value there is, which is supportable by the facts, may be measured by the amount by which the appraised value of the tangible assets exceeds the net book value of such assets.

(g) Sales of stock of a closely held corporation should be carefully investigated to determine whether they represent transactions at arm's length. Forced or distress sales do not ordinarily reflect fair market value nor do isolated sales in small amounts necessarily control as the measure of value. This is especially true in the valuation of a controlling interest in a corporation. Since, in the case of closely held stocks, no prevailing market prices are available, there is no basis for making an adjustment for blockage. It follows, therefore, that such stocks should be valued upon a consideration of all the evidence affecting the fair market value. The size of the block of stock itself is a relevant factor to be considered. Although it is true that a minority interest in an unlisted corporation's stock is more difficult to sell than a similar block of listed stock, it is equally true that control of a corporation, either actual or in effect, representing as it does an added element of value, may justify a higher value for a specific block of stock.

(h) Section 2031(b) of the Code states, in effect, that in valuing unlisted securities the value of stock or securities of corporations engaged in the same or a similar line of business which are listed on an exchange should be taken into consideration along with all other factors. An important consideration is that the corporations to be used for comparisons have capital stocks which are actively traded by the public. In accordance with section 2031(b) of the Code, stocks listed on an exchange are to be considered first. However, if sufficient comparable companies whose stocks are listed on an exchange cannot be found, other comparable companies which have stocks actively traded in on the over-the-counter market also may be used. The essential factor is that whether the stocks are sold on an exchange or over-the-counter there is evidence of an active, free public market for the stock as of the valuation date. In selecting corporations for comparative purposes, care should be taken to use only comparable companies. Although the only restrictive requirement as to comparable corporations specified in the statute is that their lines of business be the same or similar, yet it is obvious that consideration must be given to other relevant factors in order that the most valid comparison possible will be obtained. For illustration, a corporation having one or more issues of preferred stock, bonds or debentures in addition to its common stock should not be considered to be directly comparable to one having only common stock outstanding. In like manner, a company with a declining business and decreasing markets is not comparable to one with a record of current progress and market expansion.

SEC. 5.    WEIGHT TO BE ACCORDED VARIOUS FACTORS.

The valuation of closely held corporate stock entails the consideration of all relevant factors as stated in section 4. Depending upon the circumstances in each case, certain factors may carry more weight than others because of the nature of the company's business. To illustrate:

(a) Earnings may be the most important criterion of value in some cases whereas asset value will receive primary consideration in others. In general, the appraiser will accord primary consideration to earnings when valuing stocks of companies which sell products or services to the public; conversely, in the investment or holding type of company, the appraiser may accord the greatest weight to the assets underlying the security to be valued.

(b) The value of the stock of a closely held investment or real estate holding company, whether or not family owned, is closely related to the value of the assets underlying the stock. For companies of this type the appraiser should determine the fair market values of the assets of the company. Operating expenses of such a company and the cost of liquidating it, if any, merit consideration when appraising the relative values of the stock and the underlying assets. The market values of the underlying assets give due weight to potential earnings and dividends of the particular items of property underlying the stock, capitalized at rates deemed proper by the investing public at the date of appraisal. A current appraisal by the investing public should be superior to the retrospective opinion of an individual. For these reasons, adjusted net worth should be accorded greater weight in valuing the stock of a closely held investment or real estate holding company, whether or not family owned, than any of the other customary yardsticks of appraisal, such as earnings and dividend paying capacity.

SEC. 6.    CAPITALIZATION RATES.

In the application of certain fundamental valuation factors, such as earnings and dividends, it is necessary to capitalize the average or current results at some appropriate rate. A determination of the proper capitalization rate presents one of the most difficult problems in valuation. That there is no ready or simple solution will become apparent by a cursory check of the rates of return and dividend yields in terms of the selling prices of corporate shares listed on the major exchanges of the country. Wide variations will be found even for companies in the same industry. Moreover, the ratio will fluctuate from year to year depending upon economic conditions. Thus, no standard tables of capitalization rates applicable to closely held corporations can be formulated. Among the more important factors to be taken into consideration in deciding upon a capitalization rate in a particular case are: (1) the nature of the business; (2) the risk involved; and (3) the stability or irregularity of earnings.

SEC. 7. AVERAGE OF FACTORS.

Because valuations cannot be made on the basis of a prescribed formula, there is no means whereby the various applicable factors in a particular case can be assigned mathematical weights in deriving the fair market value. For this reason, no useful purpose is served by taking an average of several factors (for example, book value, capitalized earnings and capitalized dividends) and basing the valuation on the result. Such a process excludes active consideration of other pertinent factors, and the end result cannot be supported by a realistic application of the significant facts in the case except by mere chance.

SEC. 8. RESTRICTIVE AGREEMENTS.

Frequently, in the valuation of closely held stock for estate and gift tax purposes, it will be found that the stock is subject to an agreement restricting its sale or transfer. Where shares of stock were acquired by a decedent subject to an option reserved by the issuing corporation to repurchase at a certain price, the option price is usually accepted as the fair market value for estate tax purposes. See Rev. Rul. 54–76, C.B. 1954–1, 194. However, in such case the option price is not determinative of fair market value for gift tax purposes. Where the option, or buy and sell agreement, is the result of voluntary action by the stockholders and is binding during the life as well as at the death of the stockholders, such agreement may or may not, depending upon the circumstances of each case, fix the value for estate tax purposes. However, such agreement is a factor to be considered, with other relevant factors, in determining fair market value. Where the stockholder is free to dispose of his shares during life and the option is to become effective only upon his death, the fair market value is not limited to the option price. It is always necessary to consider the relationship of the parties, the relative number of shares held by the decedent, and other material facts, to determine whether the agreement represents a bonafide business arrangement or is a device to pass the decedent's shares to the natural objects of his bounty for less than an adequate and full consideration in money or money's worth. In this connection see Rev. Rul. 157 C.B. 1953–2, 255, and Rev. Rul. 189, C.B. 1953–2, 294.

SEC. 9. EFFECT ON OTHER DOCUMENTS.

Revenue Ruling 54–77, C.B. 1954–1, 187, is hereby superseded.

# REVENUE RULING 65-193

26 CFR 20.2031-2: Valuation of          Rev. Rul. 65-193
  stocks and bonds.
(Also Sections 1001, 2512; 1.1001-1, 25.2512-2.)

Revenue Ruling 59-60, C.B. 1959-1, 237, is hereby modified to delete the statements, contained therein at section 4.02(f), that "In some instances it may not be possible to make a separate appraisal of the tangible and intangible assets of the business. The enterprise has a value as an entity. Whatever intangible value there is, which is supportable by the facts, may be measured by the amount by which the appraised value of the tangible assets exceeds the net book value of such assets."

The instances where it is not possible to make a separate appraisal of the tangible and intangible assets of a business are rare and each case varies from the other. No rule can be devised which will be generally applicable to such cases.

Other than this modification, Revenue Ruling 59-60 continues in full force and effect. See Rev. Rul. 65-192.

# REVENUE RULING 68-609

SECTION 1001.—DETERMINATION OF AMOUNT OF AND RECOGNITION OF GAIN OR LOSS

26 CFR 1.1001–1 : Computation of gain or loss.      Rev. Rul. 68–609 [1]
(Also Section 167; 1.167(a)–3.)

The purpose of this Revenue Ruling is to update and restate, under the current statute and regulations, the currently outstanding portions of A.R.M. 34, C.B. 2, 31 (1920), A.R.M. 68, C.B. 3, 43 (1920), and O.D. 937, C.B. 4, 43 (1921).

The question presented is whether the "formula" approach, the capitalization of earnings in excess of a fair rate of return on net tangible assets, may be used to determine the fair market value of the intangible assets of a business

The "formula" approach may be stated as follows:

A percentage return on the average annual value of the tangible assets used in a business is determined, using a period of years (preferably not less than five) immediately prior to the valuation date. The amount of the percentage return on tangible assets, thus determined, is deducted from the average earnings of the business for such period and the remainder, if any, is considered to be the amount of the average annual earnings from the intangible assets of the business for the period. This amount (considered as the average annual earnings from intangibles), capitalized at a percentage of, say, 15 to 20 percent, is the value of the intangible assets of the business determined under the "formula" approach.

The percentage of return on the average annual value of the tangible assets used should be the percentage prevailing in the industry involved at the date of valuation, or (when the industry percentage is not available) a percentage of 8 to 10 percent may be used.

The 8 percent rate of return and the 15 percent rate of capitalization are applied to tangibles and intangibles, respectively, of businesses with a small risk factor and stable and regular earnings; the 10 percent rate of return and 20 percent rate of capitalization are applied to businesses in which the hazards of business are relatively high.

The above rates are used as examples and are not appropriate in all cases. In applying the "formula" approach, the average earnings period and the capitalization rates are dependent upon the facts pertinent thereto in each case.

The past earnings to which the formula is applied should fairly reflect the probable future earnings. Ordinarily, the period should not be less than five years, and abnormal years, whether above or below the average, should be eliminated. If the business is a sole proprietorship or partnership, there should be deducted from the earnings of the business a reasonable amount for services performed by the owner or partners engaged in the business. See *Lloyd B. Sanderson Estate* v. *Commissioner*, 42 F. 2d 160 (1930). Further, only the tangible assets entering into net worth, including accounts and bills receivable in

---

[1] Prepared pursuant to Rev. Proc. 67–6, C.B. 1967–1, 576.

excess of accounts and bills payable, are used for determining earnings on the tangible assets. Factors that influence the capitalization rate include (1) the nature of the business, (2) the risk involved, and (3) the stability or irregularity of earnings.

The "formula" approach should not be used if there is better evidence available from which the value of intangibles can be determined. If the assets of a going business are sold upon the basis of a rate of capitalization that can be substantiated as being realistic, though it is not within the range of figures indicated here as the ones ordinarily to be adopted, the same rate of capitalization should be used in determining the value of intangibles.

Accordingly, the "formula" approach may be used for determining the fair market value of intangible assets of a business only if there is no better basis therefor available.

See also Revenue Ruling 59–60, C.B. 1959–1, 237, as modified by Revenue Ruling 65–193, C.B. 1965–2, 370, which sets forth the proper approach to use in the valuation of closely-held corporate stocks for estate and gift tax purposes. The general approach, methods, and factors, outlined in Revenue Ruling 59–60, as modified, are equally applicable to valuations of corporate stocks for income and other tax purposes as well as for estate and gift tax purposes. They apply also to problems involving the determination of the fair market value of business interests of any type, including partnerships and proprietorships, and of intangible assets for all tax purposes.

A.R.M. 34, A.R.M. 68, and O.D. 937 are superseded, since the positions set forth therein are restated to the extent applicable under current law in this Revenue Ruling. Revenue Ruling 65–192, C.B. 1965–2, 259, which contained restatements of A.R.M. 34 and A.R.M. 68, is also superseded.

# REVENUE RULING 77–287

## Section 2031.—Definition of Gross Estate

*26 CFR 20.2031-2: Valuation of stocks and bonds.*
*(Also Sections 170, 2032, 2512; 1.170A-1, 20.2032-1, 25.2512-2.)*

**Valuation of securities restricted from immediate resale.** Guidelines are set forth for the valuation, for Federal tax purposes, of securities that cannot be immediately resold because they are restricted from resale pursuant to Federal securities laws; Rev. Rul. 59-60 amplified.

## Rev. Rul. 77-287

SECTION 1. PURPOSE.

The purpose of this Revenue Ruling is to amplify Rev. Rul. 59-60, 1959-1 C.B. 237, as modified by Rev. Rul. 65-193, 1965-2 C.B. 370, and to provide information and guidance to taxpayers, Internal Revenue Service personnel, and others concerned with the valuation, for Federal tax purposes, of securities that cannot be immediately resold because they are restricted from resale pursuant to Federal securities laws. This guidance is applicable only in cases where it is not inconsistent with valuation requirements of the Internal Revenue Code of 1954 or the regulations thereunder. Further, this ruling does not establish the time at which property shall be valued.

SEC. 2. NATURE OF THE PROBLEM.

It frequently becomes necessary to establish the fair market value of stock that has not been registered for public trading when the issuing company has stock of the same class that is actively traded in one or more securities markets. The problem is to determine the difference in fair market value between the registered shares that are actively traded and the unregistered shares. This problem is often encountered in estate and gift tax cases. However, it is sometimes encountered when unregistered shares are issued in exchange for assets or the stock of an acquired company.

SEC. 3. BACKGROUND AND DEFINITIONS.

.01 The Service outlined and reviewed in general the approach, methods, and factors to be considered in valuing shares of closely held corporate stock for estate and gift tax purposes in Rev. Rul. 59-60, as modified by Rev. Rul. 65-193. The provisions of Rev. Rul. 59-60, as modified, were extended to the valuation of corporate securities for income and other tax purposes by Rev. Rul. 68-609, 1968-2 C.B. 327.

.02 There are several terms currently in use in the securities industry that denote restrictions imposed on the resale and transfer of certain securities. The term frequently used to describe these securities is "restricted securities," but they are sometimes referred to as "unregistered securities," "investment letter stock," "control stock," or "private placement stock." Frequently these terms are used interchangeably. They all indicate that these particular securities cannot lawfully be distributed to the general public until a registration statement relating to the corporation underlying the securities has been filed, and has also become effective under the rules promulgated and enforced by the United States Securities & Exchange Commission (SEC) pursuant to the Federal securities laws. The following represents a more refined definition of each of the following terms along with two other terms—"exempted securities" and "exempted transactions."

(a) The term "restricted securities" is defined in Rule 144 adopted by the SEC as "securities acquired directly or indirectly from the issuer thereof, or from an affiliate of such issuer, in a transaction or chain of transactions not involving any public offering."

(b) The term "unregistered securities" refers to those securities with respect to which a registration statement, providing full disclosure by the issuing corporation, has not been filed with the SEC pursuant to the Securities Act of 1933. The registration statement is a condition precedent to a public distribution of securities in interstate commerce and is aimed at providing the prospective investor with a factual basis for sound judgment in making investment decisions.

(c) The terms "investment letter stock" and "letter stock" denote shares of stock that have been issued by a corporation without the benefit of filing a registration statement with the SEC. Such stock is subject to resale and transfer restrictions set forth in a letter agreement requested by the issuer and signed by the buyer of the stock when the stock is delivered. Such stock may be found in the hands of either individual investors or institutional investors.

(d) The term "control stock" indicates that the shares of stock have been held or are being held by an officer, director, or other person close to the management of the corporation. These persons are subject to certain requirements pursuant to SEC rules upon resale of shares they own in such corporations.

(e) The term "private placement stock" indicates that the stock has been placed with an institution or other investor who will presumably hold it for a long period and ultimately arrange to have the stock registered if it is to be offered to the general public. Such stock may or may not be subject to a letter agreement. Private placements of stock are exempted from the registration and prospectus provisions of the Securities Act of 1933.

(f) The term "exempted securities" refers to those classes of securities that are expressly excluded from the registration provisions of the Securities Act of 1933 and the distribution provisions of the Securities Exchange Act of 1934.

(g) The term "exempted transactions" refers to certain sales or distributions of securities that do not involve a public offering and are excluded from the registration and prospectus provisions of the Securities Act of 1933 and distribution provisions of the Securities Exchange Act of 1934. The exempted status makes it unnecessary for issuers of securities to go through the registration process.

Sec. 4. Securities Industry Practice in Valuing Restricted Securities.

.01 *Investment Company Valuation Practices.* The Investment Company Act of 1940 requires open-end investment companies to publish the valuation of their portfolio securities daily. Some of these companies have portfolios containing restricted securities, but also have unrestricted securities of the same class traded on a securities exchange. In recent years the number of restricted securities in such portfolios has increased. The following methods have been used by investment companies in the valuation of such restricted securities:

(a) Current market price of the unrestricted stock less a constant percentage discount based on purchase discount;

(b) Current market price of unrestricted stock less a constant percentage discount different from purchase discount;

(c) Current market price of the unrestricted stock less a discount amortized over a fixed period;

(d) Current market price of the unrestricted stock; and

(e) Cost of the restricted stock until it is registered.

The SEC ruled in its Investment Company Act Release No. 5847, dated October 21, 1969, that there can be no automatic formula by which an investment company can value the restricted securities in its portfolios. Rather, the SEC has determined that it is the responsibility of the board of directors of the particular investment company to determine the "fair value" of each issue of restricted securities in good faith.

.02 *Institutional Investors Study.* Pursuant to Congressional direction, the SEC undertook an analysis of the purchases, sales, and holding of securities by financial institutions, in order to determine the effect of institutional activity upon the securities market. The study report was published in eight volumes in March 1971. The fifth volume provides an analysis of restricted securities and deals with such items as the characteristics of the restricted securities purchasers and issuers, the size of transactions (dollars and shares), the marketability discounts on different trading markets, and the resale provisions. This research project provides some guidance for measuring the discount in that it contains information, based on the actual experience of the marketplace, showing that, during the period surveyed (January 1, 1966, through June 30, 1969), the amount of discount allowed for restricted securities from the trading price of the unrestricted securities was generally related to the following four factors.

(a) *Earnings.* Earnings and sales consistently have a significant influence on the size of restricted securities discounts according to the study. Earnings played the major part in establishing the ultimate discounts at which these stocks were sold from the current market price. Apparently earnings patterns, rather than sales patterns, determine the degree of risk of an investment.

(b) *Sales.* The dollar amount of sales of issuers' securities also has a major influence on the amount of discount at which restricted securities sell from the current market price. The results of the study generally indicate that the companies with the lowest dollar amount of sales during the test period accounted for most of the transactions involving the highest discount rates, while they accounted for only a small portion of all transactions involving the lowest discount rates.

(c) *Trading Market.* The market in which publicly held securities are traded also reflects variances in the amount of discount that is applied to restricted securities purchases. According to the study, discount rates were greatest on restricted stocks with unrestricted counterparts traded over-the-counter, followed by those with unrestricted counterparts listed on the American Stock Exchange, while the discount rates for those stocks with unrestricted counterparts listed on the New York Stock Exchange were the smallest.

(d) *Resale Agreement Provisions.* Resale agreement provisions often affect the size of the discount. The discount from the market price provides the main incentive for a potential buyer to acquire restricted securities. In judging the opportunity cost of freezing funds, the purchaser is analyzing two separate factors. The first factor is the risk that underlying value of the stock will change in a way that, absent the restrictive provisions, would have prompted a decision to sell. The second factor is the risk that the contemplated means of legally disposing of the stock may not materialize. From the seller's point of view, a discount is justified where the seller is relieved of the expenses of registration and public distribution, as well as of the risk that the market will adversely change before the offering is completed. The ultimate agreement between buyer and seller is a reflection of these and other considerations. Relative bargaining strengths of the parties to the agreement are major considerations that influence the resale terms and consequently the size of discounts in restricted securities transactions. Certain provisions are often found in agreements between buyers and sellers that affect the size of discounts at which restricted stocks are sold. Several such provisions follow, all of which, other than number (3), would tend to reduce the size of the discount:

(1) A provision giving the buyer an option to "piggyback", that is, to register restricted stock with the next registration statement, if any, filed by the issuer with the SEC;

(2) A provision giving the buyer an option to require registration at the seller's expense;

(3) A provision giving the buyer an option to require registration, but only at the buyer's own expense;

(4) A provision giving the buyer a right to receive continuous disclosure of information about the issuer from the seller;

(5) A provision giving the buyer a right to select one or more directors of the issuer;

(6) A provision giving the buyer an option to purchase additional shares of the issuer's stock; and

(7) A provision giving the buyer the right to have a greater voice in operations of the issuer, if the issuer does not meet previously agreed upon operating standards.

Institutional buyers can and often do obtain many of these rights and options from the sellers of restricted securities, and naturally, the more rights the buyer can acquire, the lower the buyer's risk is going to be, thereby reducing the buyer's discount as well. Smaller buyers may not be able to negotiate the large discounts or the rights and options that volume buyers are able to negotiate.

.03 *Summary.* A variety of methods have been used by the securities industry to value restricted securities. The SEC rejects all automatic or mechanical solutions to the valuation of restricted securities, and prefers, in the case of the valuation of investment company portfolio stocks, to rely upon good faith valuations by the board of directors of each company. The study made by the SEC found that restricted securities *generally* are issued at a discount from the market value of freely tradable securities.

SEC. 5. FACTS AND CIRCUMSTANCES MATERIAL TO VALUATION OF RESTRICTED SECURITIES.

.01 Frequently, a company has a class of stock that cannot be traded publicly. The reason such stock cannot be traded may arise from the securities statutes, as in the case of an "investment letter" restriction; it may arise from a corporate charter restriction, or perhaps from a trust agreement restriction. In such cases, certain documents and facts should be obtained for analysis.

.02 The following documents and facts, when used in conjunction with those discussed in Section 4 of Rev. Rul. 59-60, will be useful in the valuation of restricted securities:

(a) A copy of any declaration of trust, trust agreement, and any other agreements relating to the shares of restricted stock;

(b) A copy of any document showing any offers to buy or sell or indicating any offers to buy or selling the restricted shares;

(c) The latest prospectus of the company;

(d) Annual reports of the company for 3 to 5 years preceding the valuation date;

(e) The trading prices and trading volume of the related class of traded securities 1 month preceding the valuation date, if they are traded on a stock exchange (if traded over-the-counter, prices may be obtained from the National Quotations Bureau, the National Association of Securities Dealers Automated Quotations (NASDAQ), or sometimes from broker-dealers making markets in the shares);

(f) The relationship of the parties to the agreements concerning the restricted stock, such as whether they are members of the immediate family or perhaps whether they are officers or directors of the company; and

(g) Whether the interest being valued represents a majority or minority ownership.

SEC. 6. WEIGHING FACTS AND CIRCUMSTANCES MATERIAL TO RESTRICTED STOCK VALUATION.

All relevant facts and circumstances that bear upon the worth of restricted stock, including those set forth above in the preceding Sections 4 and 5, and those set forth in Section 4 of Rev. Rul. 59-60, must be taken into account in arriving at the fair market value of such securities. Depending on the circumstances of each case, certain factors may carry more weight than others. To illustrate:

.01 Earnings, net assets, and net sales must be given primary consideration in arriving at an appropriate discount for restricted securities from the freely traded shares. These are the elements of value that are always used by investors in making investment decisions. In some cases, one element may be more important than in other cases. In the case of manufacturing, producing, or distributing companies, primary weight must be accorded earnings and net sales; but in the case of investment or holding companies, primary weight must be given to the net assets of the company underlying the stock. In the former type of companies, value is more closely linked to past, present, and future earnings while in the latter type of companies, value is more closely linked to the existing net assets of the company. See the discussion in Section 5 of Rev. Rul. 59-60.

.02   Resale provisions found in the restriction agreements must be scrutinized and weighed to determine the amount of discount to apply to the preliminary fair market value of the company. The two elements of time and expense bear upon this discount; the longer the buyer of the shares must wait to liquidate the shares, the greater the discount. Moreover, if the provisions make it necessary for the buyer to bear the expense of registration, the greater the discount. However, if the provisions of the restricted stock agreement make it possible for the buyer to "piggyback" shares at the next offering, the discount would be smaller.

.03   The relative negotiation strengths of the buyer and seller of restricted stock may have a profound effect on the amount of discount. For example, a tight money situation may cause the buyer to have the greater balance of negotiation strength in a transaction. However, in some cases the relative strengths may tend to cancel each other out.

.04   The market experience of freely tradable securities of the same class as the restricted securities is also significant in determining the amount of discount. Whether the shares are privately held or publicly traded affects the worth of the shares to the holder. Securities traded on a public market generally are worth more to investors than those that are not traded on a public market. Moreover, the type of public market in which the unrestricted securities are traded is to be given consideration.

SEC. 7.   EFFECT ON OTHER DOCUMENTS.

Rev. Rul. 59-60, as modified by Rev. Rul. 65-193, is amplified.

# REVENUE RULING 83-120

## Section 2512.—Valuation of Gifts

*26 CFR 25.2512-2: Stocks and bonds.*
*(Also Sections 305, 351, 354, 368, 2031; 1.305-*
*5, 1.351-1, 1.354-1, 1.368-1, 20.2031-2.)*

**Valuation; stock; closely held business.** The significant factors in deriving the fair market value of preferred and common stock received in certain corporate reorganizations are discussed. Rev. Rul. 59-60 amplified.

## Rev. Rul. 83-120

SECTION 1. PURPOSE

The purpose of this Revenue Ruling is to amplify Rev. Rul. 59-60, 1959-1 C.B. 237, by specifying additional factors to be considered in valuing common and preferred stock of a closely held corporation for gift tax and other purposes in a recapitalization of closely held businesses. This type of valuation problem frequently arises with respect to estate planning transactions wherein an individual receives preferred stock with a stated par value equal to all or a large portion of the fair market value of the individual's former stock interest in a corporation. The individual also receives common stock which is then transferred, usually as a gift, to a relative.

## Sec. 2. BACKGROUND

.01 One of the frequent objectives of the type of transaction mentioned above is the transfer of the potential appreciation of an individual's stock interest in a corporation to relatives at a nominal or small gift tax cost. Achievement of this objective requires preferred stock having a fair market value equal to a large part of the fair market value of the individual's former stock interest and common stock having a nominal or small fair market value. The approach and factors described in this Revenue Ruling are directed toward ascertaining the true fair market value of the common and preferred stock and will usually result in the determination of a substantial fair market value for the common stock and a fair market value for the preferred stock which is substantially less than its par value.

.02 The type of transaction referred to above can arise in many different contexts. Some examples are:

(a) *A* owns 100% of the common stock (the only outstanding stock) of *Z* Corporation which has a fair market value of 10,500x. In a recapitalization described in section 368(a)(1)(E), *A* receives preferred stock with a par value of 10,000x and new common stock, which *A* then transfers to *A*'s son *B*.

(b) *A* owns some of the common stock of *Z* Corporation (or the stock of several corporations) the fair market value of which stock is 10,500x. *A* transfers this stock to a new corporation *X* in exchange for preferred stock of *X* corporation with a par value of 10,000x and common stock of corporation, which *A* then transfers to *A*'s son *B*.

(c) *A* owns 80 shares and his son *B* owns 20 shares of the common stock (the only stock outstanding) of *Z* Corporation. In a recapitalization described in section 368(a)(1)(E), *A* exchanges his 80 shares of common stock for 80 shares of new preferred stock of *Z* Corporation with a par value of 10,000x. *A*'s common stock had a fair market value of 10,000x.

## SEC. 3. GENERAL APPROACH TO VALUATION

Under section 25.2512-2(f)(2) of the Gift Tax Regulations, the fair market value of stock in a closely held corporation depends upon numerous factors, including the corporation's net worth, its prospective earning power, and its capacity to pay dividends. In addition, other relevant factors must be taken into account. *See* Rev. Rul. 59-60. The weight to be accorded any evidentiary factor depends on the circumstances of each case. *See* section 25.2512-2(f) of the Gift Tax Regulations.

## SEC. 4. APPROACH TO VALUATION—PREFERRED STOCK

.01 In general the most important factors to be considered in determining the value of preferred stock are its yield, dividend coverage and protection of its liquidation preference.

.02 Whether the yield of the preferred stock supports a valuation of the stock at par value depends in part on the adequacy of the dividend rate. The adequacy of the dividend rate should be determined by comparing its dividend rate with the dividend rate of high-grade publicly traded preferred stock. A lower yield than that of high-grade preferred stock indicates a preferred stock value of less than par. If the rate of interest charged by independent creditors to the corporation on loans is higher than the rate such independent creditors charge their most credit worthy borrowers, then the yield on the preferred stock should be correspondingly higher than the yield on high quality preferred stock. A yield which is not correspondingly higher reduces the value of the preferred stock. In addition, whether the preferred stock has a fixed dividend rate and is non-participating influences the value of the preferred stock. A publicly traded preferred stock for a company having a similar business and similar assets with similar liquidation preferences,

voting rights and other similar terms would be the ideal comparable for determining yield required in arms length transactions for closely held stock. Such ideal comparables will frequently not exist. In such circumstances, the most comparable publicly-traded issues should be selected for comparison and appropriate adjustments made for differing factors.

.03 The actual dividend rate on a preferred stock can be assumed to be its stated rate if the issuing corporation will be able to pay its stated dividends in a timely manner and will, in fact, pay such dividends. The risk that the corporation may be unable to timely pay the stated dividends on the preferred stock can be measured by the coverage of such stated dividends by the corporation's earnings. Coverage of the dividend is measured by the ratio of the sum of pre-tax and pre-interest earnings to the sum of the total interest to be paid and the pre-tax earnings needed to pay the after-tax dividends. *Standard & Poor's Ratings Guide*, 58 (1979). Inadequate coverage exists where a decline in corporate profits would be likely to jeopardize the corporation's ability to pay dividends on the preferred stock. The ratio for the preferred stock in question should be compared with the ratios for high quality preferred stock to determine whether the preferred stock has adequate coverage. Prior earnings history is important in this determination. Inadequate coverage indicates that the value of preferred stock is lower than its par value. Moreover, the absence of a provision that preferred dividends are cumulative raises substantial questions concerning whether the stated dividend rate will, in fact, be paid. Accordingly, preferred stock with noncumulative dividend features will normally have a value substantially lower than a cumulative preferred stock with the same yield, liquidation preference and dividend coverage.

.04 Whether the issuing corporation will be able to pay the full liquidation preference at liquidation must be taken into account in determining fair market value. This risk can be measured by the protection afforded by the corporation's net assets. Such protection can be measured by the ratio of the excess of the current market value of the corporation's assets over its liabilities to the aggregate liquidation preference. The protection ratio should be compared with the ratios for high quality preferred stock to determine adequacy of coverage. Inadequate asset protection exists where any unforeseen business reverses would be likely to jeopardize the corporation's ability to pay the full liquidation preference to the holders of the preferred stock.

.05 Another factor to be considered in valuing the preferred stock is whether it has voting rights and, if so, whether the preferred stock has voting control. See, however, Section 5.02 below.

.06 Peculiar covenants or provisions of the preferred stock of a type not ordinarily found in publicly traded preferred stock should be carefully evaluated to determine the effects of such covenants on the value of the preferred stock. In general, if covenants would inhibit the marketability of the stock or the power of the holder to enforce dividend or liquidation rights, such provisions will reduce the value of the preferred stock by comparison to the value of preferred stock not containing such convenants or provisions.

.07 Whether the preferred stock contains a redemption privilege is another factor to be considered in determining the value of the preferred stock. The value of a redemption privilege triggered by death of the preferred shareholder will not exceed the present value of the redemption premium payable at the preferred shareholder's death (i.e., the present value of the excess of the redemption price over the fair market value of the preferred stock upon its issuance). The value of the redemption privilege should be reduced to reflect any risk that the corporation may not possess sufficient assets to redeem its preferred stock at the stated redemption price. See .03 above.

## SEC. 5. APPROACH TO VALUATION— COMMON STOCK

.01 If the preferred stock has a fixed rate of dividend and is nonparticipating, the common stock has the exclusive right to the benefits of future appreciation of the value of the corporation. This right is valuable and usually warrants a determination that the common stock has substantial value. The actual value of this right depends upon the corporation's past growth experience, the economic condition of the industry in which the corporation operates, and general economic conditions. The factor to be used in capitalizing the corporation's prospective earnings must be determined after an analysis of numerous factors concerning the corporation and the economy as a whole. *See* Rev. Rul. 59-60, at page 243. In addition, after-tax earnings of the corporation at the time the preferred stock is issued in excess of the stated dividends on the preferred stock will increase the value of the common stock. Furthermore, a corporate policy of reinvesting earnings will also increase the value of the common stock.

.02 A factor to be considered in determining the value of the common stock is whether the preferred stock also has voting rights. Voting rights of the preferred stock, especially if the preferred stock has voting control, could under certain circumstances increase the value of the preferred stock and reduce the value of the common stock. This factor may be reduced in significance where the rights of common stockholders as a class are protected under state law from actions by another class of shareholders, *see Singer v. Magnavox Co.*, 380 A.2d 969 (Del. 1977), particularly where the common shareholders, as a class, are given the power to disapprove a proposal to allow preferred stock to be converted into common stock. See ABA-ALI Model Bus. Corp. Act, Section 60 (1969).

## SEC. 6. EFFECT ON OTHER REVENUE RULINGS

**Rev. Rul. 59-60**, as modified by **Rev. Rul. 65-193**, 1965-2 C.B. 370 and as amplified by Rev. Rul. 77-287, 1977-2 C.B. 319, and Rev. Rul. 80-213, 1980-2 C.B. 101, is further amplified.

The following cases are intended to illustrate the varied positions taken by the courts in the valuation of privately held companies. It is evident that there is nothing cut and dried here; cases have been judged on an individual basis depending on the specific circumstances of the case and the predilections of the court with respect to the appropriate valuation method.

*Central Trust* v. *United States* is considered to be among the most helpful opinions. The case discusses the applicability of the weighted average value based on earnings, dividends, and book value. Adjustments to this formula for such factors as the lack of marketability are also considered.

In *Andrews* v. *Internal Revenue Service* the use of minority shareholder discounts is discussed. *Righter* v. *United States* is an interesting case in which the court rejected comparisons with comparable public companies. In *Luce* v. *United States* the court employed book value as the sale basis for valuation.

## The Central Trust Company and Albert E. Heekin, Jr., Co-Executors of the Estate of Albert E. Heekin, Deceased v. The United States. Successor Executor and Trustee under the Will of Alma R. Heekin, Deceased v. The United States.

### U.S. Court of Claims, Dkt. Nos. 196–58, 199–58, 200–58, 7/18/62.—(305 F.2d 393.)

Thomas L. Conlan (Kyte, Conlan, Wulsin & Vogeler were on the briefs) for Plaintiffs in Dkt. No. 196-58. John W. Warrington, Cincinnati, Ohio (Graydon, Head & Ritchey were on the briefs), for Plaintiffs in Dkt. Nos. 199-58 and 200-58. Earl L. Huntington, with whom was Louis F. Oberdorfer, Asst. Attorney General, Dept. of Justice, Washington, D. C., for Defendant.

PER CURIAM: These cases were referred by the court, pursuant to Rule 45, to Saul Richard Gamer, a trial commissioner of the court, with directions to make findings of fact and recommendations for conclusions of law. The commissioner has done so in a report filed April 17, 1962. Plaintiffs in case No. 196-58 filed their notice of intention to except to the commissioner's findings and recommendations on May 2, 1962, and on June 18, 1962, moved to withdraw this notice. Plaintiffs in case No. 199-58 and case No. 200-58 filed their notices to except to the commissioner's findings and recommendations on May 1, 1962, and on June 13, 1962, moved to withdraw these notices. On June 15, 1962, the defendant filed its reply advising the court that it had no objection to the withdrawal of the notices and on June 22, 1962, the court allowed plaintiffs' motions to withdraw the notices of intention to except in all three cases.

Plaintiffs in their motions to withdraw their notices of intention to except also moved, pursuant to Rule 46(a), that the court adopt the commissioner's report as the basis for its judgment in the cases. Defendant's reply filed June 15, 1962, concurred in these motions. Since the court agrees with the recommendations and findings of the commissioner, as hereinafter set forth, it hereby adopts the same as the basis for its judgment in these cases. Plaintiffs are therefore entitled to recover and judgment is entered to that effect. The amounts of recovery will be determined pursuant to Rule 38(c).

It is so ordered.

### Opinion of the Commissioner

These suits are for the refund of federal gift taxes. They involve the common question of the value of shares of stock of the same company. A joint trial was therefore conducted.

On August 3, 1954, Albert E. Heekin made gifts totaling 30,000 shares of stock of The Heekin Can Company. The donor had formerly, for 20 years, been president of the Company and at the time of the gifts was a member of its board of directors. The gifts were composed of 5,000 shares to each of six trusts created for the benefit of his three sons, each son being the beneficiary under two trusts. Following his death on March 10, 1955, the executors of his estate filed a gift tax return in which the value of the stock was fixed at $10 a share. On October 28, 1957, however, they filed an amended gift tax return and a claim for refund, contending that the correct value of the Heekin Company stock on August 3, 1954 was $7.50 a share.

On October 25, 1954, James J. Heekin made gifts totaling 40,002 shares of Heekin Can Company stock. This donor, a brother of Albert E., had also formerly been, for 23 years, the president of the Company and at the time of the gifts was chairman of the board. The gifts were composed of 13,334 shares to each of three trusts created for the benefit of his three children and their families. Separate gift tax returns with respect to these (and other) gifts were filed by both James J. Heekin and his wife, Alma (who joined in the stock gifts), in which the value of the stock was similarly declared to be $10 a share. However, on January 21, 1958, James filed an amended gift tax return and a claim for refund, also contending that the correct value of the stock on October 25, 1954, was $7.50 a share, and on the same day, the executor of Alma's estate (she having died on November 9, 1955) filed a similar amended return and claim for refund.

On February 5, 1958, the District Director of Internal Revenue sent to James J. Heekin and the executors of the estates of Alma and Albert E. Heekin notices of deficiency of the 1954 gift taxes. Each of the three deficiencies was based on a determination by the Commissioner of Internal Revenue that the value of the Heekin Company stock on the gift dates was $24 a share.

Consistent with his deficiency notices, the District Director, on May 15, 1958, disallowed the three refund claims that had been filed, and in July 1958 payment was made of the amounts assessed pursuant to the deficiency notices. After the filing in August and September 1958 of claims for refund concerning these payments, the claims again being based on a valuation of $7.50, and the rejection thereof by the District Director, these three refund suits were instituted in the amounts of $169,876.19, $95,927.08, and $94,753.70 with respect to the Albert E. Heekin, James J. Heekin and Alma Heekin gifts, respectively, plus interest.


The Heekin Can Company is a well-established metal container manufacturer in Cincinnati, Ohio. In 1954, the year involved in these proceedings, its principal business consisted of manufacturing two kinds of containers, its total production being equally divided between them. One is known as packer's cans, which are generally the type seen on the shelves of food markets in which canned food products are contained. The other is referred to as general line cans, which consist of large institutional size frozen fruit cans, lard pails, dairy cans, chemical cans, and drums. This line also includes such housewares as canisters, bread boxes, lunches boxes, waste baskets, and a

type of picnic container familiarly known by the trade names of Skotch Kooler and Skotch Grill. On the gift dates its annual sales, the production of five plants, were approximately $17,000,000.

The Company was founded in 1901 in Cincinnati by James Heekin, the father of the donors Albert and James. In 1908, it built a six-story 250,000 square foot factory in Cincinnati, which is still its headquarters and one of its main operating plants, producing general line cans. In 1917 it acquired a plant in Norwood, a suburb of Cincinnati, which has since become entirely surrounded by the city, and entered the packer's can business. By 1954, it was a multistory plant with about 275,000 square feet, having grown irregularly throughout the years, one section having four floors, another three, and another only one.

In 1946, the Company branched out from Cincinnati and established a packer's can plant at Chestnut Hill, Tennessee, on property leased from and contiguous to the plant of its largest customer, which used the entire output of the Heekin plant. The cans were run by conveyor directly into the customer's packing plant.

In 1949, the Company built a 100,000 square foot plant in Springdale, Arkansas, to supply its customers in the Ozark area on a more competitive basis concerning freight costs, a large part of which, under the industry's freight-equalization practice, it had theretofore absorbed.

In 1952, the Company established it fifth plant, constituting an operation at Blytheville, Arkansas, similar to the one at Chestnut Hill, Tennessee. The plant was on leased property adjacent to the customer's plant, with the cans running directly into such plant. By 1954 this concept of installing can-making lines immediately adjacent to customers' packing plants was a recognized practice in the industry. Thus, the Company was progressively adapting itself to the modern practices of its industry.

From the beginning, the Heekin family has dominated the enterprise. James, the founder, was its president from 1901 to 1905. He was succeeded by his son, James J., one of the donors herein, who served as president for 23 years. In 1928, another son,

Albert E., another donor herein, then became president, serving for 20 years. He was succeeded in 1948 by still another son, Daniel M., who served for 6 years. In March 1954, Albert E. Heekin, Jr., the son of donor Albert E. and the grandson of the founder, succeeded to the presidency. A lawyer, he had served the Company up to 1950 as its legal counsel, joining the Company in that year as assistant to the president. On August 3, 1954, of the ten-member board of directors, eight were members of the Heekin family, five of whom were sons of the founder, and three his grandsons. Both donors were members of the board, James J. being chairman. On October 25, 1954, the board was similarly constituted, except for the death of one son in August. Despite this family domination, there was no indication on the gift dates that the enterprise was not capably managed or that salaries were in any way excessive.

On the gift dates, the Company had 254,125 shares of common stock outstanding, there being no restrictions on their transferability or sale. There was no other class of stock. Including the 70,002 shares involved in these cases, a total of 180,510 shares were owned by 79 persons who were related to James Heekin, the founder. Thus, the Heekin family owned approximately 71 percent of all of the outstanding stock. The remaining 73,615 shares were owned by 54 unrelated persons, most of whom were employees of the Company and friends of the family.

Six major customers accounted for almost one-half of Heekin's 1954 business. Relations with these important customers were long-standing and excellent. One of these customers, the Hamilton Metal Products Company, which placed over $2,000,000 worth of business with Heekin in 1954, and for whom Heekin manufactured the Skotch Kooler and Grill, had, prior to the gift dates, advised Heekin of its need for certain new products, and on August 3, 1954 (one of the gift dates), Heekin's board of directors authorized the expenditure of approximately $90,000 for new tooling and equipment at its Cincinnati plant for the manufacture of such products. Another major customer was the Reynolds Tobacco Company, which placed almost $1,500,000 of business with Heekin in 1954 and with whom Heekin had dealt since 1908.

As indicated, freight costs play an important part in Heekin's business. These costs are significant in two aspects. One is the cost of transporting raw material to Heekin's plants. In this respect Heekin was quite favorably located. It has a dock on the Ohio River in Cincinnati, permitting it to take advantage of inexpensive water transportation of steel shipped from Pittsburgh, with a consequent advantage over some of its competitors in the same area who receive their raw materials by rail. The other important freight aspect is, as above noted, the cost of shipping the final product to the customer, and which factor motivated the establishment of its Springdale, Arkansas, plant. The Hamilton Metal Products Company was located only 25 miles from Cincinnati, giving Heekin an important freight advantage. And also, on August 3, 1954, Heekin's board of directors authorized the expenditure of about $650,000 for new tooling, machinery and equipment for its Norwood plant so that Heekin could enter the new field of manufacturing beer cans. At that time no other company in the Cincinnati area was engaged in the production of such cans, and Heekin concluded that, with the freight advantage it would have over its competitors in serving the brewers of the Cincinnati area, a profitable new source of business would be developed.

In 1954, favorable economic conditions generally prevailed in the can-manufacturing industry, and demand was at a record level. Indeed, this was the condition throughout the container and packaging industry, and optimism generally prevailed about the continuation of the then current high demand.

But Heekin had its problems too. It is a relatively tiny factor in a highly competitive industry dominated by two giants, the American Can Company and the Continental Can Company. In 1954, these two companies, each with over $600,000,000 of annual sales produced from 76 and 40 plants respectively, together accounted for about 75 percent of the country's total can sales. Three other can manufacturing companies, the National Can Corporation, the Pacific Can

Company, and Crown Cork & Seal Co., Inc., together made about 8 percent of the sales. Heekin, with its five plants, did a little less than 1 percent of the total business. Prices in the can-making industry are for practical purposes established by American and Continental. When they announce prices, Heekin goes up or down with them. Unable to compete on a price basis, Heekin strives to give its customers better personal service, which, because it is smaller and closer knit, it can frequently do.

Probably Heekin's major problem is the age, and the resulting relative inefficiency, of a large part of its plant and equipment, and its inability to finance a large-scale program of modernization. This again is in part a problem of its small size. The relatively small amounts it can use for this purpose are generated by retained earnings, and it has consequently fallen behind the giants of the industry in erecting efficient plants and installing modern, high-speed, automatic can-making lines. During the war, Heekin was unable to buy new equipment. However, such competitors as American, Continental, and Pacific manufactured their own can-making equipment and were able to forge ahead, and such equipment as Heekin was able to buy after the war from other companies could not match American and Continental's modern automatic packer's can equipment, which produced 500 cans a minute. Heekin's older packer's can equipment could turn out only about 300 cans a minute, and even the new equipment it was able to buy after the war could attain, with difficulty, speeds of only 400 cans a minute. In 1954, about 90 percent of Heekin's equipment had been acquired in the middle 1930's or prior thereto. In all its plants, the Company had 37 can-making lines, 11 of which were very old and still hand operated.

Similarly, Heekin's Cincinnati and Norwood multistory plants, which accounted for about 75 percent of Heekin's total 1954 production, were less efficient than modern, single-story buildings. The can-making business is primarily a material-handling one, requiring a rapid and efficient flow of large amounts of material through the plant, from the receipt of the raw materials to the shipment of finished products. In a single-story building, materials can freely be moved horizontally with fork-lift trucks and conveyors, whereas in its six-story Cincinnati and four-story Norwood plants, elevators are used for the vertical movement of materials, resulting in excessive labor and handling costs and more difficult production controls. The proceeds of a $3,000,000 long-term loan which Heekin secured in 1950 were for the most part not available for such a plant and equipment modernization program.

However, the competitive disadvantage of lack of modern equipment was reflected more on the packer's can phase of its business than on the general line cans, which are produced both by Heekin and its competitors on only semiautomatic equipment. Such equipment does not lend itself as readily to the speed and automation required with respect to packer's cans. Heekin's semiautomatic lines were capable of producing around 300 cans a minute.

The Heekin stock was not listed on any stock exchange, and trading in it was infrequent. There was some such activity in 1951 and 1952 resulting from the desire of certain minority stockholders (the descendants of a partner of James Heekin, the founder) to liquidate their holdings, consisting of 13,359 shares. One individual alone had 10,709 shares. Arrangements were privately made in early 1951 by these stockholders with Albert E. Heekin and his son, Albert E. Heekin, Jr., to sell these holdings at the prearranged price of $7.50 a share. These shares were all sold, commencing March 22, 1951, and ending April 16, 1952, in 44 separate transactions, 35 of which took place in 1951 and 9 in 1952. No attempt was made to sell the shares to the general public on the open market. All sales were made to Heekin employees and friends of the Heekin family at such $7.50 price. Other than these 1951 and 1952 sales, the only sales of stock made prior to the gift dates consisted of one sale of 100 shares in 1953 by one Heekin employee to another, and one sale in 1954 of 200 shares, again by one Heekin employee to another, both sales also being made for $7.50 a share.

Against these background facts, the valuation question in dispute may be approached. Section 1000 of the Internal Revenue Code of 1939 (26 U. S. C. 1952 Ed., § 1000, 53 Stat. 144), the applicable statute, imposed a tax upon transfers of property by gift, whether in trust or otherwise. Section 1005 provided that "If the gift is made in property, the value thereof at the date of the gift shall be considered the amount of the gift."

Section 86.19(a) of the Regulations issued with respect thereto (Treasury Regulations 108, 8 Fed. Reg. 10858) defines such property value as the price at which the property "would change hands between a willing buyer and a willing seller, neither being under any compulsion to buy or to sell. * * * Such value is to be determined by ascertaining as a basis the fair market value at the time of the gift of each unit of the property. For example, in the case of shares of stock * * *, such unit of property is a share * * *. All relevant facts and elements of value as of the time of the gift should be considered." With respect to determining the fair market value per share at the date of the gift, subsection (c)(6) stated that, if actual sales or bona fide bid and asked prices are not available, the value should be arrived at "on the basis of the company's net worth, earning power, dividend-paying capacity, and all other relevant factors having a bearing upon the value of the stock."

Further, a lengthy Revenue Ruling (54-77, 1954-1 Cum. Bull. 187), entitled "Valuation of stock of closely held corporations in estate tax and gift tax returns," was in effect at the time of these gifts which outlined "the approach, methods and factors to be considered in valuing shares of the capital stock of closely held corporations for estate tax and gift tax purposes." After warning in section 3 that fair market value, "being a question of fact," depends on the "circumstances in each case," and that "No formula can be devised that will be generally applicable to the multitude of different valuation issues arising in estate and gift tax cases," and that there is ordinarily "wide differences of opinion as to the fair market value of a particular" closely held stock, section 4 goes on to enumerate the following factors which "are fundamental and require careful analysis in each case": (1) the nature of the business and its history,

(2) the general economic outlook of business in general and the specific industry in particular, (3) the book value of the stock and the company's financial condition, (4) the company's earning capacity, (5) its dividend-paying capacity, (6) its goodwill, (7) such sales of the stock as have been made as well as the size of the block to be valued and (8) "the market price of stocks of corporations engaged in the same or similar line of business which are listed on an exchange." After discussing each factor in detail, the Ruling goes on to consider such matters as (a) the weight to be accorded the various factors, concluding that, in a product selling company, primary consideration should normally be given to the earnings factor, and (b) the necessity of capitalizing the earnings and dividends at appropriate rates.

There appears to be no dispute between the parties concerning the validity, or the propriety of applying the principles, of the Regulations and the Ruling to these cases. The dispute arises from the differences of opinion which are inherent in the Ruling's statement that "A sound valuation will be based upon all the relevant facts, but the elements of common sense, informed judgment and reasonableness must enter into the process of weighing those facts and determining their aggregate significance."

Where, as in the present cases, the problem is the difficult one of ascertaining the fair market value of the stock of an unlisted closely held corporation, it is not surprising that, in assisting the court to arrive at an "informed judgment," the parties offer the testimony of experts. In such a situation, the opinions of experts are peculiarly appropriate. *Bader v. United States,* [59-1 USTC ¶ 11,865] 172 F. Supp. 833 (D. C. S. D. Ill). At the trial, the taxpayers produced three experts, and the Government one.

One of plaintiffs' experts was the senior partner of a firm of investment bankers and brokers. He felt that the limited prior sales of the stock at $7.50 warranted the consideration of the other factors listed in the Revenue Ruling applicable to closely held corporations. There were four major factors which he considered in arriving at his conclusion. The first was book value.

Utilizing the Company's balance sheet as of December 31, 1954 (a date subsequent to the gift dates), the book value came to about $33 a share. In this connection he noted that the Company's financial position at that time was sound, with a ratio of current assets to current liabilities of about 4.3 to 1. However, principally because of the age and multistoried inefficiency of the Company's two main plants at Cincinnati and Norwood, he reduced the book value factor by 50 percent. The second factor was earnings. The Company's audited annual statements for 1952, 1953 and 1954, which he accepted without adjustment, showed that the average of its earnings for these 3 years was $1.77 a share. He felt that, in the case of this Company, a price earnings ratio of 6 to 1 would be appropriate, but, recognizing that this was the most important factor, he weighted it to give it double value. The third factor was dividend yield. In said 3 years, the Company paid an annual dividend of 50 cents. Accepting this figure as the dividend the Company would be likely to pay in the future, he concluded that an investor would look for a 7 percent yield on this stock, and capitalized it on that basis. The fourth factor was the prior sales at $7.50. Adding and weighting these figures, he derived a value of $10.50 a share. However, because the stock was not listed on any exchange, and was closely held, with sales being infrequent, he discounted that value by 25 percent to reflect the stock's lack of marketability, and came out with an ultimate valuation of $7.88 a share.[1] This is the value plaintiffs now rely on in these cases. This value was applied to the entire block of 70,002 shares and to both dates, a block which, he noted, would give a purchaser only a minority position. Considering the Revenue Ruling's suggestion to investigate "the market price of stocks of corporations engaged in the same or similar line of business which are listed on an exchange," this witness felt that there were no listed companies that could properly be compared with Heekin.

Plaintiffs' second expert, a certified public accountant who had experience in and was familiar with the principles involved in valuing stocks of closely held corporations, arrived at the somewhat higher valuations of $9.50 per share for the 30,000 shares given on August 3, 1954, and $9.65 for the 40,002 given on October 25, 1954. He recognized that the previous sales of the stock in 1951, 1952, 1953 and 1954 at $7.50 could not be determinative because, being all at the same selling price, they could not have reflected the month-to-month or year-to-year fluctuations of actual value, which was the problem herein involved. He concluded that that price was predicated primarily to give a yield of 6⅔ percent based on an annual dividend rate of 50 cents, which the Company had paid each year from 1946 through 1954, except for a 1½-year period in 1950 and 1951. In 1950, the Company suffered extraordinary losses and dividends were suspended, and in 1951, only 25 cents was paid. Accordingly, he considered the situation appropriate for the application of the principles enunciated in the Revenue Ruling.

In so doing, he too concluded that the four major factors to be considered were earnings, dividend yield, book value, and the price of the prior sales. As to earnings, he computed, from the Company's audited statements for the years 1950-54, without adjustment, average annual earnings of $1.68. Using the comparative method of calculating price-earnings ratios of listed companies in the same or similar business and then correlating such results to Heekin, he selected 11 leading corporations in the container industry (only two of which, American Can and Continental Can, were can companies), and computed their average price-

---

[1] *Book value* = $33.20, less 50%........................................... $16.60
*Earnings* = Average 3 years = 1.77: price to earnings ratio = 6:1 =
    $10.62. Weighted to two factors..................... 21.24
*Dividends* = To give yield of 7% at rate of 50¢ per annum, would
    have to sell at..................................... 7.14
*Prior Sales* ............................................... 7.50

Total all factors......................................... 52.48
Divided by 5 to obtain weighted average............... 52.48 ÷ 5 = $10.50
Less 25% for lack of marketability.............................. 2.62

    7.88

earnings ratio over the similar 5-year period at 10 to 1, with 1954 alone producing a ratio of 11.6 to 1 because of the rise in prices of container industry stocks in that year.[2] However, he capitalized Heekin's 5-year average earnings of $1.68 at an earnings multiple of only eight times which he considered appropriate for a "marginal" company like Heekin. Since this produced a value of $13.44 based only on earnings, as of December 31, 1954, due to his using the figures for the full year 1954, he adjusted the figure to August 3, 1954, the first gift date, by reducing the figure by 14.1 percent, a figure derived by calculating the general rise in a relatively large group of certain other industry stocks between August 3 and December 31. Thus, on the basis of earnings alone, he calculated a value of $11.55 as of August 3.

As to dividends, this witness then calculated Heekin's average for the 5 years ended December 31, 1954, at 35 cents per share and capitalized that figure at 6 percent, which he considered to be appropriate in Heekin's case in view of the 5-year average dividend yield of 5.1 percent for the 11 leading companies in the container industry which he used as comparatives, and the even higher returns, on a 5-year average basis, afforded by general groups of leading industrials during that period. Thus, on the basis of a 6 percent dividend yield alone, he calculated a value of $5.83.

Using as factors the value figures derived as described on the bases of price earnings ($11.55) and dividend yield ($5.83) ratios, together with a book value figure of $33.23 as of December 31, 1954, and a $7.50 figure as the price of the prior sales, the witness then weighted these four factor figures, giving the earnings and dividend factors 40

percent each (i. e. each figure multiplied by 4), and the book value and prior sales figure 10 percent each (i. e. each figure multiplied by 1). This total figure was then reduced by 15 percent to reflect the stock's lack of marketability (which was equated to the underwriting cost of floating 30,000 shares) which, after dividing by the weight factor (10), gave the market price as of August 3 as $9.37,[3] which he rounded out to $9.50.

Using the same criteria and method, the witness valued the 40,002 shares given on October 25, 1954, at the slightly higher price of $9.65, the price of listed stocks having generally risen between the two dates.

The taxpayers' third expert, a senior officer in a firm specializing in valuing the stocks of closely held corporations, came out with the still higher valuation of $11.41 per share on August 3, in blocks of 10,000 ($11.76 in a block of 30,000 shares). For the shares given on October 25, however, his value was only $9.40 per share in blocks of 13,334 shares ($9.47 in a block of 40,002 shares).

This witness also used the technique of selecting comparable companies traded on a national exchange, ascertaining, by a very comprehensive study, the relationship between their market prices and their earnings, "earnings paid out," and return on invested capital (to which he added long-term debt), and then correlating the data to Heekin. Unlike the other two experts, he did not accept the exact figures of the audited statements of annual earnings, but studied them with a view to detecting and eliminating abnormal and nonrecurring items of loss or profit in order to obtain a better picture of the Company's normal operation and of what an investor, therefore, might reasonably conclude the Company's future performance would be. With such adjustments and eliminations, he thus recast the Com-

---

[2] He noted that this 10-to-1 ratio was higher than the Dow-Jones average of 9.9 for 30 industrials, the Standard & Poor average of 9.3 for 50 industrials, and the Moody average of 9.7 for 125 industrials for the same 5-year period.

|  | Weight | Total |
|---|---|---|
| [3] Price earnings ratio..................................... $11.55 | 4 | $46.20 |
| Dividend—35¢ capitalized at 6%.......................... 5.83 | 4 | 23.32 |
| Stock sales ............................................. 7.50 | 1 | 7.50 |
| Book value ............................................. 33.23 | 1 | 33.23 |
|  |  | 110.25 |
| Less 15%—amount for nonmarketability (flotation cost)... ..... | ....... | 16.51 |
|  |  | 93.74 |
| Divided by factor 10.................................. ..... | ....... | 9.37 |

pany's earnings for the years 1949-1953. He selected eight companies in both the can and glass container fields to use as comparatives.

In calculating Heekin's earnings, the witness used a 5-year average, as adjusted. One of the adjustments was to the Company's abnormal profits in 1951 as a result of the Korean war, which he eliminated and reduced to more normal levels. Another was to eliminate, as abnormal and nonrecurring, rather large losses the Company suffered in 1950, 1951 and 1952 as a result of the operations of a subsidiary which was liquidated. By applying a price-earnings ratio of 11.82, as derived from the comparative companies, he determined a value of the Heekin stock on August 3, based only on earnings, of $13.78 per share; a value based on earnings paid out (in which he included not ony dividends but also interest on long-term debt) on the capital invested in the business of $9.59 per share; and a value based on invested capital of $31.34 per share. To these three determinants of value, he added the fourth factor of $7.50 derived from the prior sales price. He too then weighted these figures, assigning a weight of 33⅓ percent each to the values based on earnings and earnings-paid-out, and 16⅔ percent each to the values based on invested capital and the prior stock sales. This gave a total weighted value of $14.26. He then too applied a 20-percent reduction for lack of marketability, which he also equated with flotation costs for blocks of 10,000 shares, resulting in the net figure of $11.41 as of August 3.[4]

The same technique produced a figure of $9.40 per share as of October 25, 1954, in blocks of 13,334 shares.[5] This lower valuation is attributable to the drop in the market prices of the comparative companies between August 3 and October 25, 1954. One of the comparatives (Pacific Can Company) which had been used for the August 3 valuation

was dropped since it enjoyed a rather atypical sharp rise after such date due to a proposed merger.

Various major criticisms can fairly be made of these three appraisals offered by plaintiffs. First, they all give undue weight as a factor to the $7.50 price of the prior stock sales. Almost all of these sales occurred in the relatively remote period of 1951 and early 1952. Only one small transaction occurred in each of the more recent years of 1953 and 1954. Such isolated sales of closely held corporations in a restricted market offer little guide to true value. *Wood, Adm. v. United States*, 89 Ct. Cl. 442; *First Trust Co. v. United States*, [59-1 USTC ¶ 11,843] 3 Am. Fed. Tax R. 2d 1726 (D. C. W. D. Mo.); *Drayton Cochran v. Commissioner*, 7 CCH Tax Ct. Mem. 325; *Schnorbach v. Kavanagh*, [52-1 USTC ¶ 10,836] 102 F. Supp. 828 (D. C. W. D. Mich.). In an evaluation issue, this court recently even gave little weight to the sale of shares on a stock exchange when the amount sold was "relatively insignificant." *American Steel Foundries v. United States*, Ct. Cl. No. 197-54, decided April 7, 1961 (slip opinion, p. 4). To the same effect is *Heiner v. Crosby*, [1 USTC ¶ 276] 24 F. 2d 191 (C. C. A. 3d) in which the court rejected stock exchange sales as being determinative and upheld the resort to "evidence of intrinsic value" (p. 194). Furthermore, the $7.50 price of the 1951 and 1952 sales evolved in early 1951 during a period when the Company was experiencing rather severe financial difficulties due to an unfortunate experience with a subsidiary which caused a loss of around $1,000,000, and when, consequently, the Company found itself in a depleted working capital position and was paying no dividends. Further, there is no indication that the $7.50 sales price evolved as a result of the usual factors taken into

---

[4] Value based on earnings—13.78 @ 33⅓%........................................................ $ 4.59
Value based on earnings paid out—9.59 @ 33⅓%................................................ 3.20
Value based on invested capital—31.34 @ 16⅔%................................................ 5.22
Value based on stock sales—7.50 @ 16⅔%.................................................... 1.25

100% ............................................................................................ 14.26
Less 20% for lack of marketability (flotation cost in blocks of 10,000 shares).... 2.85

Net value ...................................................................................... 11.41
Less 17.5% reduction if in a block of 30,000 shares......................... 11.76
[5] $9.47 per share in a block of 40,002 shares.

consideration by informed sellers and buyers dealing at arm's length. Fair market value presupposes not only hypothetical willing buyers and sellers, but buyers and sellers who are informed and have "adequate knowledge of the material facts affecting the value." *Robertson v. Routzahn,* [35-1 USTC ¶ 9124] 75 F. 2d 537, 539 (C. C. A. 6th); Paul, *Studies in Federal Taxation* (1937), pp. 193-4. The sales were all made at a prearranged price to Heekin employees and family friends. The artificiality of the price is indicated by its being the same in 1951, 1952, 1953 and 1954, despite the varying fortunes of the Company during these years and with the price failing to reflect, as would normally be expected, such differences in any way.

Secondly, in using the Company's full 1954 financial data, and then working back from December 31, 1954, to the respective gift dates, data were being used which would not have been available to a prospective purchaser as of the gift dates. "The valuation of the stock must be made as of the relevant dates without regard to events occurring subsequent to the crucial dates." *Bader v. United States, supra,* at p. 840. Furthermore, in the working-back procedure, general market data were used although it is evident that the stocks of a particular industry may at times run counter to the general trend. This was actually the situation here. Although the market generally advanced after August 3, 1954, container industry stocks did not.

Thirdly, the converse situation applies with respect to the data used by the third expert. His financial data only went to December 31, 1953, since the Company's last annual report prior to the gift dates was issued for the year 1953. But the Company also issued quarterly interim financial statements, and by the second gift date, the results of three-quarters of 1954 operations were available. In evaluating a stock, it is essential to obtain as recent data as is possible, as section 4 of the Revenue Ruling makes plain. Naturally, an investor would be more interested in how a corporation is currently performing then what it did last year or in even more remote periods. Although the use of interim reports reflecting only a part of a year's performance may not be satisfactory in a seasonal operation such

as canning, it is possible here to obtain a full year's operation ending on either June 30 or September 30, 1954, which would bring the financial data up closer to the valuation dates.

Fourth, it is accepted valuation practice, in ascertaining a company's past earnings, to attempt to detect abnormal or nonrecurring items and to make appropriate eliminations or adjustments. As shown, only the plaintiffs' expert who came out with the highest August 3 valuation attempted to do this by adjusting the excessive Korean war earnings and by eliminating the unusual losses suffered in 1950, 1951 and 1952 arising from the operations of a financing subsidiary (Canners Exchange, Inc.) that had been liquidated in 1952. The reason this is important is that past earnings are significant only insofar as they reasonably forecast future earnings. The only sound basis upon which to ground such a forecast is the company's normal operation, which requires the elimination or adjustment of abnormal items which will not recur. *Plaut v. Smith,* [49-1 USTC ¶ 9145] 82 F. Supp. 42 (D. C. Conn.), *aff'd, sub nom. Plaut v. Munford,* [51-1 USTC ¶ 9254] 188 F. 2d 543 (Ct. App. 2d Cir.). In *American Steel Foundries v. United States, supra,* the court similarly viewed the "earning prospects" of the company whose stock was being evaluated in light of its past earnings "as constructed by the accountants, eliminating or adjusting losses due to strikes or other nonrecurring events." And the court in *White & Wells Co. v. Commissioner,* 50 F. 2d 120 (C. C. A. 2d), also held that: "* * * past earnings * * * should be such as fairly reflect the probable future earnings" and that to this end "abnormal years" may even be entirely disregarded. The Revenue Ruling (sec. 4.02(d)) specifically points out the necessity of separating "recurrent from nonrecurrent items of income and expense."

Fifth, in deriving a past earnings figure which could be used as a reasonable basis of forecasting future earnings, none of plaintiffs' experts gave any consideration to the trend of such past earnings. They simply used the earnings of prior years and averaged them. But such averages may be deceiving. Two corporations with 5-year earnings going from the past to the present represented by the figures in one case of 5, 4, 3, 2, and 1, and in the other by the same figures of 1, 2, 3, 4, and 5, will have the same 5-year averages, but investors will quite naturally prefer the stock of the latter whose earnings are consistently moving upward. The Revenue Ruling specifically recognizes this in providing (sec. 4.02(d)) that: "Prior earnings records usually are the most reliable guide as to the future expectancy, but resort to arbitrary five-or-ten-year averages without regard to current trends or future prospects will not produce a realistic valuation. If, for instance, a record of progressively increasing or decreasing net income is found, then greater weight may be accorded the most recent years' profits in estimating earning power."

And further, since the most recent years' earnings are to be accorded the greatest weight, care must be taken to make certain that the earnings figures for such years are realistically set forth. For instance, in Heekin's case, profits for 1952-54 were understated because a noncontributory retirement plan for hourly employees was established in 1951 for which the costs attributable to 1950 and 1951 were borne in the later years of 1952-54. Similarly, 1954 profits were further understated because they reflected (1) a renegotiation refund arising out of excess profits made in 1951, and (2) they were subjected to a charge of $174,203.54 ($83,617.70 after taxes) as a result of a deduction from 1954 profits only of certain expenses attributable to both 1954 and 1955. This abnormal doubling up of 2 years' expenses in one year was permitted by a change in the tax laws which became effective in 1954 (and which was later revoked retroactively) which allowed taxpayers such as Heekin to change their methods of accounting so as to effect the accrual in 1954 of these 1955 expenses. If proper adjustments are made in Heekin's 1954 statements for these items, the earnings for the 1954 period prior to the gift dates would be realistically increased and given due weight insofar as earning trends are concerned.

None of plaintiffs' experts made any of these adjustments in connection with a trend study or otherwise.

Sixth, it is generally conceded that, as stated by the Revenue Ruling, in evaluating stocks of manufacturing corporations such as Heekin, earnings are the most important

factor to be considered. *Badar v. United States, supra.* Yet only one of plaintiffs' experts, who assigned double value to this factor, gave it such weight. As shown, the other two assigned the dividend factor equal weight. Some investors may indeed depend upon dividends. In their own investment programs, they may therefore stress yield and even compare common stocks with bonds or other forms of investment to obtain the greatest yields. However others, for various reasons, may care little about dividends and may invest in common stocks for the primary purpose of seeking capital appreciation. All investors, however, are primarily concerned with earnings, which are normally a prerequisite to dividends. In addition, the declaration of dividends is sometimes simply a matter of the policy of a particular company. It may bear no relationship to dividend-paying capacity. Many investors actually prefer companies paying little or no dividends and which reinvest their earnings, for that may be the key to future growth and capital appreciation.

And further, in capitalizing the dividend at 6 and 7 percent, as did two of the experts, rates of return were used which well exceeded those being paid at the time by comparable container company stocks. And still further, one of the experts used a 35-cent dividend rate as the basis for his capitalization because that was the average paid for the 5 years ended December 31, 1954. However, it seems clear that an annual dividend rate of 50 cents a share would be the proper rate to capitalize since that was the dividend paid by Heekin every year since 1945 except for the year 1950 and the first half of 1951 when, as shown, dividends were temporarily suspended. By the end of 1951 the Company had recovered from the situation causing the suspension and the normal dividend (quarterly payments of 12½ cents per share) was then resumed. By August and October 1954, Heekin's demonstrated earning capability and financial position were such that there was little doubt it would at least continue its 50-cent annual dividend, which represented only about 25 percent of its current earnings per share. To dip back into this 1950-51 atypical period to compute an "average" of dividends paid for the past 5 years is unrealistic.

Finally, the record indicates that all three experts took too great a discount for lack of marketability. Defendant disputes the propriety of taking this factor into consideration at all. It seems clear, however, that an unlisted closely held stock of a corporation such as Heekin, in which trading is infrequent and which therefore lacks marketability, is less attractive than a similar stock which is listed on an exchange and has ready access to the investing public. This factor would naturally affect the market value of the stock. This is not to say that the market value of any unlisted stock in which trading is infrequent would automatically be reduced by a lack of marketability factor. The stock of a well-known leader in its field with a preeminent reputation might not be at all affected by such a consideration, as was the situation with Ford Motor Company stock before it was listed. *Couzens v. Commissioner,* [CCH Dec. 3931] 11 B. T. A. 1040. But the stock of a less well-known company like Heekin which is a comparatively small factor in its industry is obviously in a different position. In such a situation, a consideration of this factor is appropriate, especially where, as here, only a minority interest is involved. *Bader v. United States, supra; Baltimore National Bank v. United States,* [56-1 USTC ¶ 11,576] 136 F. Supp. 642 (D. C. Md.); *Schnorbach v. Kavanagh, supra; Cochran v. Commissioner, supra; First Trust Co. v. United States, supra.* But see *Couzens v. Commissioner, supra; Estate of Katharine H. Daily v. Commissioner,* 6 CCH Tax Ct. Mem. 114.

Defendant concedes that if such a factor is appropriate in these cases, a reasonable method of determining the diminution in value attributable to lack of marketability is to determine how much it would cost to create marketability for the block of stock in question. This was the method used by the court in *First Trust Co. v. United States, supra.* The record shows that for a company of Heekin's size, and for blocks of 30,000 and 40,000 shares, which would appear to be the appropriate considerations, flotation costs would amount to about 12.17 percent of the gross sales prices. However, as shown, the discounts taken by plaintiffs' experts for this factor ranged from 15 to 25 percent.

For all the above reasons, the opinions of plaintiffs' experts are not wholly acceptable.

Defendant produced one expert, an employee of a recognized appraisal company. His primary work over may years was the valuation of intangibles, including closely held stock. His opinion was that the value of the Heekin stock in question on August 3 and October 25, 1954, was $16 and $15.25 per share, respectively. This witness also used the comparative appraisal method, considering a group of stock in the can and glass container industries. As part of a very comprehensive study, he selected eight container companies, six engaged in can production and two in glass container production, glass container enterprises being similar to those engaged in can production. He considered net assets as a key factor in the determination of a stock price, and one which keeps a stock price from declining to zero when earnings become zero or even when losses are suffered and when a price-to-earnings ratio would therefore become meaningless. He therefore developed for the comparative companies percentage ratios of profits and dividends to net worth as well as market value to net worth. In developing figures for the profits and dividends of the comparative companies for the past 5 years, he gave weight to the trends thereof. He then developed Heekin's profits over the period 1950 through September 1954, making adjustments for the retirement plan costs, the losses from subsidiaries, the renegotiation refund, and the abnormal 1951 profits, in order to reflect the more nearly normal operations over the period. Adjusted profits were developed for the 12-month periods ending June 30 and September 30, 1954. Before correlating the percentages developed for the comparative companies to Heekin, however, he concluded that only two of such companies, United Can and Glass Company and Crown Cork & Seal Company, Inc., could be considered conformable to Heekin. The others, including the giants of their industries, such as American Can, Continental Can, and Owens Illinois Glass Company which, because of acquisitions, diversification, premium investment quality position, and mere size, were not considered fairly comparable, were eliminated. Correlating the data developed with respect to such two companies, he concluded that, as of August 3, Heekin would be worth 59.5 percent of net worth, or $19.72 per share, a stock exchange equivalent of 19¾ per share. The similar method produced $18.78 per share as the value as of October 25, 1954, or a trading equivalent of 18¾.

This witness too felt that the correlation process resulted in comparing Heekin with seasoned listed stocks enjoying marketability, and that an adjustment should be made for the closely held nature of the Heekin stock with its resultant lack of marketability, especially where only a minority interest was involved. Similarly equating this adjustment to deductions a seller would experience through floating the shares through an underwriter, which he calculated to be almost 20 percent, resulted in net valuations of 16 and 15¼ as of August 3 and October 25, 1954, respectively. Since these values approximate Heekin's current assets (including inventories) less all of its liabilities, without giving any value at all to any of its plants, equipment, or other noncurrent assets, he concluded they were extremely conservative. Employing the common tests of price-to-earnings ratio and yield on the basis of the current 50-cent dividend, these values would result in a price-to-earnings ratio of 7.24:1 as of August 3, based on $2.21 adjusted net profit per share for the 12 months ending June 30, as well as a 3.13 percent dividend yield, and a ratio of 8.29:1 as of October 25, based on $1.84 adjusted net profit per share for the 12 months ending September 30, as well as a 3.28 percent dividend yield.

This witness' study has certain meritorious features. It is based on justifiable adjustments in Heekin's earnings records to eliminate abnormal and nonrecurring items (although he made no adjustment for the 1954 doubling up of certain expenses). It considers earnings trend. It disregards the prior $7.50 sales prices as a major factor. And in employing the Company's financial data going up to June 30 and September 30, 1954, it is based on its most recent performance. However, it has certain weaknesses

too, the principal one being the limitation of the comparative companies to two, one of which, Crown Cork & Seal, leaves much to be desired as a comparative because its principal business is the manufacture of bottle caps and bottling machinery, an entirely different business. Only 40 percent of its business is in can production. On the basis of size too there are great differences. At that time, Crown, including its foreign subsidiaries, was doing about $115,000,000 worth of business as against Heekin's $17,000,000. And the other comparative, United Can and Glass, presents the complication that it declared periodic stock dividends to which the witness gave no consideration, although it seems that some element of value should fairly be attributed to them.[*] Although no two companies are ever exactly alike, it being rare to have such almost ideal comparatives as were present in *Cochran v. Commissioner, supra,* so that absolute comparative perfection can seldom be achieved, nevertheless the comparative appraisal method is a sound and well-accepted technique. In employing it, however, every effort should be made to select as broad a base of comparative companies as is reasonably possible, as well as to give full consideration to every possible factor in order to make the comparison more meaningful.

Further, in compiling Heekin's financial data for correlation purposes, this witness used Heekin's average dividends for the 4½ years preceding the valuation dates, thus including the atypical period when no dividends were paid.

Defendant, considering its own expert's valuations to be unduly conservative, and disagreeing as a matter of law with any deduction for lack of marketability (and in any event with the amount deducted by its expert for such factor), now offers valuations on what it claims to be a more realistic basis. It also adjusts and redistributes Heekin's profits, including the "doubling up" expenses in 1954, the renegotiation re-

---

[*] "In theory, of course, the additional stock certificate gives him [the stockholder] nothing that he would not own without it • • •. But in actuality the payment of periodic stock dividends produces important advantages. Among them are the following: • • • 4. Issues paying periodic stock dividends enjoy a higher market value than similar common stocks not paying such dividends." Graham & Dodd, *Security Analysis, Principles and Technique* (3d ed. 1951) pp. 444-5.

fund, and the retirement plan. As comparatives, it uses for the purpose of developing a price-earnings ratio 11 can and glass container manufacturing companies, including American Can and Continental Can (although it concedes that with respect to the stock of such companies in this field, the investing public affords "some extra value coincident with size"), as well as Crown Cork & Seal and United Can. The dividend yield of seven comparative companies, based on their 1954 dividend payments, was 3.77 percent. Defendant too gives no cognizance to United Can's stock dividends, although it concedes that "stock dividends have some effect on market value." On Heekin's 50-cent dividend, the market price of Heekin stock would be $13.33, based solely on a 3.75 (the figure used by defendant) percent dividend yield.

Defendant then computes representative earnings for Heekin as $1.89 per share, based on 1953 and 1954 adjusted earnings. The average price to current earnings ratio of the 11 comparative companies in 1954 was 13 to 1. On this formula, Heekin's stock would sell for $24.57 per share if earnings were the sole factor. However, defendant reduces this figure to $22.50 for the purpose in question.

On the basis of the book value of Heekin stock being $33.15 as of June 30, 1954, and comparing the market prices of various alleged comparable companies to their book value (i. e., the stocks of 11 unidentified comparatives used by the Commissioner of Internal Revenue in making his valuation sold for 1.4 times book value), defendant concludes that Heekin stock would not sell for less than $33 per share.

The three factors of earnings, dividend yield, and book value are then weighted, earnings, considering their recognized importance for valuation purposes and the upward trend thereof, being assigned 50 percent weight, and dividend yield and book value receiving 30 percent and 20 percent respectively. On this basis, defendant arrives at a fair market value figure of $21.85 as of August 3, 1954.[1]

Since there was a slight drop in the market price of can manufacturing stocks between August 3 and October 25, 1954, defendant concludes the fair market value on the latter date would be about 50 cents less per share, or $21.35.

Thus, defendant now seeks a fair market value determination as of the gift dates of $21.85 and $21.35 respectively, in lieu of the $24 value fixed by the Commissioner of Internal Revenue.[2]

In its selection of the three basic factors to be considered in determining fair market value, the weights to be assigned to these factors, the earnings adjustments, and the use of 50 cents per annum as the proper dividend basis, this estimate has merit. However, the selection of such companies as American Can and Continental Can as comparatives—companies held in esteem in the investment world—will obviously give an unduly high result. It simply is not fair to compare Heekin with such companies and to adopt their market ratios for application to Heekin's stock. Furthermore, defendant's use of the comparatives is confusing. The employment of different comparatives for different purposes is unorthodox. When the comparative appraisal method is employed the comparatives should be clearly identified and consistently used

---

[1] Earnings ............... $22.50 × .5 = $11.25
   Dividend yield ......... 13.33 × .3 =  4.00
   Book value ............. 33.00 × .2 =  6.60
                                        ———————
                                         $21.85

[2] This $24 value resulted from a study by the Commissioner of 11 comparatives. Their price to book value ratio was 1.4; price to average earnings, 14.3; price to current earnings, 13; and price to current dividends, 31.1.

Applying these ratios to Heekin, 1.4 times book value of $33.23 as of December 31, 1954, equals $46.52 per share. Average earnings for a 5-year period of $1.68 per share times 14.3 equals $24.02 per share. Current earnings times

13 equals $17.16 a share. Price to current dividend equals $15.55 per share.

In addition, in 1954 National Can purchased Pacific Can and the Commissioner analyzed the sale price for comparative purposes. The sales price came to 12.5 times Pacific's earnings. Application of that ratio to Heekin's 1953 earnings would price Heekin's stock at $24.38 per share. Pacific's price also represented 17 times its average 1949-1953 earnings. Application of such ratio to Heekin would price its stock at $28.39 per share. Further, Pacific's price bore a ratio of 1.6 to book value. Application of such ratio to Heekin's stock would price it at $53.17 per share.

for all purposes. And the refusal to make any allowance for lack of marketability contributes further to the unrealistic nature of defendant's fair market value estimate.

To summarize, Heekin's stock has been valued as of August 3 and October 25, 1954, in blocks of 30,000 and 40,002 shares respectively, as follows: $10, originally, by two donors and the executor of the third; $7.50, in amended returns; $7.88 by one expert of plaintiffs (upon which valuation plaintiffs now stand); $9.50 and $9.65 respectively by plaintiffs' second expert; $11.76 and $9.47 respectively by plaintiffs' third expert; $16 and $15.25 respectively by defendant's expert; $21.85 and $21.35 respectively by defendant in these proceedings; and $24 by the Commissioner of Internal Revenue.

The proper use of the comparative appraisal method, applying the principles already indicated, should provide a reasonably satisfactory valuation guide in these cases.* In its application, it would under all the circumstances herein involved appear appropriate to select the three factors of (1) earnings, (2) dividends and dividend-paying capacity, and (3) book value, as being the important and significant ones to apply. *First Trust Co. v. United States, supra; Cochran v. Commissioner, supra; Bader v. United States, supra.*

As to earnings, an examination of them for the periods from 1950 to June 30 and September 30, 1954, which are the most recent periods in relation to the gift dates, would be most representative. For this purpose, the annual profit and loss statements, plus the Company's interim balance sheets, from which can be derived with reasonable accuracy the Company's earnings for the 12-month periods ending June 30 and September 30, 1954 (thus eliminating distortions due to seasonal factors), are the starting points. As stated, it would then be proper to make such adjustments therein as would be necessary to eliminate abnormal and nonrecurring items and to redistribute items of expense to their proper periods. In these cases, this normalizing process would require (a) the elimination from the years 1950 to 1952 of the abnormal, nonrecurring losses incident to its financing subsidiary, which had been completely liquidated by 1952; (b) the elimination of the abnormally large 1951 profits due to the Korean war; (c) the redistribution of the expenses attributable to the establishment subsequent to 1951 of a retirement plan, which expenses, although borne in later years, were also applicable to 1950 and 1951, thereby overstating 1950 and 1951 profits and similarly depressing 1953 and 1954 profits; (d) the shift from 1954 to 1951 of a renegotiation refund paid with respect to excessive 1951 profits; (e) the elimination from 1954 of the abnormally large charge relating to the accrual in 1954 of certain expenses actually attributable to 1955, as hereinabove explained, and which resulted in the doubling up of 2 years of such expenses in 1954, as permitted by a then recent change in the tax laws. The method adopted in making these adjustments, and the adjusted profit figures resulting therefrom, are set forth in detail in finding 47.

As indicated, it would then be appropriate to give due consideration and weight to the trend of such earnings. Greater weight should fairly be given to the most recent years and periods. The method adopted in finding 48 of assigning greater weight to the later periods is a reasonably accurate one, and indicates that as of June 30 and September 30, 1954, Heekin's reasonably expected annual earnings per share would be $1.93 and $1.79, based on average annual earnings of $491,460.86 and $454,492.82, respectively.

As to dividends and dividend-paying capacity, it has already been indicated that as of the gift dates, it could reasonably be expected that Heekin would continue to

---

* In the related estate tax area, § 2031(b) of the Internal Revenue Code of 1954 specifically provides that: "In the case of stock and securities of a corporation the value of which, by reason of their not being listed on an exchange and by reason of the absence of sales thereof, cannot be determined with reference to bid and asked prices or with reference to sales prices, the value thereof shall be determined by taking into consideration, in addition to all other factors, the value of stock or securities of corporations engaged in the same or a similar line of business which are listed on an exchange." 26 U. S. C. (1958 Ed.) § 2031(b).

pay in the foreseeable future its usual 50-cent annual dividend. Indeed, on its aforesaid earnings basis, this would appear to be a conservative distribution. However, while the declaration by the board of directors of a small increase might have been considered a possibility—a 10-cent increase would, for instance, result in a corporate outlay of only $25,412 on the 254,125 shares outstanding—it seems clear, nevertheless, that no substantially larger payment, at least for some time to come, could reasonably have been anticipated. Heekin's equipment was, as shown, not modern and the Company was in need of relatively large sums for equipment and plant modernization if it hoped to continue to be a competitive factor in the industry. For such a program, the Company would have to depend almost entirely on retained earnings. A further limitation on the Company's dividend-paying capacity was its repayment obligations on its long-term debt. Annual installments on principal of $150,000 had to be made through 1965, plus 20 percent of the net income (less $150,000) for the preceding year.

As to book value, the Company's balance sheets showed the book value per share to be, conservatively, $33.15 and $33.54 as of June 30 and September 30, 1954, respectively (findings 51-53). These statements also showed the Company to be in a current sound financial condition. As of June 30, 1954, current assets alone, amounting to almost $8,700,000, far exceeded its total liabilities of approximately $4,700,000, including its long-term debt. Its ratio of current assets to current liabilities was 3.17 to 1.

With the above basic data applicable to Heekin, it is then appropriate to select as closely comparable companies as is possible whose stocks are actively traded on an exchange, and to ascertain what ratios their market prices bear to their earnings, dividends, and book values. The application of such ratios to Heekin would then give a reasonable approximation of what Heekin's stock would sell for if it too were actively traded on an exchange.

A study of all the numerous companies considered by the experts as proper comparatives indicates that five of them, i.e., Pacific Can Company, United Can and Glass Company, National Can Corporation, Brockway Glass Co., Inc., and Thatcher Glass Manufacturing Co., Inc., are, while by no means perfect comparables, certainly at least reasonably satisfactory for the purpose in question. The detailed reasons for their selection are set forth in finding 57. In size they all fall generally into Heekin's class, and the nature of their operations is also comparable. In addition, five companies give a sufficiently broad base. Such companies as American Can, Continental Can, and Crown Cork & Seal, for the reasons already indicated, are eliminated (finding 56).

After similarly computing the earnings, as adjusted, of the comparatives for the same periods as for Heekin (finding 58), and similarly weighting them to give effect to the trend factor (finding 59), the average ratio of their market prices to their adjusted earnings as of August 3 and October 25, 1954 (the "price-earnings" ratio), was 9.45 and 9.84 to 1, respectively (finding 62). Thus, on the basis only of earnings, Heekin's stock would similarly sell for $18.24 and $17.61 per share on such dates.

Similarly, the comparatives' dividend payments for the 12 months ending June 30 and September 30, 1954, after making some allowance for United's stock dividend, show an average percent yield of 3.50 and 3.56 respectively (finding 64). Thus, on the basis only of dividend yield, Heekin's stock would similarly sell for $14.29 and $14.05 per share on August 3 and October 25, 1954, respectively (finding 65).

As to book value, the average market prices of the comparatives were 83.96 and 86.39 percent, respectively, of the book values of their common stocks on said dates (finding 66). Thus, on the sole basis of the average relationship between such book values and market prices, Heekin's comparable market prices on said dates would be $27.83 and $28.98 (finding 67).

However, since the three factors of earnings, dividends, and book value are not entitled to equal weight, it becomes necessary to consider their relative importance in the case of a company such as Heekin. In this connection, plaintiffs' contention that in these cases no factor is to be considered of greater importance than dividend yield and that no investor would reasonably be expected to buy Heekin stock at a price

which would afford a yield of less than 7 percent, cannot be accepted, not only for the reasons set forth above concerning the general relative importance of this factor but also because it is not supported by the specific data relating to the container industry as shown by the comparatives' yields. Investors were purchasing the stocks of comparable container companies which were yielding much less return than 7 percent. As shown, the average dividend yield of the five comparative companies was only around 3½ percent. Investors were purchasing Pacific Can at a price which afforded a yield of less than 3 percent. Indeed, they were purchasing National Can at more than $13 a share although it was paying no dividend at all.

Considering all the circumstances, it would appear appropriate to accept defendant's proposals in this respect and to consider earnings as entitled to 50 percent of the contribution to total value, and to give dividend yield (which in this case would appear to be substantially equivalent to dividend-paying capacity) 30 percent, and book value 20 percent, thereof. Cf. *Bader v. United States, supra*, in which the court gave 50 percent weight to earnings, and divided the remaining 50 percent equally between the dividend yield and book value factors. Book value indicates how much of a company's net assets valued as a going concern stands behind each share of its stock and is therefore an important factor in valuing the shares. As defendant's expert pointed out, this is the factor that plays such a large part in giving a stock value during periods when earnings may vanish and dividends may be suspended. However, principally because book value is based upon valuing the assets as a going concern, which would not be realistic in the event of a liquidation of the corporation, a situation which a minority stockholder would be powerless to bring about in any event, and for the additional reasons set forth in finding 50, this factor is, in the case of a manufacturing company with a consistent earnings and dividend record, normally not given greater weight than the other two factors.

On the above percentage bases, the fair market value of Heekin's stock on August 3 and October 25, 1954, would be $18.98 and $18.83 respectively (finding 69).

These prices, however, assume active trading for Heekin's stock on an exchange, as was the situation with the comparatives. As shown, the closely held nature of, and the infrequent trading in, Heekin's stock resulted in a lack of marketability which would affect its market value. Equating the proper discount to be taken for this factor with the costs that would be involved in creating a market for the stock, a method which defendant concedes is reasonable, results in a deduction of approximately 12.17 percent for a company of Heekin's size and for blocks of 30,000 and 40,000 shares. On this basis, the fair market values of the Heekin stock as of August 3 and October 25, 1954, would be $16.67 and $16.54 respectively.

These are the values resulting largely from strictly formula and statistical applications. While such use of figures and formulas produces, of course, results which are of important significance, and may in certain instances be given conclusive weight, it is nevertheless recognized that determinations of fair market value can not be reduced to formula alone, but depend "upon all the relevant facts," including "the elements of common sense, informed judgment and reasonableness." Revenue Ruling, sec. 3.01. The question of fair market value of a stock "is ever one of fact and not of formula" and evidence which gives "life to [the] figures" is essential. *Estate of James Smith v. Commissioner*, 46 B. T. A. 337, 341-2. The selection of comparatives has been a particularly troublesome problem in these cases. National Can's erratic earnings record, even though adjustments are attempted to normalize its situation (findings 57-58), and its nonpayment of dividends (finding 64), certainly weaken its position as a comparative, and suggest the desirability of an adjustment in the final market value figures set forth above. Pacific Can's sharp rise in price after August 3, 1954, justifies a similar adjustment for the October 25, 1954, valuation. While the inclusion of the glass container manufacturers with their higher dividend yields tends to neutralize somewhat the National Can situation, an adjustment downward would, in fairness to plaintiffs, nevertheless guard against their being prejudiced by the aforementioned selections of comparatives. Furthermore, while the sales of Heekin

stock at $7.50 warrant, as hereinabove pointed out, only minimal consideration, the figures derived from the above formula give them no cognizance whatsoever.

Giving important weight to the figure of $16.67 produced by the application of the comparative appraisal method as applied herein, but viewing it in light of all the facts and circumstances involved in these cases, it is concluded that the fair market value of the 30,000 shares given on August 3, 1954, was $15.50 per share.

The market for stocks of the can and glass container manufacturing companies fell somewhat between August 3 and October 25, 1954, so that ordinarily on that basis as well as on the basis of Heekin's own financial and operating positions on October 25 as compared with August 3, a slightly lower value would be justified as of October 25 (although one of plaintiffs' experts felt that, insofar as Heekin stock is concerned, the same value should be applied to both dates, and another came out with a higher value for the second date). It seems clear, however, that the brightened prospects for increased business and profits resulting from the Company's decision in August 1954 to embark upon the beer can business and to satisfy further the demands of its largest customer for new products would, in Heekin's instance, tend to neutralize the market decline and to make its stock at least as valuable on October 25 as it had been on August 3. Accordingly, it is concluded that the fair market value of the 40,002 shares given on October 25, 1954, was also $15.50 per share.

A $15.50 valuation represents a price to adjusted earnings ratio on the gift dates of between 8 and 9 percent (somewhat less than the 9-10 percent average of the comparatives (finding 62)), a dividend yield of 3.23 percent (slightly less than the 3.5 percent average of the comparatives (finding 64)), and only 46 percent of book value (considerably less than the approximately 85 percent of the comparatives (finding 66)). On these bases, it is a figure that is fair to both sides.

Plaintiffs should consider that such a valuation prices the stock only at an amount representing the difference between current assets and total liabilities, including its long-term debt, as shown by its June 30, 1954, balance sheet. Thus, at such price,

the value of the stock would be represented in whole by current assets, with no consideration whatsoever given to plant, equipment, or any other assets. As such, it would appear to be a conservative price indeed. Despite the difficulties under which it is laboring in a highly competitive industry, Heekin was, as of the valuation dates, a profitable, dividend-paying company, in sound financial condition, in an industry in which demand was at record levels, and in which it was forging ahead with relatively large investments in new fields holding bright prospects. Only a disregard of these favorable factors would warrant any lower valuation.

On the other hand, defendant should consider that such a valuation would give an investor a dividend yield of less than 3.5 percent on his investment, with little prospect of any significant increase in the foreseeable future. The fact that the Company was, on the gift dates, a relatively small one competing, with a comparatively old plant, against the giants of the industry operating at high efficiency with the most modern equipment, makes unwarranted a valuation of this closely held stock representing only a minority interest on any significantly higher basis. For these reasons also the $15.50 valuation is considered to be fair and just to both plaintiffs and defendant.

On this valuation basis, plaintiffs are entitled to recover, the amount of the recovery to be determined in accordance with Rule 38(c).

*Estate of Woodbury G. Andrews, Deceased, Woodbury
H. Andrews, Executor, Petitioner v. Commissioner of
Internal Revenue, Respondent*

*Docket No. 12465-79. Filed November 29, 1982.*

*Franz P. Jevne III, Michael S. Frost,* and *George R. A.
Johnson,* for the petitioner.
*Jeffrey D. Lerner,* for the respondent.

### OPINION

WHITAKER, *Judge*: Respondent determined a deficiency of
$160,981.67 in the Federal estate tax of petitioner. The sole
issue for decision is the date-of-death fair market value of
shares of stock held by decedent in four closely held corporations. Since this case is largely factual, we have combined our
findings of fact with our opinion.

Some of the facts have been stipulated and are so found. The
parties have stipulated that Woodbury G. Andrews (hereinafter referred to as the decedent) was a resident of Excelsior,
Minn., when he died testate on May 16, 1975. It has been
further stipulated that Woodbury H. Andrews, a son of
decedent, was appointed executor of the estate of decedent and
resided in Minneapolis, Minn., when the petition in this case
was filed.

Among the assets listed in the estate tax return of decedent
were his interests in the following four closely held corporations: (1) 54 shares of W.F. & H.H. Andrews Co. (W.F. & H.H.),
(2) 100 shares of St. Anthony Holding Co. (St. Anthony), (3) 50
shares of Green Mountain Investment Co. (Green Mountain),
and (4) 63 shares of Andrews, Inc. Decedent owned approximately 20 percent of the total outstanding shares of each of
the four corporations at the time of his death,[1] with the
remainder being owned by his four siblings in approximately
equal proportions. The stock had been held by these five
individuals since their father died in 1945. Decedent worked

[1]The exact percentages held by decedent were 20.4 percent of Andrews, Inc., 21.6 percent
of W.F. & H.H., and 20 percent of the other two corporations.

with these corporations from approximately 1927 until his death in 1975. His two brothers have been involved with the corporations since the early 1930's. Together, decedent and his two brothers constituted the entire management of all four corporations; the two sisters did not actively participate in management. There is no evidence of any significant internal management disputes or family discord.

As of the date of death, W.F. & H.H. had been in business 73 years; St. Anthony, 71 years; Green Mountain, 66 years; and Andrews, Inc., 53 years. All four corporations have been involved primarily in the ownership, operation, and management of commercial real estate properties, although they also held some liquid assets such as stocks, bonds, and cash.[2] The real estate holdings included warehouses, apartment buildings, factories, offices, and retail stores in the Minneapolis - St. Paul metropolitan area. Many of the properties were in rundown urban areas, and most of the buildings were quite old, having been acquired during the early years of the corporations' operations. Most of the properties were leased to small tenants under leases for periods of less than 5 years.

To handle their management and maintenance responsibilities, the corporations together employed approximately 22 persons in addition to the three Andrews brothers. Fourteen persons were listed as employed and paid by Andrews, Inc.; two by Green Mountain; and three, each, by St. Anthony and W.F. & H.H. However, the record discloses that many of the employees assigned to Andrews, Inc., performed services for all the corporations, which were billed on a monthly basis for their allocable shares of employee payroll and related charges. The types of employees included janitors, parking lot attendants, night watchmen, office personnel, and maintenance workers, who handled plumbing, carpentry, painting, heating,

---

[2]Based on respondent's expert's appraisal of the assets of each corporation, W.F. & H.H. had 76.6 percent of its assets invested in real estate; Green Mountain had 80.9 percent; St. Anthony had 55.8 percent; and Andrews, Inc., had 66.4 percent as of the date of decedent's death. Additionally, most of the cash held by Andrews, Inc., was attributable to a condemnation award and fire insurance proceeds, which were to be invested in real property to avoid recognition under sec. 1033. These amounts, earmarked for the purchase of real estate, should be considered as invested in real estate for our purposes, and, after making this adjustment, Andrews, Inc., should be seen as having had 89.9 percent of its assets invested in real estate.

and other maintenance and repair work.

On its estate tax return, petitioner valued decedent's stock interest in Andrews, Inc., at $56,700; St. Anthony at $45,000; W.F. & H.H. at $12,690; and Green Mountain at $13,000. In his notice of deficiency, respondent determined that petitioner had significantly undervalued these stocks, and valued Andrews, Inc., at $517,608; St. Anthony at $287,400; W.F. & H.H. at $114,264; and Green Mountain at $93,650.

Fair market value has long been defined as the price at which property would change hands between a willing buyer and a willing seller, neither being under any compulsion to buy or to sell and both having reasonable knowledge of relevant facts. Sec. 20.2031–1(b), Estate Tax Regs.; *United States v. Cartwright*, 411 U.S. 546, 551 (1973). This is a question of fact, with the trier of fact having the duty to weigh all relevant evidence of value and to draw appropriate inferences. *Hamm v. Commissioner*, 325 F.2d 934, 938 (8th Cir. 1963), affg. a Memorandum Opinion of this Court.

In determining the value of unlisted stocks, actual arm's-length sales of such stock in the normal course of business within a reasonable time before or after the valuation date are the best criteria of market value. *Duncan Industries, Inc. v. Commissioner*, 73 T.C. 266, 276 (1979). However, the stock of these four corporations has never been publicly traded, and there is no evidence of any sales of stock in these corporations at any time near the date of decedent's death. In the absence of arm's-length sales, the value of closely held stock must be determined indirectly by weighing the corporation's net worth, prospective earning power, dividend-paying capacity, and other relevant factors. *Estate of Leyman v. Commissioner*, 40 T.C. 100, 119 (1963), remanded on other grounds 344 F.2d 763 (6th Cir. 1965); sec. 20.2031–2(f), Estate Tax Regs.[3] These

---

[3] Sec. 20.2031–2(f), Estate Tax Regs., provides:

(f) *Where selling prices or bid and asked prices are unavailable.* If the provisions of paragraphs (b), (c), and (d) of this section are inapplicable because actual sale prices and bona fide bid and asked prices are lacking, then the fair market value is to be determined by taking the following factors into consideration:

(1) In the case of corporate or other bonds, the soundness of the security, the interest yield, the date of maturity, and other relevant factors; and

(2) In the case of shares of stock, the company's net worth, prospective earning power and dividend-paying capacity, and other relevant factors.

factors cannot be applied with mathematical precision. Rather, the weight to be given to each factor must be tailored to account for the particular facts of each case. See *Messing v. Commissioner*, 48 T.C. 502, 512 (1967).

Both parties relied upon experts' valuations derived from analyses of intrinsic factors. However, because of fundamental differences in approach between respondent's and petitioner's experts, particularly with respect to the weight to be placed upon net asset value as opposed to earnings or dividend-paying capacity, the amounts arrived at in the valuations were extremely far apart. The following chart, which was used on the estate tax return, lists the different values arrived at by petitioner's primary expert, Sigurd Wendin; petitioner's second expert, Orville Lefko; and respondent's expert, Edward Bard:

|  | *Andrews, Inc.* | *St. Anthony* | *W.F. & H.H.* | *Green Mountain* |
|---|---|---|---|---|
| Mr. Wendin | $56,700 | $45,000 | $12,690 | $13,000 |
| Mr. Lefko | 55,755 | 46,500 | 12,204 | 12,250 |
| Mr. Bard | 570,843 | 260,000 | 113,832 | 97,800 |

Respondent's first witness, James M. McKenzie, performed an appraisal of the assets held by the corporations. He valued each real property using three commonly accepted approaches to valuation—comparable sales, replacement costs, and income-producing capacity. After correlating the values found under each of these approaches, he arrived at the following total values for the assets held by the corporations:

---

Some of the "other relevant factors" referred to in subparagraphs (1) and (2) of this paragraph are: the good will of the business; the economic outlook in the particular industry; the company's position in the industry and its management; the degree of control of the business represented by the block of stock to be valued; and the values of securities of corporations engaged in the same or similar lines of business which are listed on a stock exchange. However, the weight to be accorded such comparisons or any other evidentiary factors considered in the determination of a value depends upon the facts of each case. In addition to the relevant factors described above, consideration shall also be given to nonoperating assets, * * *

| | Andrews, Inc. | St. Anthony | W.F. & H.H. | Green Mountain |
|---|---|---|---|---|
| Real estate | $2,780,700 | $1,239,800 | $677,500 | $645,500 |
| Cash, stocks, and bonds | 1,405,024 | 808,230 | 56,700 | 151,682 |
| Miscellaneous assets | 121,313 | 174,105 | 149,388 | --- |
| Total | 4,307,037 | 2,222,135 | 883,588 | 797,182 |
| Liabilities | 116,493 | 2,667 | 696 | 515 |
| Net asset value | 4,190,544 | 2,219,468 | 882,892 | 796,667 |

Petitioner has not attacked Mr. McKenzie's valuations of the underlying assets. However, the executor has argued that in arriving at overall net asset value, adjustments should have been made to reflect costs that would have been incurred if the corporations had liquidated all their real estate properties and placed them on the market at one time. The adjustments sought by petitioner are for blockage, capital gains tax to the seller, real estate commissions, and real estate taxes and special assessments constituting a lien against the real estate. We disagree with this argument. Both parties have agreed here that there was no reasonable prospect of liquidation, and the evidence clearly supports this finding. When liquidation is only speculative, the valuation of assets should not take these costs into account because it is unlikely they will ever be incurred. See *Estate of Piper v. Commissioner*, 72 T.C. 1062, 1087 (1979); *Estate of Cruikshank v. Commissioner*, 9 T.C. 162, 165 (1947); *Estate of Huntington v. Commissioner*, 36 B.T.A. 698 (1937).[4]

Respondent's second expert, Edward Bard, a financial analyst employed by respondent, initially used three approaches to value the stock of each corporation: Earnings and dividend-paying capacity, linear regression analysis, and net asset valuation. The former two methods produced values far lower than valuation based on net asset values. For instance, the values he computed for Andrews, Inc., based upon capitaliza-

---

[4]See also *Estate of Thalheimer v. Commissioner*, T.C. Memo. 1974-203, affd. on this issue and remanded without published opinion 532 F.2d 751 (4th Cir. 1976); *Gallun v. Commissioner*, T.C. Memo. 1974-284.

tion of earnings and dividends ranged from $1.1 million to $1.5 million,[5] the value based on linear regression analysis was $1.6 million but the value based on net asset value was $4.1 million.[6] He concluded that the former two values should be disregarded because they were unrealistically low, even though his computations did show that the corporations' yields on investment had consistently been exceptionally low.[7] Thus, his starting point for valuing each of these corporations was the net asset values derived from Mr. McKenzie's appraisals. Because he saw the corporations involved here as holding passive items, he believed they were comparable to closed end mutual funds, which are also corporate entities holding investment properties. He found that shares of mutual funds generally traded at a 25-percent discount from the value of the assets held by such funds, and accordingly, applied a 25-percent discount to the net asset values of the corporations. To this amount, he then applied a lack of marketability discount, varying from 11.9 percent to 20.74 percent to reflect each corporation's costs of flotation if the stock were to be publicly offered.[8]

Respondent argues that Mr. Bard was correct in ignoring earnings and dividend-paying capacity because all four corporations should be classified as investment companies not involved in the active operation of a business. He believes that a willing buyer would recognize that the value of his investment would be in his right to share in the value of the corporations' underlying net assets, regardless of their low

---

[5]To arrive at these figures, Mr. Bard computed the price-earnings ratios of publicly owned real estate enterprises, primarily real estate investment trusts, that he considered comparable to the corporations involved here. The corporations selected as comparables had price-earnings ratios on a 3-year average of approximately 11 percent, price cash flow earnings of approximately 6.4 percent, and dividend income that averaged 9.6 percent. He applied these percentages to the earnings of Andrews, Inc., to arrive at an income valuation of $1,393,990 based on the latest 3-year average earnings; $1,134,214 based on the latest 3-year average cash flow earnings; and $1,452,073 based on dividend-paying capacity.

[6]All these values were prior to any discount for lack of control or marketability.

[7]Dividing net assets by net income for each corporation showed yields on investment of 3.1 percent for St. Anthony, 3.6 percent for Andrews, Inc., 3.5 percent for W.F. & H.H., and 4.1 percent for Green Mountain.

[8]At trial and on brief, respondent, in light of Rev. Rul. 81-253, 1981-2 C.B. 187, has taken the position, which we discuss later in this opinion, that neither of these discounts should be allowed.

earnings and dividend-paying capacity. Petitioner attacks respondent's characterization of these corporations as investment companies, stressing that the corporations employed 25 employees and actively performed real estate management and maintenance functions.[9] Characterizing these corporations as operating companies, petitioner believes greater weight should be placed on earnings and dividend-paying capacity than on net asset values.

We believe, however, the corporations here cannot be characterized for valuation purposes as solely investment companies or solely operating companies. The cases cited by respondent,[10] which involved corporations holding only cash, commercial paper, or marketable securities, are readily distinguishable on the ground that the corporations involved here were actively engaged in the real estate management business. But cases dealing with corporations owning factories and other industrial or commercial operations are also not directly on point.[11] Unlike many industrial companies, where the value of the manufacturing equipment and plant is tied to the nature of the manufacturing operation, here, the value of the underlying real estate will retain most of its inherent value even if the corporation is not efficient in securing a stream of rental income. It seems reasonable to assume, as we did in *Estate of Heckscher v. Commissioner*, 63 T.C. 485, 493 (1975), that a—

---

[9]As we found earlier, although employees other than the three Andrews brothers were assigned to only one corporation for bookkeeping purposes, many of them actively performed services for all the corporations.

[10]The following cases were cited by respondent: *Estate of Cruikshank v. Commissioner*, 9 T.C. 162 (1947); *Gallun v. Commissioner, supra; Estate of Thalheimer v. Commissioner, supra; Estate of Cotchett v. Commissioner*, T.C. Memo. 1974–31; and *Richardson v. Commissioner*, a Memorandum Opinion of this Court dated Nov. 30, 1943, affd. 151 F.2d 102 (2d Cir. 1945). *Estate of Lee v. Commissioner*, 69 T.C. 860 (1978), in which we used net asset values in arriving at the value of a close corporation that held primarily real estate is likewise distinguishable because the real estate was not rental property but rather undeveloped property that offered no immediate prospects for taxable income to the corporation.

[11]See *Waterman v. Commissioner*, T.C. Memo. 1961–225, in which we rejected both respondent's valuation based solely on net asset values and petitioner's valuation based solely on earning capacity as inappropriate for a corporation holding improved rental property; and *Estate of Tompkins v. Commissioner*, T.C. Memo. 1961–338, in which we rejected similar contentions with respect to a corporation holding unimproved real estate.

potential buyer would have to forego some current return on his investment in exchange for an interest in a net worth much more valuable than the price he pays for the stock, and the seller would have to be willing to part with an equity interest in the company for much less than its indicated value in return for something that would produce a greater yield on his investment. * * *

Furthermore, regardless of whether the corporation is seen as primarily an operating company, as opposed to an investment company, courts should not restrict consideration to only one approach to valuation, such as capitalization of earnings or net asset values. See *Hamm v. Commissioner*, 325 F.2d 934 (8th Cir. 1963), affg. a Memorandum Opinion of this Court; *Portland Manufacturing Co. v. Commissioner*, 56 T.C. 58, 80 (1971); *Estate of Schroeder v. Commissioner*, 13 T.C. 259 (1949); *Hooper v. Commissioner*, 41 B.T.A. 114 (1940).[12] Certainly, the degree to which the corporation is actively engaged in producing income rather than merely holding property for investment should influence the weight to be given to the values arrived at under the different approaches but it should not dictate the use of one approach to the exclusion of all others.

The regulations[13] call for all relevant factors to be examined and, in a case such as this, we believe values arrived at under all the accepted valuation methods should be considered. We therefore believe respondent's expert was incorrect to simply reject earnings and dividend-paying capacity valuations because they produced too low a result. Certainly, a prospective buyer would not so reject one particular type of valuation. A buyer of stock in these corporations would necessarily look to the earning capacity for part of his return on his investment. Nevertheless, this would not be the only factor that he would consider. Undoubtedly, he would also give substantial weight to each corporation's underlying net asset value even though

---

[12] See also *Estate of Dooly v. Commissioner*, T.C. Memo. 1972–164; *Lippman v. Commissioner*, T.C. Memo. 1965–73; and *Wallace v. United States*, an unpublished opinion (D. Mass. 1981, 49 AFTR 2d 82–1482, 82–1 USTC par. 13,442), in which the court stated:

"The 'willing buyer' and 'willing seller' * * * test the experts' advice, and the formulas the experts advance to bolster their advice, against common sense. The willing buyer and willing seller are not limited to choosing one formula or another among competing formulas advanced by experts. [49 AFTR 2d 82–1482.]"

[13] See sec. 20.2031–2(f), Estate Tax Regs.

he would have no ability to directly realize this value by forcing liquidation.

Respondent argues that there is a particular reason why only net asset values should be used in this case. Mr. McKenzie's determination of the values of the real estate properties held by the corporations was arrived at through a computational method that considered, among other factors, the projected earning capacity of the properties. Respondent contends that in valuing each corporation it is therefore appropriate to use only the underlying net asset value, which is the sum of the appraised real estate values plus the values of other assets held by the corporation, such as stocks and bonds, minus all the corporation's liabilities.[14] However, to do so would ignore the corporate entities. If the properties had been held directly by decedent, respondent would undoubtedly be correct, but here we are not faced with the question of finding a value for the properties themselves; rather, we must find the value of shares of the corporations that held the properties. The corporations are businesses, engaged in the maintenance and management of these real estate properties. Thus, some of the value attached to the corporations must be based upon the operating nature of the businesses, with attention paid to their earnings and dividend history, management, and prospects for growth.

We turn now to analyze petitioner's experts' valuations, which we also find to be markedly deficient, largely because of their adopting approaches that minimize the importance of the value of the underlying assets.

Petitioner's first expert, Sigurd Wendin, selected as comparables four large publicly traded real estate management corporations, although he recognized that there were differences in size, financing, number of employees, and types of activities carried on. Based on his analysis of these publicly traded corporations, he assigned price earnings multiples to

---

[14]Because the corporations followed a very conservative policy of avoiding substantial debt, St. Anthony, W.F. & H.H., and Green Mountain had virtually no liabilities, and the liabilities of Andrews, Inc., equaled only 2 percent of the value of its assets.

the corporations involved here of five for future earnings, four for current earnings, five for the average of the last 3 years' earnings, and seven for the average earnings for the period 1970 through 1973. These multiples were somewhat lower than those obtained from the comparable companies because of the difficulty in marketing nonpublicly traded shares. He then applied these multiples to net operating income during the applicable periods, and applied a minority discount for lack of marketability of 40 percent based on his overall experience with the amount of such discounts commonly allowed.

For dividend capitalization purposes, Mr. Wendin assumed a 10-percent rate, based upon the fact that corporate bond yields were around 9 percent to 11 percent. He believed bond yields were better comparables than the yield rate on stocks because the assets involved here were frozen and stock yields had been quite variable during this time period. He applied this 10-percent rate to the last year dividend and to his estimate of the future dividend that could be expected. Again, he discounted these amounts by 40 percent for lack of marketability.

Mr. Wendin also looked at the corporate balance sheets showing net assets and liabilities of the corporations. He did not have Mr. McKenzie's or any other appraisal of underlying assets so he looked at book values instead of net asset values. He reduced the book values to 80 percent based on the market-to-book-value ratio here found in analyzing his four "comparables."[15] To this he applied a 40-percent discount for lack of marketability.

In combining all of these factors to arrive at an overall valuation of each corporation, Mr. Wendin minimized the impact of the adjusted book value per share. He believed this approach was necessary because there were no plans to liquidate and because a minority stockholder would have had no ability to force liquidation. Listed below as an example are the weights given to each factor, the values per share, and the overall average value arrived at for Andrews, Inc., stock:

---

[15]Exactly how he arrived at this 80-percent figure is not clear since the ratios for three of the selected "comparables" were 51 percent, 79 percent, and 92 percent, and for the fourth "comparable" an astounding 3,007 percent.

| | Per share | Weight | Amount |
|---|---|---|---|
| Future dividend capitalization | 900.00 | 5 | $4,500.00 |
| Last year dividend capitalization | 770.76 | 4 | 3,083.04 |
| Future earnings capitalization | 1,167.00 | 3 | 3,501.00 |
| Last year earnings capitalization | 940.34 | 2 | 1,880.68 |
| Three-year average earnings capitalization | 963.57 | 1.5 | $1,445.36 |
| 1970–73 year average earnings capitalization | 998.07 | 1.5 | 1,497.11 |
| Book value | 2,345.11 | 1 | 2,345.11 |
| | | 18 | 18,252.30 |
| | | Average | 1,014.02 |

To this $1,014.02 value per share he applied an additional discount to reflect specific negative factors such as deterioration of areas, strategic location, rising inflation, taxes, future maintenance costs, and the ability to quickly adjust rentals. He ended up with an estimated value for Andrews, Inc., of $900 per share. The values for the other three companies were determined in equivalent manners. In no case was book value given more than a one-ninth weight in determining the current value.

We find Mr. Wendin's valuations to be seriously flawed because they did not take into account each corporation's net asset value, i.e., the total value of its assets less liabilities. Although he attempted to approximate net asset values by using adjusted book values,[16] which were arrived at by reducing book values by a market-to-book ratio, the figures so computed bore no reasonable relation to actual net asset values. Mr. Wendin used a market-to-book ratio of 80 percent, but a comparison of book values to the appraised values determined by Mr. McKenzie shows the ratio was actually near 300 percent. Moreover, even if the adjusted book values had been close to actual net asset values, Mr. Wendin assured they would be of little importance in his overall computations

---

[16]Mr. Wendin apparently recognized that unadjusted book values are often unreliable for valuation purposes because they may have little relation to the assets' fair market values at the date of valuation. With an asset that appreciates in value (and thus has investment value), such as real estate, book value may be far below current fair market value. See *Estate of Poley v. Commissioner*, a Memorandum Opinion of this Court dated Mar. 7, 1947, affd. per curiam 166 F.2d 434 (3d Cir. 1948).

by assigning insubstantial weights, varying from one-ninth to one-eighteenth, to them. As discussed earlier, a prospective buyer of stock in these corporations would undoubtedly give substantial weight to net asset values.

Another problem with the Wendin valuations was that he applied to his adjusted book values a 40-percent discount for lack of marketability and control. We believe this was improper because lack of control was also reflected (excessively) in the weighting of factors considered in computing an overall valuation.

Petitioner's second expert, Mr. Orville G. Lefko, was retained to prepare an analysis after the McKenzie appraisals had been made available to petitioner. Mr. Lefko employed an approach somewhat different than Mr. Wendin but still minimized the importance of net asset values and arrived at figures quite close to those computed by Mr. Wendin.

Mr. Lefko felt that both net asset value and earnings capability were not very important in comparison to dividend projections for purposes of valuing corporations such as the ones at issue here. Although the dividend history of each of the corporations had been irregular, Mr. Lefko came to the conclusion that each corporation had the ability to pay a regular dividend. To arrive at a rate of dividend capitalization, he looked at seven equity real estate investment trusts, which he selected as comparables. These "comparables" yielded a 12-percent dividend capitalization rate, which he increased to between 15 and 17 percent because he believed that real estate investment trusts involved lower risks due to factors such as professional management, geographical diversity, and size. After applying the dividend capitalization rate to projected dividends, he applied a 45-percent discount for lack of marketability.

Mr. Lefko did not entirely dismiss the net asset value of the corporations but attempted to factor into his overall value a liquidation probability value, to reflect the buyer's prospect of realizing on liquidation a share of the underlying asset values. First, he adjusted the appraised value of the corporation's assets. He decreased the values of real properties by anticipated liquidation costs of stocks and bonds by handling charges, and receivables by a bad debt allowance. This gave him a net realized value per share of each corporation. Next, he projected when a purchaser of shares that had been held by decedent might reasonably expect to obtain his share of the underlying assets through liquidation. Because of the corporation's long history of continuing operations and no prospect of imminent liquidation, Mr. Lefko believed there was no chance of liquidation within 5 years, a 5-percent chance in 10 years, a 10-percent chance in 15 years, a 35-percent chance in 20 years, and a 50-percent chance in 25 years. He multiplied the net realized value per share by each of these percentages and then discounted the resulting amounts because of the lost time value of money prior to the assumed future liquidation. He thereafter added together all the discounted amounts and applied a 45-percent illiquidity discount. In this manner, he computed a liquidation probability value for each corporation, equal to approximately 3 percent to 5 percent of the fair market value of the underlying assets. This liquidation probability value was added to the previously determined dividend capitalization value of each of the corporations.[17]

We find the liquidation probability approach to be highly speculative at best. Moreover, we believe the computation improperly reduced asset values on account of lost use of money. This discounting for lost use of money is unrealistic because it fails to recognize that the underlying assets will themselves appreciate, most probably, at a rate similar to that applied as a discount. Another problem with Mr. Lefko's valuation was his use of real estate investment trusts (REITs) as comparables. These entities are not truly comparable to the corporations involved here because of the requirement that REITs must pass through 90 percent of earnings as dividends and because REITs are generally highly leveraged while the corporations here were virtually debt free.

---

[17]We note that it is highly unusual in a valuation to add together the values derived through two independent estimates of valuation, here the liquidation probability approach and the dividend capitalization approach. Theoretically, each approach should result in computation of the entire value of the property and although averaging of the different computations might be necessary, it would not be appropriate to add together separate valuations.

Petitioner's third expert, Thomas C. O'Connell, based his valuation solely upon an approximation of cumulative future dividends of all the corporations. He started with the total average dividend for all the corporations over the 3-year period from 1972 through 1974. To this amount he applied a dividend capitalization rate of between 18.75 percent and 25 percent. He explained that this capitalization rate was arrived at based upon his belief that an investor would require a return of 150 to 200 percent of the prime rate because the companies had certain negative factors such as a low return on invested capital, a low rate of cash flow, very conservative management, fragmented management control, and a lack of consistent policy in prior years. He also stressed that there was no public market for the shares, a low return on net worth and a lack of any long-term plan or growth strategy. Applying the dividend capitalization rate to the prior 3-year total average dividend, he computed a value for the four corporations of between $605,000 and $807,000. For the 20 percent of the shares involved here, he estimated the value of $121,000 to $161,000 total.

We have accorded little weight to Mr. O'Connell's valuation for several reasons. Most importantly, he did not consider earnings and took no account whatsoever of the net asset values of the corporations. Furthermore, in selecting a dividend capitalization rate, he did not examine comparable companies but simply expressed his relatively unsubstantiated opinion that an 18.75- to 25-percent rate of dividend capitalization would be desired by a willing purchaser. In the absence of more facts showing why this specific rate was chosen, it is difficult for the Court to determine whether the rate was simply an educated guess or whether he really had a substantial basis for concluding that it was appropriate. Another problem with Mr. O'Connell's approach was that in applying the dividend capitalization rate to the average dividends received for the prior 3-year period, he did not differentiate among the corporations but considered them as if they were only one single entity. Thus, there is no way in which his valuation can be used directly to arrive at the value of any particular corporation involved here.

In Mr. Bard's valuation report and in computing the amount of deficiency, the net asset values of the four corporations were each reduced first by a 25-percent discount based on a comparison with publicly traded closed end mutual fund shares, and then by discounts ranging from 11.9 percent to 20.74 percent based on Securities Exchange Commission flotation rates. These discounts were designed to reflect the shares' restricted marketability and lack of control.

Rev. Rul. 81–253, 1981–2 C.B. 187, was published by respondent after the statutory notice was issued, and it sets forth respondent's current position concerning the allowance of minority discounts in valuing stock of closely held family corporations. Based on Rev. Rul. 81–253, respondent now argues that no discounts for lack of control or restricted marketability should be applied, although he has not asserted a deficiency greater than that asserted in the statutory notice. Thus, respondent argues that discounts should not be applied to the extent they would result in reducing the values below those asserted in the notice of deficiency.

Petitioner has questioned whether it is proper for respondent to now argue against allowing a minority discount even though he allowed a discount in computing the deficiency in the statutory notice. However, this is not a case where petitioner was surprised at trial by respondent's introduction of a new issue. It is clear that petitioner was prepared for the minority discount question being raised at trial, and has devoted large portions of its briefs to rebutting respondent's position that no minority discount should be allowed. Therefore, we find no merit to petitioner's claim that the minority discount issue has been improperly raised by respondent. See *Llorente v. Commissioner*, 74 T.C. 260, 269 (1980), modified on other grounds 649 F.2d 152 (2d Cir. 1981).

Respondent argues that no discounts should be allowed because all the shareholders in the four corporations, including decedent, shared in control. According to respondent's argument, the hypothetical "willing seller" used in arriving at valuation of the stock must be presumed to be one of the five family members, including decedent, who held stock in the corporations and shared an element of control. Respondent reasons further that such a willing seller would not have sold his shares except as part of the controlling family interest, unless to another family member or the corporations, themselves. If the shares were sold in this way, respondent contends they would retain their control value, and no minority discount would be justified.

In their arguments, neither petitioner nor respondent clearly focuses on the fact that two conceptually distinct discounts are involved here, one for lack of marketability and the other for lack of control.[18] The minority shareholder discount is designed to reflect the decreased value of shares that do not convey control of a closely held corporation. The lack of marketability discount, on the other hand, is designed to reflect the fact that there is no ready market for shares in a closely held corporation. Although there may be some overlap between these two discounts in that lack of control may reduce marketability, it should be borne in mind that even controlling shares in a nonpublic corporation suffer from lack of marketability because of the absence of a ready private placement market and the fact that flotation costs would have to be incurred if the corporation were to publicly offer its stock. However, the distinction between the two discounts is not crucial for purposes of this case. Because respondent's basis for opposing both discounts is the same—that the hypothetical willing buyer must be seen as a family member—our subsequent discussion, like the parties' briefs, will consider the two discounts together.

The leading case dealing with this question is *Estate of Bright v. United States*, 658 F.2d 999 (5th Cir. 1981) (en banc), in which the court recognized that a minority interest in a corporation should not be seen as having any control value, even though the family unit had control of the corporation. The case involved whether a minority discount should be allowed in valuing a decedent's undivided one-half interest in

---

[18]See Fellows & Painter, "Valuing Close Corporations for Federal Wealth Transfer Taxes: A Statutory Solution to the Disappearing Wealth Syndrome," 30 Stan. L. Rev. 895, 920 (1978).

the control block of 55 percent of the stock of a corporation, where the other one-half interest in the control block was owned by the husband of the decedent (who was also executor of the estate and subsequently trustee of the testamentary trust that received the stock in issue). Two major bases for its decision were explained by the court. First, it found that established case law did not support any type of "family attribution" in which the control of the corporation was attributed among family members. The Fifth Circuit noted that the Tax Court, since at least 1940, has uniformly valued a decedent's stock for estate tax purposes as a minority interest when the decedent, himself, owned less than 50 percent of the stock regardless of whether control of the corporation was in the decedent's family.[19] The court also cited two District Court opinions that took the same position,[20] and it stated that it had found no estate tax cases supporting respondent's position. The court found further that case authority in the analogous gift tax area also supported the taxpayer's position, although not unanimously.[21]

The second major reason cited in the *Estate of Bright* opinion for applying a minority discount was based upon the concept of the hypothetical willing-buyer, willing-seller rule. Section 20.2031–1(b), Estate Tax Regs., sets forth the following

---

[19]The following Tax Court cases were cited by the Fifth Circuit for this proposition: *Estate of Zaiger v. Commissioner*, 64 T.C. 927 (1975); *Estate of Leyman v. Commissioner*, 40 T.C. 100, 119 (1963); *Estate of DeGuebriant v. Commissioner*, 14 T.C. 611 (1950), revd. on other grounds 186 F.2d 307 (2d Cir. 1951); *Hooper v. Commissioner*, 41 B.T.A. 114 (1940); *Estate of Kirkpatrick v. Commissioner*, T.C. Memo. 1975–344; *Estate of Stoddard v. Commissioner*, T.C. Memo. 1975–207; *Estate of Thalheimer v. Commissioner*, supra; *Estate of Maxcy v. Commissioner*, T.C. Memo. 1969–158, revd. on other grounds 441 F.2d 192 (5th Cir. 1971); *Estate of Katz v. Commissioner*, T.C. Memo. 1968–171. We agree with the Fifth Circuit that these cases show our established view that a decedent's stock in a family controlled corporation should be seen as a minority interest whenever the decedent individually did not have control.

[20]The two District Court opinions cited by the court were *Obermer v. United States*, 238 F. Supp. 29 (D. Hawaii 1964); and *Sundquist v. United States*, an unpublished opinion (E.D. Wash. 1974, 34 AFTR 2d 74–6337, 74–2 USTC par. 13,035).

[21]Cases cited by the court for the proposition that minority discounts were allowed for gifts of stock in family controlled corporations included *Meijer v. Commissioner*, T.C. Memo. 1979–344; *Koffler v. Commissioner*, T.C. Memo. 1978–159; *Estate of Heppenstal v. Commissioner*, a Memorandum Opinion of this Court dated Jan. 31, 1949; *Whittemore v. Fitzpatrick*, 127 F. Supp. 710 (D. Conn. 1954); *Clark v. United States*, an unpublished opinion (E.D. N.C. 1975, 36 AFTR 2d 75–6417, 75–1 USTC par. 13,076).

rule, which has been universally applied by the courts and respondent:

The fair market value is the price at which the property would change hands between a willing buyer and a willing seller, neither being under any compulsion to buy or to sell and both having reasonable knowledge of relevant facts. * * *

The Fifth Circuit saw this language from the regulation as indicating that the "willing seller" is a hypothetical seller rather than the particular estate. Thus, the willing seller should not be identified with the decedent, and the decedent's stock should not be included as part of a family unit for valuation purposes. Nor was it proper, according to the Fifth Circuit, to place any weight upon the identity of the parties that actually received the stock after distribution from the estate. For purposes of valuation, one should construct a hypothetical sale from a hypothetical willing seller to a similarly hypothetical willing buyer.

In *Propstra v. United States*, 680 F.2d 1248 (9th Cir. 1982), the Ninth Circuit followed *Estate of Bright* and discounted the value of an undivided one-half interest in real estate held by the decedent and his wife as community property at the time of death. The Ninth Circuit noted that Congress has explicitly directed that family attribution or unity of ownership principles be applied in other areas of Federal taxation, and felt that in the absence of any legislative directive, it should not judicially require such principles to be applied in the estate tax area. Furthermore, the court emphasized the advantage of using an objective hypothetical willing-buyer, willing-seller standard, instead of a subjective inquiry into the feelings, attitudes, and anticipated behavior of heirs and legatees, which might well be boundless.

Respondent argues that the Fifth Circuit misinterpreted the concept of the hypothetical willing seller and willing buyer. In his briefs, he relies primarily upon three cases to support his proposition that a minority discount should not be applied if family members control a corporation. *Richardson v. Commissioner*, a Memorandum Opinion of this Court dated November 30, 1943, affd. 151 F.2d 102 (2d Cir. 1945), involved a family holding company whose assets were readily marketable securities. On appeal, the Second Circuit upheld the value established by us but questioned whether we had used the correct standard of valuation. Our *Richardson* opinion must be read narrowly in view of the long series of subsequent cases in which we have allowed discounts in valuing shares of family corporations that held operating as well as investment assets. *Blanchard v. United States*, 291 F. Supp. 348 (S.D. Iowa 1968), contains language supportive of respondent's position. But the court stressed that it was dealing with a unique situation involving a planned sale of all the family's shares of stock in the corporation. At first blush, *Rothgery v. United States*, 201 Ct. Cl. 183, 475 F.2d 591 (1973), seems to support respondent. But even though its valuation was phrased in terms of seeing the willing buyer as a particular person (the family member who already held almost 50 percent of the shares of the corporation), the court also explicitly found that there would have been other potential buyers for the decedent's shares of the stock at the same price if the stock had been offered for sale to persons outside the Rothgery family. Thus, despite analyzing the hypothetical sale in terms of the sale to a particular person, the court evidently attributed no premium to the fact that the family member would assure himself of control by obtaining these shares.

Three cases provide at best weak support for respondent's position that no discounts should be applied here. Opposed to this meager case law in favor of respondent is the large number of cases allowing such discounts, which were discussed in the *Estate of Bright* opinion. We see no reason to depart from such established precedent but follow the Fifth Circuit's well-reasoned and thoroughly researched opinion. Respondent's approach would have us tailor "hypothetical" so that the willing seller and willing buyer were seen as the particular persons who would most likely undertake the transaction. However, the case law and regulations require a truly hypothetical willing seller and willing buyer. We must assume these hypothetical parties exist even though the reality of the situation may be that the stock will most probably be sold to a particular party or type of person. Certainly, the hypothetical sale should not be constructed in a vacuum isolated from the actual facts that affect the value of the stock in the hands of decedent, but we do not see any actual facts in this case that require the stock to be valued as anything other than minority interests in each corporation.

We have pointed out above the defects of the approaches used by both parties' experts. Having taken diametrically opposed views as to the factors to be weighed in valuing the stock involved in this case, the parties "failed successfully to conclude settlement negotiations—a process clearly more conducive to the proper disposition of disputes such as this." *Messing v. Commissioner*, 48 T.C. 502, 512 (1967). Because we have concluded that none of the experts gave appropriate weight to net assets as well as earning and dividend-paying capacity, we must necessarily make our own best judgments of value. While we have considered the valuation reports of Messrs. Wendin, Lefko, and Bard, we have also weighed all other relevant factors such as the extremely conservative business attitudes and practices of the management, the nature of the real estate holdings, the amount of cash and other liquid assets held by the corporations, and the business climate on the valuation date, both overall and for these corporations in particular. We have discounted the values because of the restricted marketability of the shares and the lack of control a hypothetical willing buyer of these minority shares would be able to exercise. Based on all these factors and on the entire record, we conclude and find as a fact the following date-of-death fair market values for the stock held by decedent:

| | |
|---|---:|
| Andrews, Inc | $302,400 |
| St. Anthony | 158,000 |
| Green Mountain | 56,000 |
| W.F. & H.H | 64,800 |

*Decision will be entered under Rule 155.*

# In the United States Claims Court

*Luce v. the United States No. 519-81T, filed December 13, 1983.*

---

| | |
|---|---|
| ALBERT L. LUCE, JR., FRANCES C. LUCE, GEORGE E. LUCE, WILLOUISE B. LUCE, JOSEPH P. LUCE AND MARILYN S. LUCE <br><br> v. <br><br> THE UNITED STATES | ) Gift tax; valuation <br> ) of the shares of a <br> ) closely held corpora- <br> ) tion; minority in- <br> ) terest. <br> ) <br> ) <br> ) <br> ) |

---

<u>Theodore M. Forbes, Jr.</u>, Atlanta, Georgia, attorney of record for plaintiffs. <u>Robert D. Strauss</u> and <u>Gambrell & Russell</u>, of counsel.

<u>Israel D. Shetreat</u>, Washington, D. C., with whom was Assistant Attorney General <u>Glenn L. Archer, Jr.</u>, for defendant. <u>Theodore D. Peyser</u> and <u>Robert S. Watkins</u>, of counsel.

---

OPINION <u>*/</u>

MILLER, <u>Judge</u>:

This is a suit for refund of gift taxes paid with respect to gifts of stock of the Blue Bird Body Company, made in 1976 by the three Luce brothers, Albert L., Jr., George E. and Joseph P., who are the controlling stock-holders of that company. On September 30, 1976, Albert gave 19,000 shares to a trust for his daughter. There-after, on October 29, 1976, Albert gave 2,000 additional

---

*/ Since all of the pertinent findings of fact are contained in this opinion, pursuant to Rule 52(a) no separate findings will be filed.

shares directly to his daughter, and George and Joseph each gave 38,000 shares both directly to members of their families and to trusts for their benefit. There were a total of 16 gifts, consisting of 97,000 shares, 83,000 of which were in nine trusts with a common trustee, the Citizens and Southern National Bank of Macon, Georgia. The 97,000 shares represented 17 percent of the total of 582,000 shares which were outstanding.

Each donor filed a gift tax return valuing the shares at $39.31, which is equal to their book value as of September 30, 1975, the end of the prior fiscal year.

After filing appropriate claims for refund, plaintiffs 1/ brought timely suit and now claim that the fair value of the gifts should more properly have been computed at $26 per share.

The Blue Bird Body Company was founded in 1927 by A. L. Luce, Sr., plaintiffs' father. By 1947 its shares were owned one-fourth by A. L. Luce, Sr., and his wife, and one-fourth by each of the three plaintiffs. Plaintiffs' father died in 1962, and by 1966 the three plaintiffs had acquired 100 percent of the shares.

Starting in 1969 Blue Bird initiated a policy of selling some of its stock to executive employees and officers other than members of the Luce family. In March 1969 it sold 10 shares to Corbin J. Davis, an officer. Preliminary to such sale it amended its by-laws to provide that no stockholder or his heirs, personal representatives or assigns may sell, pledge or otherwise dispose of any shares until he first offers to sell them to the corporation at their book value as of the end of the next preceding fiscal year. If the corporation fails to repurchase the shares within 45 days, he is to offer them to the other stockholders pro rata at the same price. If any of the other stockholders fails to exercise his purchase rights, he is to assign them to the remaining stockholders. Only if the other stockholders fail to make the purchase, may the stock be sold to outsiders.

Thereafter, from 1969 through the corporation's fiscal year ending October 30, 1976, sixteen managerial and executive employees acquired a total of 33,429 shares

---

1/ Although the wives are necessary parties to the suit by virtue of their election to treat the gifts as made by both husbands and wives, the term plaintiffs will be used hereinafter to refer exclusively to the husbands because they paid the taxes.

of Blue Bird at book values as of the end of the fiscal years preceding their acquisitions. Some shares were sold to such employees for cash; others were issued as additional compensation. Blue Bird has bought back shares from the estate of one such employee and from two others who left its employment -- always at book value as of the end of the preceding fiscal year.

In 1972 the three plaintiffs gave 139,320 shares of Blue Bird stock to eight trusts for their children and grandchildren, naming themselves as co-trustees with the Citizens and Southern National Bank of the trusts of which they were grantors.

Following the 1976 gifts, Blue Bird's stock was owned:

| Owner | Shares | Percentage |
|---|---|---|
| Plaintiffs | 312,251 | 53.6 |
| Plaintiffs' children | 14,000 | 2.4 |
| Citizens and Southern National Bank as trustee or as co-trustee with plaintiffs | 222,320 | 38.2 |
| Non-family executives | 33,429 | 5.8 |
| | 582,000 | 100.0 |

Section 2512(a) of the Internal Revenue Code of 1954 provides that for gift tax purposes, "If the gift is made in property, the value thereof at the date of the gift shall be considered the amount of the gift." Treasury Regulations on Gift Tax (1954 Code) § 25.2512-1, (26 C.F.R.)), states that such value is "the price at which such property would change hands between a willing buyer and a willing seller, neither being under any compulsion to buy or sell, and both having reasonable knowledge of relevant facts."

One of the more difficult property valuation problems is the appropriate method and measure of valuation of the shares of the stock of a closely held corporation, which are not ordinarily traded on an open market. See Righter v. United States, 194 Ct. Cl. 400, 407, 439 F.2d 1204, 1207 (1971). Section 2031 of the Code, relating to the estate tax, provides:

> (b) Valuation of unlisted stock and securities.--In the case of stock and securities of a corporation the value of which, by reason of their not being listed on an exchange and by reason of the absence of sales thereof, cannot be determined with reference to bid and asked prices or with

reference to sales prices, the value thereof
shall be determined by taking into consideration, in addition to all other factors,
the value of stock or securities of corporations engaged in the same or a similar line
of business which are listed on an exchange.

While no similar provision appears in the gift tax
sections of the Code, gift tax Regulations § 25.2512-2(f)-
provides that where selling prices or bid and asked prices
are unavailable, the valuation of shares of stock is to be
determined by taking into consideration the company's net
worth, prospective earning power, dividend-paying capacity, goodwill, economic outlook in the industry, the company's position in the industry, its management, the
degree of control of the business represented by the block
of stock, the value of securities of corporations engaged
in similar lines of business which are listed in a stock
exchange, and other relevant factors. See also Penn Yan
Agway Cooperative, Inc. v. United States, 189 Ct. Cl. 434,
446, 417 F.2d 1372, 1378 (1969); Arc Realty Co. v. Commissioner, 295 F.2d 98, 103 (8th Cir. 1961).

In 1976 Blue Bird was primarily a manufacturer and
seller of school bus type vehicles, plus a limited number
of small urban transit buses and luxury motor homes. As
previously noted, the enterprise had been founded in 1927
by Mr. A. L. Luce, Sr. After their return from military
service in World War II, his three sons, the plaintiffs,
entered the business with him and have been in control of
the business since their father's death in 1962. The
business has grown steadily. In 1945 Blue Bird manufactured 750 bus bodies, in 1946, 1,000. By 1976 Blue
Bird was producing 10,000 buses per year.

Approximately 56 percent of Blue Bird's 1976 sales
revenue were derived from the sale of buses for which the
chassis and engines were provided by the truck manufacturers, such as Ford, GM or International Harvester. The
manufacturers inventoried their trucks on Blue Bird property, and Blue Bird's only obligation was to maintain insurance on them. Blue Bird built the bodies, including
seats, electrical wiring and all other appurtenances,
installed chassis and engines and shipped the finished
buses to the customers. An additional 30 percent of Blue
Bird's revenues came from the sale of  buses for which
Blue Bird manufactured the chassis as well as the bodies,
installing, however, engines manufactured by such engine
manufacturers as Ford, GM, Cummins or Caterpillar. The
remaining 14 percent of sales volume was about evenly
divided between urban transit buses and the motor homes.

Blue Bird's domestic sales are generated primarily through corporate or distributor competitive bidding for state, county, and local government sales. Approximately 20 to 30 percent of Blue Bird's revenues result from state purchases by competitive bid. The other source of domestic sales for Blue Bird comes from its distributor network. In 1976, this network was comprised of 54 distributors and five direct factory representatives. A distributor may sell on the basis of competitive bids or through negotiations with school boards or with contractors to school boards at the county level. In 1975 and 1976, Blue Bird was also very active in the export market, and, during that time, the export market was very strong. Large orders from Middle Eastern countries contributed to the 1975-76 growth in export sales.

Many of Blue Bird's distributors have been with the Company from 20 to 30 years. Many distribute solely Blue Bird products; however, some sell, in addition, trucks, autos, or other school equipment.

Although the school bus industry is highly competitive and school bus manufacturers generally have had the capacity to produce twice as many buses as the market demand, in 1976 Blue Bird was one of the top two or three companies in unit sales in the industry. It supplied 22.4 percent of the school buses sold in the United States, 45 percent of the school buses sold in Canada and approximately 25 percent of the school buses used for such purpose in all the other countries. It was a half-century old well-established company with a good, solid, basic market. Its facilities and machinery and equipment were in good condition and well maintained. Its principal executives had been with the company for substantial periods of time, its employees were well paid, and its labor relations were good. It had no significant long term debt and it had a good line of credit. It had a network of franchises and qualified salesmen selling its products in the United States, Canada, and in the international markets. Its sales, production, and profits were on the rise, and its competitors had a difficult time competing with it. It had generally and consistently been a successful and profitable business; and its management had plans and expectations for boosting its profits by increasing its unit sales to 25 percent of the domestic market by 1980, which would give it the number one spot. In fact, it achieved this goal by 1978 or 1979.

Plaintiff produced, as an expert witness to testify with respect to the fair market value of the gifts of stock at issue, Mr. Charles B. Shelton, III, First Vice President in the corporate finance department of The Robinson-Humphrey Company, Inc., a member of the New York,

American and Midwest Stock Exchanges and a full-service
investment banking and brokerage house.

He determined that, based on information provided by
management and a review of market conditions in the fall
of 1976, the difference in the values of Blue Bird's common stock on September 30 and October 29, 1976, when the
two sets of gifts were made, was negligible, and accordingly valued them both as of the latter date.

He accepted as correct and without further investigation the financial information concerning the company
provided by Blue Bird's management. Included were
audited financial statements of Blue Bird for the fiscal
years ended in October 1971 through 1975, but not for
1976. Because the financial statement for October 30,
1976, was not yet available on October 29, 1976, he substituted the company's earnings projection for the fiscal
year ending October 30, 1976, made by the company in the
summer of 1976. And he added a forecast for fiscal 1977,
also made in the summer of 1976. He summarized the
earnings record for 1971-75 as follows:

| (000's omitted) | 1971 | 1972 | 1973 | 1974 | 1975 |
|---|---|---|---|---|---|
| Net Sales | $32,008 | $36,888 | $40,649 | $55,123 | $78,886 |
| Earnings | 2,125 | 2,520 | 2,507 | 2,071 | 6,381 |
| Earnings Per Share | 3.75 | 4.45 | 4.38 | 3.56 | 10.98 |
| Net Profit Margin | 7% | 7% | 6% | 4% | 8% |

He set forth the 1976 and 1977 estimates comparatively
with the actual results for 1974 and 1975 as follows:

| | 1974 | 1975 | 1976 Est. | 1977 Est. |
|---|---|---|---|---|
| Units Sold | 7,701 | 9,566 | 8,995 | 10,221 |
| % Increase (De-crease) in Units Sold | | 24.2% | (6.0)% | 13.6% |
| Earnings (000's omitted) | $2,071 | $6,381 | $5,932 | $3,670 |
| % Increase (De-crease) in Earnings | | 208% | (7.0)% | (38.1)% |

He also noted that the company's net worth as of November 1, 1975, was $22,839,000 (or $39.24 per share), and,
after subtracting goodwill, that tangible net worth was
$22,503,000 (or $38.73 per share).

In order to determine the value of the 97,000 shares which were the subject of the gift, he first found it necessary to value 100 percent of the equity in the company, which was represented by 582,000 shares of stock.

Mr. Shelton's report and testimony discussed various measure of value for the stock of the entire company but he ultimately relied on only one.

He rejected the market comparison approach, which arrives at the value of a closely held company by applying to it the ratios which the market price of the stock of a publicly owned company in the same industry bears to its earnings, dividends and net book value, on the ground that he was unaware of any publicly traded company whose business was similar to that of Blue Bird in product, size and scope.

He rejected an asset appraisal approach to value on the ground that Blue Bird was a going concern and its management had no intention of liquidating the assets.

He found the book value of Blue Bird's net assets, or net worth, was $22,838,818 or $39.24 per share on November 1, 1975, and an estimated $28,189,000, or $48.43 per share on October 29, 1976 (after giving effect to a $1.00 per share dividend declared October 25, 1976), but rejected that too.

The only method he discussed to arrive at value on the basis of objective comparative data with respect to other companies was the capitalized excess earnings method of valuation. Under this method the average return of a company on its tangible net worth (the book value of tangible assets less liabilities) over a number of years is compared to that of its industry. To the extent that the company's average return on its tangible net worth is at a rate in excess of that prevailing in the industry generally, it is assumed that such excess earnings indicate it has intangible value (or goodwill) in excess of the value of its tangible net worth. To ascertain what that value is, that portion of the earnings is capitalized at a suitable rate commensurate with the investment risk. The product is then added to the value of the tangibles to determine total value.

In making this comparison, Mr. Shelton used the average net book value of Blue Bird's tangible assets for the years 1972-76 and the average earnings for the same years. For the industry comparisons for return on net worth, he used Annual Statement Studies for 1977, by Robert Morris Associates, covering eleven companies of similar asset size as Blue Bird, primarily engaged in manufacturing automobile bodies, or assembling complete passenger cars, trucks, commercial cars, buses and special purpose vehicles, with fiscal years ending in 1976; Standard & Poor's Automobile Index; Standard & Poor's Automobile Index excluding General Motors; Standard & Poor's Automobiles-Trucks & Parts Index and Standard & Poor's 400 Industrial Index. The comparison was as follows:

BLUE BIRD BODY COMPANY
COMPARISON OF RETURNS ON NET WORTH RATIOS
(Using Tangible Net Worth, Net of Goodwill)

Blue Bird Body Company
Return on Net Worth

| | |
|---|---|
| 1976 | 20.9% Est. |
| 1975 | 28.4% |
| 1974 | 12.2% |
| 1973 | 16.1% |
| 1972 | 18.4% |
| Average 1972–1976 | 19.2% |

Robert Morris Associates
Industry Median Return
On Net Worth

| | |
|---|---|
| 1976 | 15.40% |
| 1975 | 9.13% |
| 1974 | 7.98% |
| 1973 | 11.72% |
| 1972 | N.A. |
| Average 1973–1976 | 11.06% |

Standard & Poor's
Automobile Index

| | |
|---|---|
| 1976 | 17.33% |
| 1975 | 5.74% |
| 1974 | 6.05% |
| 1973 | 16.94% |
| 1972 | 16.61% |
| Average 1972–1976 | 12.53% |

Standard & Poor's Automobile
Index Excluding GM

| | |
|---|---|
| 1976 | 12.78% |
| 1975 | Def. |
| 1974 | 3.82% |
| 1973 | 12.89% |
| 1972 | 12.86% |
| Average 1972–1976 | 8.47% |

| Standard & Poor's Automobiles-Trucks & Parts Index | |
|---|---|
| 1976 | 14.28% |
| 1975 | Def. |
| 1974 | 8.60% |
| 1973 | 11.07% |
| 1972 | 6.57% |
| Average 1972-1976 | 8.10% |

| Standard & Poor's 400 Industrial Index | |
|---|---|
| 1976 | 14.02% |
| 1975 | 12.11% |
| 1974 | 14.17% |
| 1973 | 14.15% |
| 1972 | 11.71% |
| Average 1972-1976 | 13.23% |

Although over the preceding 5 years Blue Bird had earned a rate of return on tangible net worth substantially in excess of that earned by each group of comparables, nevertheless he applied a relatively low multiple, five times earnings, to the excess yield. Despite the low multiple, however, this method resulted in a total value of $32,373,000 for the whole company, equivalent to $55.62 per share.

All of the foregoing, however, appears to have been mere padding. Mr. Shelton disregarded the $39.24 and $48.43 book values, for the stated reason that the shares of some publicly held companies in the automotive industry in some years sold at prices below their book values and because he was of the opinion that earnings are generally the most important factor bearing on the value of a going concern. Also, after having gone to the trouble of making all of the foregoing calculations and comparisons, Shelton then repudiated the $55.62 value he determined by the capitalized excess earnings method of valuation because the industries whose rates of return were used were broader than Blue Bird and not largely confined to school buses, because Blue Bird's average rate of return was inflated by its 1975 high earnings level, and because the method did not consider all relevant factors.

Mr. Shelton arrived at his valuation of the company by a modified capitalization of earnings method. He averaged Blue Bird's reported earnings for 1972-75 together with the estimate for 1976 and the projection for 1977, and obtained an average earnings base of $3,847,000. Dividing this earnings base by the 20 percent capitalization rate (or applying a multiple of five times earnings) resulted in a total value for the company under this approach of $19,235,000. He then added to that figure a sum sufficient to increase the $19,235,000 to $21,500,000, without explanation other than that it was a matter of judgment. Dividing this figure by the 582,000 outstanding shares arrives at a per share value of $37 for the whole company.

Shelton then reduced the $37 per share by 30 percent to $26, for the 97,000 shares which were the subject of the gifts, because they represented in the aggregate only a 17 percent minority interest, which lacked an established market for sale to the public, and absent such a sale they were subject to the will of the controlling stockholders, who could use the corporation to benefit themselves at the expense of other stockholders.

Mr. Shelton's method of valuation is subject to criticism in several respects. First, the earnings he used are not necessarily representative of the earning capacity of the business. As the court stated in Central Trust Co. v. United States, 158 Ct. Cl. 504, 530, 305 F.2d 393, 409 (1962), in using reported earnings as a basis for stock valuation, it is "proper to make such adjustments therein as would be necessary to eliminate abnormal and nonrecurring items and to redistribute items of expense to their proper periods."

Blue Bird's 1974 earnings had been reduced by approximately $787,000 as a result of a one time change in the company's method of accounting. By converting from first-in first-out to last-in first-out inventory accounting in that year, Blue Bird decreased its closing inventory and pre-tax income by $1,430,800. Restoration of this sum less the offsetting tax savings attributable thereto (at the 45 percent rate used by Shelton) results in additional representative after-tax earnings of $787,000 for the year. Applying this increase to Shelton's capitalized average earnings computation results in a $1.13 per share increase in his valuation of the company.

The 1976 earnings estimate used in Mr. Shelton's earning's base, $5,932,000, was short of the earnings reported for that year, $6,381,000, by $449,000. The estimate relied on was made during the summer of 1976. However, monthly financial statements were available, and Mr. Pennington, Blue Bird's independent auditor, testified that by the end of September 1976 they would have enabled determination of the annual income with 80-90 percent accuracy. Plaintiffs have not shown that as the valuation date at issue, October 29, 1976, only one day prior to the close of the fiscal year, Blue Bird's auditors could not have furnished Mr. Shelton a closer approximation of actual earnings for the year than that made during the summer. Adjustment of the earnings base for this increase results in an additional increase of $0.64 per share in Mr. Shelton's valuation for the whole company.

The reported earnings were after reduction each year by approximately 10 percent for contributions to a private charitable trust (The Rainbow Fund) of which the three Luce brothers were the trustees. In 1976 the contribution was $575,000. It is difficult to understand why the earnings base for valuation of a company should be reduced by such a voluntary diversion of earnings which was not shown to benefit the corporation. Mr. Shelton argued that since the siphoning off of earnings by controlling stock-holders was adverse to a minority interest, an adjustment for this annual sum should not increase the value of the gift shares. However, it is a proper item for adjustment of the earnings base in determining the value of the entire corporation prior to computing the value of a minority interest; otherwise the witness' discount for a minority interest is duplicated. More important, once there is a significant unrelated minority interest, a serious question arises as to the right of the controlling stockholders to continue to divert a substantial share of the corporate earnings to their private charitable founda-tion without the consent of all of the stockholders. See A. P. Smith Manufacturing Co. v. Barlow, 13 N.J. 145, 98 A.2d 581 (1953); Annot. 39 A.L.R. 2d 1192 (1955); 19 Am. Jur., Corporations § 1015; and H. Ballantine on Corpora-tions (Rev. Ed.) § 85 at 228.

Mr. Shelton included in his earnings base a forecast of earnings for 1977, which had been prepared by the company in the summer of 1976. Although the forecast was for $3,670,100 in earnings and the actual 1977 earnings turned out to be $3,883,600, the propinquity of the fore-cast to the actual results (6 percent below) does not necessarily show the soundness of the forecast. It actually appears to be happenstance. The forecast was made in the summer of 1976, up to 5 months before the beginning of the 1977 fiscal year. The projection was for substantially increased sales, both in units and dollars, over prior years. The forecast of reduced earnings was based on projections of increased inflation rates and correspondingly higher material and labor costs generally, and was thought by Albert Luce to be a single year's break in the trend of increased earnings. The June 1980 report of a company official responsible for the forecast ex-plains that the 1977 results were close to the forecast because "cost increases were not quite as great as anticipated", but "On the other hand price increases were not as great as anticipated."

The use of an earnings forecast made months prior to the start of the year, and which is based on predictions of the general inflation rate with respect to raw material and labor costs generally, as a base for capitalization of earnings is subject to great error. The unreliability of such an initial estimate may be inferred from the fact that the corresponding initial forecast for 1976 was for $2,985,800 in earnings, while actual earnings turned out to be $6,189,000, more than 100 percent higher. The risks associated with such forecasts of future earnings are more properly a function of the capitalization rate than the earnings base. To reflect a forecast of a possible earnings decrease for a single future year in both the base and the rate results in an exaggeration of the effect of such a forecast.

On November 5, 1981, Mr. Shelton prepared another valuation report for the plaintiff on the entire Blue Bird stock as of August 10, 1981, for purposes of a proposed recapitalization of the company. This did not involve a tax problem. In it he followed the same general method of valuation. However, for the average earnings base he used the results of the 1976 through 1980 years and the estimate for 1981. The latter he derived from the results for the 7 months ending in May 1981. He did not include any forecast for 1982.

In addition, in constructing the earnings base in the 1981 valuation report, Mr. Shelton used a method of averaging which emphasizes the importance of the most recent experience. He used the sum of the digits method, which places greatest weight on the most recent years, to arrive at average earnings for 1976 to 1980, and then weighed that at 40 percent and the estimated whole year 1981 earnings at 60 percent to arrive at the average for 1976-81. Had he applied that method to his 1972-76 earnings the earnings base would have been much higher, to wit:

| Year | Earnings | Weight Factor | Weighted Earnings |
|------|----------|---------------|-------------------|
| 1972 | 2,519,845 | x 1/10 | 251,984 |
| 1973 | 2,507,003 | x 2/10 | 501,401 |
| 1974 | 2,071,386 | x 3/10 | 621,416 |
| 1975 | 6,381,385 | x 4/10 | 2,552,554 |
|      |          | 10/10 | 3,927,355 |
|      | x weight factor of |  | 40% |
|      |          |  | 1,570,942 |

1976        5,931,800 x weight factor of 60% = 3,559,140
Weighted Earnings Base                        $ 5,130,082

This compares to the average earnings base of $3,847,000 he actually used to value the entire company as of October 29, 1976.

In Central Trust Co. v. United States, 158 Ct. Cl. at 522, 305 F.2d at 404, the court pointed out that mere averages may be deceiving since they equate both increasing and decreasing earnings without regard to their trend, and that "the most recent years' earnings are to be accorded the greatest weight."

For the foregoing reasons, Mr. Shelton's average earnings were not a wholly reliable base for the capitalization of earnings method of valuation.

Second, Mr. Shelton's valuation of Blue Bird at $37 per share as of October 29, 1976, is unacceptable because it is almost a fourth less than the book value of its net assets less liabilities, $48.98, as of October 30, 1976, even though all but one percent of that book value was represented by tangible assets, cash and receivables. Indeed, an appraisal of the tangible assets at Blue Bird's main plants, made for insurance purposes as of December 12, 1975, established that the replacement cost of such assets less sustained depreciation was far in excess of their book value and that had it been substituted for the book figures the book value per share would have been increased to $61.65.

If a company's net worth consists of substantial write-ups of intangible value acquired in mergers or corporate acquisitions, if it has paid inflated prices for its assets, or if its machinery and equipment are obsolete, and it has consistently been unable to obtain a fair return on its investment, then the fair market value of the company may understandably be less than its book value. But the undisputed evidence here is that as of the valuation date Blue Bird's ownership had been in the same family since it was organized, its net worth was not inflated by any substantial intangible value, and its plant and equipment were in good condition and enabled it to be a dominant company in its industry. Moreover, Mr. Shelton's own computations showed that the company's returns on its tangible net worth ranged between 16.1 and 28.4 percent, with an average of 19.2 percent, over the preceeding 5 years, returns far in excess of those earned in the closest comparable industries Mr. Shelton could find. A seller could hardly have been expected to be willing to accept 25 percent less for the company than the cost of duplicating the net depreciated tangible assets alone, without regard to its value as a going concern with goodwill, qualified personnel, an established national distributors' organization and high earning capacity; and a hypothetical buyer could also hardly have expected that he could obtain it for that price. 2/ In such circumstances, it is reasonable to conclude that book value is at the least a floor under fair market value, which an appraiser may not properly ignore. Cf. Schwartz v. C.I.R., 560 F.2d 311, 316-17 (8th Cir. 1977); Hamm v. C.I.R., 325 F.2d 934, 937, 941 (8th Cir. 1963), cert. denied, 377 U.S. 993 (1964); City Bank Farmers Trust Co. v. Commissioner, 23 B.T.A. 663, 669 (1931).

Third, the most serious weakness in Mr. Shelton's valuation of the company lies is in his failure to supply a rational objective basis for the key element thereof, the capitalization rate he applied to Blue Bird's average earnings. He testified that in his judgment "a buyer of such securities of the risks inherent in Blue Bird would look for a 20 percent return." However, he was unable to furnish any objective data with respect to any comparable situations underlying that judgment, so as to enable the court to determine whether it was soundly based. Nor could he supply any objective data which would tend to support a judgment that a knowledgeable seller would be willing to dispose of the Blue Bird stock at a price so low as to be no more than he would have received in just 5 years of its average earnings or 3 years of its most recent earnings. When pressed, Mr. Shelton fell back on his "experience"; but he conceded he was not an expert on the market for school buses and had never sold stock of any company which manufactured or sold buses, and could not identify a single contemporaneous purchase or sale of the stock of any company in his experience which was the basis of his judgment. Nor, even omitting the names of the participants, could he describe the circumstances of any comparative purchase or sale. Assuming (without necessarily deciding) the good faith of Mr. Shelton's testimony, it must be concluded that his judgment in this regard was merely intuitive and the basis therefor was not susceptible of rational or objective examination or evaluation by the court. 3/

---

2/ This is also supported by the fact that the controlling stockholders contemporaneously sold shares of stock and gave bonuses to executive employees at book value as of the end of the prior year and deemed the price to be at least fair to the employees.

3/ In support of the 20 percent capitalization rate, plaintiff argues that the government's expert witness used a 5.3 multiple of earnings which is not very far from Shelton's. The fact is, however, that the government's witness used a multiple of 7.7 times the 5 year average for 1972-76 and 5.3 times 1976 earnings, to arrive at a

Nor is Mr. Shelton's judgment that $2,265,000 should be added to the capitalized earnings base any more rationally founded. It is self-evident that it was added to raise the $19,235,000 to $21,500,000 in order to reach a predetermined round figure. It may also be inferred that it is in recognition that the other methods of valuation reached considerably higher figures. But why $21,500,000 rather than some other figure? It must be concluded that the witness' judgment in this regard is equally intuitive and not based on objective facts or reasoning susceptible of objective examination or evaluation.

Plaintiffs argue in their brief that "The value of expert opinion testimony lies in the qualifications of the witness" and that it is not the court's role to reason why. But however difficult, the law has never deemed the valuation of the stock of a closely held company to be an arcane or occult craft beyond the ken of courts, which must be content to evaluate only the credibility of the expert witness. "[L]ike any other judgments, those of an expert can be no better than the soundness of the reasons that stand in support of them." (Fehrs v. United States, 223 Ct. Cl. 488, 508, 620 F.2d, 255, 265 (1980).) The opinion of an expert witness is "no better than the convincing nature of the reasons offered in support of his testimony" (Potts, Davis & Company v. C.I.R., 431 F.2d 1222, 1226 (9th Cir. 1970).) "Opinion evidence, to be of any value, should be based either upon admitted facts or upon facts, within the knowledge of the witness, disclosed in the record. Opinion evidence that does not appear to be based upon disclosed facts is of little or no value." (Baliban & Katz Corp. v. Commissioner, 30 F.2d 807, 808 (7th Cir. 1929).) 4/ "[I]n order for the opinion to have any value it must be based on assumptions which the trier of facts can find to have been proved", (Rewis v. United States, 369 F.2d 595, 602 (5th Cir. 1966).) A court "is not required to surrender its judgment to the judgment of experts." (Hamm v. Commissioner, 325 F.2d 934, 941 (8th

---

3/ cont'd.

value of $54 per share. As noted hereinafter, the court finds it unnecessary to rely on the government's expert testimony.

4/ Also quoted with approval in Continental Water Co. v. United States, 49 A.F.T.R. 2d 82-1070, 1080 (1982), (Trial Judge, Court of Claims), adopted per curiam 231 Ct. Cl. ___, 50 A.F.T.R. 82-5128 (1982).

Cir. 1963).)    Andsee also The Conqueror, 166 U.S. 110,
131-33 (1897); Pumice Supply Co. v. C.I.R., 308 F.2d 766,
769 (9th Cir. 1962); and Gloyd v. Commissioner, 63 F.2d
649, 650 (8th Cir.), cert. denied, 290 U.S. 633 (1933).

Finally, plaintiff's reliance upon Shelton's
determination that the fair market value of the 97,000
shares which were the subject of the gifts should be
reduced by 30 percent, to $26 per share, because as a
minority interest without an established market they could
not be sold to the public except at a substantial
discount, is based on a misconception of both the law and
the facts. First, under the law, the applicable market in
which the hypothetical willing buyer may be found need not
be one which includes the general public. It is sufficient if there are potential buyers among those closely
connected with the corporation.

In Rothgery v. United States, 201 Ct. Cl. 183, 189,
475 F.2d 591, 594 (1973), there was at issue the valuation
for estate tax purposes of 50 percent of the stock of an
automobile dealership, the remaining 50 percent being
owned by the decedent's son. Since there was no public
market for the shares, the court found the value of the
entire stock from the book value and appraisals of the
underlying assets less the liabilities, and then allocated
that value on a per share basis. The court responded to
the estate's argument that the pro rata allocation was
excessive because there was no public market for the
decedent's shares and because the 50 percent interest of
the estate was not a controlling interest, by finding that
the decedent's son would have been a willing buyer of the
shares from any hypothetical seller; that the son intended
to continue the corporate business after his father's
death; that he wished to have control of the corporation,
so that his own son might have a place in the business;
that this objective required the acquisition of the
decedent's stock interest in the corporation; and that the
evidence warranted the inference that the son would have
been willing to pay -- and from a business standpoint
would have been justified in paying -- for the decedent's
half-interest in the corporation an amount equal to half
the value of the corporation's assets. This was a market
sufficient to negate any need for a discount to sell the
shares.

In Couzens v. Commissioner, 11 B.T.A. 1040 (1928),
the Board of Tax Appeals was required to find the value of
the Ford Motor Company stock on March 1, 1913, in order to
determine the late Senator Couzen's gain on the sale of
his stock in 1920. Prior to the 1920 sale only ten
individuals were the sole stockholders, there was no
public market for the stock, and there was a restriction
on the certificates giving existing shareholders the prior

right to purchase the stock at the price at which it was offered to an outsider. The Commissioner argued that the limited market for the shares under such circumstances depressed the value of a minority interest below the fair market value of the shares as a whole and would have necessitated a substantial discount to make them saleable to a willing buyer. In rejecting this contention, the court stated (11 B.T.A. at 1164):

> We do not construe a fair market as meaning that the whole world must be a potential buyer, but only that there are sufficient available persons able to buy to assure a fair and reasonable price in the light of the circumstances affecting value. 5/

On cross-examination, Mr. Shelton likewise concurred that if the company or its controlling stockholders pursued a policy of buying back shares from persons who were not family members or executive employees, that fact could put a greater value on the shares by providing a potential market for them.

The record in this case establishes that there was indeed an available market for the shares at issue within the company or among persons associated with the company. Plaintiff Albert L. Luce testified 6/ that it was company and Luce policy that all shares of Blue Bird's stock remain in the ownership of members of the Luce family, of trusts for their benefit, and of executive employee. This purpose motivated the adoption of the by-law in 1969, when shares were first offered to executive employee Corbin Davis, requiring any stockholder desiring to dispose of his shares to offer them first to the corporation and then to the remaining stockholders at book value. Thereafter, whenever shares were offered to an employee, Albert Luce personally told him that the company would repurchase the

---

5/ Accord: Estate of Goldstein v. Commissioner, 33 T.C. 1032, 1037 (1960), affirmed on another issue, 340 F.2d 24 (2nd Cir. 1965); Smith v. Commissioner, 46 B.T.A. 340-41 (1942), mod., sub. nom., Worcester County Trust Co. v. Commissioner, 134 F.2d 578 (1st Cir. 1943).

6/ Neither of the other plaintiffs testified. Joseph Luce was hospitalized at the time of trial, but no explanation was given for George's absence, nor was any effort made to obtain Joseph's testimony at another time. It is assumed therefore that there was no divergence as to the facts and Albert spoke for all three.

shares at book value if he left the company, died or desired to dispose of the shares for any other reason; and the company has in fact followed this practice.

The company's purpose for the by-law and commitment was explained by Albert as follows:

> As we offered the stock to other members, other than the Luce family, and to some of our top executives, we did not want them to dispose of their stock to our competitors or someone we would not want to know more details about our operation or our business.

He elaborated on this theme that they wanted control of the company to remain in the family and that it was their intent that no shares be held by strangers generally. Accordingly, no shares have ever been sold to outsiders.

The same intent prevailed with respect to the shares given to the trustee for the benefit of other members of their family. Luce testified that had the trustee desired to sell any of the shares on the open market he would not have allowed it, but would have bought it back, because, as a major stockholder, he wanted to retain control of the block of stock, he wanted it to remain in the family, and he had no intention of allowing it to go to outsiders. Furthermore, he conceded he would even have paid "a premium over whatever the fair market value might be not to let any Blue Bird shares get outside the Luce family and the executives or corporate management."

Even without regard to the personal funds of the Luce brothers and their families, it is clear that as of October 29, 1976, Blue Bird had the financial resources to pay for the 97,000 shares at the $39.31 1975 book value at which they were reported on the gift tax returns if they were offered to it by the trustee or by a willing buyer from the trustee. The cost of such a purchase would have been $3,813,070. The company's financial report as of October 30, 1976, shows it had net current assets (less current liabilities) of $13,375,405, of which cash and receivables were $4,697,151, and, in addition, it owned $3,480,597 in cash value of life insurance on the lives of its officers, against which it could borrow at will. It also had a good line of credit and substantial borrowing capacity, its long term liabilities being no more than $1.7 million, which was less than 6 percent of equity.

In addition to the corporation itself and its controlling stockholders there was a further market for the shares among the other managerial employees of Blue Bird. Corbin Davis, the company's vice-president for marketing, testified without contradiction that since 1976 fifteen to twenty other managerial employees who were offered stock in the corporation at book value took the opportunity to purchase it and that there were 200 other employees in the management team, every one of whom would have been eager to purchase shares at the same price if it had been offered to him.

Thus, there was no occasion for a 30 percent discount in order for the hypothetical seller to find a willing buyer.

In a suit for refund of federal income taxes, the taxpayer bears the burden of proving that he has overpaid his taxes. This means that not only must he establish that the assessment was erroneous, but also the amount which is correct. United States v. Janis, 428 U.S. 433, 440 (1976), Helvering v. Taylor, 293 U.S. 507, 514 (1935); Lewis v. Reynolds, 284 U.S. 281 (1932); E. I. DuPont De Nemours & Co. v. United States, 221 Ct. Cl. 333, 349-50, 608 F.2d 445, 454 (1979), cert. denied, 445 U.S. 962 (1980); Dysart v. United States, 169 Ct. Cl. 276, 340 F.2d 624 (1965). Since plaintiffs paid gift taxes on their gifts of 97,000 shares on the basis of a $39.31 per share value, plaintiffs are only entitled to a refund if they can demonstrate the extent to which such value was excessive. Plaintiffs have failed to prove by their evidence that any portion of the $39.31 per share was excessive. 7/ Accordingly, it is unnecessary to review the testimony of defendant's valuation witnesses and defendant's other arguments, such as the argument that the prices the employees paid for their stock and the deductions the corporation took on its tax return for the stock bonuses are actual transactions more persuasive than opinions on hypothetical facts.

Wherefore, the clerk is directed to enter judgment for the defendant and to dismiss the complaint.

---

7/ Indeed, to the contrary, a fair inference may be drawn that on October 29, 1976, no hypothetical informed seller with knowledge of the results shown in the monthly audit reports would have been willing to sell his shares at the $39.31 book value as of the end of the prior year, when, by waiting only one or two additional days, in all probability he could have commanded a $48.98 price, the book value as of October 30, 1976.

# APPENDIX 3:
## Acquisition Takeover Glossary

**Asset play**[1] A firm whose underlying assets are worth substantially more (after paying off the firm's liabilities) than the market value of its stock.

**Bear hug** An unnegotiated offer, in the form of a letter made directly to the board of directors of the target company. The price and terms are sufficiently detailed so that the directors are obliged to make the offer public. The offer states a time limit for a response and may threaten a tender offer or other action if it is not accepted.

**Black knight**[1] A potential acquirer that management opposes and would prefer to find an alternative to (that is, a *white knight*).

**Breakup value**[1] The sum of the values of the firm's assets if sold off separately.

**Crown jewel option**[1] The strategem of selling off or spinning off the asset that makes the firm an attractive takeover candidate.

**Four-nine position**[1] A holding of approximately 4.9 percent of the outstanding shares of a company. At 5 percent, the

---

[1] From the *AAII Journal*, April 1986, published by the American Association of Individual Investors, 625 N. Michigan Avenue, Chicago, IL 60611.

holder must file a Form [13d] with the SEC, revealing the position. Thus, a four-nine position is about the largest position that one can quietly hold.

**Going private**[1] The process of buying back the publicly held stock so that what was heretofore a public firm becomes private.

**Golden handcuffs**[1] Employment agreement that makes the departure of upper level managers very costly to them. For instance, such managers may lose very attractive stock option rights by leaving prior to their normal retirement age.

**Golden handshake**[1] A provision in a preliminary agreement to be acquired in which the target firm gives the acquiring firm an option to purchase its shares or assets at attractive prices or to receive a substantial bonus if the proposed takeover does not occur.

**Golden parachute**[1] Extremely generous separation payments for upper level executives that are required to be fulfilled if the firm's control shifts.

**Greenmail**[1] Incentive payments to dissuade the interest of outsiders who may otherwise seek control of a firm. The payment frequently takes the form of a premium price for the outsiders' shares, coupled with an agreement from them to avoid buying more stock for a set period of time.

The firm bears the cost of the payment. The stock price generally falls after the payment and the removal of the outside threat.

**In play**[1] The status of being a recognized takeover candidate.

**Junk bonds**[1] High-risk, high-yield bonds that are often used to finance takeovers.

**LBO**[1] A leveraged buyout. A purchase of a company financed largely by debt that is backed by the firm's own assets.

**Loaded laggard**[1] A stock of a company whose assets, particularly its liquid assets, have high values relative to the stock's price.

**Lockup agreement**[1] An agreement between an acquirer and target that makes the target very unattractive to any other acquirer; similar to a *golden handshake.*

**Mezzanine financing** Debt financing subordinate to the claims of the senior debt. This financing often has equity participation in the form of stock options, warrants, or conversion to cheap stock.

**Nibble strategy** A takeover approach involving the purchase in the public market of minority stock position in the target company and a subsequent tender offer for the rest of the target stock.

**PacMan defense**[1] The tactic of seeking to acquire the firm that has targeted your own firm as a takeover prospect.

**Poison pill**[1] A provision in the corporate bylaws or other governance documents providing for a very disadvantageous result for a potential acquirer should its ownership position be allowed to exceed some preassigned threshold. For example, if anyone acquires more than 20 percent of Company A's stock, the acquirer might then have to sell $100 worth of its own stock to other shareholders at $50.

**Raider**[1] A hostile outside party that seeks to take over other companies.

**Saturday night special** A seven-day cash tender offer for all of the target firm's stock. It is usually launched on a Saturday on the assumption that the target company will have difficulty mobilizing its key advisors in reaction to the offer.

**Scorched earth defense**[1] A tactic in which the defending company's management engages in practices that reduce their company's value to such a degree that it is no longer attractive to the potential acquirer. This approach is more often threatened than actually employed.

**Senior debt financing** The issuance of debt instruments having first claim on a firm's assets (secured debt) or cash flow (unsecured debt).

**Shark repellent**[1] Anti-takeover provisions such as the poison pill.

**Short swing profit**[1] A gain made by an insider (including anyone with more than 10 percent of the stock) who holds stock for less than six months. Such gains must be paid back to the company whose shares were sold.

**Standstill agreement**[1] A reciprocal understanding between a company's management and an outside party that usually owns a significant minority position. Each party gives up certain rights in exchange for corresponding concessions by the other party. For example, the outside group may agree to limit its stock purchases to keep its ownership percentage below some level (for instance, 20 percent). In exchange, management may agree to a minority board representation by the outsider.

**Swipe** An unnegotiated offer to purchase the shares of a target company's stock made after the target's board has announced its intention to sell the company (usually in a leveraged buyout to management). The swipe price is higher than that initially proposed by the board of directors.

**Tender offer** An offer by a firm to buy the stock of another firm (target) by going directly to the stockholders of the target. The offer is often made over the opposition of the management of the target firm.

**13d**[1] A form that must be filed with the SEC when a single investor or an associated group owns 5 percent or more of a company's stock. The form reveals the size of the holding and the investor's intentions.

**Two-tier offer**[1] A takeover device in which a relatively high per-share price is paid for controlling interest in a target and a lesser per-share price is paid for the remainder.

**White knight defense**[1] Finding an alternative and presumably more friendly acquirer than the present takeover threat.

**White squire defense**[1] Finding an important ally to purchase a strong minority position (for example, 25 percent) of the potential acquisition's stock. Presumably this ally (the "white squire") will oppose and hopefully block the efforts of any hostile firm seeking to acquire the vulnerable firm.

# Index